DAN ADAMS

READ AND DESTROY

SKATEBOARDING THROUGH A BRITISH LENS '78 TO '95

ACC ART BOOKS

24
39
42
48
50
54
56
60
8
12
38

oLLieFINgerF
lipFeeBLE-an
DRechtNO-CoM
plYDISASTer-
DeMOinDyeGGp
LANt-

e reading, now go out and
ceptions: shred, rage,
ur eyes and your mind.
This is not a practice run.

RAD

Magazine

anYO
oLL
lip
DR
pl
De

CONTENTS

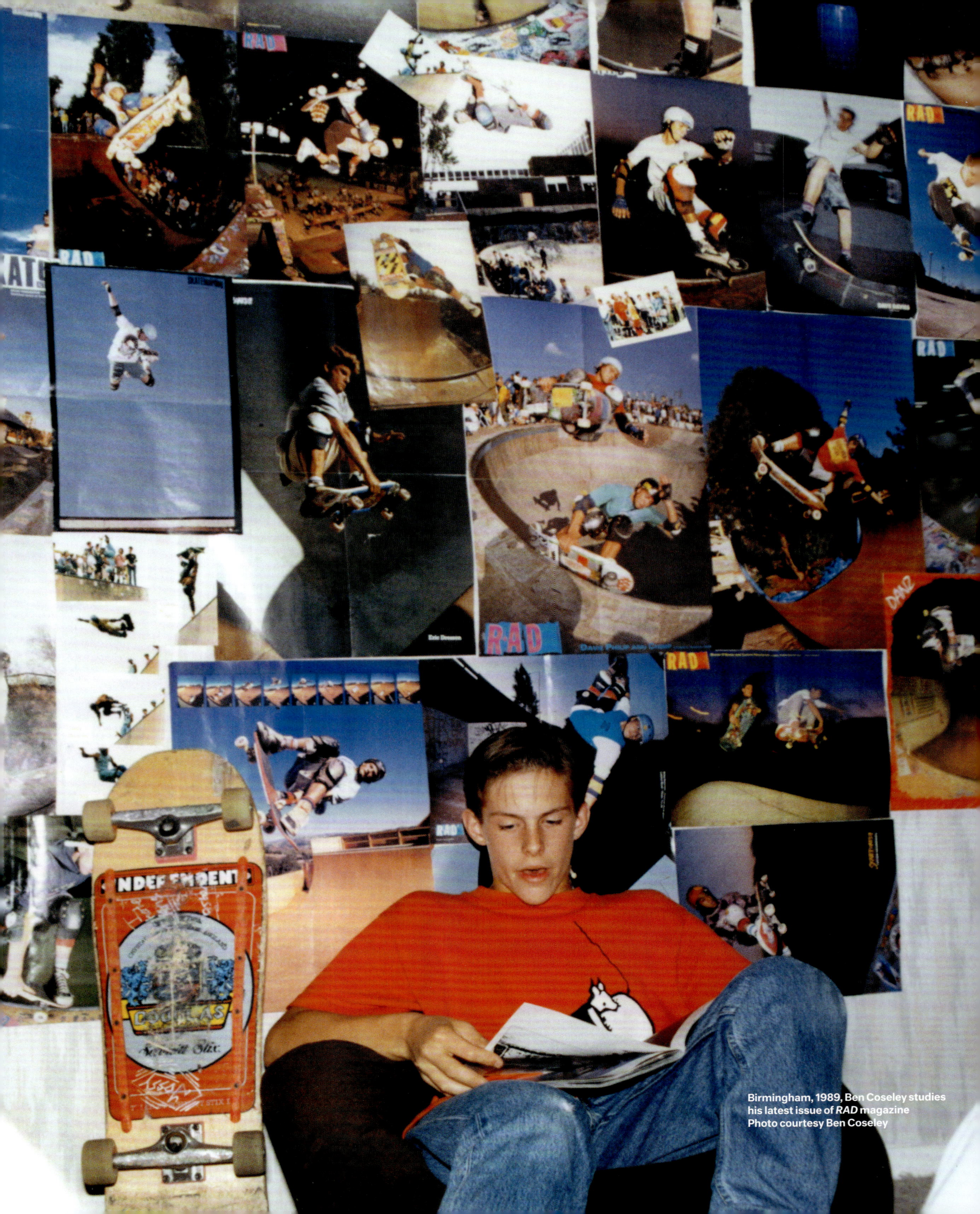

Birmingham, 1989, Ben Coseley studies his latest issue of *RAD* magazine
Photo courtesy Ben Coseley

FOREWORD

I've always had pangs of envy at the people in punk documentaries who were lucky with timing—the ones who were the 'right' age when punk broke. The energy must've been amazing—that feeling of being a part of something exciting and new, actively participating in a golden era.

But I recently realised something that I hadn't considered at the time—I had experienced some perfect timing too. I was an enthusiastic participant in a different golden era; I was part of the *Read And Destroy* generation. I was just perfectly ready for it and effortlessly part of it. In fact, I felt as though I had been waiting for it. And though skateboarding was a tiny subculture (and the British proponents of it therefore formed an exponentially tinier subculture) *RAD* magazine has always had huge significance for those of us who were of the right age and mindset. Ripples still felt, and all that.

The magazine entered my life subtly. Growing up in the New Forest, it made sense to ride BMX when that first entered my psyche in the early 1980s; there were lots of bumps and jumps around. It was fun. Oh, and there, on the shelves of the newsagent—a magazine—*BMX Action Bike*? Cool. Perhaps a bit dry, a bit 'sporty', what with all those races and things, but then along came the freestylers. They started out innocuously enough. Routines and such. But soon, something interesting started to happen. A new breed of freestyler. They didn't wear the regulation jerseys and helmets, and they did tricks in unregulated places, places where surely it must be illegal? A subversive feel was building... And then, slowly at first, the skateboarders appeared in the pages. Not the long-haired, bare-footed kind. No short-shorts or hang-tens here. Neon shirts, ripped jeans, chequered canvas shoes, wild hair, these big wide boards with skulls on! And they weren't gliding round the slopes at skateparks, they were in the streets—wild in the streets. They were jumping off benches!

Something happened to the magazine then. It entered its golden era. It became edgy, it became exciting. It became *RAD*. I devoured that mag every month. Growing up in the middle of nowhere, it was—cliché imminent—my Bible. I still remember captions from 35 years ago. That's ridiculous. The energy was bursting out of that thing every issue. Boneless ones off planters, BMX wallrides, punkish collages. The jarring juxtaposition of neon berets and shorts with drab British car parks. This was a unique moment.

In the mid-1980s, street skating was just blossoming. The first street pro-model skateboards were coming out; it was Gonz and Natas over Hosoi and McGill. And frankly, there was no contest. It seems so obvious in retrospect. Of course street skating would take over—it's accessible. No vert ramp required. All it did require was imagination. Skateboard culture was exploding and evolving and *RAD* was right there, all the way, documenting the UK scene and fuelling the fire. The American skaters undeniably led the way at this point, and so the US magazines were hugely important. They portrayed an idyllic far-off land. One with sun! One where skaters seemed to be an accepted—or at least acknowledged—part of life. Things were different on our drizzly isles though. Skating seemed somehow more surreal in these environs. And we may not have had the smooth sidewalks of SoCal, but as a nation, we've always been good at 'making-do', at adapting. So while the US magazines did dictate, they didn't quite translate. Not only did *RAD* speak to this curious breed, the British skater, it was also, significantly, much easier to find, and much cheaper than the American magazines.

At the time, skate magazines—and later, but much less frequently, skate videos—were hugely important for communication. Skateboarding has always progressed very fast—much faster than most things by comparison. Monthly magazines could barely keep up. And I don't suppose I need to outline the progression of skateboarding since that era—presumably you already know all about it if you are holding this book in the first place. And if you don't, I suppose you could just flip through the pages and get a good general idea. Because *RAD* was always on top of things. From a how-to on cutting down your skate shoes, to the rave-era 'Get a Clue' sticker, to those dreadful-quality video-grab sequences of dreadful triple-pressure-flips or whatever; *RAD* always knew what was up. And then, quite suddenly it changed. The original editorial staff left, making way for the all-too-brief *Phat* magazine which, if pressed, I would describe as a British *Big Brother*, only less deliberately controversial. And then, that... was that.

Skateboarding is on television now. Most human beings in the Western world under 60 years old have heard of Tony Hawk. Today you'll walk past a dozen people wearing 'skate shoes' but never give them a second glance because you already know they aren't skaters. Paradoxically, you may well actually skate in shoes made by a major sports brand. Things have changed, of course. It's the 2020s for goodness' sake; we all live in 'the future' now. The golden era I speak of is long, long gone. But—and another cliché races towards us—its influence is still being felt.

Such is the generational nature of things (and especially of skateboarding), that those kids who were pictured in the pages of *RAD* doing boneless ones off Tesco shopping trolleys and chink-chinks on suburban mini-ramps, some of them anyway, now own the skate shops, run the board companies, or have been absorbed into the Californian skateboarding industry. Or not. Some have gone on to do other things entirely—some of them exceptional. Because to be a skater then, especially in a small place like England, meant that you probably were exceptional in some way. A black sheep maybe; a weirdo probably; a free-thinker definitely. I've always maintained that skateboarding doesn't 'matter' in the grand scheme of things, but how much richer it has made some of our lives. *RAD* magazine was, for a few golden years, a lifeline for the outsider skaters of the UK. Thank you Tim Leighton-Boyce and everyone else. We really appreciate it.

RICHARD HART
Photographer and Editor, *Push Periodical*

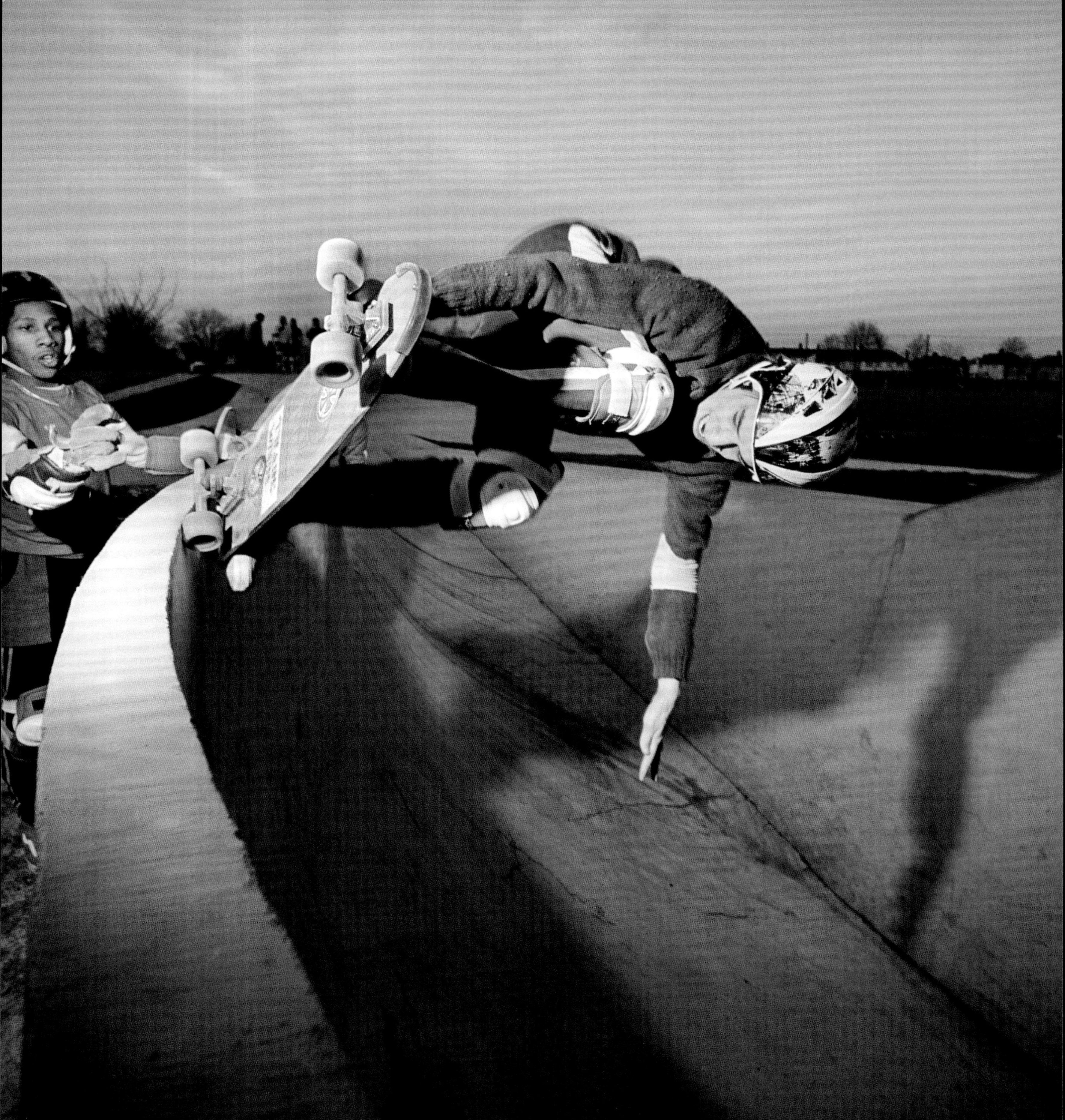

THE ROUTES TO RAD

MAKING IT HAPPEN 1978–1980

When *RAD* magazine launched in 1987 it arguably spearheaded a re-birth of skateboard media and a re-energised skateboard culture in Britain. It arrived after almost a decade that was once proclaimed as the death of skateboarding by wider society—often described as 'The Dark Days'. The established skateboard magazines had ceased publication, boom-era skateparks had closed and equipment manufacturing contracted. In the words of Tim Leighton-Boyce (TLB), *'In retrospect it had already boomed and collapsed on Boxing Day 1977 after poorer than expected Christmas sales.'*

Inspired by the innovation and power of skateboarding, the photographers who instigated *RAD* magazine had strived, in the shadows, to document this supposedly 'dead' activity. With few or no skate magazines in Britain or Europe, their photographs found visibility in cheaply produced zines and newsletters at home, and abroad in underground US magazines *Thrasher* and *Transworld Skateboarding*, as those publications sought to connect with a wider global skateboarding community. One of the earliest and perhaps most pioneering of these photographers (and the eventual editor of *RAD* magazine) to emerge from this 'dead' period was Tim Leighton-Boyce. In the absence of any viable skateboard media, it had become his quiet yet determined mission to document the diminished British skate scene. He used the power of the photograph and small-scale, lo-fi publishing to communicate with and bring together the disparate pockets of skateboarders in Britain.

RAD magazine was the culmination of almost a decade of building—connections, ideas, networks, friends, photography and a culture. The domestic skateboard scene was more than ready for a regular magazine to promote and reflect the activities of its own lively community. Indeed, by this point it had been almost eight years since a skateboard-focused magazine had been published and circulated in Britain.

In the formative years of skateboarding, it was primarily the specialist magazines that provided the window into this new world. They quickly became the essential building block of the new culture as it evolved. They featured dynamic photography that heightened the action, writing that made legends of the young, bold, innovative practitioners, alongside advertisements with rich, colourful displays of new, exotic, hard-to-source equipment. These elements conspired to be an intoxicating, heady mix for their youthful audience. Despite their commercial ambitions, these magazines established themselves as the go-to source of communication and knowledge for anyone keen to initiate themselves in the arrestingly new, constantly evolving culture of skateboarding. The startling visual experience that these magazines provided sowed the seeds for the development of a culture that placed visceral visual expression at its core.

When the second wave of skateboarding had arrived in Britain in the mid-1970s the appeal was immediate. Here (according to what could be seen in the American magazines) was a striking and apparently rule-free physical activity performed by impossibly youthful, sun-kissed deities. The strong surfing associations of the time suggested a romantic, free-wheeling Californian lifestyle so utterly different from life anywhere in Britain in 1976.

The modernity and apparent democratic appeal of skateboarding cut through the class and social associations of the established and traditional rule-based sports that were the usual rites of passage for the young in Britain. Here was a new, non-conformist activity that might free the participant from any youthful disaffection with the predictable outlets for teenage physical energy: cricket, football, rugby or smashing windows. Skateboarding presented an image that was unashamedly urban, positively aggressive, progressive, free and inclusive.

Along with the new skateboards from America came the specialist skateboard magazines. First, in the mid-1970s, *Skateboarder*—the de facto publication for the newly minted skateboard enthusiasts—then *Skateboard World* arrived from America, with monthly exotic depictions of blue skies, other-worldly sculptural terrain and dynamic never-before-seen athleticism. Skin Phillips, *RAD* contributor and one-time editor-in-chief of *Transworld Skateboarding,* remembers:

'Being 11 or 12 and a friend of mine had been in the States for the summer. He'd brought back an issue of Skateboarder *which he showed me on the first day of school and I was like "Fuckin' hell!". It blew me away. At the time I didn't even realise that an American scene existed—which is hard to imagine now but back then seeing that magazine really was like looking at another planet.'*

Paul Sunman, founder of Slam City Skates in London, was similarly inspired by the evocative images in these publications:

'Every so often we'd pick up the American magazines—but that was quite rare. It was fantastic to see those pictures, it was like a utopia: blue skies, everyone wearing shorts and tube socks and all the concrete looking so smooth. It seemed like America had the smoothest concrete on the planet—in our town centre everything was covered in paving slabs.

'I was interested in the photography in those magazines because the images were so glorious; all that sun and light looked fantastic. They were a driving force for me to think "How can I recreate that on the two weekends a year that it's sunny here, to make it look like California?"'

These new, alluring publications spawned a slew of copycats across Europe, imitative titles rarely capable of matching the quality of photography seen in the American magazines. Few rose to the challenge of the high standard of photography established by the likes of Warren Bolster, James Cassimus, Jim Goodrich, Craig Fineman, Wynn Miller, Ted Terrebonne, Craig Stecyk and Glen E. Friedman in *Skateboarder* and Bill and Stan Sharp in *Skateboard World*.

Shooting skateboarding delivered a challenge potentially as exciting as mastering a skateboard itself. The intrinsic importance of these skate-focused photographers was key to the way skateboarding was displayed in—and then absorbed through—the pages of the magazines. A dedicated skate photographer became embedded, capturing the culture and positively defining the moment. With the ceaseless, month-on-month progression that skateboarding made, the skate photographers honed their feel for the manoeuvres and became as skilled as the riders themselves in defining these new tricks. For the initiates of the new booming cult the right photograph captured up-close critical details—more than a documentarian, the skate photographer placed the viewer right at the heart of the action.

As skateboarding has evolved it is the photographers who have given it form, capturing insanely fleeting, radical moments to describe physical shapes and exploits that other skaters then seek to emulate. The decisive moment par excellence. These captured body shapes and visual descriptions of new tricks speak volumes to fellow practitioners and fans alike. Images that sharply define and describe the skateboarders' aims and objectives, desires and aspirations. These photos could powerfully communicate the 'stoke' of skateboarding—the inherently aggressive, triumphal emotion of an edgy manoeuvre pulled off with stylish skill, power and finesse. In 1978, speaking in the BBC documentary, *Skateboard Kings* (Horace Ové, producer), the US *Skateboarder* magazine publisher David Dash expressed:

'As far as photography [goes], we tend to accentuate the radicalness or curves of manoeuvres sometimes because of the types of lenses we use...'

The skate photograph quickly established itself as the primary tool for disseminating the practice and lifestyle of skateboarding globally

'Jeremy Henderson, Neil Harding, Rodga Harvey—they all taught me how to take skate pictures—giving me feedback on the slide shows we used to do' TLB

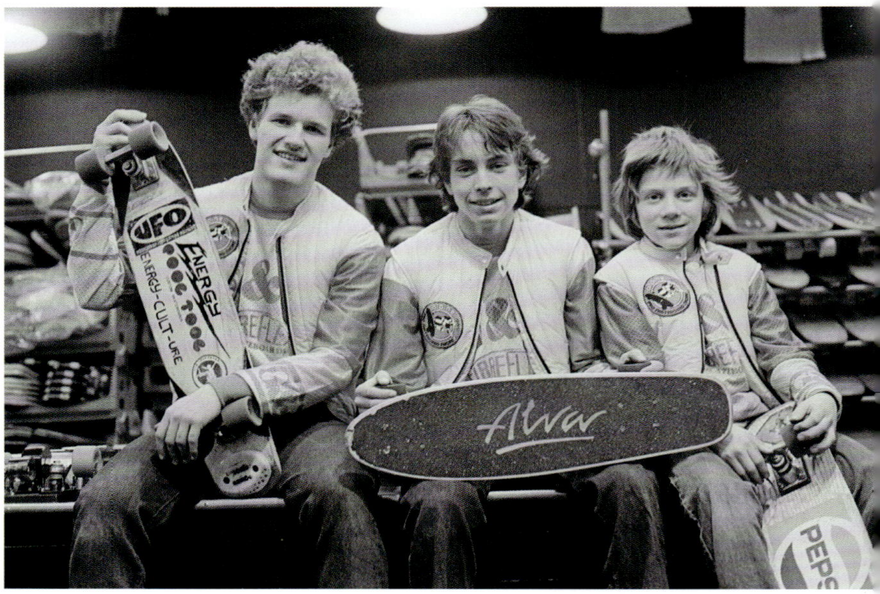

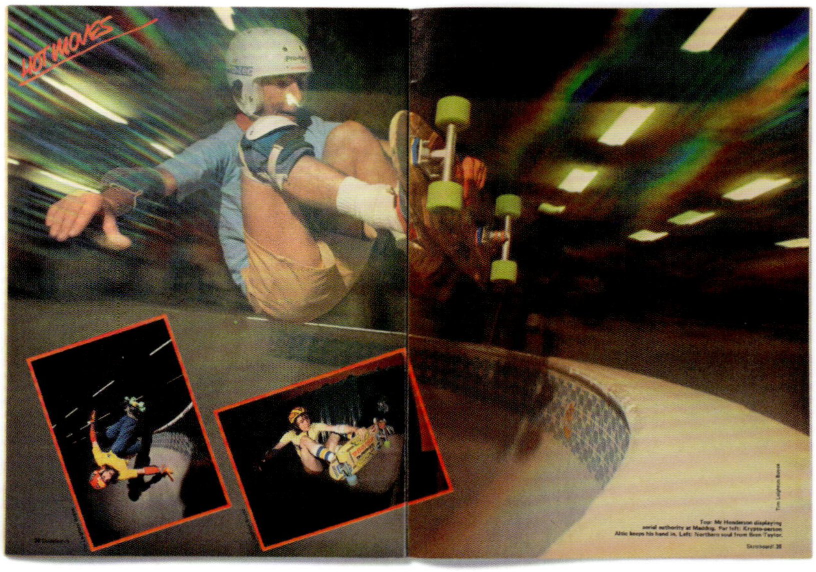

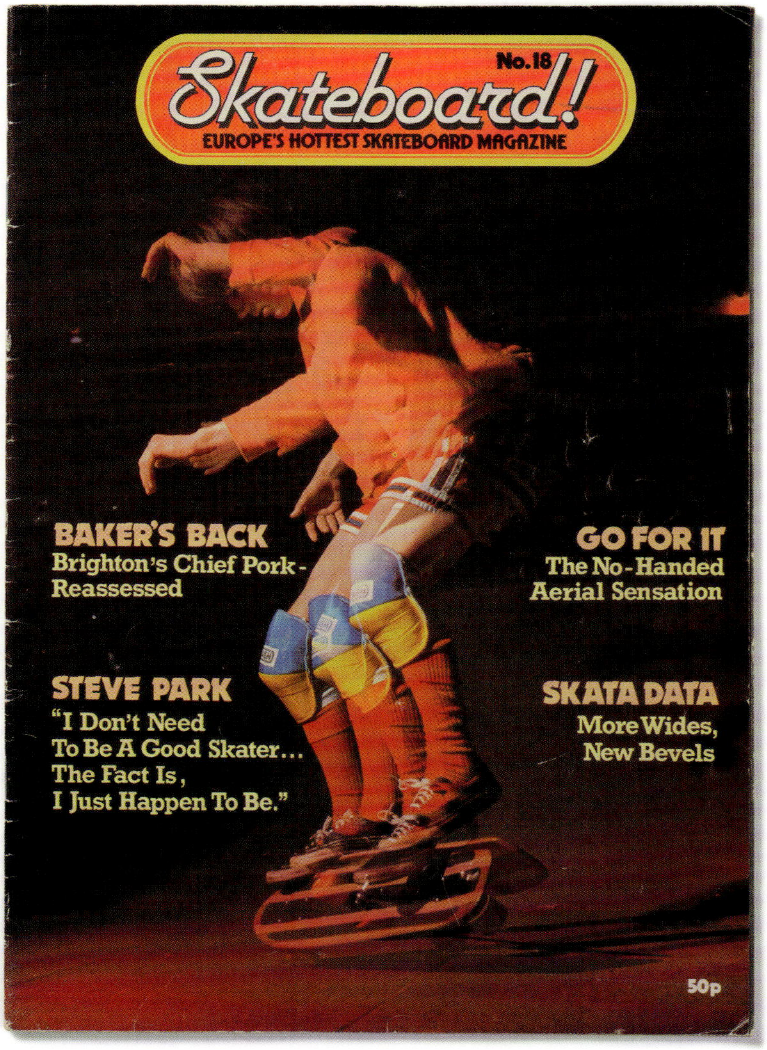

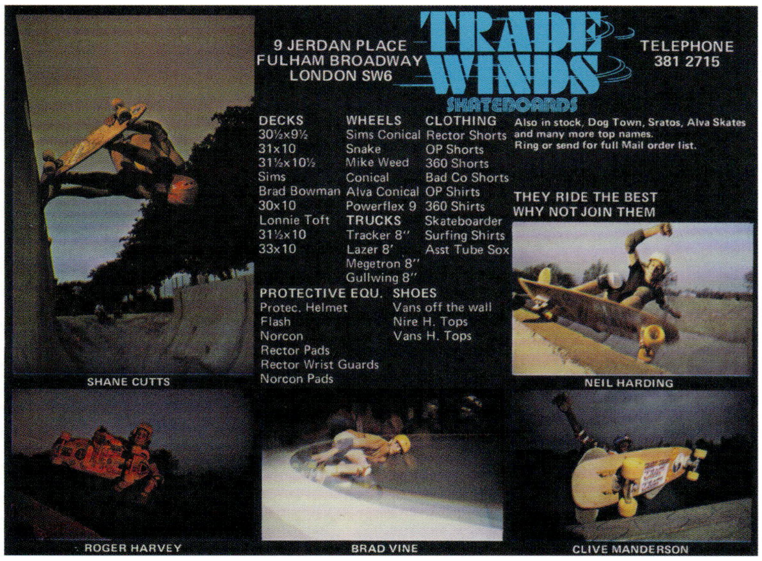

Previous spread: Shane Cutts, Harrow skatepark performance bowl, London, 1978 **Opposite top:** Members of the Alpine Sports skate team (from left): Simon Tuck, Bradley Vine and 'Baby' Ben at the Knightsbridge store, London, 1978 **Opposite bottom:** Double page spread from *Skateboard!* Issue 19, June 1979 featuring Jeremy Henderson at London's Mad Dog Bowl skatepark

Top: Front cover of *Skateboard!* Issue 18, March 1978 featuring Dom Thrupp **Above:** Quarter page ad for Tradewinds skateboards as featured in *Skateboard!* Photographed at Gillingham and Harrow skateparks. All original transparencies now missing **All photos:** TLB

(until the later arrival of video, then digital film and now the social media clip). The photographers—and therefore the magazines—have shaped, even elevated the practice and are an intrinsic part of the evolution of skateboarding. As the only source to view these evocative and instructional photographs, the skateboard magazine was the vital conduit to a quickly evolving, highly influential pop culture for the most part hidden from view in mainstream media.

As the global skateboard craze boomed, European publishing houses were quick to follow the American skate magazines, seeing an opportunity to capitalise on the advertising revenues offered by the explosion in popularity of the new phenomenon and the slew of products that rapidly appeared in its wake. Into this world stepped Tim Leighton-Boyce, eager to commit skateboarding to film and develop a career as a professional photographer. For a few busy months in 1978/9, TLB's photos appeared in what was then Britain's foremost skateboarding publication, *Skateboard!*

LEARNING TO SHOOT

In the late '70s TLB was a budding photographer looking to further an already keen interest in capturing the city and life around him on film. He had embraced the camera at the age of five (thanks to a generous birthday gift from a neighbour), and as a teenager his photographs were an attempt at deconstructing the cityscape and capturing movement through space. Whilst studying English and cinema, university friends dabbled with skateboarding and he began photographing their four-wheeled exploits. Tapping into earlier interests, TLB was attracted by the free-flowing movement through the built environment that the new phenomenon of skateboarding offered.

After graduating, an apparently random chain of events secured him a job at London's then premium skateboard retailer Alpine Sports and in this immersive skateboarding environment TLB developed connections that would further enable his interest in skateboard photography:

'I started taking pictures of skaters and most of the time we would go to Harrow skatepark. I think that's where I really started to learn. The owners of Harrow brought over an American, Jim Rennie, to manage the park. He was living in this extraordinarily posh flat, God knows how; it had a damn grand piano in it! The significance of that was that we used to go to Harrow, take pictures, and then organise slide projector sessions at his flat where I would show the shots. I was shooting slides then because I already wanted to get pictures in magazines and I knew you had to shoot slides to do that. Everyone—Brad Vine, John Sablosky, Neil Harding, Jules Gayton, Paul Sully and Rodga Harvey—was there looking at the pictures. From that, I learned what people wanted and what they liked.

'So it's from that little crew of people there—that's how I learnt to do it. Obviously I was also looking at American magazines all the time and was hugely influenced by them too—Wynn Miller was an influence and Raúl Vega, who did the Alva ads that I loved— but it was that crew who gave me immediate feedback.

'I was taking pictures and doing slide shows, basically hanging out with that crew of skaters, becoming their pet photographer. Then Tradewinds [skate shop] invited me on a trip to Paris to La Villette skatepark. They took some of my photos from that trip and showed them to Skateboard! *Next thing Bruce Sawford [*Skateboard! *editor] rings and says "Where have you been all my life?" He asked me to go and talk, so I went and he gave me my first commission. He basically told me how to do it—he said "Everybody goes along and takes all those colour pictures, but you've got to make sure we have coverage of all the scene. You've got to have half as much black and white because half the mag is in black and white, loads of general background stuff, overviews of the park etc."*

'Not only did he tell me how (and what) to shoot, when I had done it he showed me how to invoice. He put the paper in the typewriter and said "Now, what's your name and address?" and typed it all up! He was the person who got me started. Showed me how to do it. There's been a whole series of mentors throughout this process including Richard Grant and Nigel Thomas at Action Bike, but he got me started.'

'I shot photos for the original Skateboard! *from issues 16 to 19 and I think there was maybe one more unpublished issue, that we had proofs of.'*

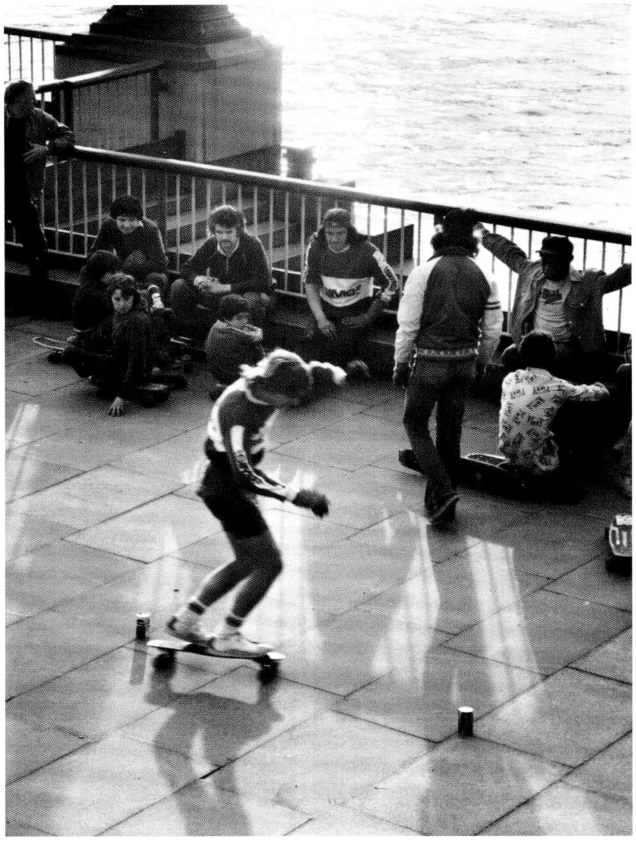

Left: Tim Panting slalom racing together with a group of early skateboard colonisers of the public spaces beneath London's Southbank Centre, 1978
Below: Visiting American professional skateboarder, Russ Howell gives an impromptu demonstration at the Southbank undercroft, 1978
Photos: TLB

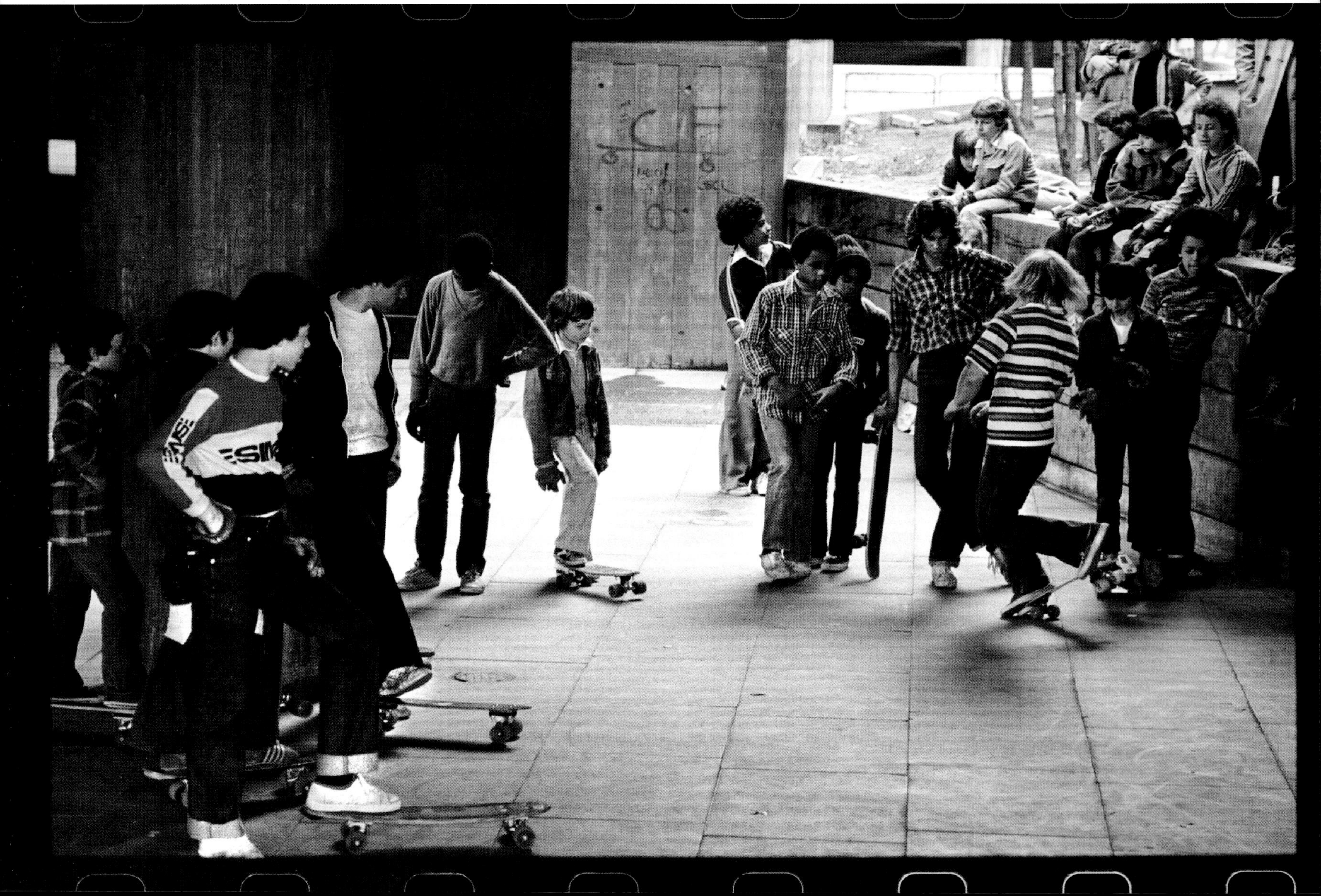

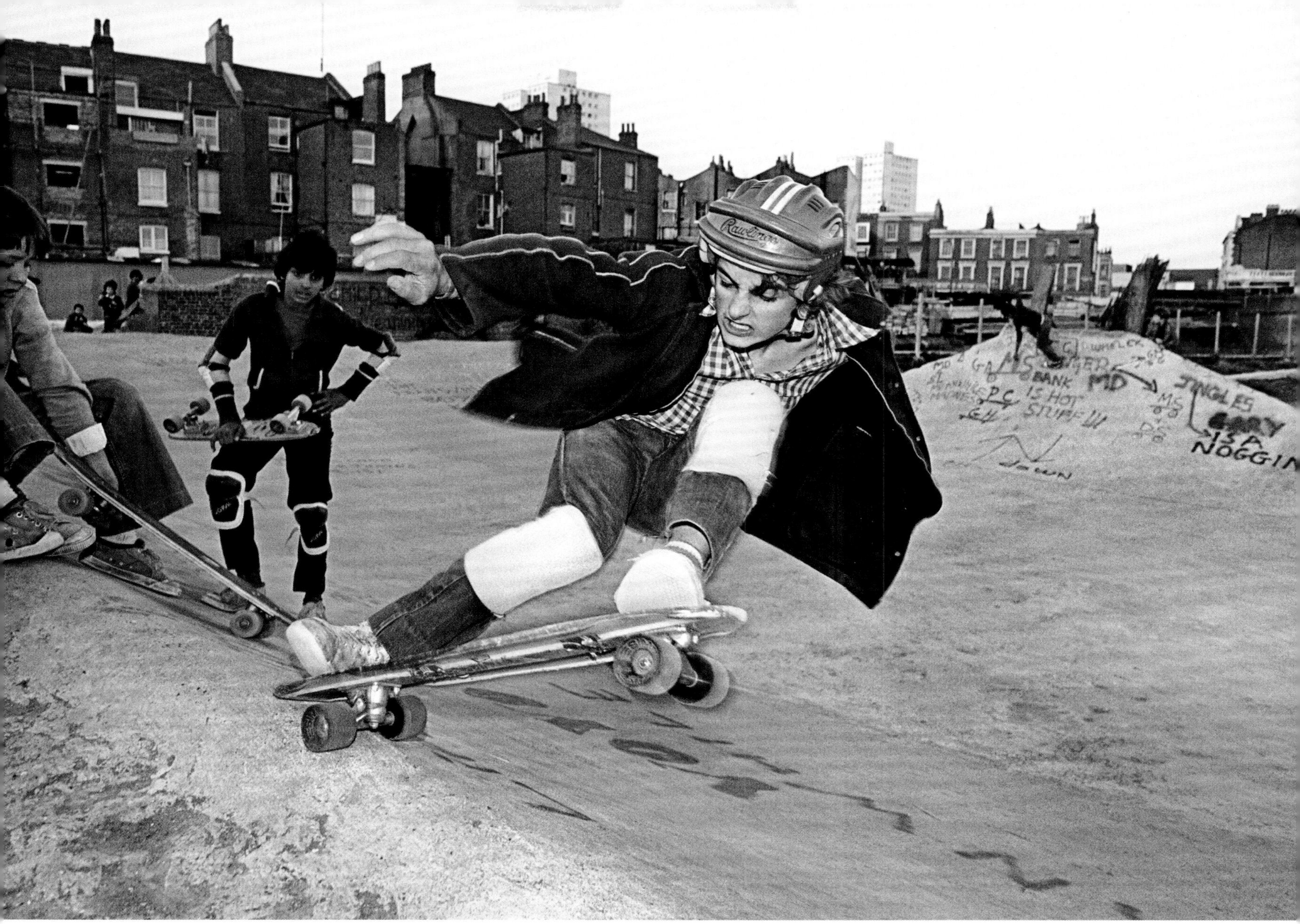

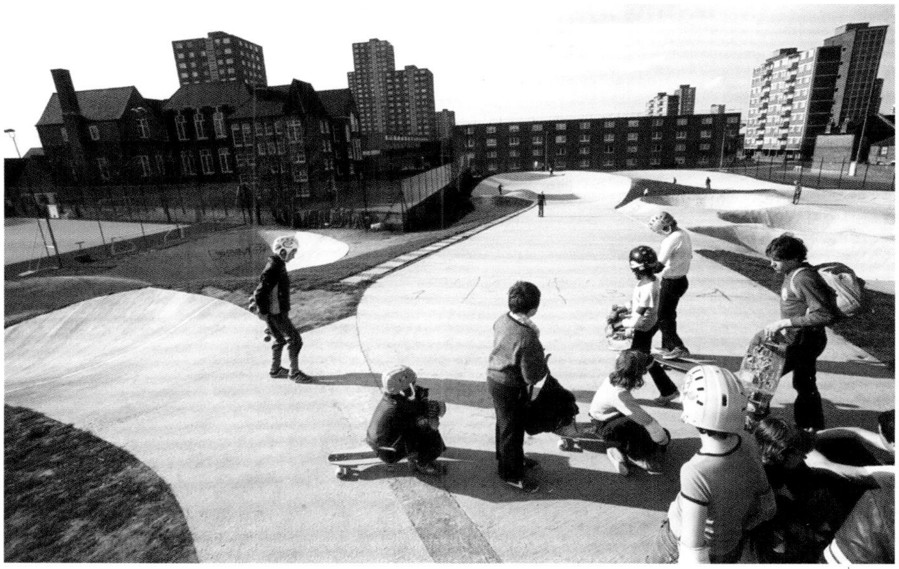

Above: Hugo Carey, Meanwhile Gardens, London, 1978 **Right:** Fordham Park, New Cross, London, 1978 **Photos:** TLB

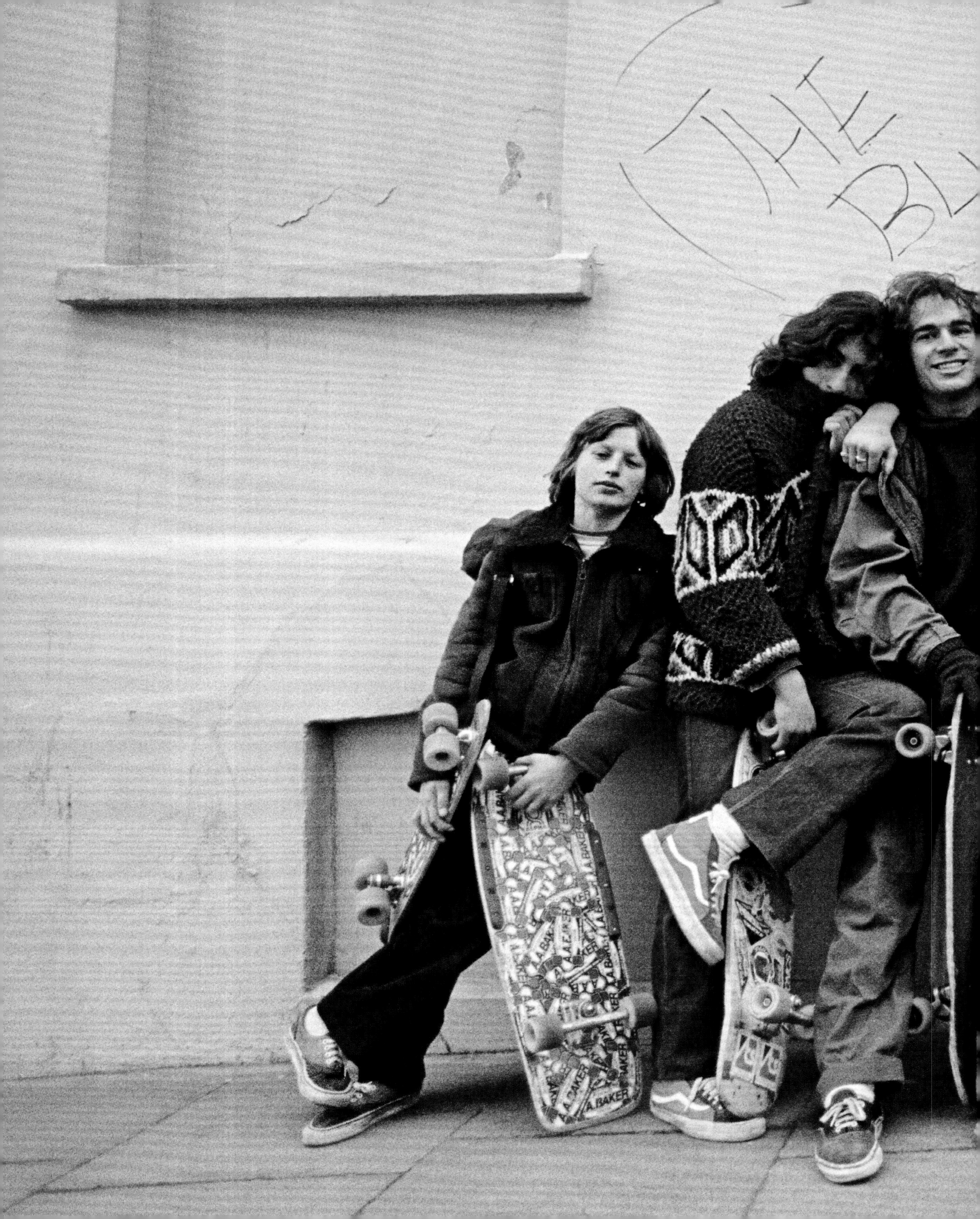
THE
A.BAKER

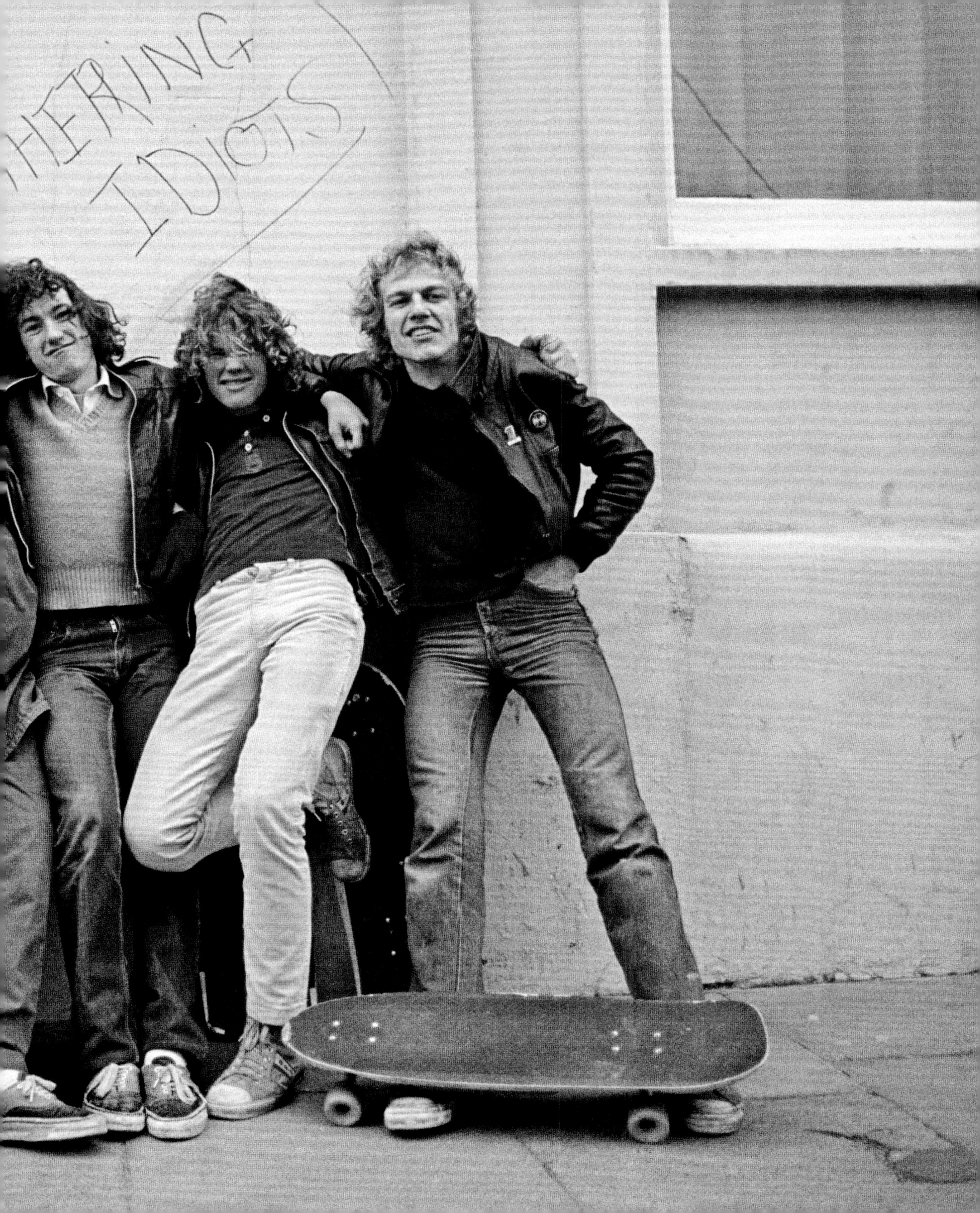
HERING+
IDIOTS

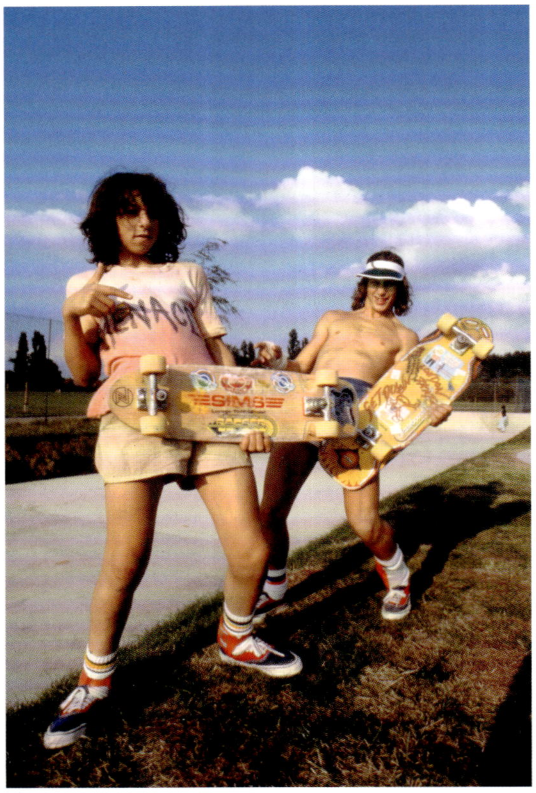

Previous spread: Brighton skate crew, 1978 (left to right): Steve Kellner, Steve Karous, Tim Dunkerley, Twiggy, Theseus Gerard and Neil Allen
Left: Karl Preston and Rodga Harvey, Harrow skatepark, 1978
Below and opposite: Brighton's 'Mad' Mark Baker, Cage skatepark, Brighton, 1978 **Opposite below:** The Pig City DIY board workshop, Brighton squat, 1978 (left to right): Neil Allen, Chris Sullivan, Steve Kellner, Steve Karous (behind), Tim Dunkerley, Mark Baker, Twiggy and Theseus Gerard **All photos:** TLB

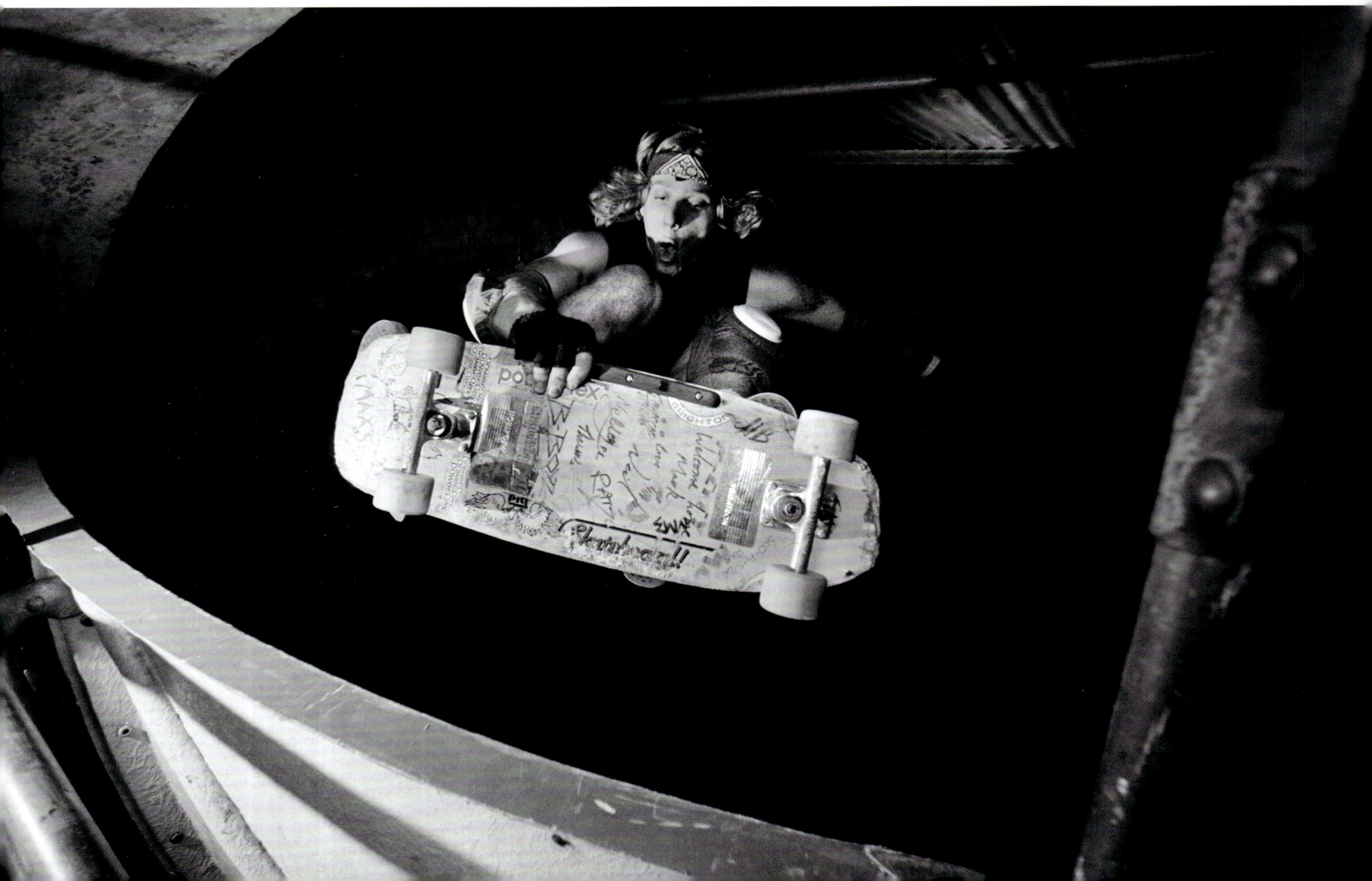

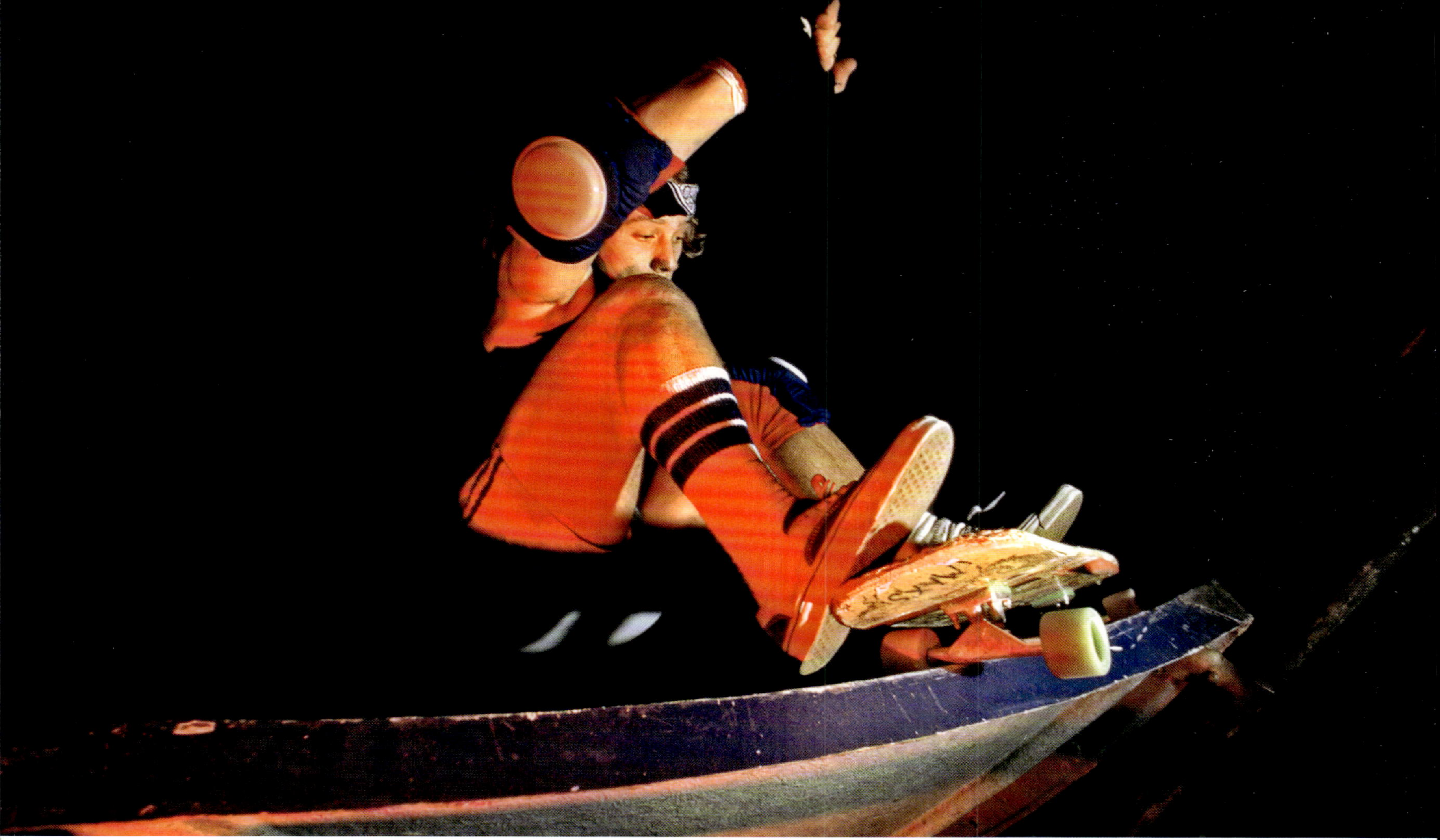

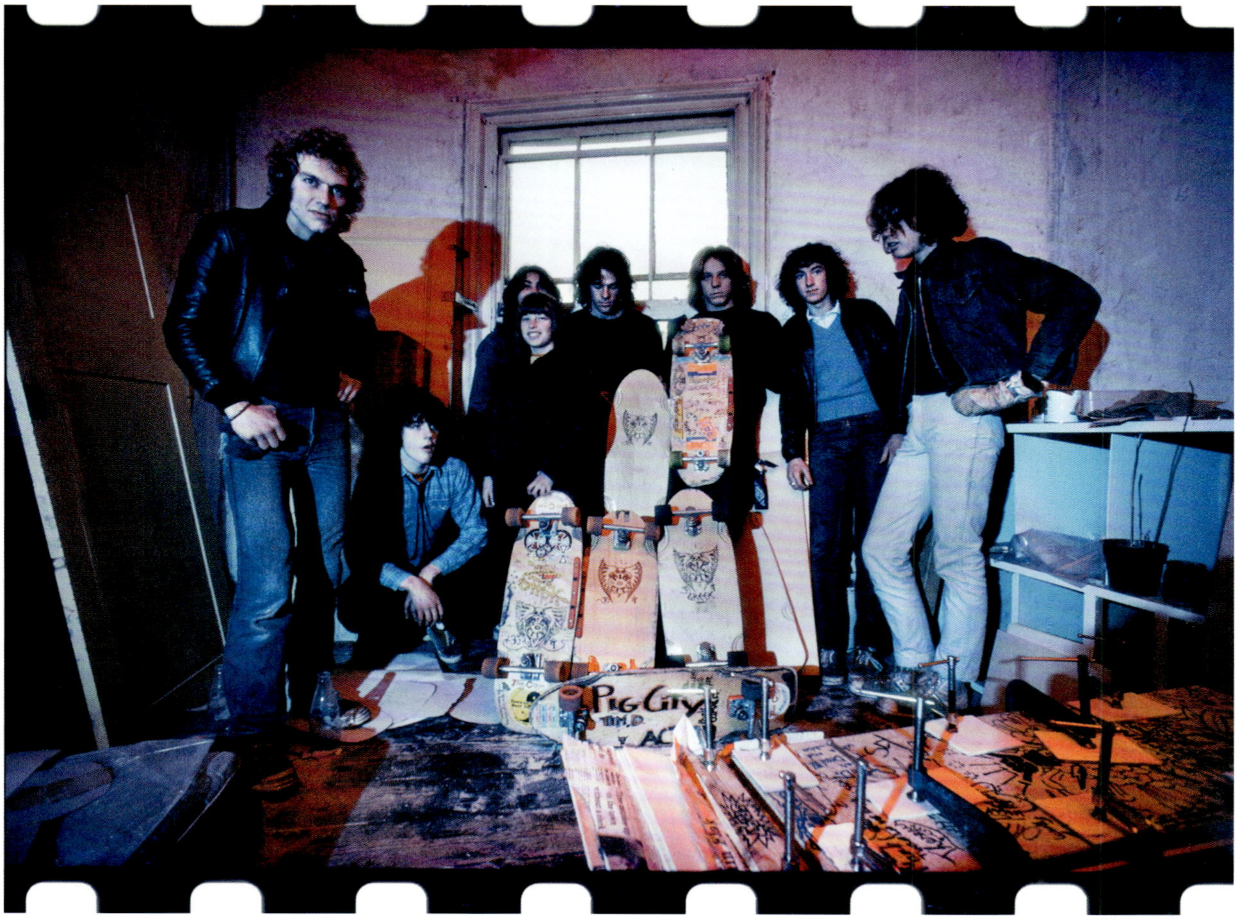
Pig City

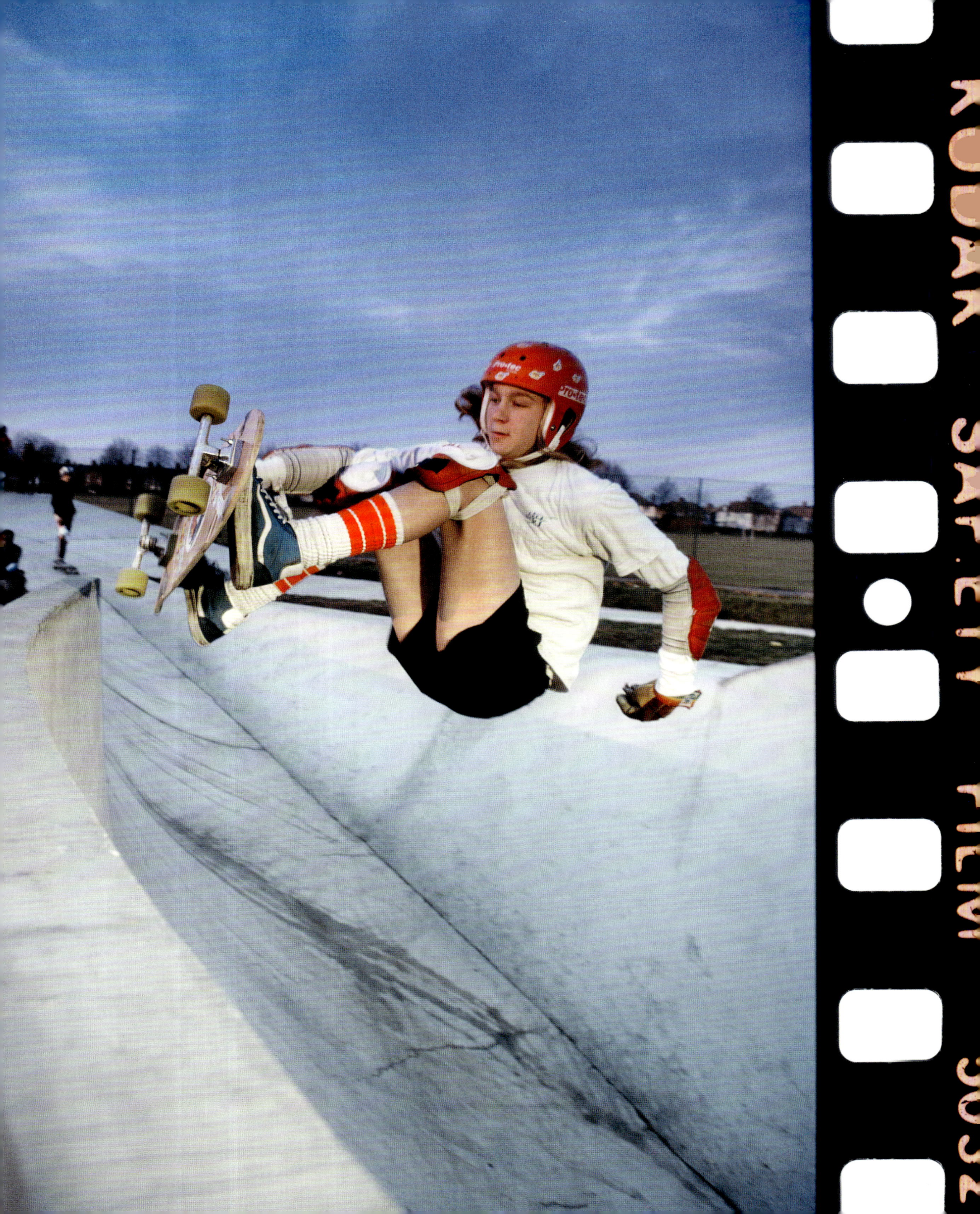
KODAK SAFETY FILM 5063

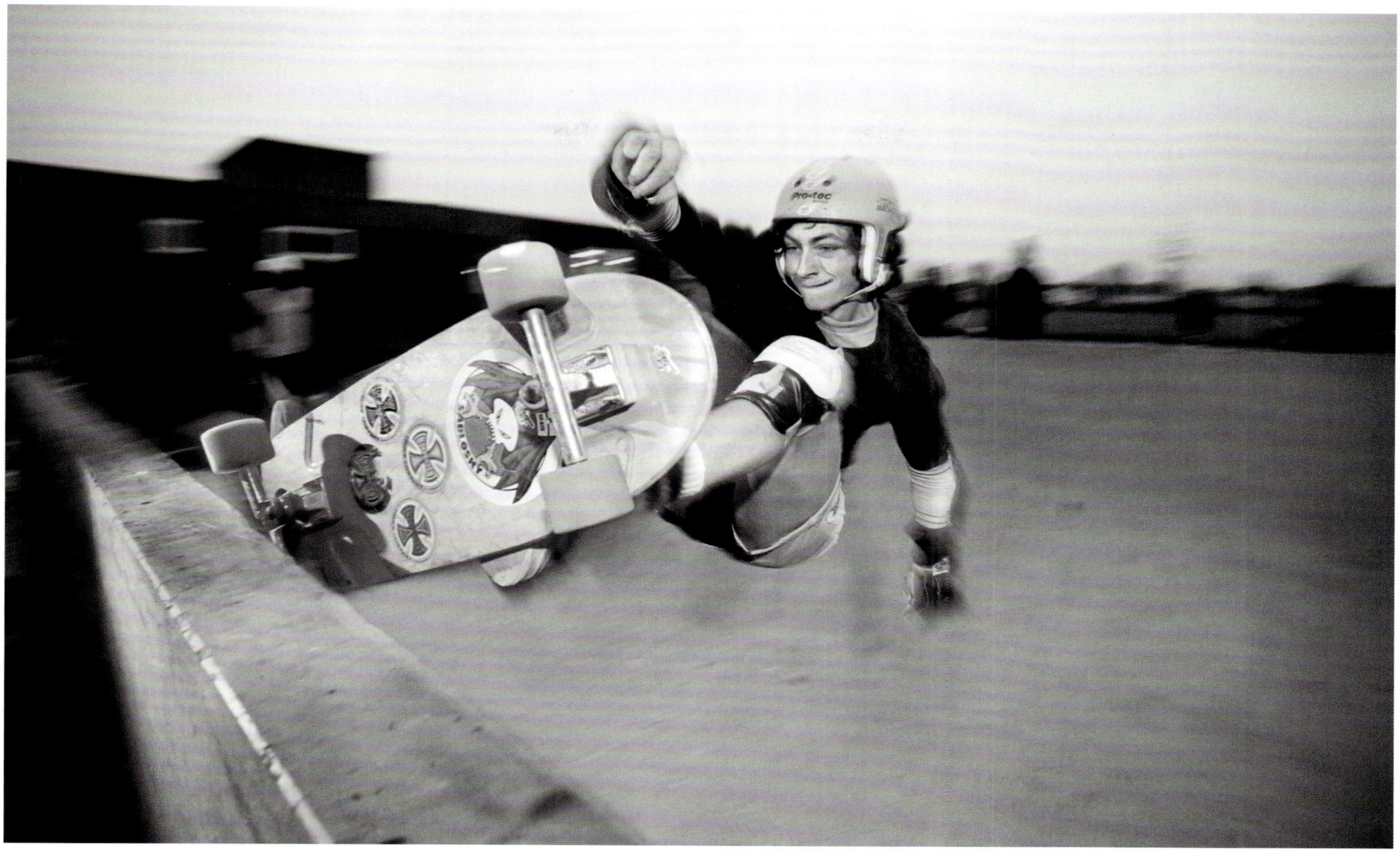

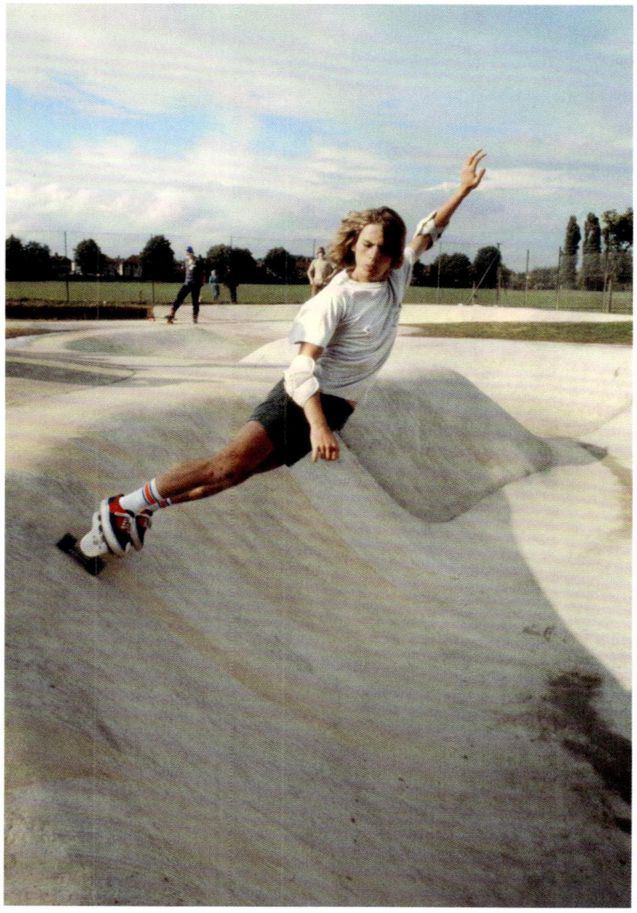

Opposite: John Sablosky in the legendary 14-foot-deep Harrow skatepark performance bowl, 1979 **Above:** Jules Gayton, Harrow skatepark, 1979
Right: Tim Panting, taking a slalom racing board through the Harrow skatepark transitions, 1978
Photos: TLB

Keith Laing, Cage skatepark, Brighton, 1978 **Photo:** TLB

‘In retrospect it had already boomed and collapsed on Boxing Day 1977’ TLB

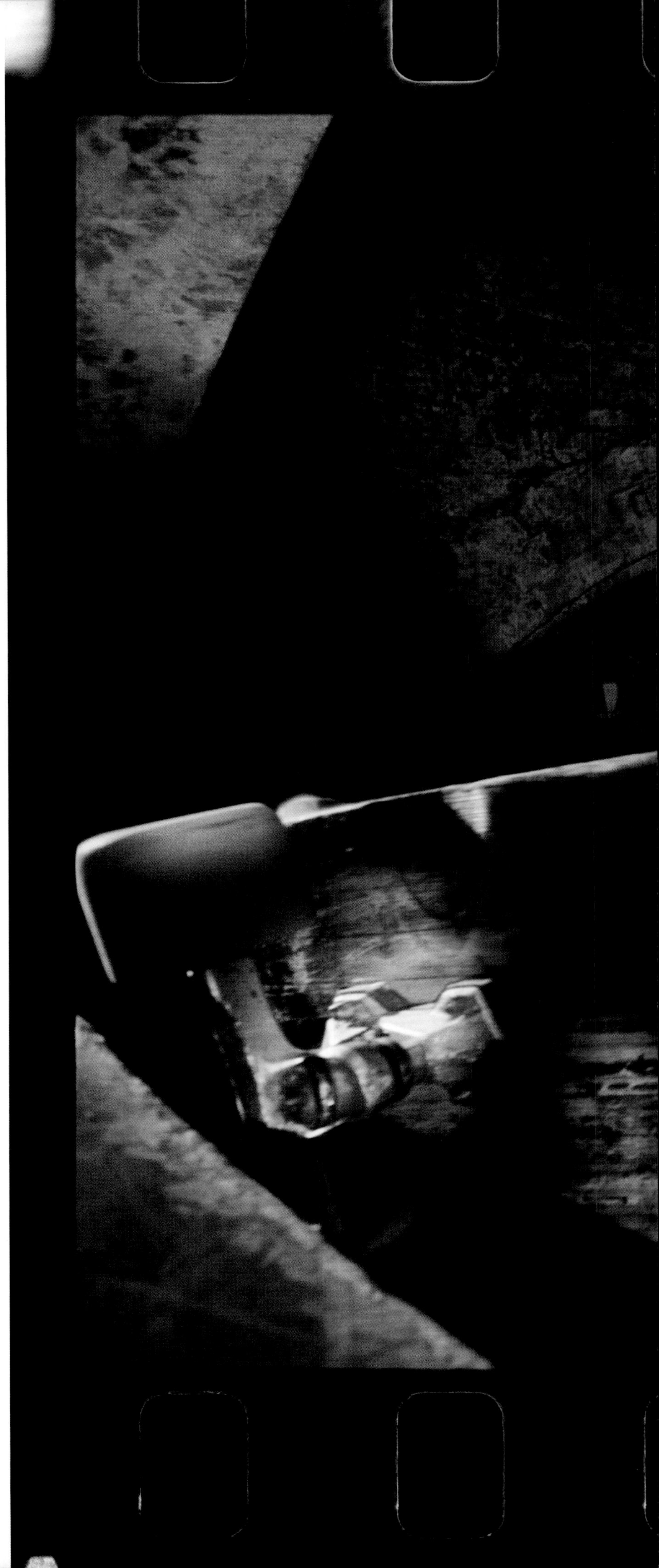

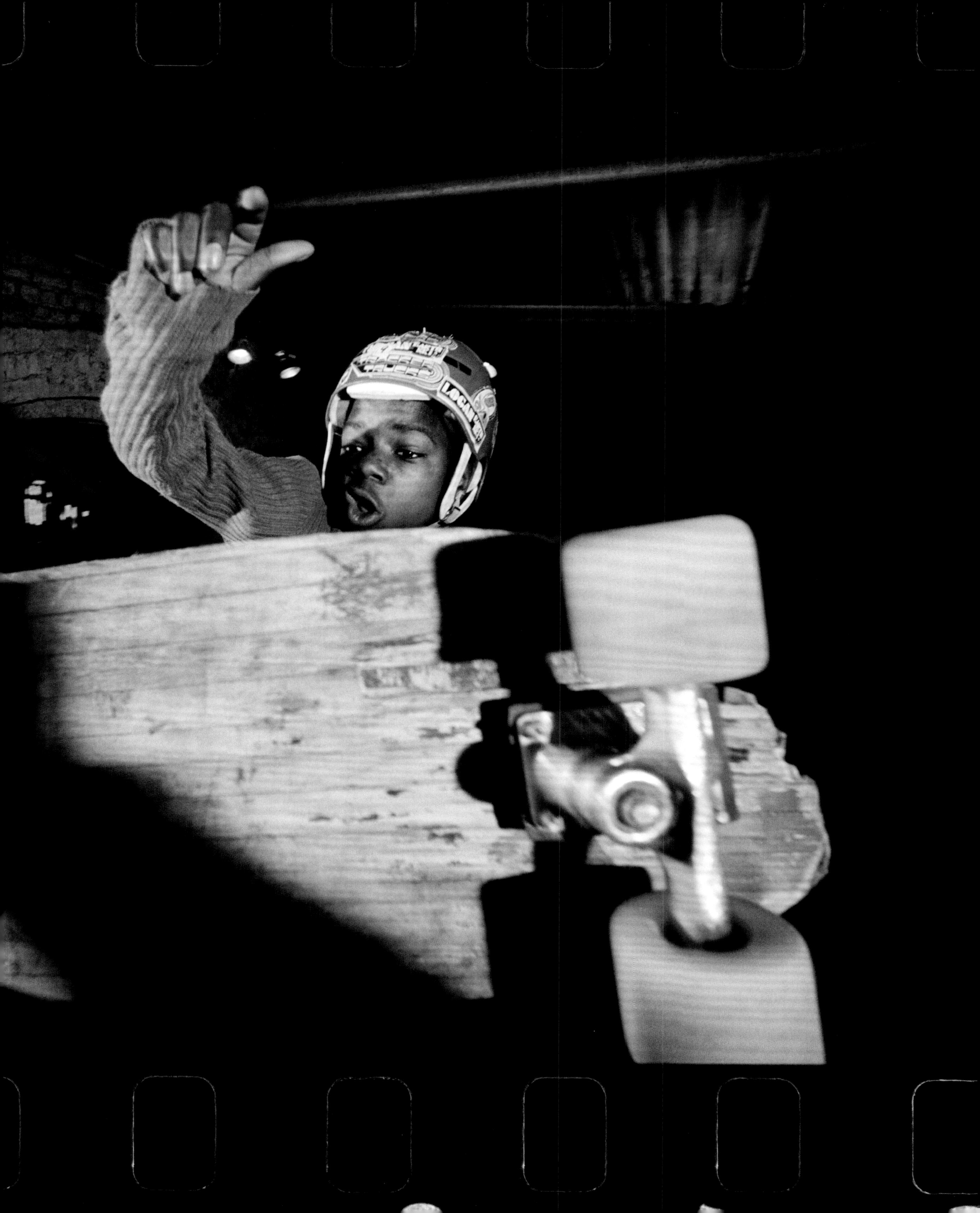

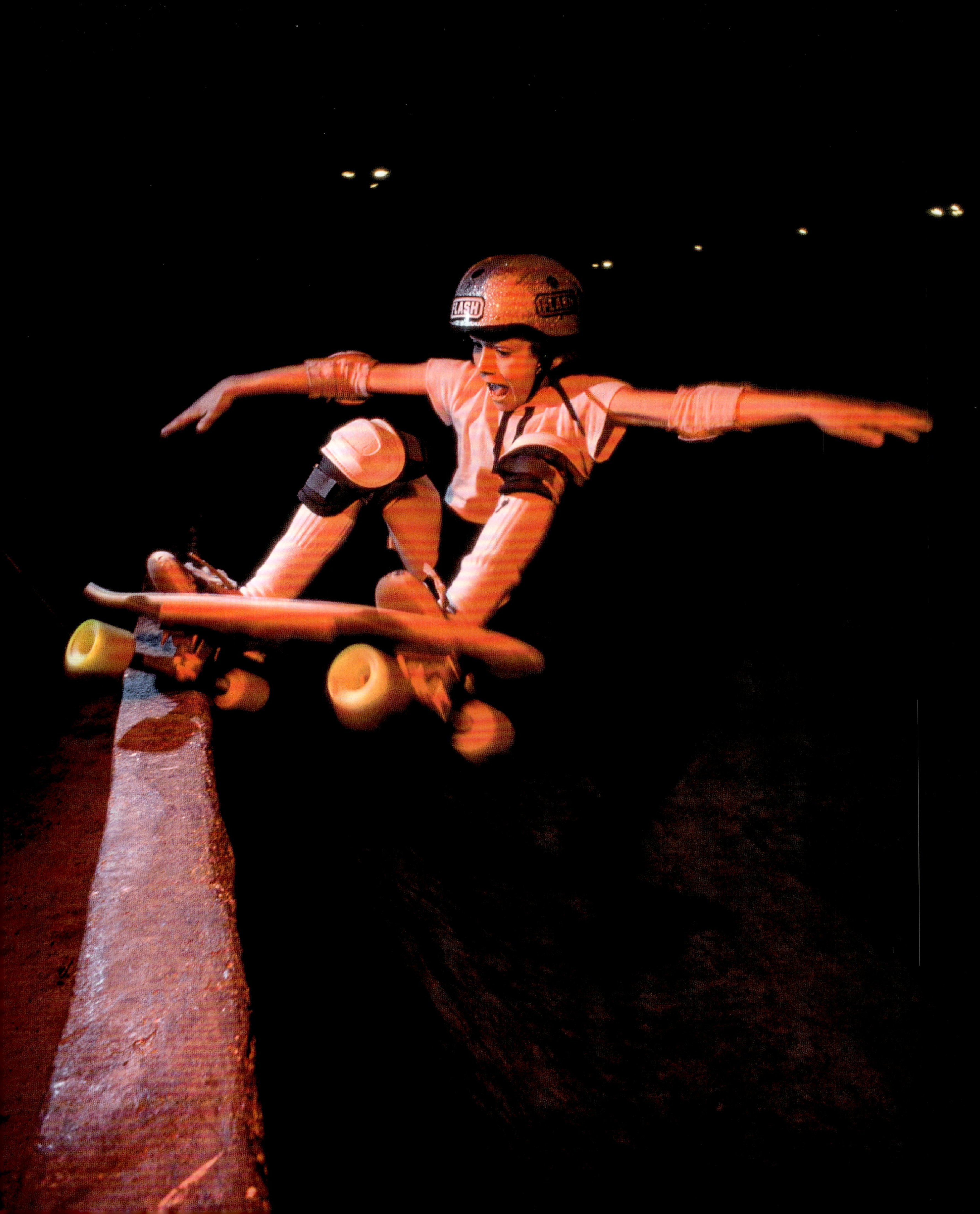
FLASH

The short lifespan of these early magazines meant that by 1979, after just 19 issues, any notion of a viable British skateboard media had been well and truly extinguished. The few remaining specialist retailers of the time drip-fed a limited supply of US publications to their customers. These expensive and hard-won magazines were a lifeline for the die-hard followers of the shrinking British skateboard scene.

As the skate business evolved at Alpine Sports and sales challenges arose, TLB found opportunities within the company to explore his photography together with hitherto untapped writing abilities:

'*Skateboard!* basically fizzled out and I was then aware of a complete absence of any channel of communication [for the skate scene]. At that point I was running the skateboard mail order department at Alpine. I started turning the humble price list (which is what got posted out to customers) into a sort of newsletter. It progressed from being just a printed list and gradually gained more and more content. At some point I started putting photographs into it.*

'With magazines gone there was an awareness of an audience out there; people who had a need for a communication channel. You'd get letters from kids, talking about what's going on in their part of the world, wanting to know what was happening. And famously what I think really tipped it over the edge was that people were ordering Rector safety pads, and the shipment didn't come on time. So we had a lot of back orders and I thought "Well I've got to tell customers what's going on", so I made a sort of mail-out that went to everyone. We had a user need, right then, which was about communication.'

Before the arrival of revolutionary desktop computers and design software in the mid to late 1980s the cost of printing and reprographics prevented the production of anything more ambitious than simple black-and-white newsletters or broadsheets. Despite the simplicity of these very basic documents they were a lifeline for the dwindling number of skateboarders keen to stay connected and informed about other satellites of the culture they had become so immersed in.

'They were made on my weekends and evenings, produced on an electronic typewriter, so if I made a mistake I had to Tippex it out or re-type it. I was literally typing all this stuff up myself. I did the typesetting and the layout. I had my whole family folding these up for posting—they did it, it wasn't Alpine.

'Issue 4 may be the first time we put photographs in it. For the text, I would tell encapsulated stories of things that happened, and if you were actually to monitor the amount of time taken, all the other stuff took up far more effort than photography. But what I wanted to do was take the photographs—it was all about the photographs... and going to visit places. What I really liked very much about this period was clocking up insane mileage every week, just going all over the place and seeing huge parts of the country.

'In the RAD days, before the web was invented, I'd already started experimenting with online skate stuff via Usenet. After RAD, one of the first things we did when I joined the pioneering web team at State51 was to publish the online directory of places to skate as "Knowhere". But the roots of all that were in these Alpine newsletters. So at this point, back in '79 or whenever, I'm already starting to compile a list of all the skate places. There was no other way of getting information, particularly in the British scene at that time.

'In retrospect I recognise now how limited information was. There was this scene that I was part of and that seemed to be everything that was going on at the time; it felt like a tiny, tiny world. Although in reality, even in the UK, that world was slightly bigger than I knew—communication was so hard that pockets could exist in isolation.'

The late 1970s skateboarding downturn saw a winding-down of skate-related business for Alpine. They had begun diversifying into BMX equipment alongside skateboards—the greater income soon coming from bike sales. In order to return the focus to their original mountain sports business, a decision was made, involving a small group of staff fiercely committed to skateboarding, to physically break away the skateboard and BMX business. Taking the name Alpine Action (from the TLB-authored store newsletters) the new specialist shop opened in Notting Hill Gate, London in 1981.

Alpine Action quickly established itself as arguably the hippest skateboard outlet of the time, due in part to the disappearing competition and certainly due to the personas of those involved in the business. They were aided by sharp graphic design and modest but savvy direct marketing to their loyal fans. Ads frequently made a play on the fact that they were selling products for an activity already deemed old hat or even dead: 'Skate with the UN-DEAD' and 'The only shop in which to be seen dead' ran two notable headlines. Although not directly connected to the shop—remaining at the original Alpine Sports until bankruptcy struck—TLB was always in close contact with the staff, stepping in to take photographs when required.

As the 1980s unfolded, Alpine Action, like the few other stores of its kind dotted around the country, had a new, growing market for BMX and rollerskate equipment. In some ways, a reversal of history had occurred—bike shops keen to cash-in on a new craze had been some of the earliest stockists of skateboards when they first appeared. The change was in part due to a real need to bolster falling revenues from skateboard sales but also because these imported US cultures (following hard on the heels of skateboards) had collided with, and were beginning to share, the same spaces physically and mentally as skateboarding. It's perhaps the earliest phase of what by the mid-1990s came to be known as 'extreme sports culture'—the X Games seed.

BMX bikes were the latest hip import from America and a necessary accessory for city and suburban thrill seekers keeping up with the cool in the lively, shifting sands of 1980s outsider youth culture. As their local skateparks had closed or their fellow riders drifted away, many skateboarders had switched to these new imported bikes in their continued search for an adrenaline rush. A sometimes fluid, sometimes confrontational relationship between skateboarding and BMX evolved throughout the decade. But it was a fertile mix—arguably the first phase of a cross-pollination that bubbled up in the 1970s, evolved during the 1980s and was certainly the cocktail that informed the development and early content of *RAD* magazine.

Opposite: John Turner, Rolling Thunder, London, 1979 **Photo:** TLB
Below: Alpine Action newsletters, 1979–81

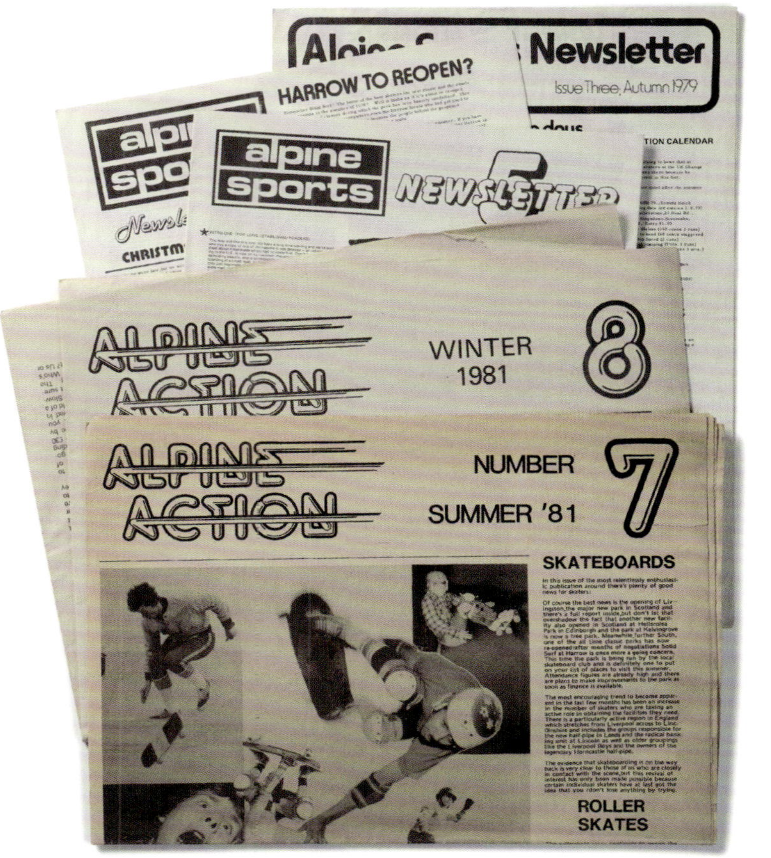

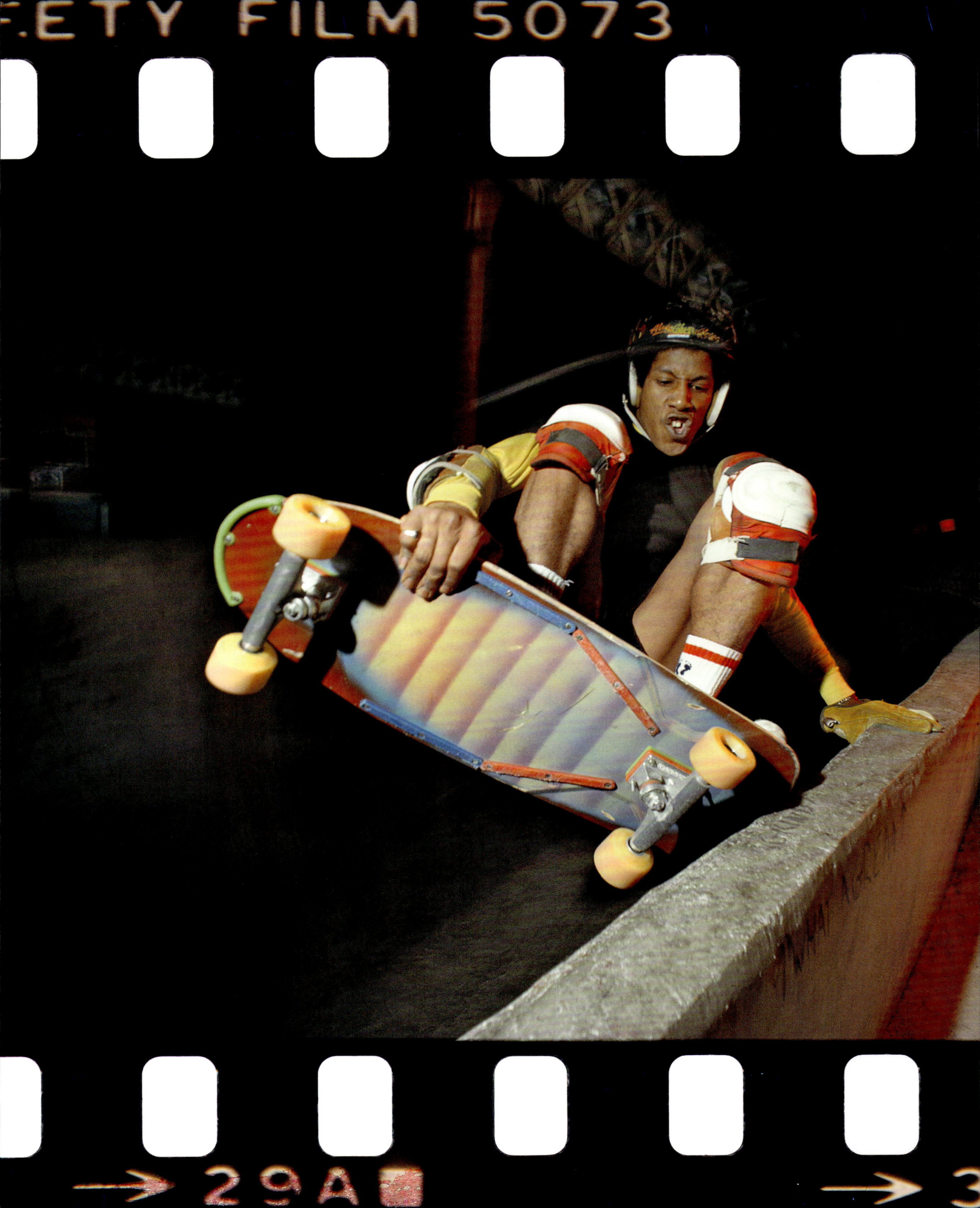

ETY FILM 5073
29A

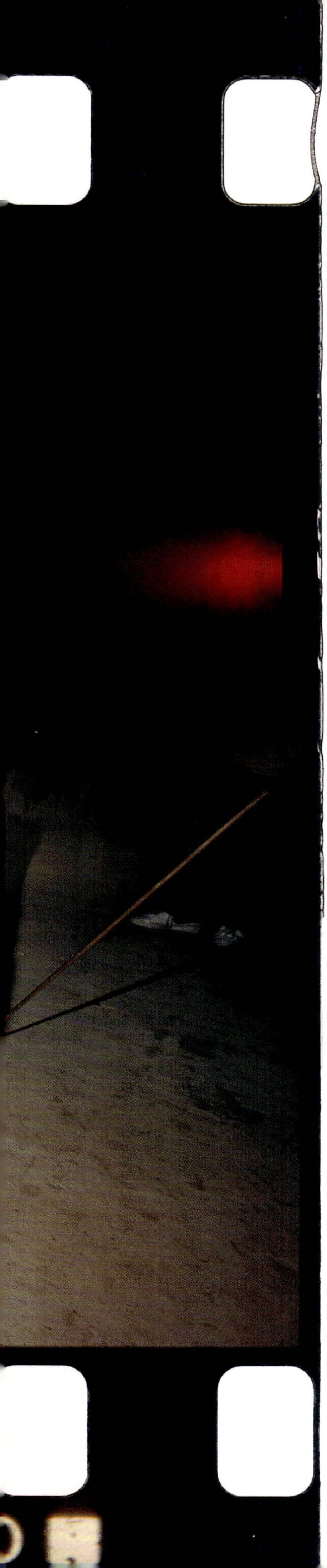

'There was this scene that I was part of and that seemed to be everything that was going on at the time; it felt like a tiny, tiny world' TLB

As the skate downturn bit, TLB's lens made a gradual shift towards BMX, beginning when the publisher of *Skateboard!* magazine pulled that title and TLB was offered a gig to photograph off-road motorbikes.

'So off I went on my first off-road motorbike shoot with this guy jumping over a tree, and I put up coloured flash guns and got out my 17mm lens; the pictures came out all lit up in colour—really stupidly close. So there was a little period there where I used to do mad off-road motorbike stuff using the same techniques I'd developed photographing skateboarding.' TLB

From here it was a short step to covering races for *BMX Action Bike*—the publication that would eventually morph into *RAD* magazine. These foundational experiences were an important phase of Leighton-Boyce's evolution into a significant cultural documentarian, advocate of skateboarding and eventual magazine editor and chief photographer. Despite the twists and turns of an evolving career as a photographer, TLB continued—undeterred and unpaid—to shoot skateboarding when and where he could. He also continued his efforts to document and promote the small British scene through any channels available—continuing the vital job that he'd started with the Alpine newsletters, recording and communicating to the disparate band of skate fanatics.

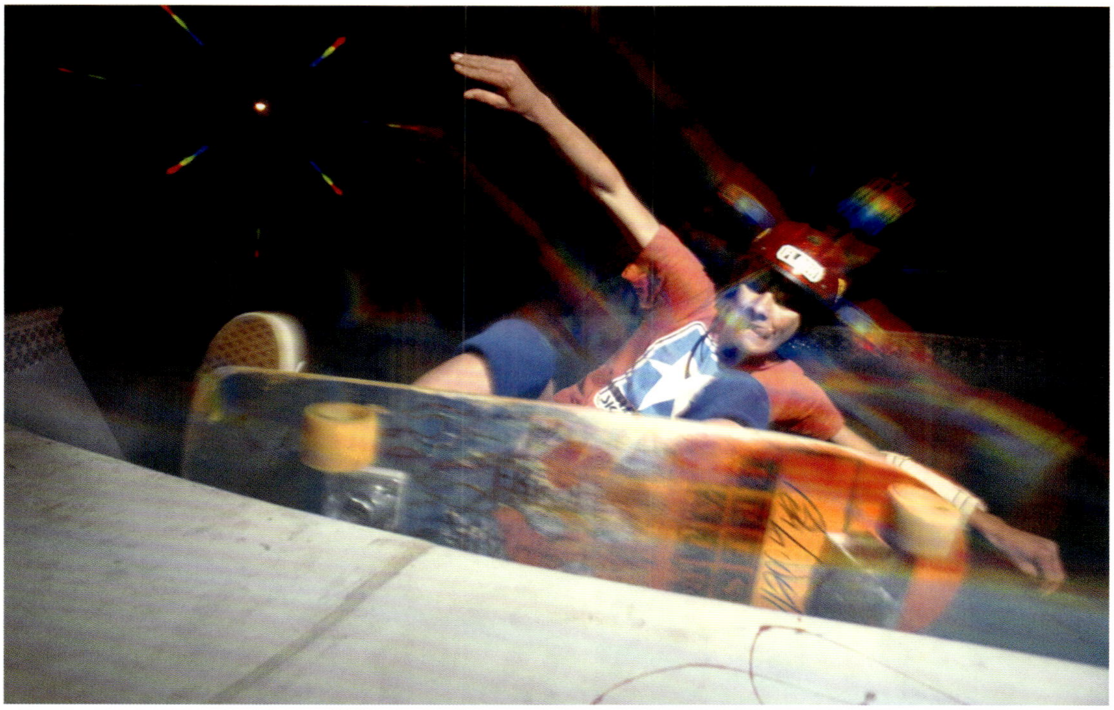

Left: Derek 'Jingles' Jhingoree, Rolling Thunder skatepark, London, 1979 **Above:** John Finch, Mad Dog Bowl skatepark, London, 1978 **Photos:** TLB

'I was interested in time and space. Flow and arcs. I was doing multiple exposure and flash and blur pictures of my friends to try to show time in a still picture before skateboarding. I also liked the shapes of urban architecture. I was taking pictures of the South Bank before skateboarding, particularly the Hayward Gallery when the high-level walk-ways were still open.'

TLB

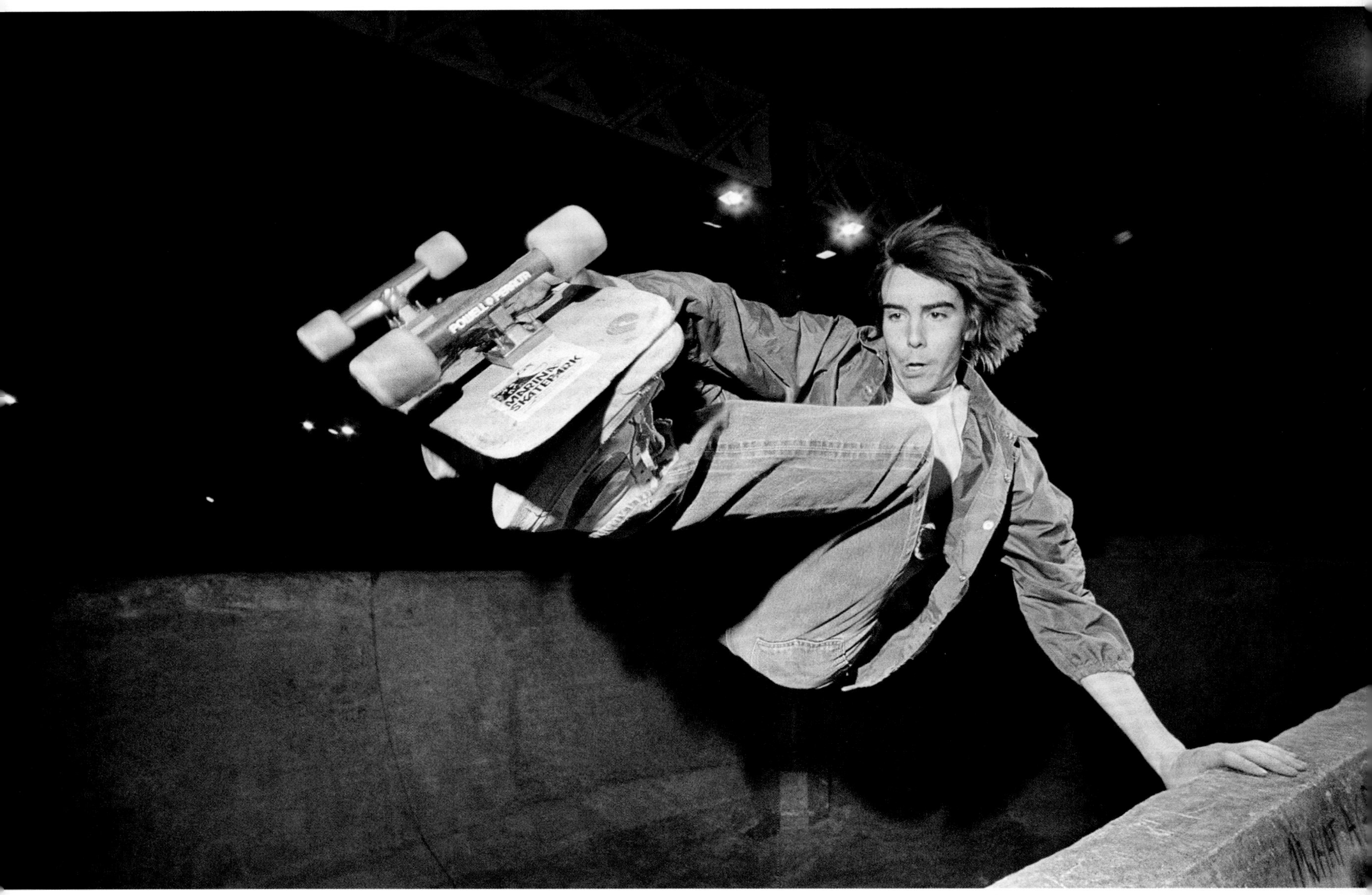

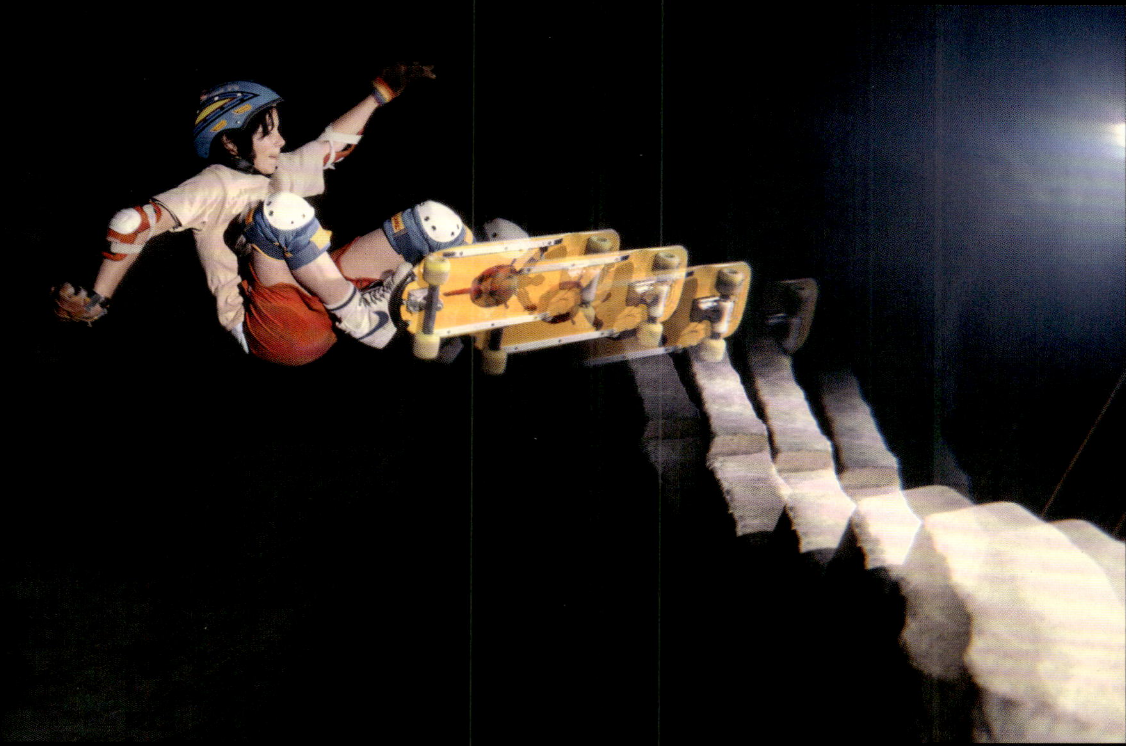

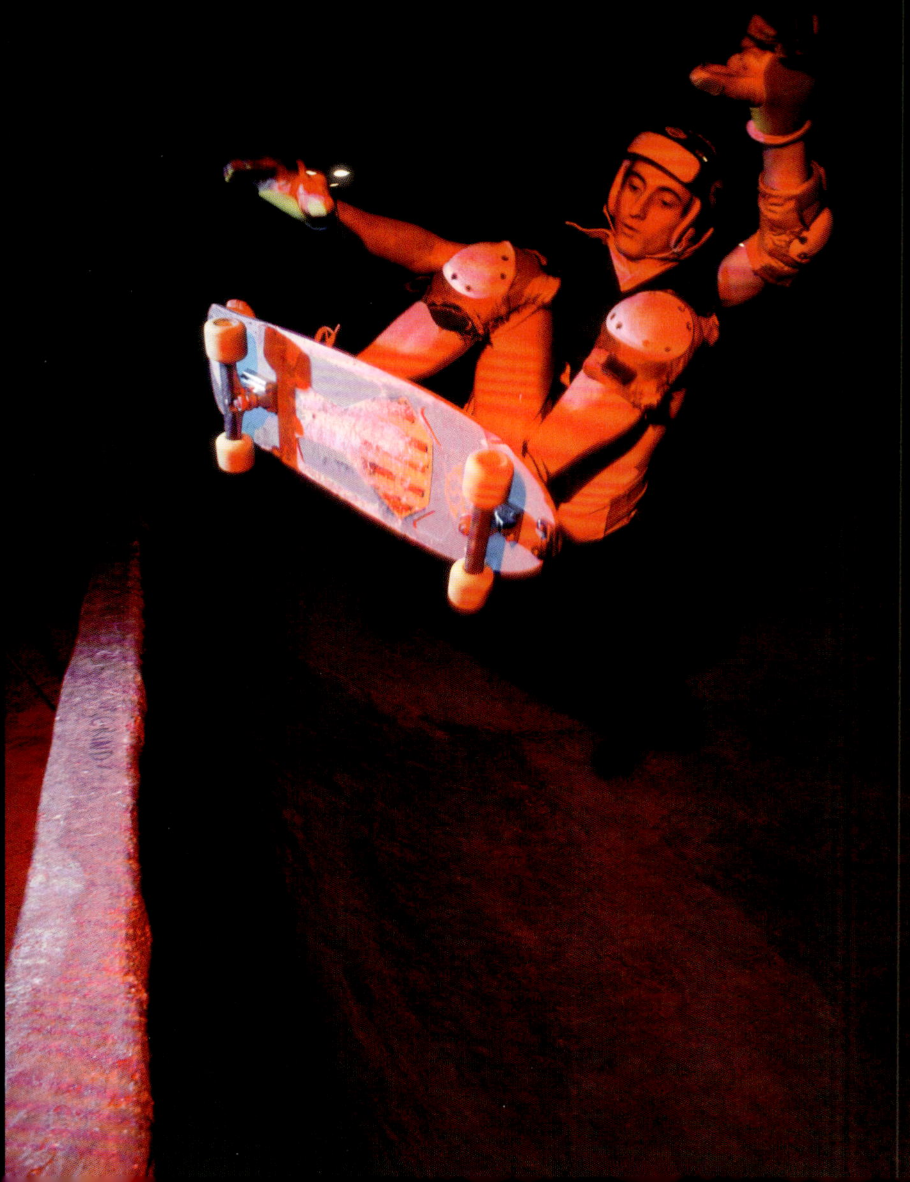

Opposite: Jeremy Henderson
Above: Rolling Thunder skatepark
Left: Brian Murray, Rolling Thunder, London, 1979 **Photos:** TLB

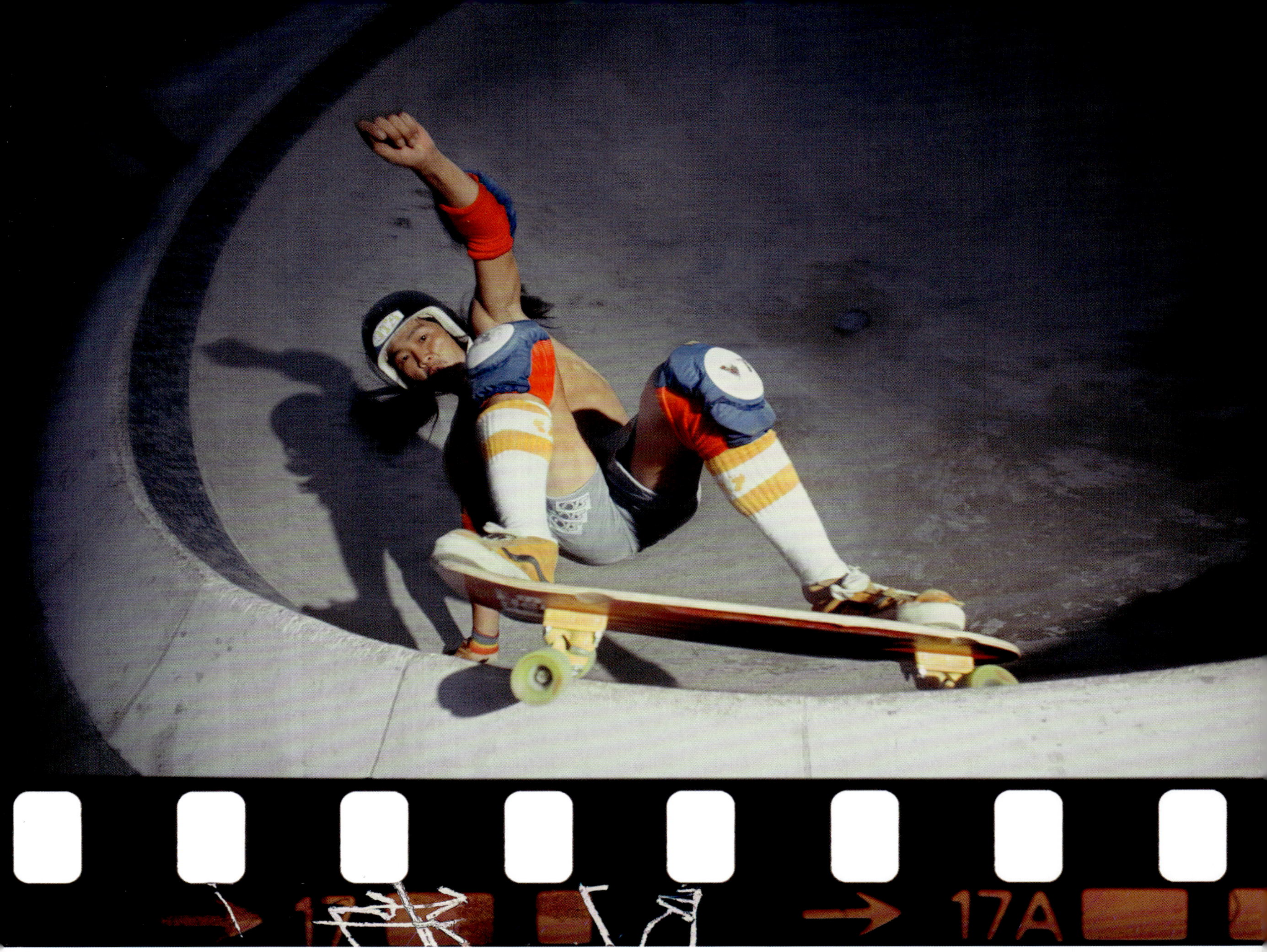

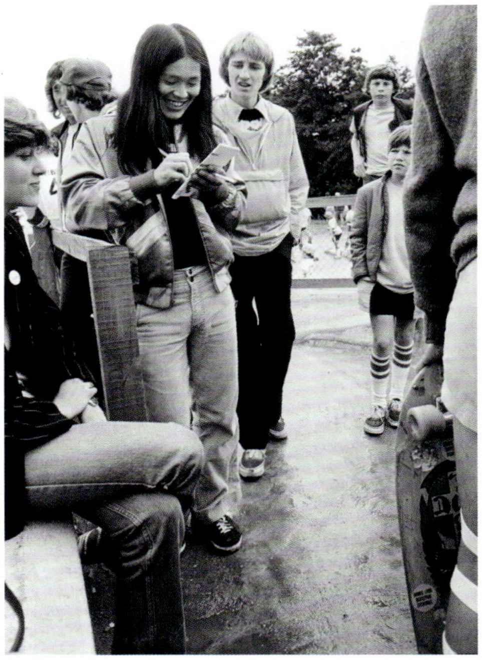

'The dynamics of action photography have helped to popularise the sport and given the young skaters their own heroes' *Skateboard Kings*, BBC documentary, 1978

A steady flow of American professional skateboarders visited Britain from 1977 onwards. The influential Shogo Kubo came in 1979 and stayed for a year; declared 'MIA' by his sponsor **Opposite and below:** Harrow skatepark, 1979 **Opposite below:** Skate Star skatepark, Guildford, 1979 **Photos:** TLB

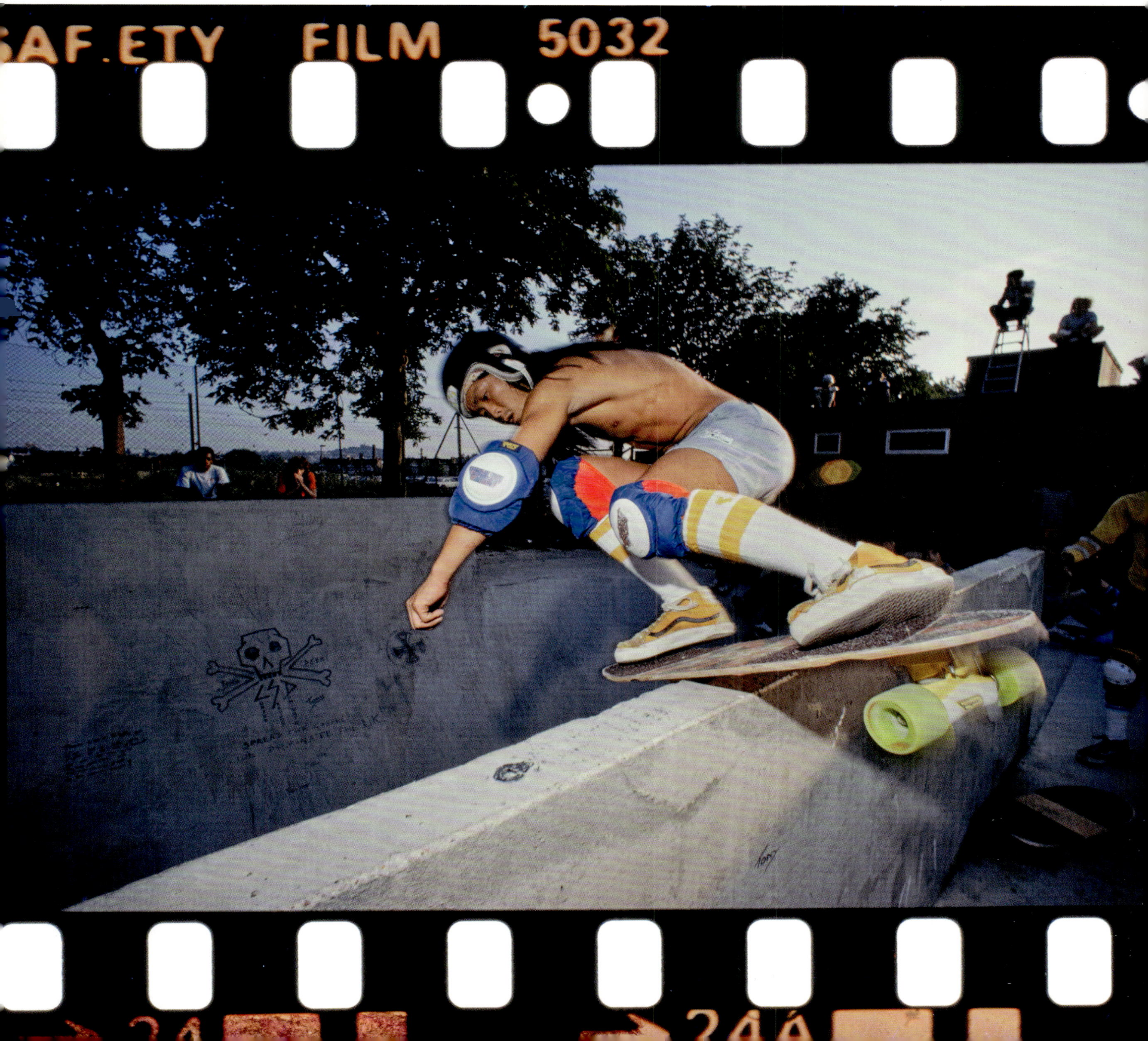

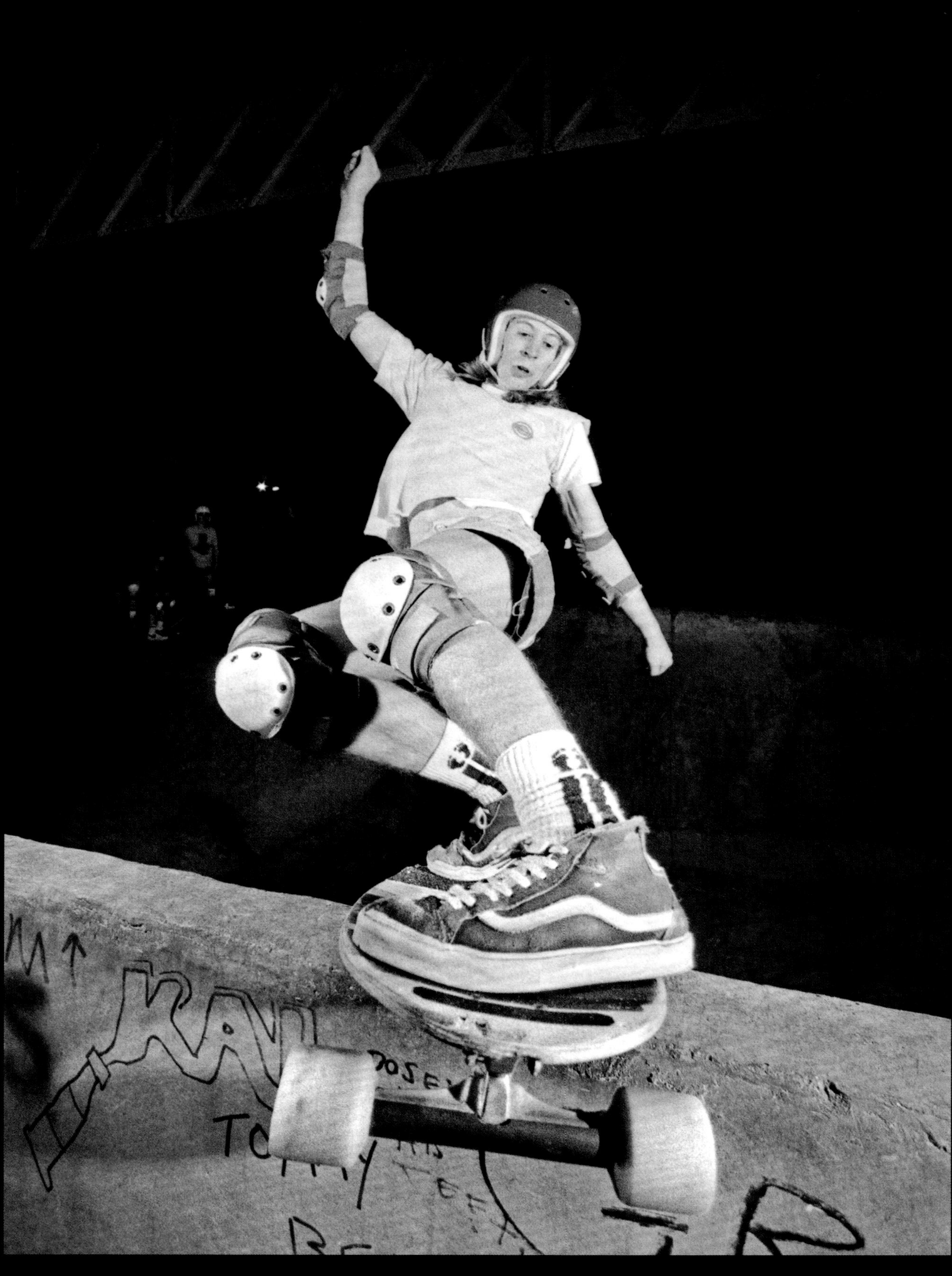

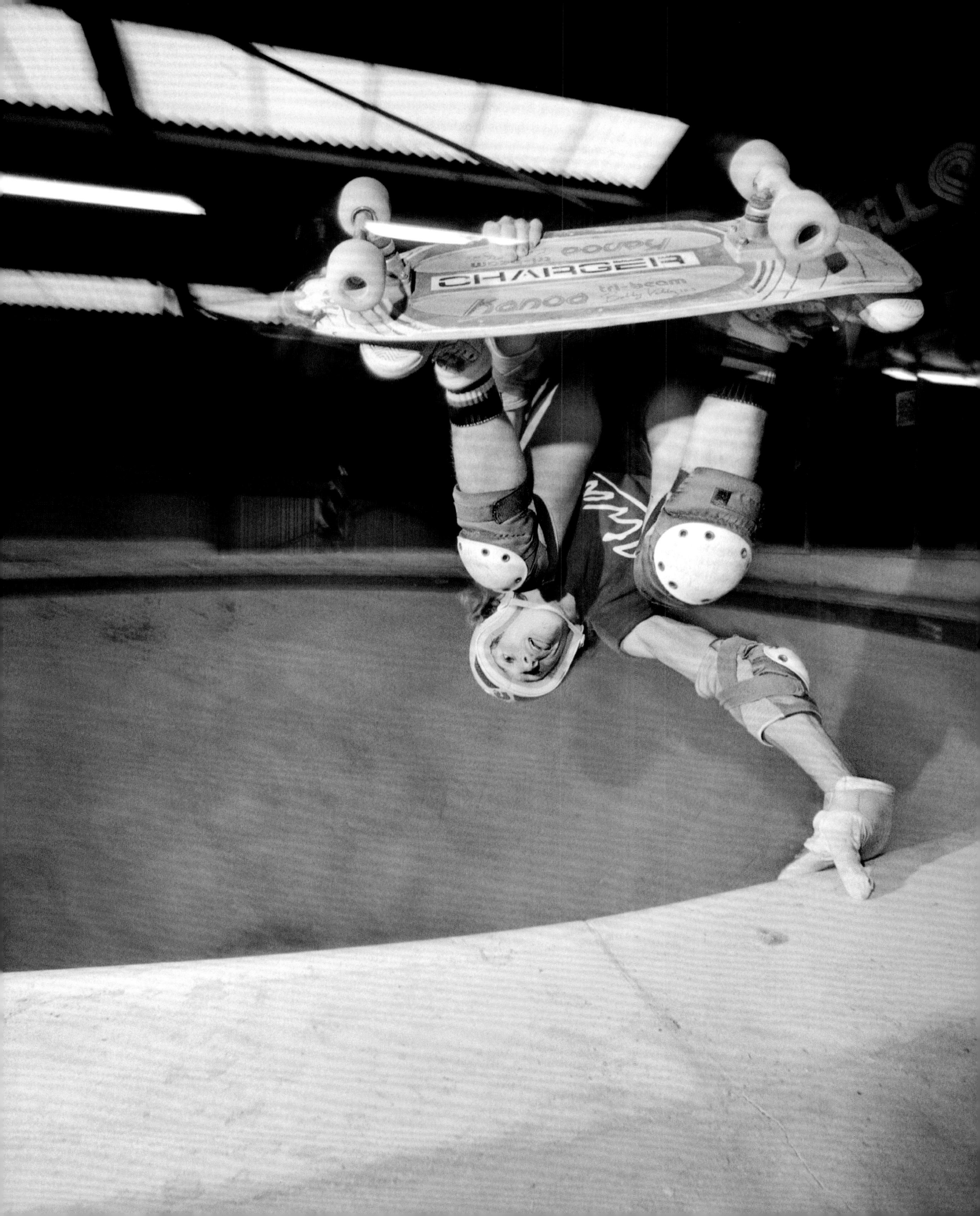
CHARGER
Kanoa
tri-beam

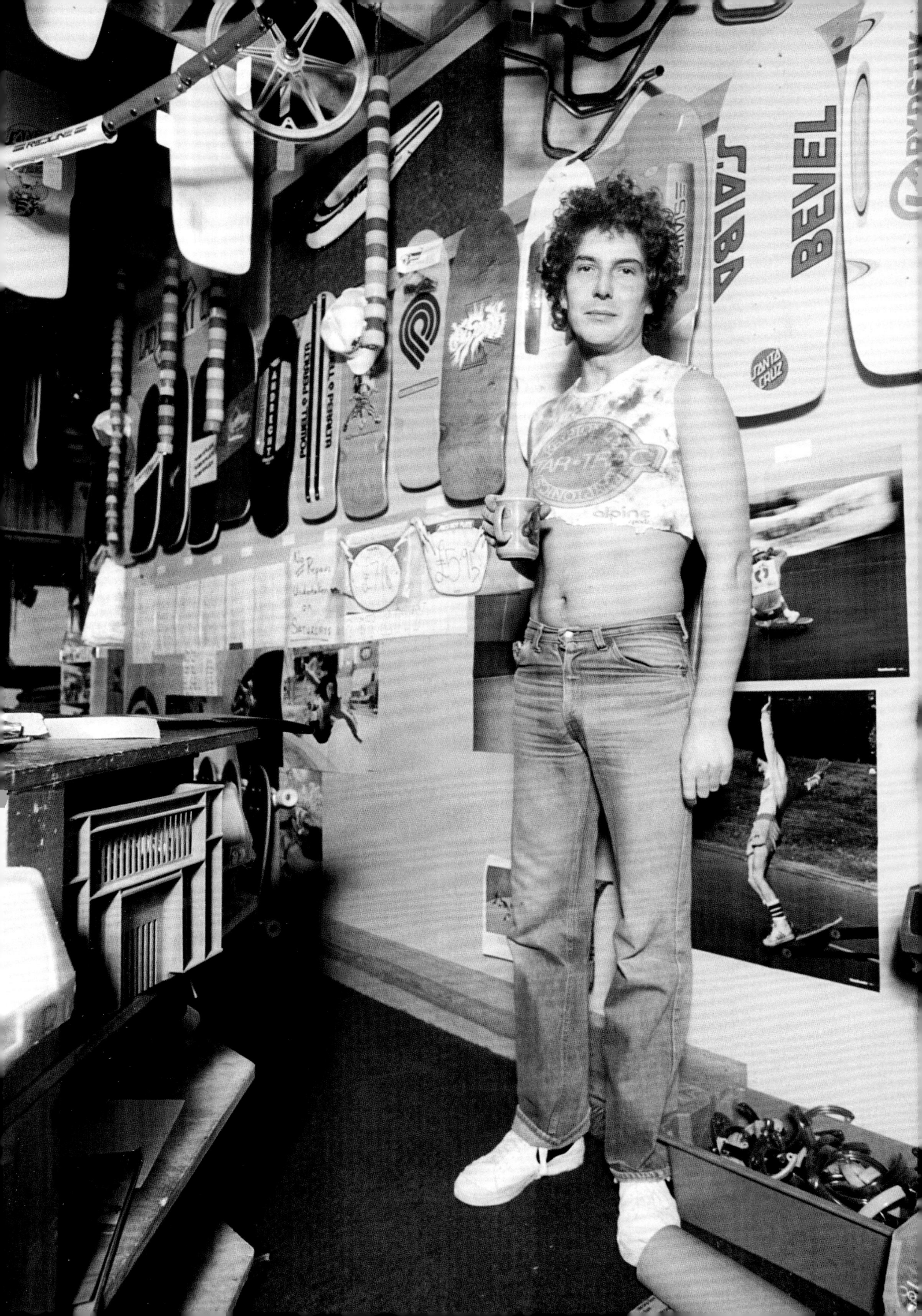
S.ALBA
BEVEL
SANTA CRUZ
No Repairs Undertaken on Saturdays

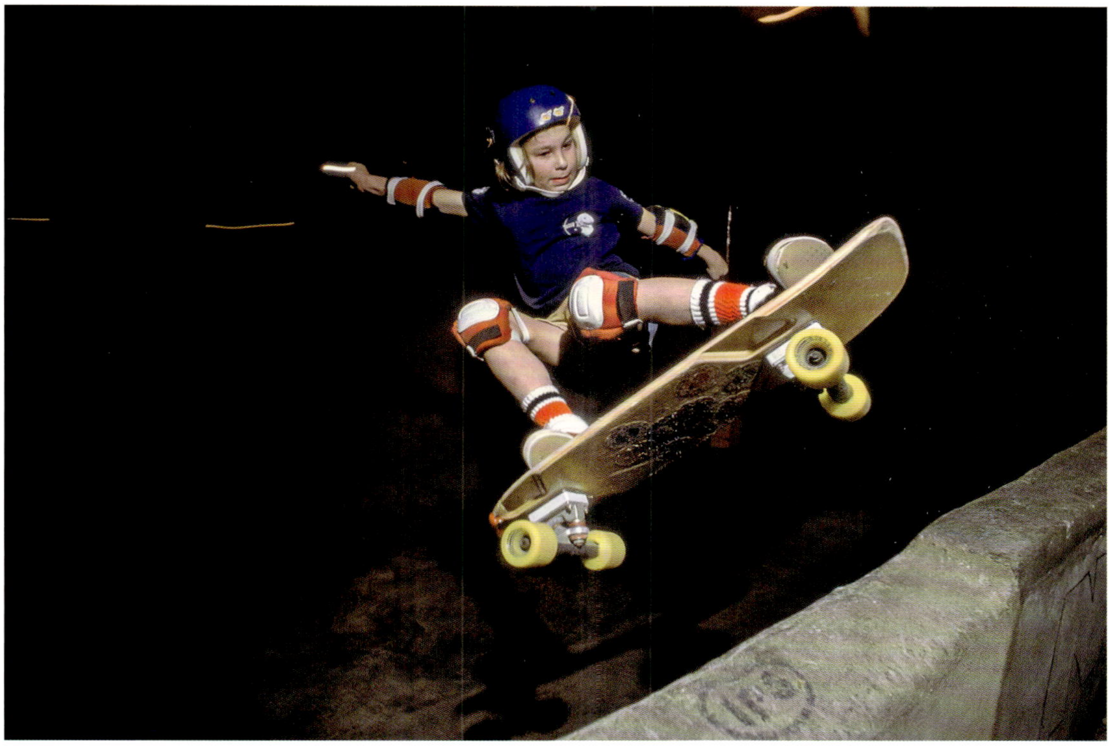

Previous spread left: Neil Harding, Rolling Thunder, London, 1979, and **right:** Steve Gratton, Colne skatepark, Lancashire, 1979 **Opposite:** Alpine Action partner Ray Abbott, London, 1980 **Right:** Mark 'Floater' Maunders, Rolling Thunder, London, 1979 **Below:** Knebworth skatepark, 1979 (left to right): Mark Abrook, unknown, Jeff Lockwood **All photos:** TLB

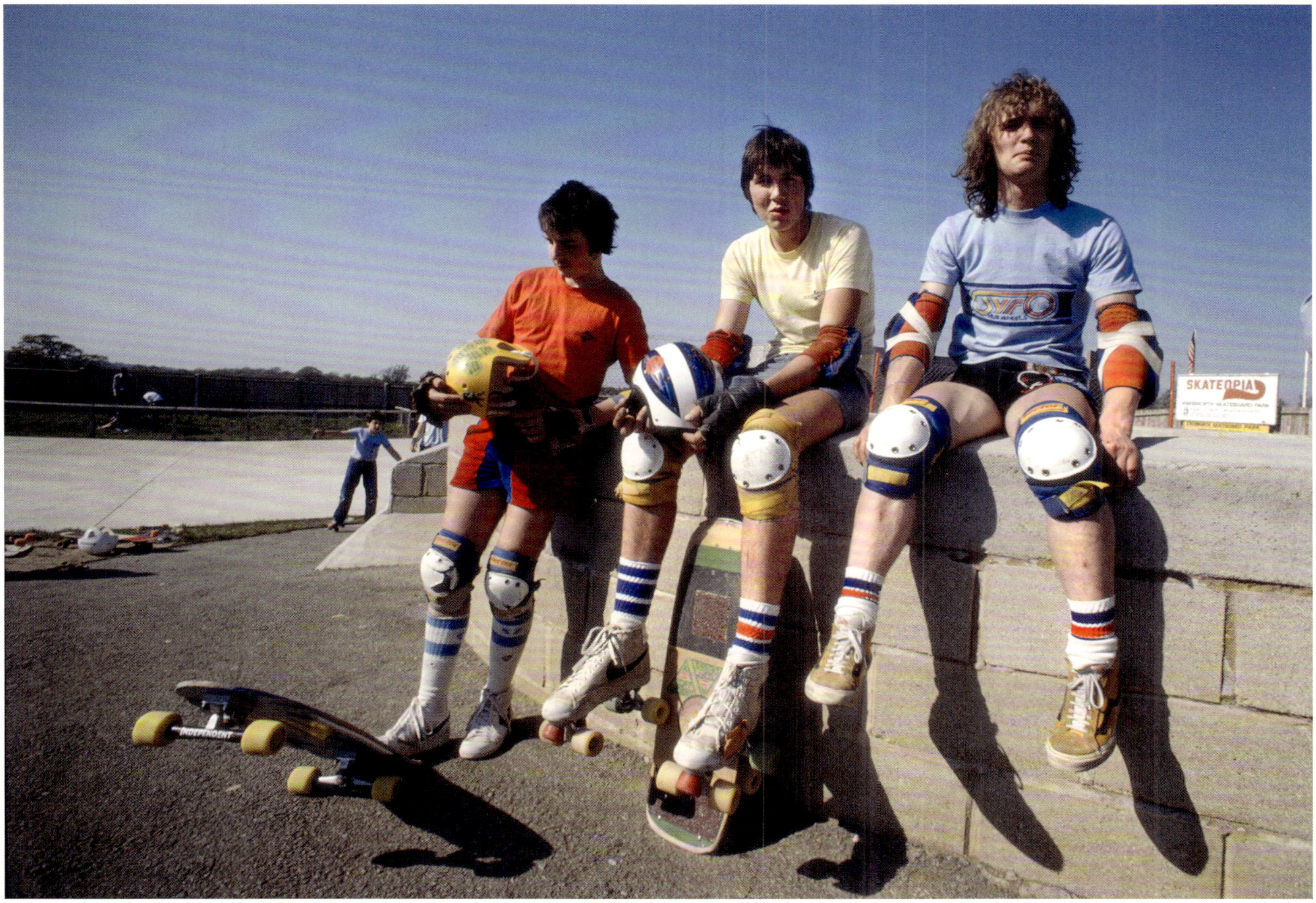

DEATH & REBIRTH

SCENES AND ZINES 1980–1986

'After Skateboard! *died at the end of the '70s, that left a really small group of people who continued a chapter of development, and that formed the British scene. That seems very important to me. I think the fact that skateboarding died out on a mainstream level is the thing that helped it boil down and form into an underground culture. Maybe that wouldn't have happened if it had stayed massively popular.'* Ged Wells

Writers, artists and musicians of the 1960s generation often cite the end of 'deference'—the submission to the elders of a higher, more cultured society and social order—as a liberating force to their ground-breaking creativity. By the 1970s this sentiment of new freedoms had begun to infiltrate a developing culture of urban physical pursuits. No longer beholden to sporting exploits in the 'playing fields of England', once firmly rooted in empire and the public school system, the 'kids' were busily inventing new forms of performative physical expression and 'combat' (as opposed to competition). Skateboarding, BMX, breakdancing and all their off-shoots emerged in the late 1970s to become a vital crucible of creativity for the youth of the 1980s and into the subsequent decades.

Circling around the edge of these creative physical and cultural experiments were parents and adults seeking to shape skateboarding through the norms of competition and organised 'sport' (and so it continues). The more business minded among them sought to profit from the organised constructs by establishing commercial skateparks and manufacturing companies; but it was the 'kids' themselves who were shaping the new frontiers and developing the forms. And it was the magazines that disseminated the new standards they were setting.

TLB sought to hold up a mirror to the groundbreaking activities of the skateboard scene and his efforts to document and promote skateboarding meant that by the early '80s he had become a well-known, integral part of the wider British skateboard scene. Intentionally or not, he now found himself as a sometime spokesperson for the culture; credentials which propelled him into a short-lived tenure as secretary of the fledgling English Skateboard Association (ESA). Despite a natural aversion to competitive sports, TLB found himself in the slightly uncomfortable position of actively promoting a national circuit of skateboard contests. These events were, in reality, little more than social get-togethers for the die-hards under the guise of competition. Happily for TLB the experience was short-lived and he passed on responsibility for the competitive circuit—which flourished during the 1980s—to the more enthusiastic guidance of Derry Thompson.

Competitions in Britain took their structure and inspiration from the skatepark events covered in the US skate magazines of the late '70s and early '80s. The US events were in some ways an attempt at drumming up interest and patronage for their own economically challenged skateparks, but the competitions also helped to hold together the dwindling scene—attempting to arrest any further decline in skateboarding's popularity.

Just as in the US, competetive events in Britain took place across the nation, quickly forming the backbone for a shrinking, tight-knit scene. The annual skate contest circuit provided a place to meet, catch up, talk shop, forge friendships, revel in their culture and commit the action and lifestyle to film. Despite the unquestionable usefulness and pleasure in pulling skaters together to celebrate their fanaticism, TLB's antipathy to organised competition endured.

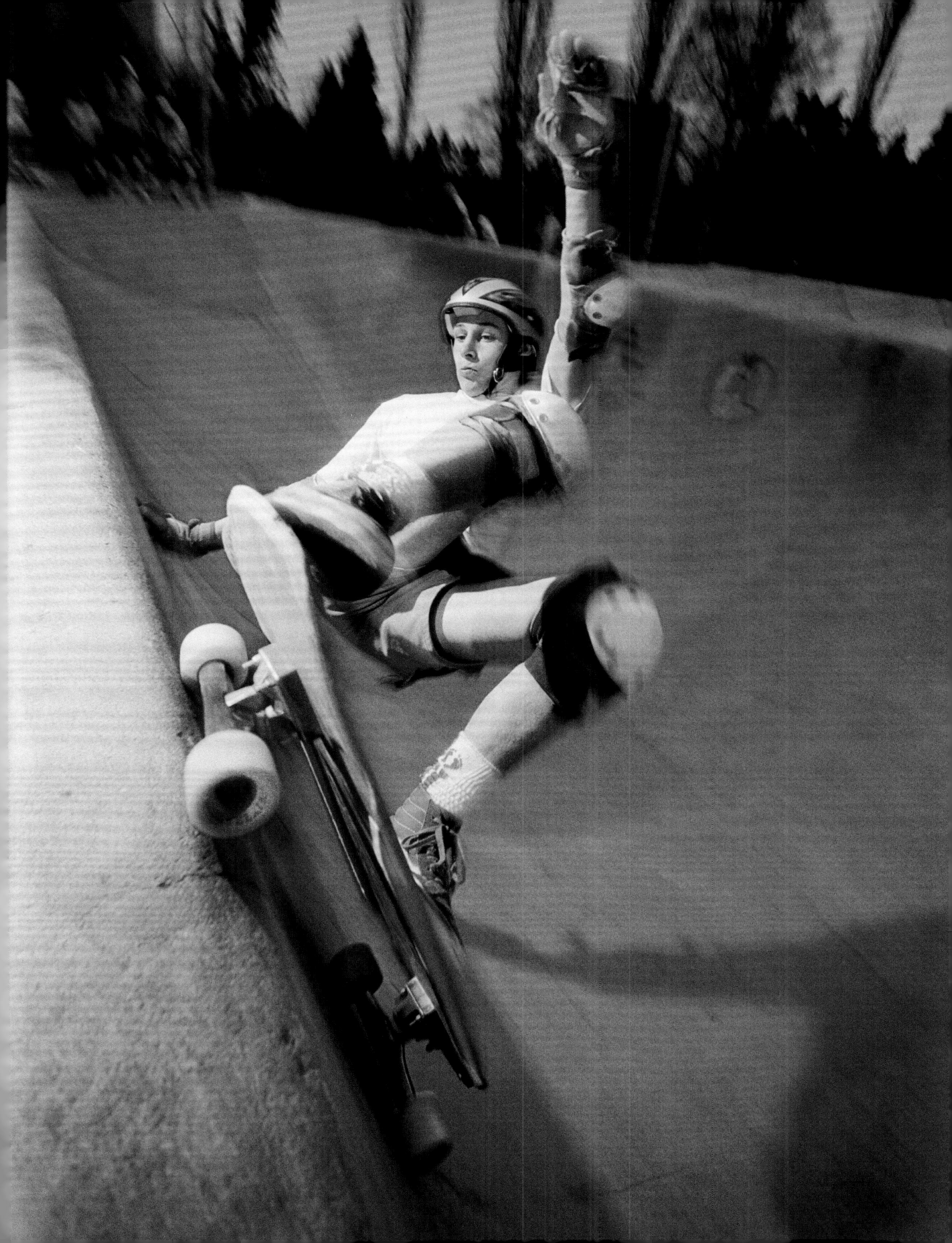

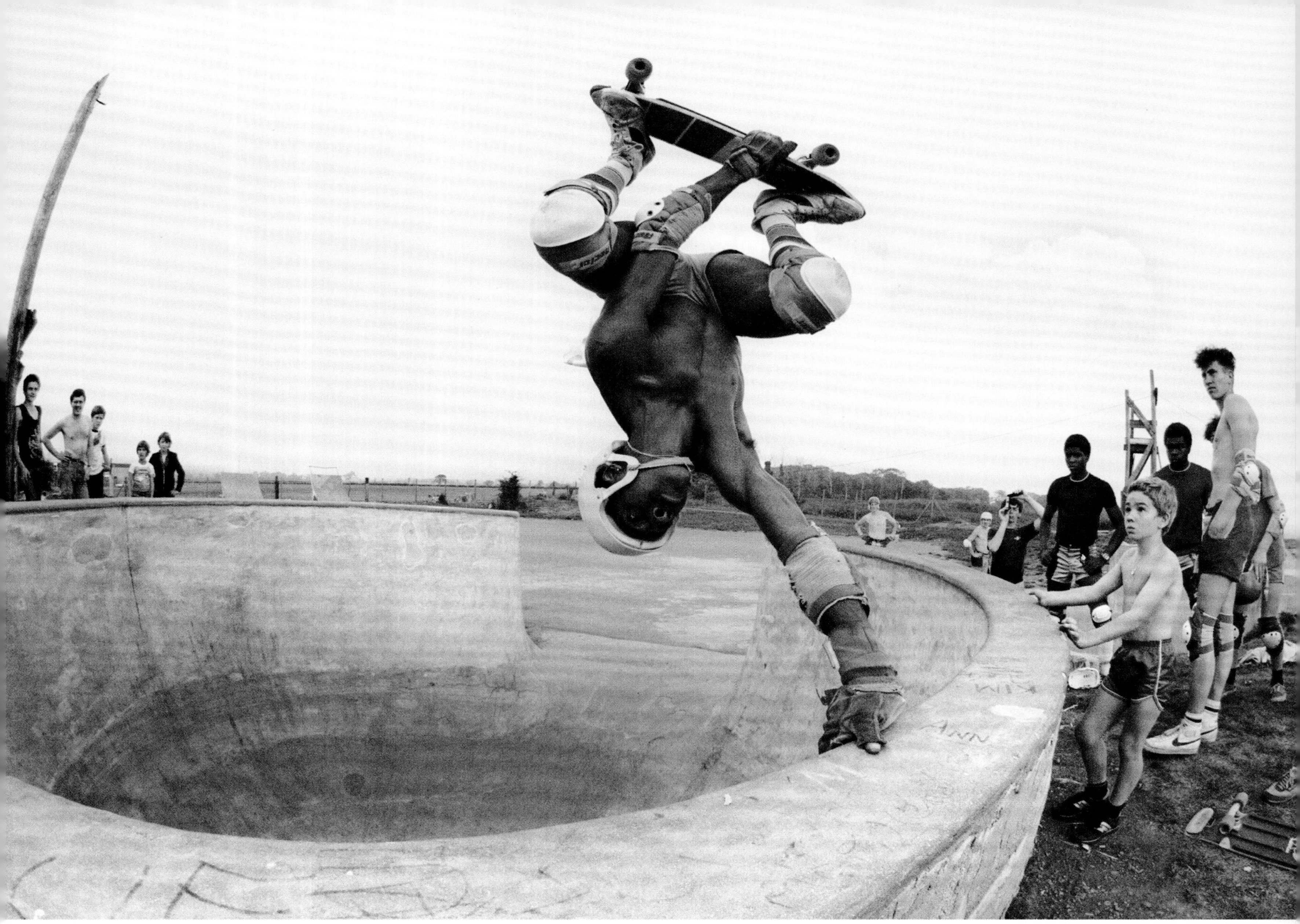

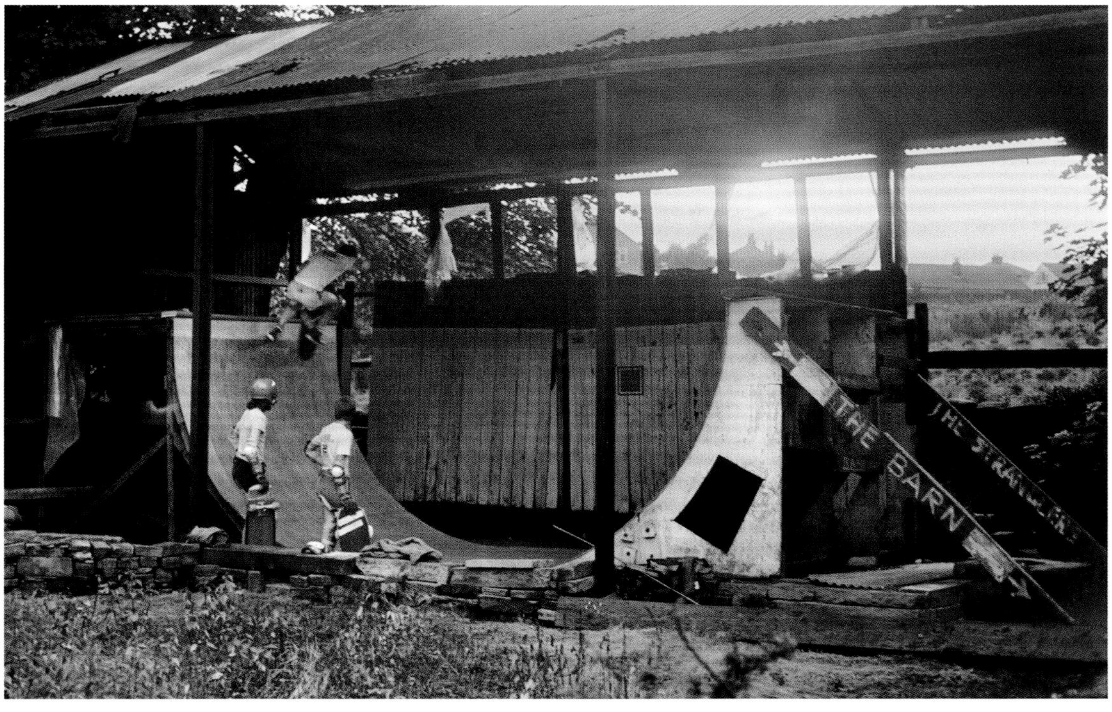
THE BARN

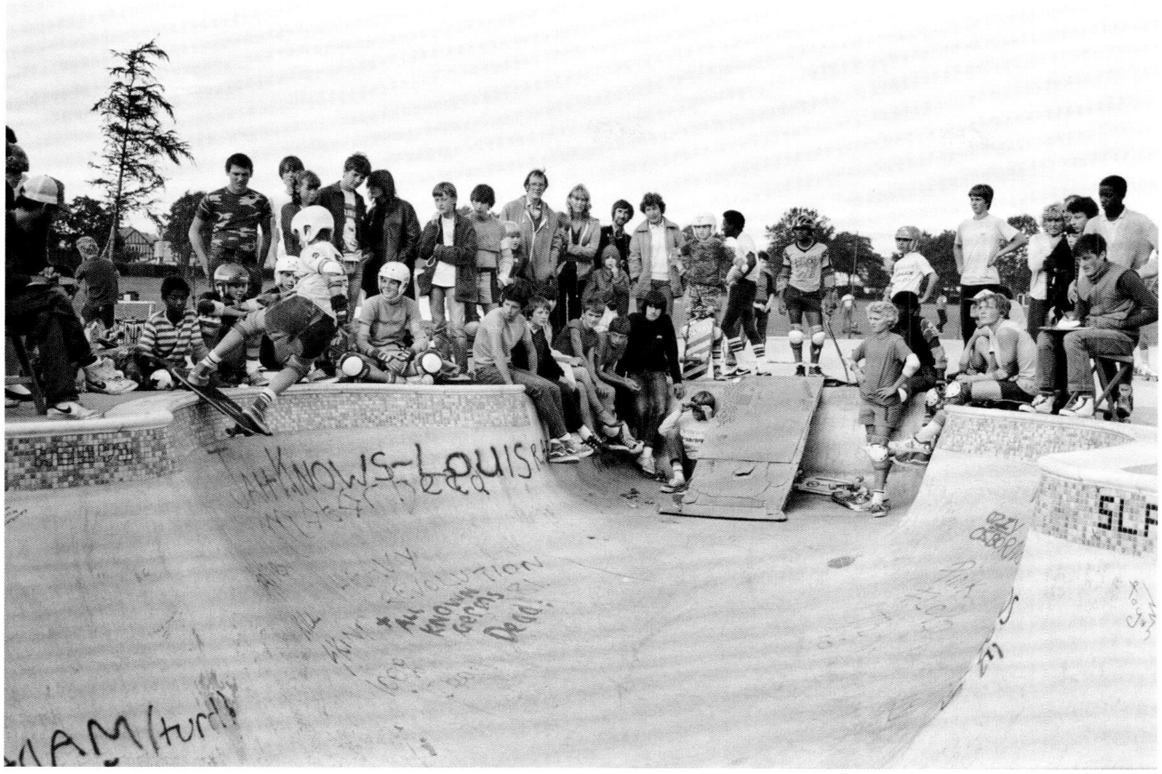

Previous spread: Rodga Harvey, Bowes Lyon skatepark, Stevenage, 1980 **Opposite page top:** Neil 'Danz' Danns, Lockleaze, Bristol, 1981, and **bottom:** Private ramp, North England, 1982 **Left:** Steve Douglas, Harrow skatepark, ESA contest, 1981 **Below:** Lockleaze, Bristol, 1981 **All photos:** TLB

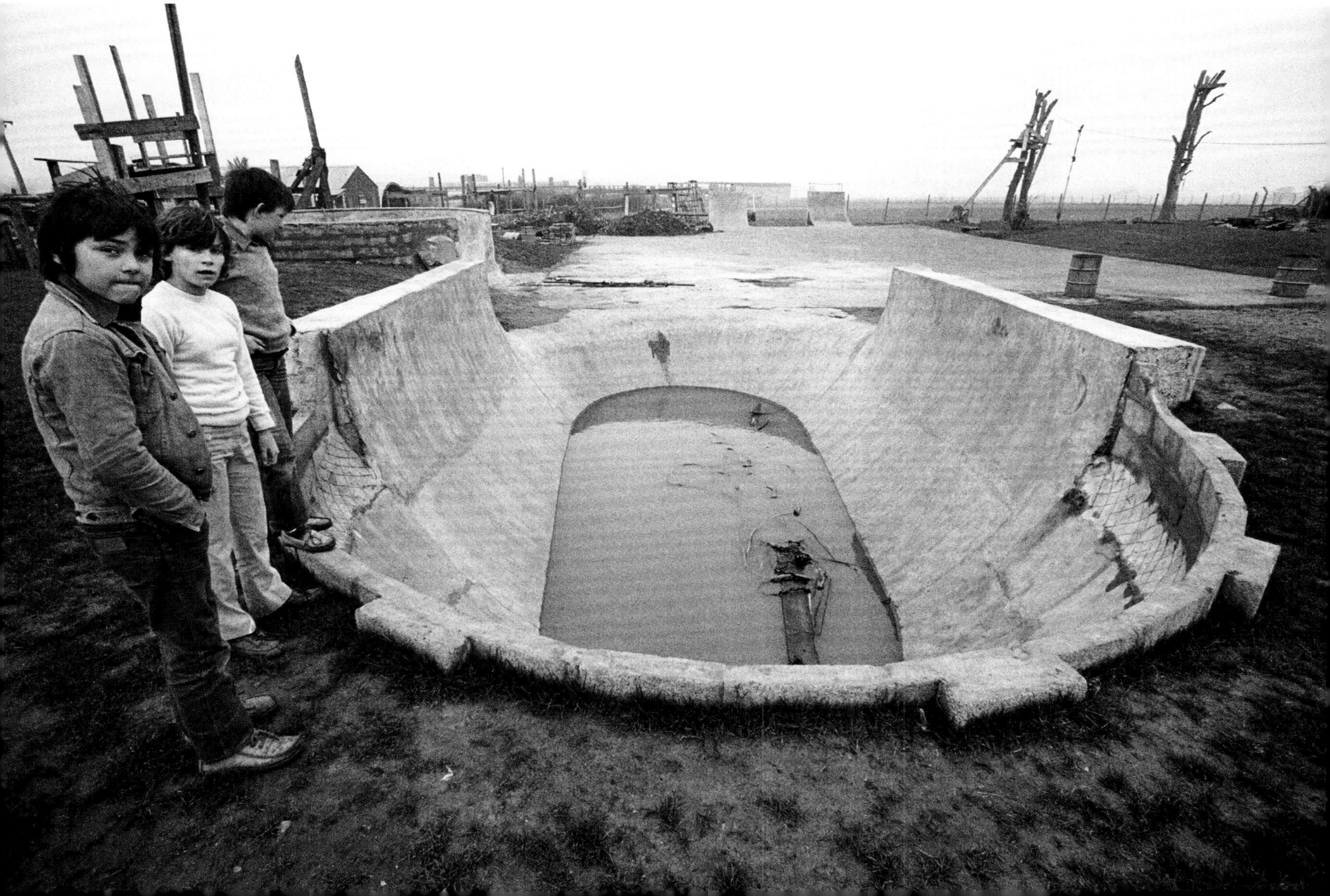

'Southbank was an institution that became my life and photography became an interesting way to document what was going on'

Paul Sunman

'Skateboarding doesn't need competitions. Organisers have always tried to push skateboarders into competitive events to give skateboarding a status which it doesn't necessarily need. The mags like competitions too, it gives them something neat to hang themselves around.

'I'm fully aware that this will upset people who have put a lot of time into creating skateboarding as a fully accepted conventional sport for "the kids", but I've always been convinced that it wasn't necessary.' TLB

Despite personal misgivings about the usefulness of competition in skateboarding, TLB recognised the important social aspect of these events as a way to encourage the culture's future development.

'TLB got me into the comps—because I didn't know about them. I went to my first event and I loved it, I met all these different people—a whole other world of skaters who were travelling around the country to those contests and it was so amazing to me. I remember coming back and saying to the Harrow boys "Guys, you have to go to these events". I was like "There are people out there like us, but they're from Andover, Liverpool, Southsea, Scotland" and they were like "Fuck off, Steve" [laughter].' Steve Douglas

The ESA communicated these vital, national gatherings through printed newsletters—undeniably primitive in appearance and content, but very effective in reaching and pulling together their small devoted audience. TLB's involvement delivered the added highlight of professional-quality photography, included alongside the all-important information.

As the post-boom skate scene hunkered down into the 1980s, working out new ways to celebrate the scene and cement its future, a new group of would-be photographers and writers began to emerge. This younger group of photographers were as eager as TLB to document the culture they were all so excited by and committed to. In emulation of the skateboard magazine and keen to share their photographs with fellow enthusiasts, they utilised what was then the only readily available tool of publication and communication—the photocopied zine.

Punk and new wave music of the 1970s and '80s was already the soundtrack and visual influence of skateboarding, crashing hard into skating's Californian surf origins and sending it careering towards a more aggressive urban future. Punk had popularised the zine as an accessible communication tool for the underground scene. Cheap, quick to produce and easy to circulate wherever skaters congregated, the zines of the '80s were an effective stand-in for the full-colour specialist magazines of earlier times.

The authors of these dynamic, often irreverent publications turned to typewriters, tape, glue and photocopiers to broadcast news and connect their scenes. And no zine of any worth appeared without photographs—the influence of those extinct colour magazines still powerful. The authors took their own photos or turned to skate photographer friends to provide images for their titles. And once again, the vital symbiotic relationship between skateboarding and photography bore out.

Wherever pockets of skateboarding clung on, cameras were being picked up to record their scenes and transmit images to the wider fraternity via these very limited channels. No contest, event or gathering was complete without an eager cluster of skate photographers vying to capture the action.

Acting as a glue, binding together the small groups of local scenes around the world, these zines were unwittingly fuelling the incipient revival of a commercial skate media—some of the most prominent and capable British zine and image makers of this era would go on to become key players in the *RAD* magazine age.

Without a skate magazine to be published in, the few skate photographers active in early 1980s London honed their skills and made their mark contributing to the zines. As their confidence grew, photo submissions were made to *Transworld* and *Thrasher*, the US magazines keen to connect with as wide an audience as possible in their culture-building efforts.

'There still wasn't a UK skate magazine, but I knew the players involved here and as the British skaters got sponsored I began sending shots to American manufacturers and some of those pictures got used in adverts that ran in Thrasher. *So that was good for me, even though most of the time I was getting paid in boards and wheels, shots were starting to get published.'* Mike John

The nucleus or congregation point of the early 1980s London skate scene was the Southbank undercroft, a visible open-access meeting place, colonised by skateboarders from far and wide since the earliest days of skateboarding in Britain. Other notable London spots at Meanwhile 2, Crystal Palace ramp or Harrow and Rom skateparks were all important satellites where the scene would congregate to skate, exchange information and compete.

The close-knit Southbank scene, like so many other small, isolated skate crews of the early 1980s, skated, travelled and competed together at events and gatherings all over the country and abroad. Travelling across the city and around the country became an essential part of skate culture's connective tissue along with the zines and photography. All important connections for skateboarding's future global development were made on trips to the US, Sweden, Germany and beyond, as British skaters and photographers travelled to meet and compete with fellow skateboarders, documenting the faces and places as they went.

Alongside travel, a strong sense of trial and error, learn-by-doing and DIY became a dominant cultural mindset as skateboarding discovered its inner strength. The need to work out, from scratch, how to perform a new trick with no prior instruction other than looking at a still photo meant that the average skateboarder quickly developed an empowering sense of experimental can-do. Paul Sunman, skateboarder, photographer and later shop owner from the London scene explains:

'For all of us in that period it was hard; you didn't volunteer to be a skateboarder because it was easy. Therefore everybody had that mentality of "no one else is going to do it for us; we have to build our own ramp, we have to design our own zine, open our own shops and take our own photographs." So from the late '70s when everything collapsed right through to the mid '80s, if you were a skateboarder you were classed as a weirdo who was out there and the general attitude was "What do you want to do that for?" That time was an immensely creative period though, where skating developed and a new industry formed around it.'

Equipped with this capacity for learning on the job in a supportive tight-knit community, the small dedicated band of London skate photographers quickly developed the skills required to capture the dynamic images they wanted to create. The like-minded skateboarding scene of the early 1980s harboured sympathetic relationships among its participants, and with a keenness to share knowledge—how to do a new trick, the location of a new skate spot or how to take the best photos—a pool of knowledge and connections developed.

Southbank regulars Paul Sunman and Mike John had both picked up cameras as an effective tool for capturing their excitement and love for skateboarding. The open and supportive nature of the scene that they were a part of meant that sharing both photos and technique was a regular interaction amongst this small group. Mike John recalls an early connection with TLB that would ultimately lead to having his own photos published first in *BMXAB* and then *RAD* magazine:

'In 1982 when [US pro skaters] Steve Caballero and Mike McGill came to Crystal Palace in London, I saw Tim down there taking pictures and I'd seen him before up at Harrow. Later on, I saw the pictures he'd taken—maybe in the Alpine Action newsletters—and the next time I saw him, I approached and said "I really like those shots you took; how did you get that blurred effect on the images?" and he was kind enough to explain. I thought "Wow, he's taking time out to talk to me and to give me advice" and that gave me confidence.'

With Southbank acting as such a focal point for the London scene and where much of the connecting and knowledge-sharing took place, its importance to the scene was in no doubt. The legacy of the spot already ran deep; TLB had taken some of his earliest skate photos there in the late 1970s (and architectural photos before that). Mike and Paul, keen to record the world that had become integral to their lives, began experimenting with skate photography in the early '80s. Skaters Bod Boyle and Steve Douglas and later BMXer Nick Philip (the first designer of *RAD*) were also mainstays of the ever-present mid '80s Southbank crew. At a time when channels of communication were extremely limited, skateboarders visiting London could pass through Southbank, with the knowledge that there would likely be other like-minded individuals there to make all-important connections with.

'I think those guys were influential in the sense that it was a very small scene then and each member of our small scene contributed just by being there and being part of it. The fact that we had people interested in photography and being creative, as well as skateboarding—that all went hand-in-hand with the culture. It was serendipitous, you know.' Bod Boyle

'We were always the square pegs in the round holes. If you look back at a spot like Southbank, you had a complete mixture of people there: different races and different classes. The thing that brought them together was the skating and the attitude. It isn't a team sport where you have to go out and practise or follow certain rules—it was free. And that's why I think it attracted creative people, because it's a blank canvas to work with. Then they take that attitude back out into other areas of life.' Mike John

The web establishing itself amongst the community forged relationships that would have lasting impact on the future of British skateboarding and so, too, on the individuals involved. Bod Boyle, arguably one of the most successful British professional skateboarders of the late '80s, had his first skate photos taken by Mike John and his first published magazine photos by TLB. The photographers, as much as his fellow skateboarders, recognised and encouraged Bod's prowess on a board. He and fellow British professional skateboarder Steve Douglas—whose all important *GO FOR IT!* zine had been a significant communication platform in the early '80s for the future *RAD* contributors—both went on to become influential figures in the global skateboard industry.

'There's benchmarks in life, right? I remember going to Southbank and going, "Oh my God, there's a scene, I want to be part of that scene. Will they let me in?" And then I'm in. And then the graduation to Crystal Palace. And each one of them was, you know, "Oh my God, I can't believe that I'm skating with these people and a part of this crew. I feel like I'm a part of something."' Bod Boyle

As the underground London scene flourished, ramps were built, contests organised, national and international trips undertaken, photographs shot and zines made; all helping to establish greater connectivity and a stronger culture in the process. This formula was being played out in small pockets all over Britain and abroad. The building blocks and attitude for a future British magazine were taking shape. The ever-present goal amongst those keen documentarians was to find a way to convey all this rich activity in their own full-colour magazine—a possibility frustratingly out of reach at the time.

Throughout this haphazard but hugely enjoyable period of evolution for British skateboarding and alongside his efforts to document skate culture, TLB continued working as a photographer for *BMX Action Bike*. Ultimately, a cross-fertilisation between BMX and skate culture, and in particular the changing tastes and development of the new freestyle BMX, meant that TLB found ways to *'sneak skateboarding into the magazine* [BMXAB]*...'*, his enthusiasm for skateboarding undulled:

'There was a contest at Meanwhile 2 and I vividly remember Tim walking around and being very excited—he was saying "It's happening, it's happening". And I was like, "What?" "It's happening! Look, there's people here, it's happening." It was almost like this premonition for Tim. This must have been '84 or '85 when Tim was saying "skateboarding is actually growing. It's a THING and people ARE interested." He was a great believer in the act of skateboarding, right? I mean he really, really was.' Bod Boyle

Tim wasn't alone in sensing that interest in skateboarding was on the rise. Fellow enthusiast and photographer Paul Sunman, influenced by the much-missed Alpine Action store, felt that the time could be right for a new skateboarding retail venture in London:

'I opened Slam City Skates in '86, and it was the only London skate shop back then. I'd talked to Tim about the idea before we did it and he suggested meeting with Ray (Abbott) from Alpine Action to discuss opening a shop. Ray said "You're mad, are you sure you want to do it? It's really, really hard."

'Tim and I shared the view that "things are picking up here" and we knew others skaters felt it at that time too. You could sense that there was increased interest.'

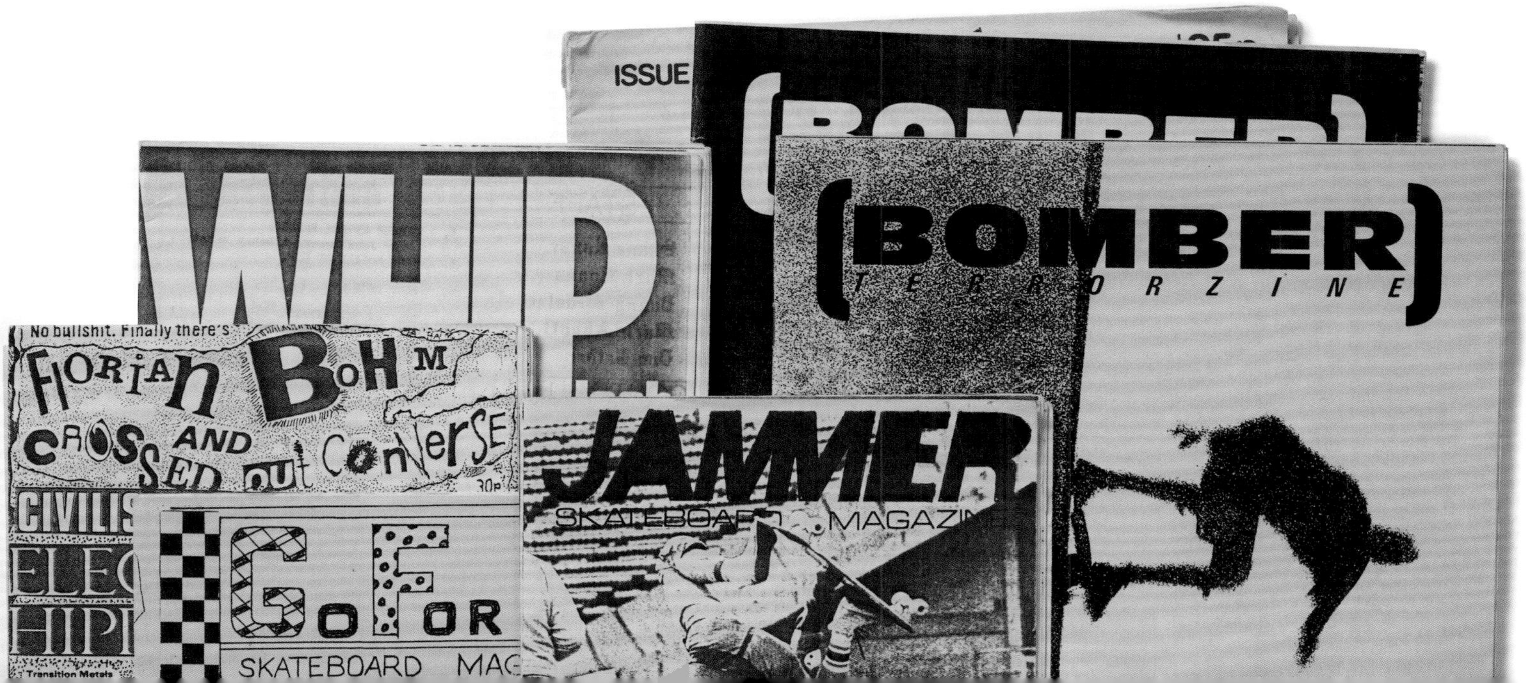

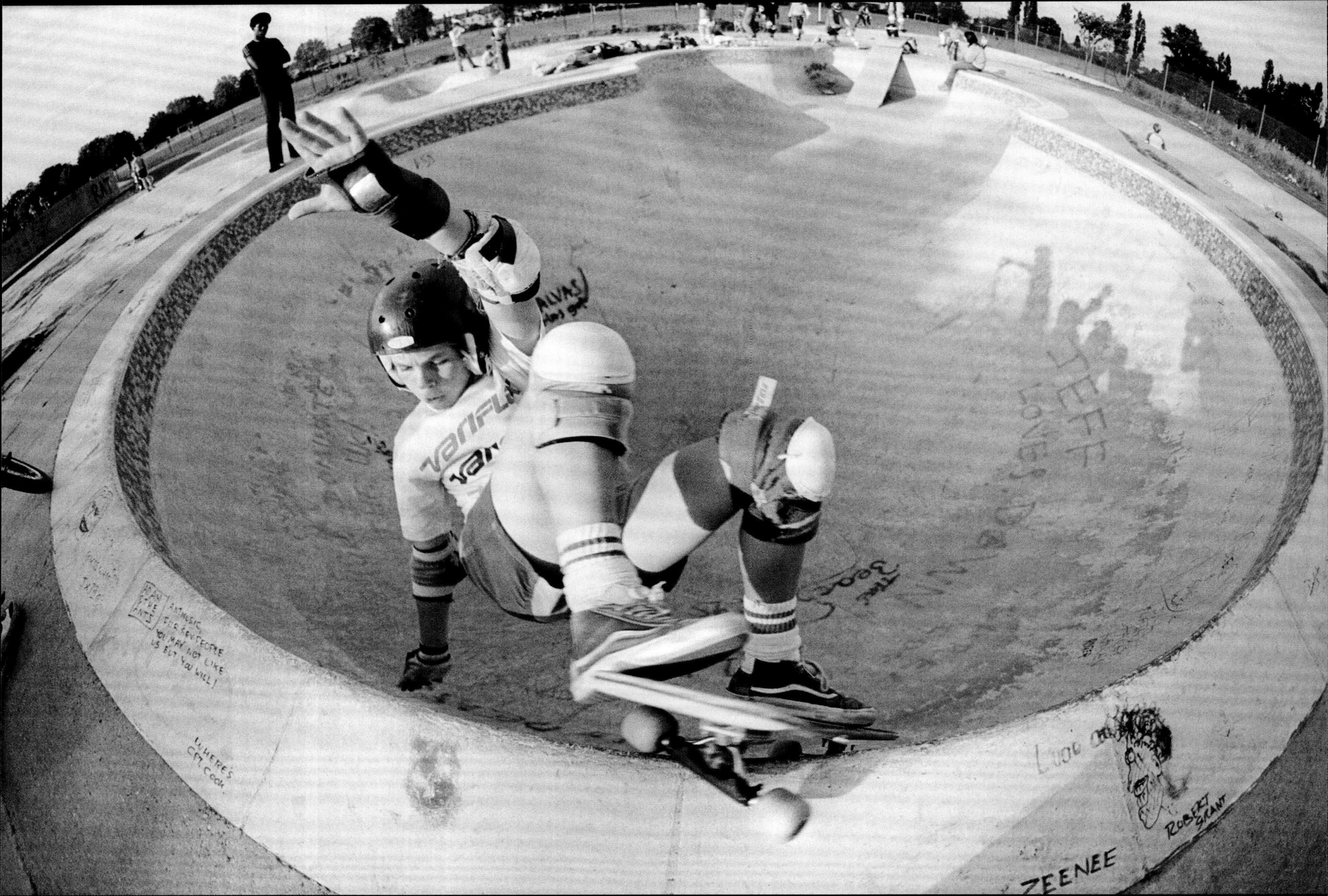

Above: Steve Douglas, Harrow skatepark, 1981. *'TLB was a huge influence in my life—introducing me to those contests and meeting all those people; it made me realise that there was another world out there. I must have got to know about 99% of the skaters who were active in Britain.'* **Photo:** TLB

Previous spread: A selection of early to mid-1980s British skate zines **Below:** Rodga Harvey, Harrow skatepark performance bowl, 1981 **Overleaf left:** Steve Caballero and Mike McGill, Crystal Palace ramp, London, 1982, and **right:** Wullie McKay, Livingston skatepark, Scotland, 1982 **Photos:** TLB

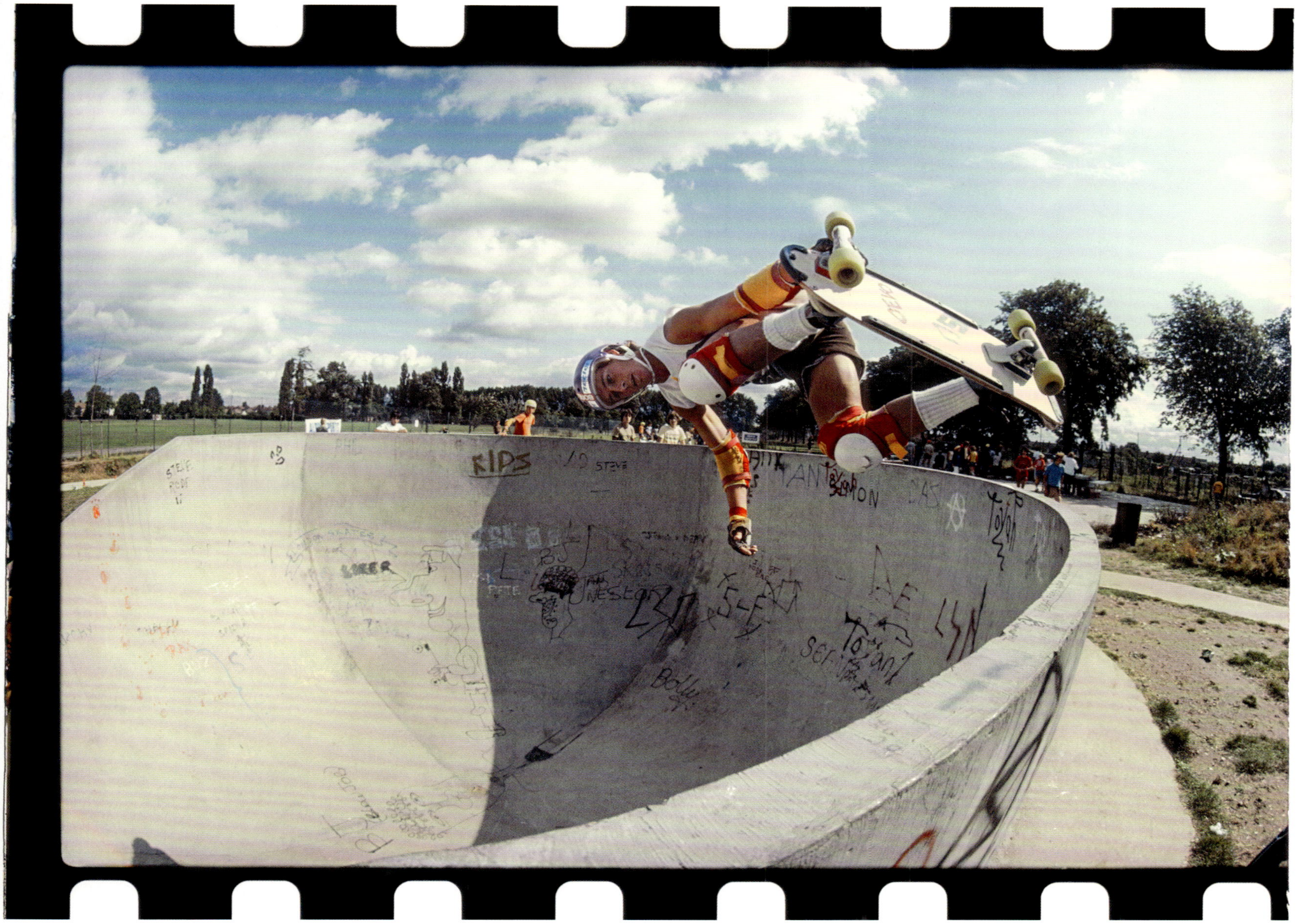

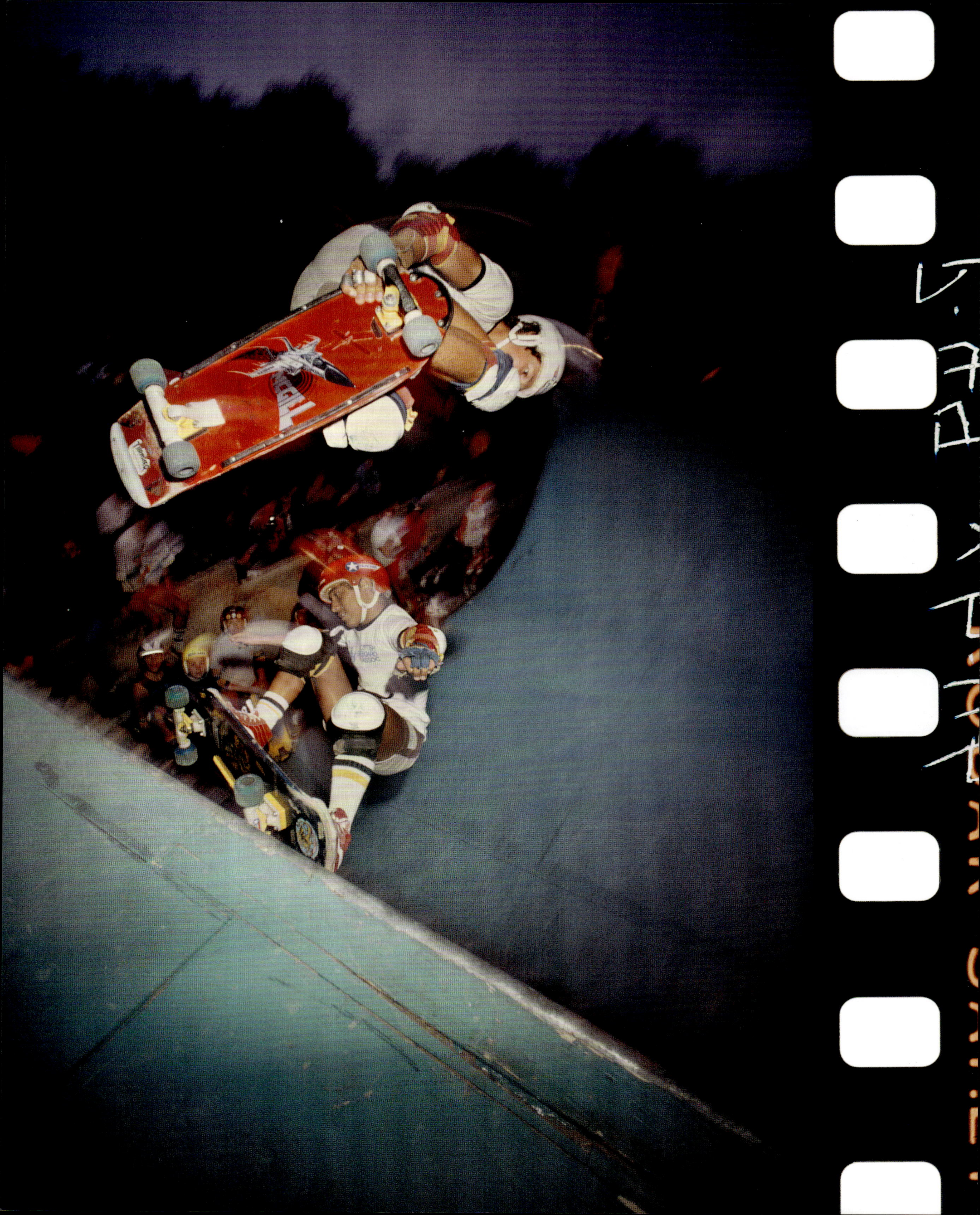

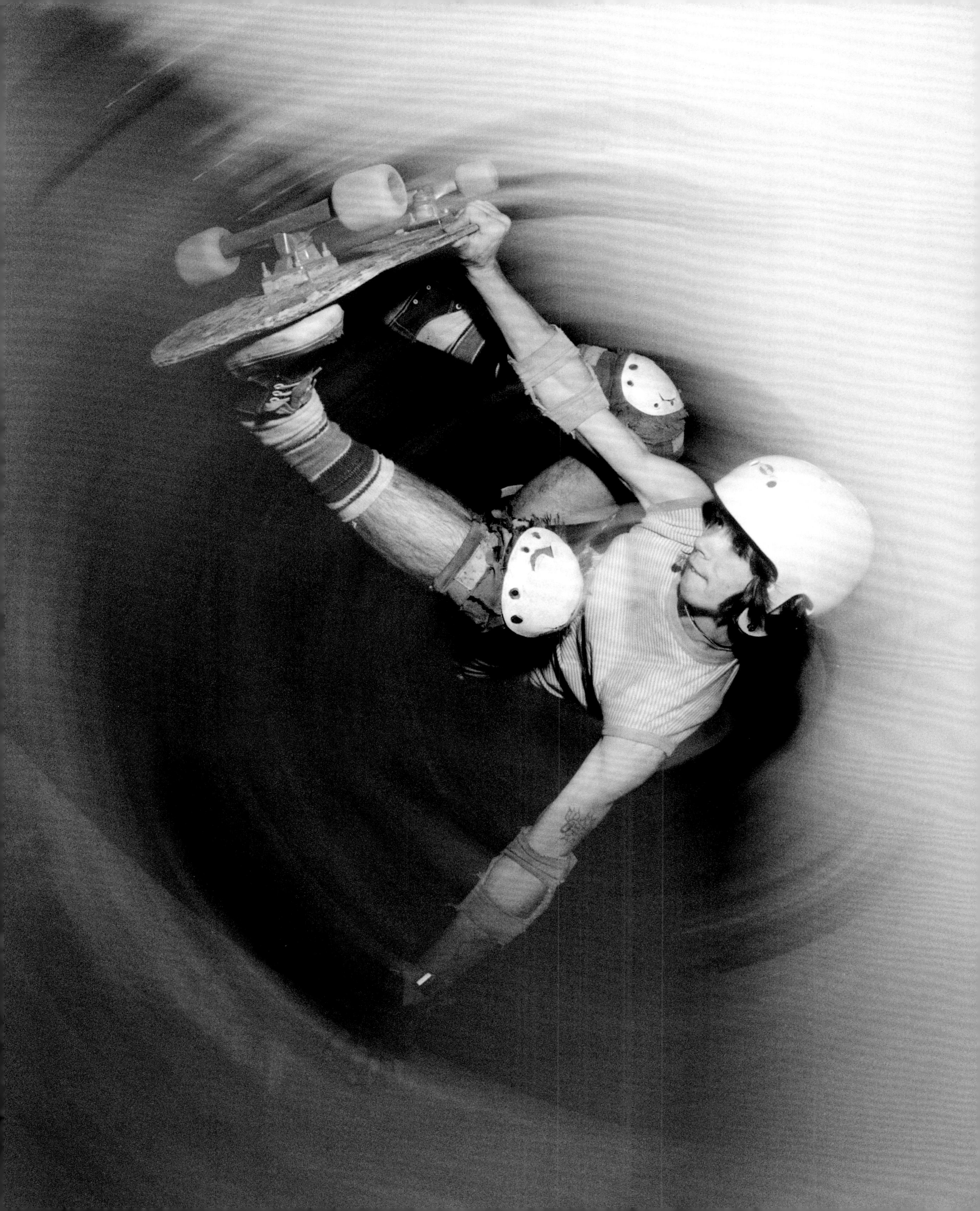

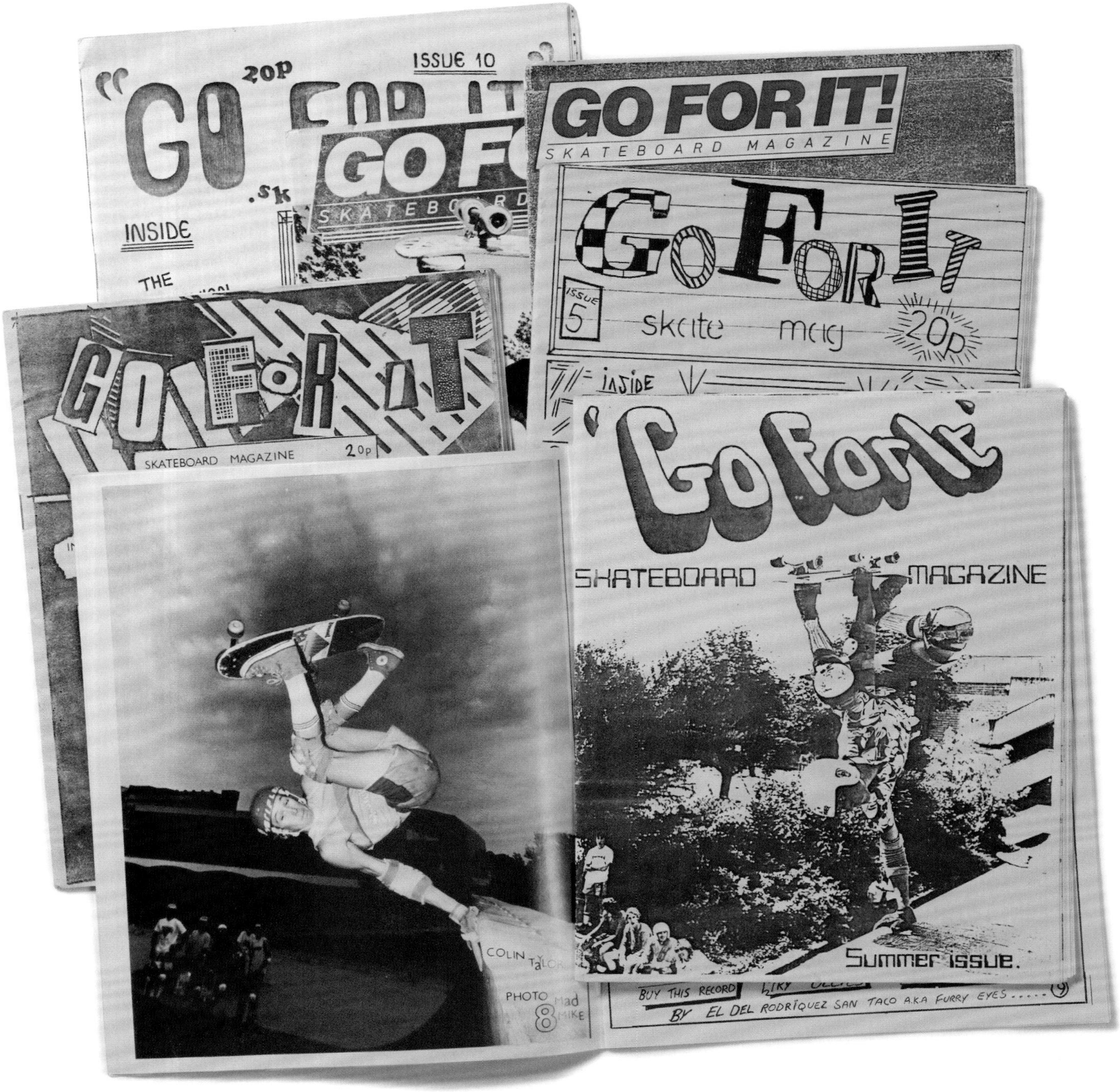

Above: A selection of Steve Douglas's mid-1980s *GO FOR IT!* skate zines including photos by Mike John
Opposite: Steve Douglas, Southbank, London, 1984 **Photo:** Paul Sunman
Overleaf: Surrey Skateboards shop, board wall display, Woking, mid-1980s
Photo: TLB

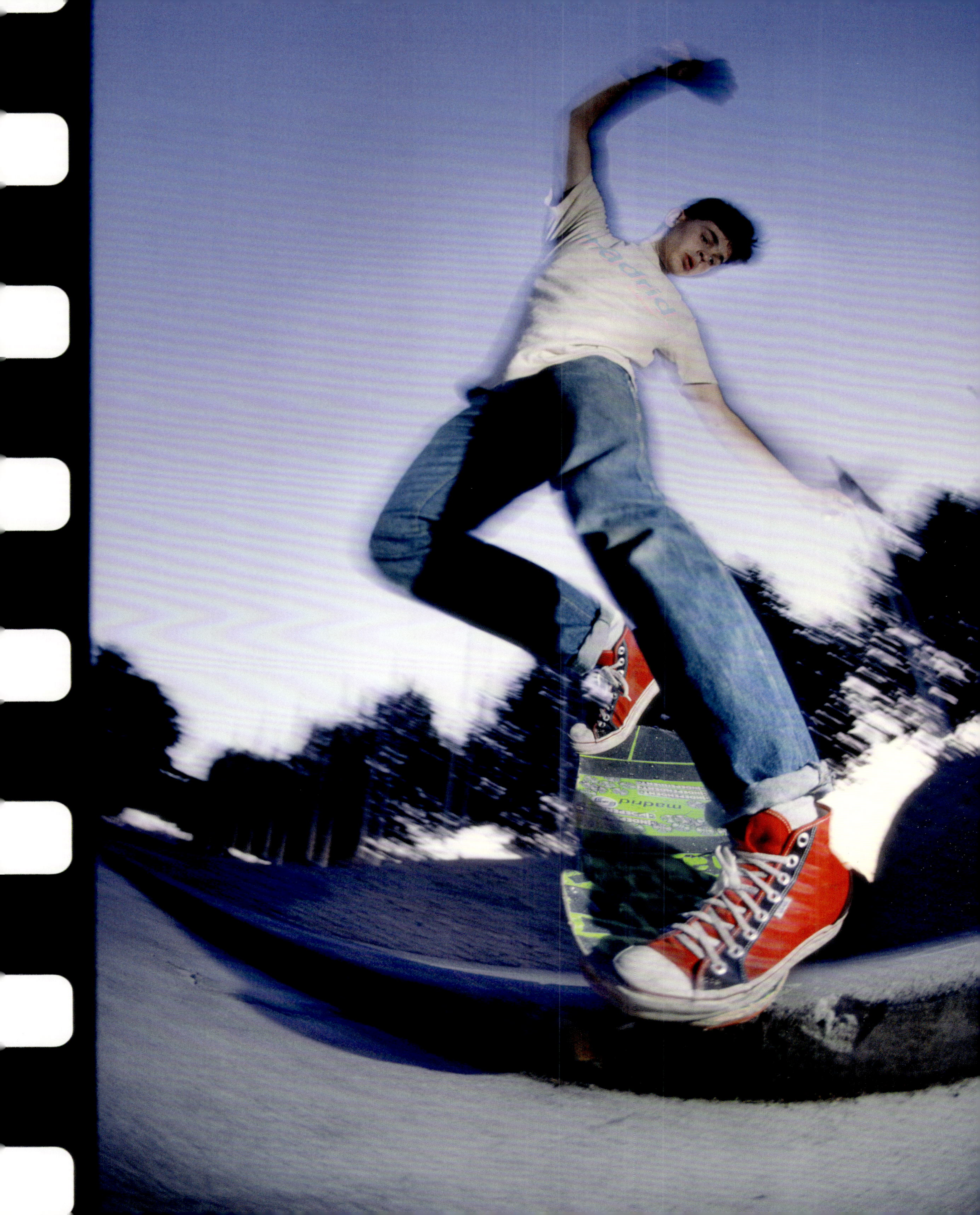

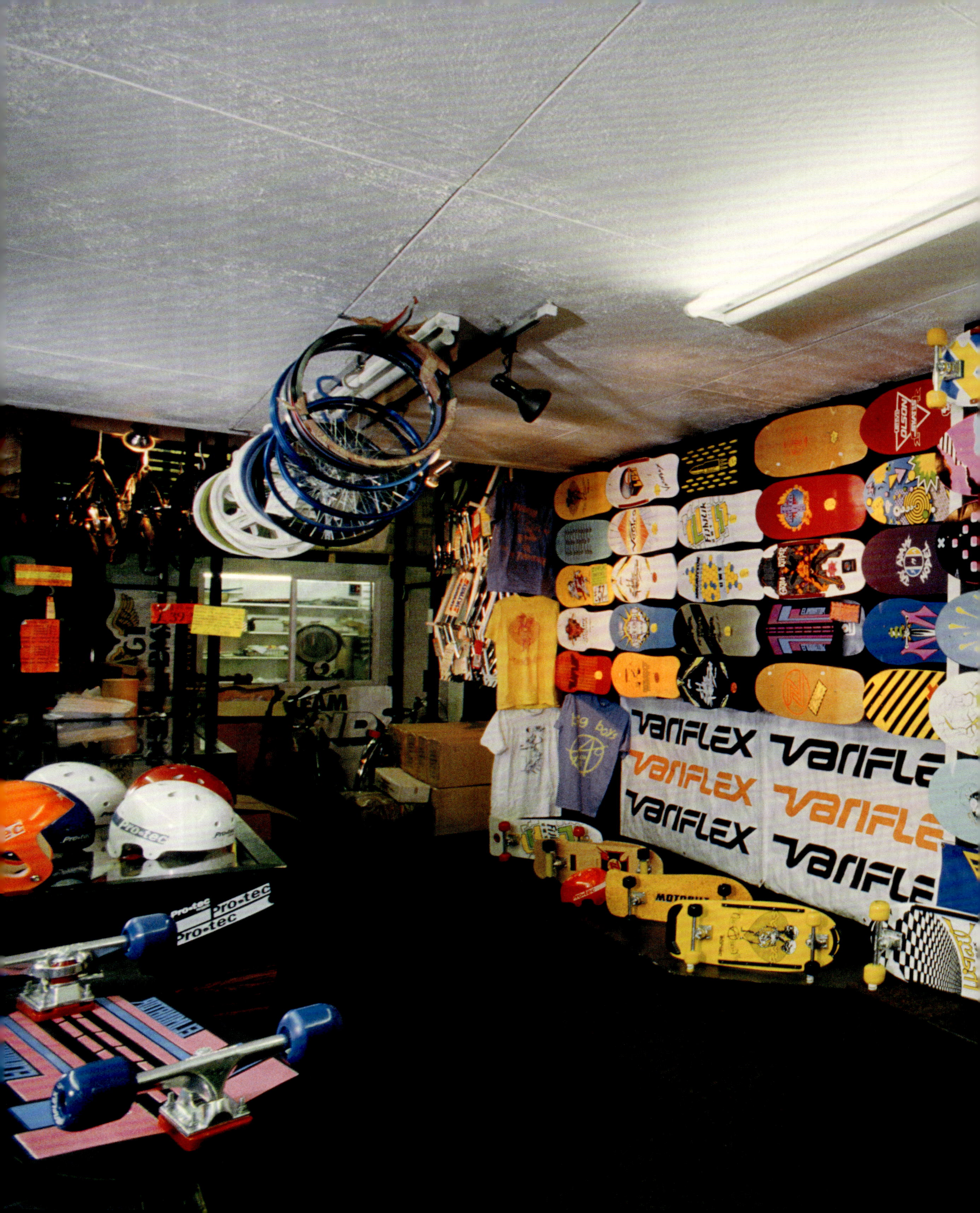
Variflex
Variflex
Variflex
Pro-tec
Pro-tec
Pro-tec

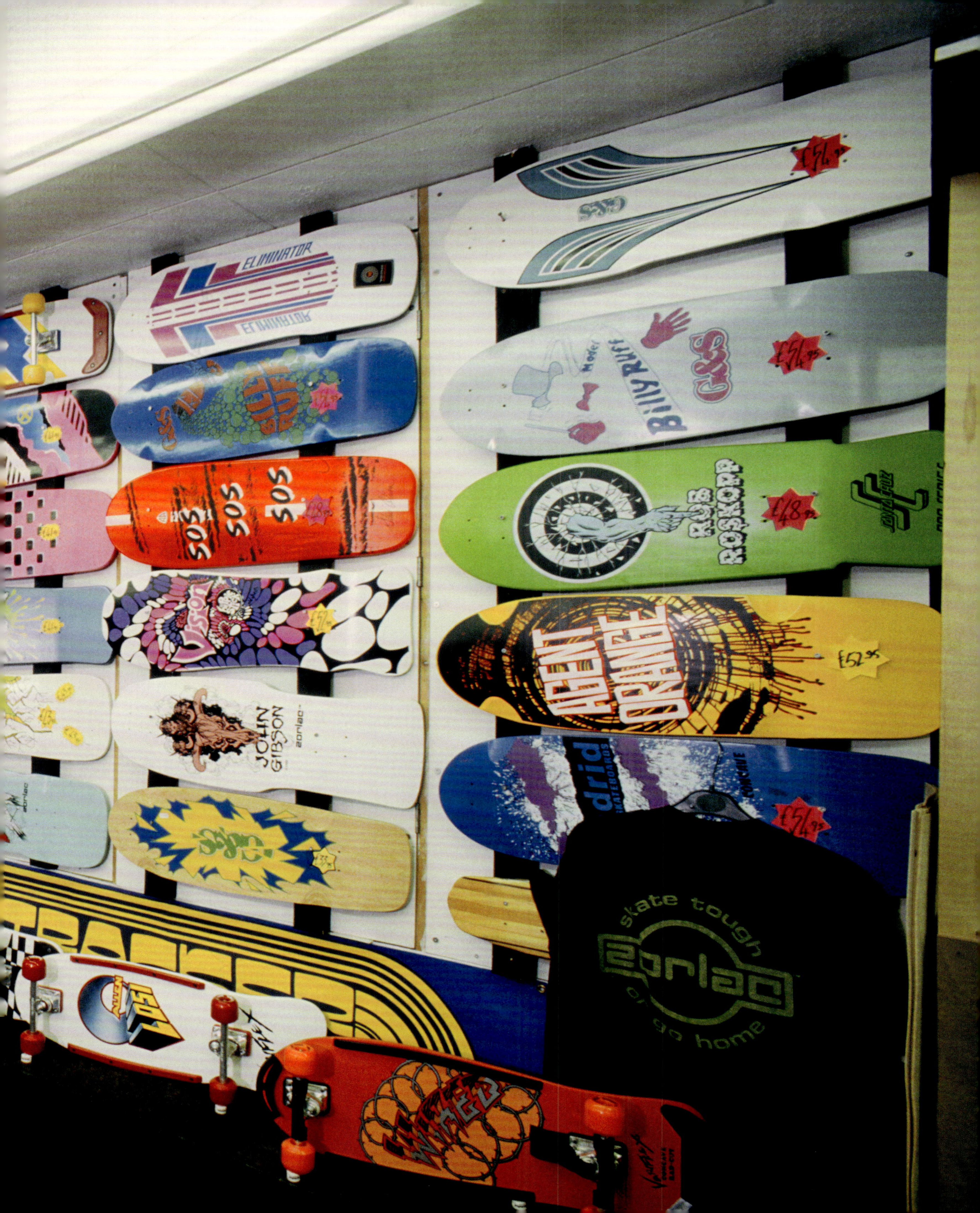
ELIMINATOR
SOS SOS SOS
JOHN GIBSON
zorlac
Billy Ruff
Model
ROB ROSKOPP
AGENT ORANGE
skate tough
zorlac
or go home

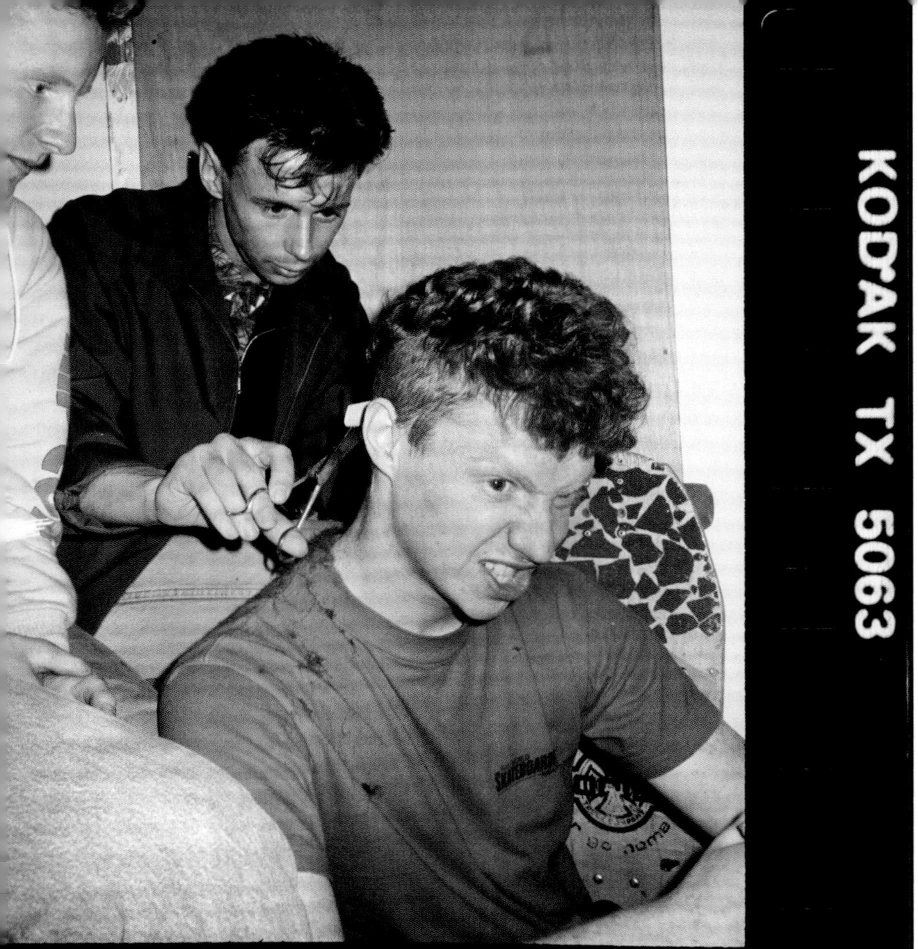

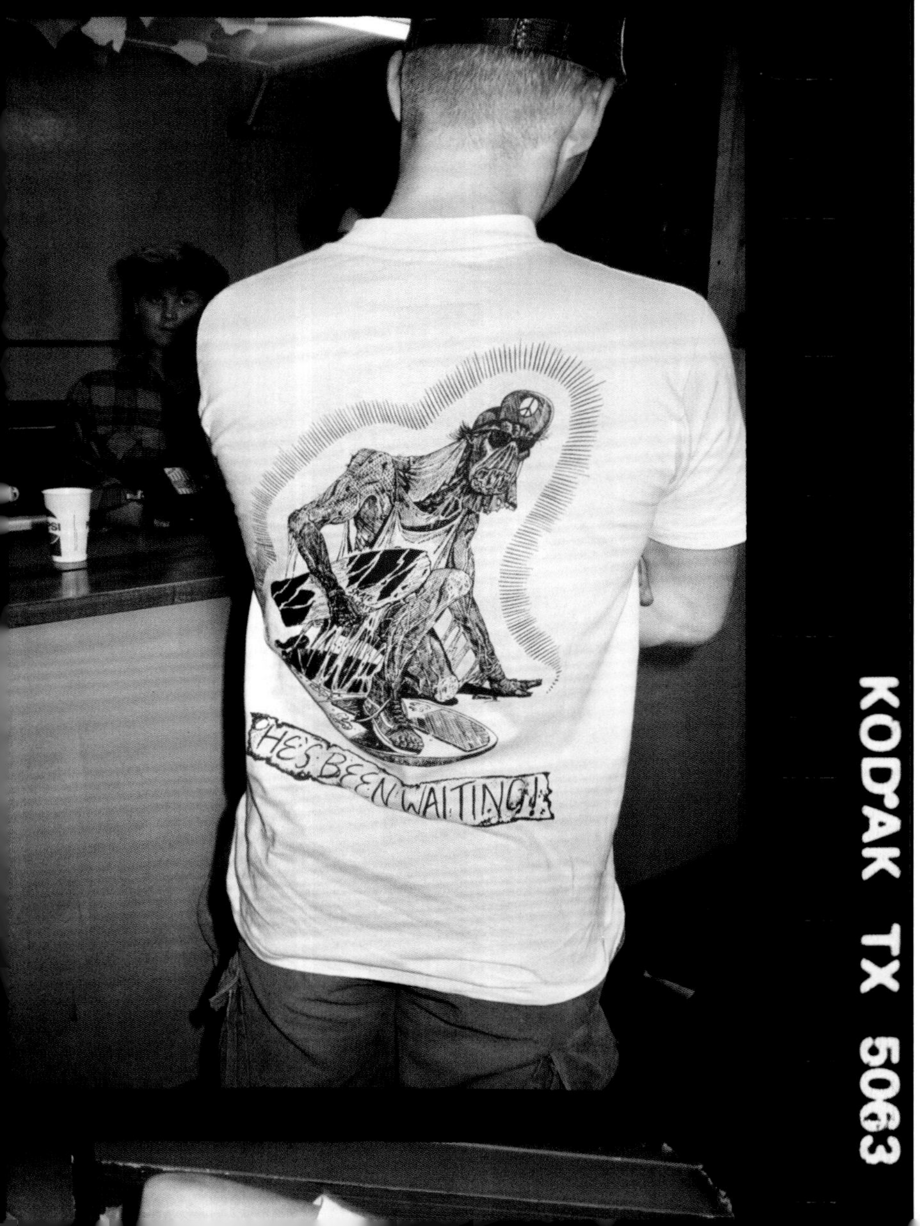

'The love of skating motivated me and I just wanted to capture it. I realised pretty early on that I wasn't going to be a brilliant skater myself, even though I enjoyed it, but another way I could be really involved in the scene was by taking pictures. I really wanted a ticket to keep me involved; something to get me up on the half-pipe platform—but you had to earn that. If people know you could come up with the shots, you were allowed to be there. So photography became my ticket.'

Mike John

Above: Contest backstage capers: Pete Rogers with scissors, Tim Hughes sitting **Left:** Sean Goff dressed in a 'HE'S BEEN WAITING' Skate Mutant tee shirt, drawing by Doug Cameron, Warrington Empire Skate Building, 1985 **Photos:** TLB **Opposite:** Phil Burgoyne, Crystal Palace ramp, 1985 **Photo:** Mike John

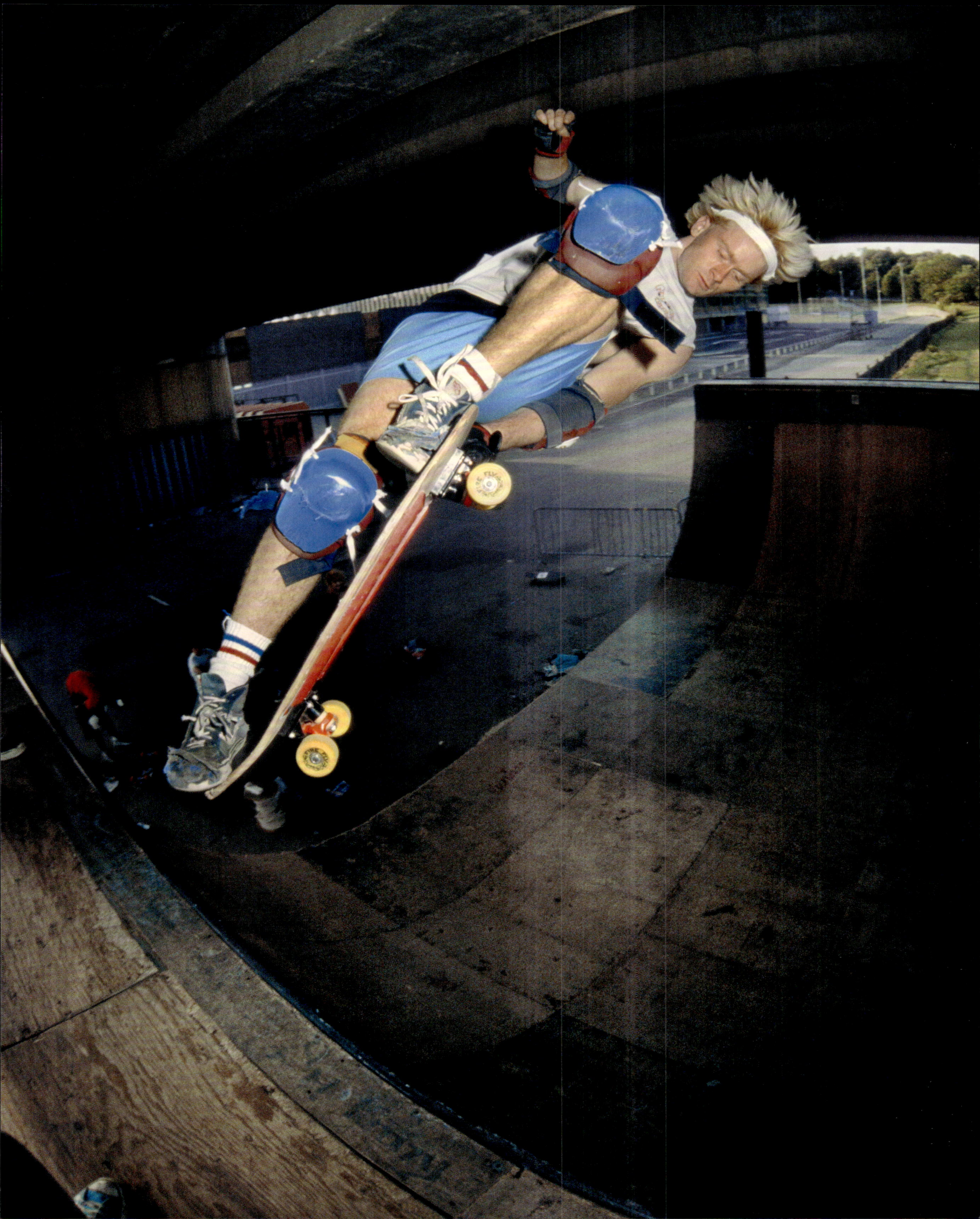

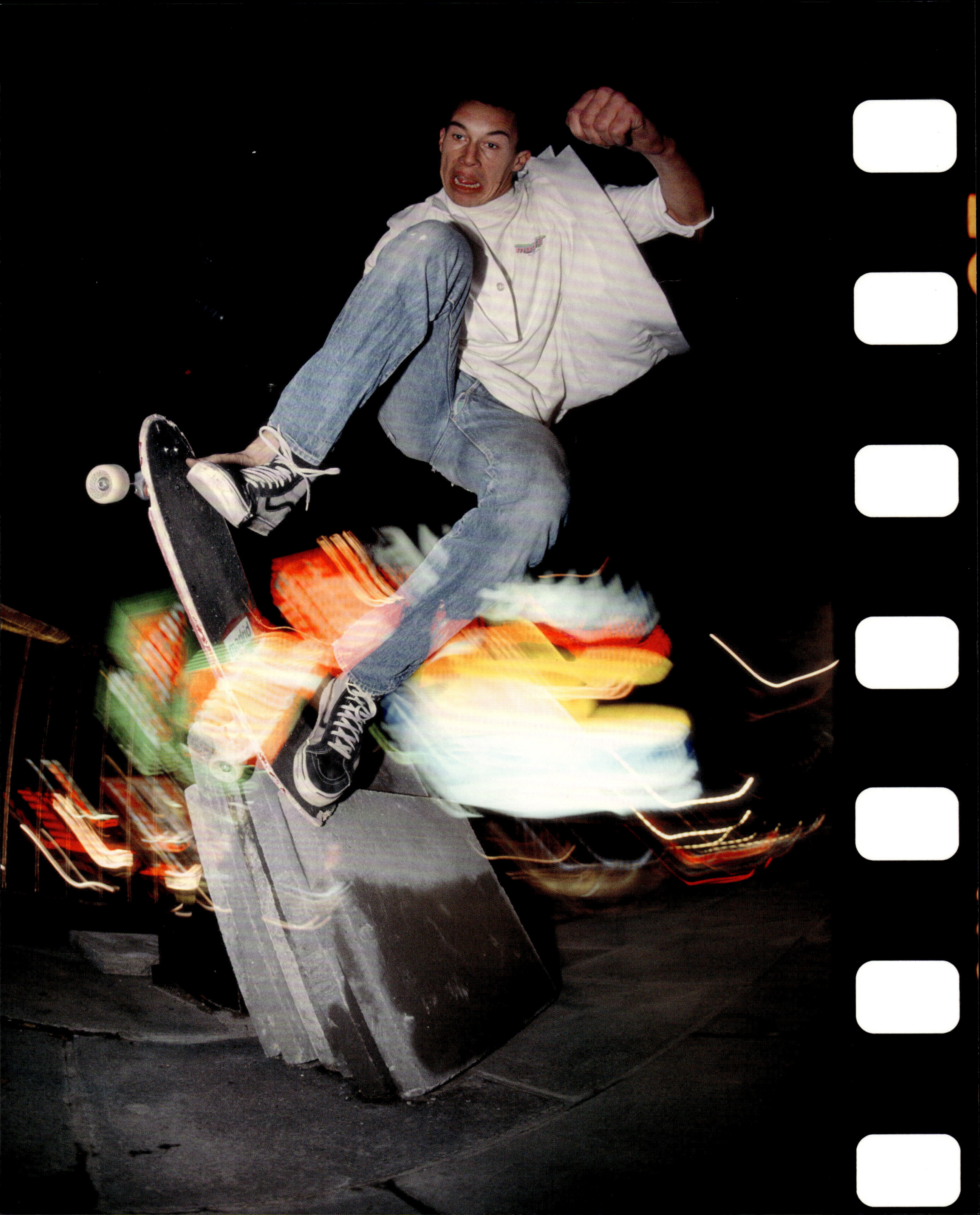

Opposite: Crispin Robinson, Leicester Square, London, 1985 **Photo:** Paul Sunman **Right:** Bod Boyle, Crystal Palace, London, 1985 **Photo:** Mike John

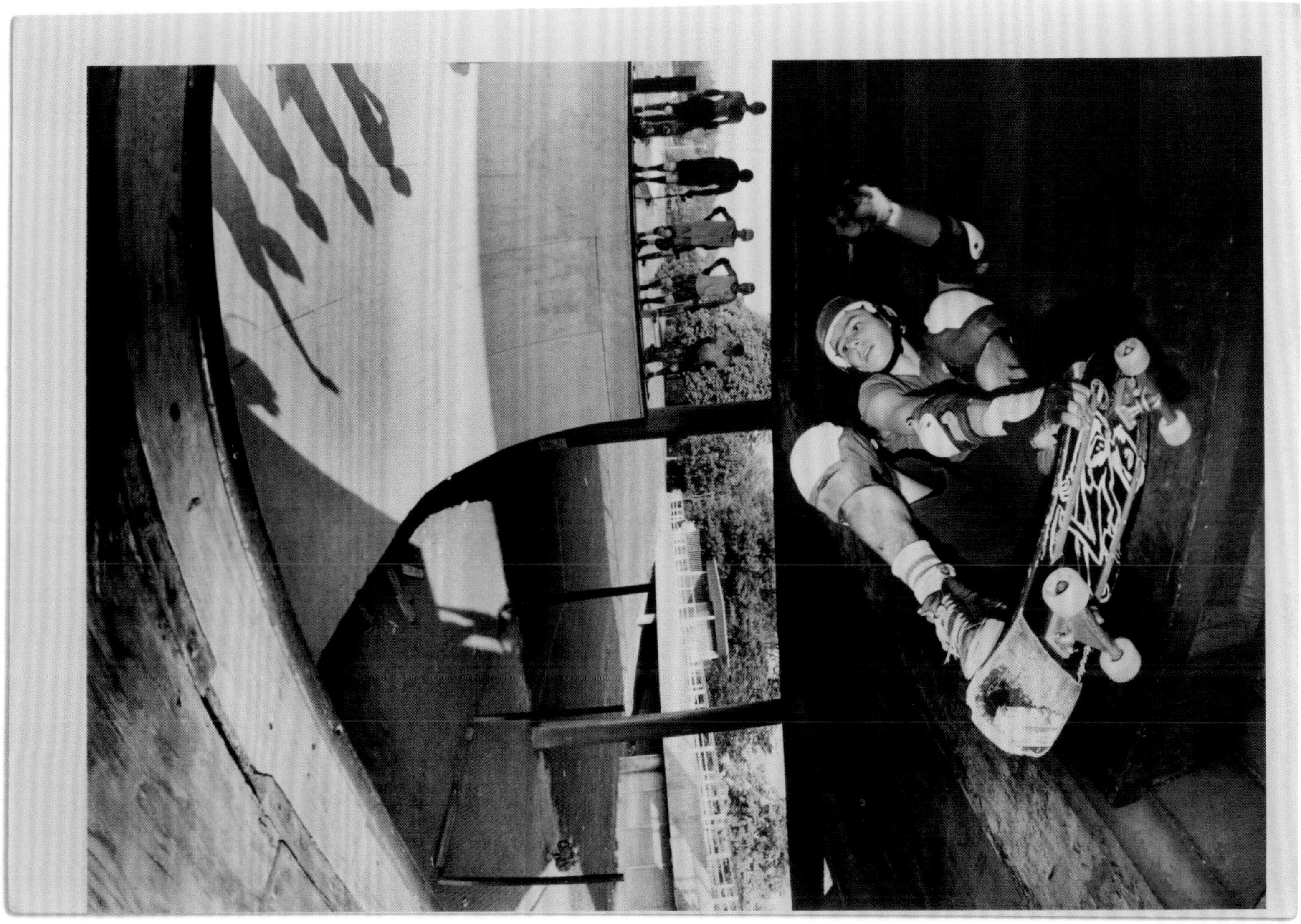

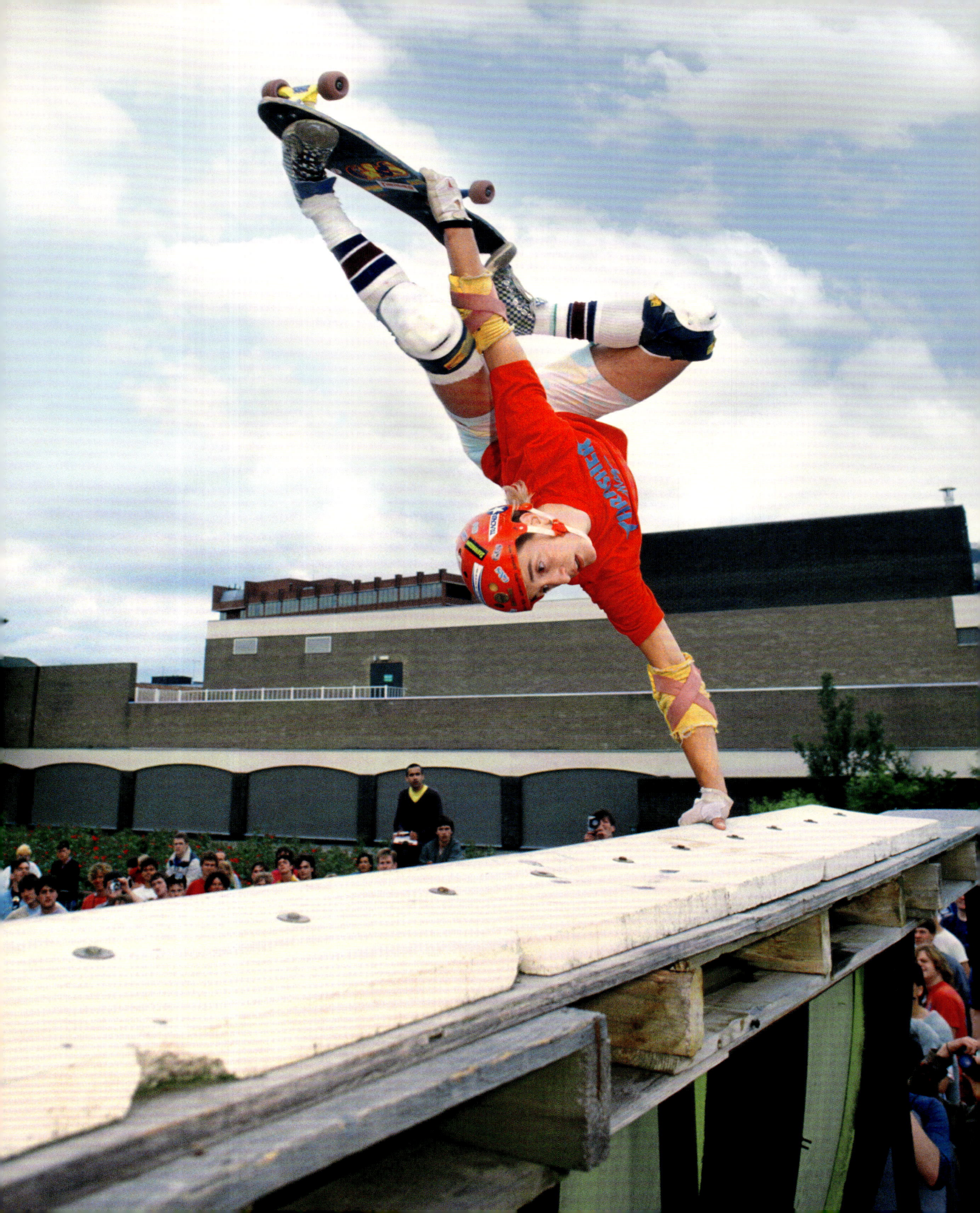
THRASHER

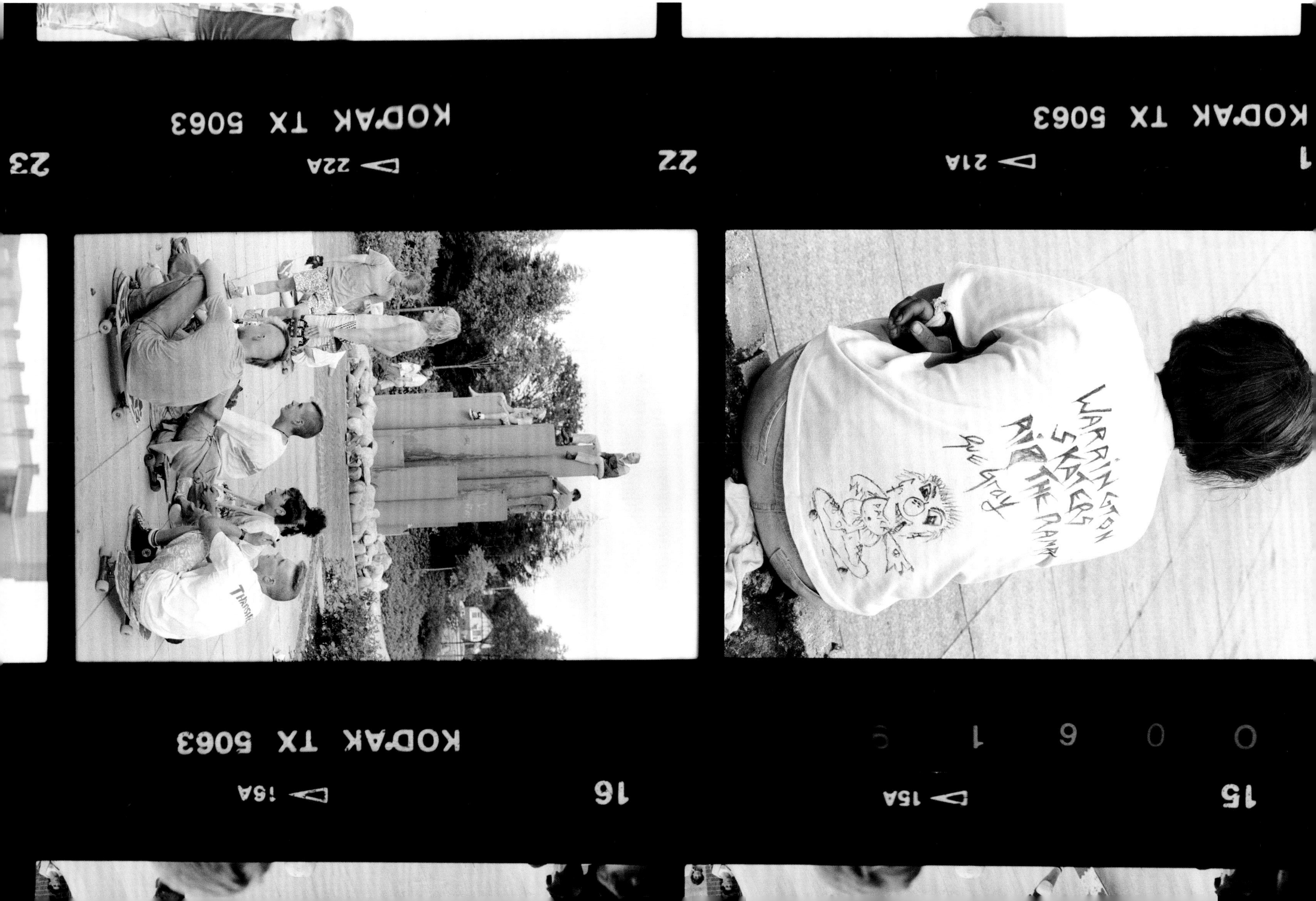

Opposite: Danny Webster, Farnborough, 1985 **Right:** Fans gather at a contest, Farnborough, mid-1980s **Photos:** TLB

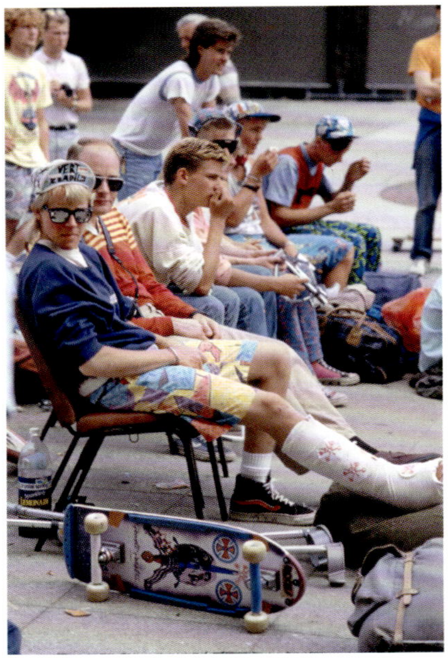

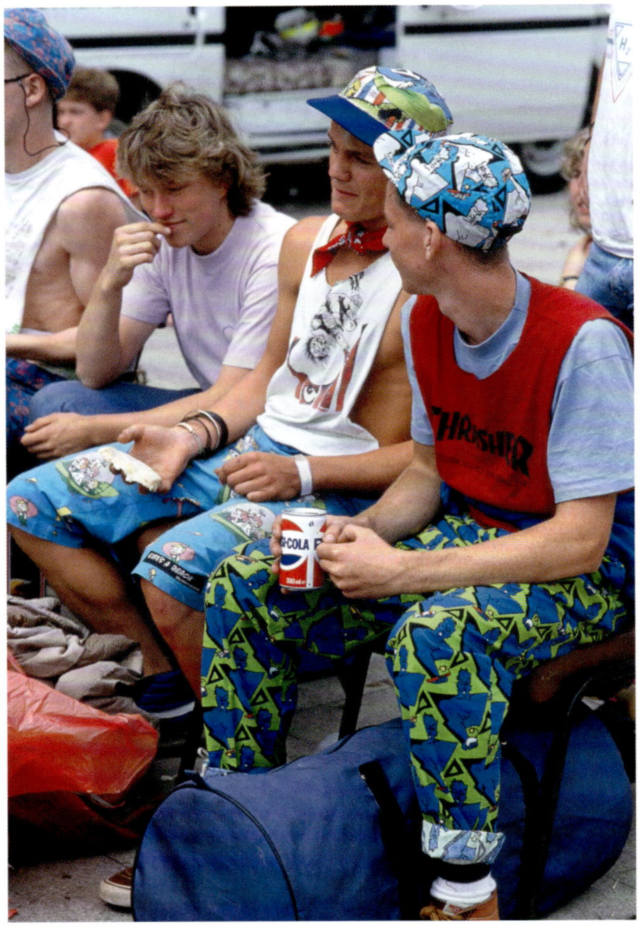

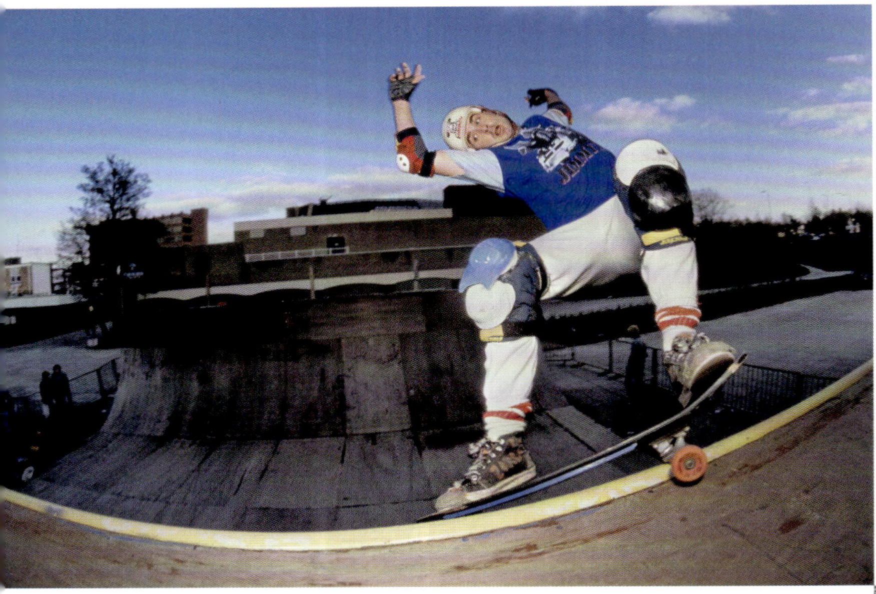

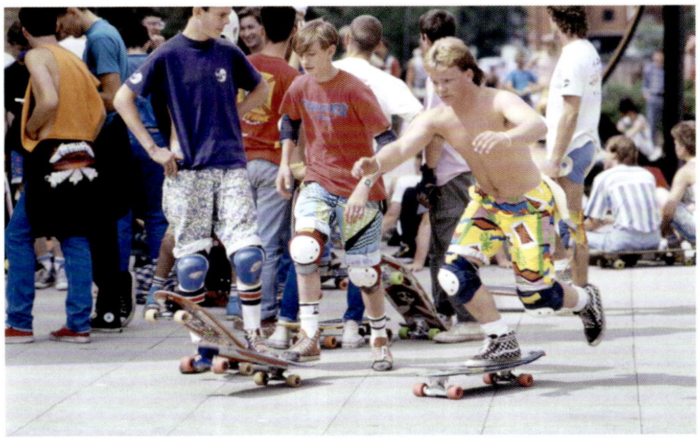

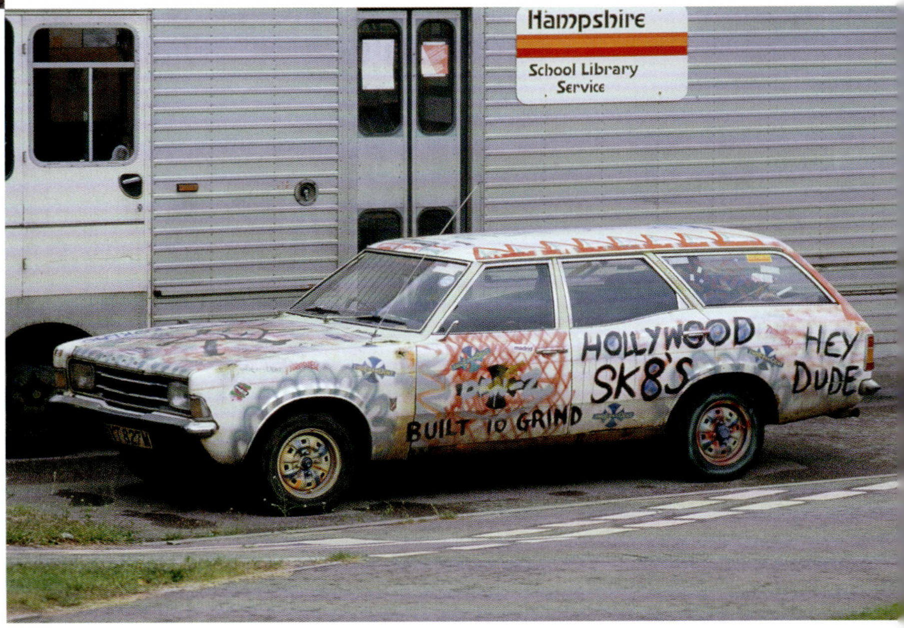
Hampshire
School Library
Service
HOLLYWOOD
SK8'S
HEY
DUDE
BUILT TO GRIND

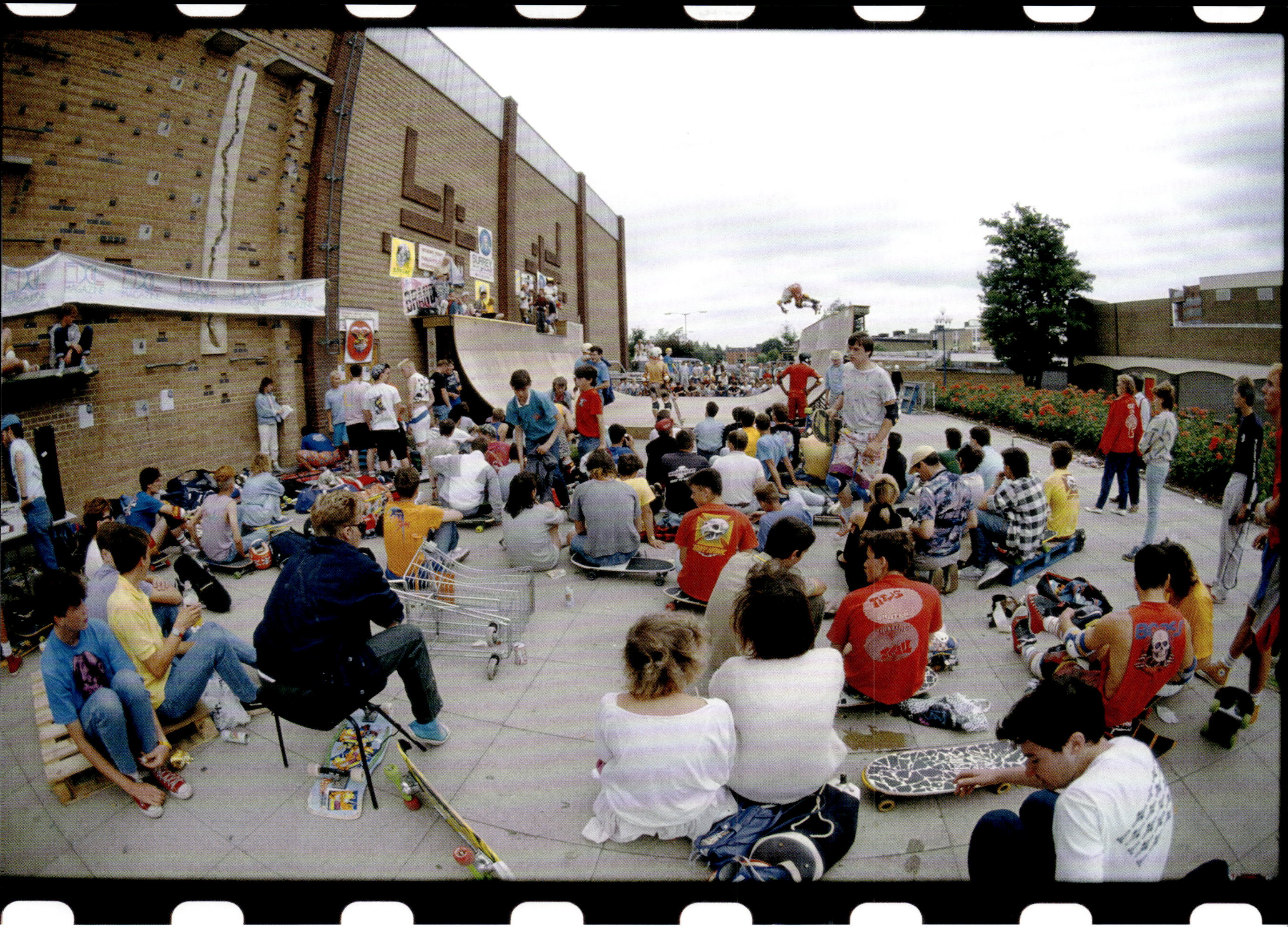

The Farnborough, Hampshire skate community maintained a 1980s contest-standard half-pipe and provided a venue for many lively events during the mid to late 1980s. Photos from various events 1985–1986 **Opposite middle left:** Mark Abrook, Farnborough, and **bottom right:** The Abrook brothers' personalised skate car **Overleaf:** Post-contest sticker toss, Farnborough, 1986 **All photos:** TLB

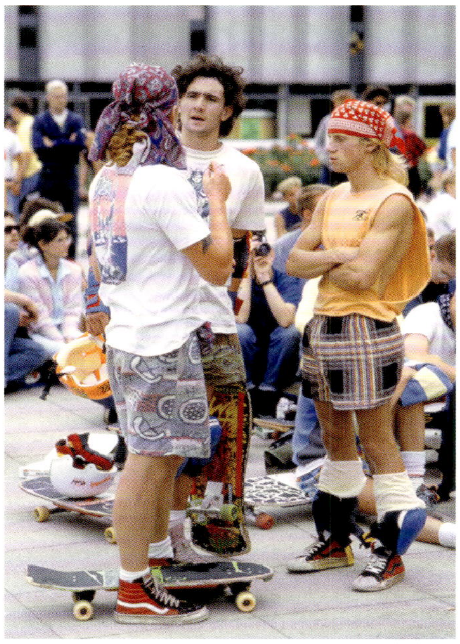

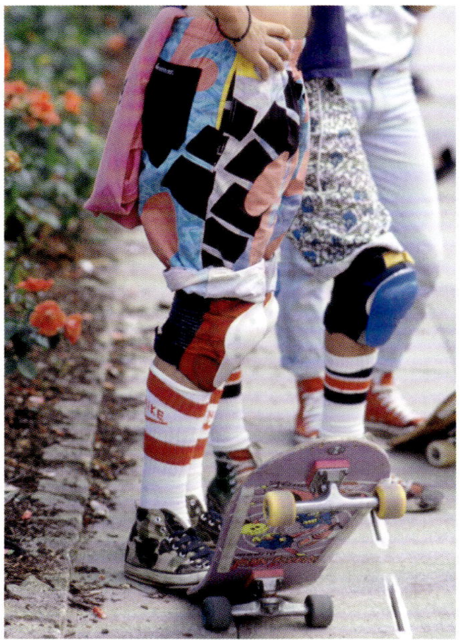

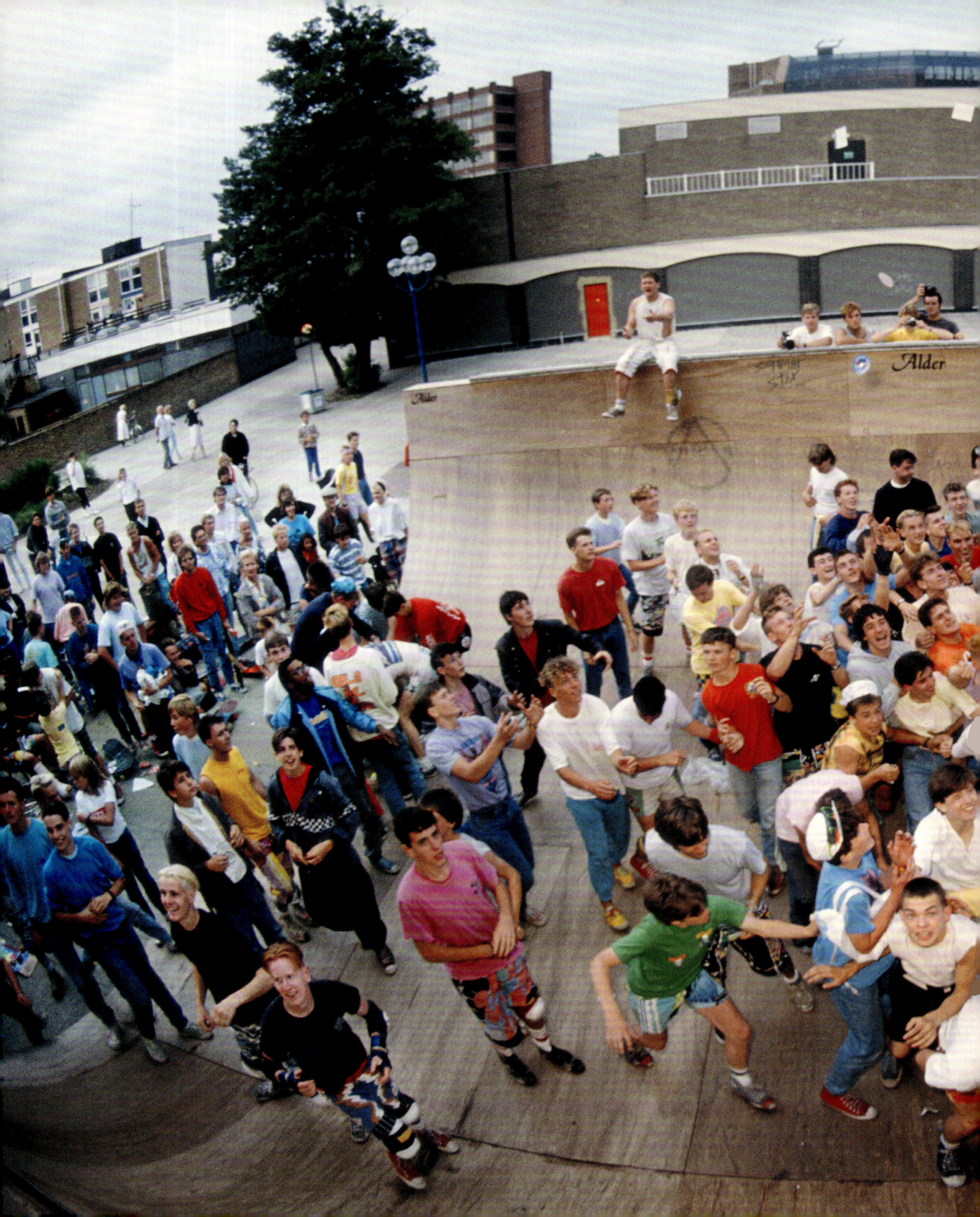
Alder

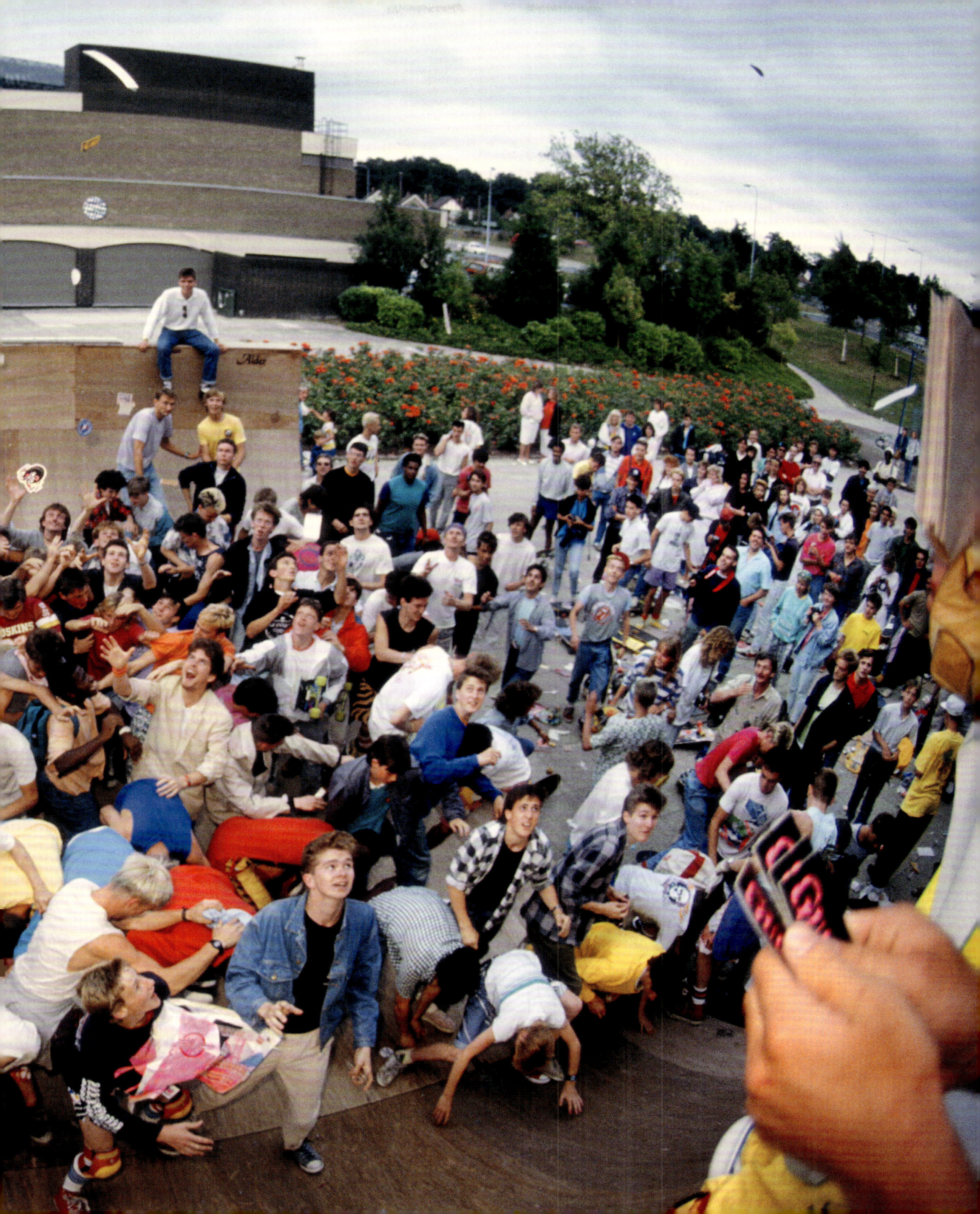

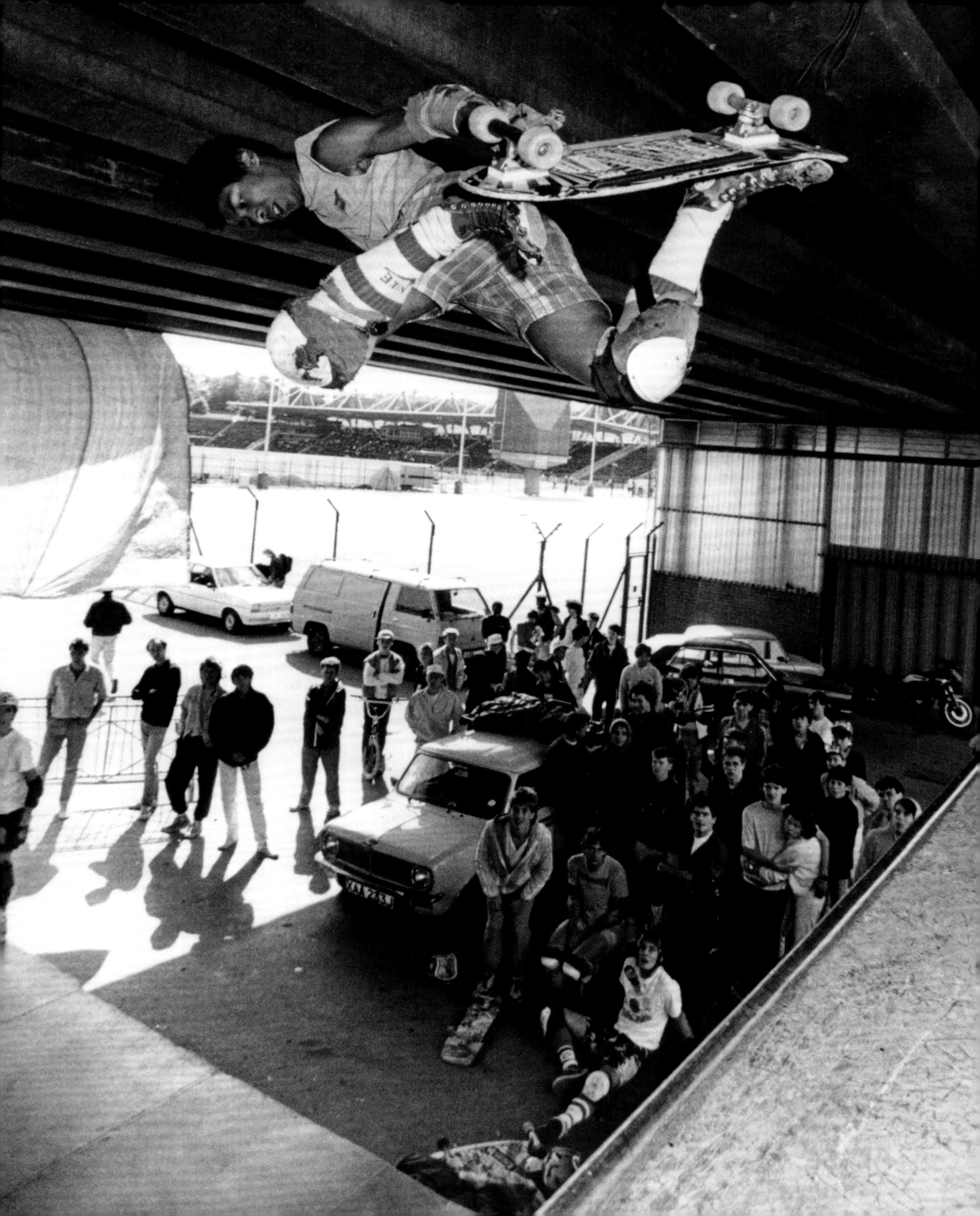
NIKE

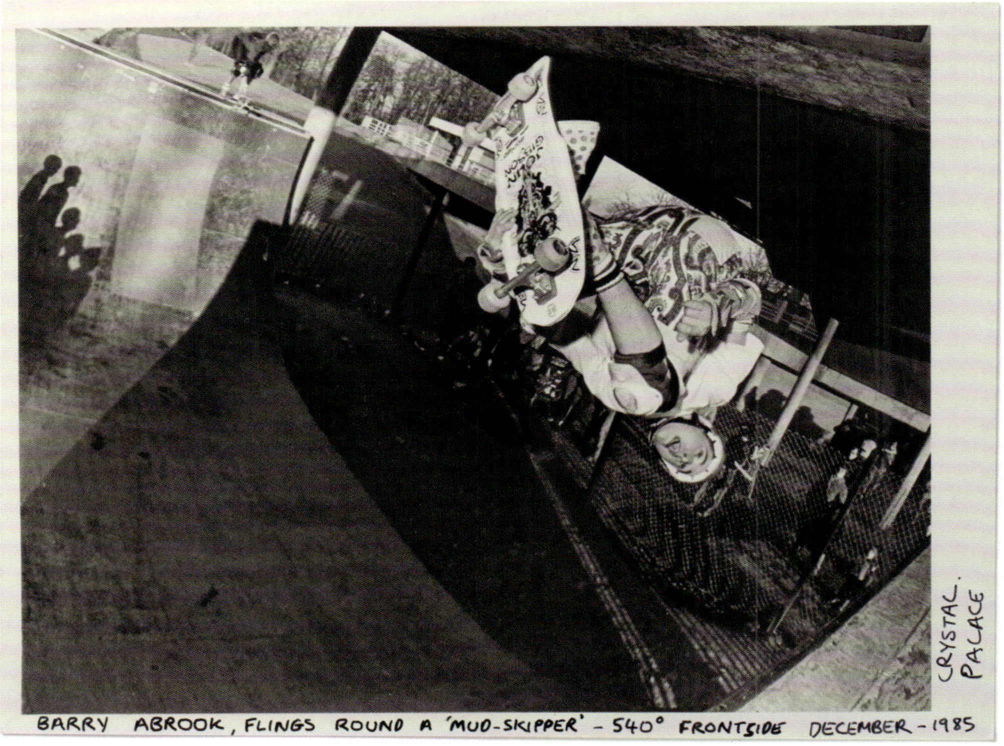

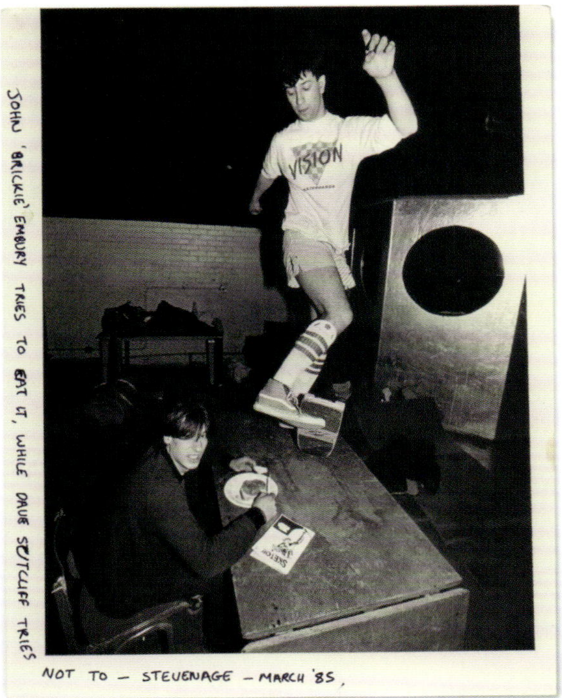

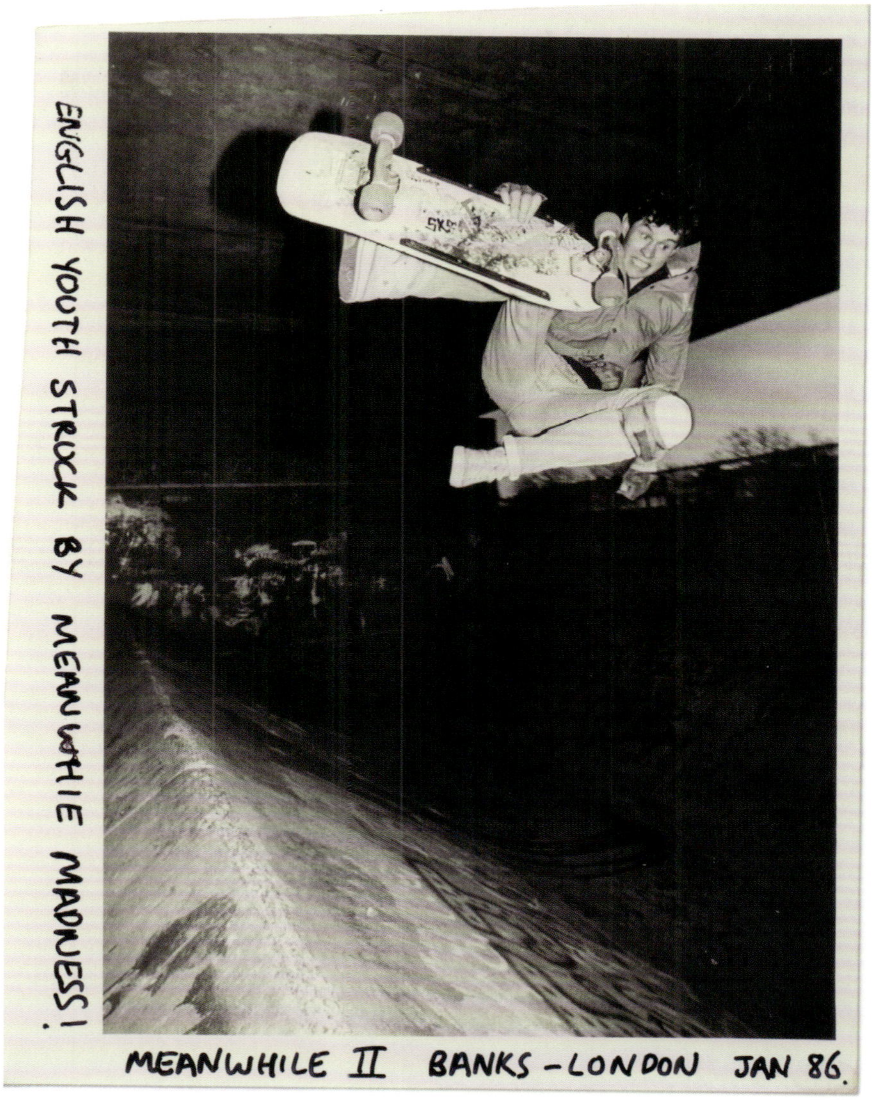

This page: All photos, prints and captions, Mike John 1985–86 **Opposite:** Lucian Hendricks, Crystal Palace fun contest, 1986 **Photo:** Mike John **Overleaf left:** Sam Davis, King's Cross underground tunnels, London, 1984 **Photo:** Mike John, and **right:** US visitor Adrian Demain, Mon Barbour's ramp, Oxfordshire, 1986 **Photo:** TLB

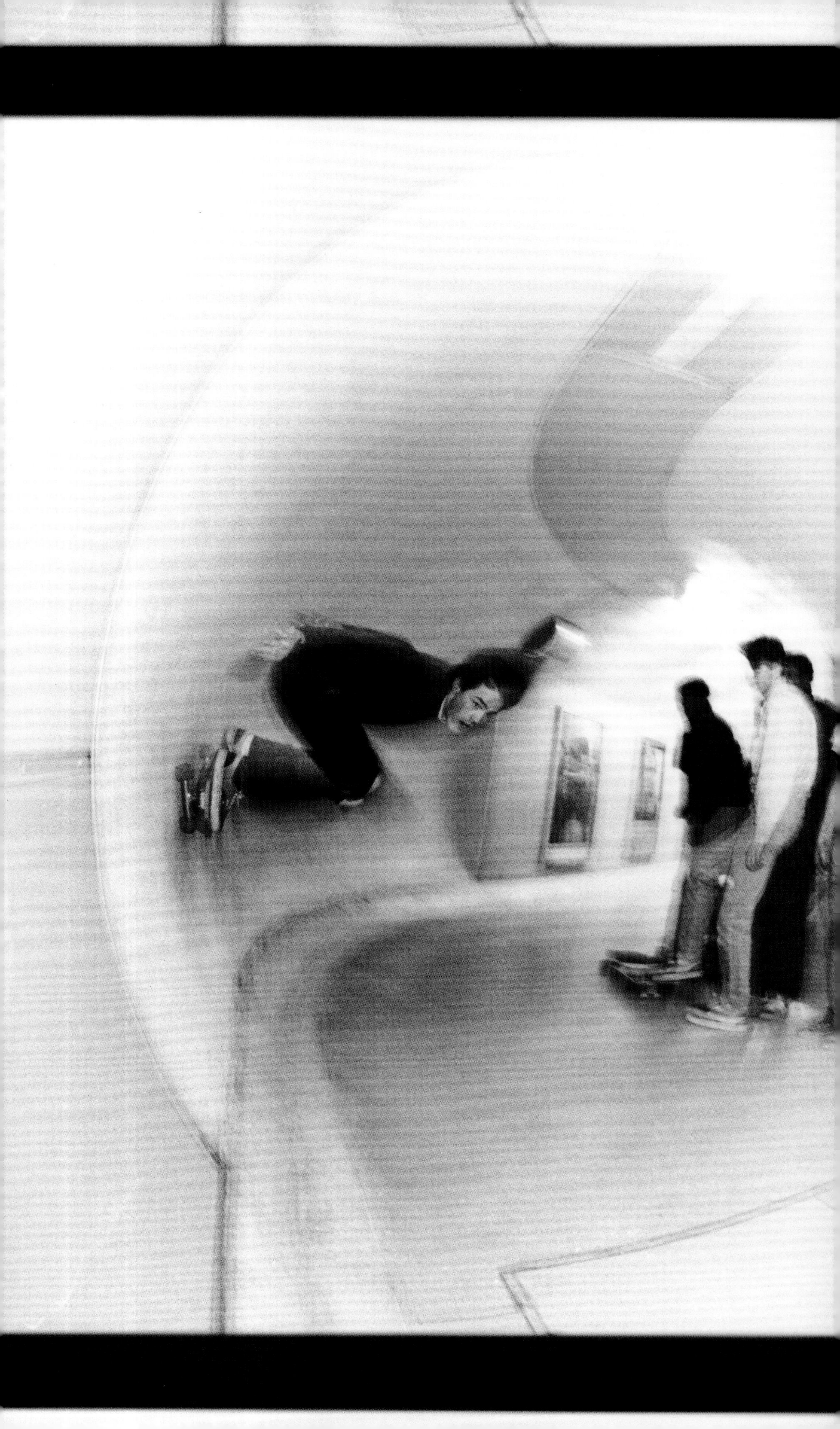

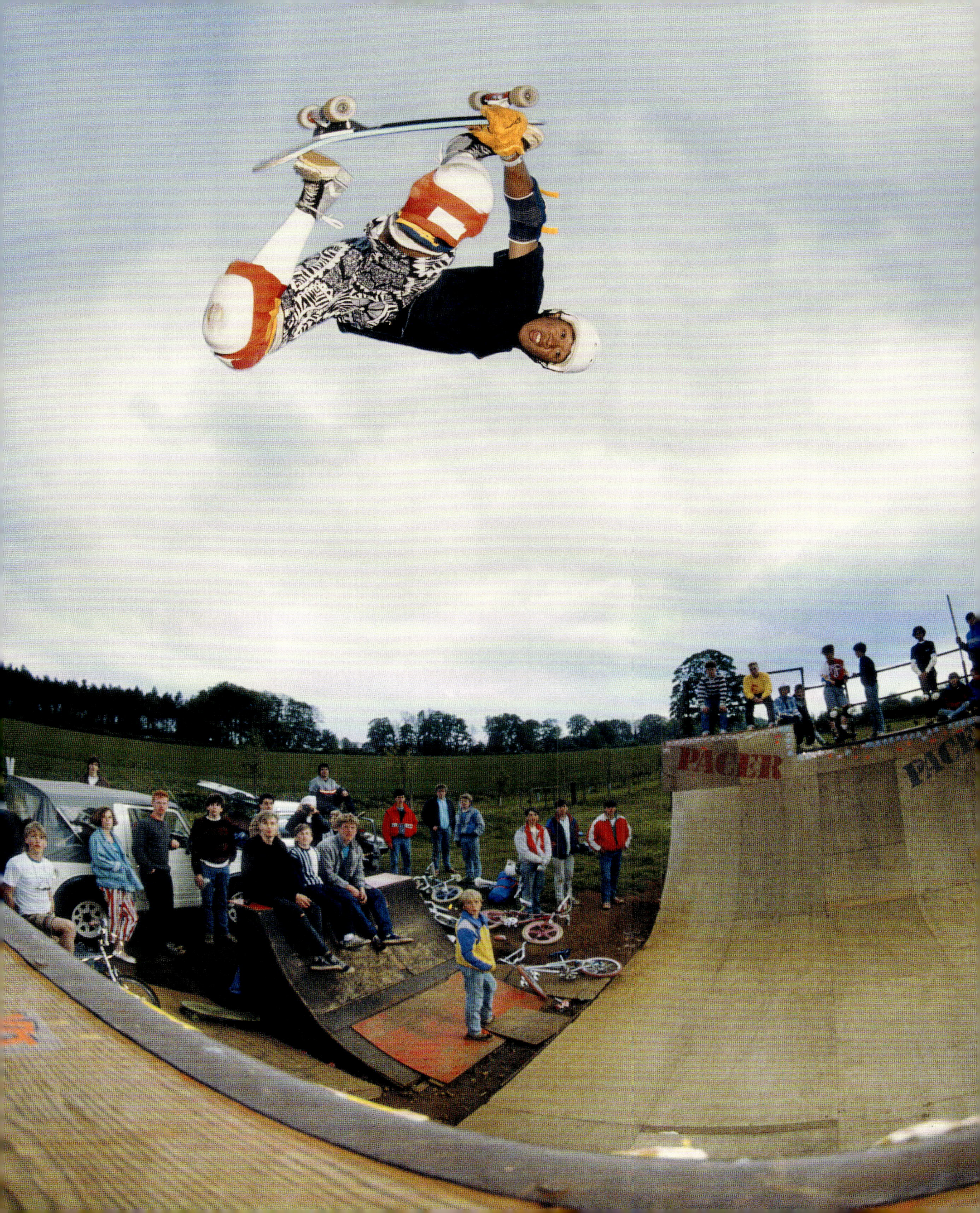
PACER
PACER

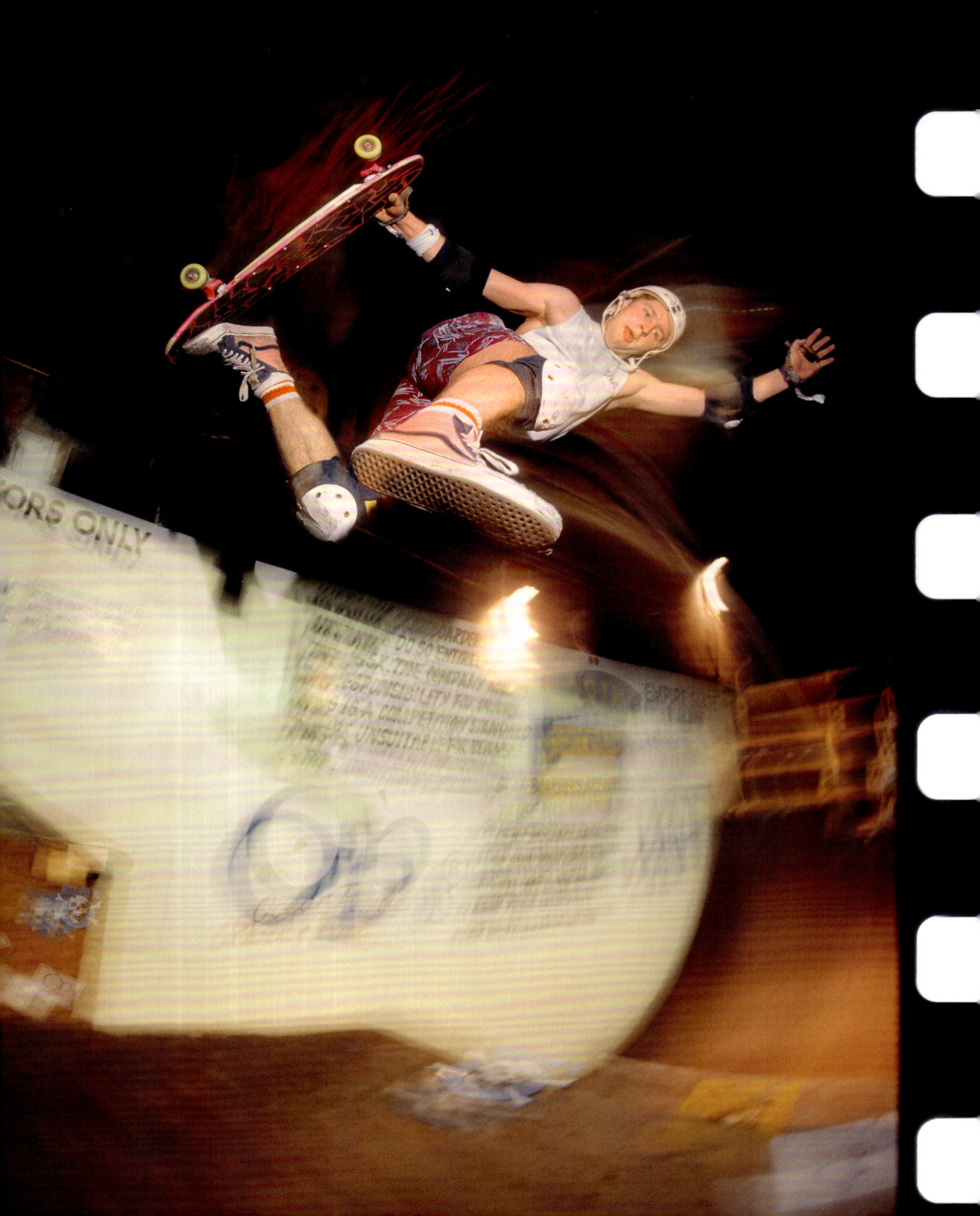

Opposite: Gary Lee **Photo:** Paul Sunman **Right:** Neil 'Danz' Danns, Empire Skate Building, Warrington, 1985 **Photo:** Mike John

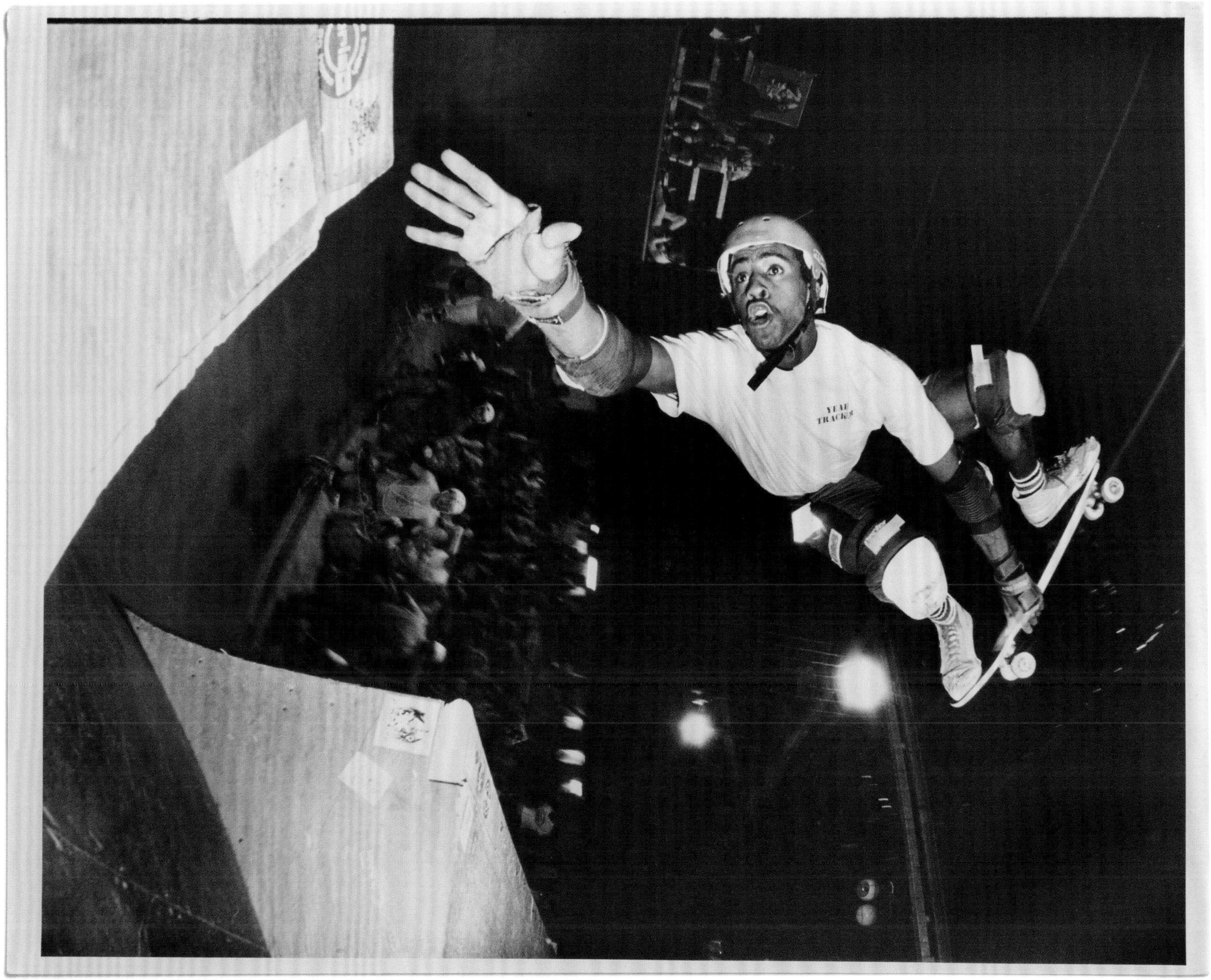

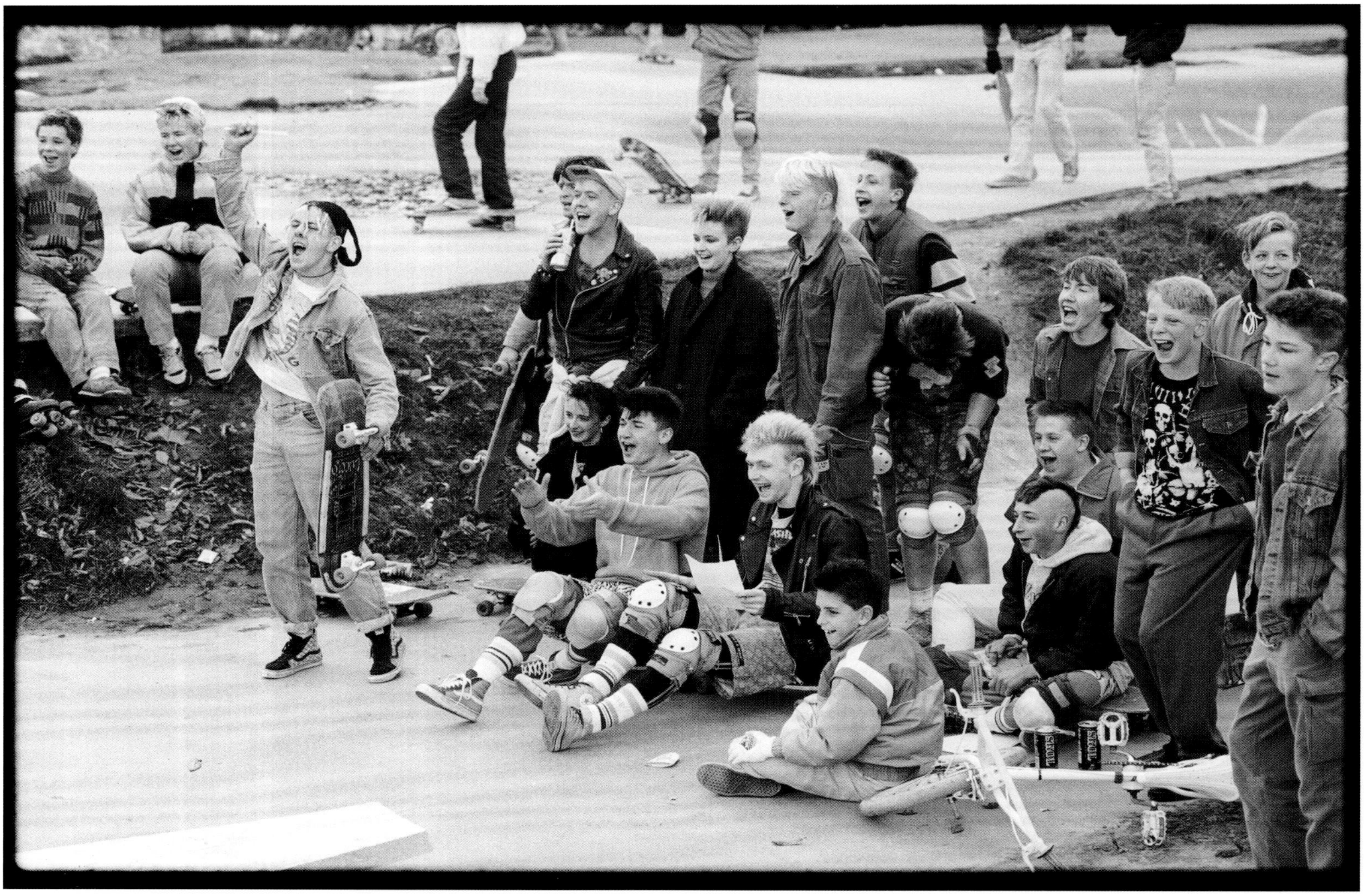

Above: Harrow skatepark fun contest, 1986 **Photo:** TLB
Opposite: Barry Abrook, Empire Skate Building, Warrington, 1985
Photo: Paul Sunman
Overleaf: Sean Goff, Swansea, Wales, 1986 **Photo:** TLB

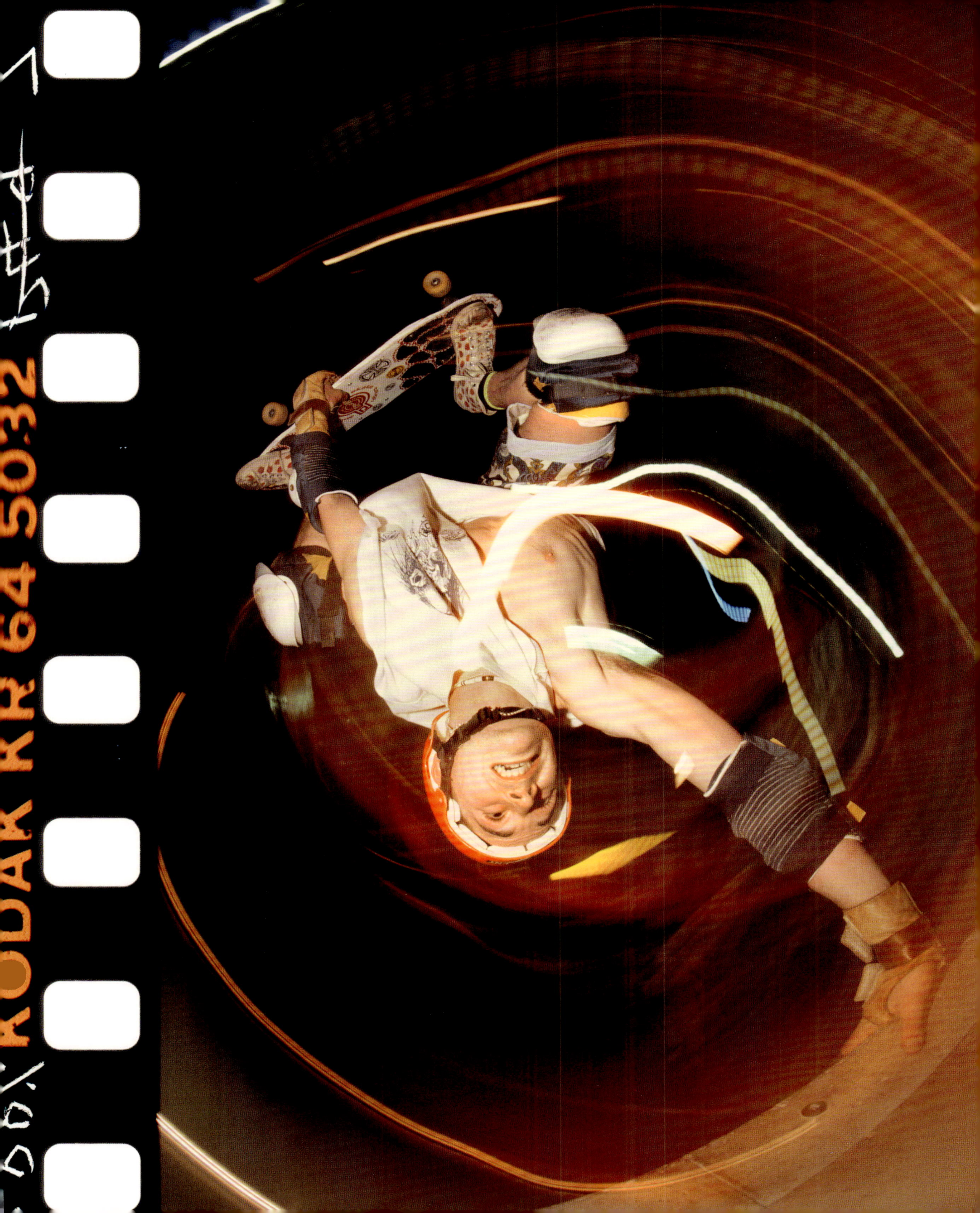
KODAK RR 64 5032

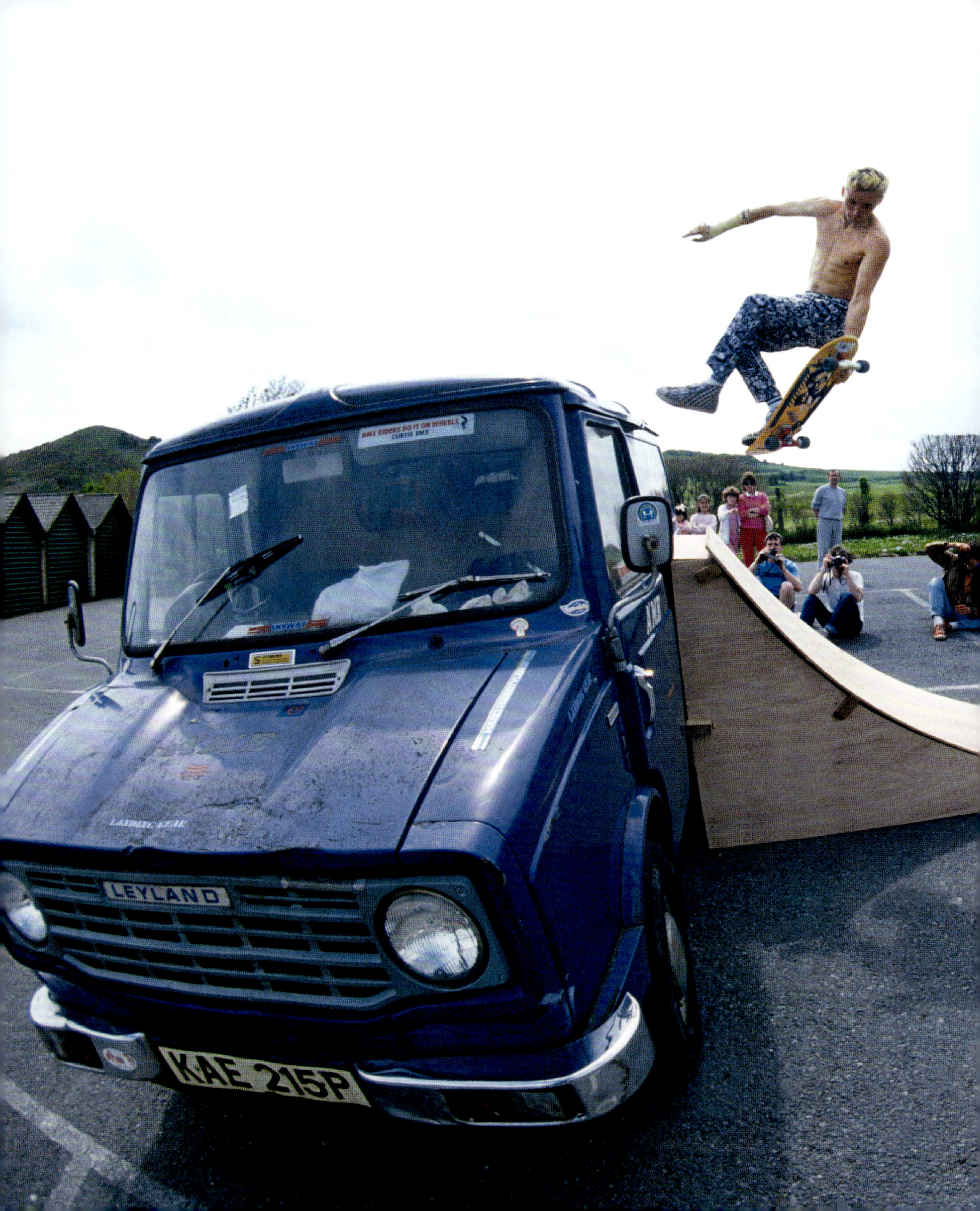
BMX RIDERS DO IT ON WHEELS
CURTIS BMX
LEYLAND
KAE 215P

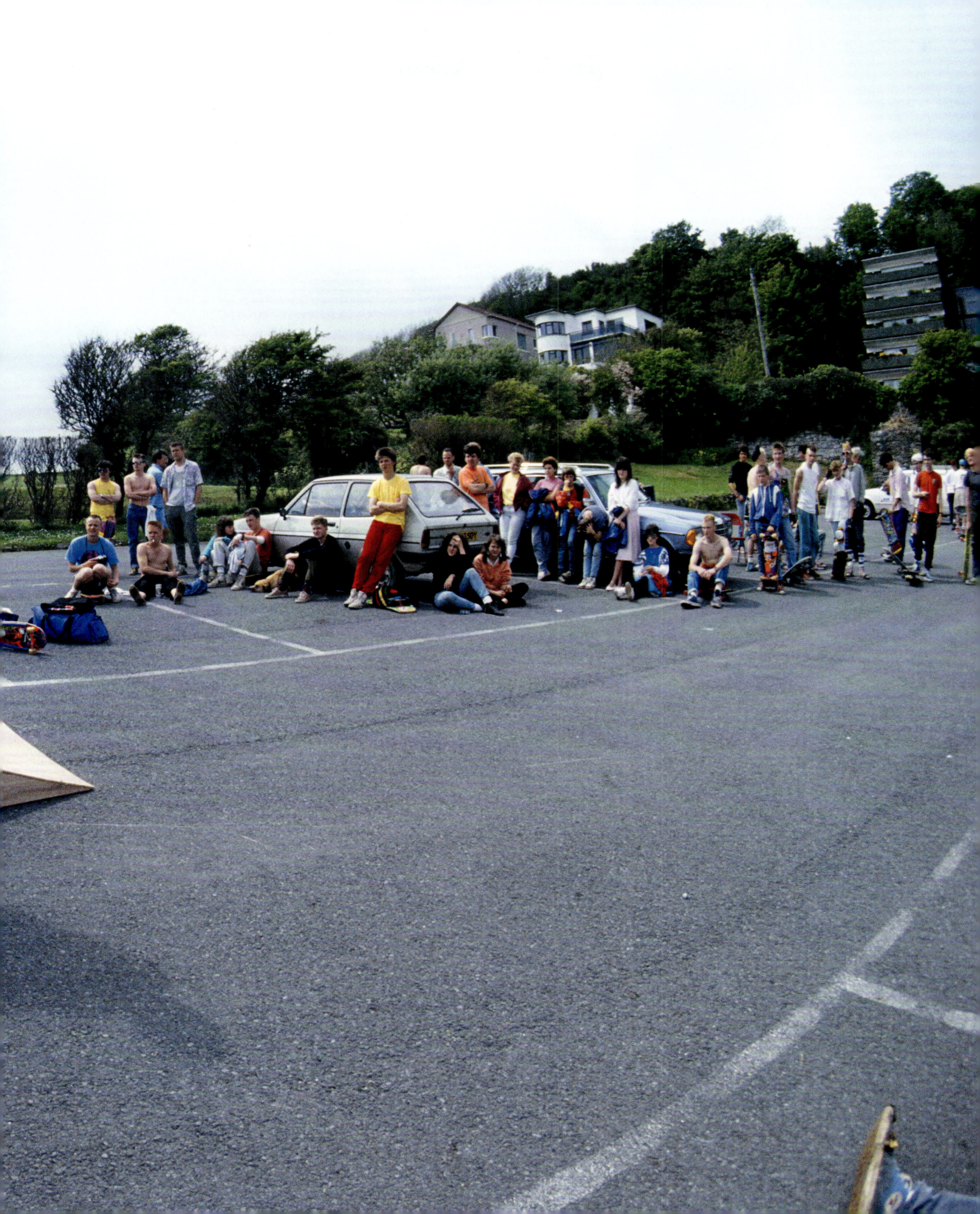

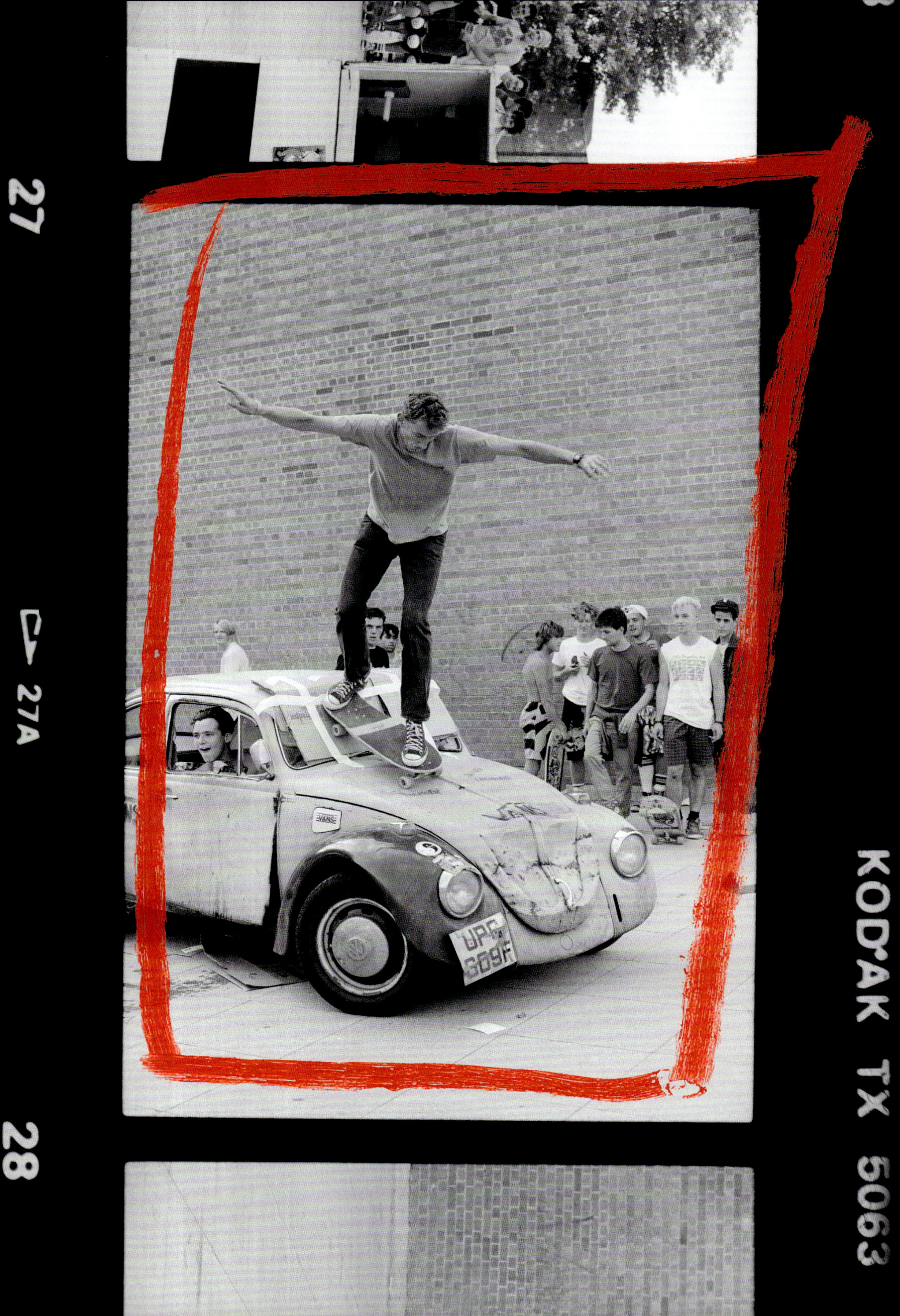

Left: Ian Deacon, Farnborough Street Jam, 1986 **Opposite:** Bod Boyle, Mon's ramp, Oxfordshire, 1985 **Photos:** TLB

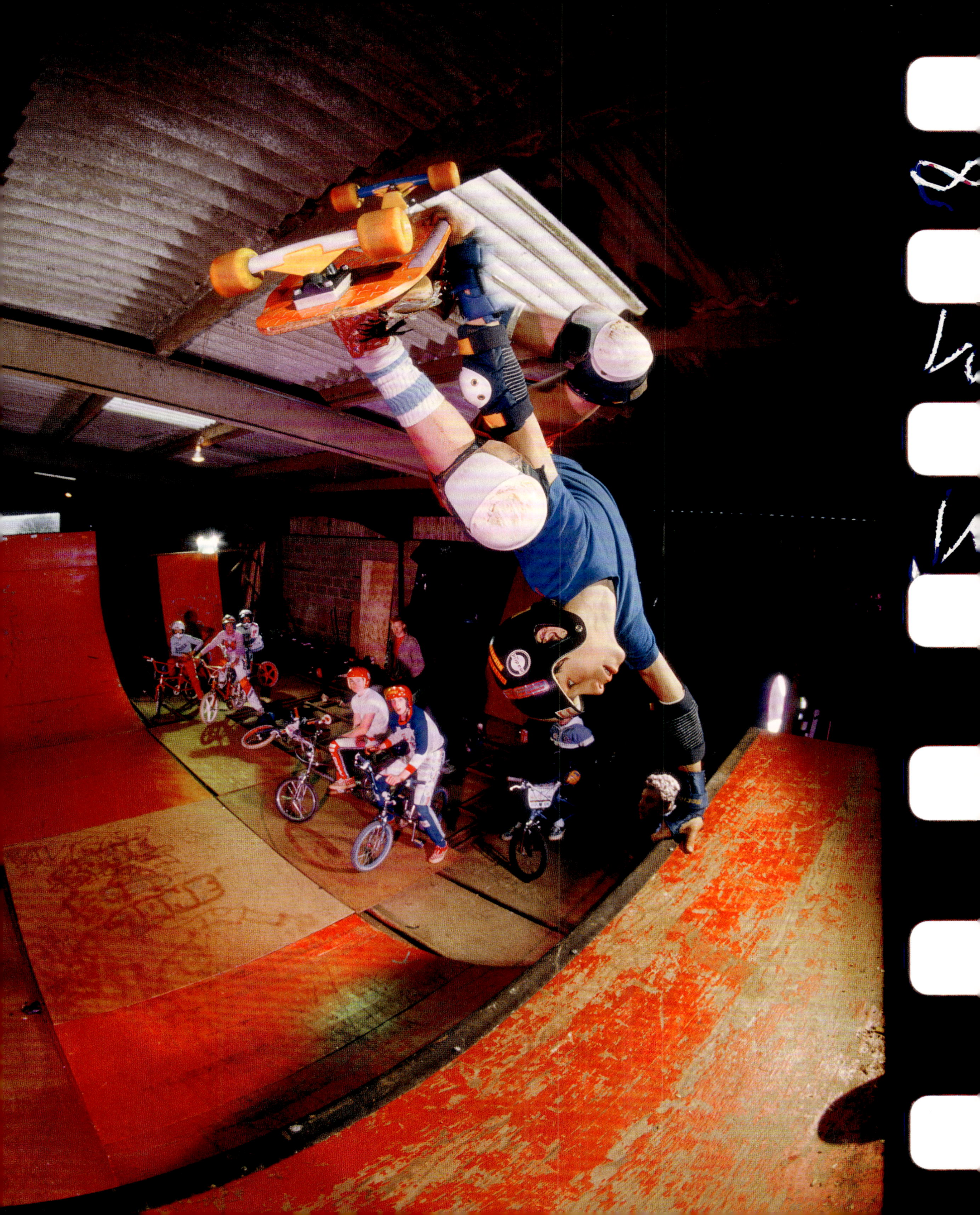

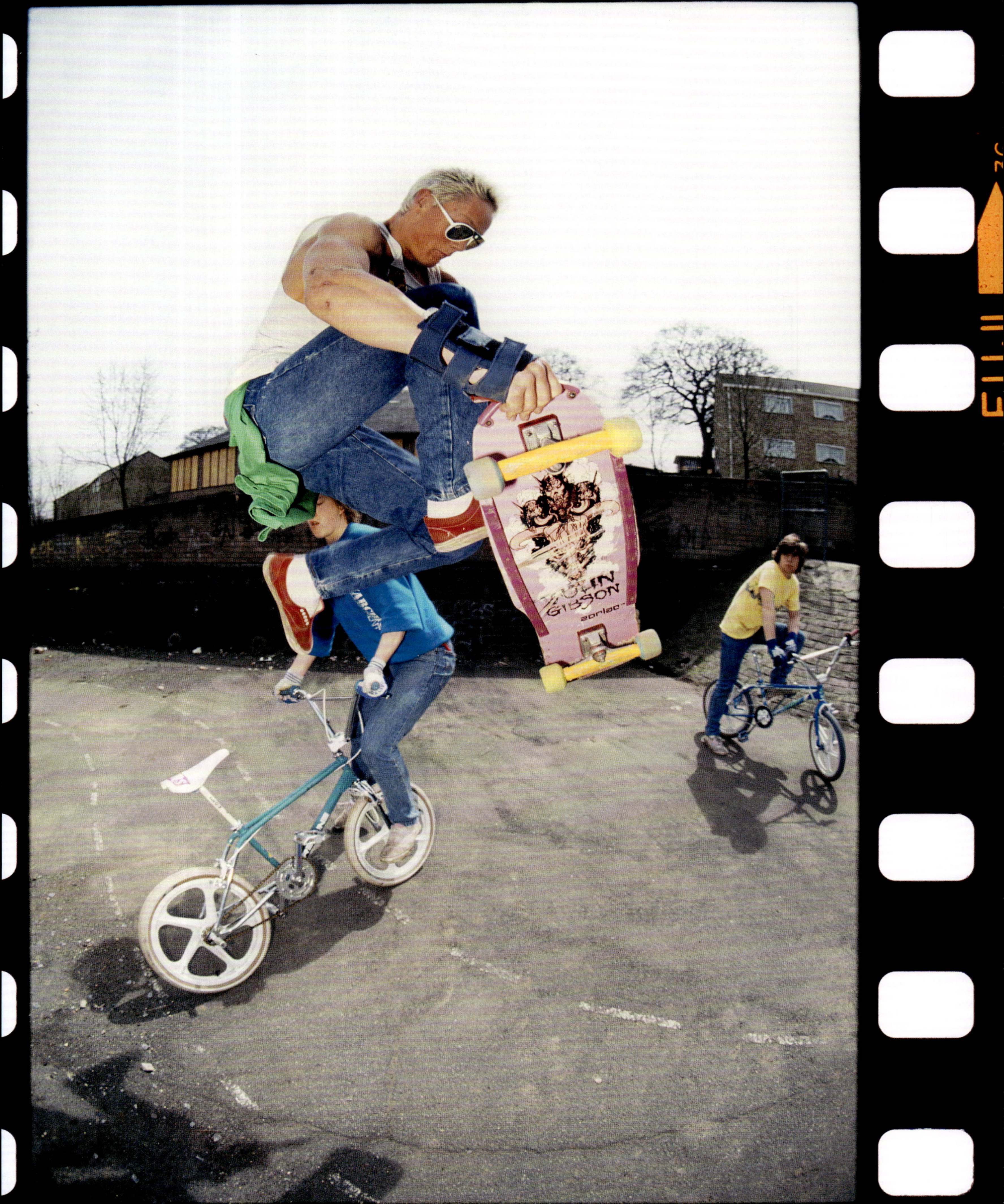
GIBSON
zorlac

IN FULL COLOUR

ZINES TO MAINSTREAM 1987–1993

'During the '80s, skateboarding outgrew the sanitised confines of commercial skateparks and was looking to lay claim to any shreddable surface that presented itself. The magazines' infectious enthusiasm for skate culture and "what if...?" approach to graphic design captured skaters' imaginations and hot-wired a street-skating revolution across the UK. Staffed by the very same skaters, riders and "vandals" the magazine celebrated, RAD *adopted a partisan DIY skate zine aesthetic in a bid to replicate the exhilaration of a grinding truck or bike frame along a concrete edge.'* Joel Lardner

In 1987, the building blocks finally fell into place. The long-awaited opportunity to publish a full-colour magazine with British skateboarding at its heart, had arrived. As TLB remembers: *'In the "dark ages" of skateboarding, nobody would have believed that you could release a magazine about skateboarding. That really wasn't on anyone's radar. But as soon as it was offered I grabbed at the chance.'* Fortuitously, TLB had been given an opening to allow him to continue the job of documenting and promoting the British skate scene, now via a prominent, full-colour platform.

'There was a strong desire to try and do a proper skate mag—it was totally a goal, right the way through. This was a mission to get a skateboard magazine. We subverted that magazine [BMX Action Bike]*. And I do feel awkward—because I knew what it felt like as a skater in the skateboard community when a magazine disappeared. But then I did that to another community, I stole their magazine I suppose. It feels bad; that's the way it's described at least.'* TLB

This move had not been a calculated, pre-meditated overthrow of any existing order—trying to force the hand of an unwilling audience. The evolution of the magazine came about in many ways by accident, but the change also captured the zeitgeist:

'Everyone saw the BMX industry beginning to contract and BMX Action Bike *were sensing this because advertising revenue was drying up. One of their biggest advertisers, Shiner Distribution in Bristol, knew that a resurgence in skateboarding's popularity was happening in America. They wanted to fund a skateboarding supplement for the BMX mag (to advertise the skate products that they were selling). The* SK8 Action *mag-within-a-mag was the result and it went down relatively well, encouraging further skate coverage in* BMX Action Bike *during that period.'* TLB

It was not just industry insiders who could see change on the horizon. The established die-hard skate community was dumbfounded when, seemingly out of the blue, Hollywood delivered two movies—*Back To The Future* in 1985 and *Thrashin'* in 1986—with skateboarders as the main protagonists. Who could predict that the jokey teen adventure movie *Back To The Future* would be the spark to ignite the passions of a whole new generation of skate enthusiasts, discovering fun on four wheels instead of two. By 1987, commercial and media interests had skateboarding firmly fixed in their sights and joined Hollywood in introducing skateboarding to a whole new audience.

Two key events in '87 clearly illustrated that major changes in the fortunes of British skateboard culture were underway. London's annual commercial BMX extravaganza, Holeshot, chose for the first

Previous spread: Paul Wright, 1987 **Photo:** TLB **Below:** March 1987's call to action as *BMX Action Bike* magazine begins its evolution to *Read And Destroy*

'In the early days of *RAD* there were two of us sharing a single desk in the corner of someone else's office. Nick defined the future of the mag just as much as I did' TLB

time to showcase some of America's most important professional skateboarders alongside the usual gathering of top international BMX riders. A pumped crowd of skate and bike enthusiasts took inspiration from none other than Mark Gonzales, Christian Hosoi, Steve Alba, Jeff Grosso and Jason Jesse. To witness such luminary figures of 1980s skateboarding live in Britain was a BIG deal.

In the same year, Britain's top skateboarders had their own chance to fire up an avid crowd with a half-pipe demo at London's Wind and Surf trade show. All of those involved, both in front of and behind the scenes, were astounded at the enthusiastic packed house of fans, apparently there purely for the skateboard demo. Hard evidence of skateboarding's nascent resurgence.

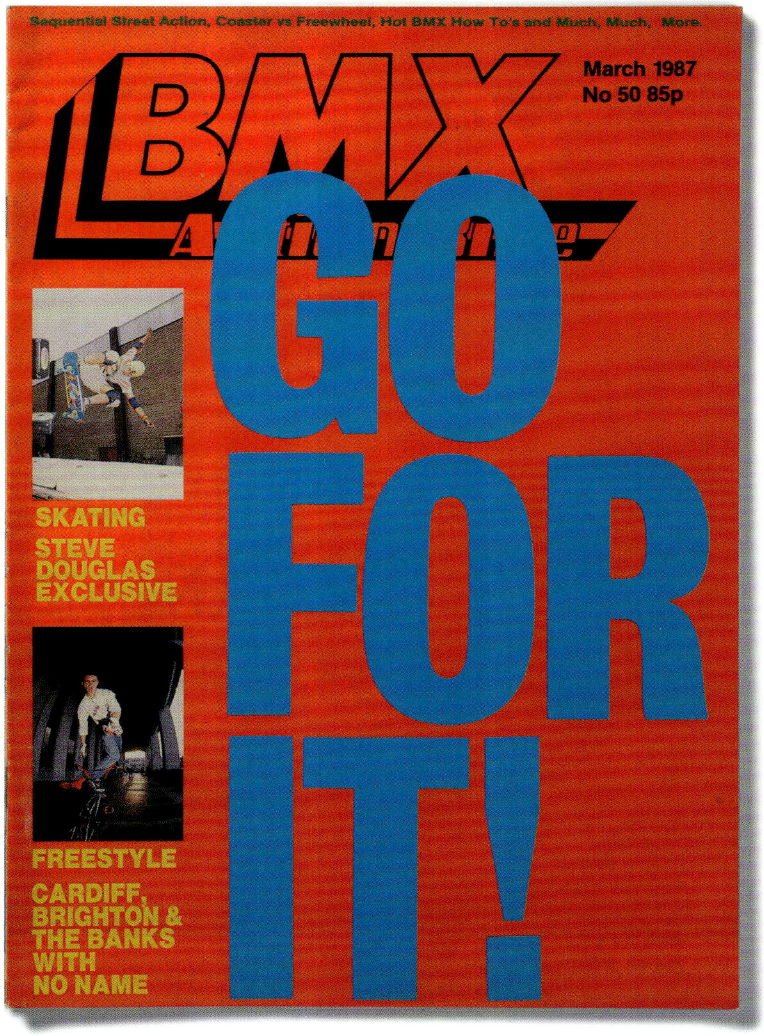

With this increased activity, mainstream media took to rediscovering skateboarding, amazed that a 'dead 1970s kids' craze' had evolved into a major underground culture. The revolving door of post-punk British youth cultures provided endless fascination to media outlets in their attempts at deciphering the latest youth phenomena. Now skateboarding, so long hidden from view, was being thrown into the mix—the next 'cool' thing. It was clear that the skateboarding enthusiasts of the 'dark days' had successfully built themselves a visceral, three-dimensional culture that offered great promise to anyone interested enough to take notice.

Clearly the time was right for a revival in the fortunes of British skateboarding publications—synchronicity would play its part. With *RAD*'s inception, a hungry, youthful audience, keen to connect with and learn about this newly discovered dynamic culture, had found their communication channel. Knowledge could of course be gleaned from the pages of *Thrasher* and *Transworld Skateboarding*—both firmly established in America as the leading voices of 1980s newly booming skate culture. But like the pioneering American skate magazines of the 1970s, these were impossibly faraway, idealised voices—not to mention difficult to find and expensive to buy. How could you discover and connect with the who, what, where of British skateboarding from the small suburban towns and villages across the nation?

Under TLB's editorship *RAD* magazine chose to address this need and reported from local perspectives, an approach which struck a chord with its hungry new audience:

'What TLB did was the hardest thing to do—because he had a super-tight budget—he had the vision to realise that there was a starved culture out there and he decided to give it a voice.' *RAD* contributor, Ged Wells

'Tim didn't want to be complacent and have an easy life. He wanted to inspire people to get out there and ride and he wanted kids to interact...' *RAD*'s second designer, Ian Roxburgh

The striking graphic appearance of this new magazine was developed by Nick Philip, the 'kid' who sought to bring the rule-breaking exploits of his progressive freestyle BMX riding to his graphic design. Already well-known at the Southbank and much influenced by the skateboarders he'd met there, he was part of the small London network of progressive DIY BMX riders and skateboarders.

As a sometime lurker at the *BMX Action Bike* offices, Nick walked into the role of designer / art director / layout artist, to work alongside photographer—and now editor—TLB to establish the voice and tone of the new magazine. Attacking the task at hand with a naive enthusiasm, what quickly evolved was a vivid, brash, counter-cultural visual language for *Read And Destroy*.

'Nick turned up as a kid producing a T-shirt company he called Anarchic Adjustment and wanted to take an advert out in the magazine. They had to explain to him how you made adverts, and very quickly he graduated from making his own adverts to being someone brought in to help with the design. The magazine was in the middle of a change of ownership and the new publisher came up with this arrangement where they'd have me doing all the words and pictures and Nick doing the paste up. So—two people producing the entire magazine, literally off a single desk.' TLB

'I didn't know anything about anything. There was this transition [in ownership] going on and they [the BMXAB publishers] were sort of like: "Yeah, you've got a bit of an eye, why don't you just art direct this whole magazine—see ya." And I have a feeling they thought, well, you know, the ship's going down so it doesn't really make that much difference if we give it to this kid and he fucks up.' Nick Philip

The publishers by and large chose to take a hands-off approach to the evolution of the new magazine. As editor, TLB was able to provide Nick with a *'non-didactic'*, supportive partnership and the creative space for him to experiment—and fail—trusting that the outcome would be honest and appropriate to the need.

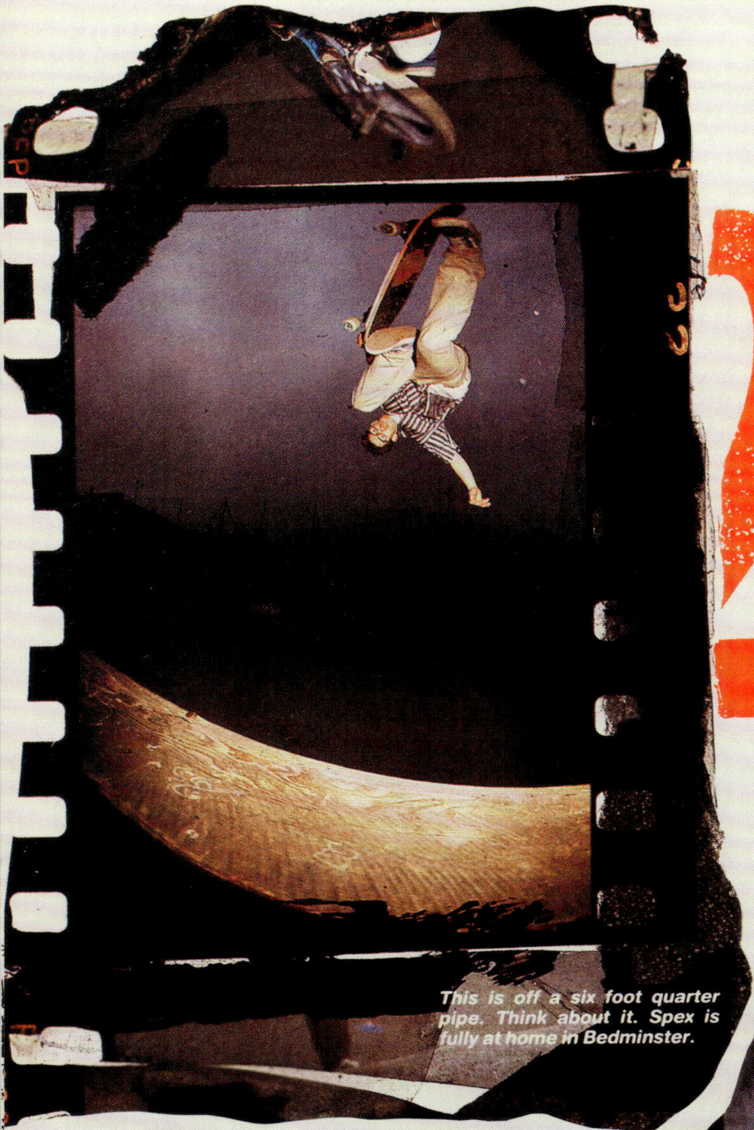

This is off a six foot quarter pipe. Think about it. Spex is fully at home in Bedminster.

This was probably built with some carving notion in mind in the days when skating was thought to be about hacking down hills on poly-props with granny-bowling in mind. Who knows? It's the most heavily sessioned place in the park.

The repertoire of moves is huge. Spex has probably got most. When we were there he was into sundry airs but there was a time when he used to do nothing but stalled inverts. And of course there's all the sliding and grinding and rock-n-rolling and laying back that such banks are so hot for. On this occasion the gnarly lip type stuff was provided by a bloke called Adam who certainly knows how well hard wheels, trucks and concrete go together.

Running down the whole side of the hill is a weird cross between a snake run (remember?) and an old-style tight concrete half-pipe. What the designers had in mind is anybody's guess. Carving round the snakey side??? Fortunately time and the skater's imagination have come up with lots of fun things to do. The locals have some innovative lines. They use the fact that one side goes up into a high bank to get speed for some staggering air over the hips of the snake side. Then again you can use the bowl type bits for some gnarly lip work.

That's one of the great things about Bedminster: in the age of the wooden ramp and the bona fide street it's easy to forget the attractions of skating or purpose built curved concrete. (You know — kinks, surface as rough as pizza tape...)

When places like Bedminster were built everyone shunned them for the attractions of the commercial parks, like the country club one in Bristol. Now nearly all the big parks have gone, but with them all the preconceptions about what is and what isn't skateable. The free parks remain, and they've come into their own now that skaters have got rid of their blinkers and learnt to explore the possibilities of everything around them — including places actually built for skating.

That's why Bedminster is a bank skater's paradise. Those who seek vert are not catered for. Well, there is a tinny old 6 foot quarter pipe facing a bank, but a REAL ramp skater would just laugh at it. Until he saw Spex at play. On our way out he treated us to a mind numbing display of just about anything you would expect to see on a full sized ramp. And that included staggering amounts of air as well as a hefty variety of lip tricks within the confines of the skinny twiglet. You have to see it to believe it.

Next stop was in the middle of town outside the Norwich Union building. This is where Dressen did the Ollie to 50/50s on a rail featured last month. Until then it was considered good for Rock'n'Roll slides. There's also a paving stone bank on a slope which is good for dossing around on. Only problem is that this pace is right next to a fairly busy road, and on a hill. Watch that expensive new board...

The problem at the next spot was of a different nature. Another nearby office building with excellent big, steep banks. And away from the traffic too. Trouble is this one's private and comes equipped with security men who don't like skaters. So it's back to the streets, I suppose.

Not necessarily. Bristol's got roots and a long history of skating: too much to ignore. As a result the council have come up with more in the way of facilities than just Bedminster. On a hill on the outskirts is Lockleaze. We didn't visit it this time, and it doesn't get sessioned very much because of where it is, but it's interesting. Lockleaze is in an adventure playground and it's another concrete job, built at the end of the last craze. There's a capsule type half-pipe, but it's been messed up with a half finished extension. Then there's the bowl — the more interesting feature of the two. It's strange: small and tight and sunk half-way into the ground. That means the run-in is half way up the wall from where you have to climb up to the lip. And climb's the word. There's now an extension on this for those who want to use it as a drop-bowl/ quarter-pipe. Talking of quarter-pipe's, there are also two ramps. Both are meant to be quarter-pipes, but one's more of an overgrown jump.

Back to the guided tour. It was getting dark when we made it to the wheels park at StGeorges. This is mellow and big. All the bank/bowl stuff you could want. Plus a bridge and a tunnel (that's not supposed to be a full-pipe is it?) There was a lot of grommet bike activity here. In fact they objected to the arrival of skaters on the grounds that the park was built during the BMX craze period and was meant for bikes only. Does it really matter? StGeorge's looks good for a doss, but it was a bit hard to tell by now because it was dark and starting to rain. We sat in the mini pipe, ran a tape on Dressen and went home.

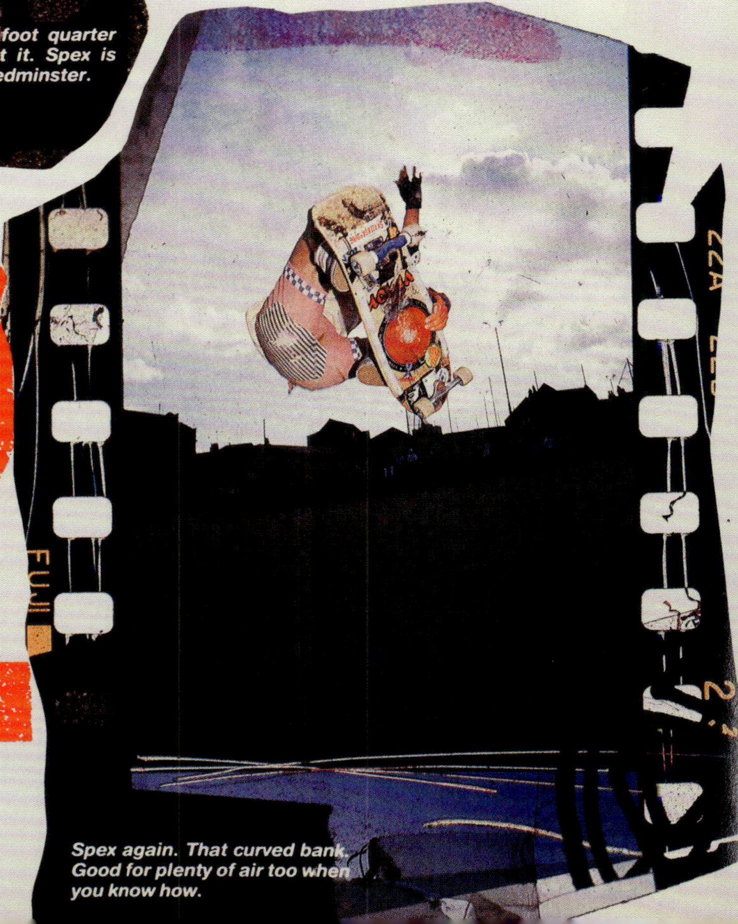

Spex again. That curved bank. Good for plenty of air too when you know how.

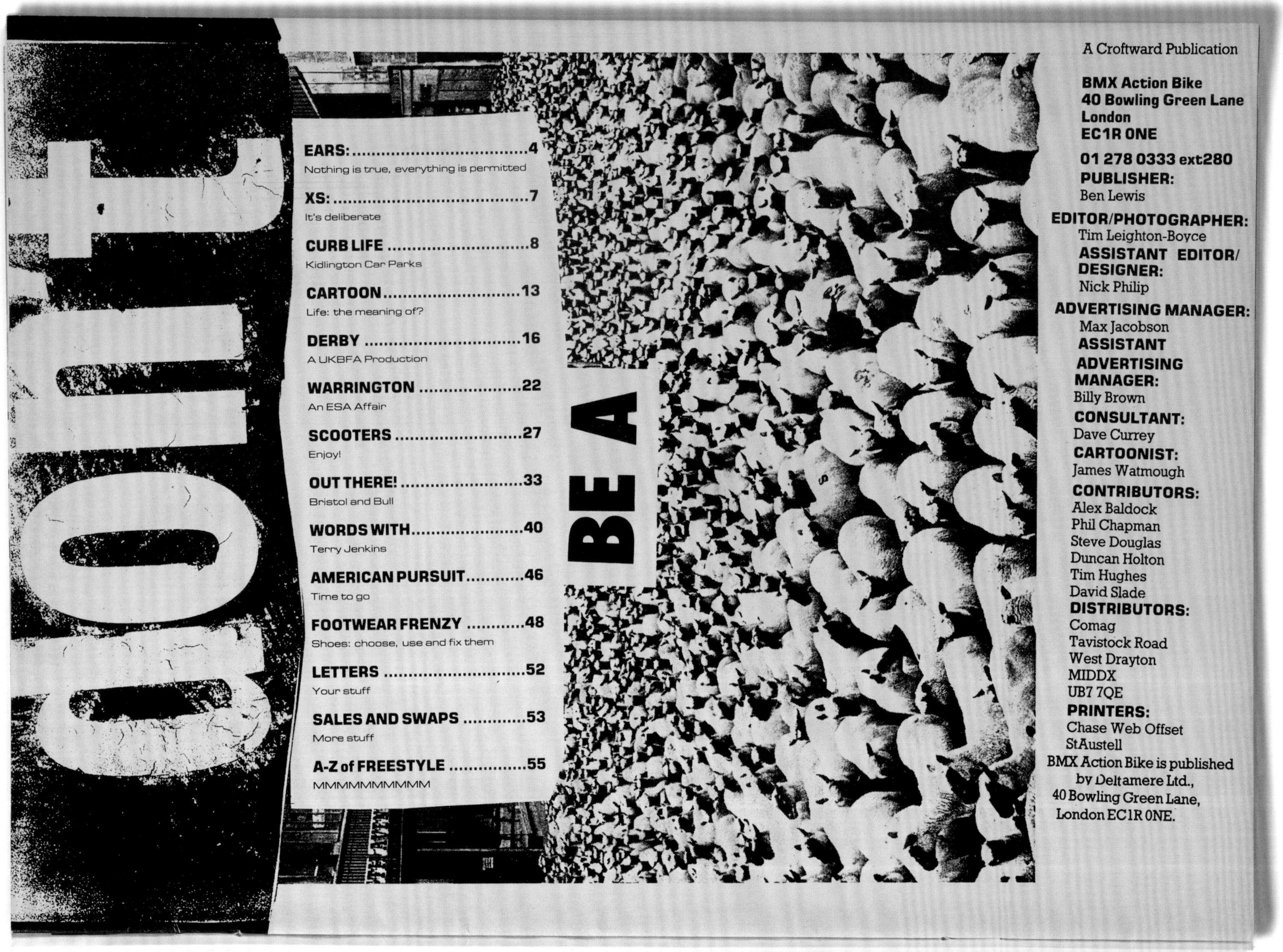

dont
EARS: 4
Nothing is true, everything is permitted
XS: 7
It's deliberate
CURB LIFE 8
Kidlington Car Parks
CARTOON 13
Life: the meaning of?
DERBY 16
A UKBFA Production
WARRINGTON 22
An ESA Affair
SCOOTERS 27
Enjoy!
OUT THERE! 33
Bristol and Bull
WORDS WITH 40
Terry Jenkins
AMERICAN PURSUIT 46
Time to go
FOOTWEAR FRENZY 48
Shoes: choose, use and fix them
LETTERS 52
Your stuff
SALES AND SWAPS 53
More stuff
A-Z of FREESTYLE 55
MMMMMMMMMM
BE A
A Croftward Publication
BMX Action Bike
40 Bowling Green Lane
London
EC1R ONE
01 278 0333 ext280
PUBLISHER:
Ben Lewis
EDITOR/PHOTOGRAPHER:
Tim Leighton-Boyce
ASSISTANT EDITOR/ DESIGNER:
Nick Philip
ADVERTISING MANAGER:
Max Jacobson
ASSISTANT ADVERTISING MANAGER:
Billy Brown
CONSULTANT:
Dave Currey
CARTOONIST:
James Watmough
CONTRIBUTORS:
Alex Baldock
Phil Chapman
Steve Douglas
Duncan Holton
Tim Hughes
David Slade
DISTRIBUTORS:
Comag
Tavistock Road
West Drayton
MIDDX
UB7 7QE
PRINTERS:
Chase Web Offset
StAustell
BMX Action Bike is published by Deltamere Ltd., 40 Bowling Green Lane, London EC1R 0NE.

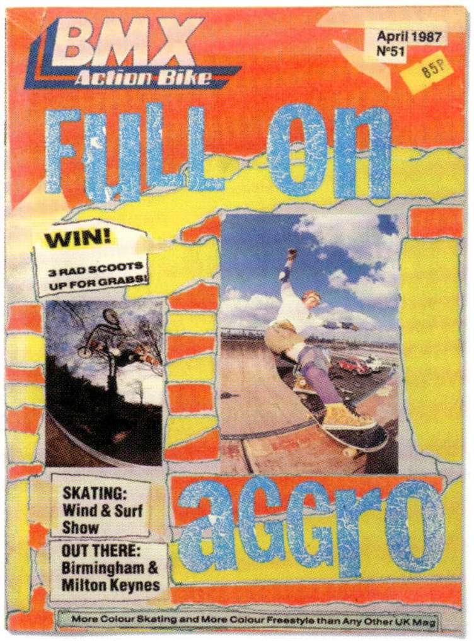

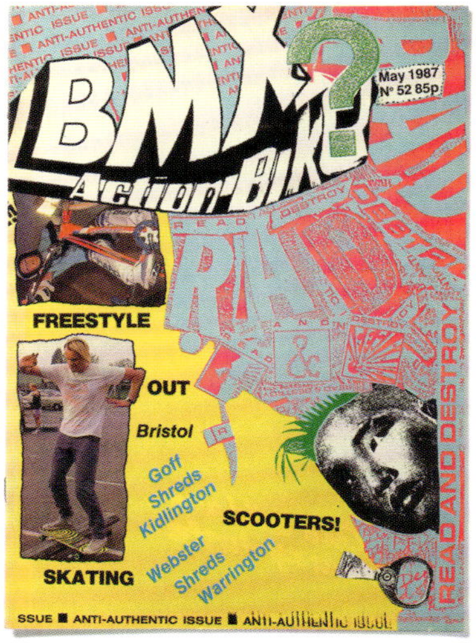

Opposite: 1987 contents page artwork by Nick Philip **Left:** Cover transitions from *BMX Action Bike* to *RAD*. Issue 51, Nick Philip design. Issue 52, Nick Philip and Dave Currey graphic design **Right:** Issue 53, Nick Philip graphic design **Below:** Pushing the envelope, Nick Philip translates the skateboarder's wallride to BMX **All photos**: TLB

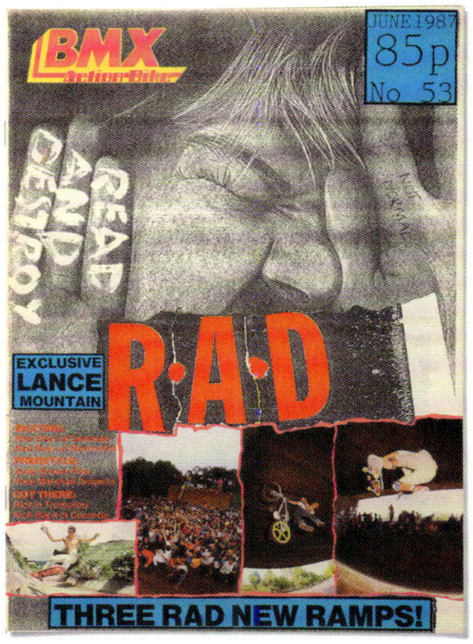

'So it was this situation where I had the possibility to do anything—which ended up being making loads of mistakes, right? I was just, have-at-it with whatever I had in front of me—if that was a PMT camera, if that was a Xerox machine, if that was a slide transparency that I could scratch into or throw a bit of bleach on, whatever—putting grip tape through the scanner. So it was a lot of mistakes and trial and error. The things that worked would never really have seen the light of day I think if I hadn't been given so much freedom.' Nick Philip

'Nick didn't know anything about type fitting (amongst other things). He was doing this multi-page layout and got to page three of it or whatever and he'd used up all the text on the first two pages, so he just hand wrote across it "No more words after this", as in—I've run out of them. And I thought that was brilliant, just his mad approach to doing it.' TLB

And so, in an open, experimental environment, a dynamic clash of bikes, skateboards and street culture was erupting. A combined 'radical' culture was taking shape—a chaotic mash-up of thrill-seeking, wheeled endeavours, with skateboarding at its core. The sentiments expressed were driven very much by the underground DIY survival ethos that the skateboarding community had built for themselves throughout the preceding years of the early 1980s.

Without doubt, for hard-core purists from the established BMX and skateboarding communities, this new culture clash was an unseemly chimera. However, there was a newer generation that accepted, even relished this beast with enthusiasm:

'It ended up that we were able to make this transition and redirect the magazine so that we could be aligned with skateboarding and the street culture that was emerging.' Nick Philip

It was clear from the outset that Nick's dynamic visual approach and feisty counter-cultural attitude struck a chord with the outsider mindset of the skateboard community *and* the evolving freestyle BMX world. His graphic exploits at the magazine and forays into clothing and print design had just the right amount of punky, rebel-without-a-cause attitude to find fans in both camps.

The shared 'uniform' of the mid-1980s freestyle BMX, surf and skateboarding scenes was a major unifying element—a visually wild mixture of loose, layered shapes in electric colours emblazoned with bold graphics and all-over prints. Shoes designed for and marketed to skateboarders had long since crossed over into BMX culture. Whether featured in visually arresting ads from the likes of M-Zone and Anarchic Adjustment or conveyed in the magazine's photography, this brash, technicolour soup of surf, skate, bike and DIY clothing brands all transposed from the bright blue skies of California to the grubby, grey streets of Thatcher's Britain was a very visible characteristic of the magazine's early years.

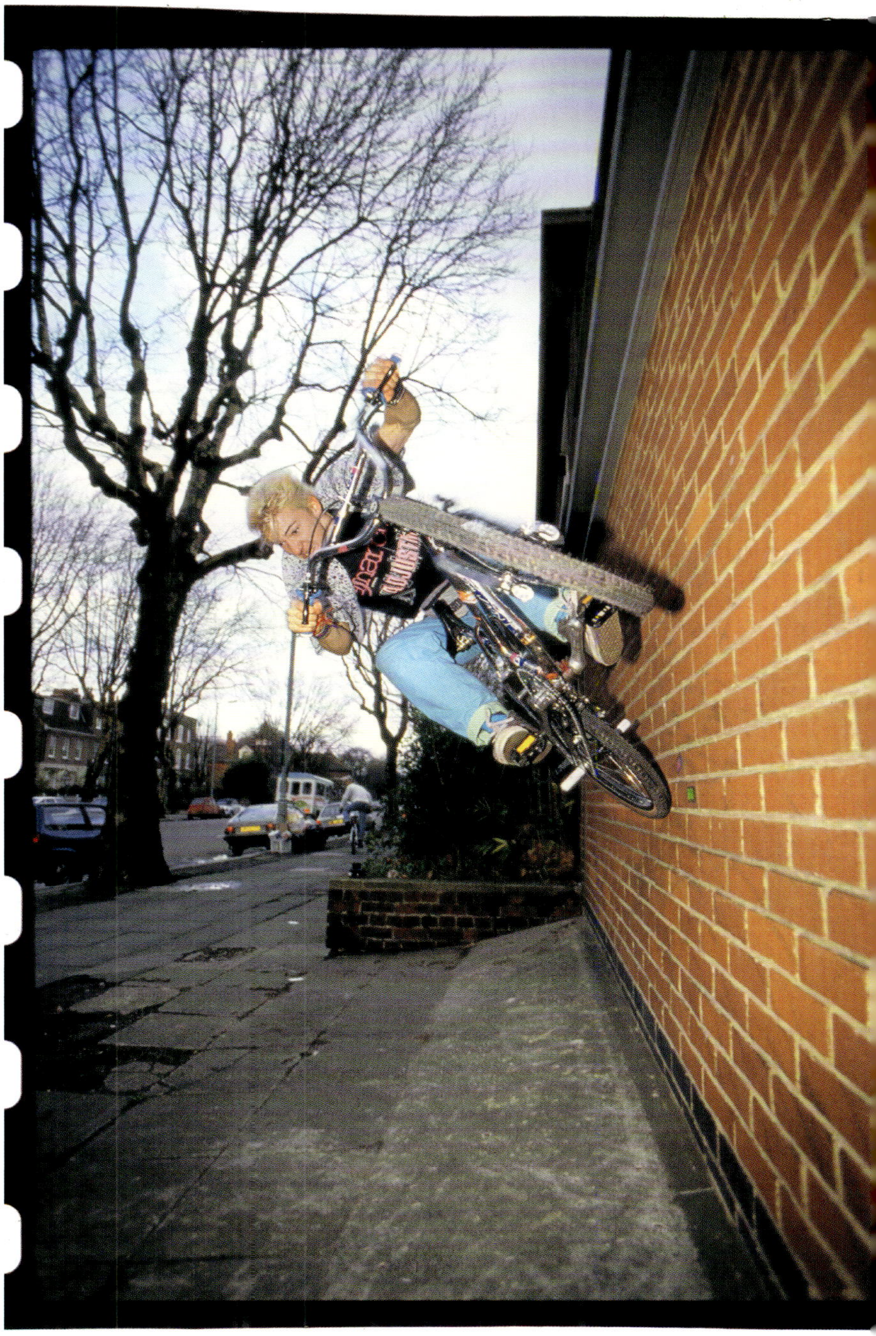

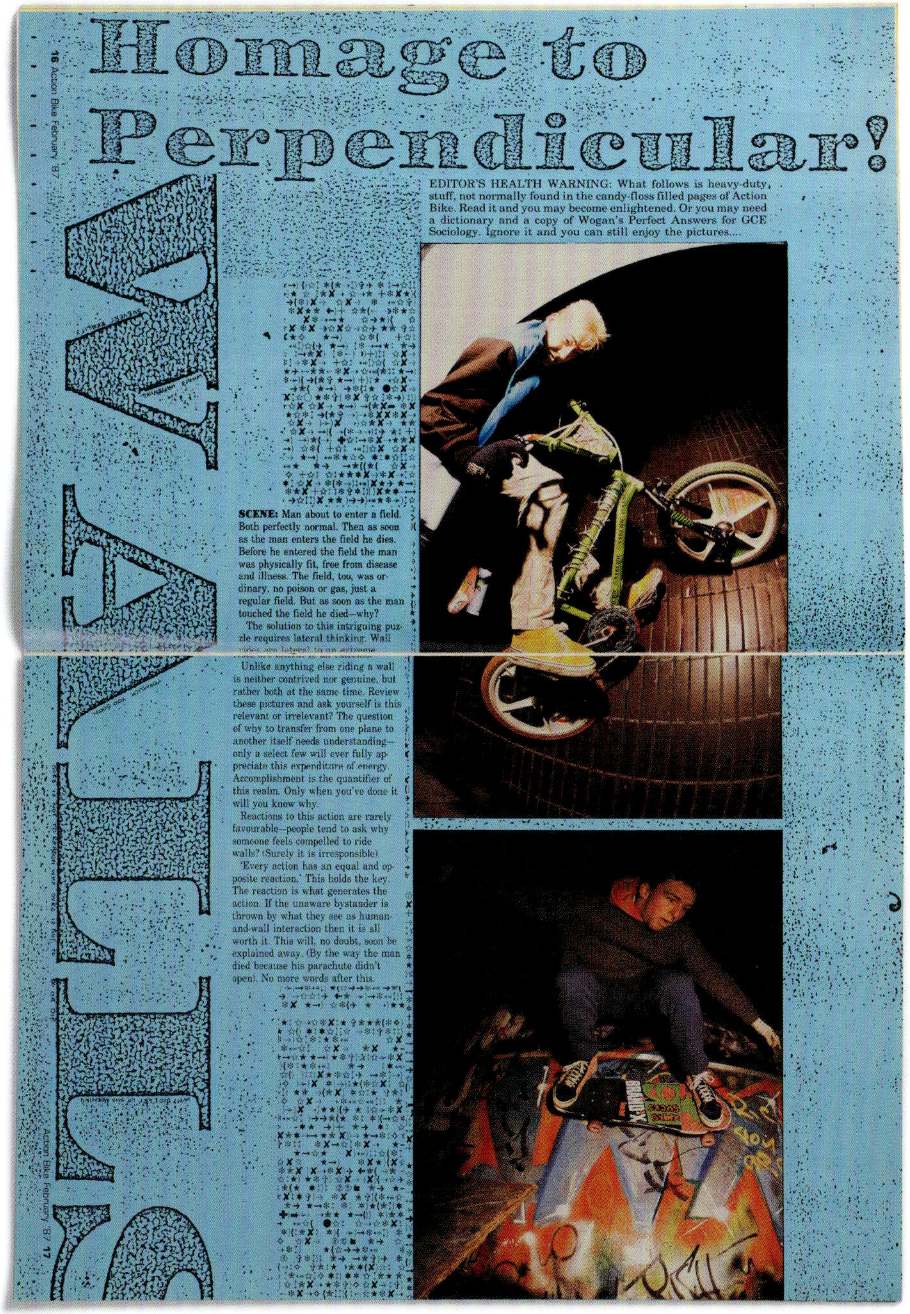

Homage to Perpendicular!

EDITOR'S HEALTH WARNING: What follows is heavy-duty, stuff, not normally found in the candy-floss filled pages of Action Bike. Read it and you may become enlightened. Or you may need a dictionary and a copy of Wogan's Perfect Answers for GCE Sociology. Ignore it and you can still enjoy the pictures....

WALLS

SCENE: Man about to enter a field. Both perfectly normal. Then as soon as the man enters the field he dies. Before he entered the field the man was physically fit, free from disease and illness. The field, too, was ordinary, no poison or gas, just a regular field. But as soon as the man touched the field he died—why?

The solution to this intriguing puzzle requires lateral thinking. Wall

Unlike anything else riding a wall is neither contrived nor genuine, but rather both at the same time. Review these pictures and ask yourself is this relevant or irrelevant? The question of why to transfer from one plane to another itself needs understanding—only a select few will ever fully appreciate this *expenditure of energy*. Accomplishment is the quantifier of this realm. Only when you've done it will you know why.

Reactions to this action are rarely favourable—people tend to ask why someone feels compelled to ride walls? (Surely it is irresponsible)

'Every action has an equal and opposite reaction.' This holds the key. The reaction is what generates the action. If the unaware bystander is thrown by what they see as human-and-wall interaction then it is all worth it. This will, no doubt, soon be explained away. (By the way the man died because his parachute didn't open). No more words after this.

16 Action Bike February '87

Action Bike February '87 17

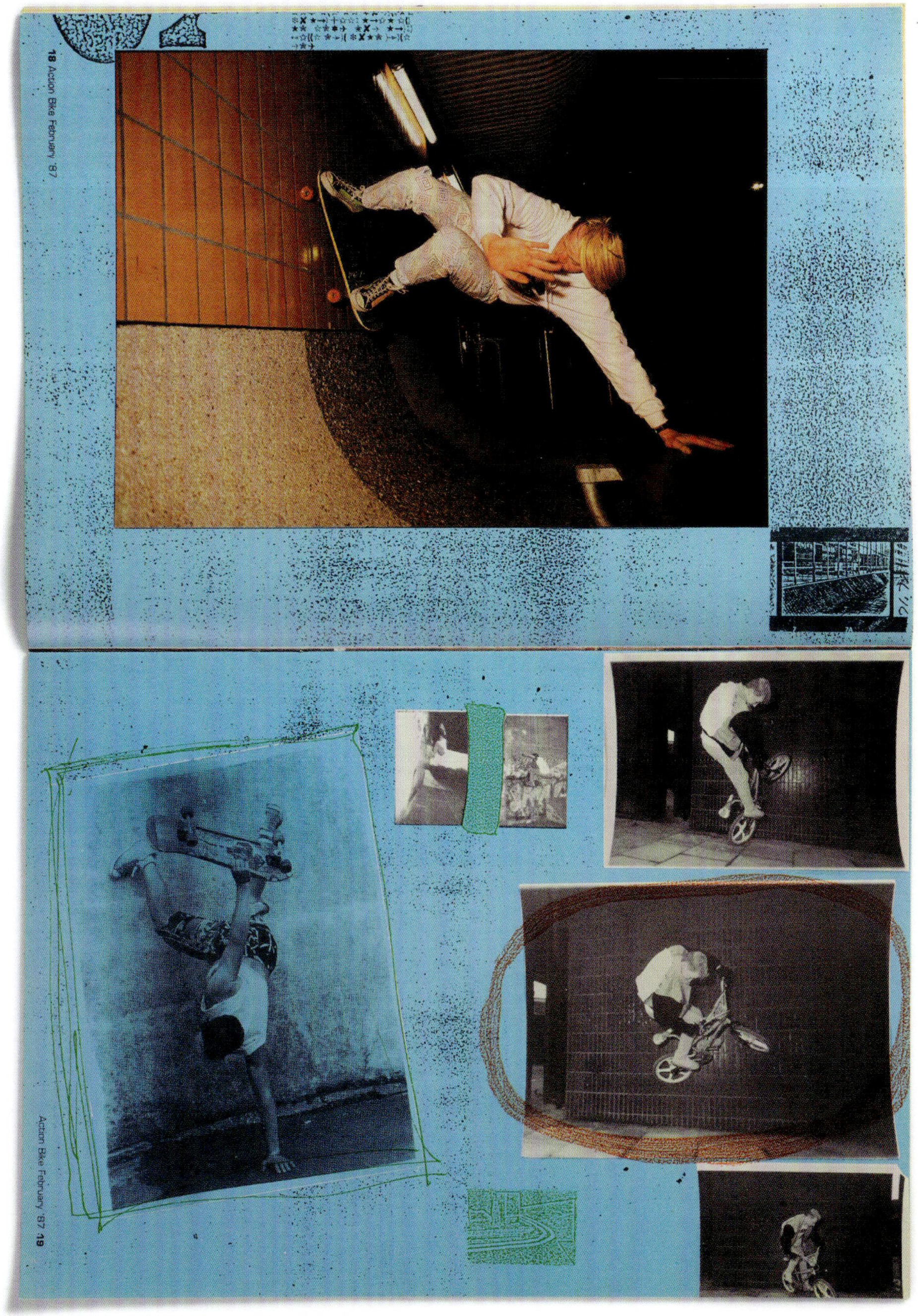

18 Action Bike February '87

Action Bike February '87 19

Left: Nick Philip artwork, *BMXAB* Issue 49, February 1987 **Photos:** TLB **Opposite:** Dave Glover, Birmingham, 1987 **Photo:** TLB

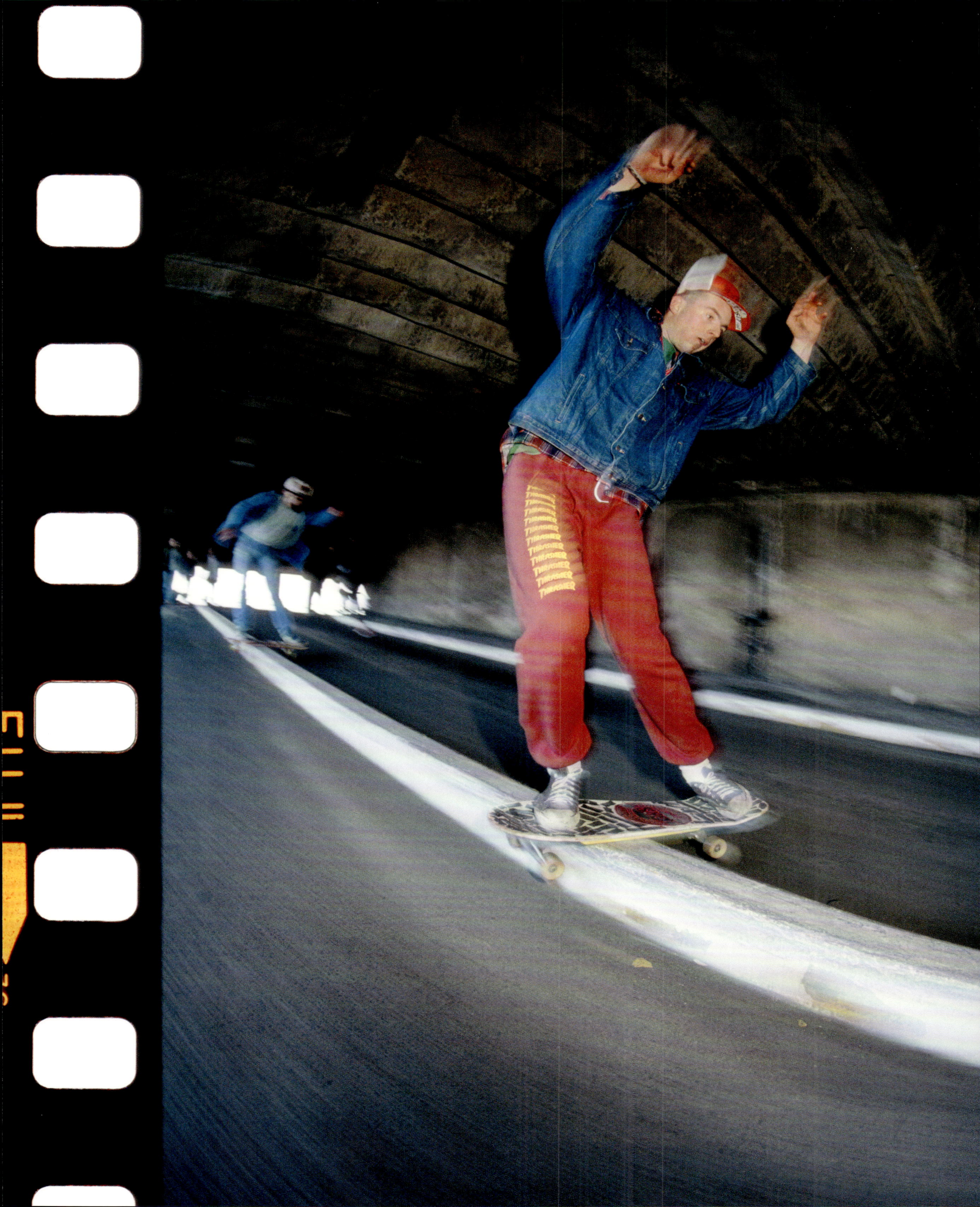
THRASHER

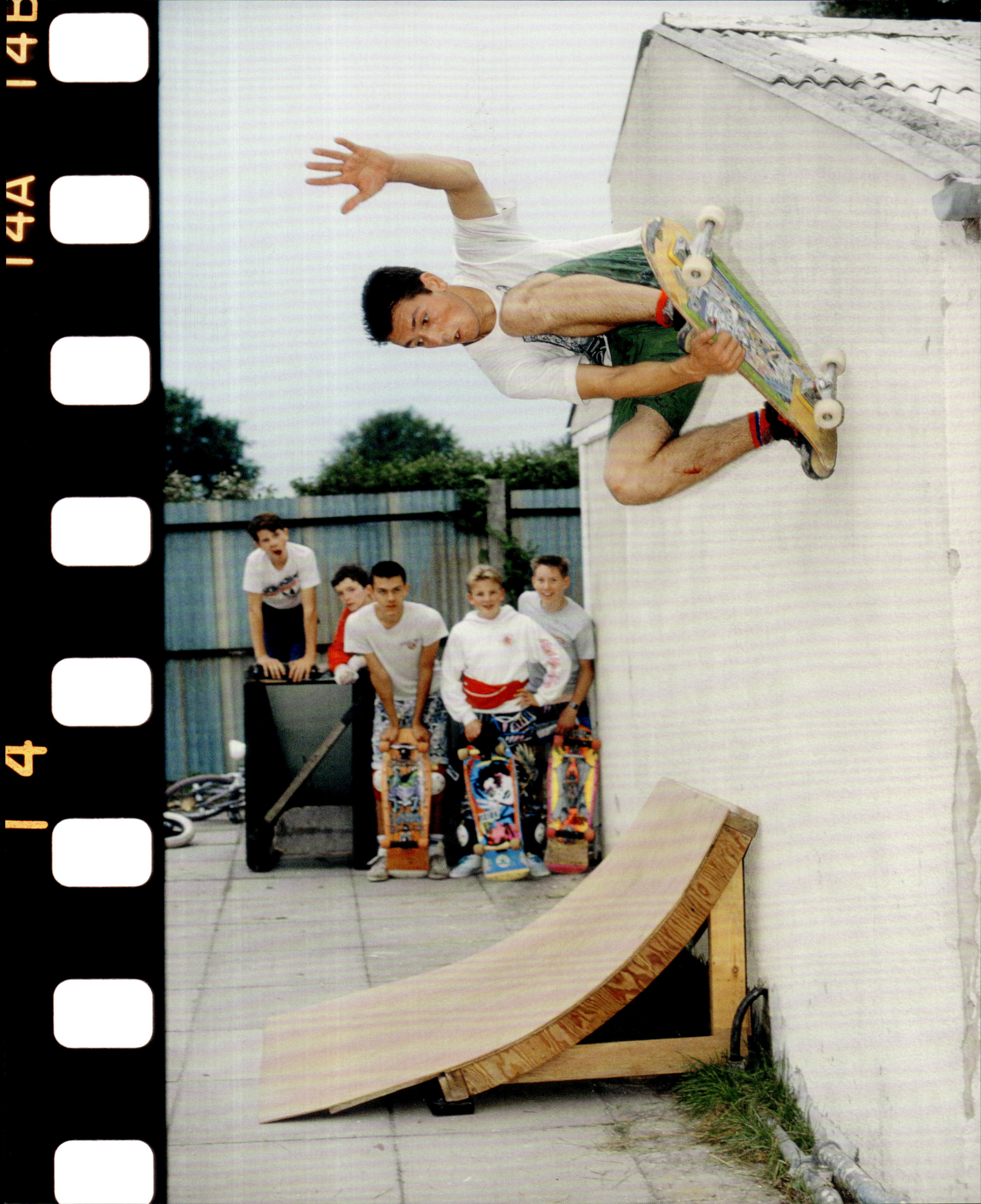
14A
14

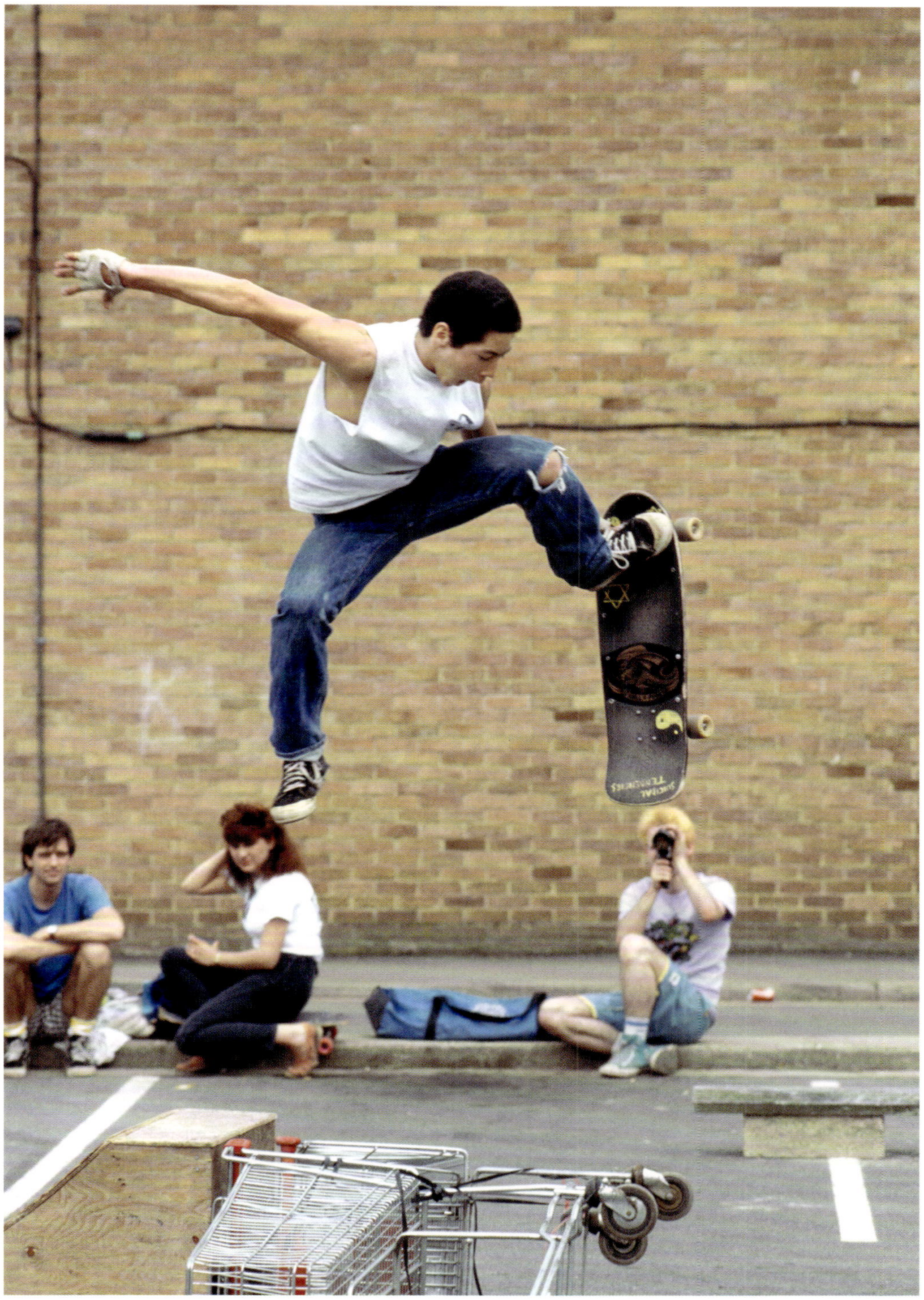

Opposite: Ged Wells, Southsea skatepark, 1987 **Right:** Andy Shohara, Kidlington, 1986 **Overleaf left:** Don Brider, Meanwhile 2 contest, 1987 **Photos:** TLB

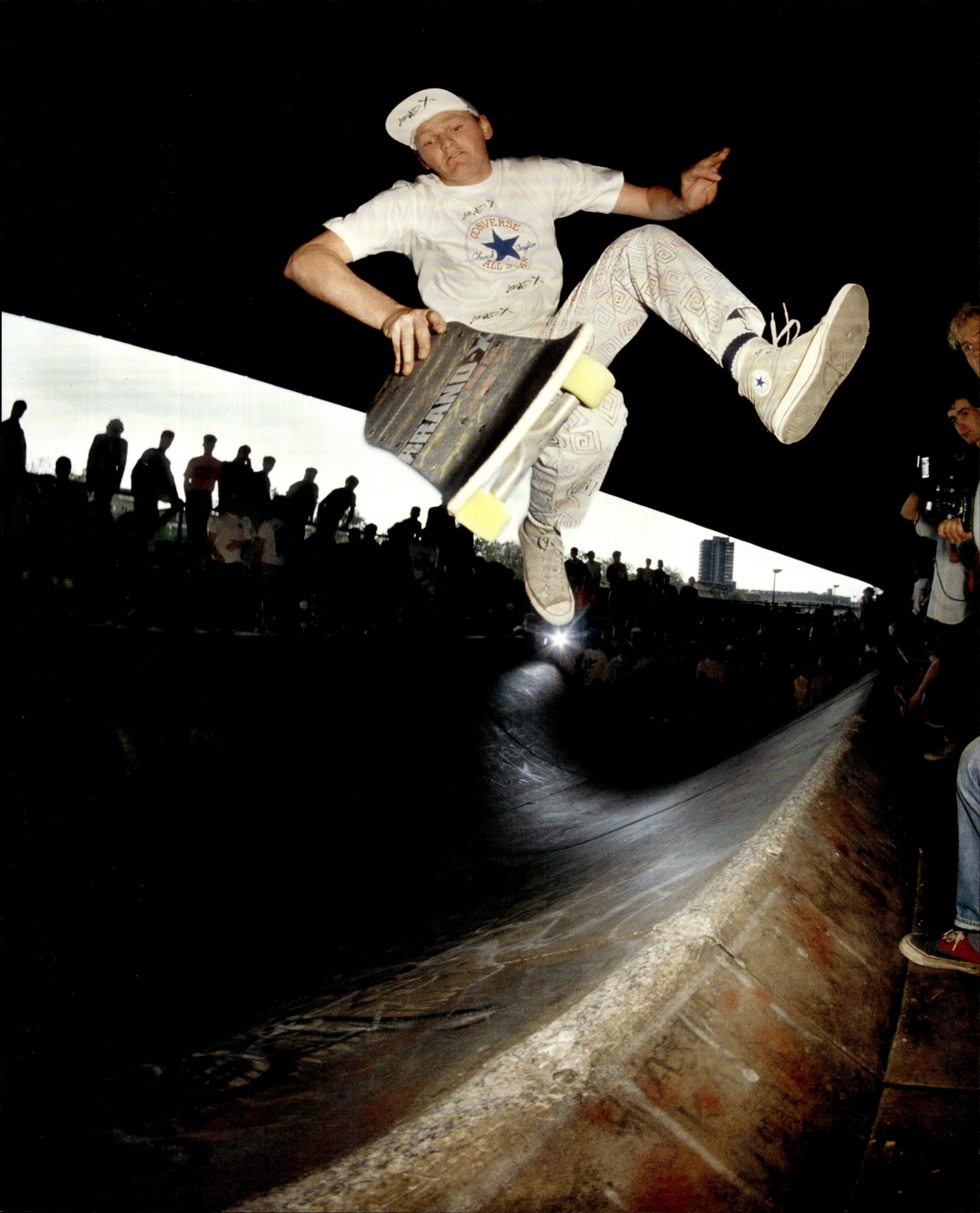
CONVERSE
Chuck Taylor

PLEASE READ (THIS TOOK ME SOME TIME TO WRITE SO DON'T IGNORE IT)

COME ON BMX ACTION BIKE/RAD. OR WHAT EVER YOUR GOING TO CALL YOUR SELVES GET YOUR ACT TOGETHER FIRST OF ALL YOU DO A LITTLE SKATE ACTION. SOON YOUR PUTTING IN MORE AND MORE AND THEN YOU SAY YOUR TRYING TO COVER THE TWO EQUALLY. THEN IN THIS ISSUE YOU GO AND AND PRINT 24 PAGES OF SKATING AND ONLY 10 PAGES OF FREESTYLE AND RACING.

IF YOUR GOING TO TURN THIS INTO A SKATE MAG THEN SAY SO AND GET RID OFF THE FEW TOCKEN

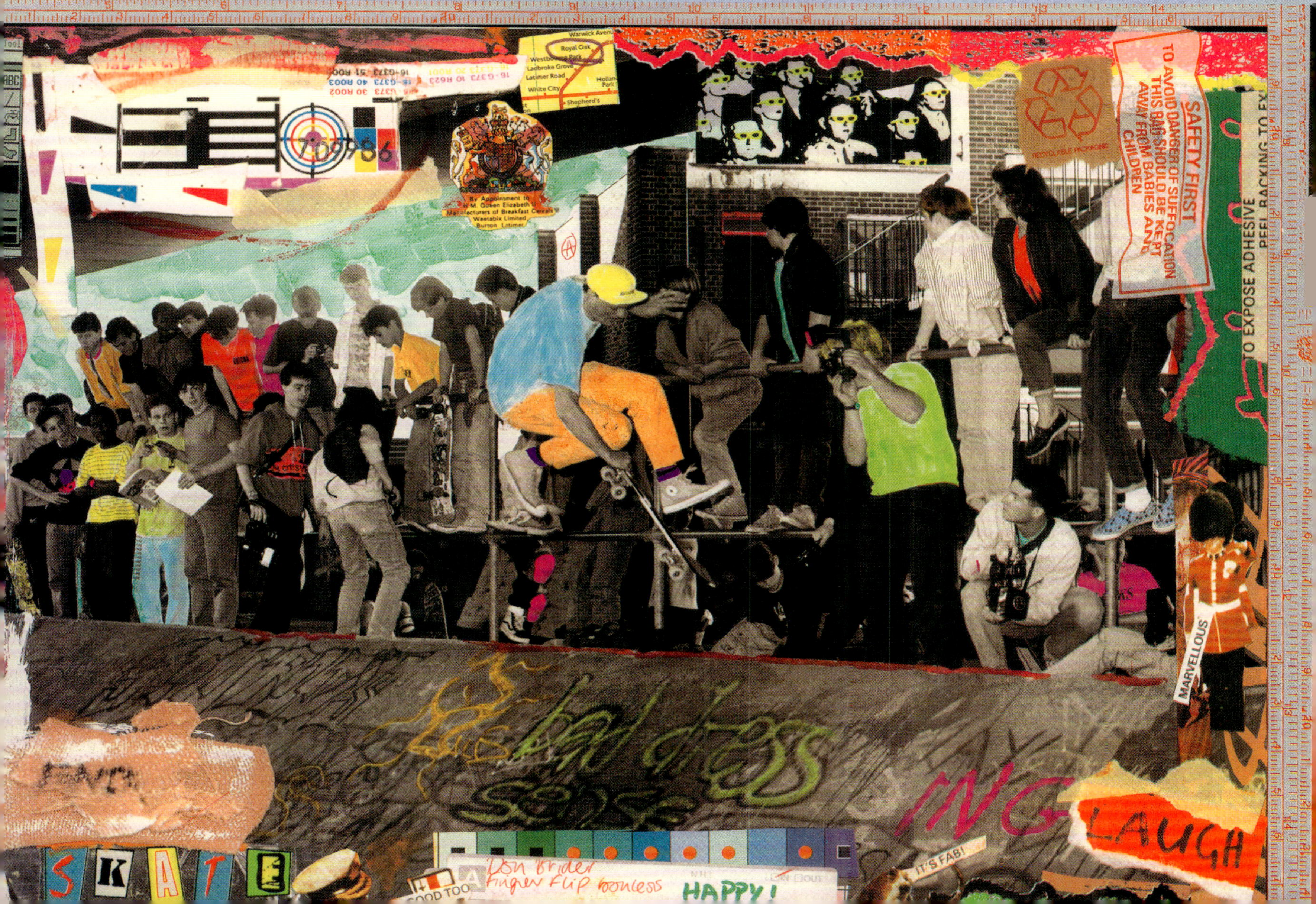

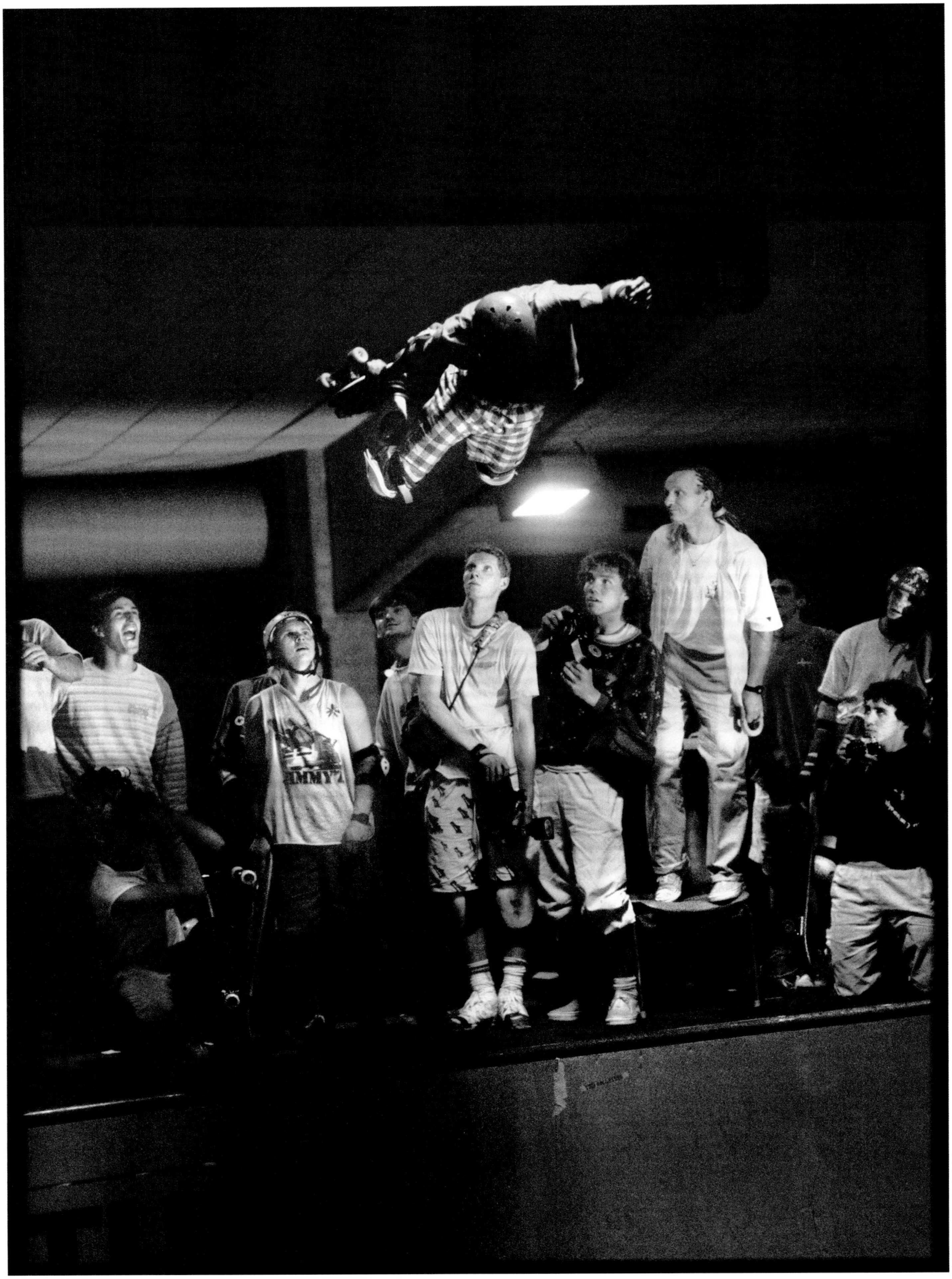

Previous page: Nick Philip collage, Issue 53, June 1987. Reader's letter, 1987 **Left:** Steve Caballero, Munster, Germany, 1987 **Opposite:** Mark Gonzales, Latimer Road, London, 1987 **Photos:** TLB

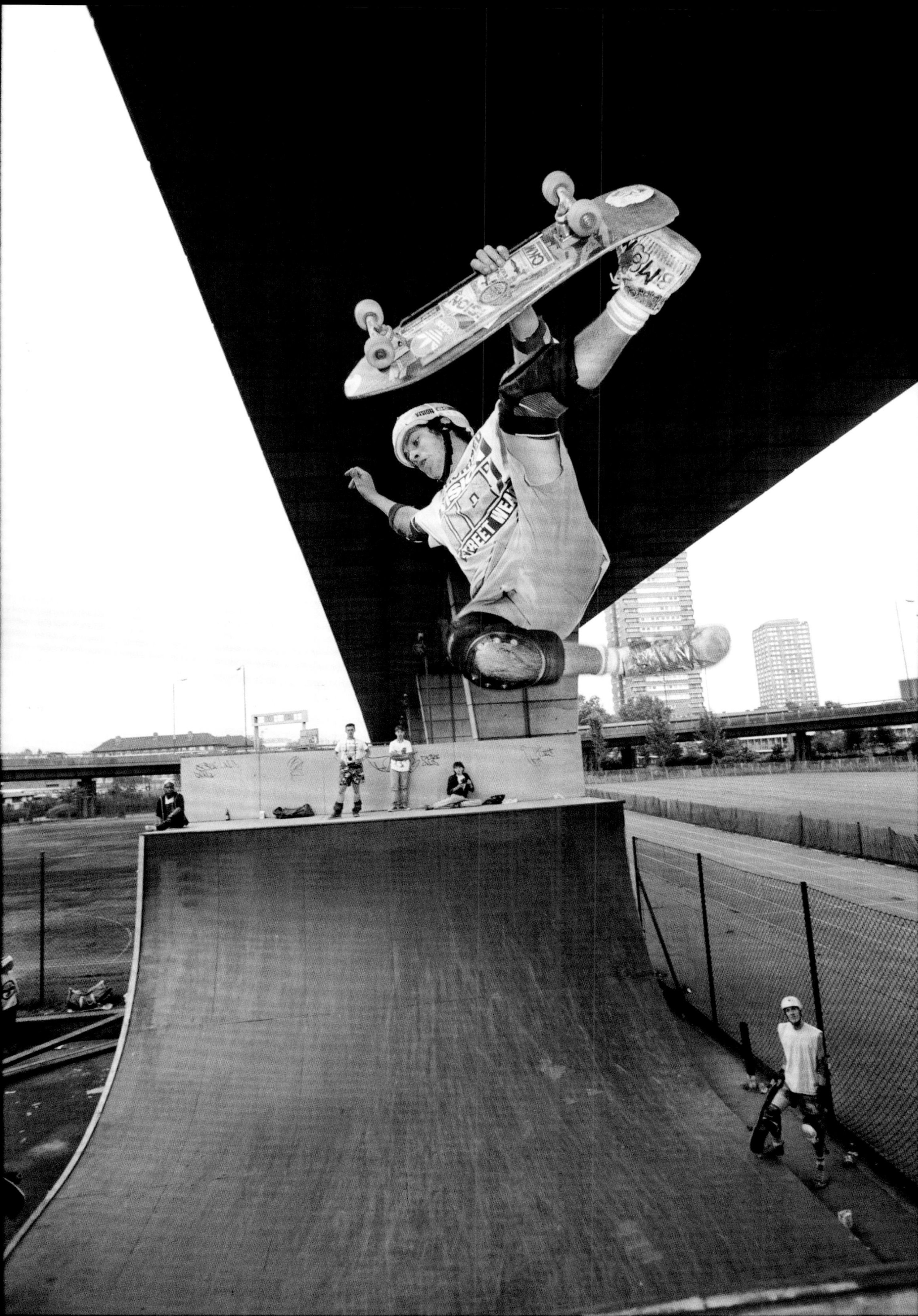
VISION

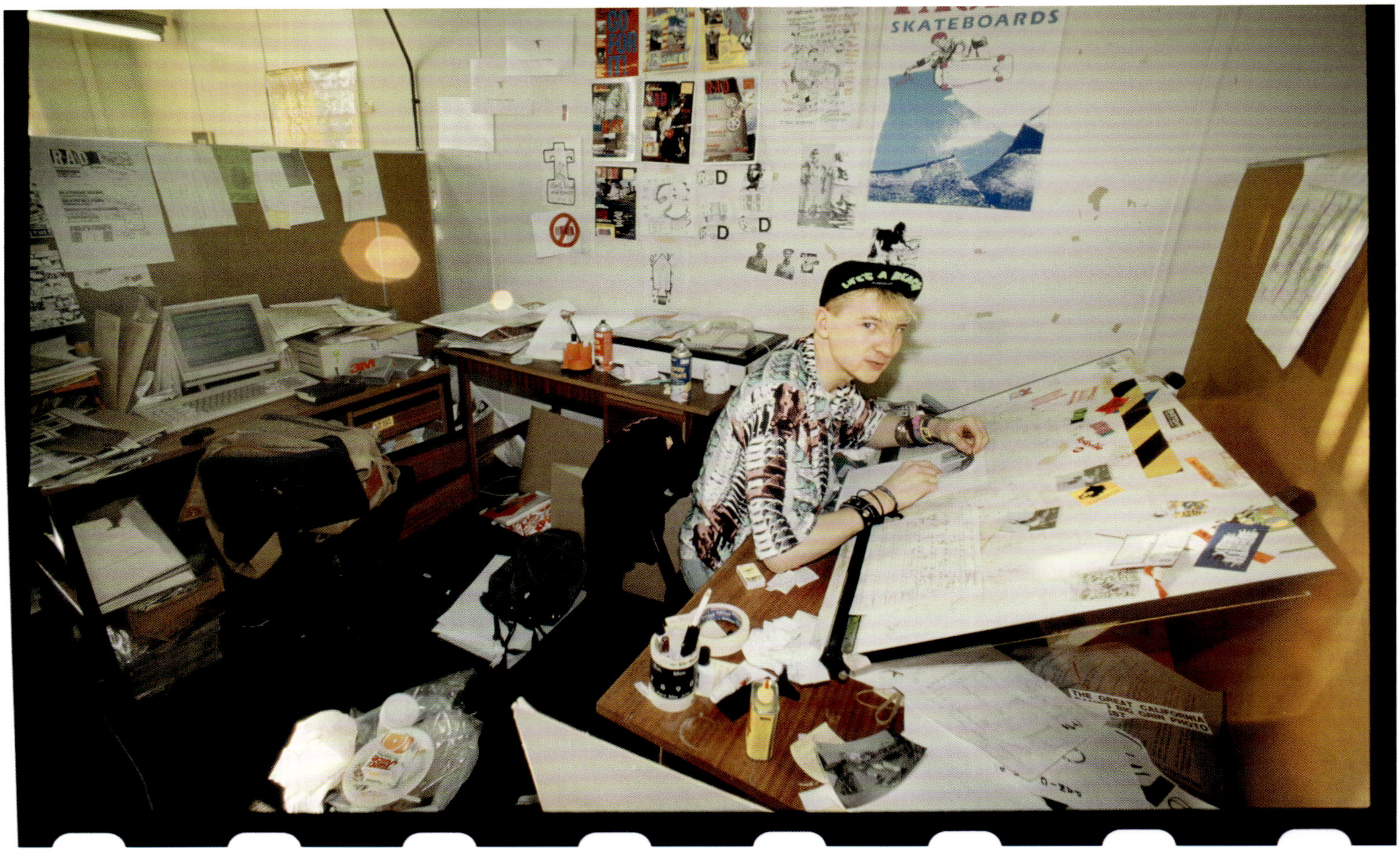

This cultural mash-up of bikes, skateboards, exuberant new 'street' fashions and surf wear was by no means isolated to Britain. After just a year of experimenting with *RAD* magazine, Nick travelled to America and was drawn into the orbit of Wizard publications. This BMX-focused publishing house had made similar transitions in content—featuring skateboards in its *Freestylin'* bike magazine sometime around 1986. Wizard was also home to two of America's most notable BMX to skateboard crossover creatives, Spike Jonze and Andy Jenkins—significant influencers of both cultures. By 1988, Wizard was about to launch *Homeboy* magazine, a new bike / skate / radical lifestyle publication.

Nick left Britain to pursue other endeavours in the USA, but not before having made his mark at *RAD* magazine, setting a visual tone for its future evolution in the hands of subsequent designers.

CUTTING AND PASTING

Photography is the key visual element if not the driving force of any skateboard publication, but it is the words and graphic design that lend character and personality and ultimately forge allegiance with the readers. Through words and photography TLB wished to establish and communicate a sense of empowerment, inclusion and free thinking for the readers—a sense of can-do—the very essence of skateboarding. Nick was packaging these ideas and images in expressive layouts, looking to the zines of the day for his inspiration. In that period of paste-up graphic design, the photocopier and scalpel were Nick's tools of choice to create the visual texture and energy that he was reaching for.

'It was a progression of the DIY aesthetic—of punk and Jamie Reid and what he'd done with the Sex Pistols graphics. And what was happening with i-D *magazine at that time. I would say Jamie Reid and Terry Jones [i-D magazine's original art director] were the kind of people that I was looking at, influenced by and interested in. And also the fact that everybody was making Xerox zines, right? I was looking at a lot of zines and it was like, how can we reproduce this feeling of roughness and rawness in a more mainstream published, full-colour magazine, you know? I felt that would give it a visual language that had an authenticity—that would talk to the people who were creating these zines and relating to them.'* Nick Philip

This visual energy was expressed first and foremost in the new masthead that Nick developed—an enduringly popular logo—graphically encapsulating in one succinct form, everything that he was experimenting with. *'The* RAD *logo was actually stapled together. I stapled it with a stapler—cut it out, tore it up and stapled it. And however the photocopier interpreted it then that was how it was.'* Nick Philip

With uncertainty about its distribution or how readers would accept the new title, it took several issues for this new logo to take full prominence on the cover. There was a gradual overlap, as the old tentatively made way for the new masthead. This transformation was most flamboyantly expressed on the cover of Issue 52—a graphic collaboration between Nick and fellow freestyle BMX pioneer Dave Currey as they searched for graphic solutions for where the magazine might be heading.

'READ AND DESTROY *is what Tim came up with—"Read and Destroy Your Preconceptions". It ended up getting a bit complicated because some "worried from Worthing" mothers were like, "Oh, 'destroy', you're just going to encourage the kids to wreck shit and fuck stuff up" and Tim was like: "No—it's about destroying your preconceptions, it's more metaphorical". So that was where he decided that we didn't call it* Read and Destroy *explicitly—it should be called* R.A.D. *With this cover* [see page 73]*, which was a significant transitional issue,* "Read and Destroy" *is more explicitly on there, written. I think we pulled back a little bit from that destroy thing after that because the distributor was concerned that there might be some problems if we pushed too hard on it.'* Nick Philip

The punchy logo, suggestive title and Nick's playful, even anarchic approach to design had an immediacy that captured the readers' interest.

Opposite: Nick Philip at his desk in the first *RAD* office, autumn 1987 **Below:** Nick Philip (right), art directs and features in a photo shoot for *BMX Action Bike*. From left: Paul Wright, Damon Nichols and Nick Philip **Photos:** TLB
This page: Fragments of original photocopied artworks used in page layouts by Nick Philip and Ian Roxburgh

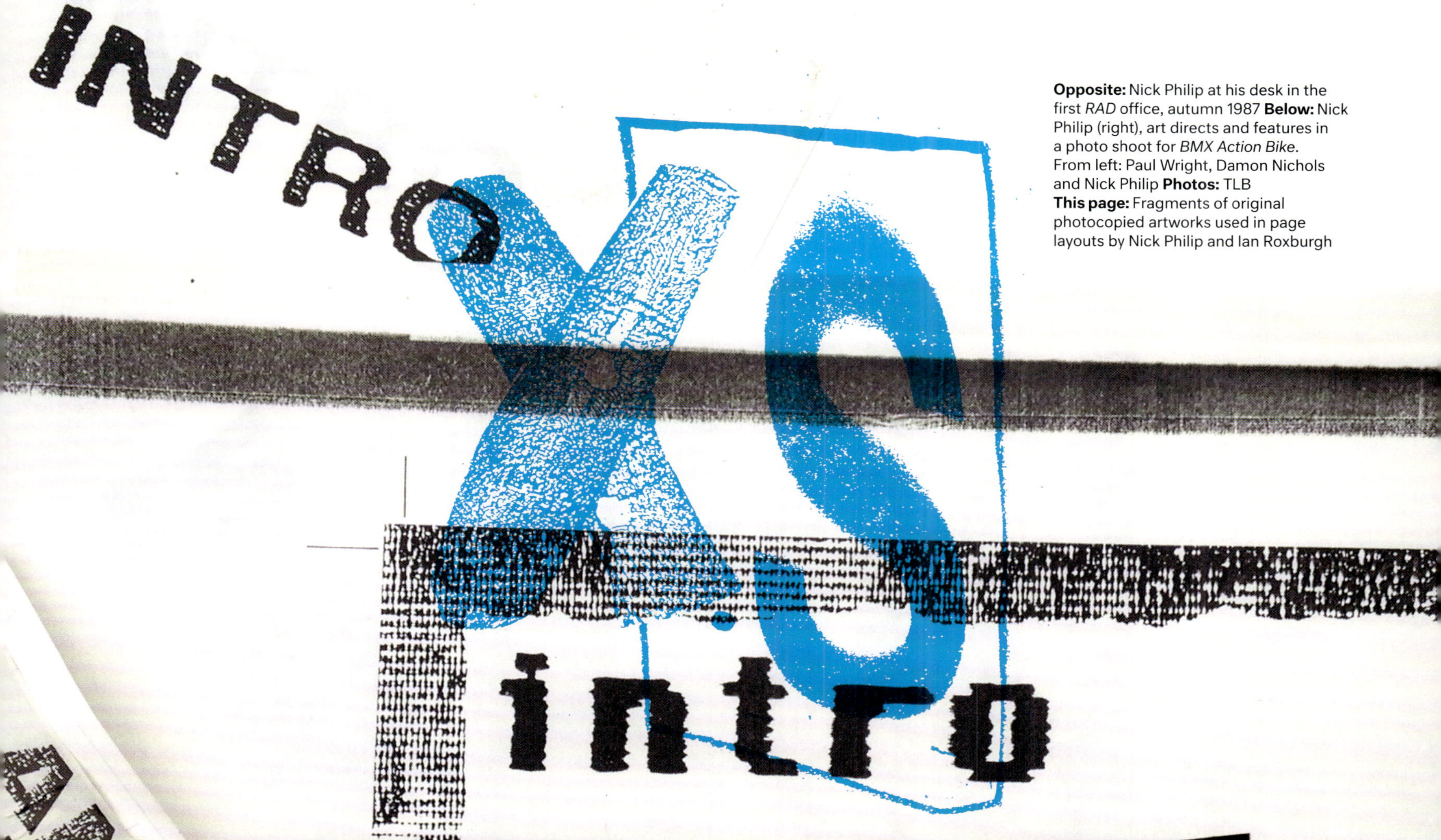

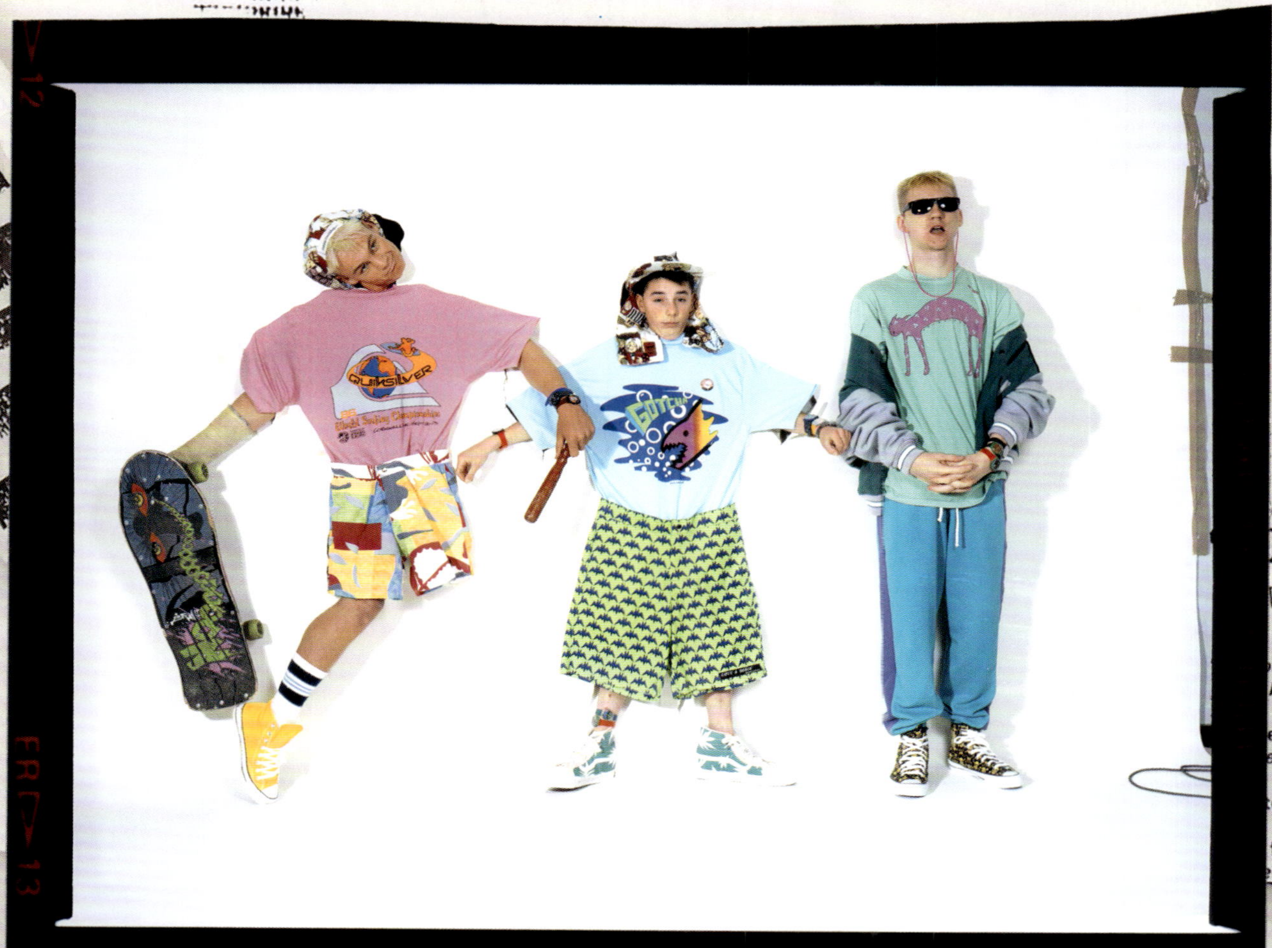

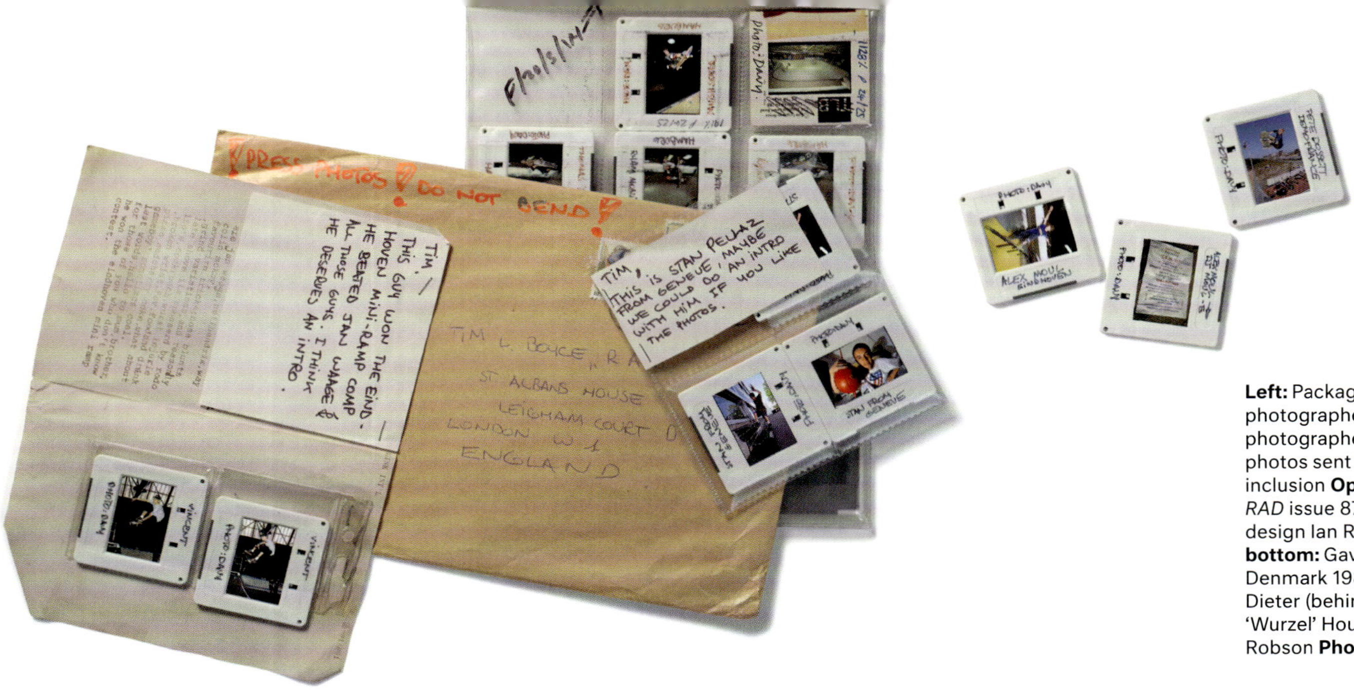

Left: Package from Belgian photographer Davy Van Laere. A typical photographer submission of original photos sent by post to the magazine for inclusion **Opposite top:** Spread from *RAD* issue 87, May 1990. Graphic design Ian Roxbrugh **Photos:** TLB, and **bottom:** Gavin Hills (seated centre) in Denmark 1989 surrounded by Aaron Dieter (behind), Ged Wells, Duncan 'Wurzel' Houlton and Paul 'Rocker' Robson **Photo:** Jay Podesta

With the personality of the magazine established, the second (and longest serving) designer, Ian Roxburgh, chose to work in a similar vein. His skateboarding background drew on a pool of influences and energies much the same as those explored by Nick:

'I loved the use of Xerox machines—I couldn't use any of that in my previous work—so all of a sudden I had the freedom to go mental. All my traditional art-working tools could now be used in a different way—I started using my pens and brushes to create expressive borders and textures.

'We had a basic desktop printer to print typeset headlines and I'd then take them downstairs to enlarge on a photocopier, which gave it that certain look.' Ian Roxburgh

With relatively limited resources Nick and then Ian sustained an energetic approach to the design of the magazine—a visual attitude which continued to influence future designers as layout methods and technologies changed over time. The original, trusting, non-didactic approach established between Nick as designer and TLB as editor allowed for continued freedom of expression and creative exploration for the magazines' designers who wanted to experiment.

In the early 1990s, when affordable graphics computers became the norm and the desktop digital design revolution took over from manual paper-and-glue paste-up layouts as the means of production, *RAD* designer number four, Steve Hicks, continued to experiment with the layered, textural energy first explored by Nick Philip:

'Holy Fuck; what were we doing!? What I notice when I look now at the design of the magazine is that we had an idea to abuse technology for the sake of design. For me, that began with Nick and Ian's original approach to using a photocopier: "What can we do with this to create something fresh and new?" So I decided that I wanted to continue that tradition but with technology that was new to me at that time.

'I was typing headlines and photographing them from the monitor. The photos were printed and I was scanning those back into the computer. So this was definitely a period where the craft of making magazines was transitioning between the physical method of production and the digital world. A lot of things we did used early versions of Photoshop and we were maybe the first magazine to run spreads straight out of Photoshop. So opening the magazine when it came back from the printers was a scary—and exciting experience [laughter] because you didn't know what it was gonna look like! But it was a really glorious experiment in using that technology in its very early, nascent stages.

'Some years ago I saw Malcolm McLaren give a lecture and I believe he said "All creativity is an act of failing gloriously" and when I think about Tim's role, it was about him letting that happen and giving me the freedom to fail. There are lots of examples of where that happened. He would see these things and say "It's OK, it doesn't matter, these things happen, it's a skateboard magazine, let's keep pushing forward."

'Tim was an amazing force in that way; he'd stand behind you, letting you fail and letting you find your own path.'

So with an ever-evolving display of photography, graphics and words in a chaotic and exciting visual collision, the structure of the magazine generated an energy that kept it moving forward at pace. The open, free flowing working methods of Nick and TLB, laid the foundations for a loose, open-door policy allowing for easy collaboration and free-thinking input to the magazine's content.

The nationwide skate network that had evolved over the previous decade now had a lively, colourful mouthpiece, primed to report on the developing culture. This 'open forum' meant space for direct interaction with readers and as a result an inclusive two-way dialogue developed: *'It was their magazine, not mine...'* TLB

CONNECTIVITY

Alongside establishing a dialogue with the readers, encouraging participation and creating opportunities were central to TLB's (and hence the magazine's) ethos. For him, if *RAD* magazine couldn't serve as the connective tissue to help bind together the culture, it would not be doing its readers justice. Open access for communication and even the chance of being included in the magazine were key components to its success in connecting with readers. An important element in fostering this participation was The Wall, a page of messages that readers could send in for publication:

'I wanted to create a level playing field where anyone could contribute. It's quite hard to write a letter to a magazine, let alone think you might be able to contribute to it. So the idea behind The Wall was to make that process easy; a simple form that you filled out and sent in. I'd then type them all up and put them in the magazine.' TLB

'The Wall was a major lifeline for us, you know. That led me to meeting people and putting on events, if you missed the deadline it was well gutting. My little cryptic statements on that page started bringing more people (in my freestyle BMX scene) together. And people would write to me to maybe buy a T-shirt or it could help you strike up a conversation.' Tim Goldie, of Ceramic Rabbit (DIY bike/skate events) fame

With limited resources, *RAD* did its best to be as comprehensive a conduit for the British skate scene and connect together as many of its disparate voices as possible. For TLB this meant that many hours of calling, questioning, driving, searching and photography were undertaken to fill each issue. The challenge, particularly in the early days with just two people and one shared desk, of creating all this visual energy and delivering informative, engaging news and editorial content, cannot be underestimated.

'I travelled around Europe with Gavin because somehow he managed to blag InterRail tickets. I spent a month or so with him in the sketchiest fucking circumstances, with no money, living by selling stickers...' Ged Wells

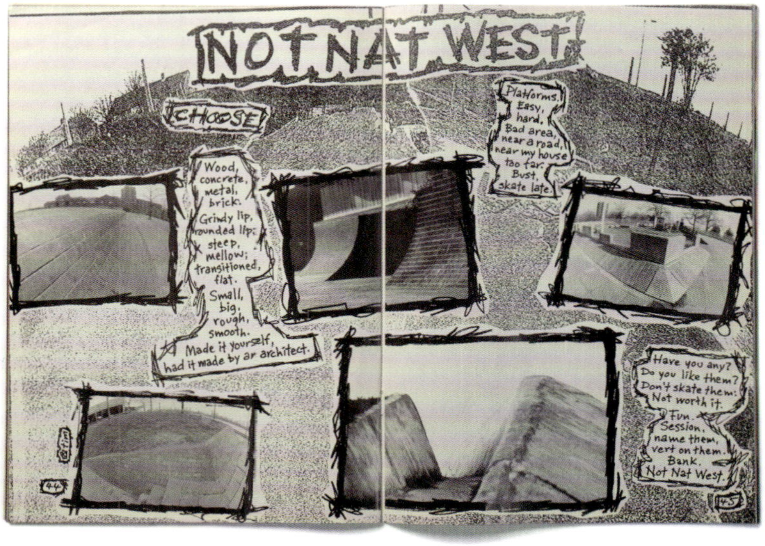

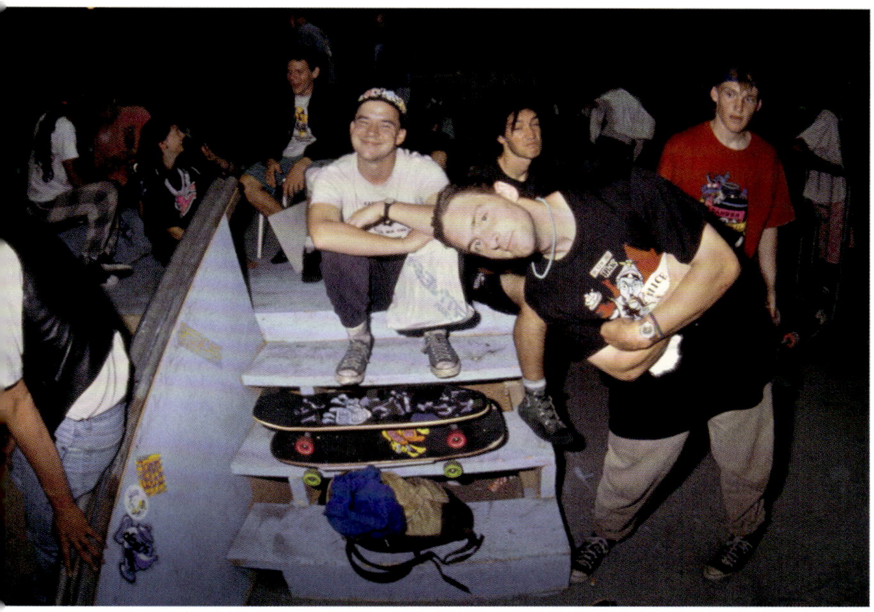

THE CONTRIBUTORS

As confidence and resources grew, the editorial and photographic scope widened through an evolving network of contributors—TLB never afraid to take on new voices:

'He was always looking for new people to write and wasn't making a situation where people got a job for life; he piloted a more transient vehicle than that. Tim wanted to keep things changing and include more people to represent the culture that was forming and I think he was always conscious it was a growing, British thing.' Ged Wells

'Ideas were encouraged but no one thought they owned it; the magazine was a mouthpiece and vehicle that everyone was using. Tim would always ask other people's opinions or if they had ideas about content. The whole thing was very democratic, never autocratic. He always wanted more people involved, was always looking out for new people to contribute and he didn't want it to follow a set pattern, repeating the same shit.' Ian Roxburgh

Ged Wells was an early collaborative voice, contributing fluid interpretive ideas and editorial that TLB had an immediate affinity with. He had, in Tim's words, *'a fundamental influence'* on the early direction of content and was *'pushing at an open door'*. Wells took advantage of the space given to him for the imagination to wander.

'I had no credentials to do shit and when I started working for the magazine, I didn't really know what my role was [laughter]. I would go to competitions and think about how we could show it in a way that would inspire people and really bring them right into the feature. Otherwise one comp would just look like any other.

'I remember talking ideas with Tim and we went down to a park in South London where he wanted to re-enact a scene from the Antonioni film Blow-Up *[which had been shot there]. It was all about capturing movement in the environment. We definitely went to unusual architectural places to shoot as well.'* Ged Wells

'Tim used to say "The architect is the skateboarder's friend". I think that's something Ged and Tim had in common: the idea that anything could be ridden.' Ian Roxburgh

'It's about inspiring progression. Building a perfect ramp only gets you the ability to do a perfect air—so let's put a kink in it instead. That's the skater's thing: whatever you find you'll use and that will bring new things forward.' Ged Wells

Amongst the evolving list of contributors, overlapping with Ged was Gavin Hills, who quickly became a consistent and prominent voice of the *RAD* cocktail. He came to the magazine together with Vernon Adams AKA Jay Podesta, both avid skate fans and committed zine makers (images for their *Bomber Terrorzine* had already featured photos by Mike John and Paul Sunman). They had been working together as journalists and looked to *RAD* as an opportunity to combine their interests and professional activities.

'Gavin would do the writing and I'd just concentrate on taking the pictures and in some ways that was an easier way to work because when we first started at City Limits *and at* RAD, *we'd originally write pieces together. We'd both write the same feature then I'd read what he'd written and he'd read what I'd written and we'd pick the best bits from each other's text and literally combine them to make the finished piece by chopping them up and putting them together.'* Vernon Adams

As chief photographer and the editor responsible for so much of the factual, newsworthy content of the magazine, TLB left space for these other voices to create more relatable, open, experiential and sometimes whimsical editorial. In Gavin's hands, words were delivered with an expressive, questioning, sometimes cynical, often humorous and rebellious energy.

This spirited, occasionally neurotic outsider writing easily caught the imagination of the often like-minded readers. Ryan Monihan, sponsored US skateboarder on an extended Euro couch tour—describing himself and fellow traveller Arron Deeter as *'nobody, loser kids from Seattle, coming to Europe'*—certainly related to the spirit and attitude that Gavin

'I sent a review of the local kerb to *RAD*, for the Where? guide. It felt amazing being able to "contribute" to that magazine and I know and appreciate now just how important that was for TLB too—to have the readers involved in the magazine's content'

Neil Macdonald AKA Science versus Life

brought to the magazine. Inspired to ignore a personal lack of journalistic experience, Monihan saw an opportunity to contribute his own expressive content (occasionally co-writing with Hills) to *RAD*.

'Gavin was such a driven person that he was a madman. He was just so excited about it. And I think part of it is because he wasn't good at this stuff [skateboarding] so he cared about it even more and was so impressed with just how great the scene was—all of these creative people doing these crazy, mad things. He was an enthusiast—an enthusiast about everything, you know. And yeah, he was the best. So, he was the energy, Tim was the organisation and then all these other people fleshed it all out with their stuff.' Ryan Monihan

Following Hills, a younger and no less prominent creative voice that would have a strong impact on the magazine's legacy was skateboarder Simon Evans. He had harboured hopes of one day becoming a writer before he connected with *RAD*, and these early ambitions found ample opportunity with Gavin's influence and TLB's encouragement:

'I grew up with stars in my eyes about RAD. *It was the holy British skate magazine—everything. And then the next thing you know, I'm part of it and it was amazing. I mean, I was just a dweeb. [Gavin] was fully formed. He was just such a brilliant... He was destined—I mean it's so tragic that he died so early—he was destined for great things. And he was an amazing writer, person; just a great guy. I was just there listening—he was like a fully formed creative being and on his way.'* Simon Evans

Whilst amongst the most visible, Ged, Gavin and Simon were by no means the only contributors of words for the magazine to lend character and expression. Written perspectives from a cross section of voices were an important and considered part of the recipe:

'"The words are just a trick to get people to look at the pictures." Did I manage to sneak that into the mag as a caption? I borrowed it from a Brian Eno point about lyrics. It wasn't true, I was just having a bit of fun. The words were hugely important and I cared a great deal about being a communication channel and connecting people in an age just before the digital.' TLB

GETTING OUT THERE

During skateboarding's lean times and with too few opportunities close at hand, it had been essential for skateboarders to travel, discover and connect—meeting new skaters and checking out new spots became an established feature of the skater's life. TLB's long-standing efforts (going back to the Alpine newsletter days) to catalogue and document skate spots, reaching out to as much of the nation as possible, was the legacy of the Out There articles that became an established, regular feature in the magazine. These stories acted as a vicarious skateboarder's travel experience, connecting the reader with new faces and places and a sense that your local scene or face might be next to appear in the magazine.

'Tim always wanted to get out there—because he didn't want to be focused only on London. He'd always have his ear to the ground, listening for people's suggestions: "come and check out this scene" in Basingstoke, Hull or wherever. Then we'd plan a road trip, taking in a few other places on the way.' Ian Roxburgh

'Tim driving people round—taking them to shoot photos—was creating all of these connections and joining the dots in many ways. And that was before it was a skateboard magazine—but he was still doing it.' Bod Boyle

'The mileage we clocked up doing all this was astonishing. I remember one feature—that Simon wrote—which we based around the A1 motorway. I don't think we went much beyond Newcastle, but we spent weeks driving up and down it and when I totalled up the money we'd spent on that, I realised we could have flown to California instead. I was very determined to try and cover the whole of the UK...' TLB

'That's what I liked about going on the road with Tim; we did sessions all over the place. At one spot he took photos of everyone and one of the local guys got on the cover of the magazine. I thought that was great, that Tim would showcase anybody. If you were good, he'd take your picture, whether you were known or not and I think that helped things grow; people could think "Maybe I can get in the magazine too." So they'd get in touch with Tim to see if he wanted to cover their scene and it all created a snowball effect. You didn't have to be one of the in-crowd to get in RAD.*'* Sean Goff

The perceptibly un-American, or more specifically un-Californian experience that articles like the Out There reports expressed often made for a more relatable magazine in Europe and further afield than some of the hard-to-get American titles. The more 'local' reporting and photographs of unknown skaters (rather than American mega-stars) gave a sense of something more attainable, whilst no less valid.

'Growing up in a Dutch shitty little village when I was young, RAD *was my saviour and window to a world of unknown brilliance. Because of* RAD, *I stuck with skating in those fickle young years where I could have easily quit and my life would have turned out so much different.'*
Piet Parra, artist and co-founder of Tired Skateboards

Reaching out to document unknown local skate scenes and publish the details in the magazine was more often than not a powerful rite of passage to be remembered long after the day—and a vicarious experience for the readers. A 1991 visit to the country village of Southrop by the *RAD* entourage was a meaningful and memorable experience for the locals:

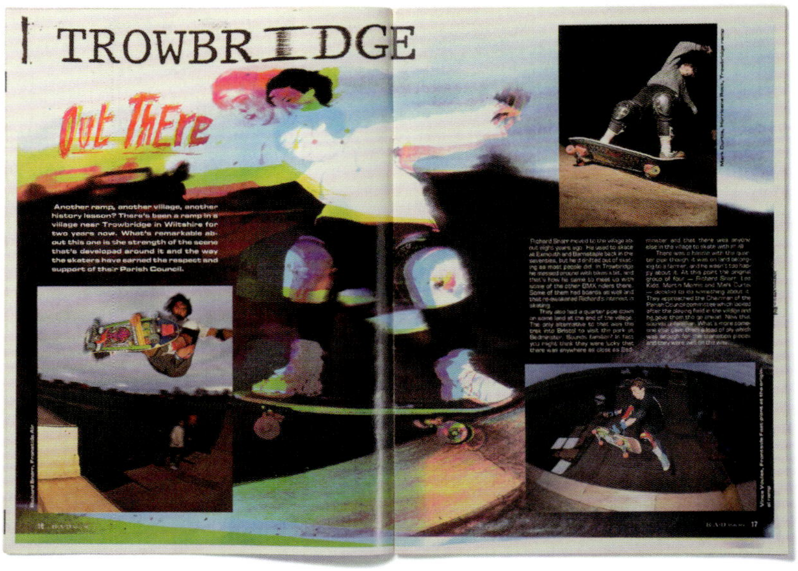

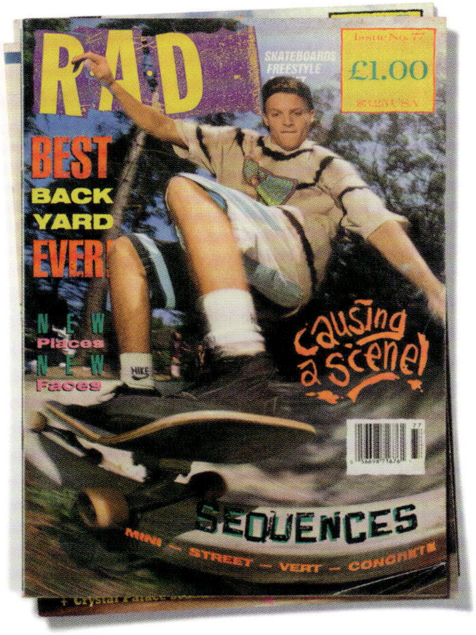

Opposite: Ian Roxburgh-designed spread utilising colour Xerox image treatments, Issue 75, May 1989 **Left:** Ian Roxburgh cover artwork with black-and-white Xerox, type treatments and hand-drawn headlines. Issue 77, July 1989 **Photos:** TLB

'Agog—and with badly feigned nonchalance—we greeted these quasi-fictitious superstars and discovered a humble and friendly band. Quirky, erudite, curious and talented, the happy visitors blended immediately into the bizarre rural scene of teenage skateboarders hosting a 1920s-themed skateboard competition / 18th birthday party in an antique barn.

'TLB snapped away as nerves were activated, stage fright battled and stunts pulled. None of us had even witnessed a skate photographer in action let alone been the target of one. We could scarcely believe this experience, this undeniable feeling that we were mid-transit from definitely nothing to maybe something by just a few clicks of the shutter.' James Davis

NEWS FROM THE SOURCE

The attention given to local and accessible experiences in no way excluded international and more specifically American news and photography from *RAD*. No skate magazine of any worth at that time could or would have ignored the leading-edge developments coming from the USA—California was still very much THE source. Skateboarding communities outside the USA were yet to find full confidence in their own identities and abilities and remained understandably enthralled with the West Coast scene and its vibrant, pioneering skateboarding personalities, manufacturers, and trick development.

In the lean times preceding *RAD,* a handful of British photographers, Tim, Paul Sunman and Mike John amongst them, had established connections with, and had photos published in America via *Transworld* and *Thrasher*. Now it was the turn of leading American photographers to be published in Britain. A tight-knit global network of skate photographers including J. Grant Brittain, Spike Jonze, Chris Ortiz, Steve Keenan, Dave Swift and Tobin Yelland made regular and welcome contributions to *RAD*.

Steve Douglas, the *Go For It!* zine maker, had recently relocated to California in pursuit of his professional skateboarding career. Through Steve, American skate scene news and connections came thick and fast, adding currency and a global dimension to the features and news sections in *RAD* magazine:

'TLB completely trusted me and knew that wherever I was I would always send through a handwritten fax with any hot news I'd heard about. My life was 24/7 skating—Bod was the same—skating was our only world. So it was easy for me to contact photographers and speak to people because I was totally immersed in the scene. My fax would always have the latest info on it; we'd go right to the deadline but I always came through.

'That meant the news that came out in RAD *was actually the most up to date anywhere in the world.* Thrasher *and* Transworld *were printing on much longer schedules, so it was great to know we were ahead of them. I would take notes during the whole month before I submitted copy and it never felt like a job. I was so into the world around skating it just seemed easy, almost like doing* Go For It! *[zine] in a way.'*

PHOTOGRAPHY

'TLB was a great collector of people and he was good at spotting individuals who turned out to be quite talented. He didn't have much to offer financially, but he did give them the chance to focus on skateboarding and apply their talents editorially, graphically and photographically in the magazine—TLB used the magazine to facilitate a lot of creativity.' Paul Sunman

The initial and essential photographic backbone of the magazine was provided mostly by TLB. Additional early contributions came via Paul Sunman, Mike John and then Jay Podesta (photographer alter ego of Vernon Adams). The earlier zine-era network was now functioning to full effect in providing content for the new magazine.

*'*RAD *gave us a framework to experiment in and become skate photographers and TLB didn't expect specific results from us. It's not his style to pressurise people that way. He enabled me to decide what I wanted to take pictures of. We were a fairly tight little unit and the motivation wasn't financial. We got a page rate for images and that helped us to cover the cost of film and travelling. It was more about being part of a community centred around Southbank and* RAD*. So there was fierce loyalty around that crew of people.'* Paul Sunman

Until the revived *Skateboard!* and later *Skate Action* magazines appeared, *RAD* was considered *the* place for any aspiring British skate photographer to be published—a desirable proving ground for those keen to join the growing party. Several upcoming photographers of the time who went on to have great impact on skateboarding photography in later decades took inspiration from *RAD* and its already-established photographers. This new breed was stepping up—eager, like Tim, Paul, Mike, Jay and others before them, to capture skateboarding's progressive development, creating memorable images on film in the process. Several of this 'second wave' of photographers had their first published photos in *RAD* and, like TLB and his experience at *Skateboard!* in the late 1970s, having photos in print fuelled their confidence and future photographic endeavours:

'This was a big, BIG moment—getting a picture published in RAD*. The magazine's story is so important to me: it tracks my life from early teenage years, from bikes to boards and on to having my first picture published within those hallowed pages.'* Wig Worland

'I first sent pictures to RAD *in '91—of the scene in Milton Keynes—and they published a three-page feature. That was the first time I had images published. I just sent some shots of me and my friends skating with a little letter and TLB put them in the mag! We were beyond stoked.'* Leo Sharp

'The first photograph I had in RAD*, in a photo annual—a shot of Pete Dossett—was the first picture I ever had published. It was a massive deal. Within skating Tim was really influential for me. He was important because he gave other people a chance. And he didn't just do that for me, he did it for people like Gavin and all the guys that were involved; he got 'em in and said "You do the magazine, you write it and I'll just help pull it all together". He didn't hold on to the whole thing and say "This is mine". He let everyone in and that was really important because we got to see how editorial worked because he showed us. There were some of us who'd never been to college or university and Tim gave us a chance, through skateboarding, to get our stuff published—which was huge, y'know.'* Skin Phillips

'The Paris [Bercy contest] was different. My friends and heroes were all there and I had unlimited access. I had a wide-angle lens and a big flash. Being in a pretty comfortable place, I took lots of pictures and some of them were all right. Those I sent to TLB, and he used them and said "Send an invoice". (Actually he probably sent some money and a pre-printed receipt to sign and return to him…) A key day—my sketchy lifelong "career" as a photographer, writer and printer of stuff began.' James Hudson

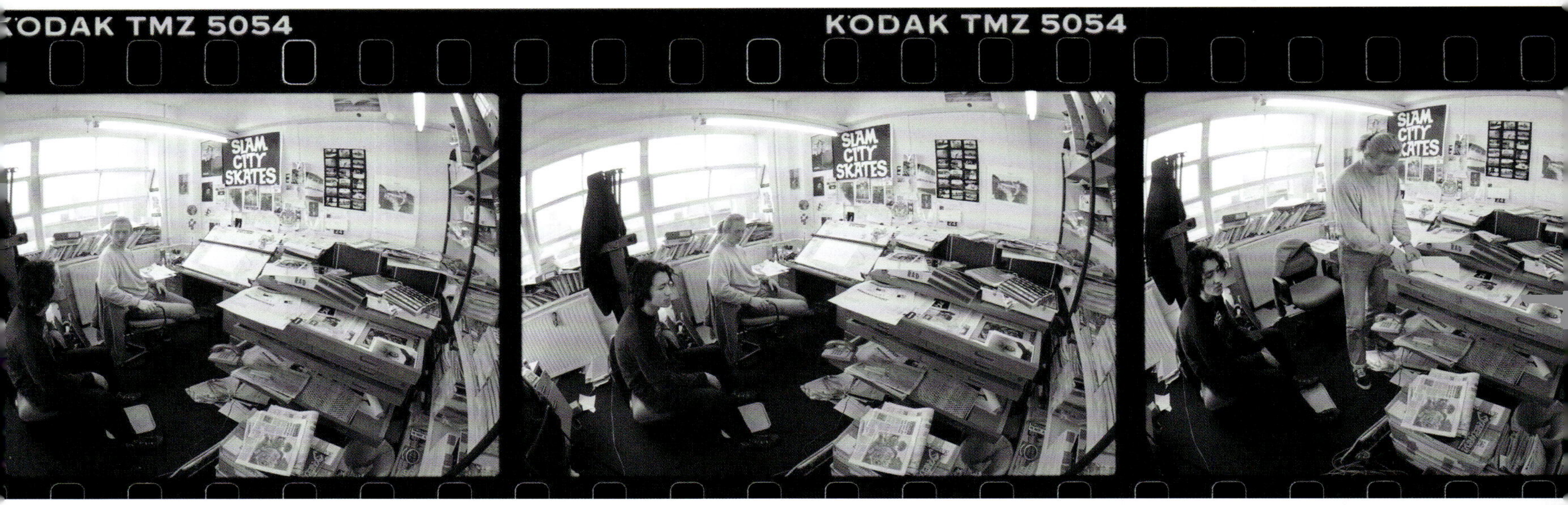

FILM TO VIDEO AND BACK AGAIN

Harking back to those early days of 35mm slide shows at Harrow skatepark with photographic critique from the skateboarders themselves, choosing photos for publication in the *RAD* magazine features was always a collaborative process.

'The photos would come back from the developers and whoever was in the office would grab them—you'd have two or three heads over the light box all at once looking at them. Vern would always look at his photos himself first, but with Tim's shots, Shane O'Brien would be straight in there and so would I, smelling the chemicals!

'We did two photo annuals, 1988 and '89, and it was a hell of a process putting those things together. We had everyone in the room: Vernon, Mike, Tim, Ged, Gav, Shane—all trying to decide which images would go in. We had a slide projector and chose images that way. Each person filled a carousel with transparencies and then we went through them, making short lists. Maybe we'd get halfway through the process and Paul's photos would turn up, making it even harder because we wanted to use all of them! For Tim that whole thing about choosing pictures was a nightmare, so he was like "I'll leave it up to you lot."' Ian Roxburgh

'Oh yeah. [TLB] *wouldn't do it. He would just be, "Oh I don't know what's good anymore."'* Simon Evans

Despite the high level of commitment to capturing skateboarding on film, TLB remained insecure about the appropriate criteria for selecting images for publication. He had enough experience to understand that skateboarders, as skateboarding rapidly evolved, had their own very specific viewpoints when judging images, and he had no wish to interfere.

'It occurs to me that as a non-skater I did not fully understand the power of the stills. I had my personal instinctive feel for the aesthetics but not the skater's ability to relate to and interpret them. I assumed that sequences were better for understanding tricks. I underestimated the skater's ability to interpret the stills.' TLB

Photographic sequences of tricks being performed—how-to's—were a tried and tested ingredient of the skateboard magazine from the early days of skate publications. *Skateboarder* magazine had pioneered this method of un-boxing new skateboard tricks and this—like so many other aspects of the skateboard magazine formula they had established—became a feature that no future skate magazine would fail to include. As the tricks became more complicated, and with methods and terrain less tried and tested, shooting these sequences became an increasingly challenging—and often expensive—experience for the photographers.

Above: *RAD* offices in 1989, Ged Wells left, and Ian Roxburgh at his paste-up board **Right:** Efforts to promote skateboarding went beyond the pages of *RAD*; Skateboarding feature by Tom Hodgkinson in *Midweek* magazine (1990) with a TLB photo of Rodney Mullen visiting London's South Bank **Below:** an article on skateboarding's resurgence written by Andy Darling in London's *City Limits* magazine (1987) with a TLB photo of Mark Abrook at Farnborough on the cover **Opposite:** Original *RAD* layout (detail) by Nick Philip from Issue 50, March 1987, Jasper Chalk, Brighton **Photo:** TLB

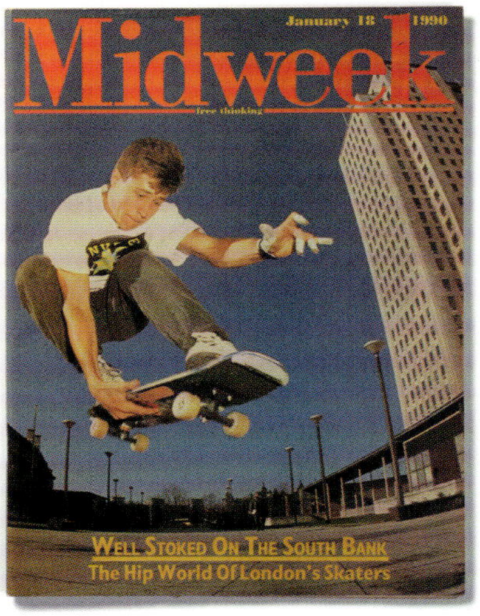

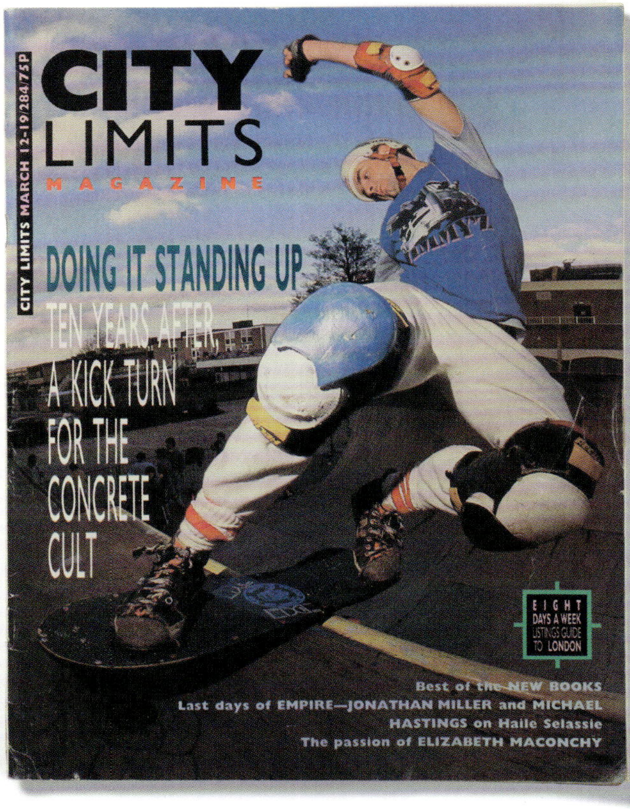

Out There

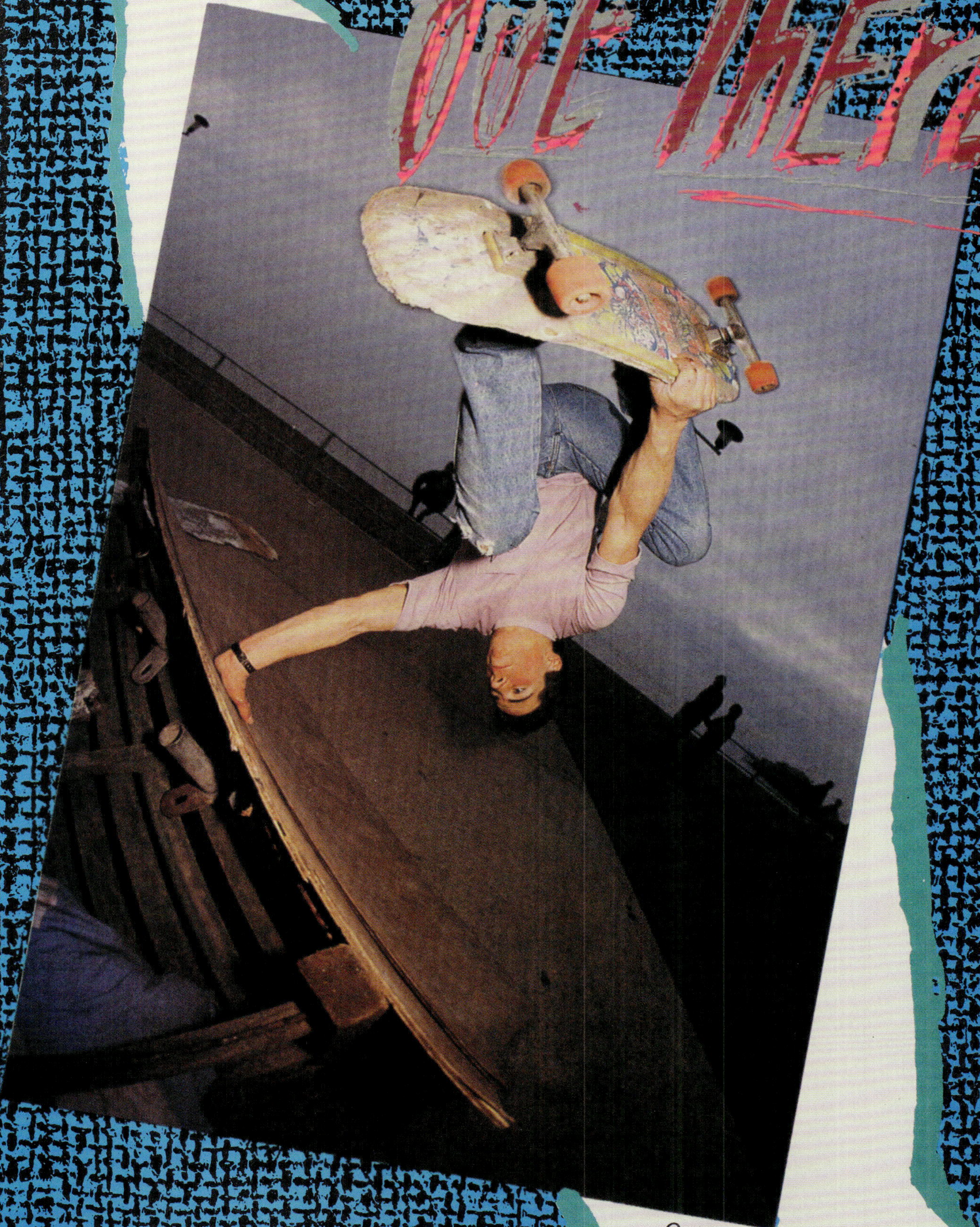

On any Sunday. Jasper Chalk hand-plant on an authentic Brighton street ramp. But it could be your home town. And it could be you. Just do it.

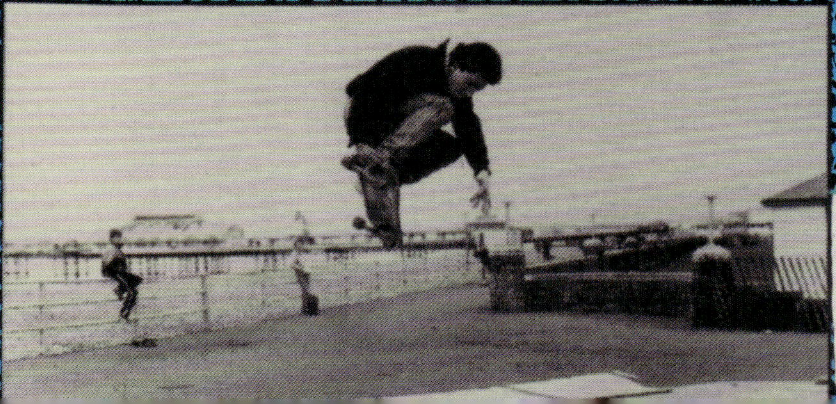

Essential action. The first and some would say the best thing you can do with a street ramp is fly out of it. Ignore all purists who say that street ramps are a contradiction. They're not. They're fu…

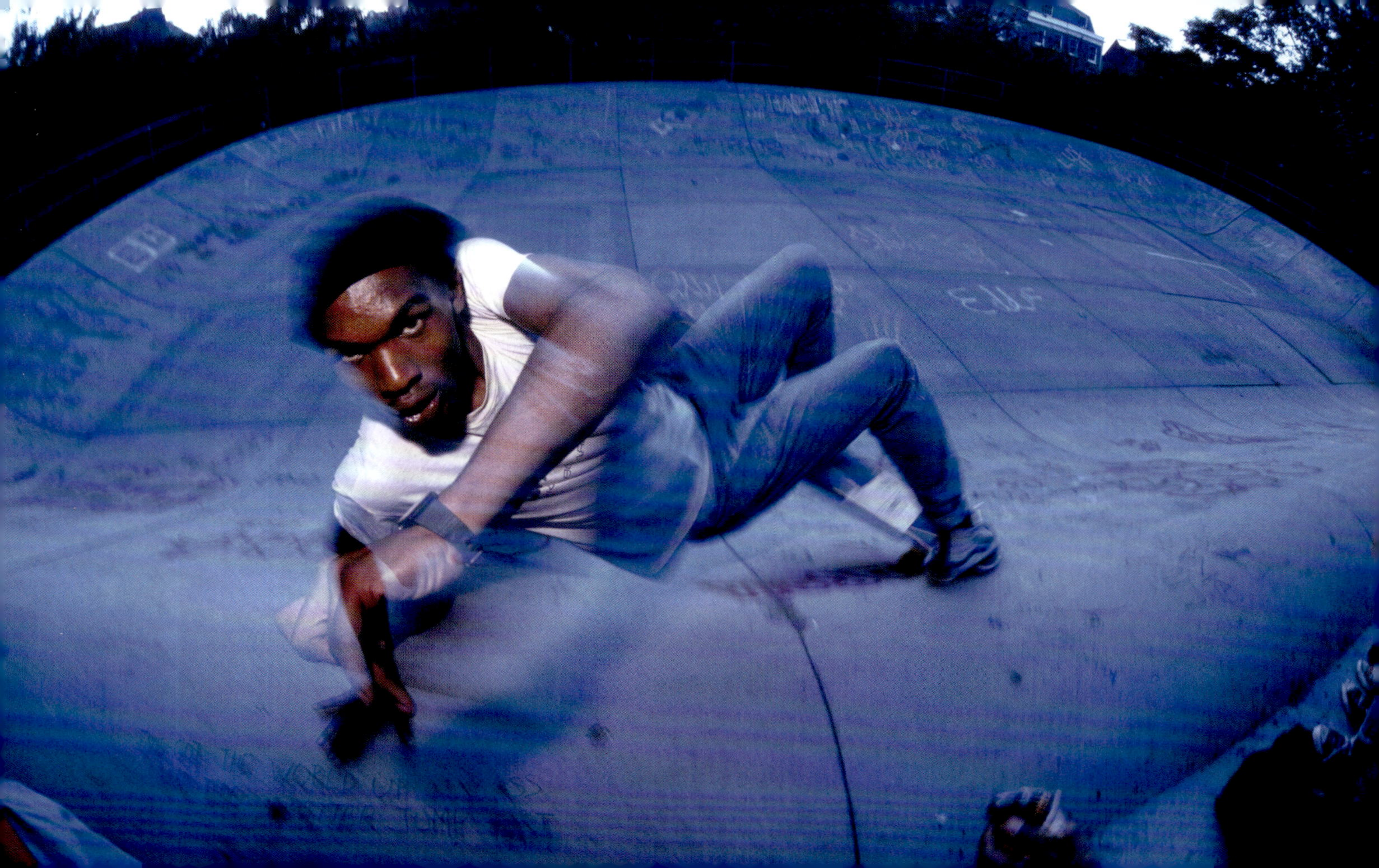

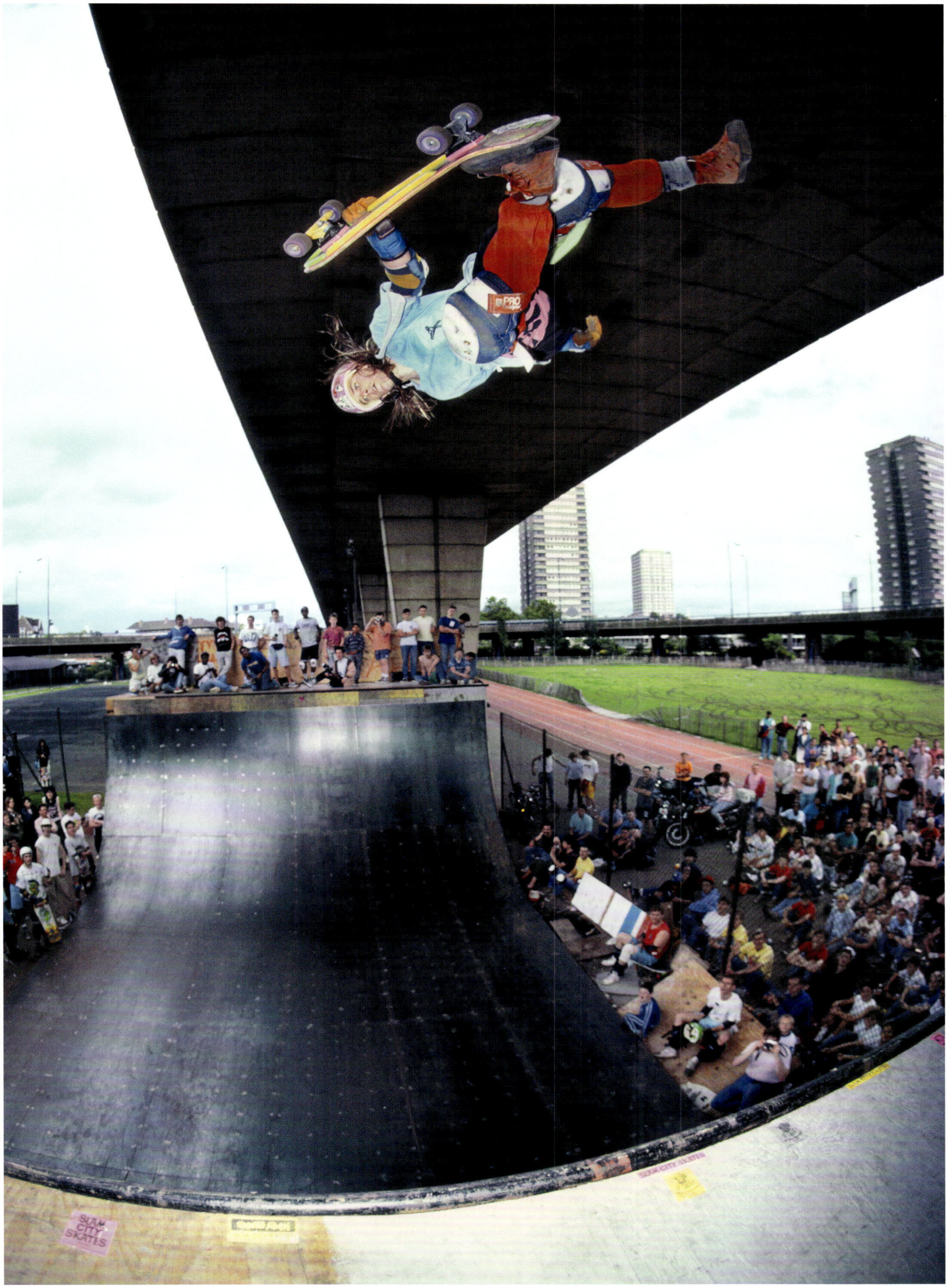

Opposite: Dean Bennett, Kennington, London, 1987 **Photo:** Mike John **Right:** Kevin Staab, Latimer Road ramp, opening contest, 1987 **Photo:** Paul Sunman

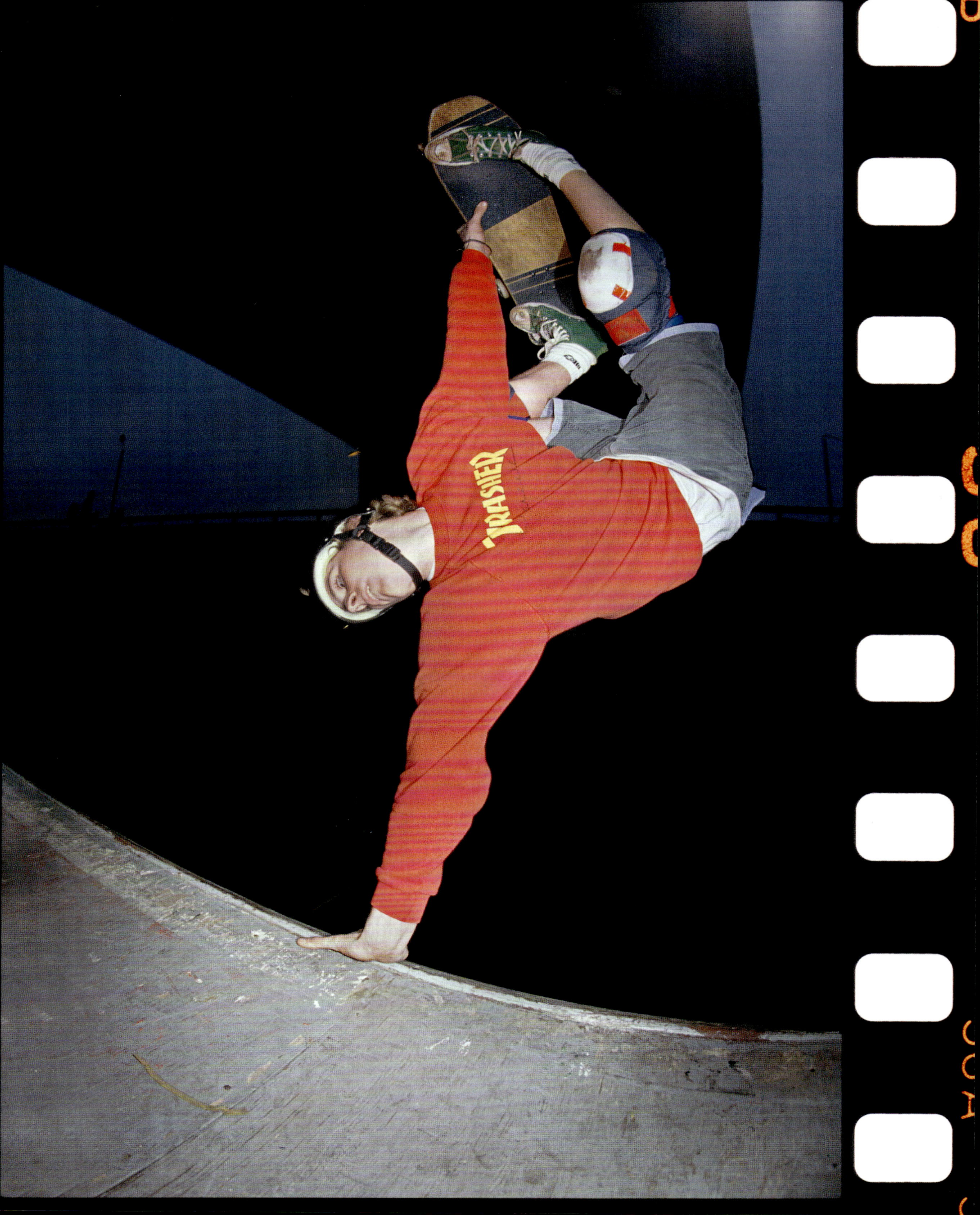

Opposite: Jeff Grosso, Latimer Road ramp, London, winter 1987 **Photo:** TLB
Below: Mark Gonzales, Munster, Germany, 1987 **Photos:** Paul Sunman

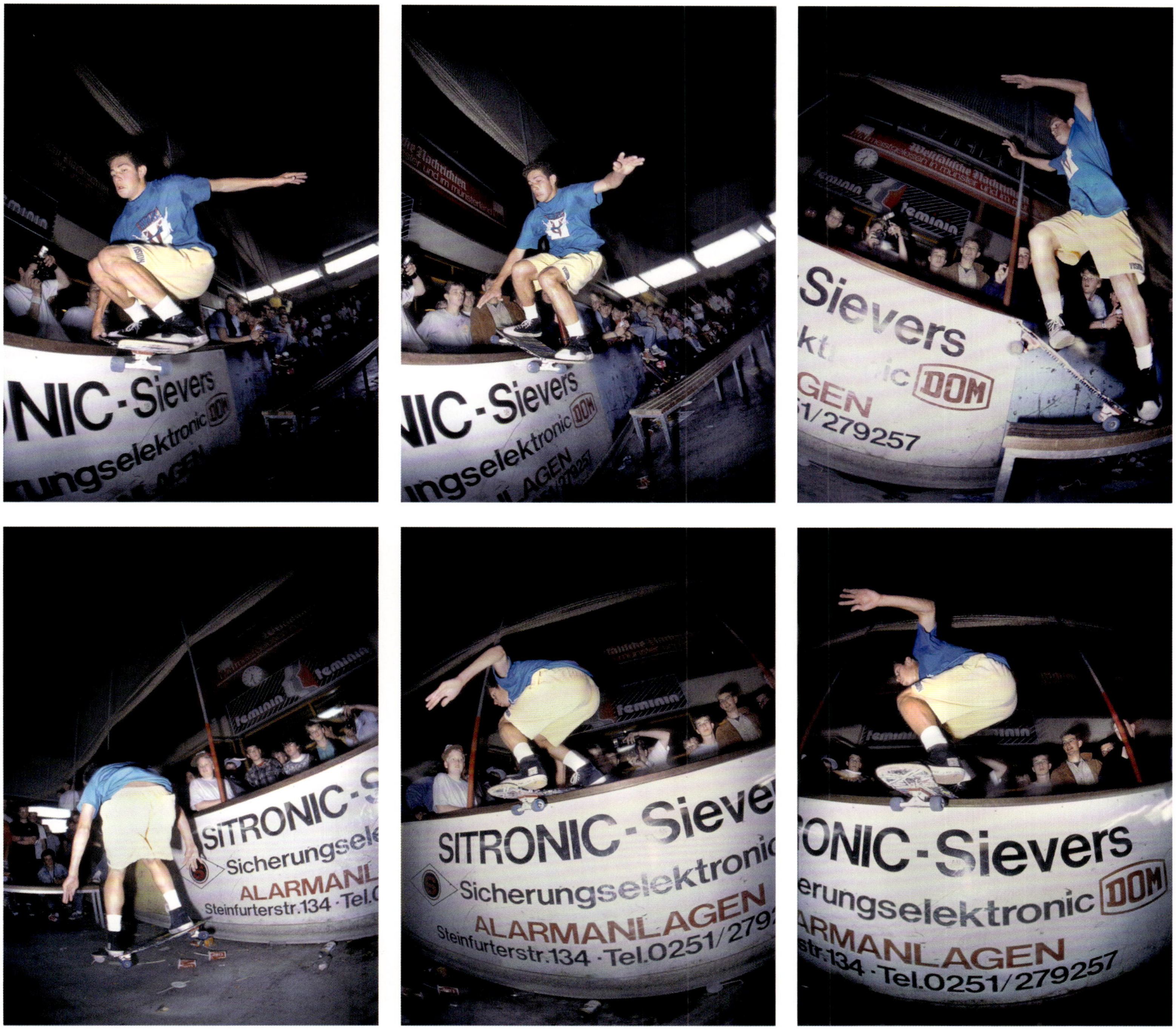

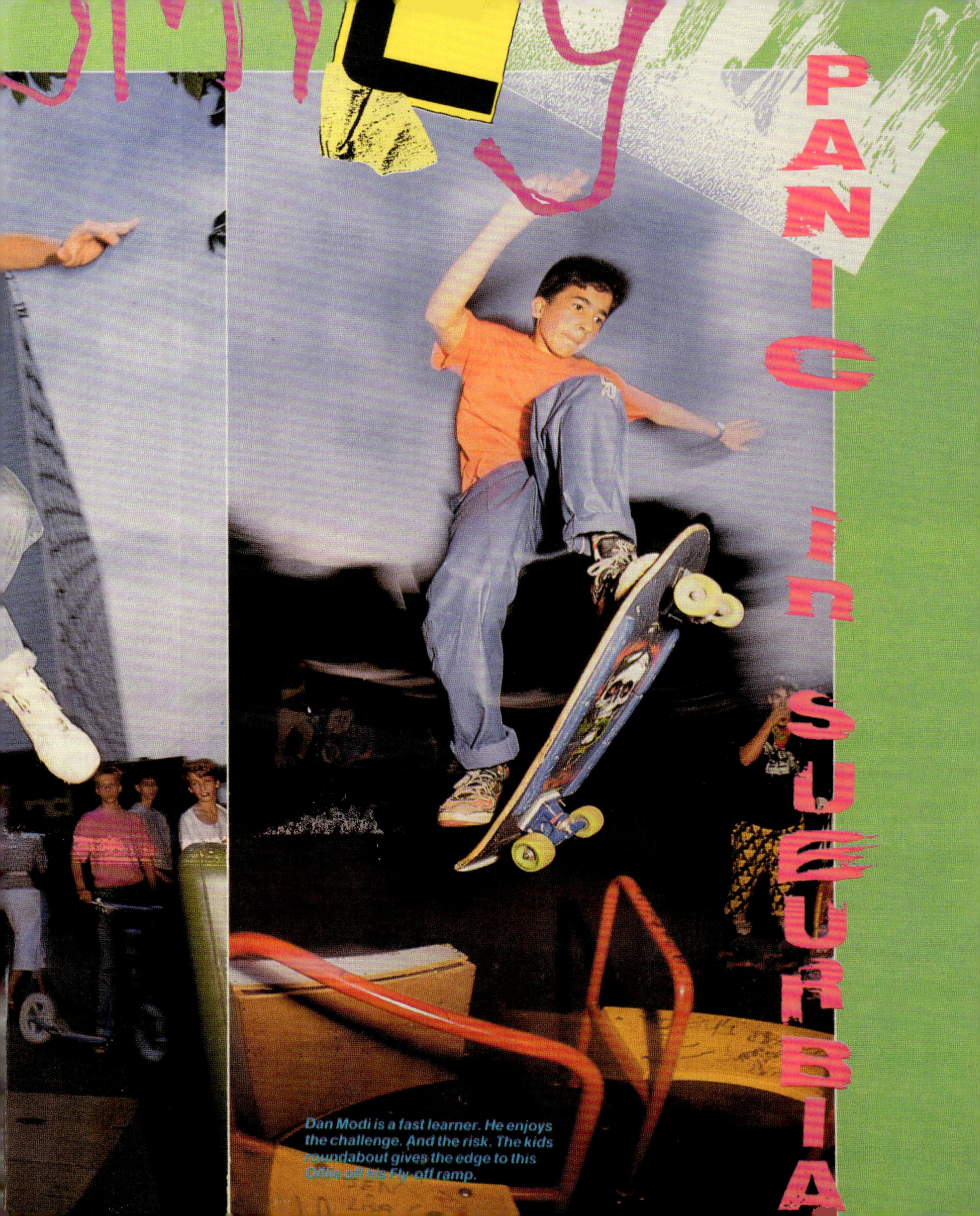

Dan Modi is a fast learner. He enjoys the challenge. And the risk. The kids roundabout gives the edge to this Ollie off his Fly-off ramp.

Opposite: Dan Modi featured in an Out There article from Issue 56, September 1987. Artwork by Nick Philip **Photo:** TLB

'I shot a lot of sequences and unfortunately people bailed a lot, so there were times when I shot a roll of film, found the next bin and tossed it, because I knew there was nothing on it. We shot a lot of sequences on cheaper film for that reason. We also used colour film and scanned them as black and white to cut the cost. There were no contact sheets either; we just went straight to prints which were then pasted straight onto board, to be scanned as a single image [to save costs].' Vernon Adams

A potential answer to the frustration of wasting vast amounts of money trying to capture trick sequences on film came via increasingly easy access to new video filming technologies and then, digital image capture. With the birth of the skate video phenomenon, the dominance of analogue film and stills photography began a slow descent from pole position as the primary image capture and communication system for skateboarding. The new, visceral, three-dimensional experience of watching feature-length skate videos presented a very real challenge to skate magazines everywhere.

With video footage in ascendancy, magazines now existed in an in-between world, vying with the increasingly frequent releases of skate videos to present skateboarding in an enticing format.

'At the start, we were in the world where everything hinged around the still photograph because there was nothing else. By the end we were in a different context and video had become a new, other way of spreading trick development. And those more complex tricks, the flippy sequential type, I was struggling to encapsulate successfully in a single still image. Hence the less than satisfactory experiments with video frame grabs.' TLB

'The screen grab era was wrong—it was bad. That was a "solution" that had presented itself and then you realised it wasn't the right thing. Yeah, they [the video frame grab images] weren't attractive—weren't very aesthetic.' Simon Evans

The image capture experiments which attempted to document and communicate the complex trick evolution now taking place, meant expensive investments in new technology. The images that developed from these experiments weren't always greeted with approval. *'I had an interview and it had video grabs. You couldn't... like "what the fuck IS that"? They just looked like squares of camouflage!'* Danny Wainwright

With questionable, even unsatisfactory results, TLB pressed on with exploring the possibilities that new technology could deliver, foreseeing that filmed footage would one day likely eclipse stills photography and print magazines in illustrating progressive skateboarding manoeuvres:

'Tim was certainly part of 411 Video Magazine *starting. We were sitting in a pub and he said "So, what's Rocco gonna do next? Is he going to start a video magazine?" Tim's question stuck in my mind.'* Steve Douglas

Despite the progression and increasing prominence of video footage—and the image capture experiments that grew out of it—the power of the still skate photo and magazines continued to have influence.

Stills represented a version of skateboarding that video and sequences couldn't. In looking at a still photograph a mental process of filling in gaps takes place; imagining the before and after and establishing a narrative around the image. The stills had an aesthetic edge that digital sequences couldn't replicate. Photographers had helped skateboarding to establish a language of particular body shapes and trick 'best practice'—a hand needs to be there and a foot should be positioned like that—forms that might have gone unregistered had they not been described so clearly in the photographers' considered captures. *'We were just like, REALLY into skateboarding and imagining—I always think about that now—how our bodies looked in sequence.'* Simon Evans

CONFIDENCE AND INDEPENDENCE

RAD magazine evolved into an engaging sum of its creative parts. A successful combination of differing voices and visuals that had earned itself a loyal following. Skateboarding is, and in the late 1980s and early 1990s most definitely was, a fast-moving beast. Being open to change and collaboration with new views and voices meant that *RAD* successfully moved with the times. Huge chunks of the vibrant British skate culture and its movers, shakers and ideals would have gone unrecorded and unseen had it not been for the efforts of its dedicated contributors.

'Tim always had a massive emotional attachment to the magazine and he saw it as a kind of responsibility to get it right. Just doing a magazine could be pretty easy, if you don't give a shit—if anything he cared about it too much, that's why he was good at it.' Ged Wells

The creative influence from the likes of Ged Wells, Gavin Hills and Simon Evans, coupled with photographic talents, both established and new, local and international; as well as exciting, unexpected design and editorial; up-to-date news and a sense of open connectivity; had forged a highly relatable publication with a discernibly strong personality. The magazine served as an important post on which British skateboarding could proudly fly its freak flag—an effective mirror and feedback loop to the culture it was reporting on while also acting as a guidebook of sorts.

'*RAD* cast a spell on us; a spell of confidence and independence, of focused removal of preconceptions. A spell of participation and creativity, of sound defence of our emerging values, of healthy critique of the paths we were meant to follow. A spell of positive interference in our town and cityscapes. Most of all was cast a spell of consciousness; both of our place in the world and the wherewithal to do something about it.'

James Davis

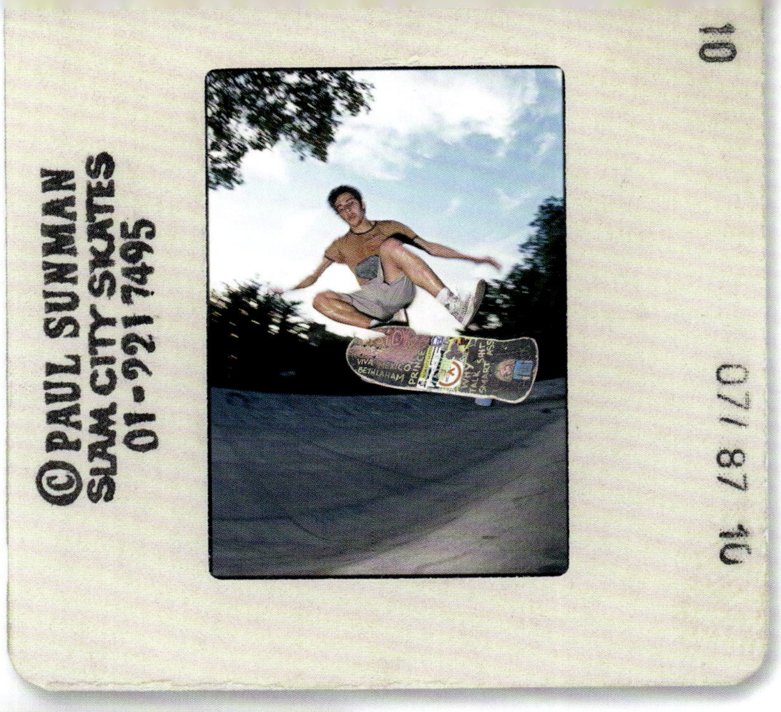

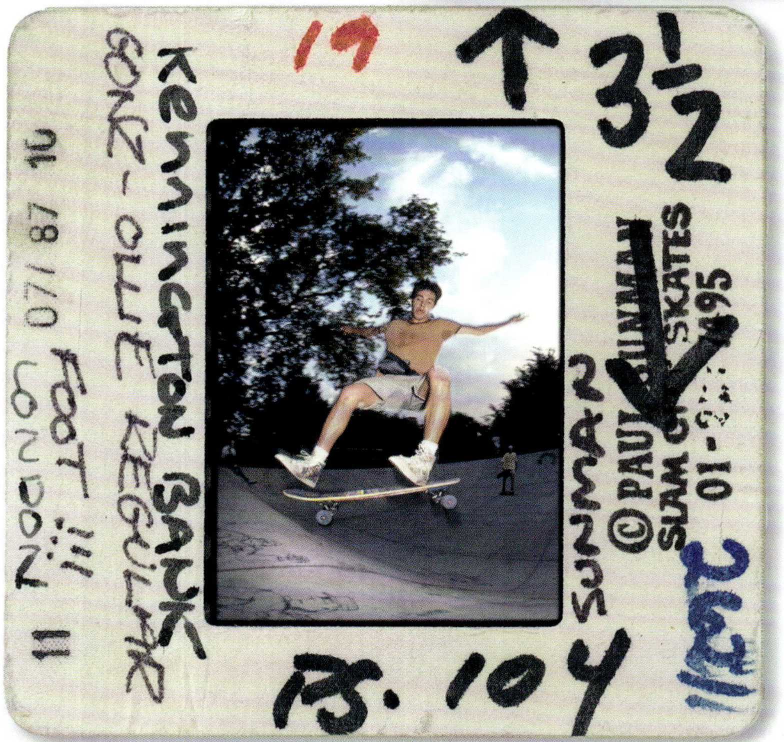

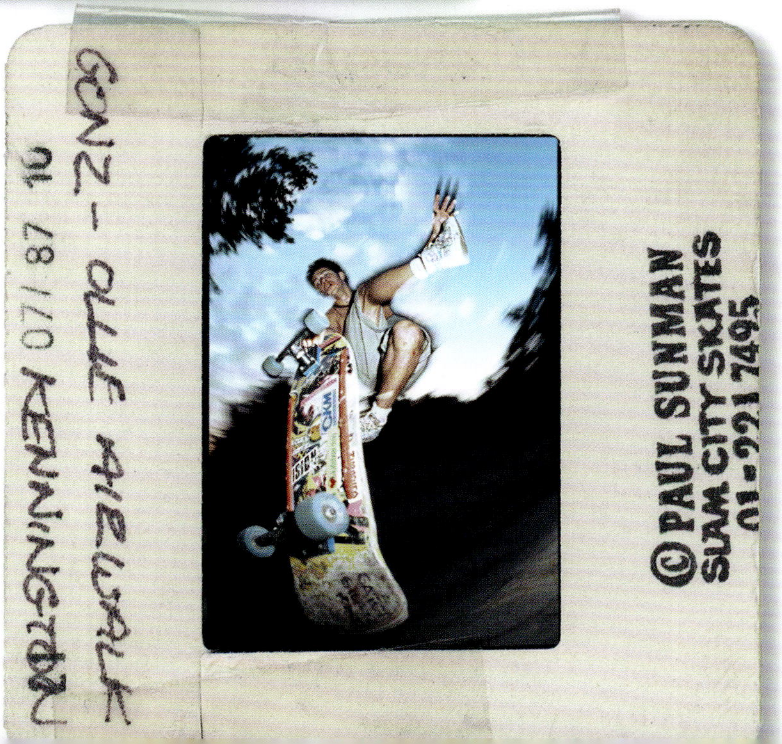

Left and opposite: Mark Gonzales, Kennington, London, summer 1987 (note comments on slide mounts)
Overleaf left: London's Meanwhile 2 earns the 'Gonz Gap' title thanks to groundbreaking moves from Mark Gonzales, summer 1987, and **right:** Contact sheet from the same session, all that remains of this iconic and groundbreaking moment, now that the negatives have gone missing
All photos: Paul Sunman

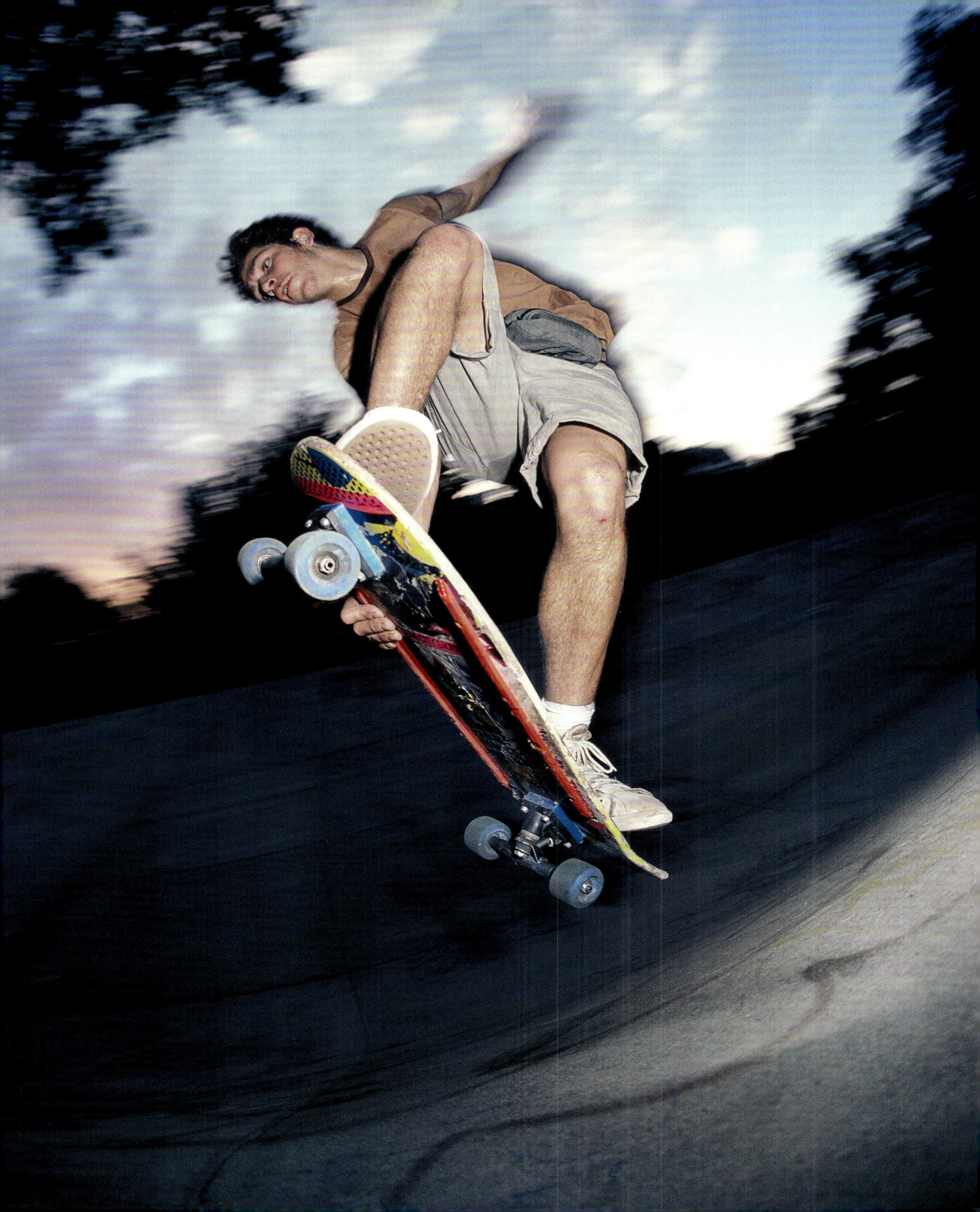

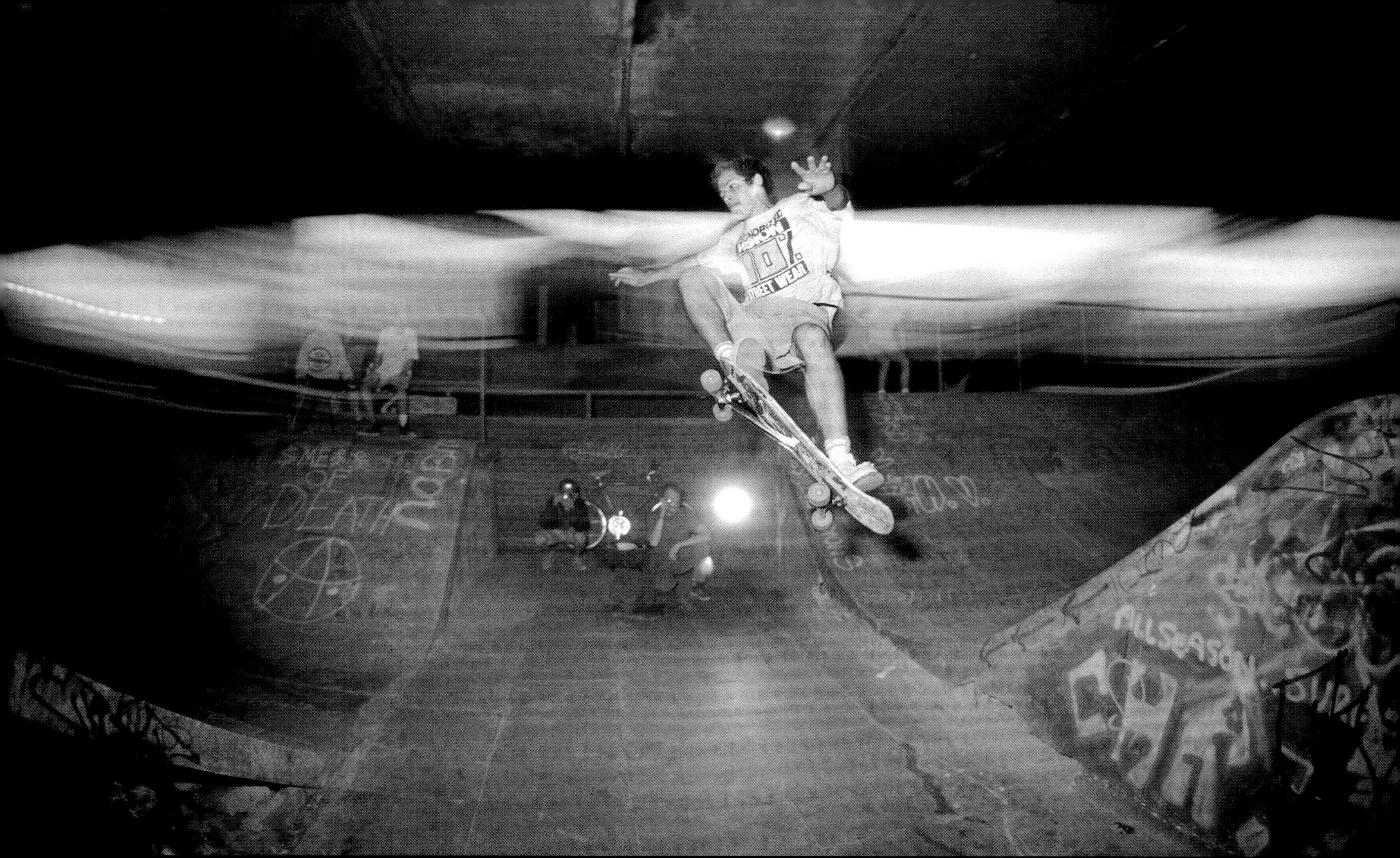
STREET WEAR
OF
DEATH
ALL SEASON

‘I’d been around Mark in a few different sessions, so that gave some understanding of how he approached things. I’d set myself up in the gap [at Meanwhile 2] because I realised he was going to try to ollie it. I’d watched him practising his line up to it, stepping off just before he got to the edge.

‘I remember fiddling with the camera, trying to work out how to get enough flashes to catch the sequence and then he did it and by some miracle the flash kept up with it and I got the sequence of him going across the gap. I think he only did it once. That turned out to be an iconic moment—Gonz turned up and brought a totally fresh attitude to a spot that people had been skating since the 1970s.’

Paul Sunman

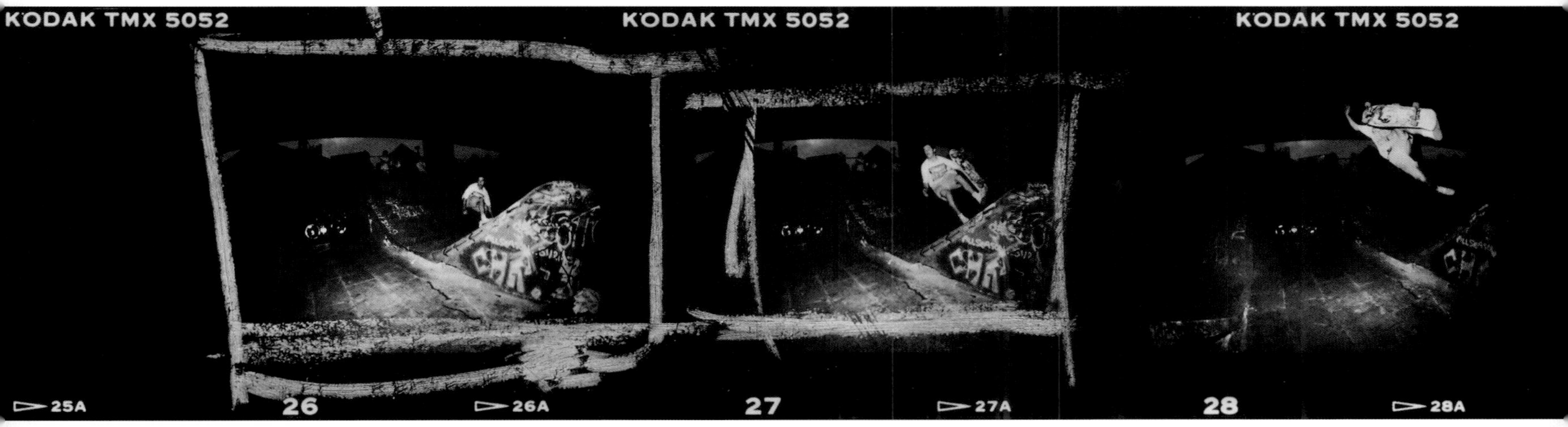

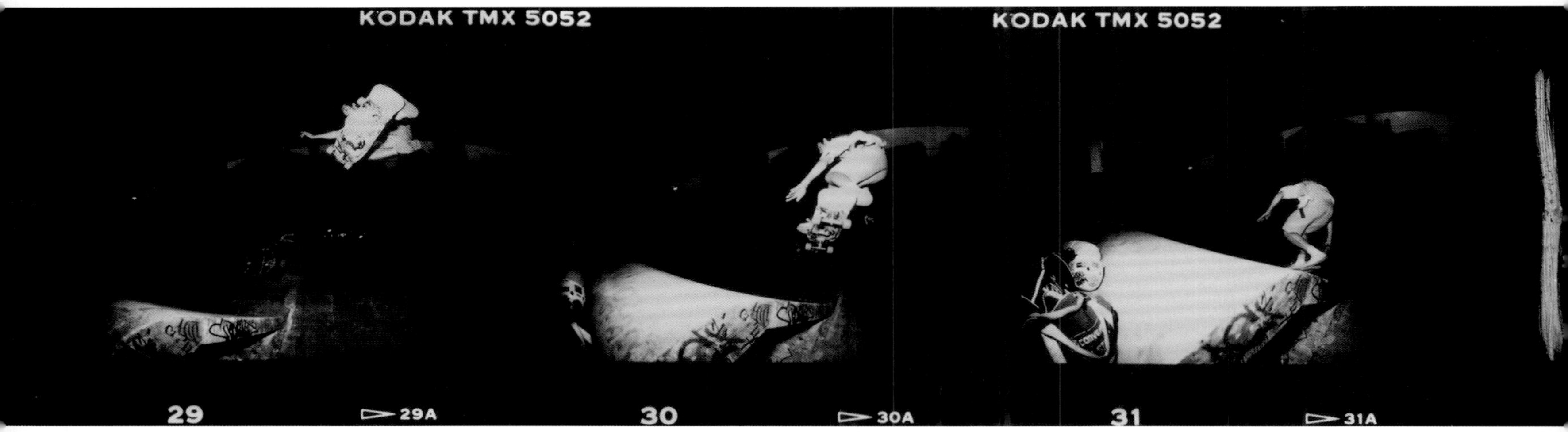

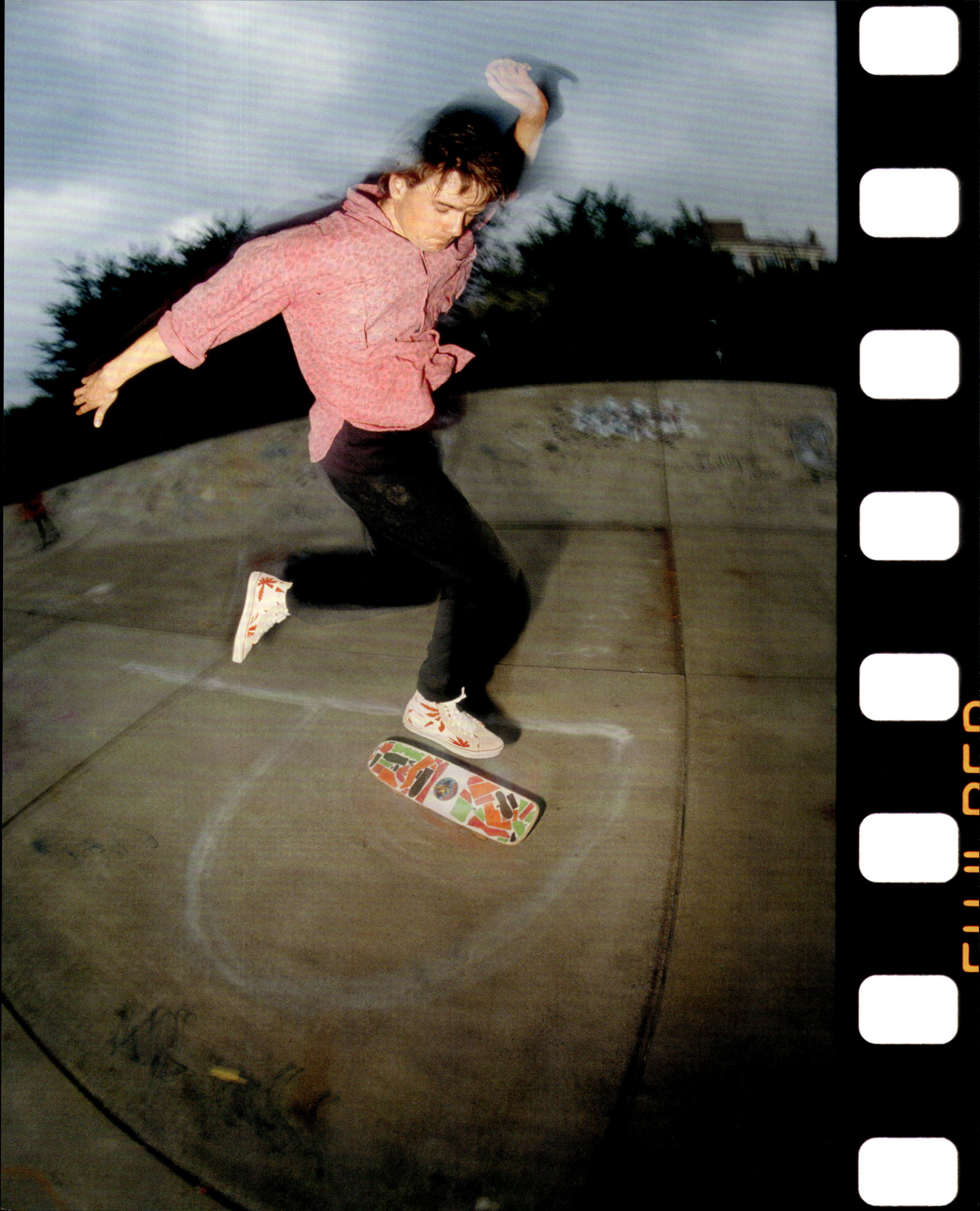

Opposite: Graham 'Mac' McEachran, Kennington, London, 1987 **Below:** Lucian Hendricks, Latimer Road, 1987 Mike John standing, camera in hand **Overleaf left:** Paul 'Rocker' Robson, Southsea skatepark, 1988, and **right:** Don Brider, Meanwhile 2, London 1988 **All photos**: TLB

'Their photography was also a reflection of their personalities. I remember Mike was wild—running around shooting his arm out, not looking through the lens, just capturing it, which is kind of how he rode a skateboard. He was a total wild card, right?'

Bod Boyle

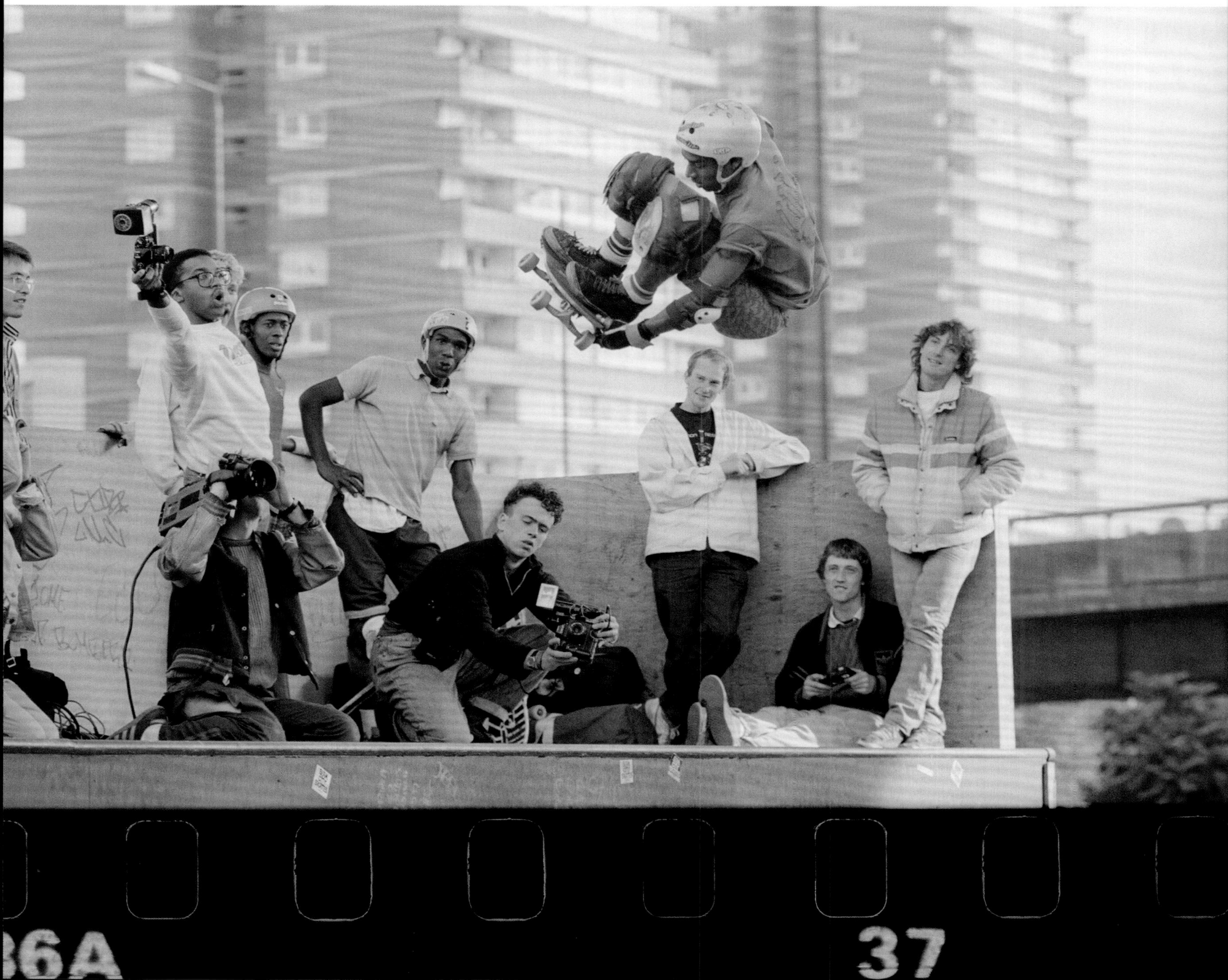

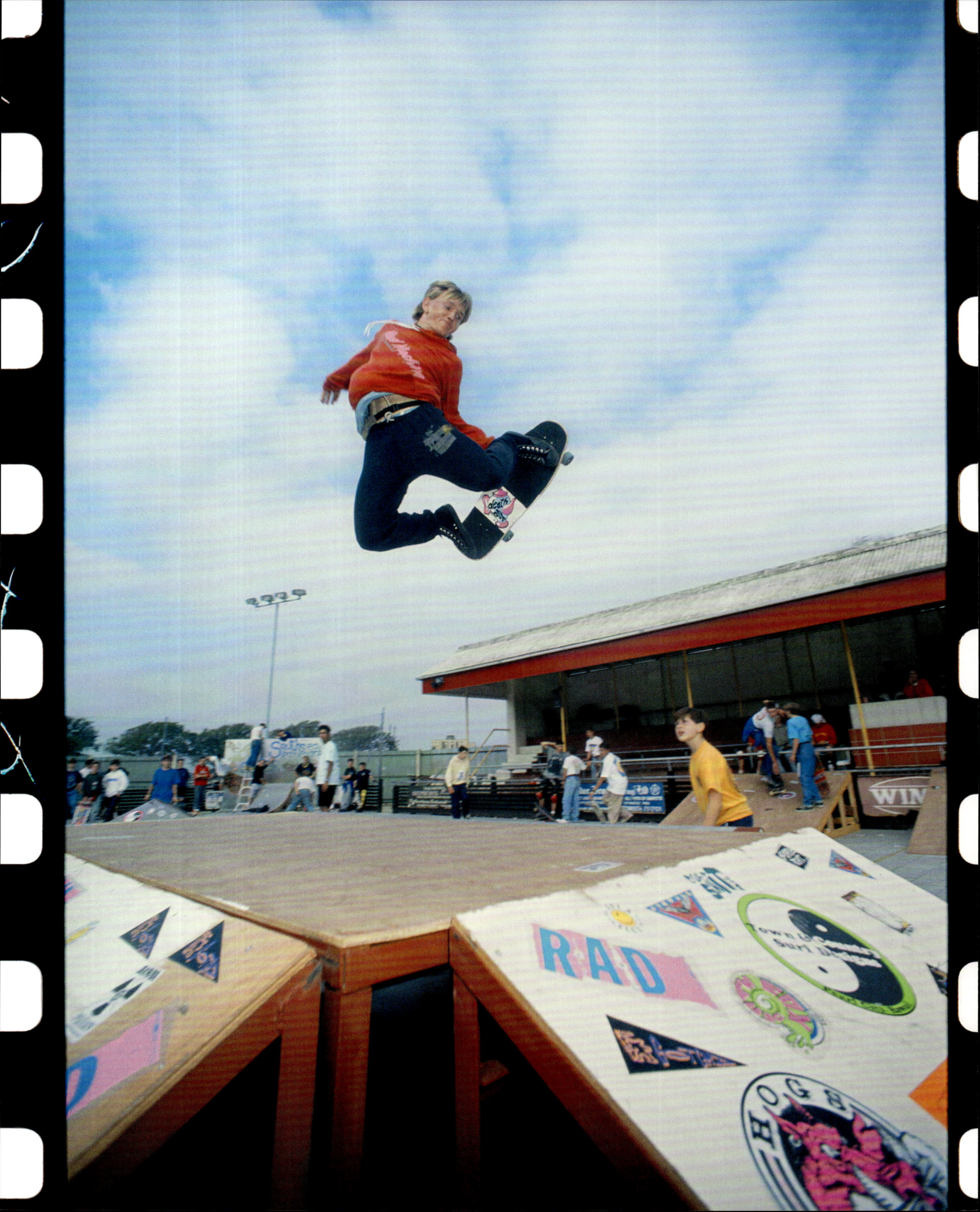
RAD
WIN

Cirencester

dear ED

I writing from the depths of the wacky countryside to ask of some assistants.Where i live there is no skate parks ,no radical shops,nothing. What is the best way to find out about where i can skate ?!You may have thought that we country bumkins don't get radical at times ,but we do.

please help the deprived skaters of the country.OH !! ,i am sure all the BMXers are pissed off with skateing articles in their mag,so print a skate board mag that is BRITISH and not American.

hope to hear from you soon

keep up the good work

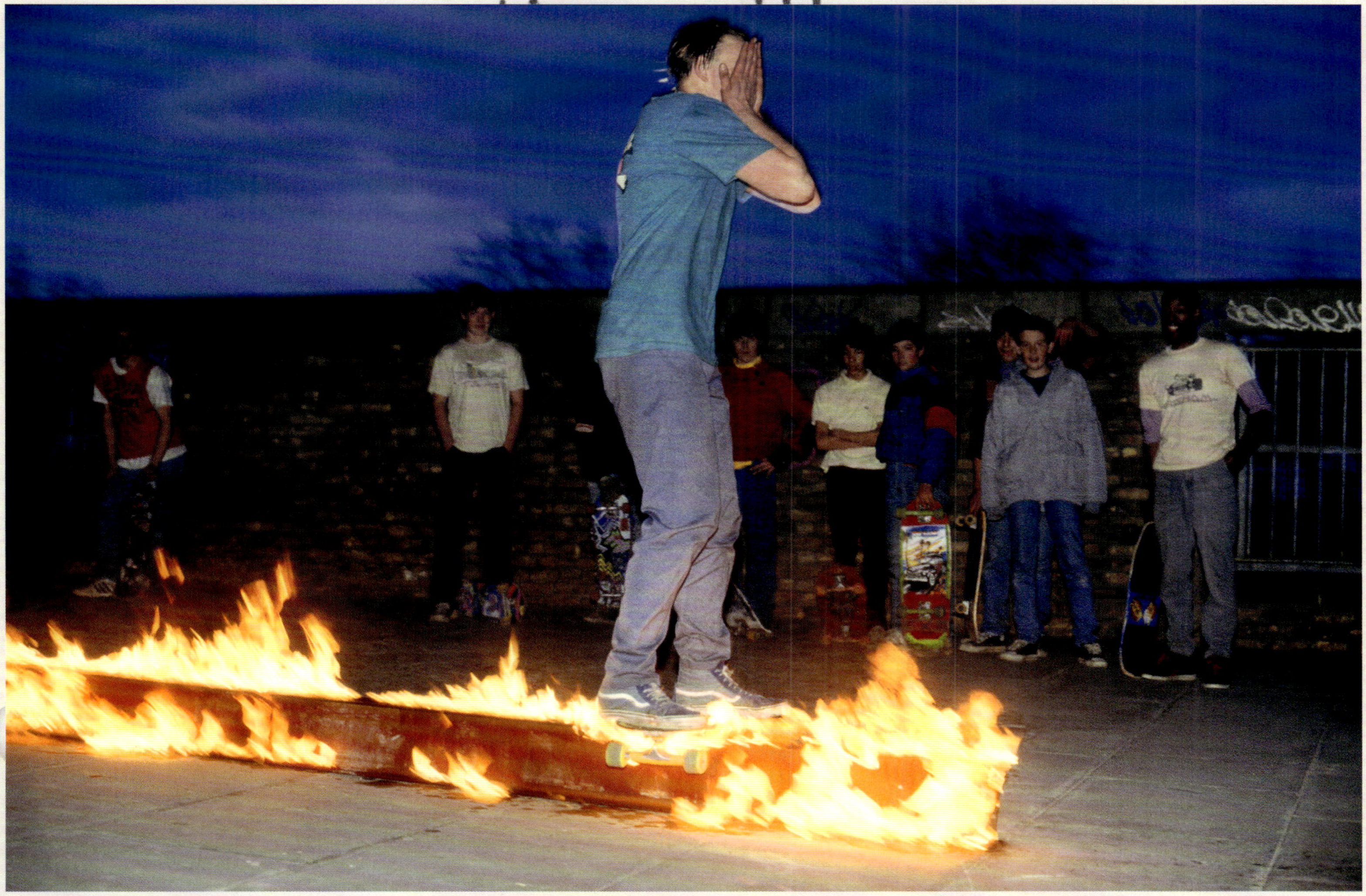

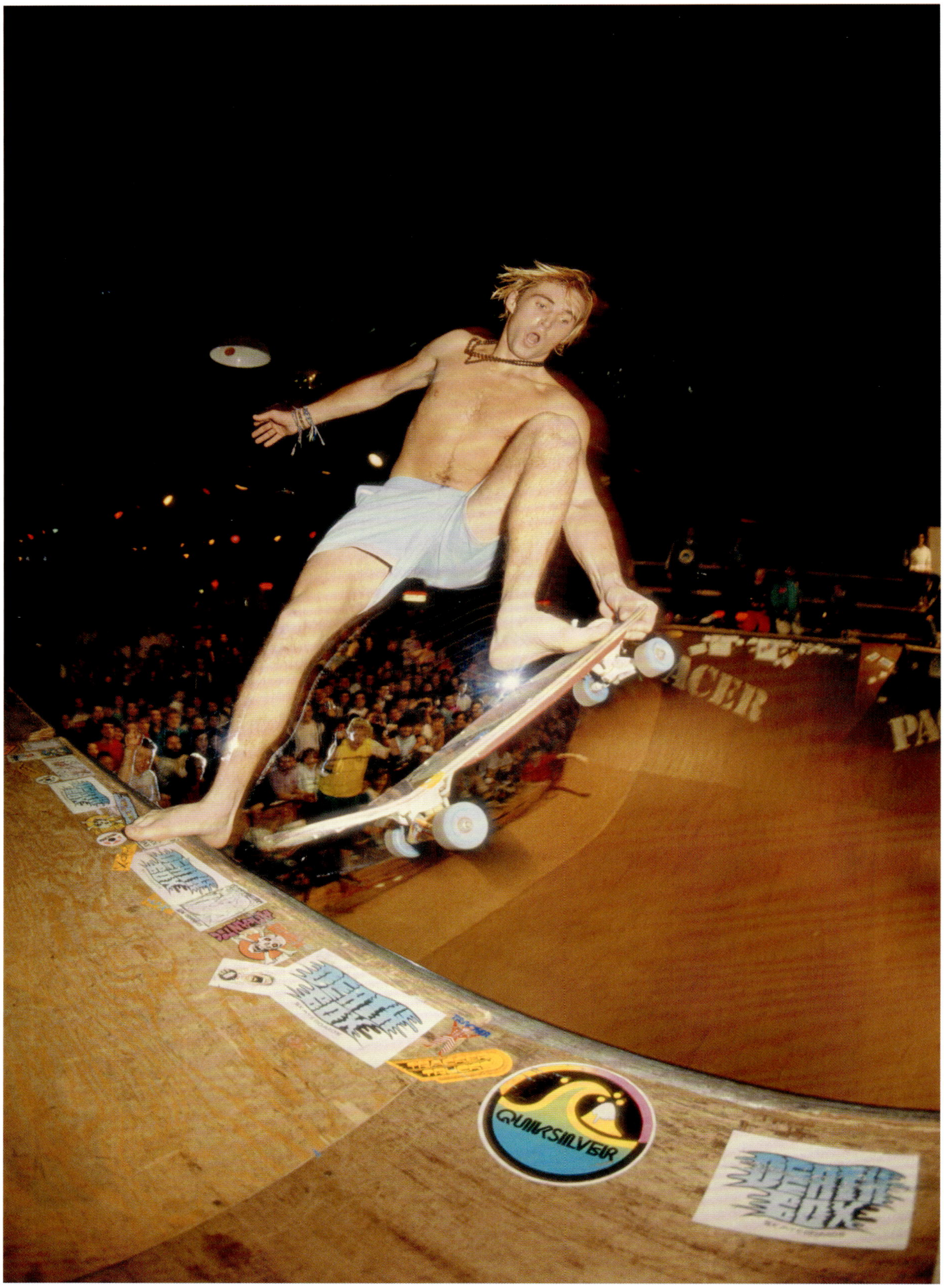

Left: Sean Goff, Warrington, 1988 **Opposite:** Pete Dossett, Southsea skatepark, 1988 **Photos:** TLB

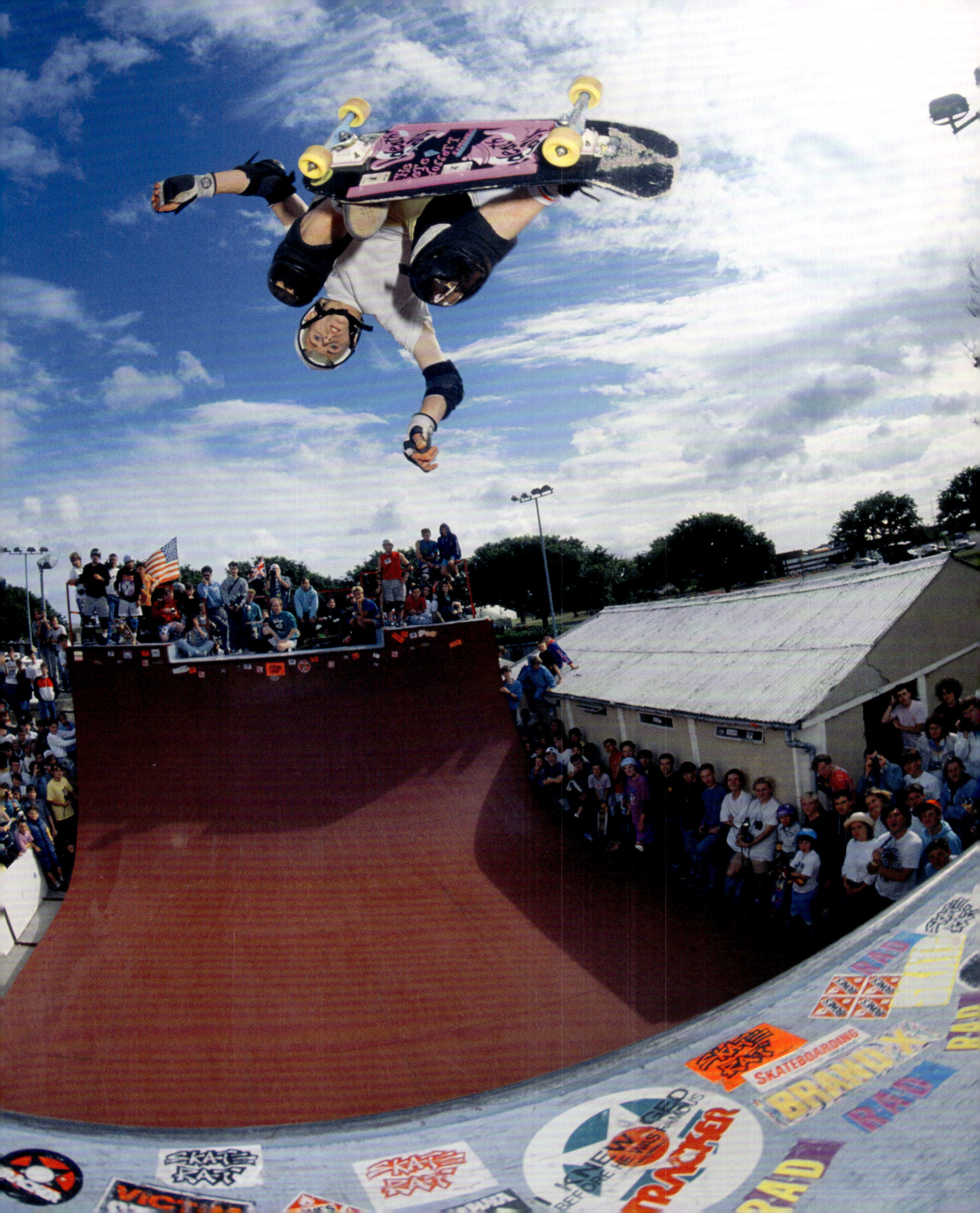
SKATEBOARDING
BRAND-X
RAD
TRACKER
SKATE RAT

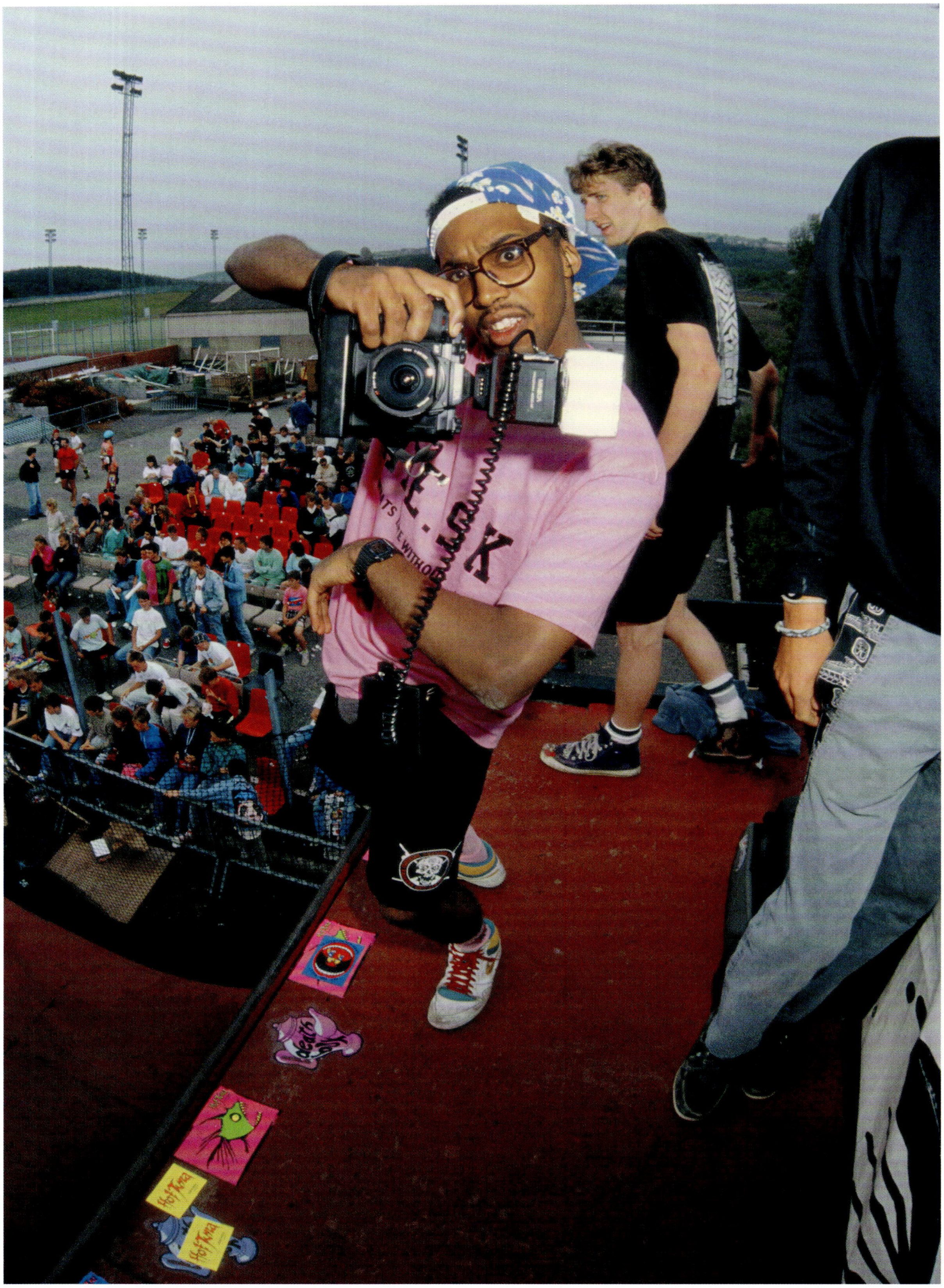

Left: Mike John, Swansea, 1988 **Photo:** Jay Podesta **Opposite:** Claus Grabke, Belgium, 1988 **Photo:** Mike John

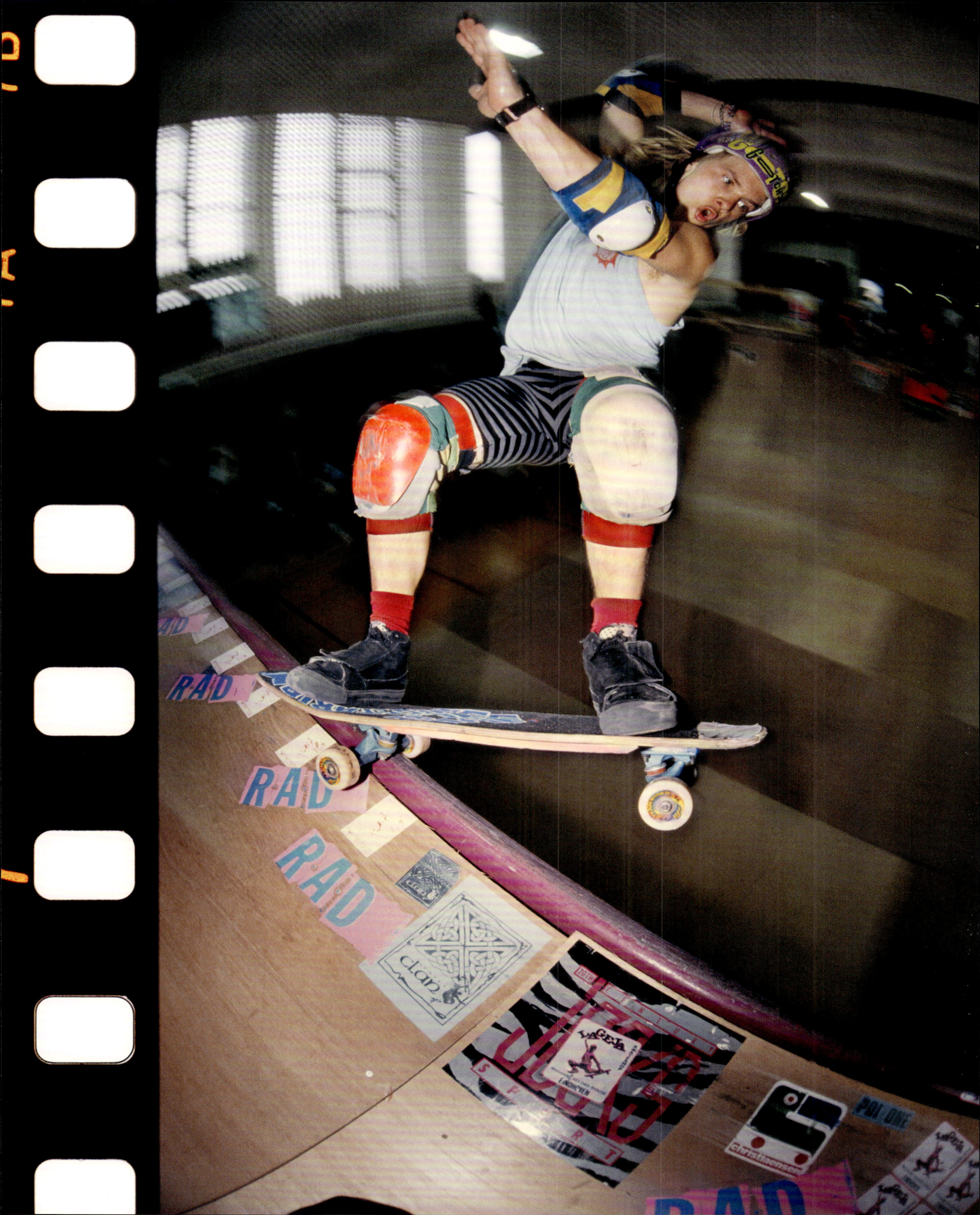
RAD
RAD
RAD
clan
christiaensen

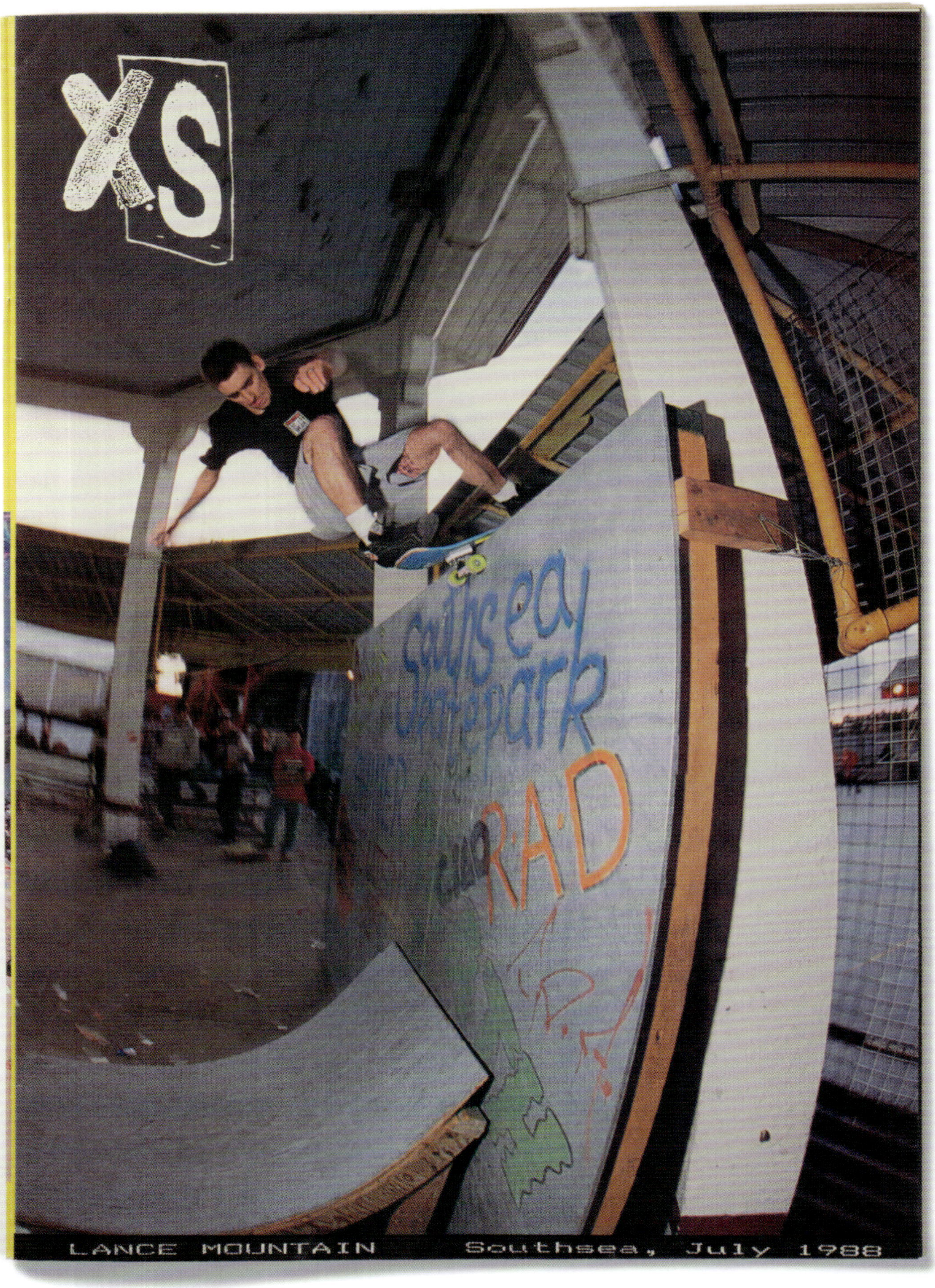

Left: Lance Mountain, Bones Brigade demo, Southsea skatepark, 1988 **Opposite:** Southsea skatepark **Photos:** TLB

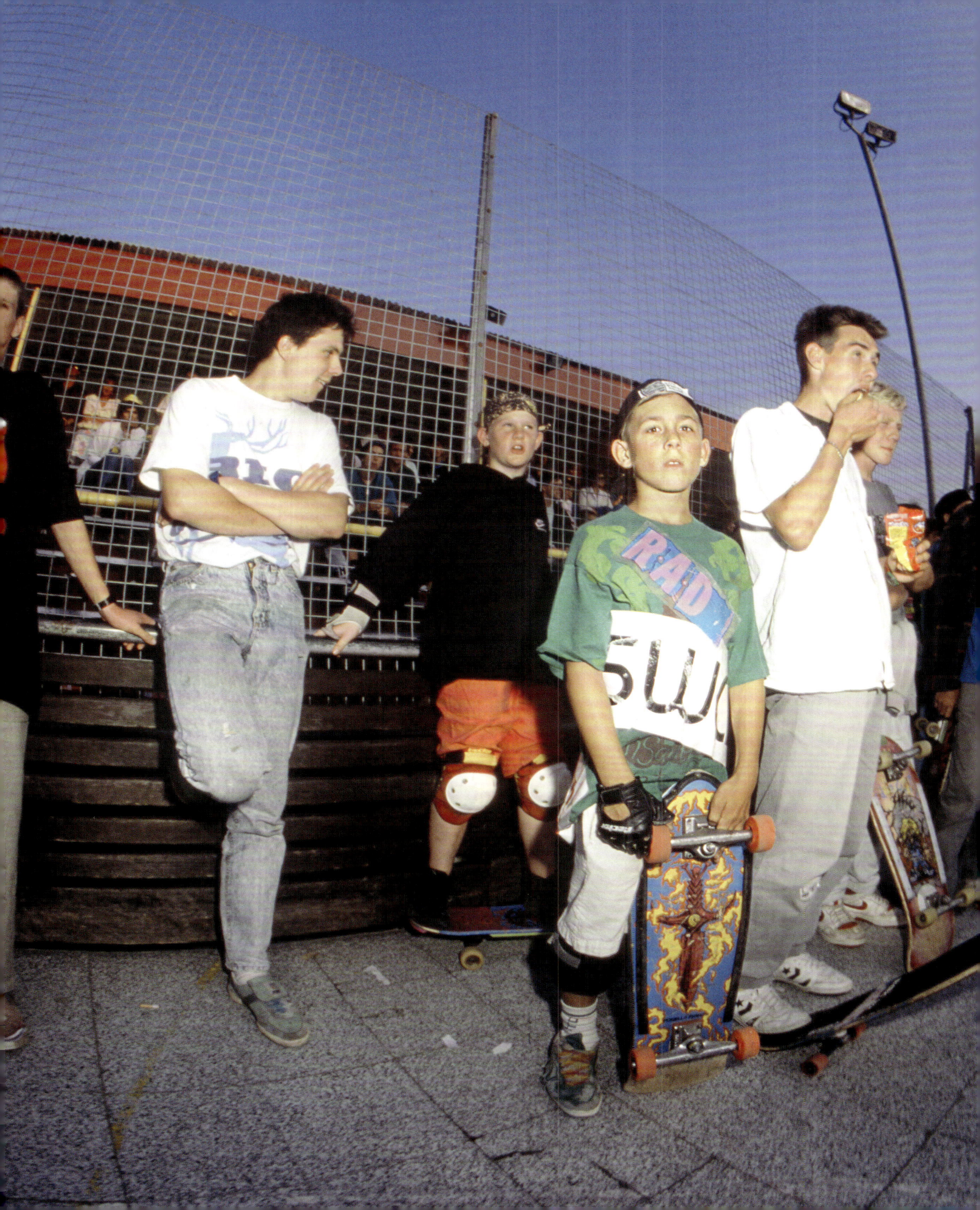
R.A.D

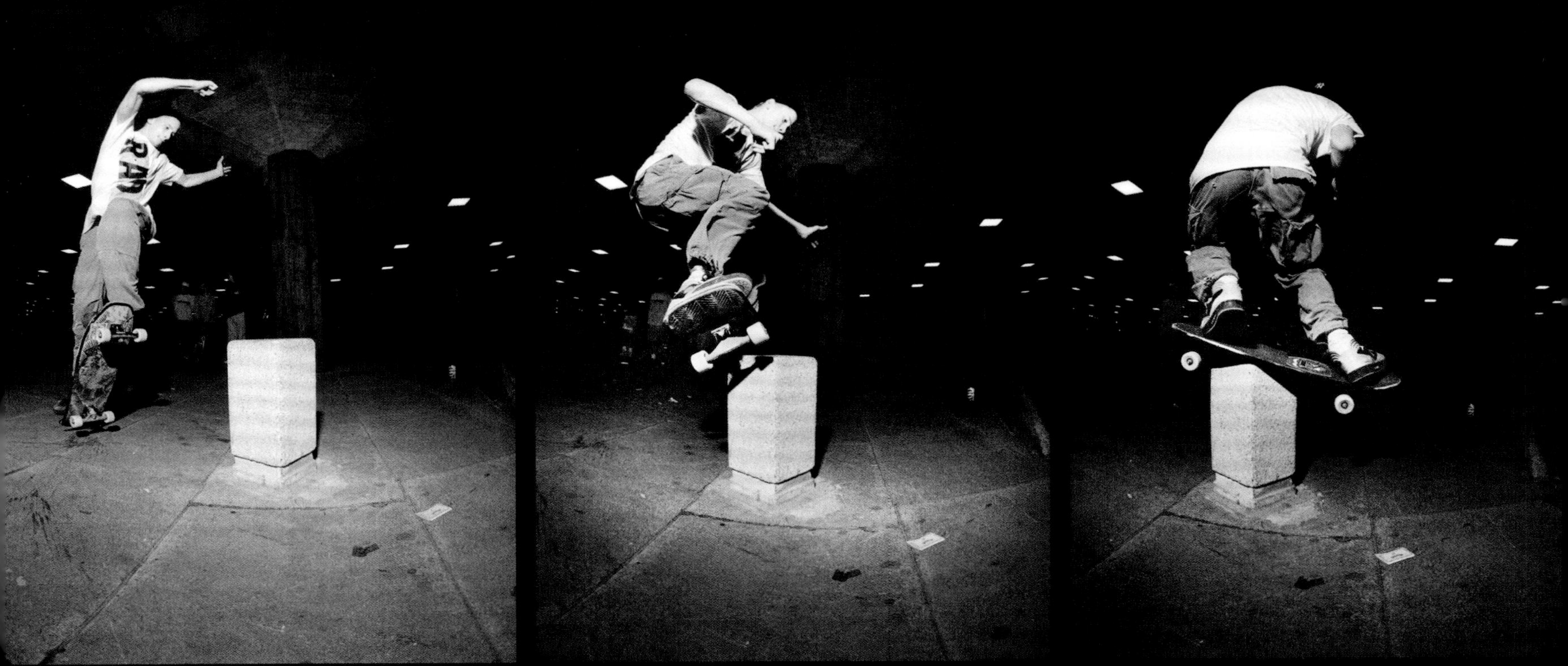

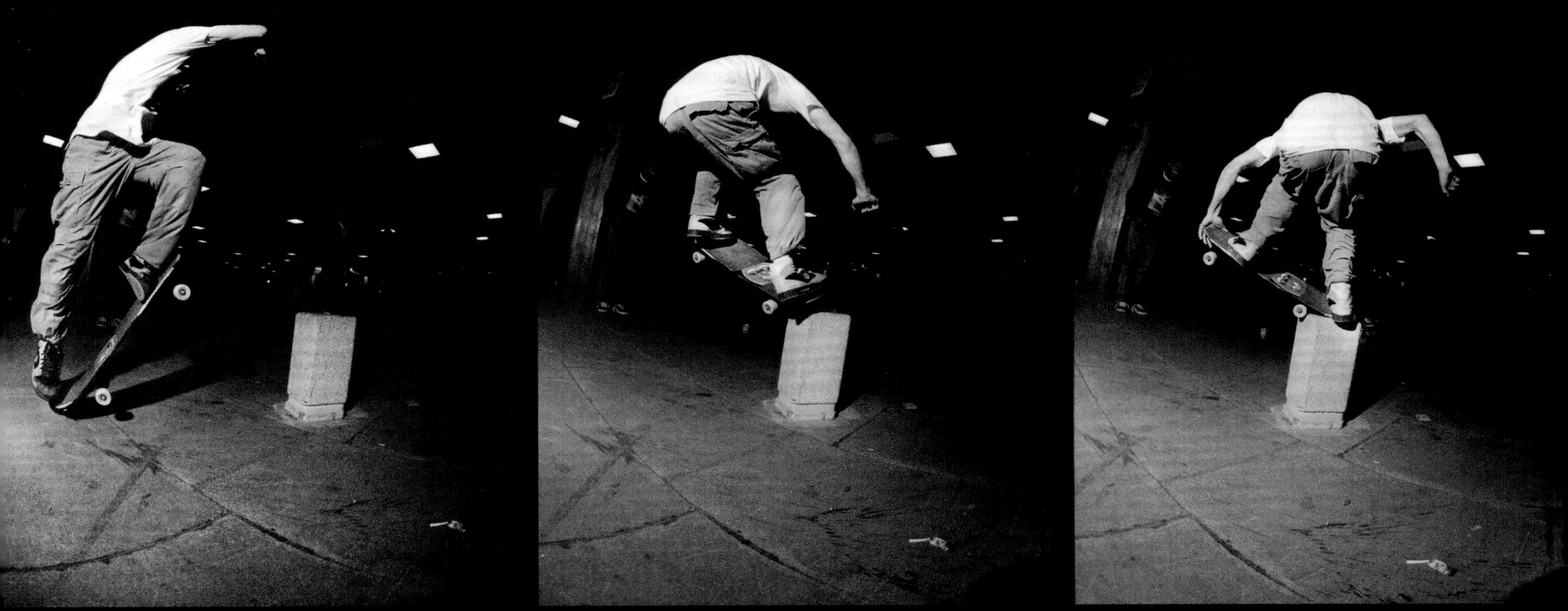

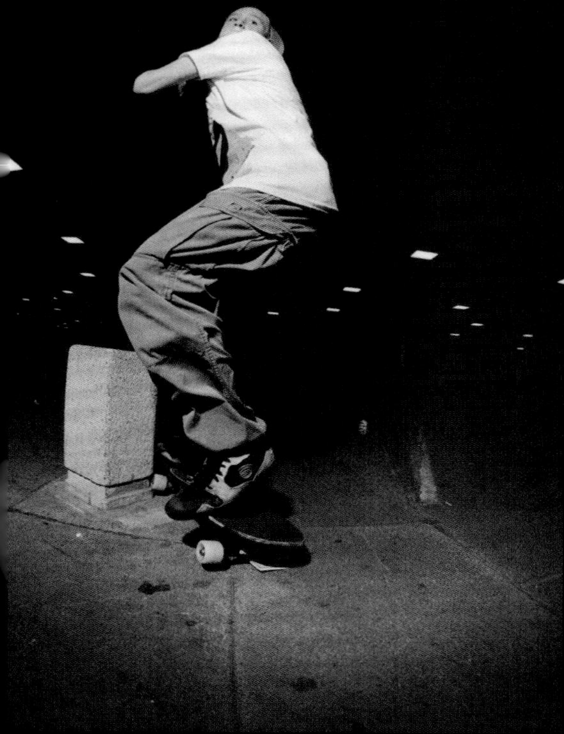

‘...one of the greatest tours I’ve ever been a part of... UK, 1988. Probably some of the best vert skating I ever did as well. On the road with legends and heroes’

Mike Vallely, 2015

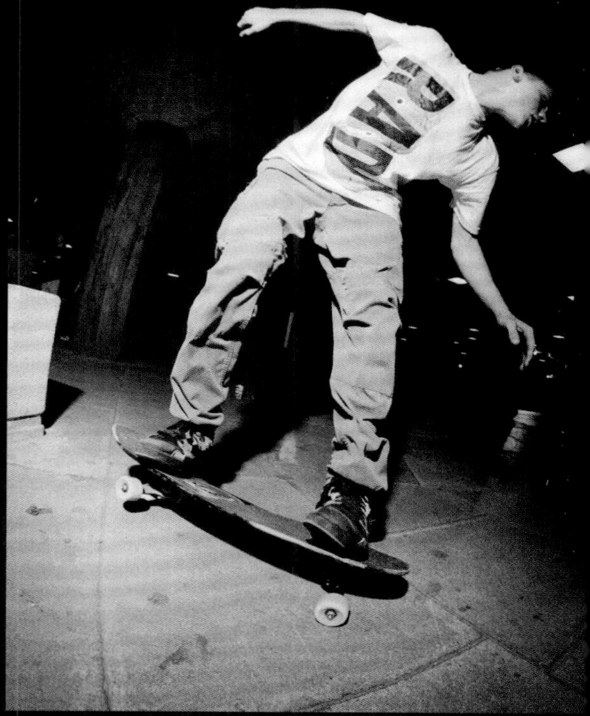

Mike Vallely, Southbank, 1988
Photos: TLB

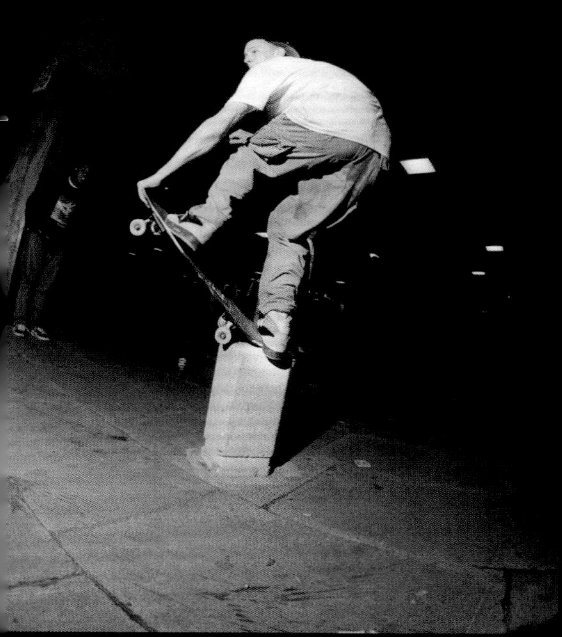

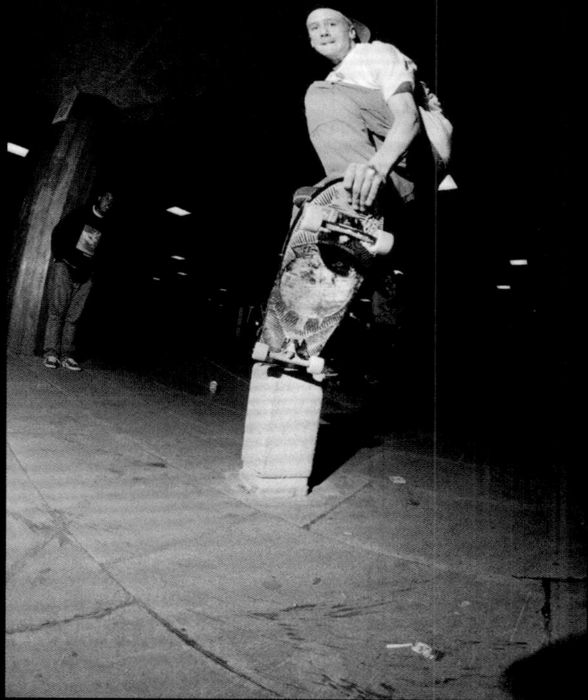

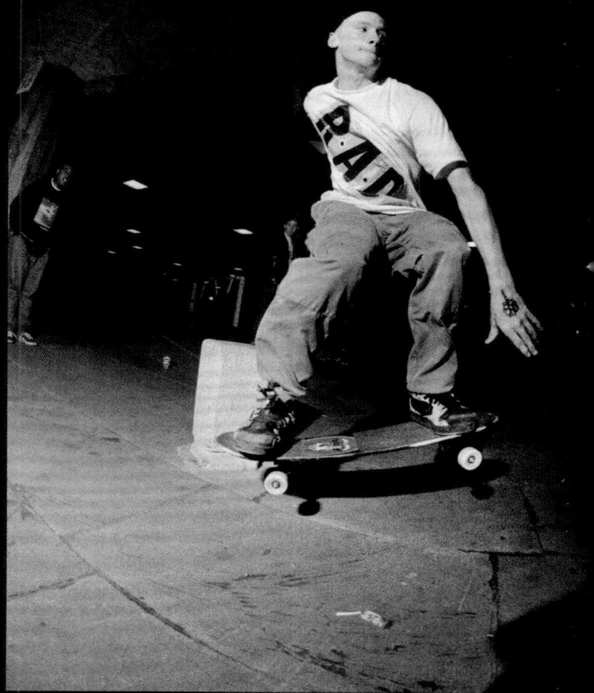

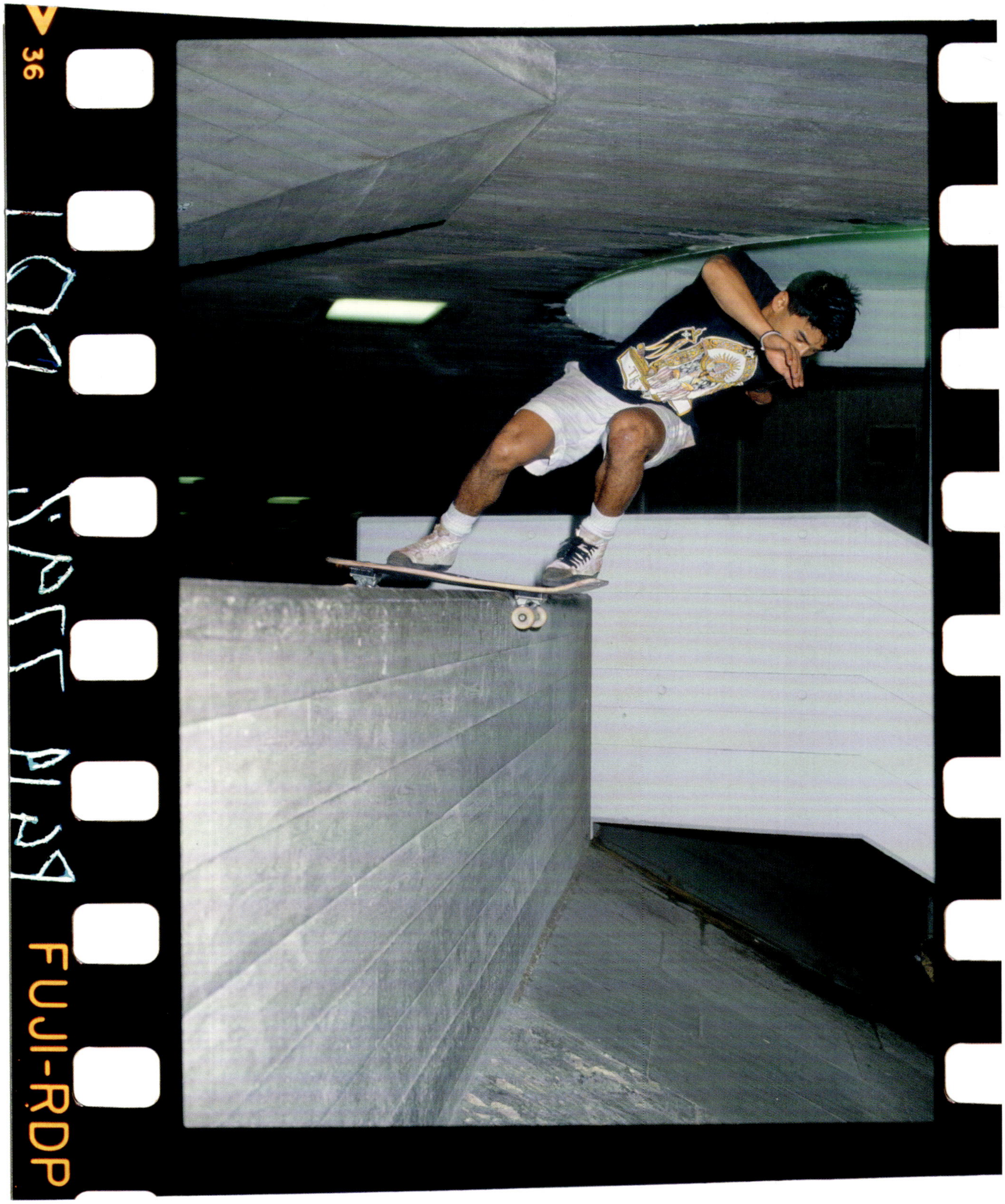

Left: Steve Caballero, Bones Brigade tour, Southbank, 1988 **Opposite:** Femi Bukanola, Manchester, 1988 **Photos:** TLB

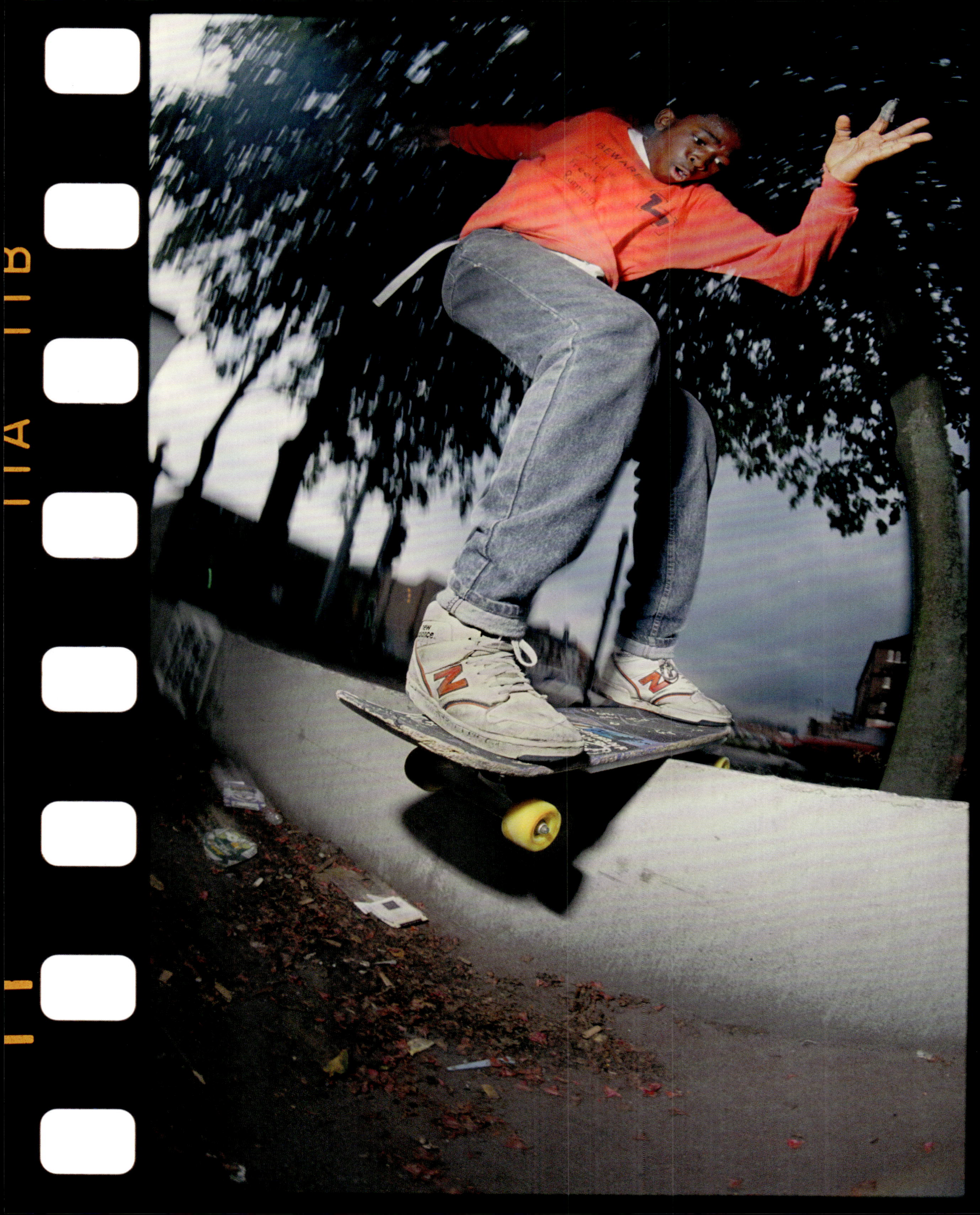

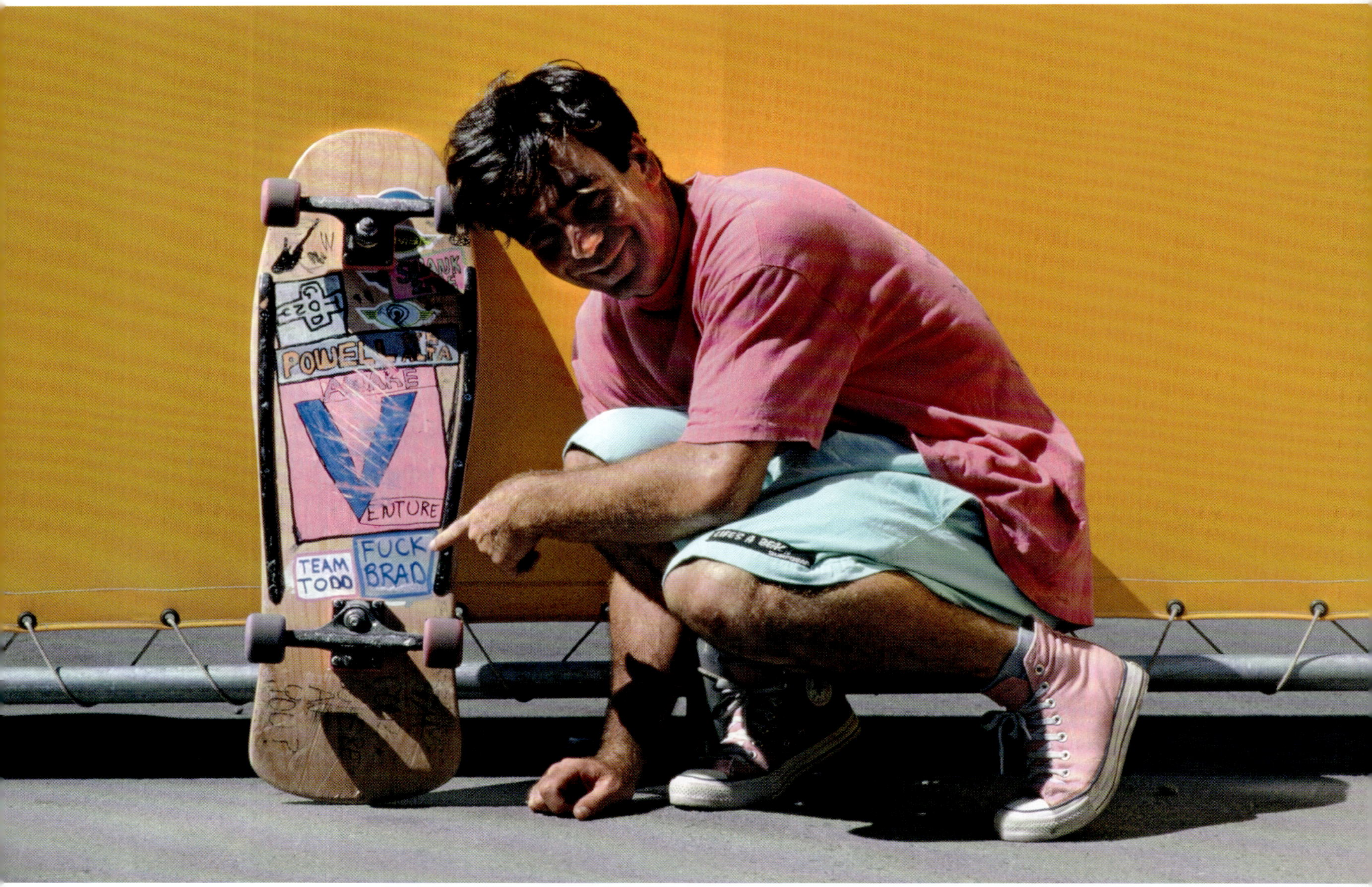

Above: Skateboarding's Disruptor-in-Chief Steve Rocco, California, 1988
Photo: Paul Sunman

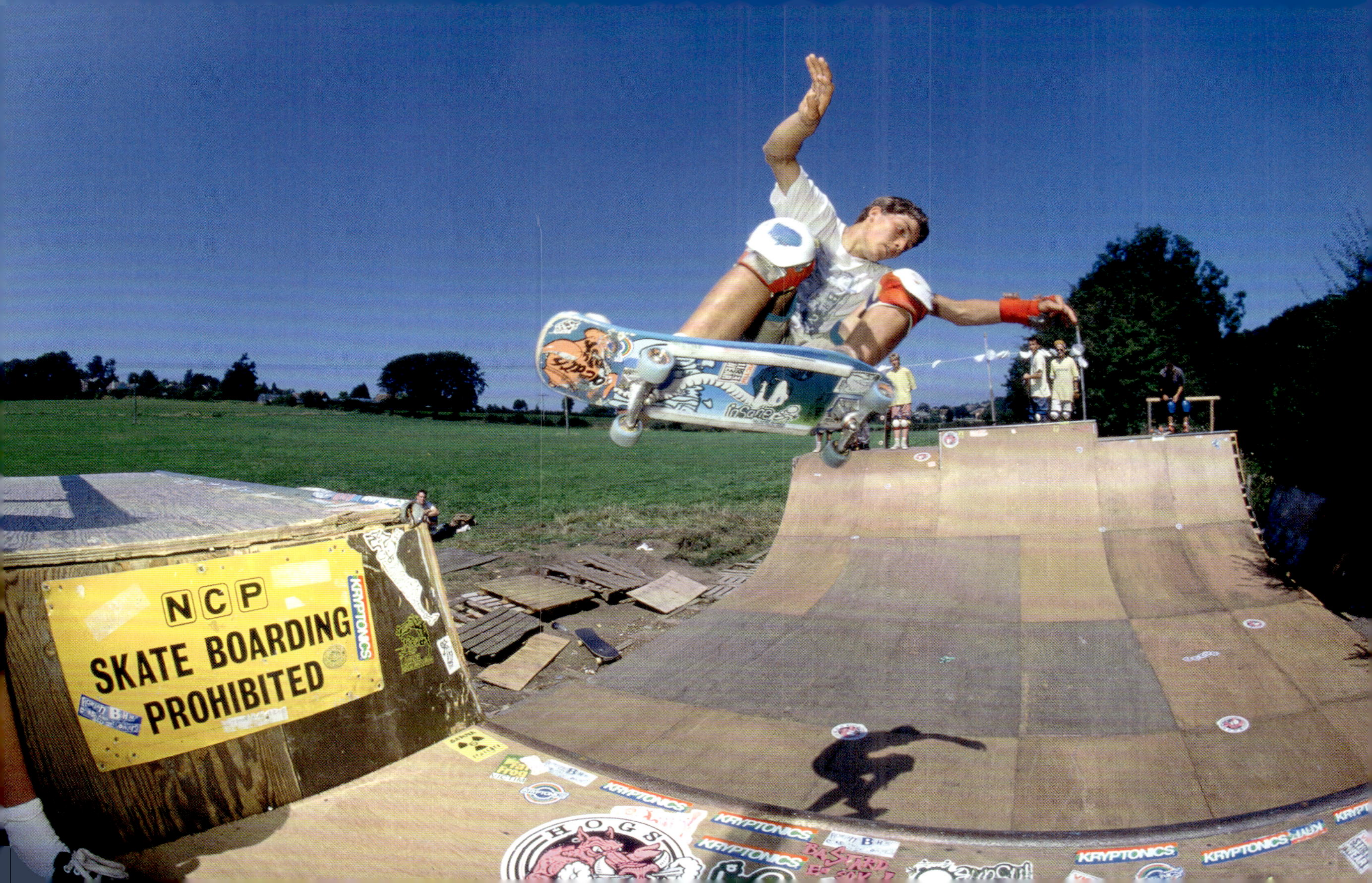
NCP
SKATE BOARDING
PROHIBITED
KRYPTONICS

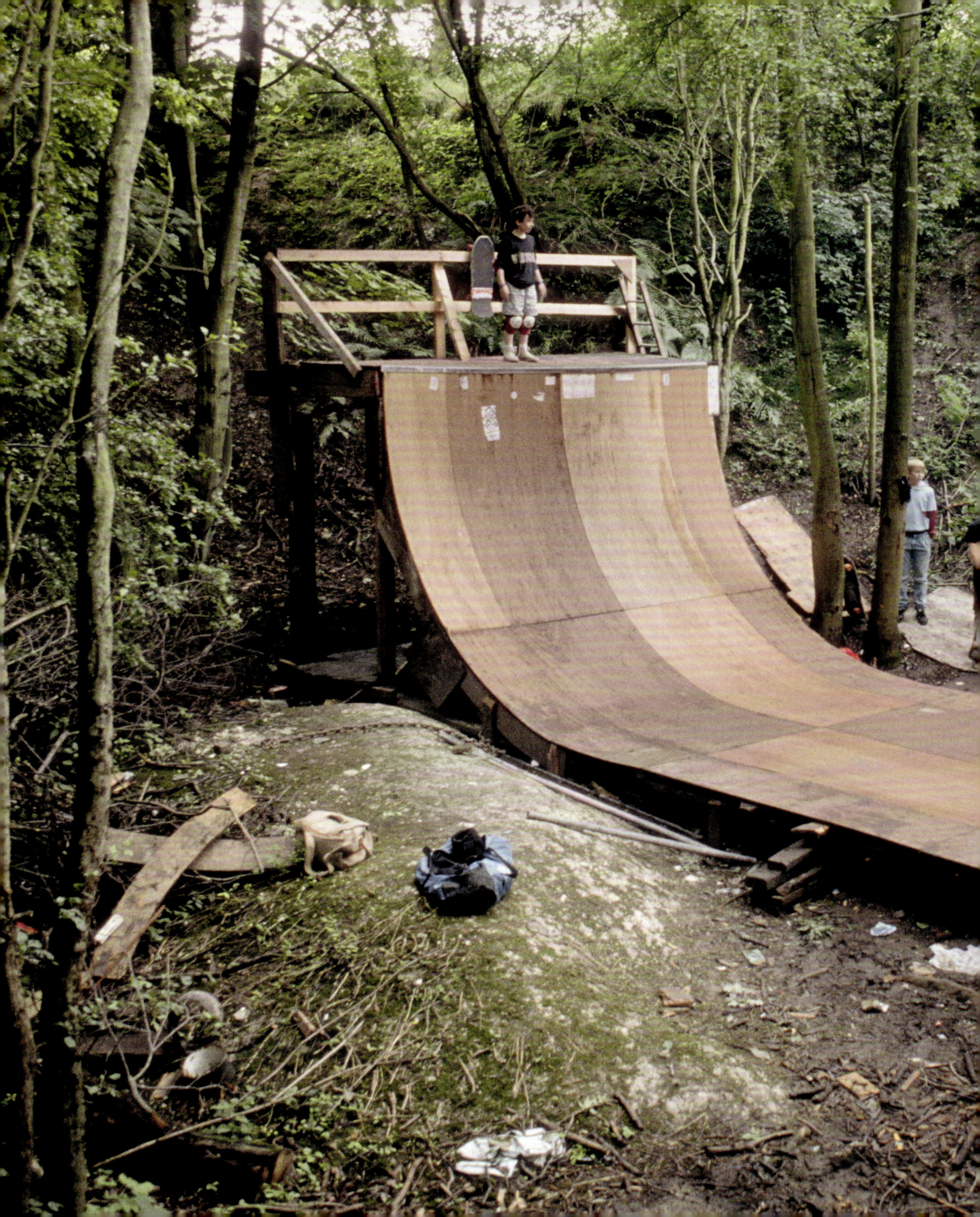

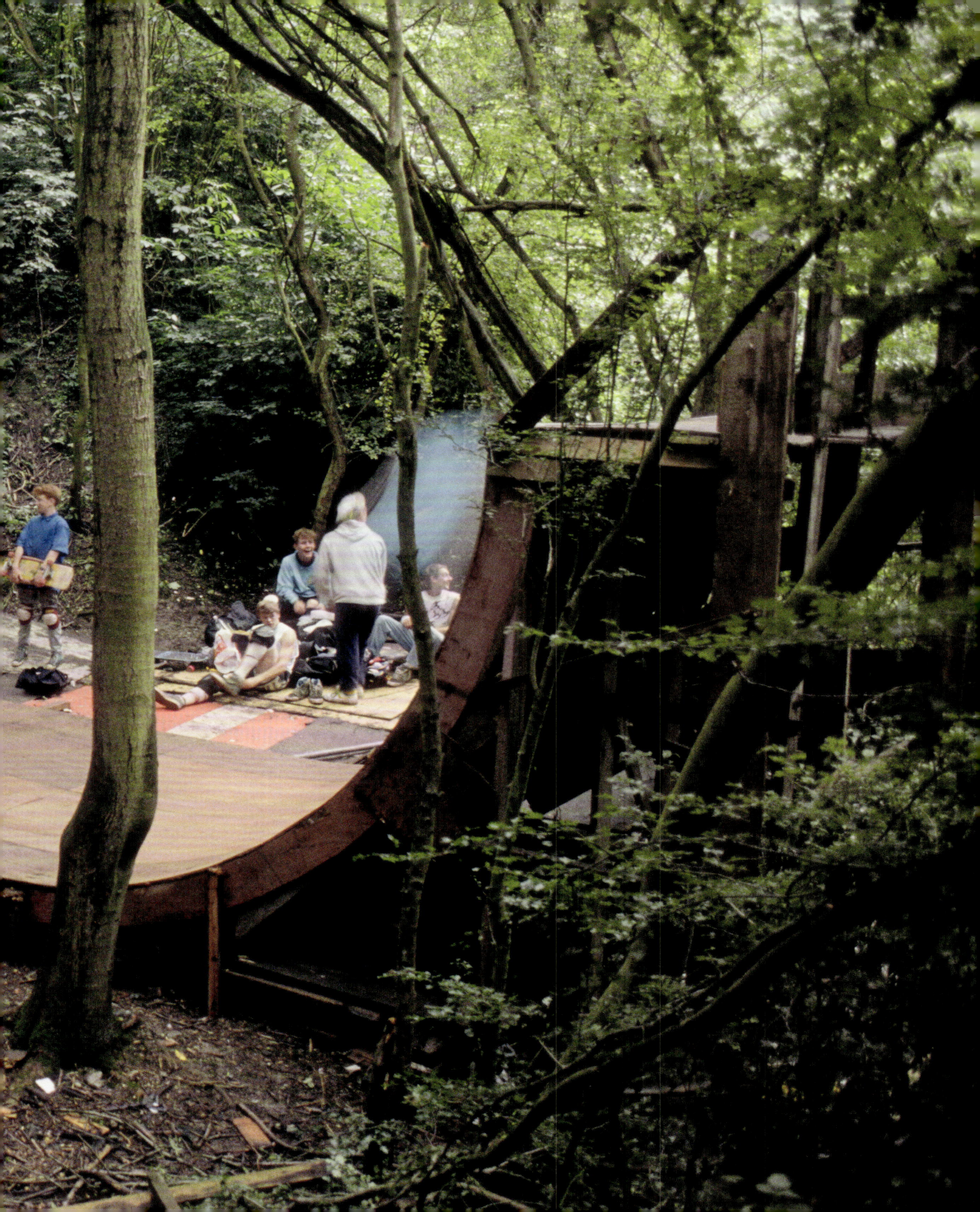

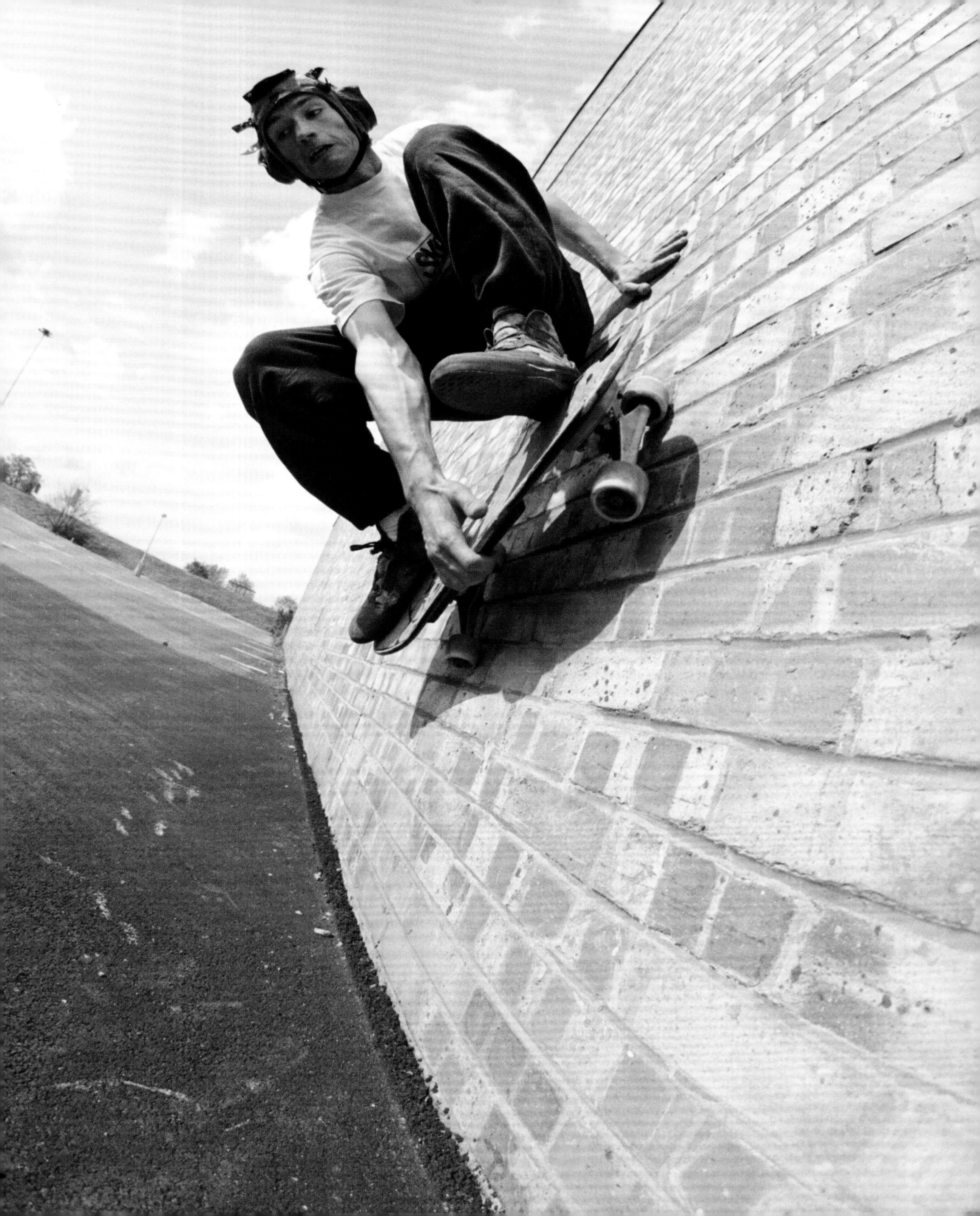

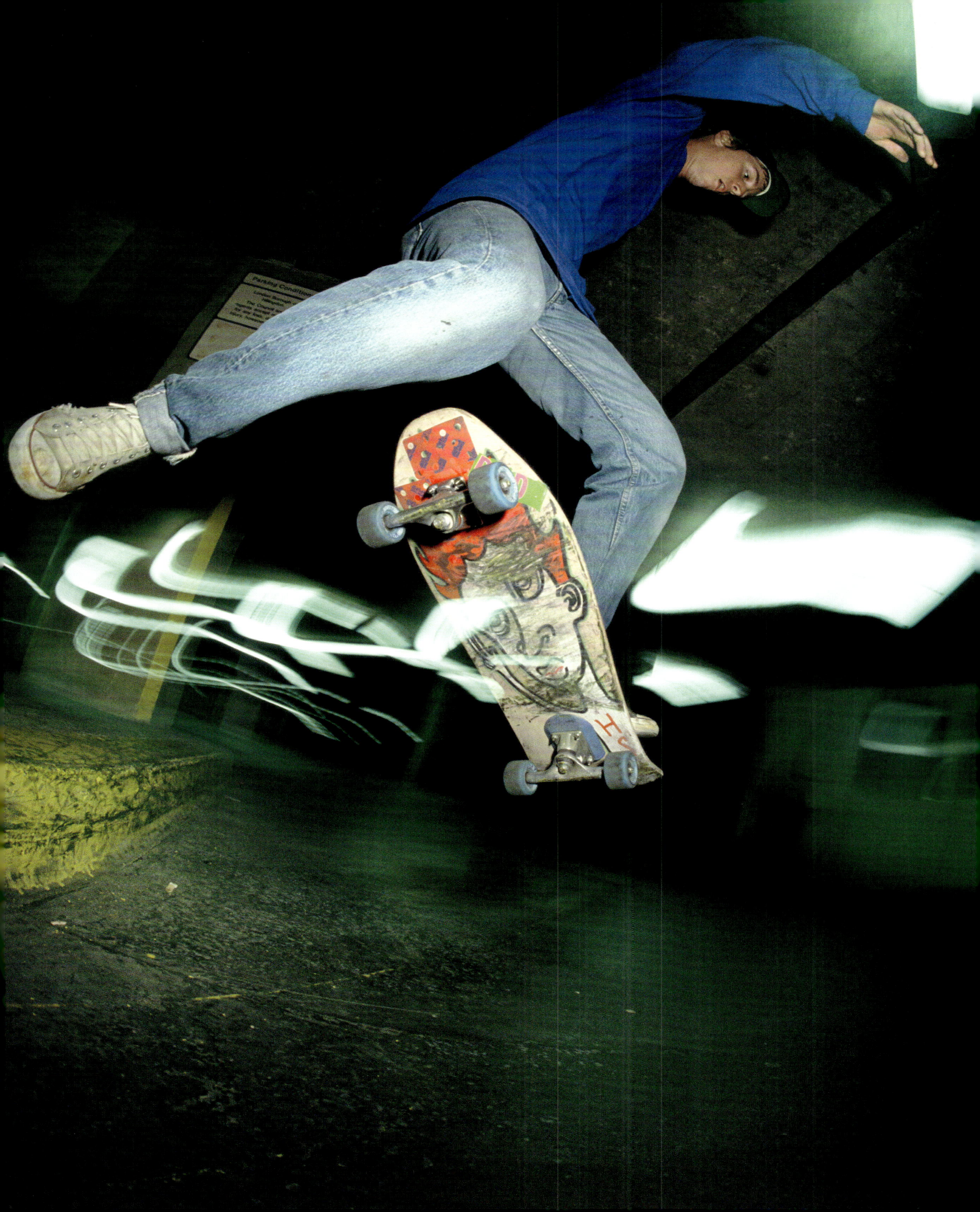

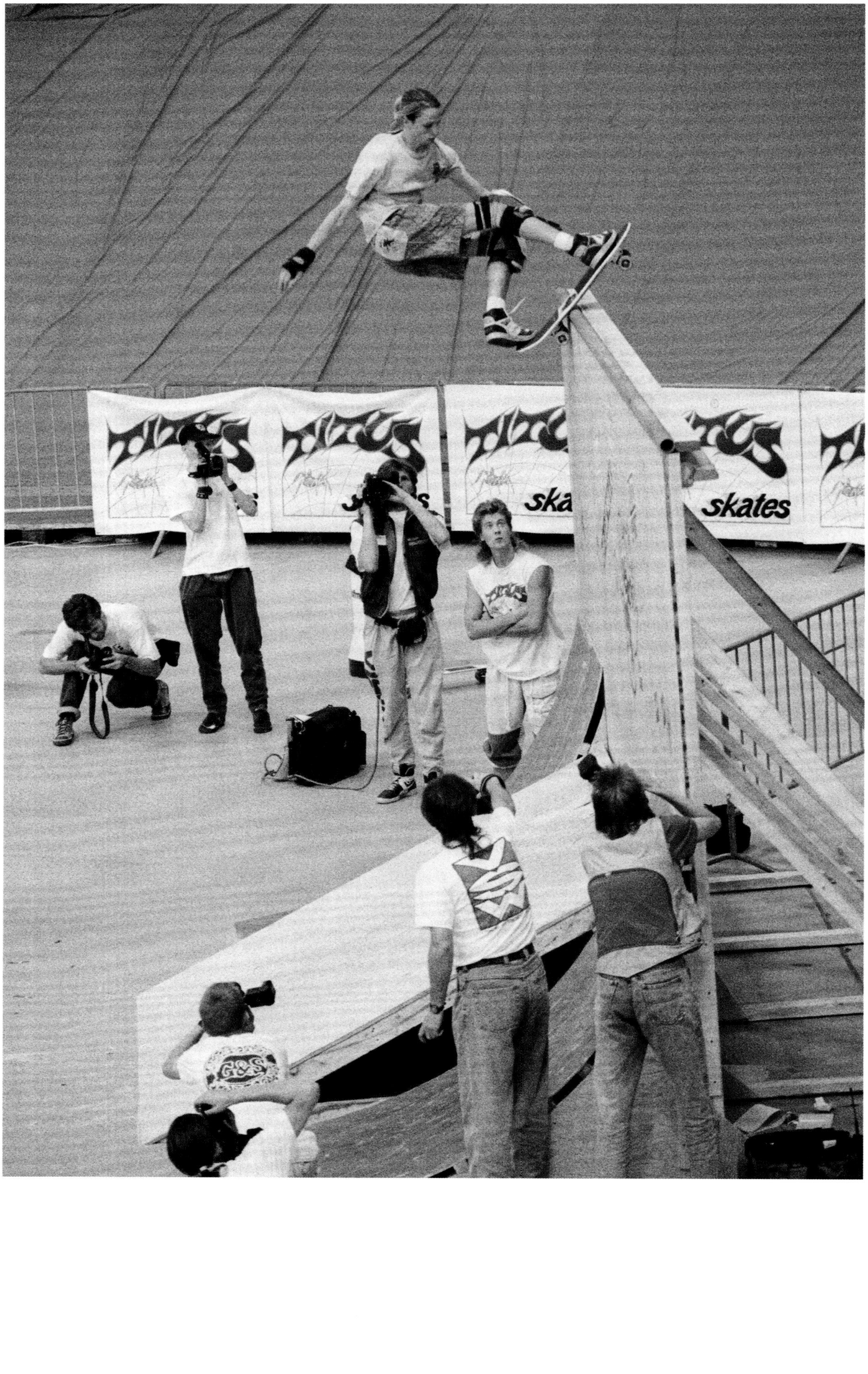

Previous spread left: Ged Wells and **right:** Jeff Klindt, London, 1988 **This page:** Tony Hawk, Copenhagen, 1988 **Photos:** TLB. **Opposite:** Mike Vallely, Carson City USA, 1987 **Photo:** Paul Sunman

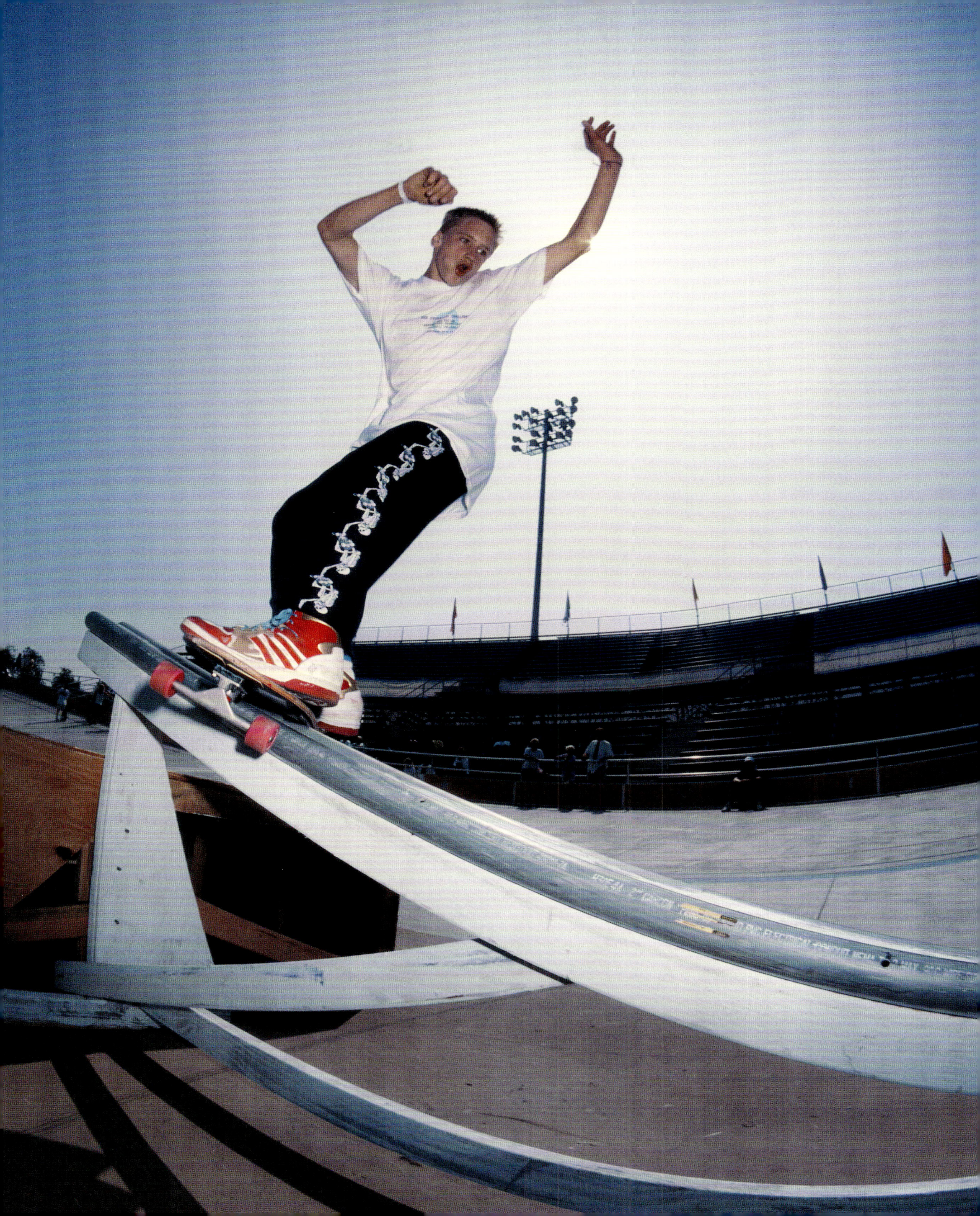

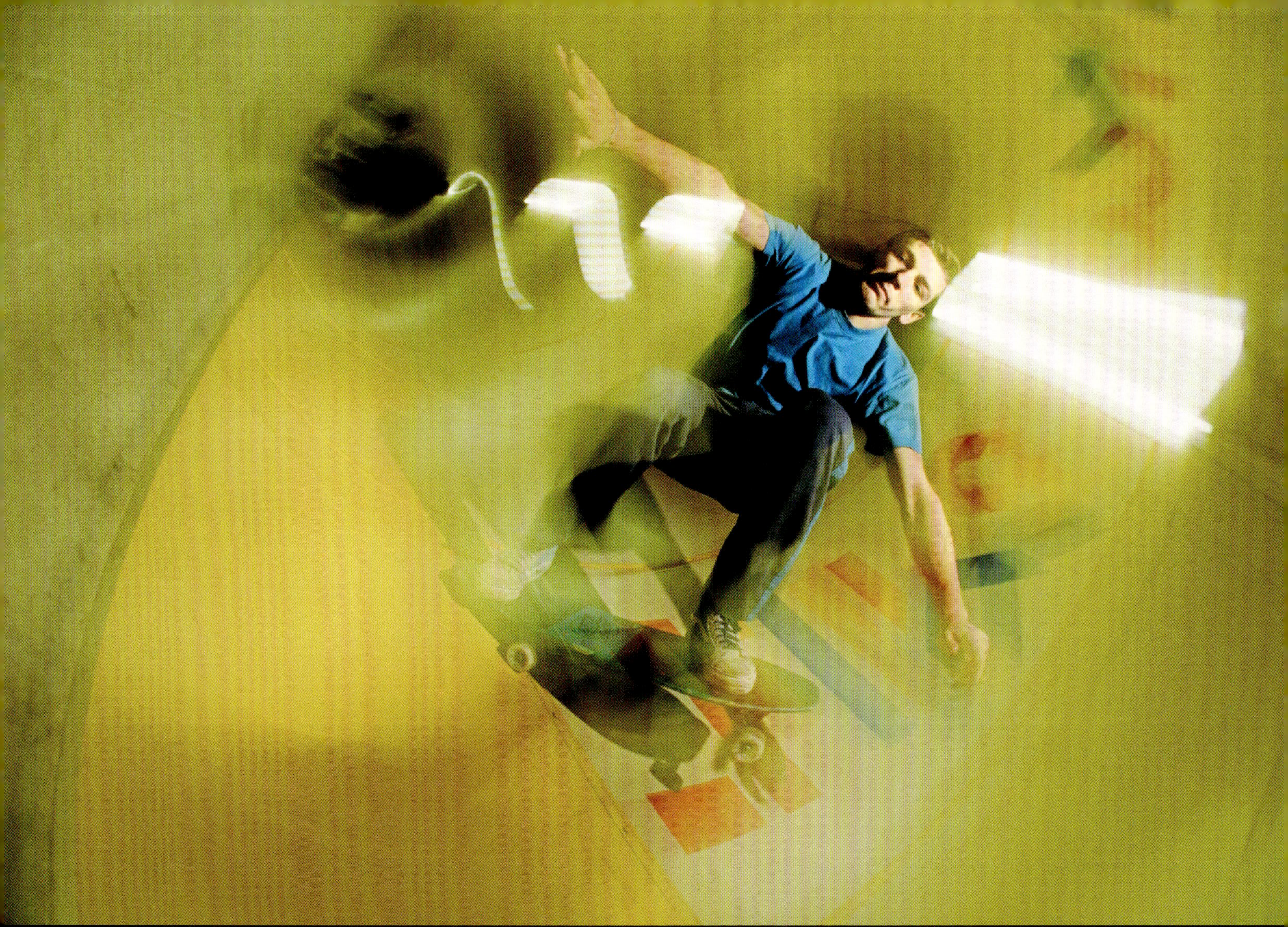

Left: Shane O'Brien, Kings Cross, 1988 **Photo:** Paul Sunman **Opposite:** Nicky Guerrero, Latimer Road, 1988 **Photo:** TLB

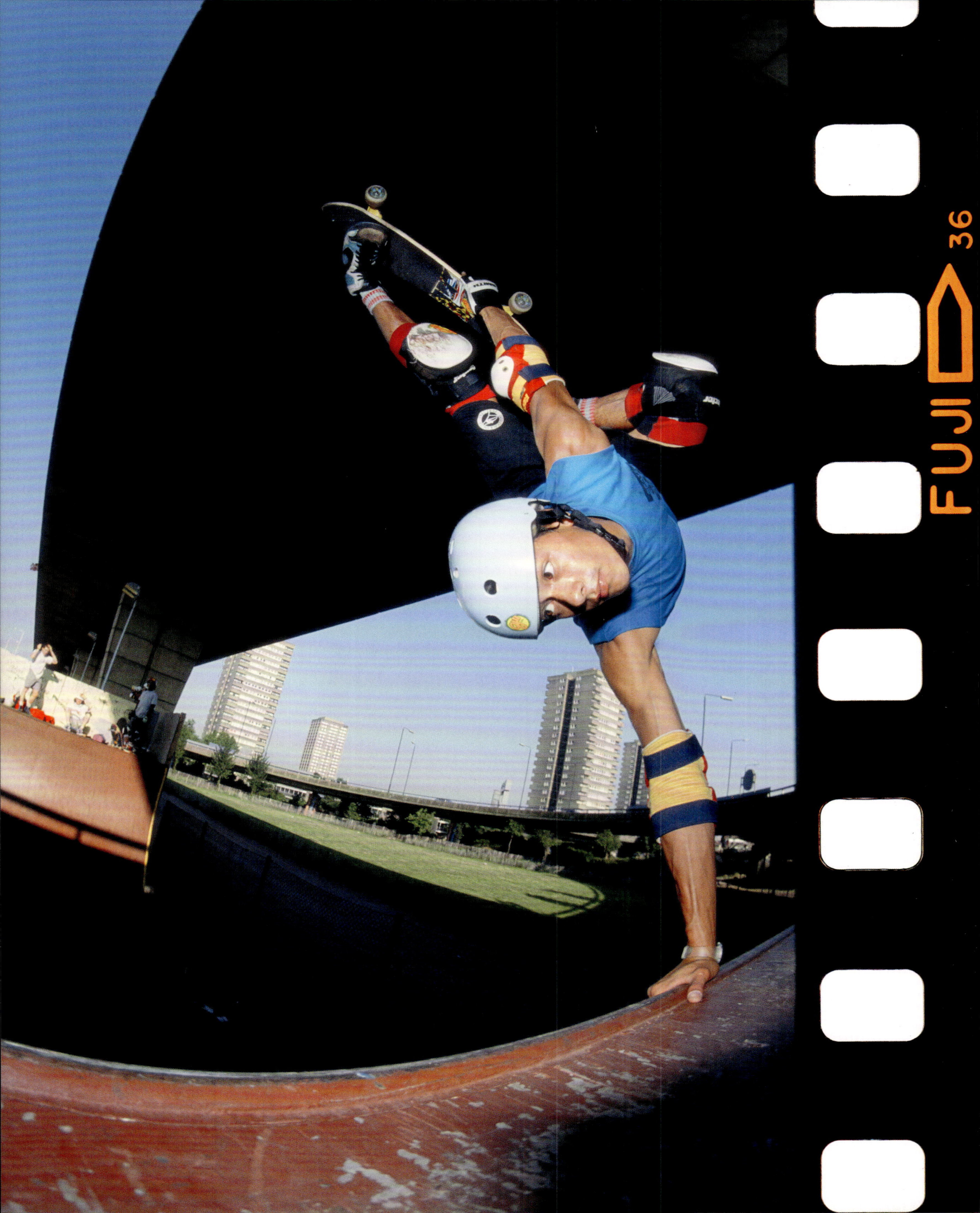

FUJI
36

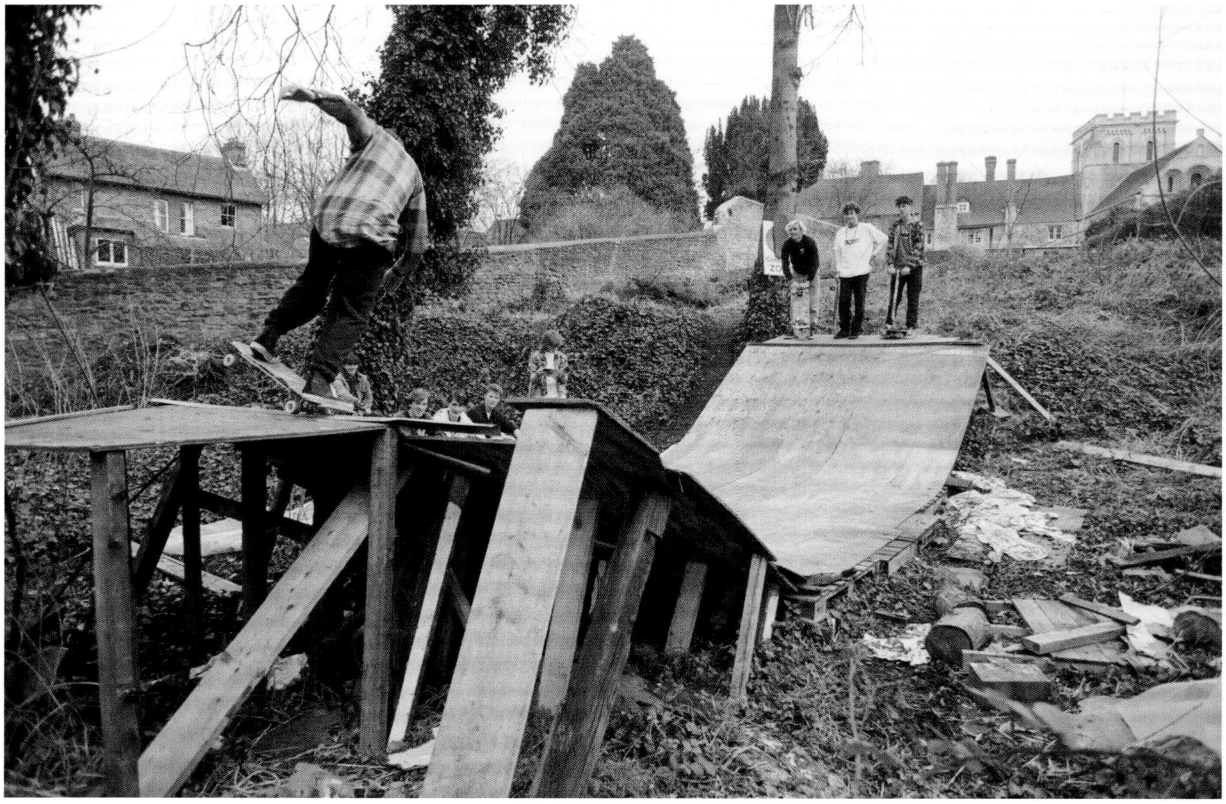

Above: Tim's ramp, Iffley, Oxfordshire, 1988 **Below:** Ashland flood defence, Milton Keynes, DIY mini ramp, 1988 **Photos:** TLB

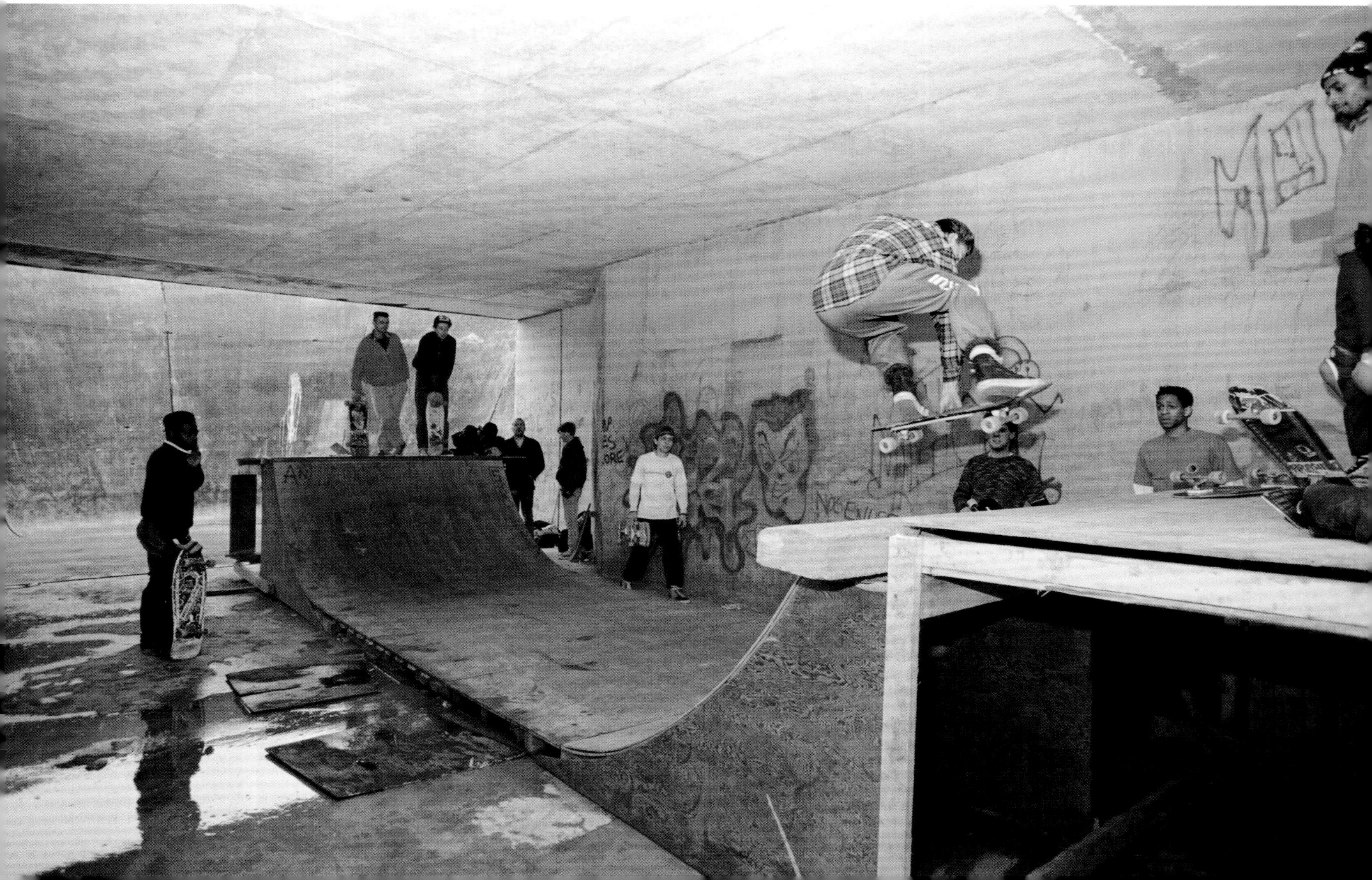

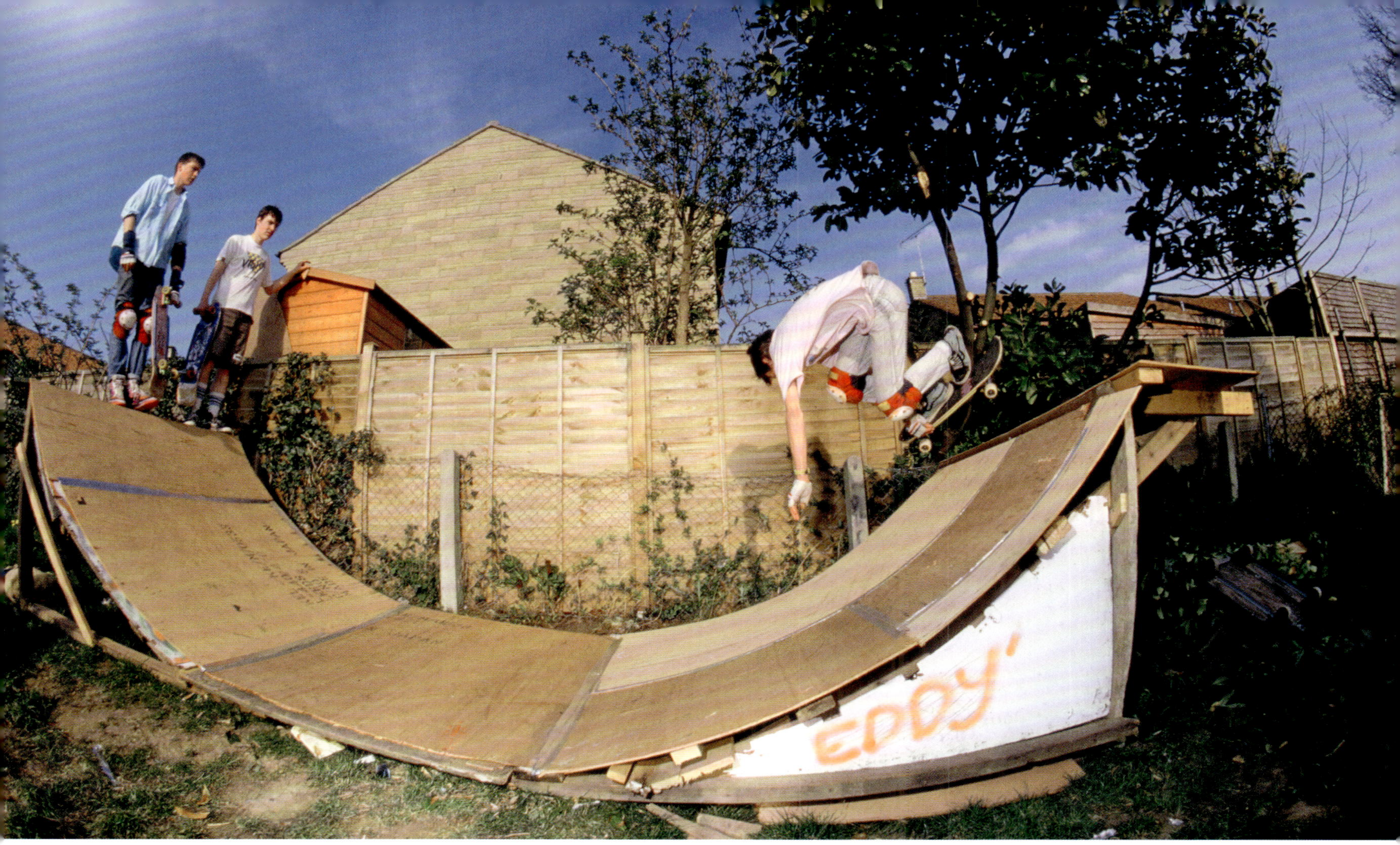

Above: Illegal roadside DIY ramp, Yeovil UK, 1988 **Below:** Billy's Ramp, Cambridge, 1988. **Photos:** TLB

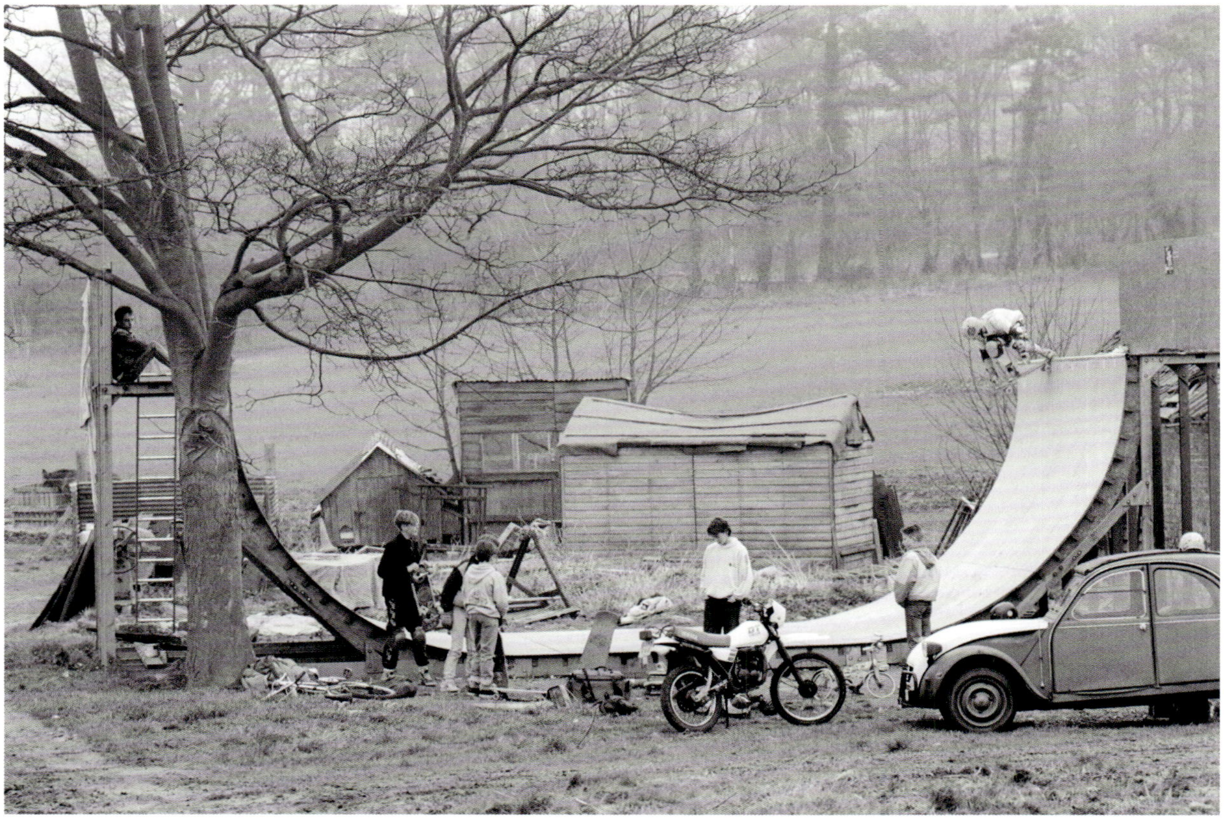

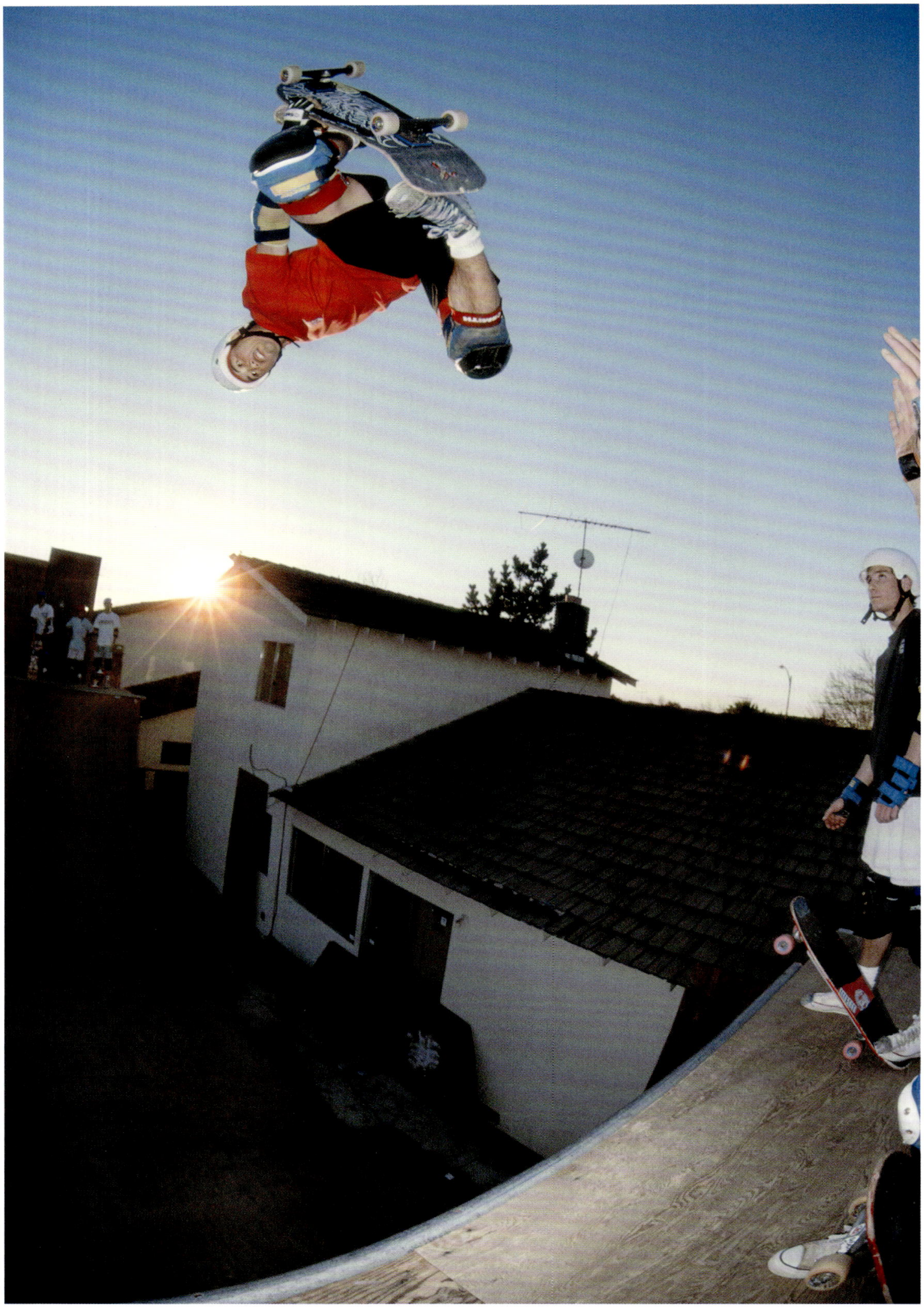

Left: Jim Namba, Louie's ramp, San Jose, California, 1988 **Photo:** Mike John **Opposite:** Natas Kaupas, Dean Lane, Bristol, UK, 1988 **Photo:** Paul Sunman

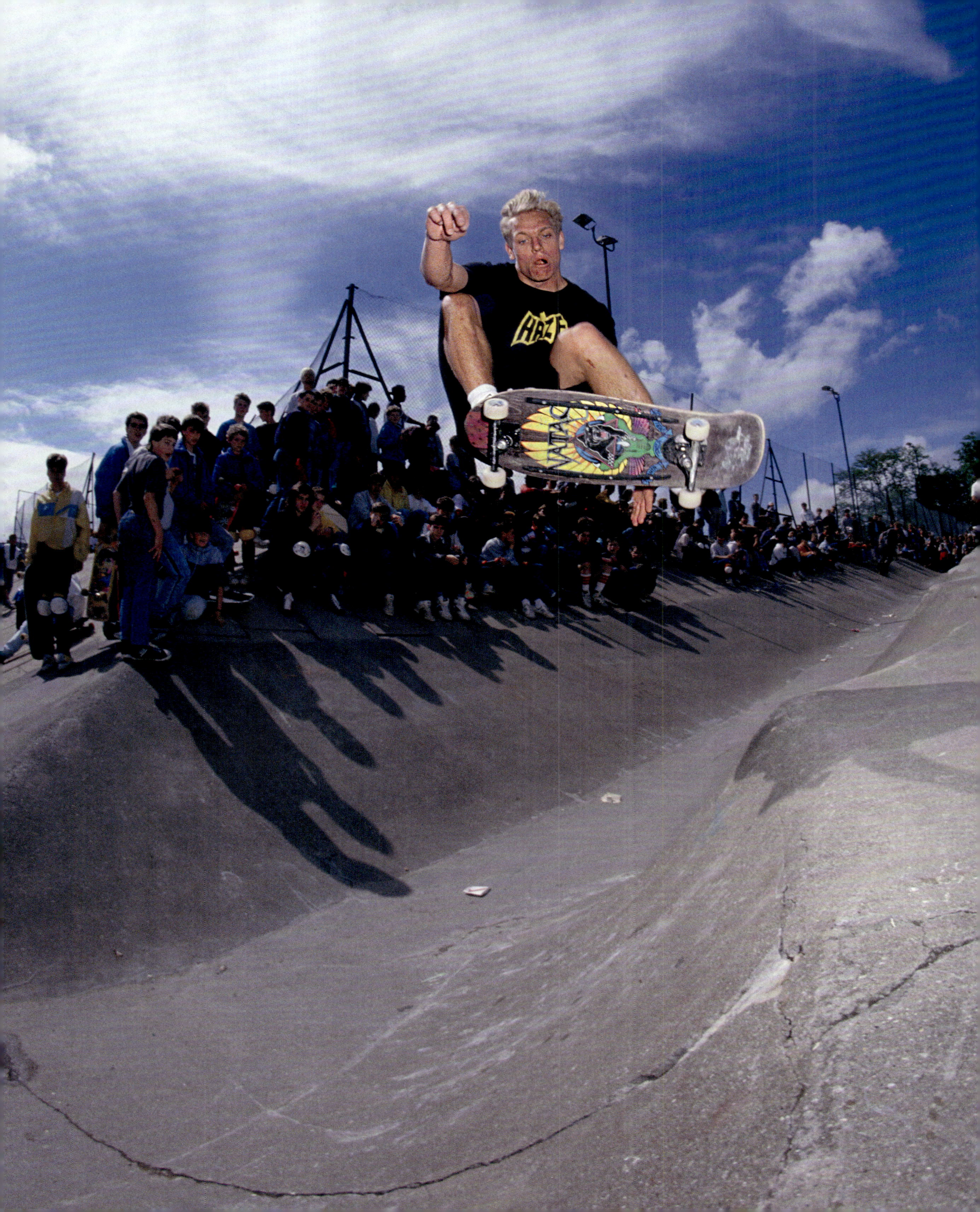

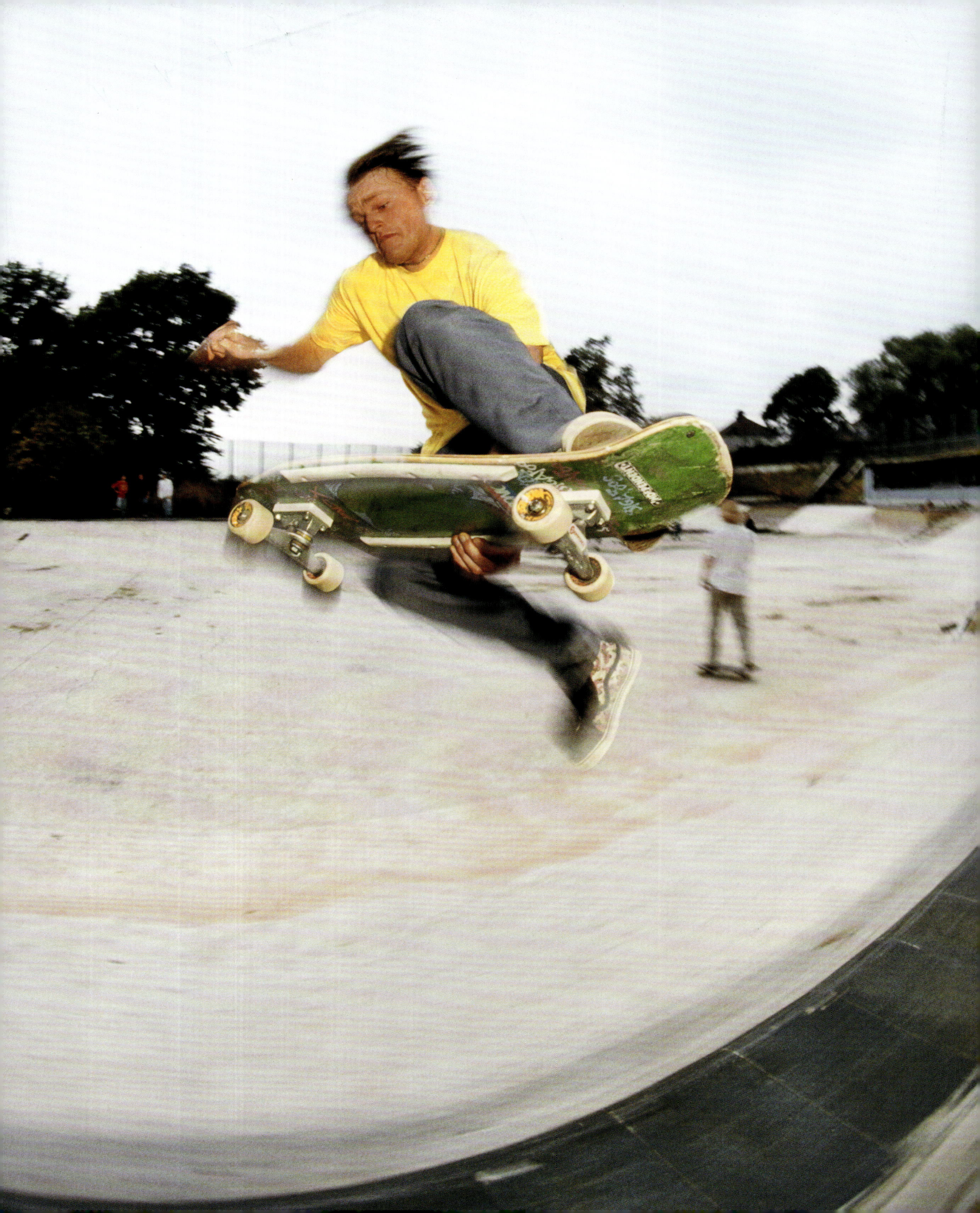

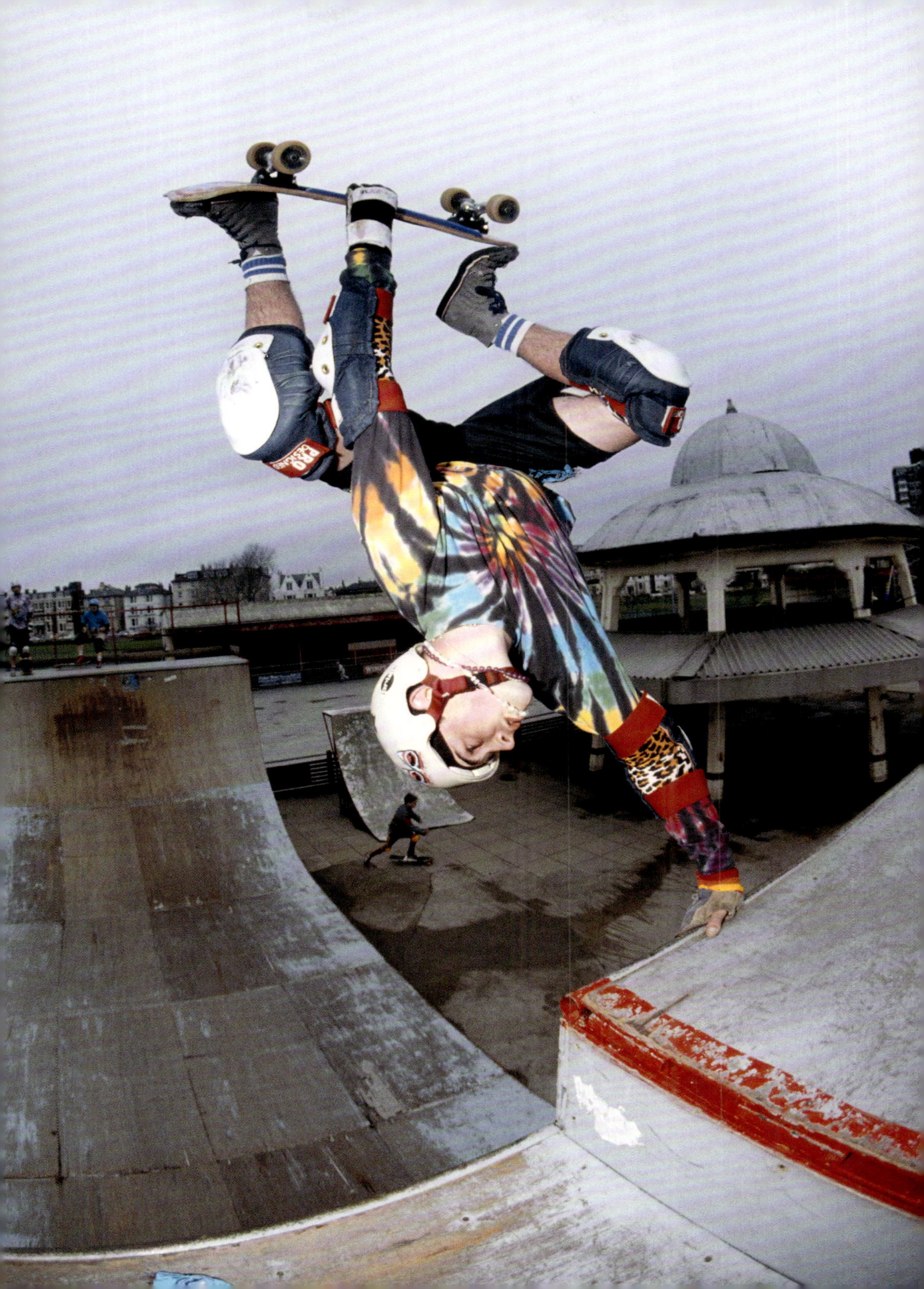

Right boyz,

Me names mad snoz, and am I gonna get it together or what. If you skate in or around Leeds than get in touch. I know your there cos I've seen you. Conference centre sessions in Harrogate, pipe partys in Bradford and ramp to wall jamming in Leeds. Wether its private garage station at home or mega alley-oop egg plants down at Warrington lets get it on. Please please ge [illegible] only lead to bigger [illegible]

A J [illegible] ad Snoz

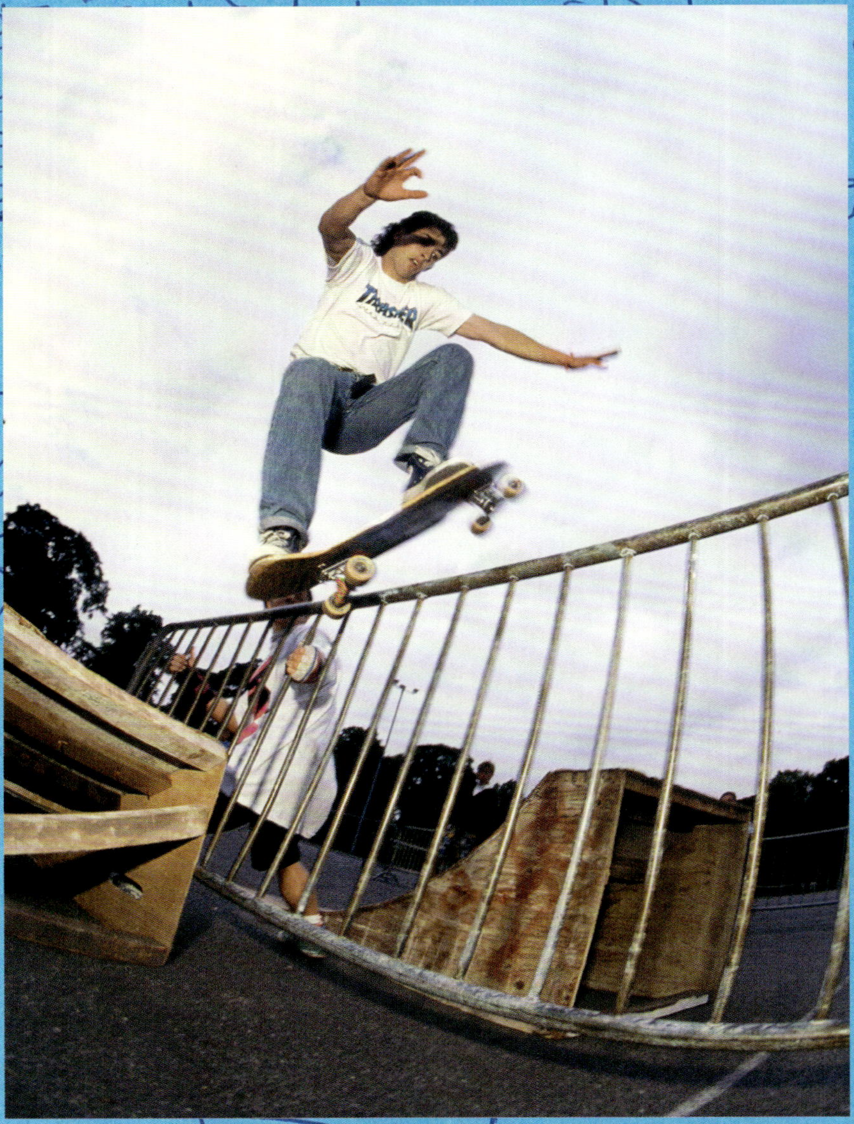

Left: Dino Squillino **Opposite:** Mark 'Mad Snoz' Snowball, Sheffield, 1989 **Photos:** TLB

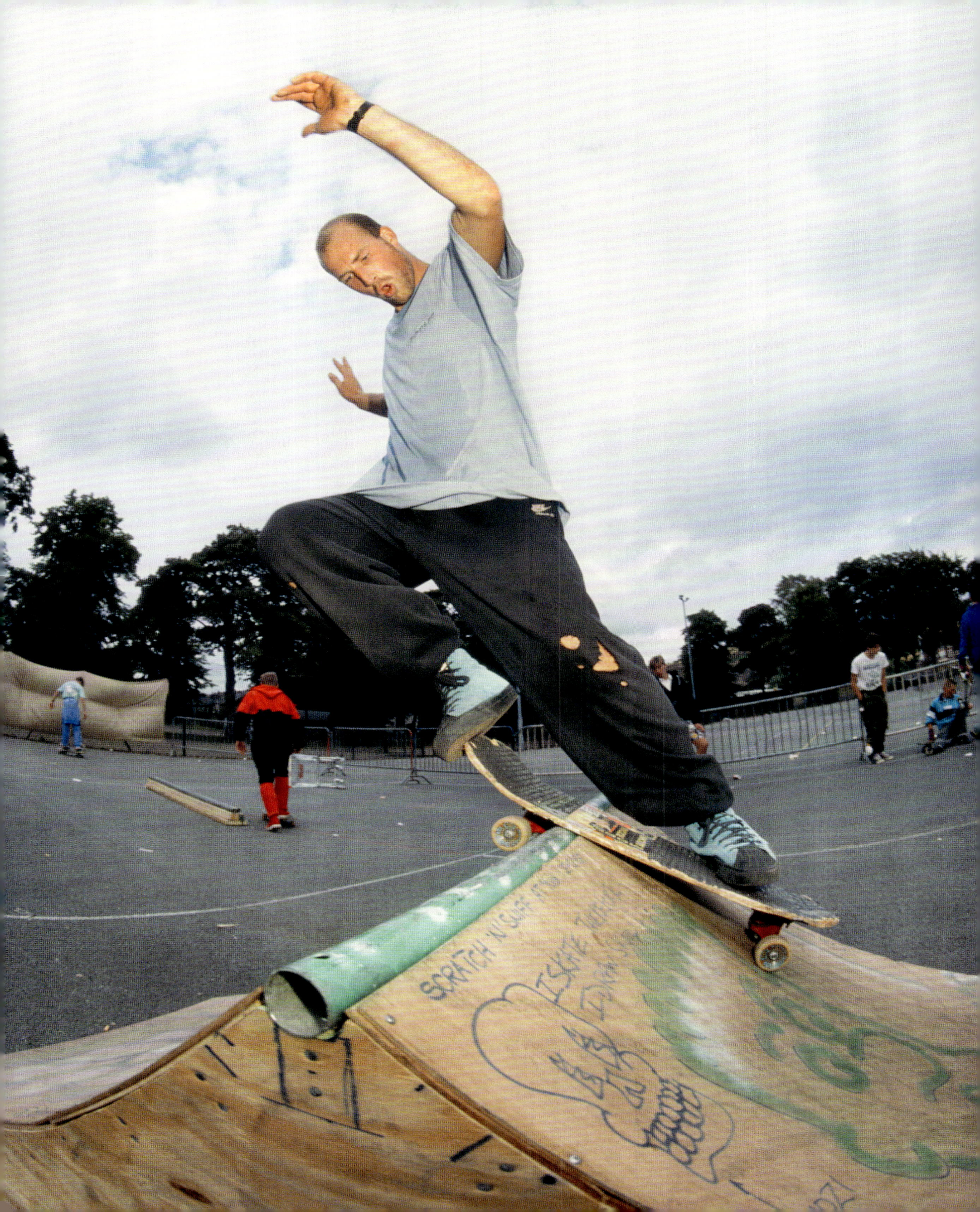

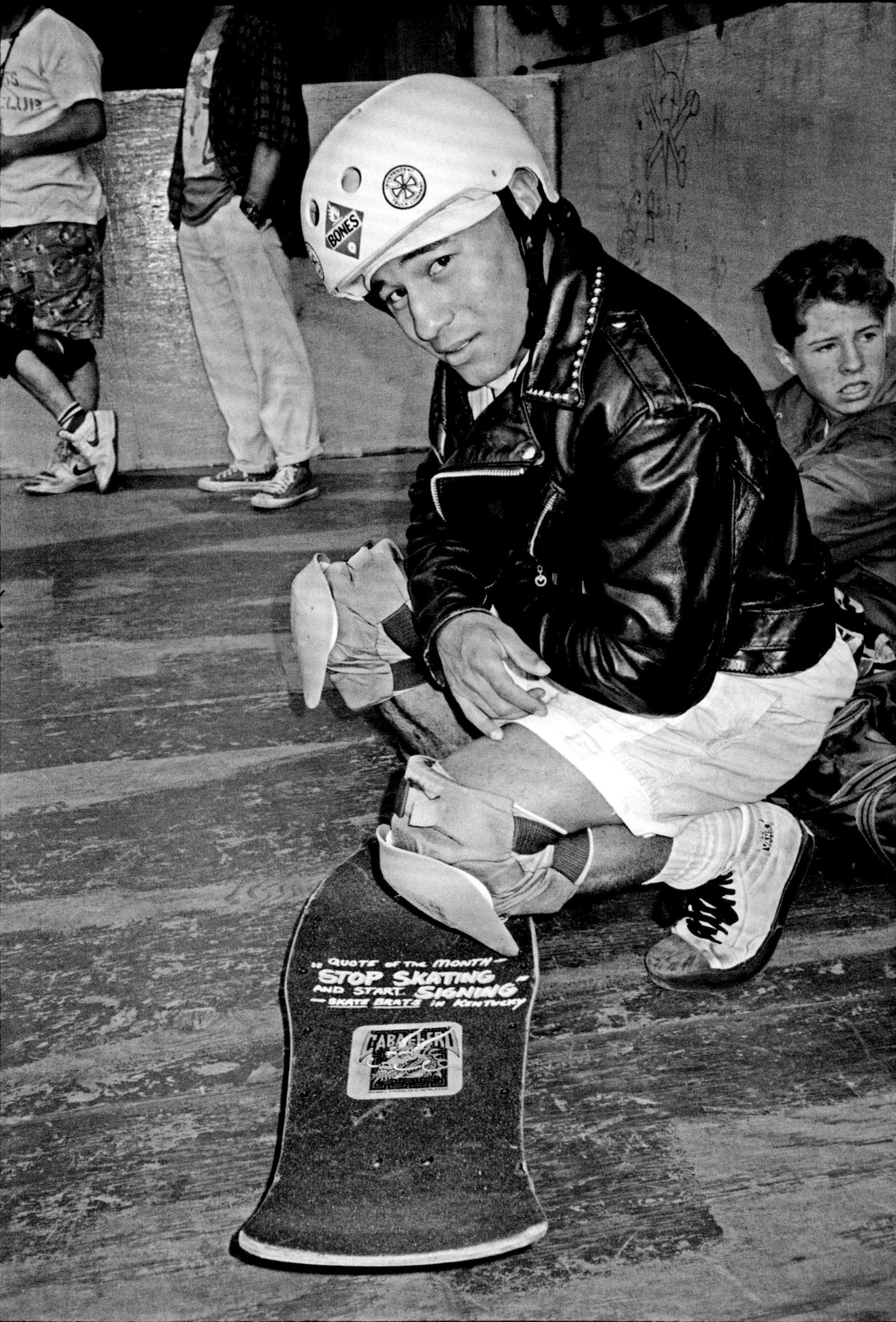

Left: Steve Caballero Latimer Road, London **Opposite:** Tommy Guerrero, Southsea skatepark, Bones Brigade UK tour, 1988 **Photos:** TLB

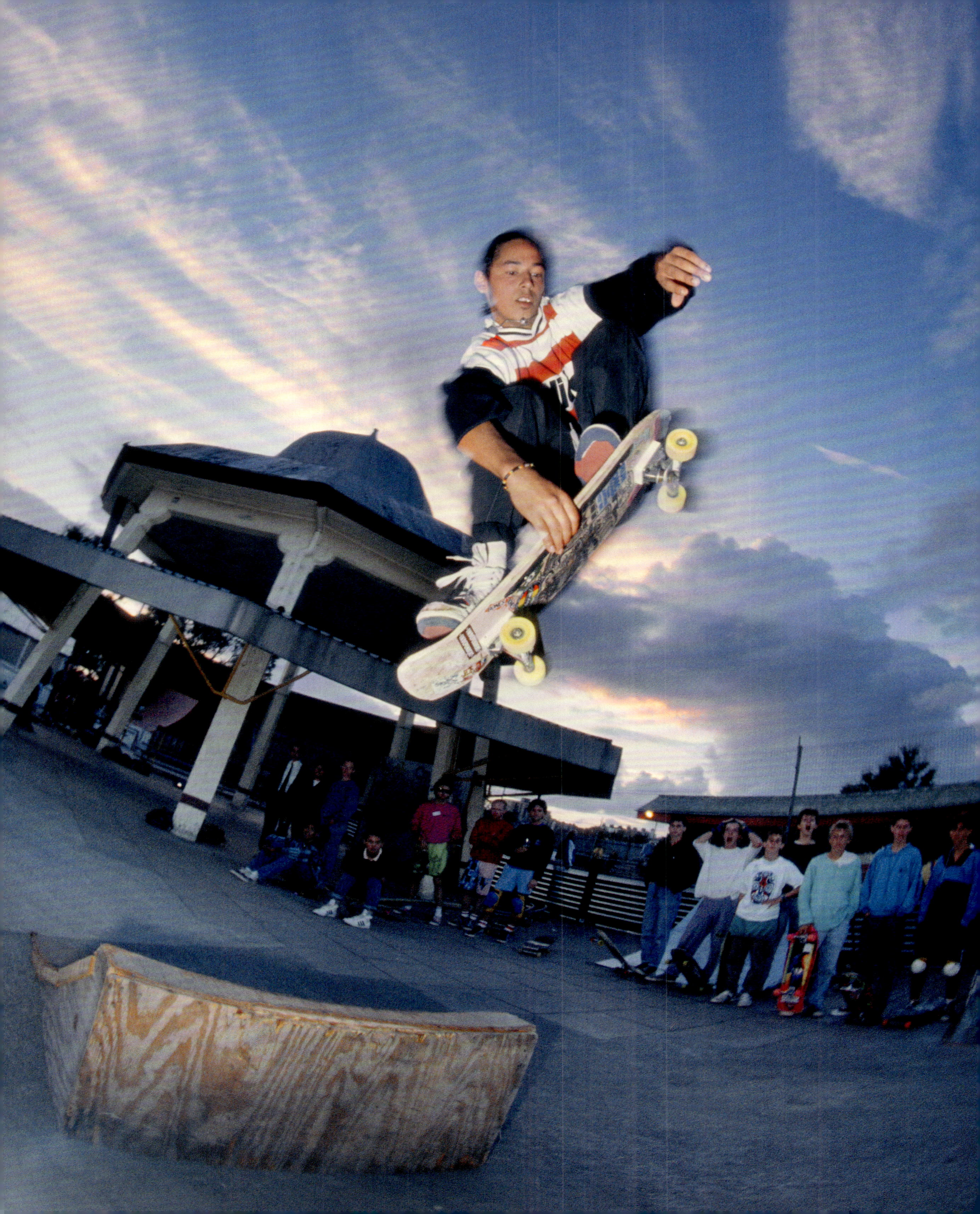

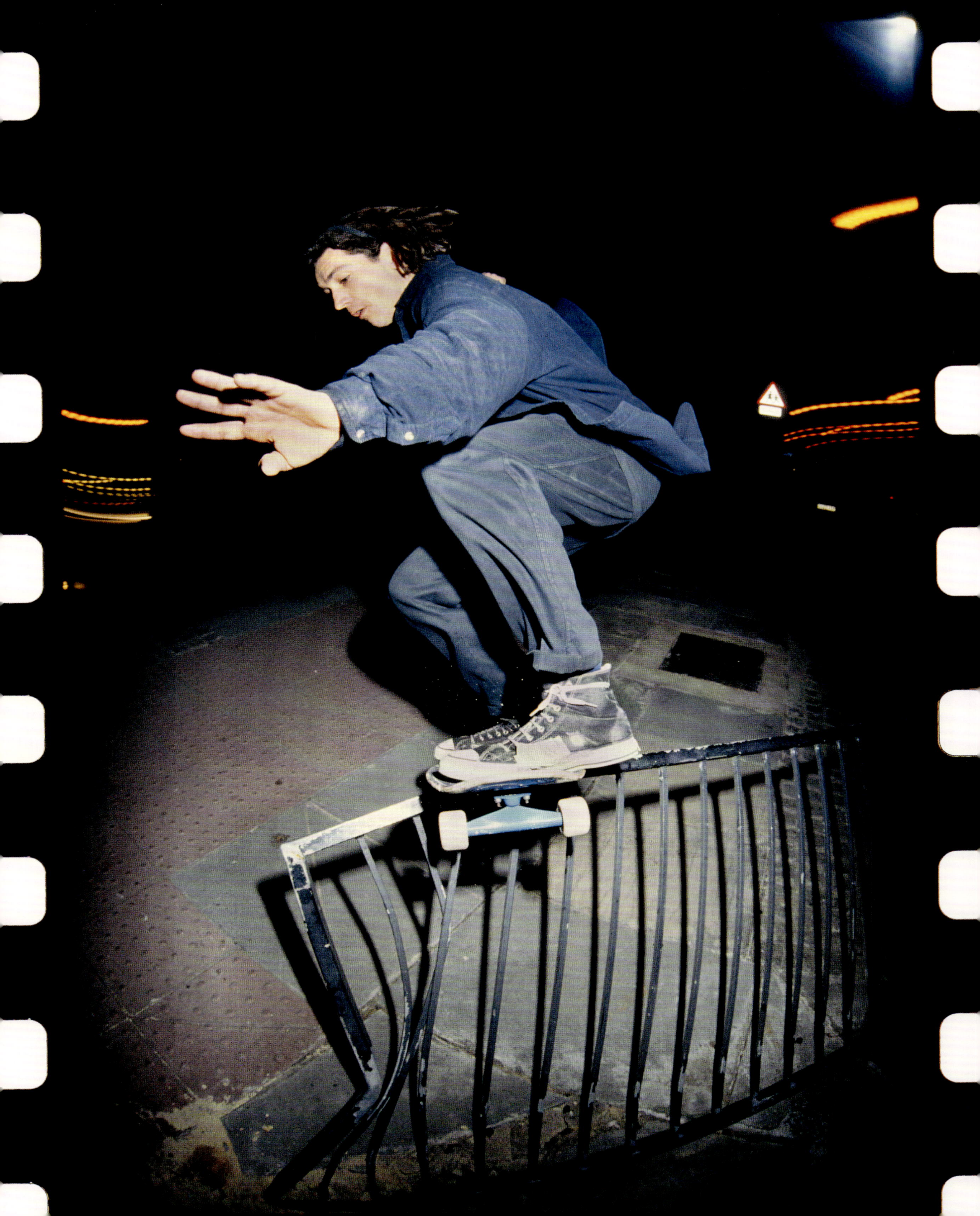

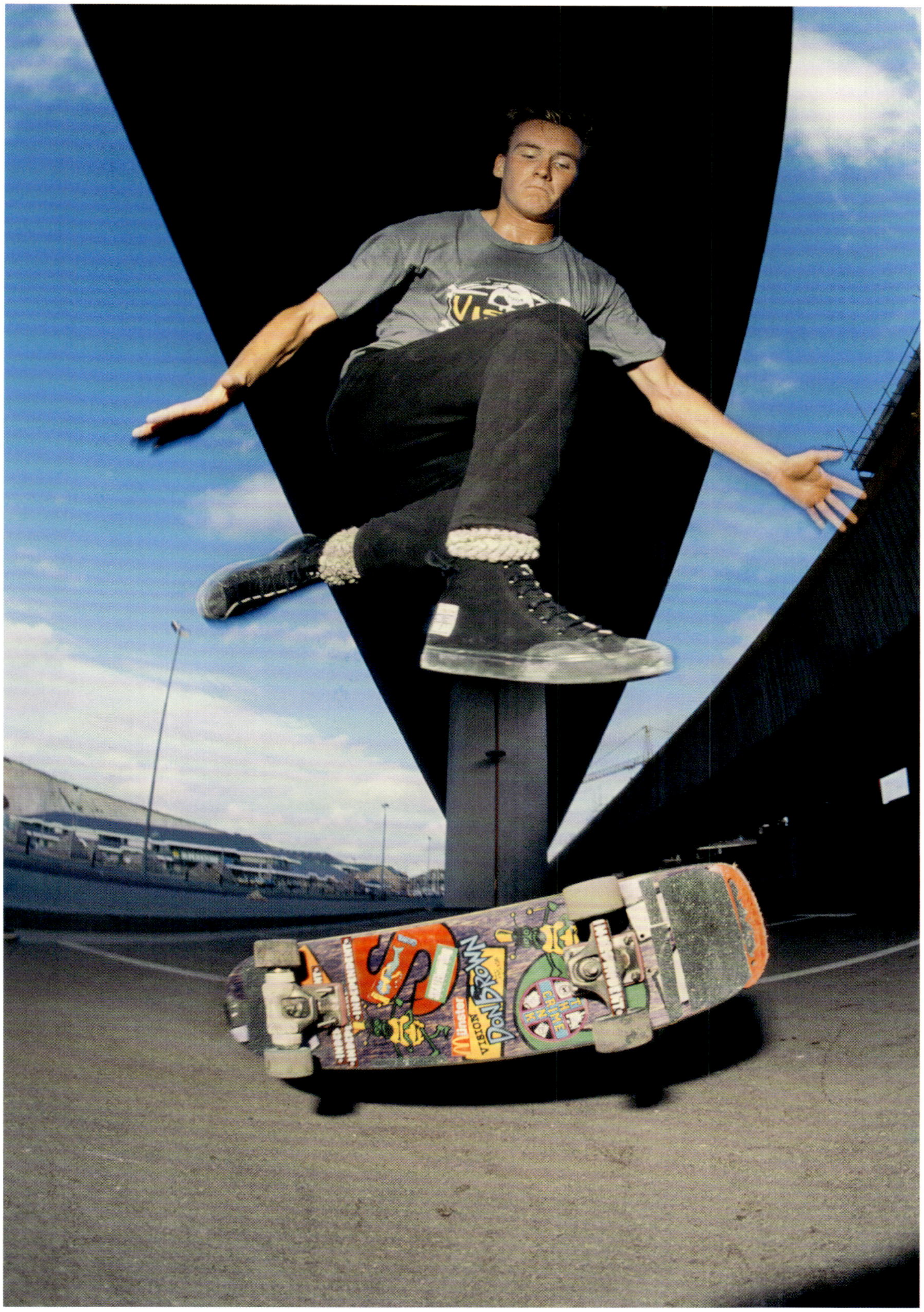

Opposite: Ged Wells, London, 1988 **Photo:** Jay Podesta **Right:** Don Brown, Brighton, 1988 **Photo:** TLB

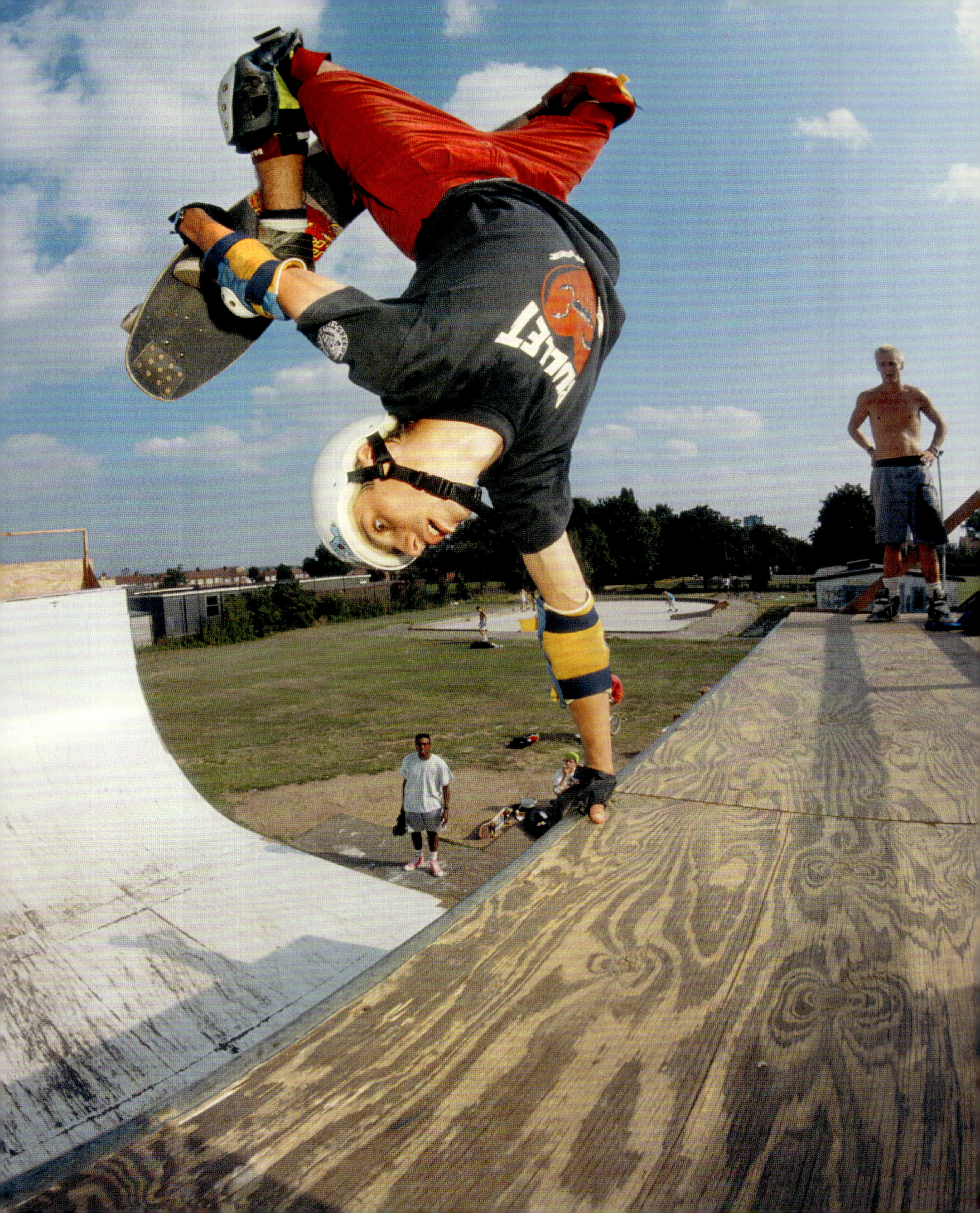
BULLET

'I remember sitting with Lee Ralph in Bod's mum's house looking at a Santa Cruz video of Tom Knox skating some curbs. Lee said "Imagine these guys talking in years to come about that concrete block they used to skate" and we were laughing but now that's totally true. Street at that time wasn't considered the thing you should be doing if you were pro, it was something you did for a laugh.' Mike John

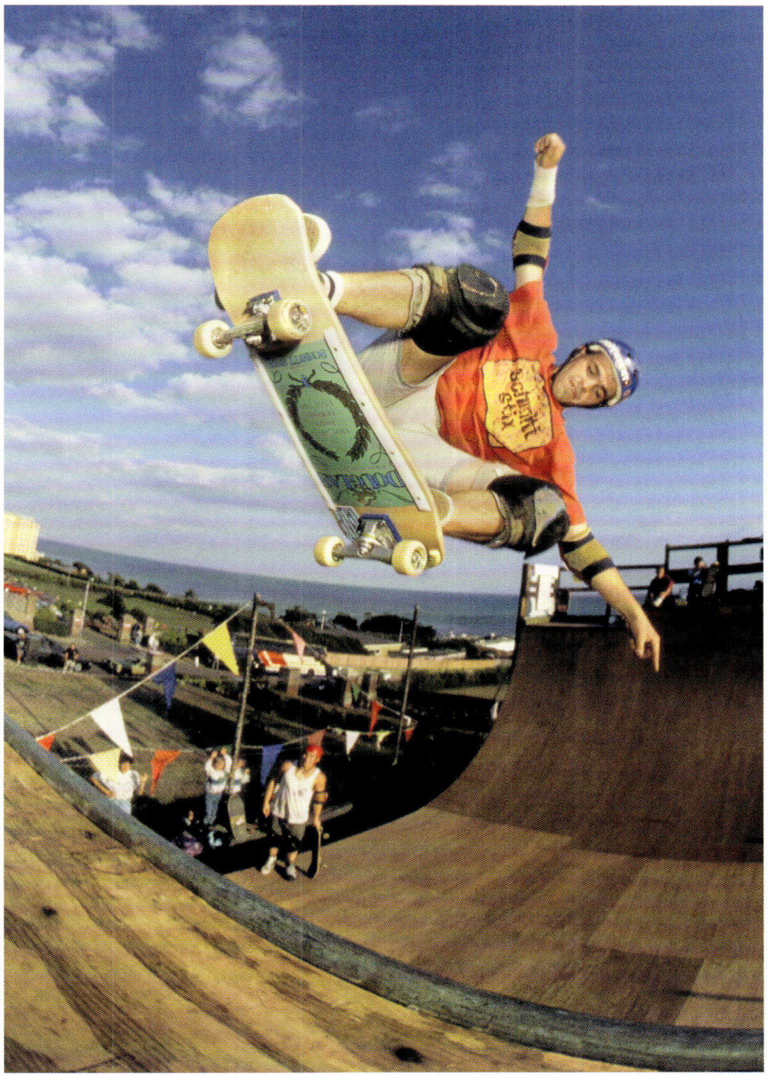

Opposite: Hugh 'Bod' Boyle, Chingford, London, 1989 **Right:** Steve Douglas **Below:** Lee Ralph, vert ramp opening demo, Hastings UK, 1989 **Photos:** TLB

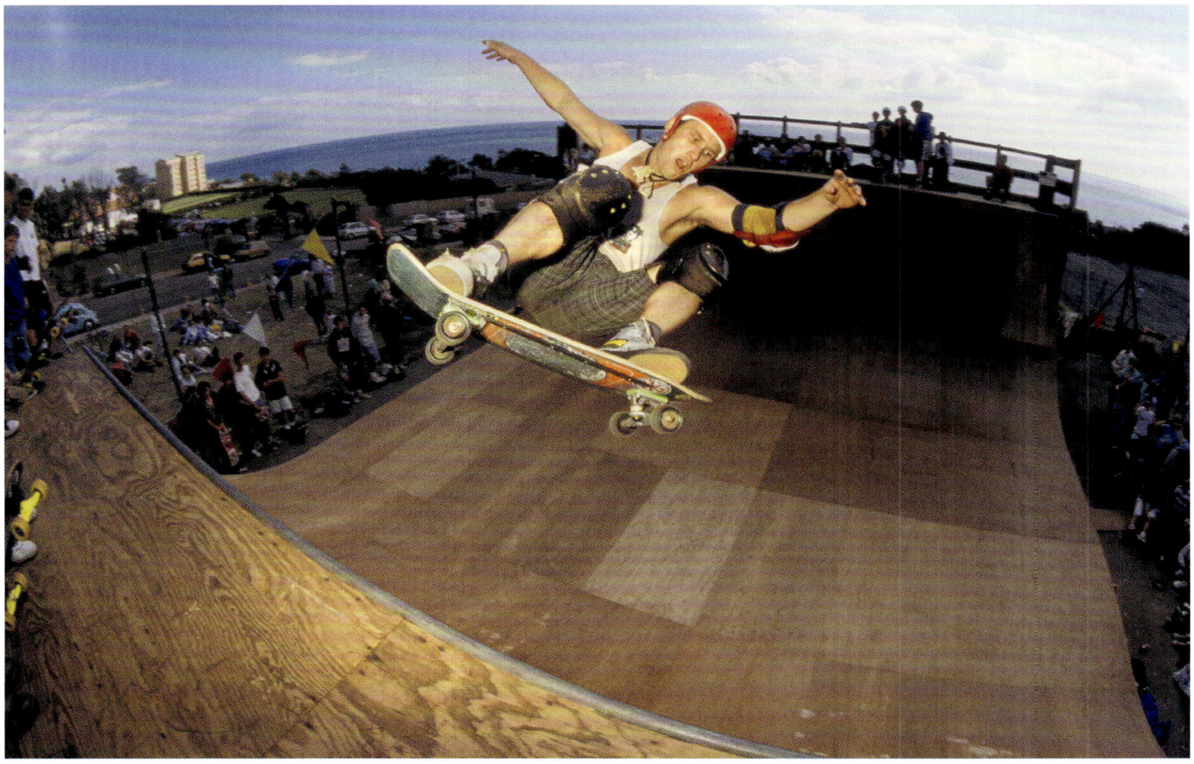

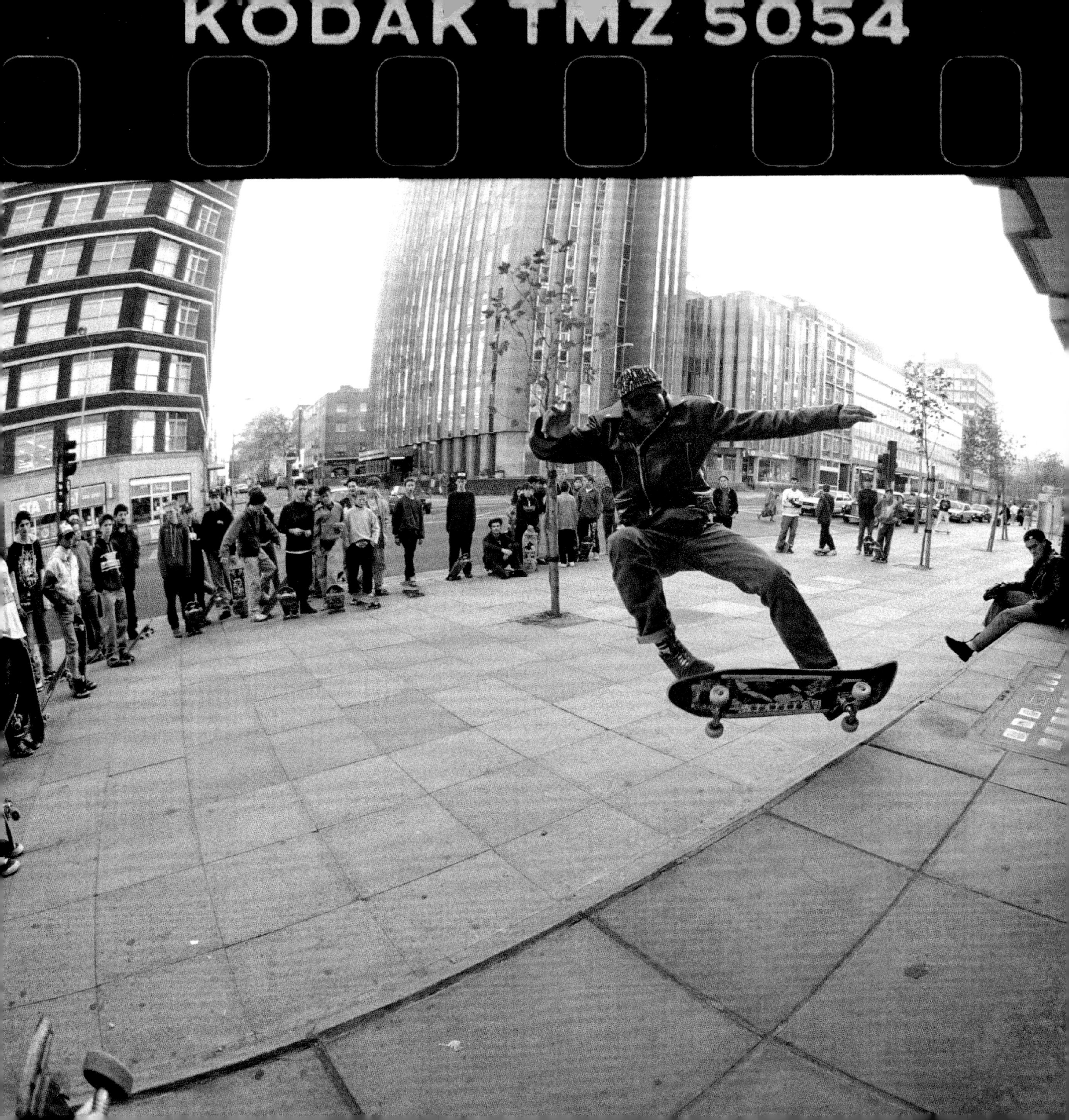
KODAK TMZ 5054

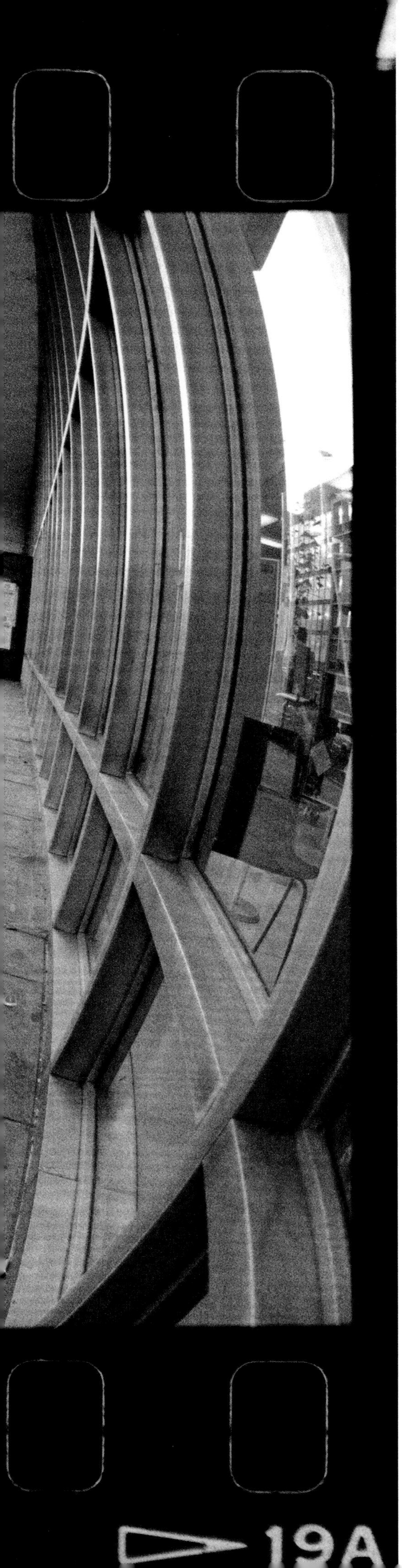

'For as long as I can remember, I had wanted to take photographs. It's true that as a kid I had laboriously produced newspapers on a type-writer, but photography was the thing that felt like a deep part of me. I wanted to take really good pictures. In order to do that I had to do a lot of other stuff to make a magazine to put them in.' TLB

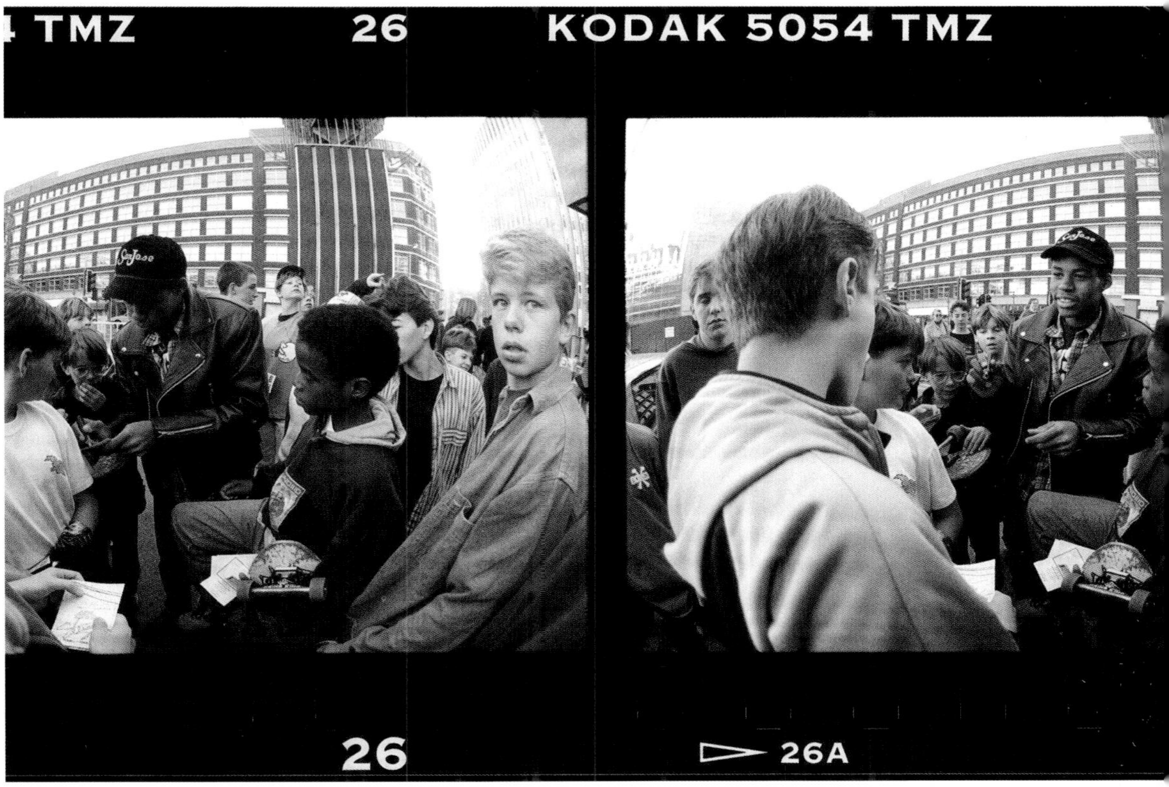

Left and above: Ray Barbee together with Steve Saiz (sitting, right) in London to promote Powell Peralta's *Ban This* video. Euston Road, 1989 **Photos:** TLB

Below: Martin Wager, Scott Wilson, Steve Jolliffe, Steve Pannell, Don Brider, Paul 'Sketchy' Browne, Lee Mockler and the law, City of London, 1989 **Opposite top:** Ged Wells assisted by Mark Abbott and Jeremy Fox, Knebworth, 1989, and **bottom:** Car park DIY, 1989 **Photos:** TLB

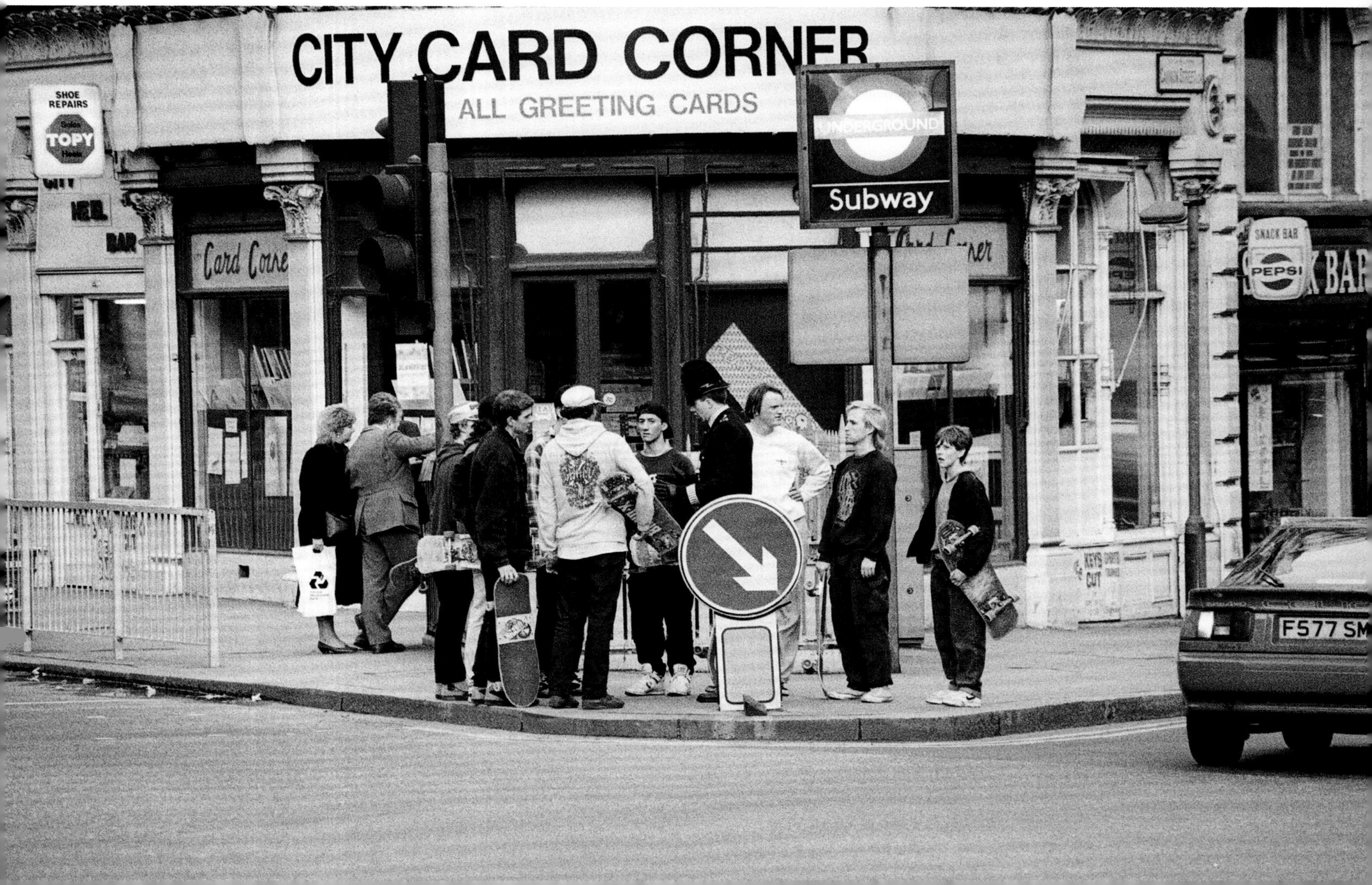

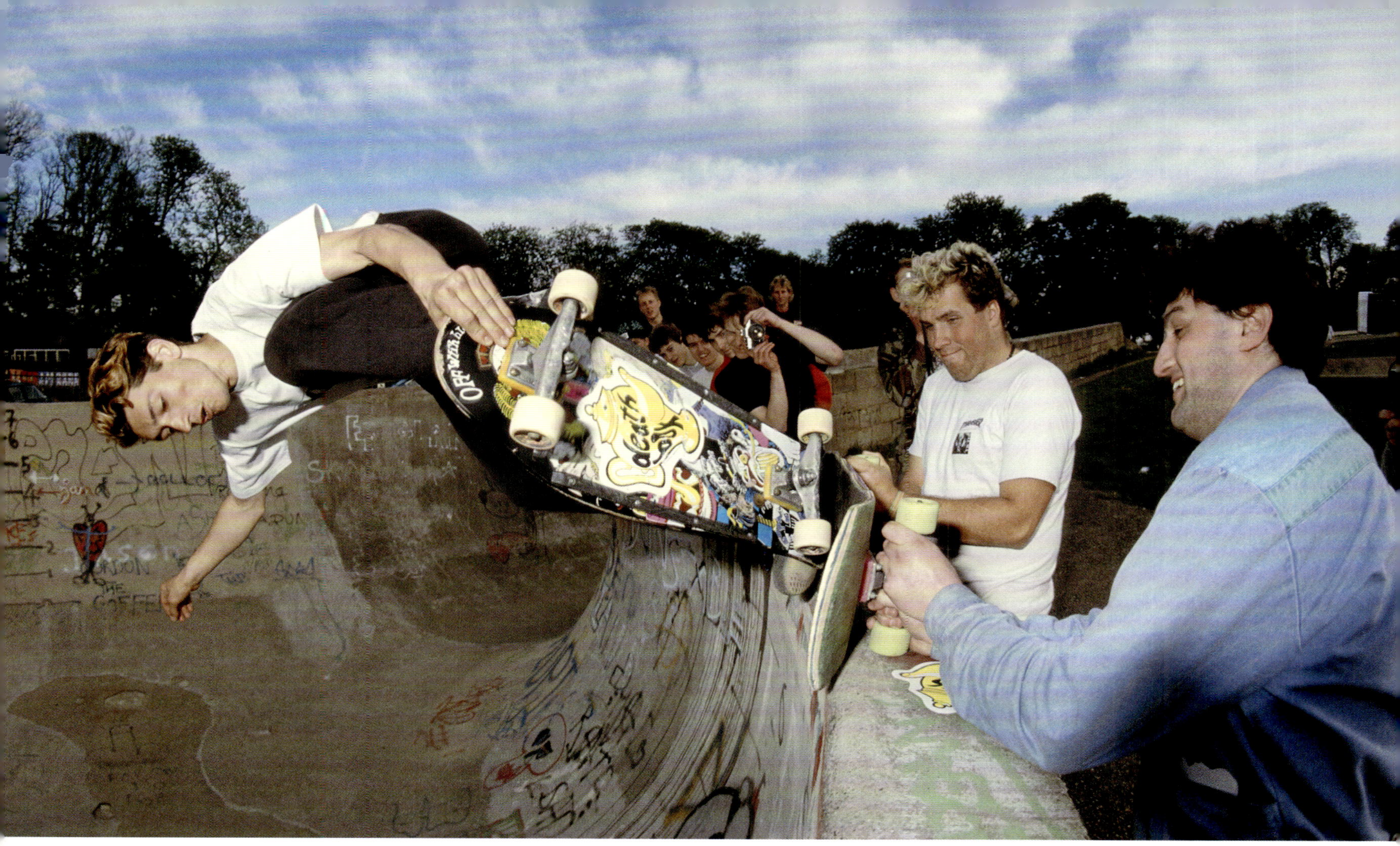

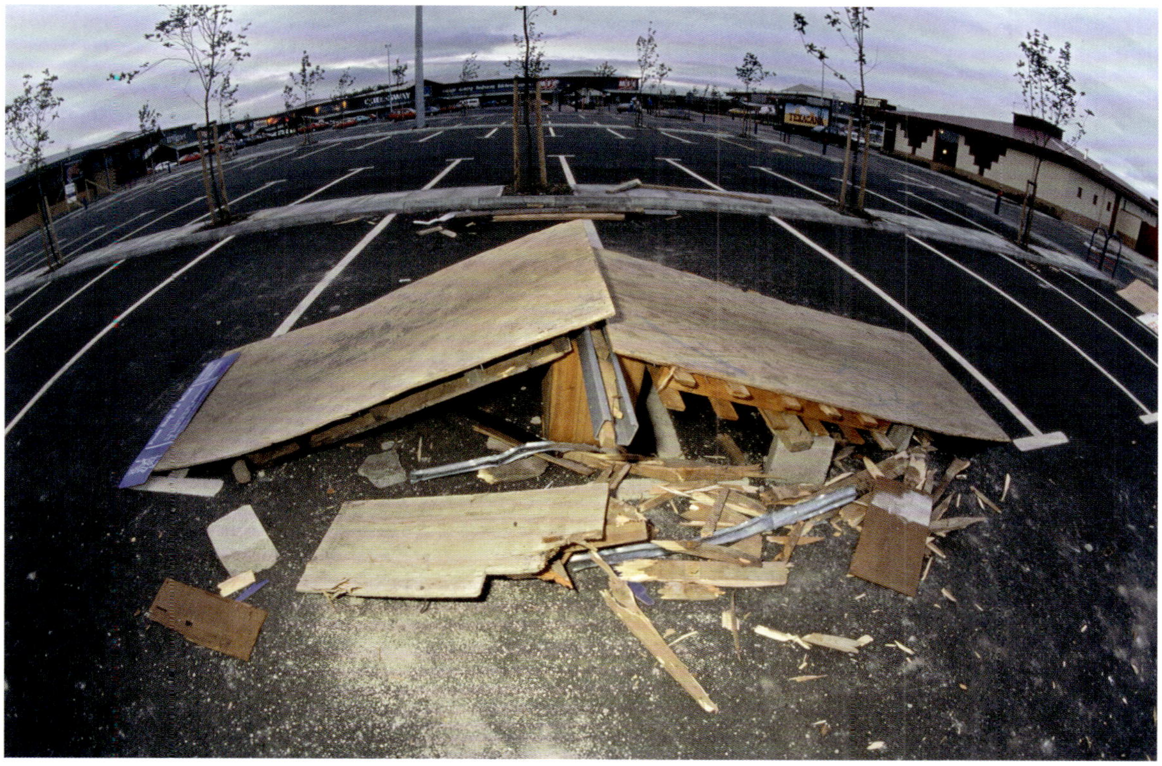

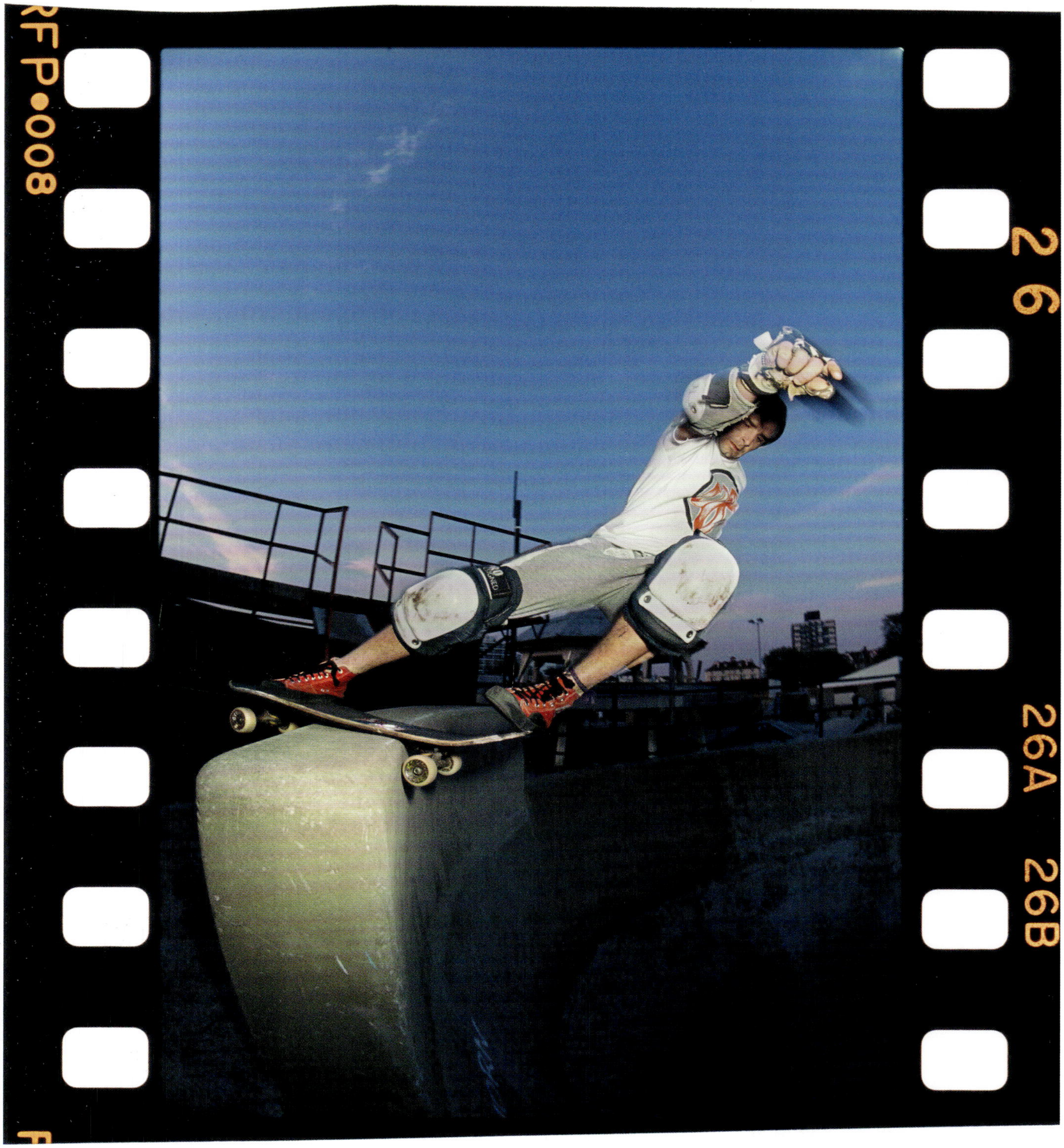

Above: Mark Abrook, Southsea skatepark, 1989 **Photo:** TLB **Opposite:** Steve Schneer, Southsea skatepark contest, 1990 **Photo:** Paul Sunman

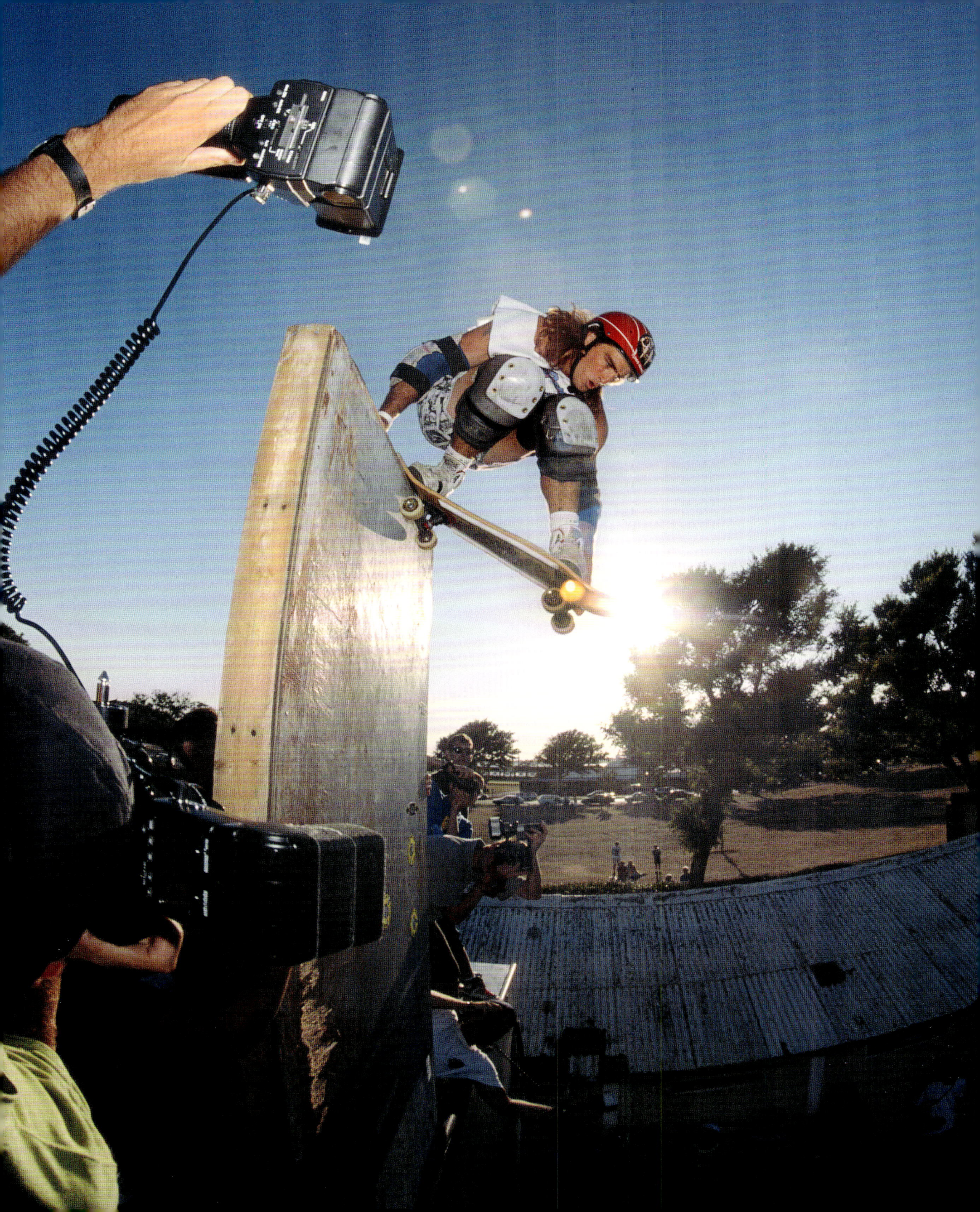

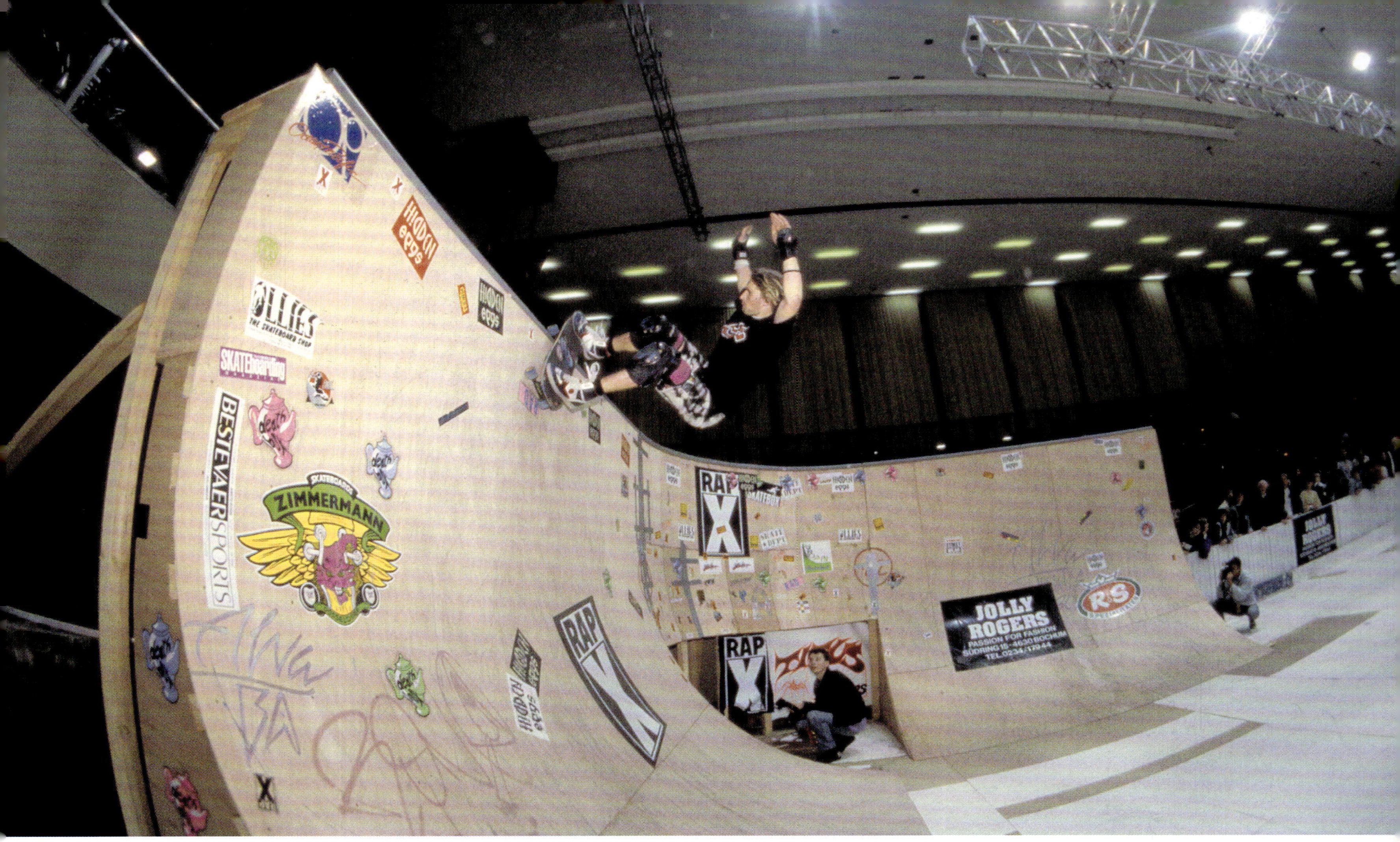
ZIMMERMANN
BESTEVAERSPORTS
RAP X
JOLLY ROGERS
PASSION FOR FASHION

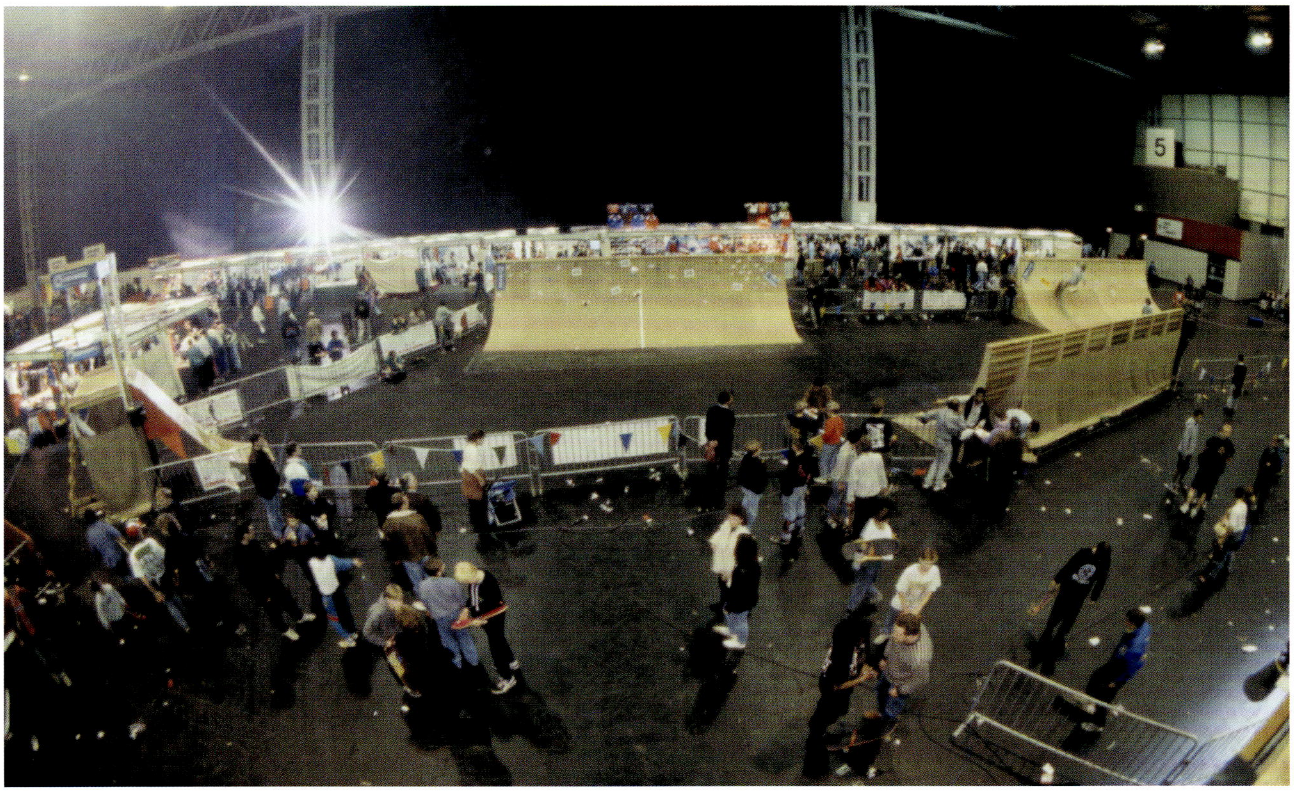

Opposite top: Sean Goff, Essen contest, Germany, 1989 **Photo:** TLB, and **bottom:** Birmingham UK contest, 1989 **Photo:** TLB **This page top:** Essen contest overview, 1989 **Photo:** Jay Podesta, and **bottom:** Duncan 'Wurzel' Houlton, Aberdeen contest, 1989 **Photo:** TLB **Overleaf left:** Matt Hensley, Munster, 1989. Magazine detail, artwork by Ian Roxburgh **Sequence photos:** Jay Podesta **Inset photo:** TLB **Overleaf right:** Matt Hensley, Munster, 1989 **Photo:** Jay Podesta

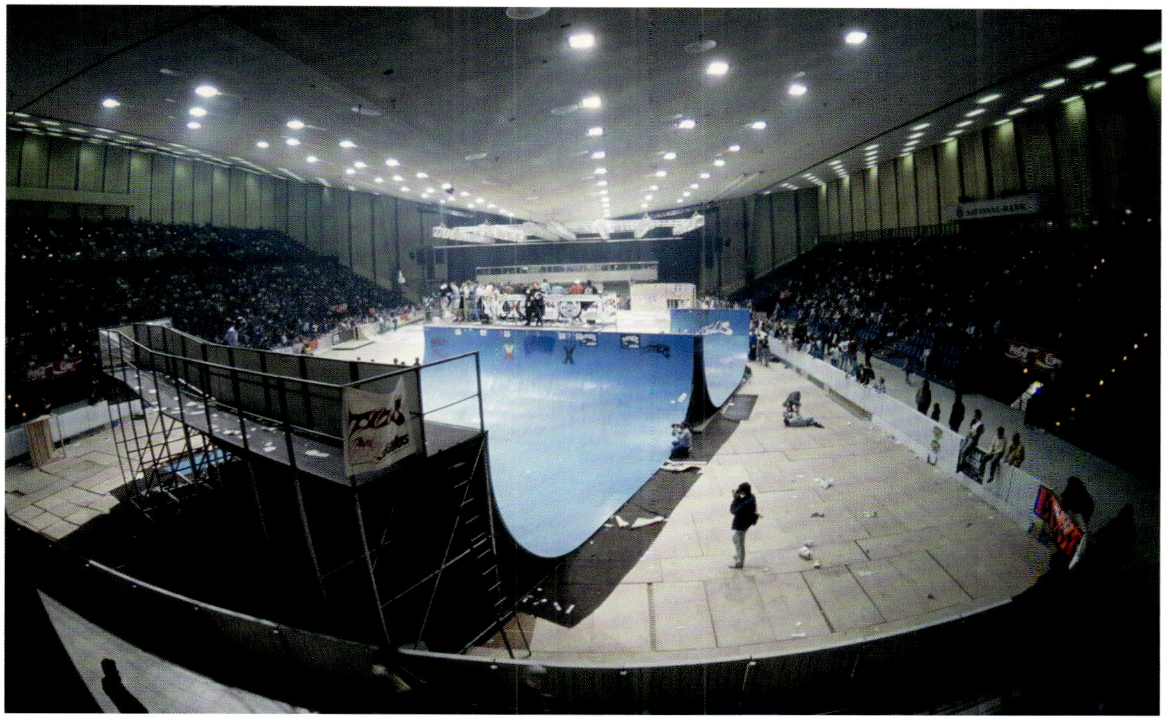

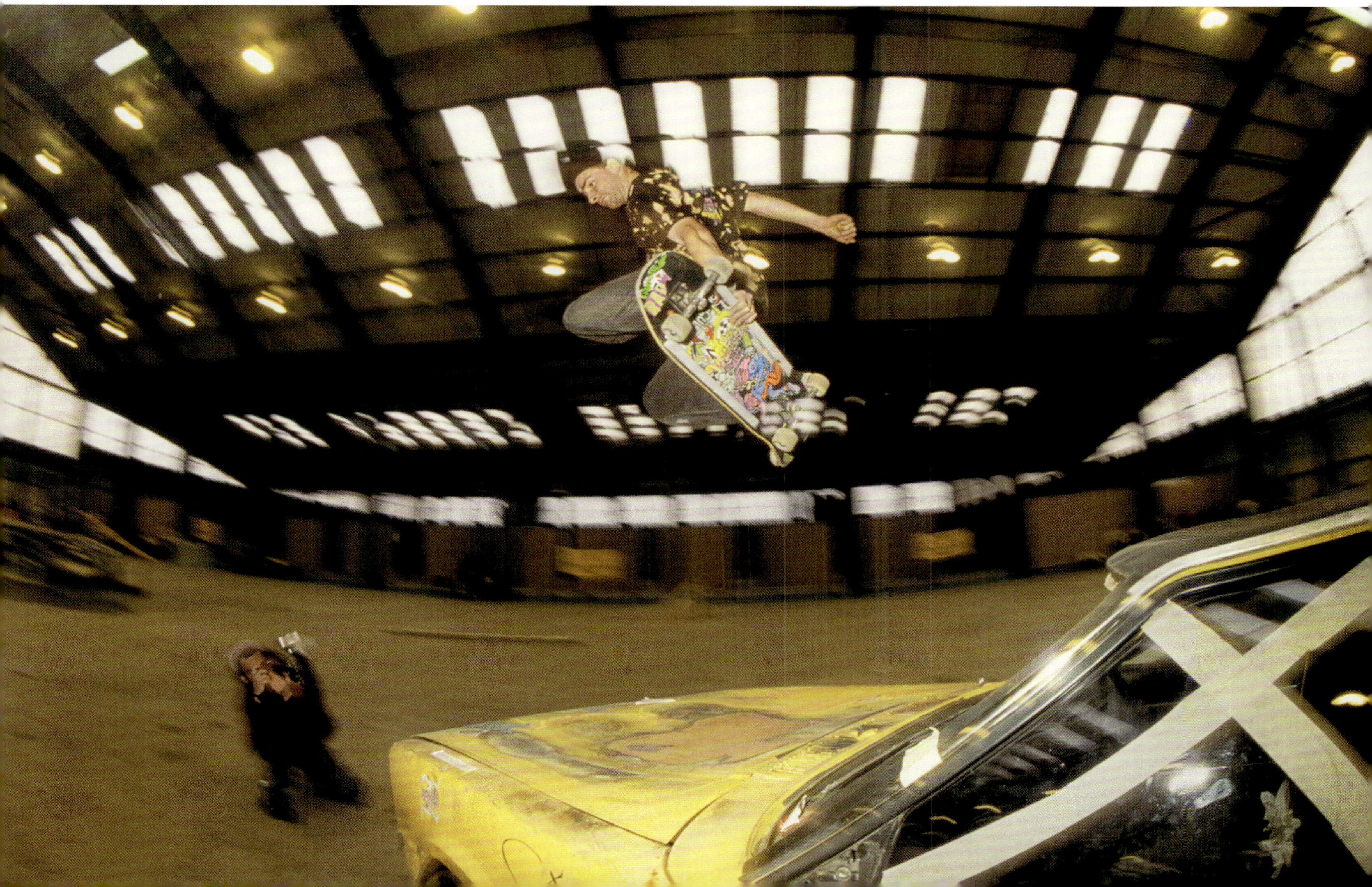

CONTRIBUTORS:
Dan Adams
Alex Baldock
Angry Brown
Jamie Cameron
Rodga Harvey
Radek Kalhous
Shane O'Brien
Jay Podesta
Skin
Twiss

254
3 x261/286
i90459

DISTRIBUTORS:
Comag
Tavistock Road
West Drayton
MIDDX
UB7 7QE

'ING

PRINTERS:
Chase Web Offset
StAustell

AGER:
TISING

Published by
Deltamere Ltd
40 Bowling Green Lane
London EC1R 0NE

UCTION:
MENT
GER:

SUBSCRIPTIONS: UK £12; Europe and USA (Air) £20; Elsewhere £30. Send stirling cheque or money order payable to 'Deltamere Ltd' or Access/ Mastercharge card number, cardholder's name, signature and address to Subscriptions Manager, R·A·D Magazine, 120-126 Lavender Ave., Mitcham, Surrey, CR4 3HP

BACK ISSUES: Some back issues are available at £1 including postage and packing from Back Issues, R·A·D Magazine, 40 Bowling Green, London, EC1R 0NE

ER
APHERS
ENT
NG DEPT

euPLANdc
NkiLLer-
eFINgerF
eeBLE-an
chtNO-CoM
DISASTer-
OinDyeGGp
t- RAD

Contents

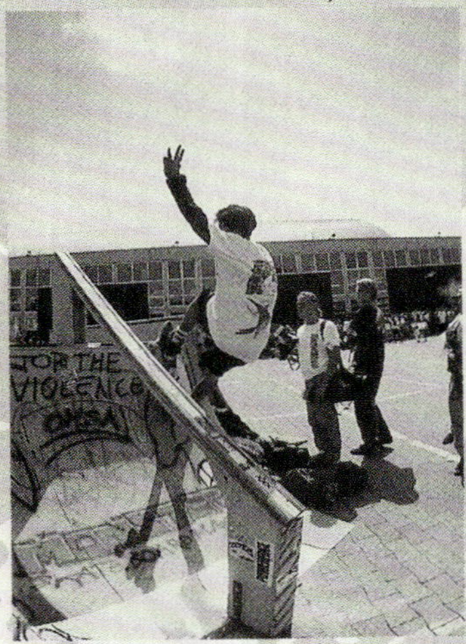
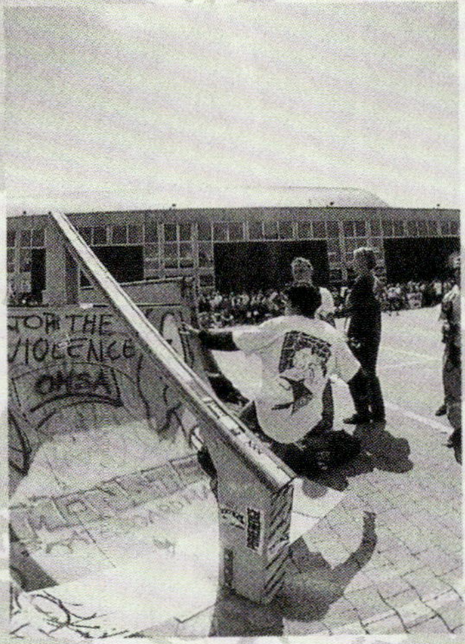

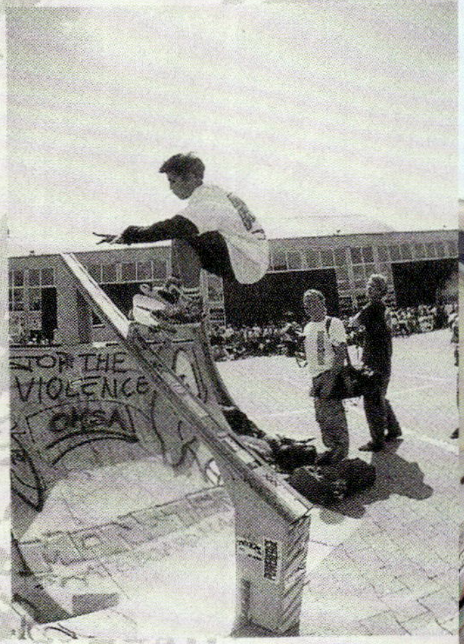
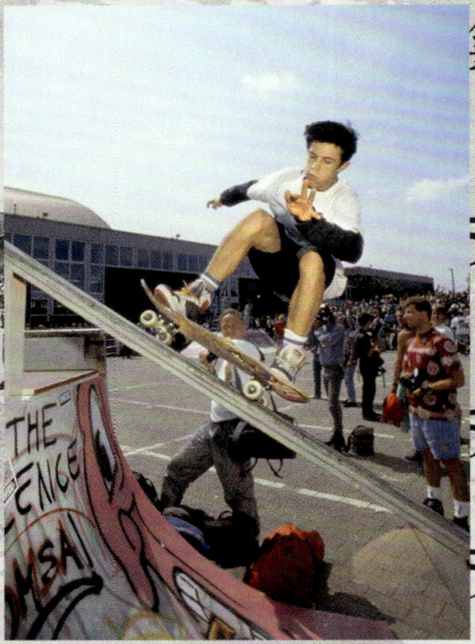

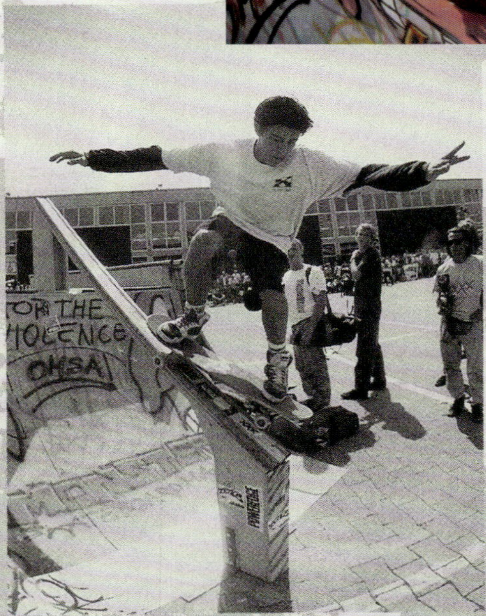

Cover: Lee Ralph at Hastings

This page: Matt Hensley in Munster

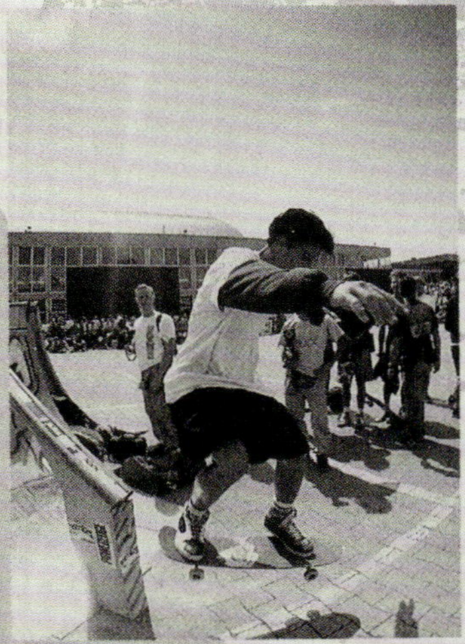
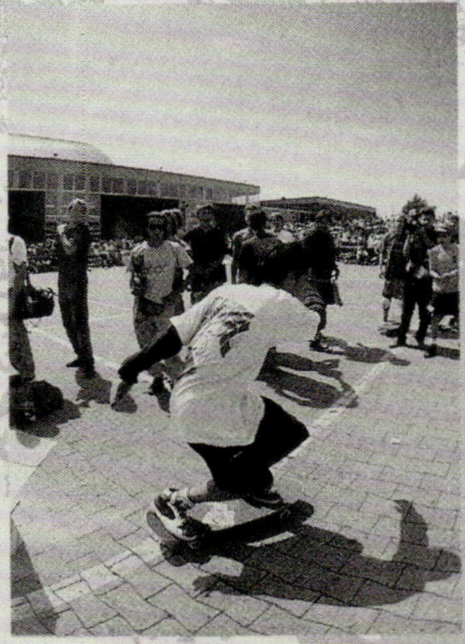
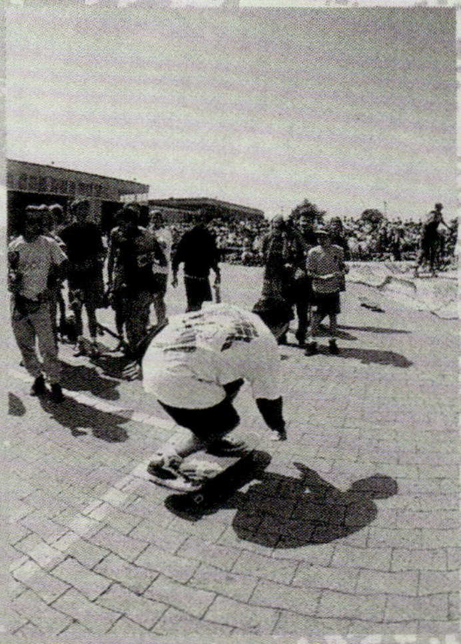

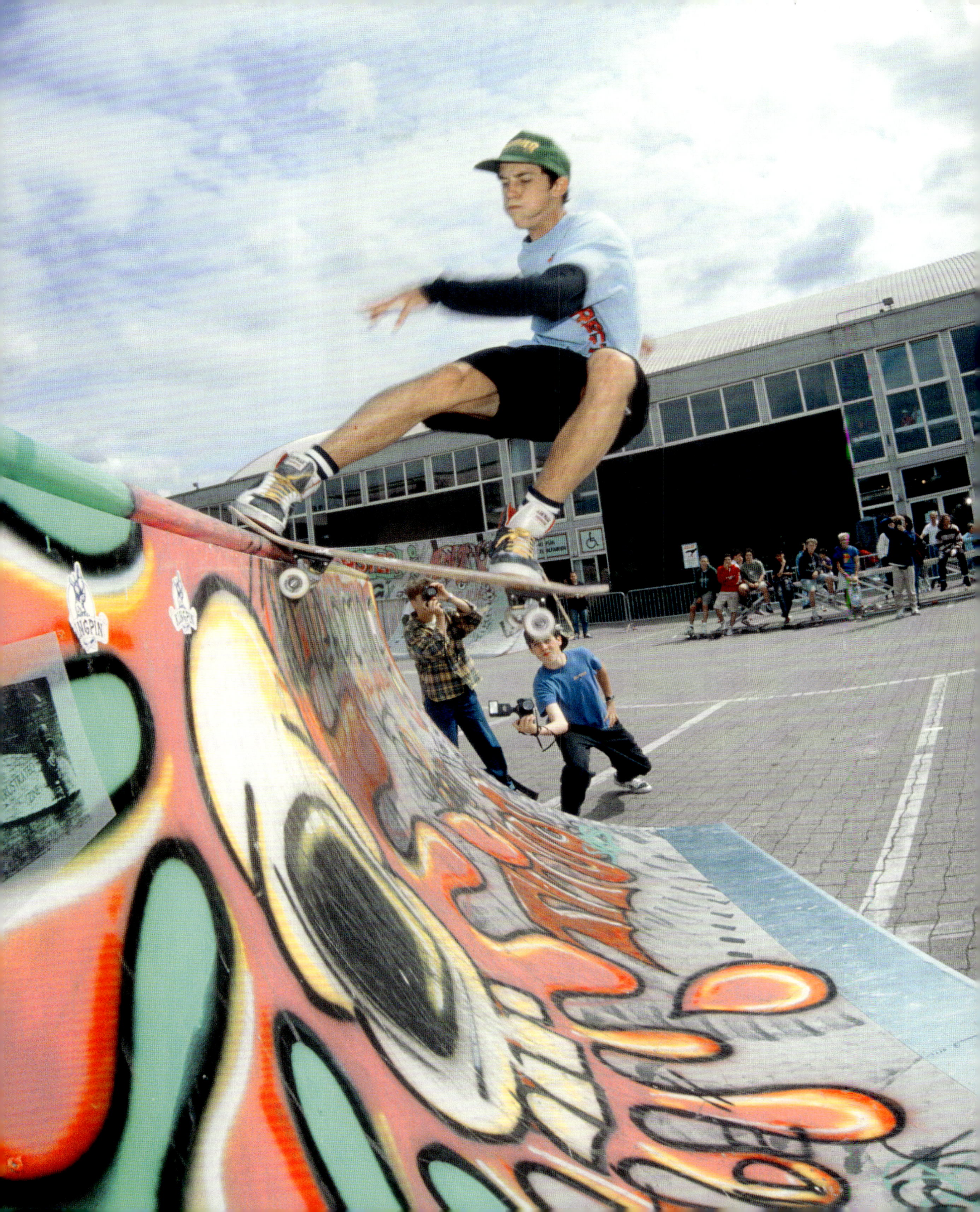

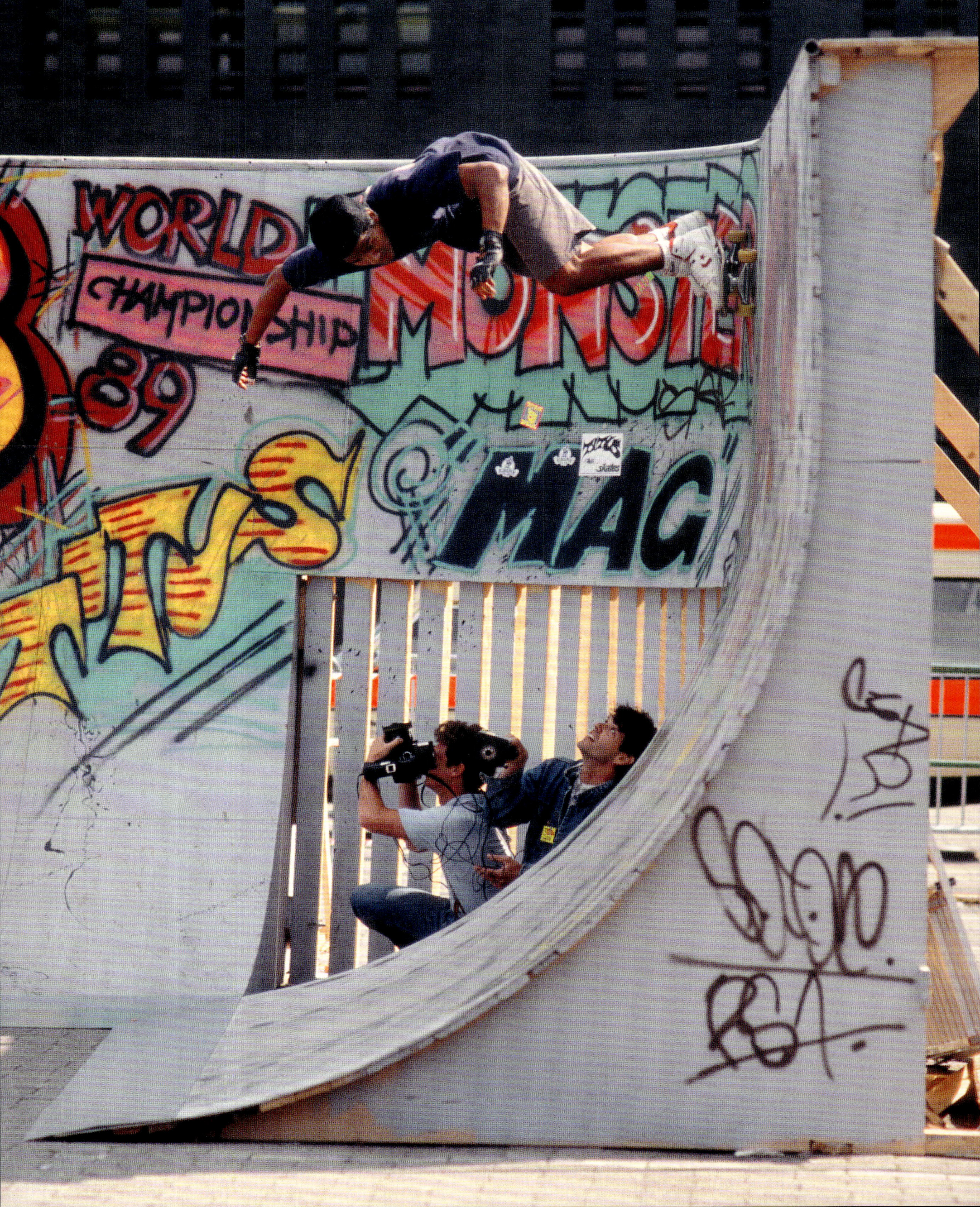
WORLD
CHAMPIONSHIP
89
MONSTER
MAG

Munster contests, Germany
Opposite: Pat Ngoho, 1989
Photo: Mike John **Clockwise from right:**
Lee Ralph, 1989 **Photo:** Paul Sunman.
Street contest overview, 1989 **Photo:**
TLB. Lee Ralph (foreground), Bill Danforth
looking on, 1990 **Photo:** Jay Podesta

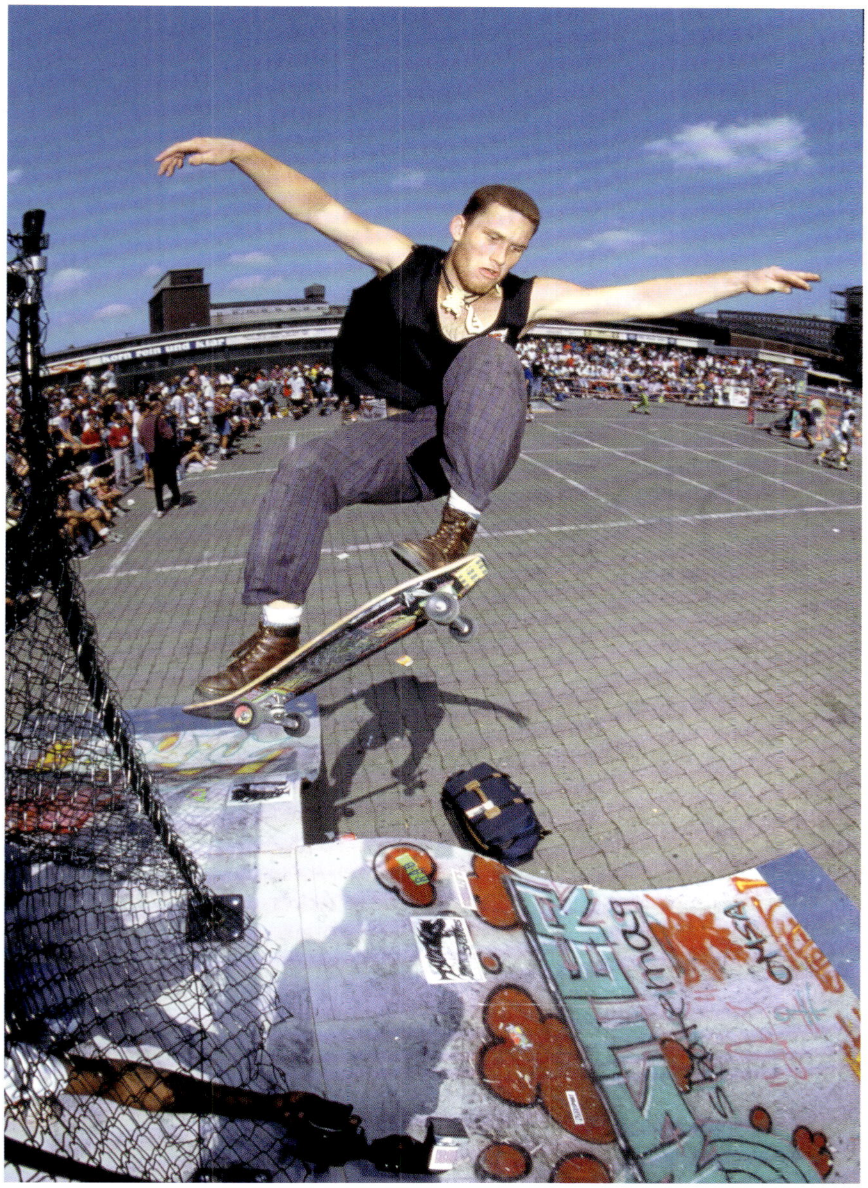

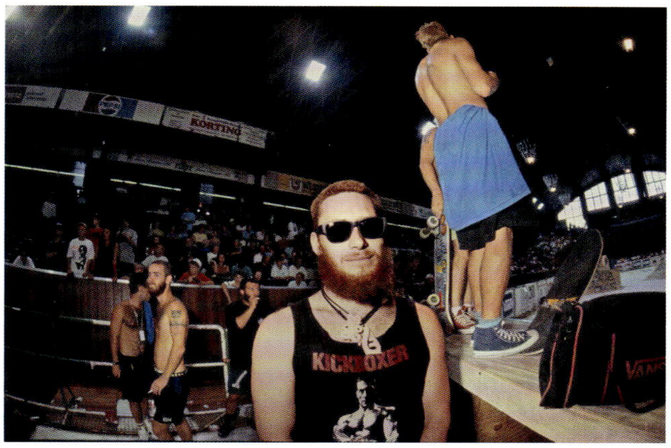

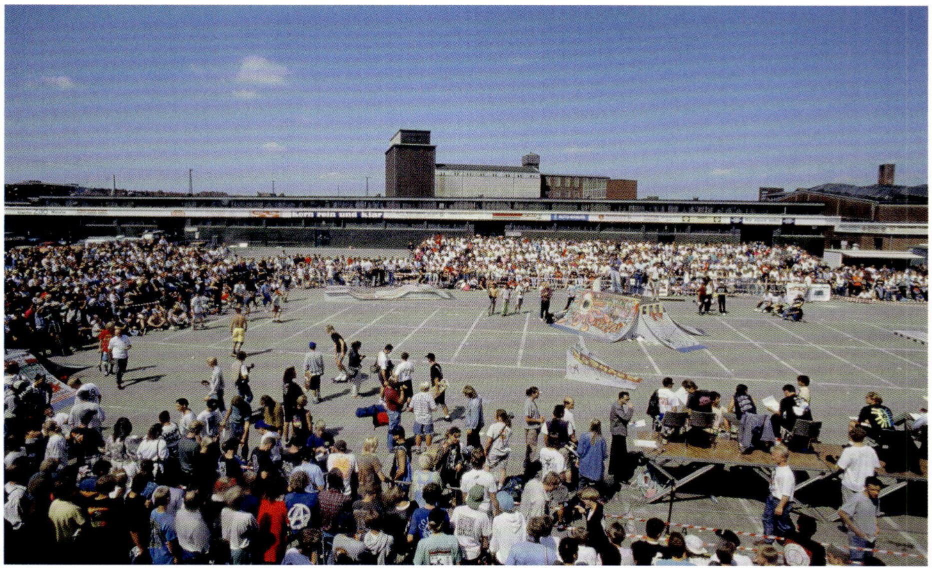

'I got a phone call from the police or the port authorities, "We've got this bloke here and he's just arrived at the border—he's from New Zealand and he hasn't got a passport or any money or any clothes, but he's got your magazine with him and he's asked us to give you a call" [laughter]. I think someone had stolen all his stuff on the ferry. Anyway, I must have said the right thing because they let him in.'

TLB

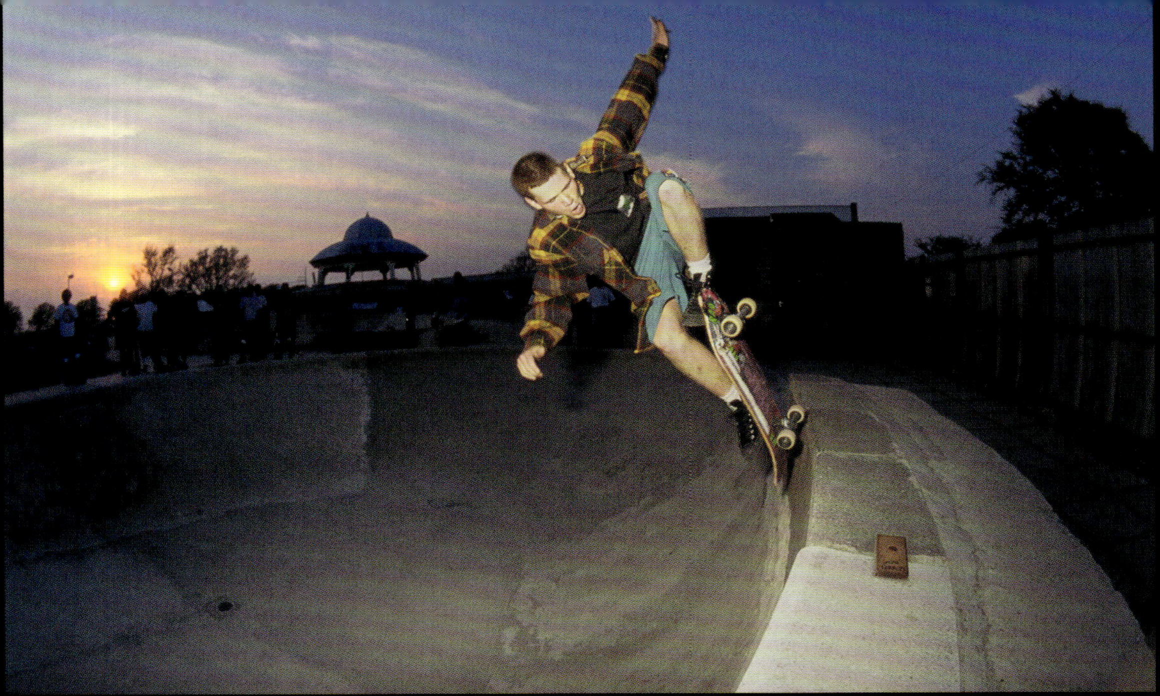

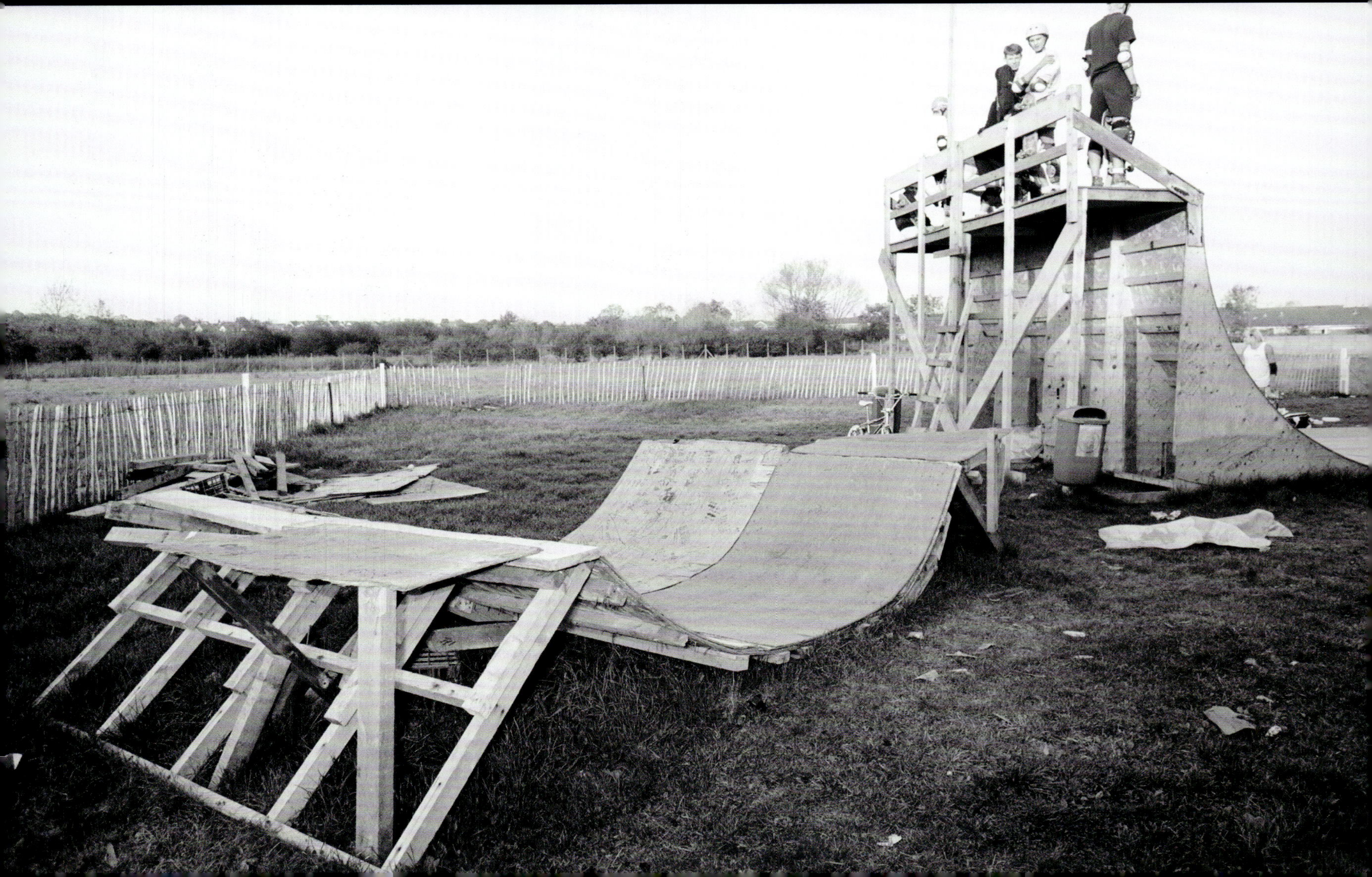

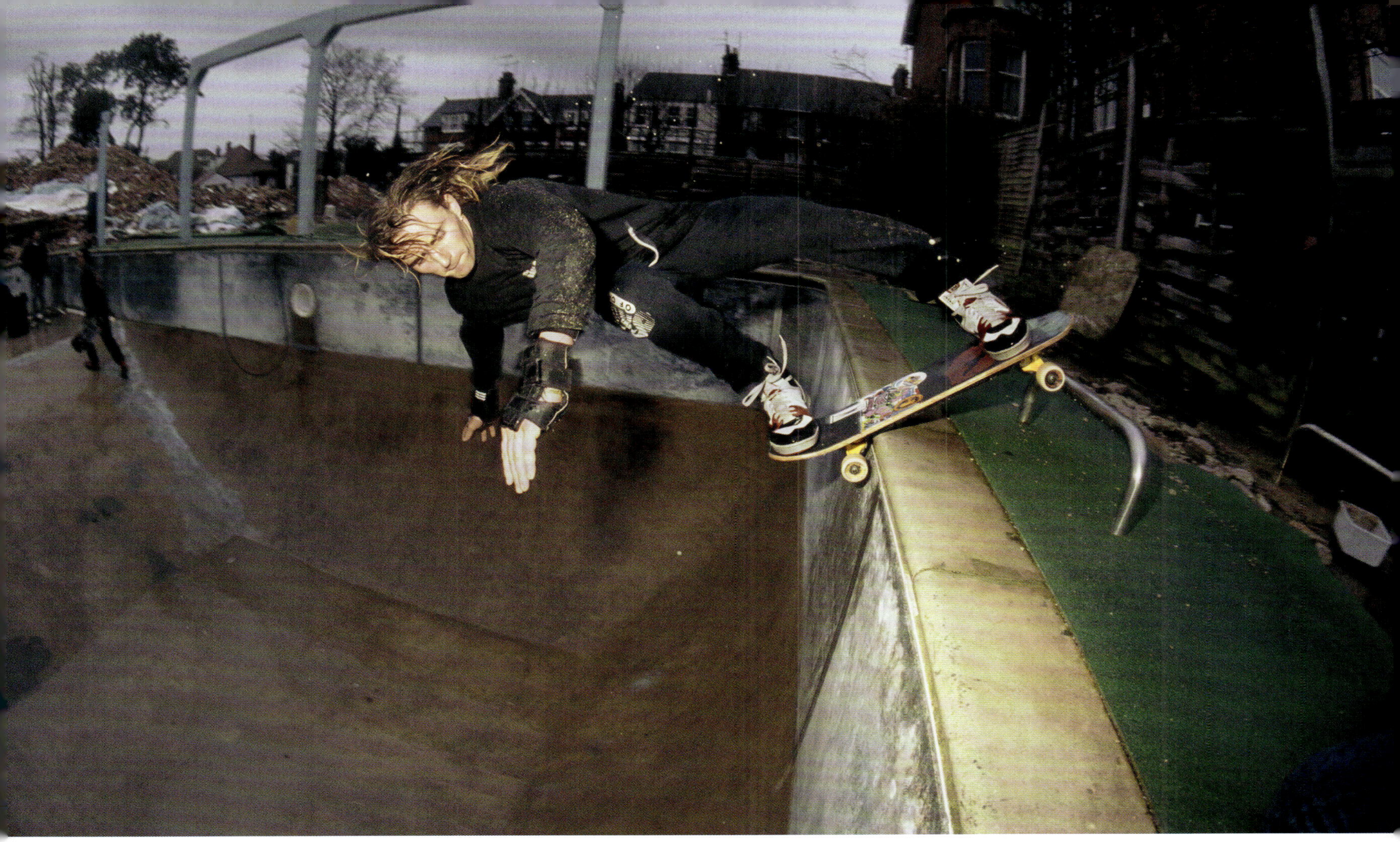

Opposite top: Aaron Dieter, Southsea skatepark, 1989, and **bottom:** Essex, UK, 1989 **Above:** Sean Goff, Cromer, Norfolk, 1989 **Below:** Paul Dixon, Woodland ramp, Evesham, 1989 **Photos:** TLB

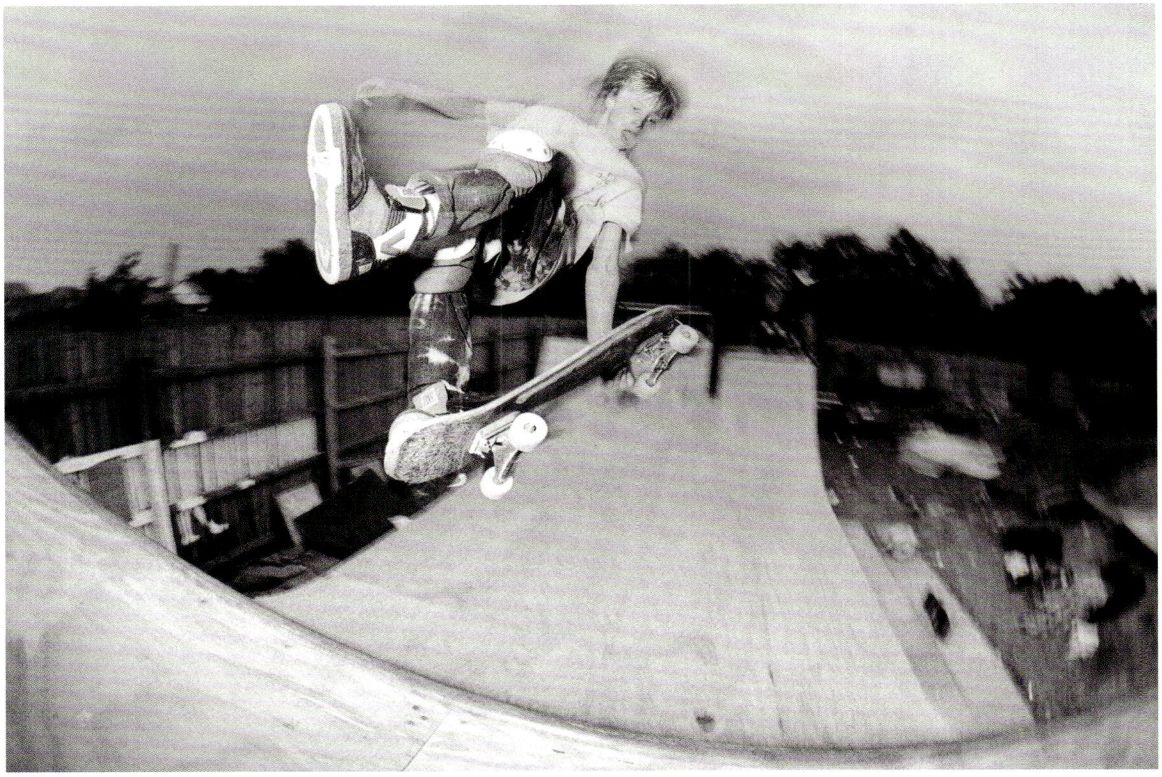

Below: Jim Murphy, Rom skatepark, 1989 **Photo:** Jay Podesta **Opposite:** Jimmy Boyes, Wigan contest, 1989 **Photo:** TLB

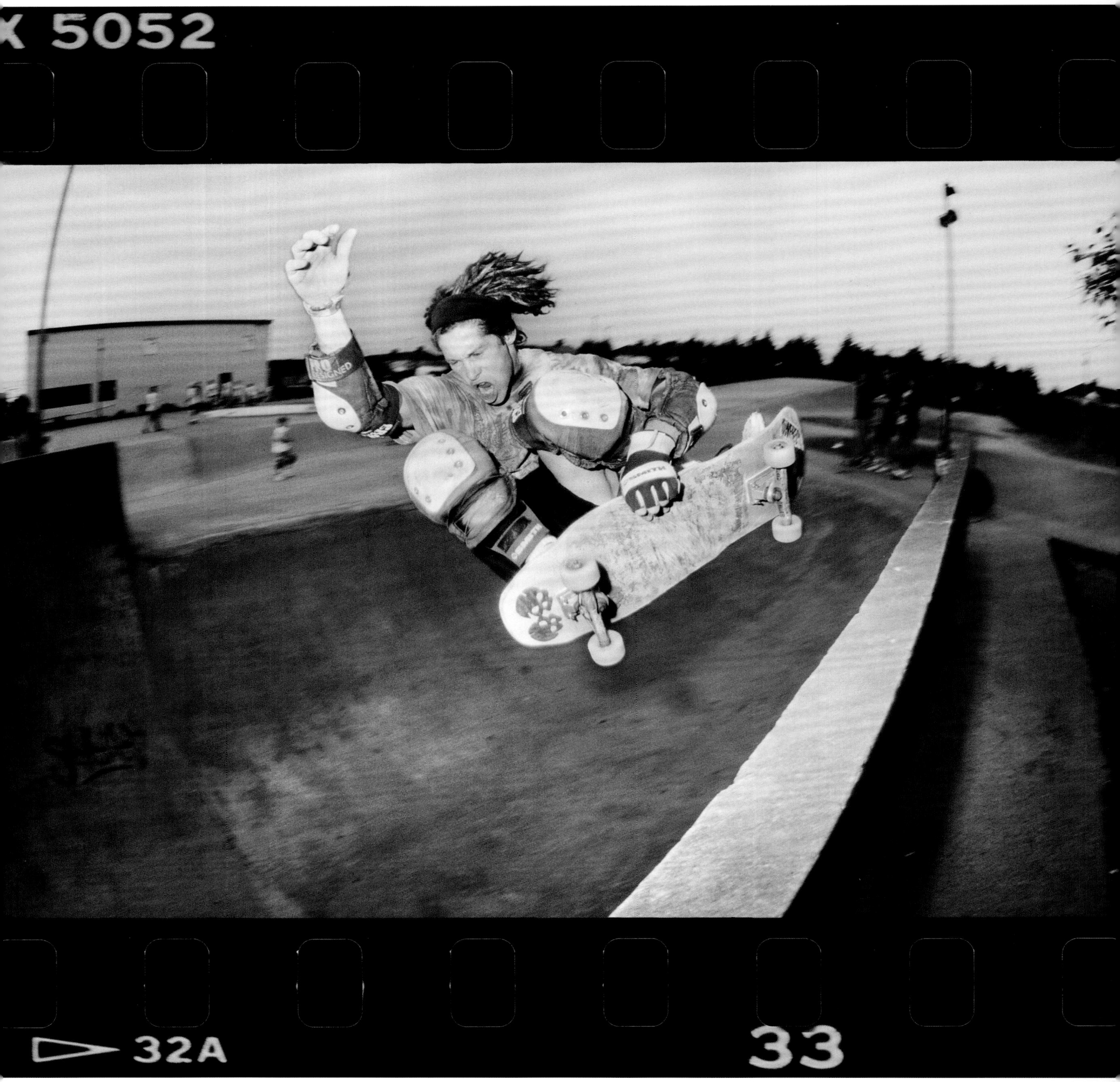

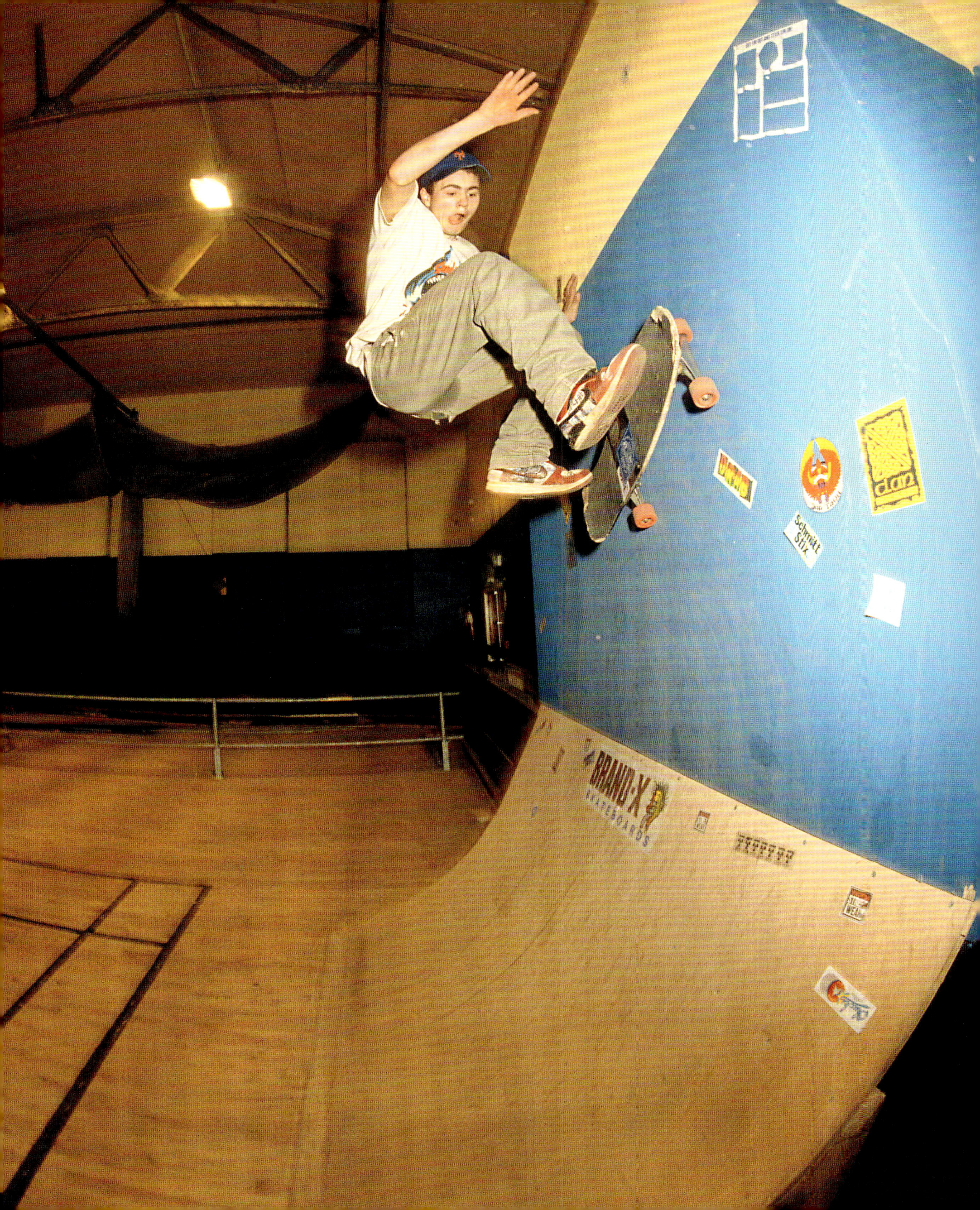
clan
Schmitt Stix
BRAND-X
SKATEBOARDS

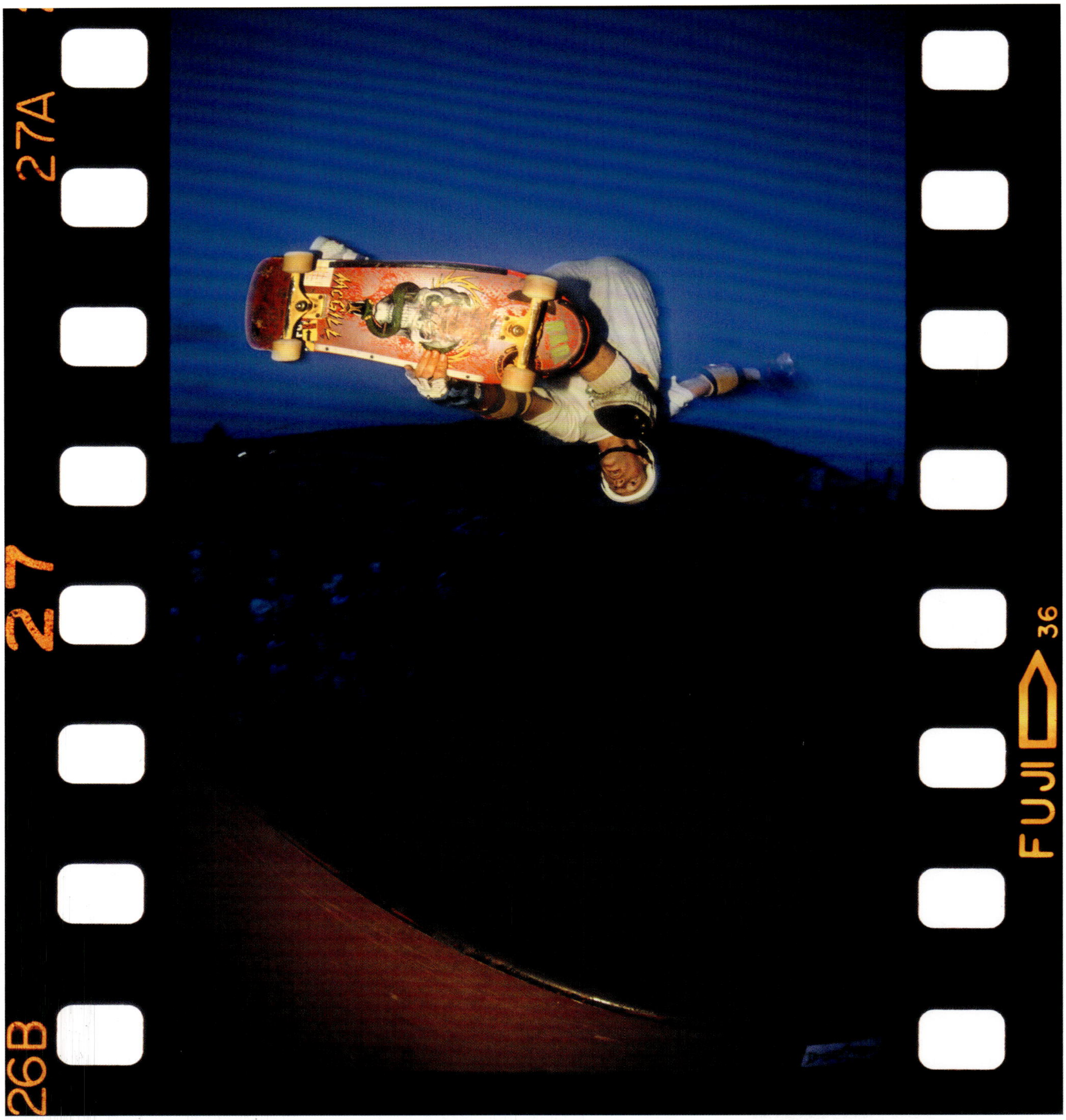

Left: Mike McGill, Bones Brigade UK tour, 1989 **Photo:** Mike John **Opposite:** Craig Johnson, Glasgow contest, Scotland, 1988 **Photo:** TLB

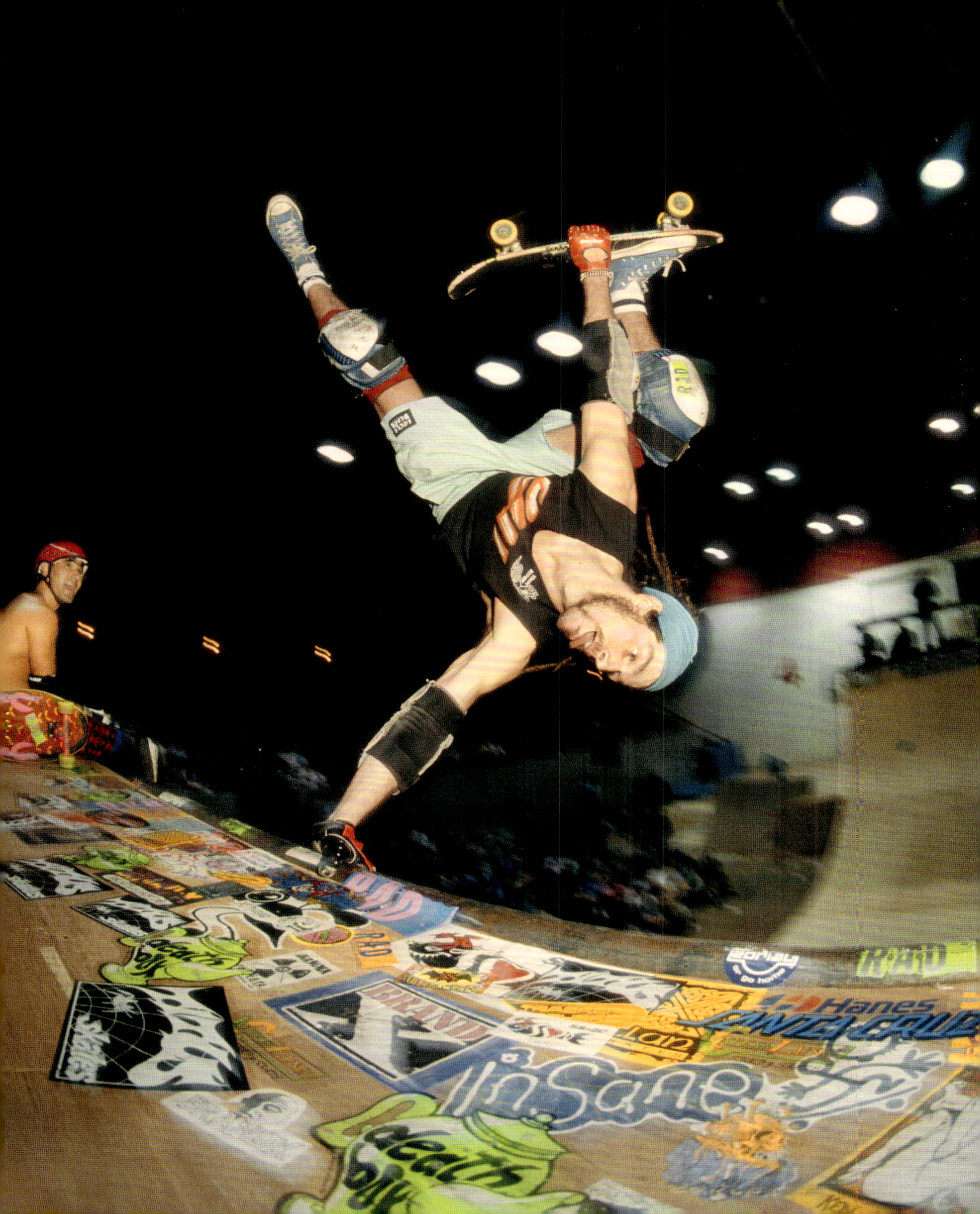

Hanes
In.Sane

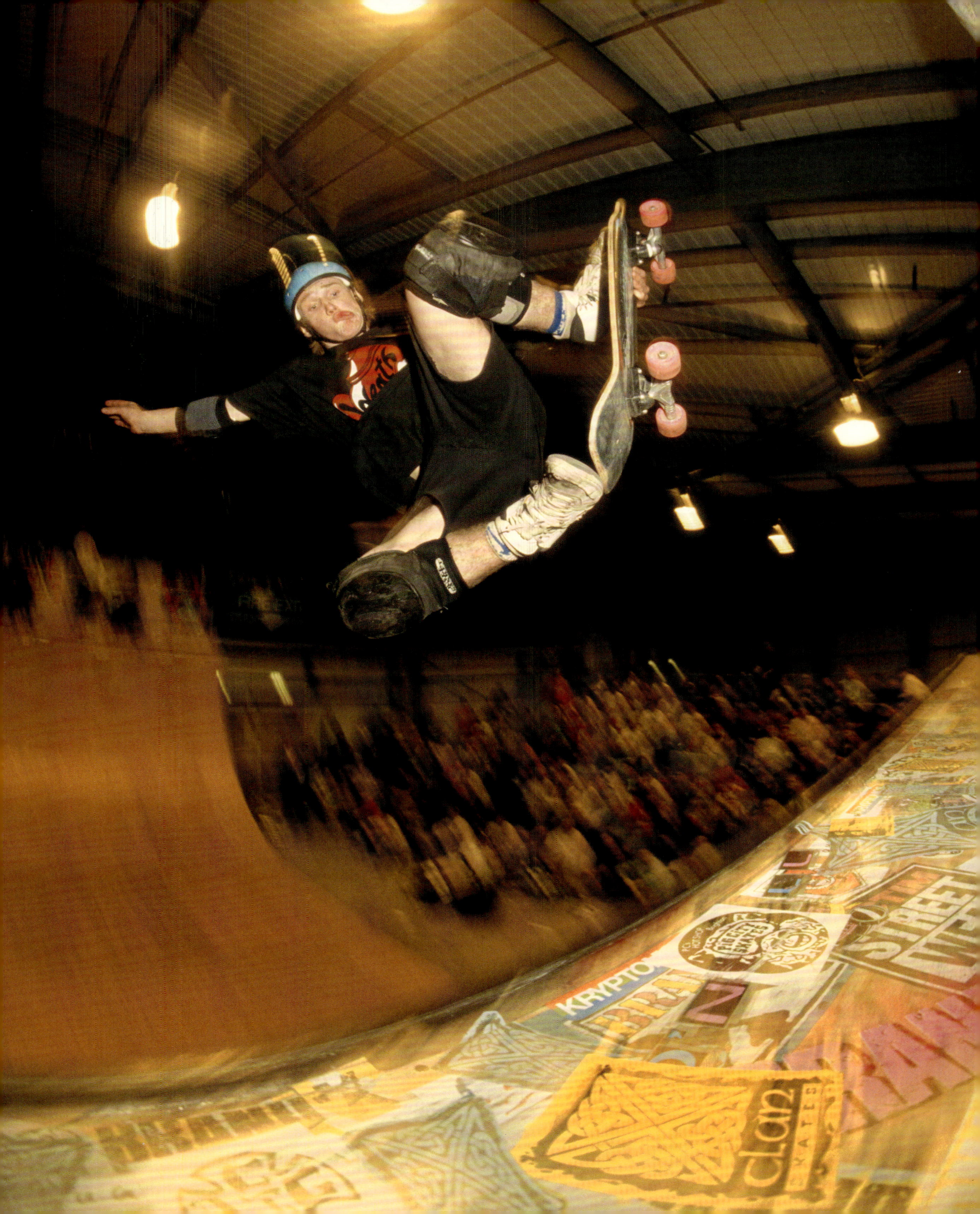
KRYPTO
STREET
clan

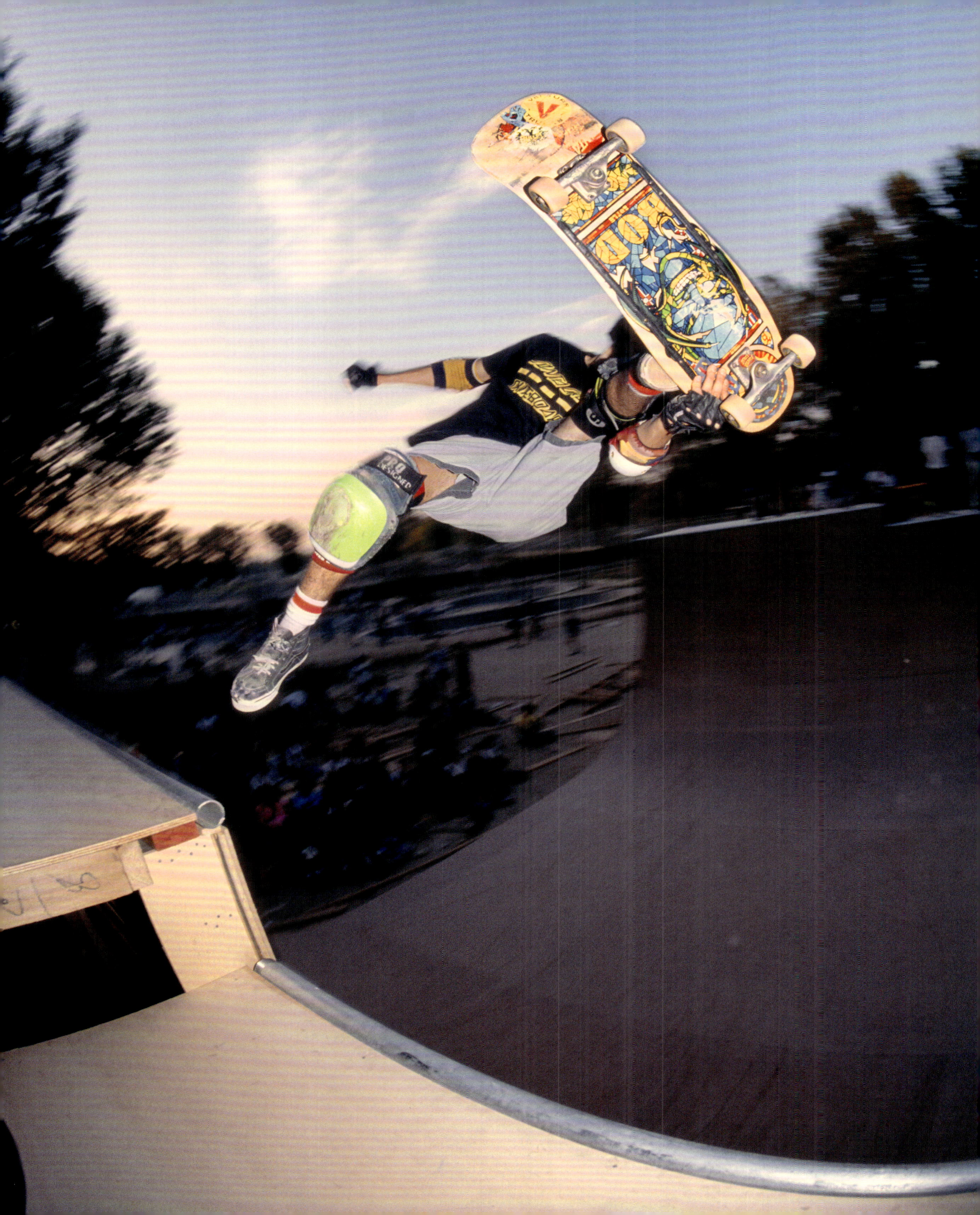

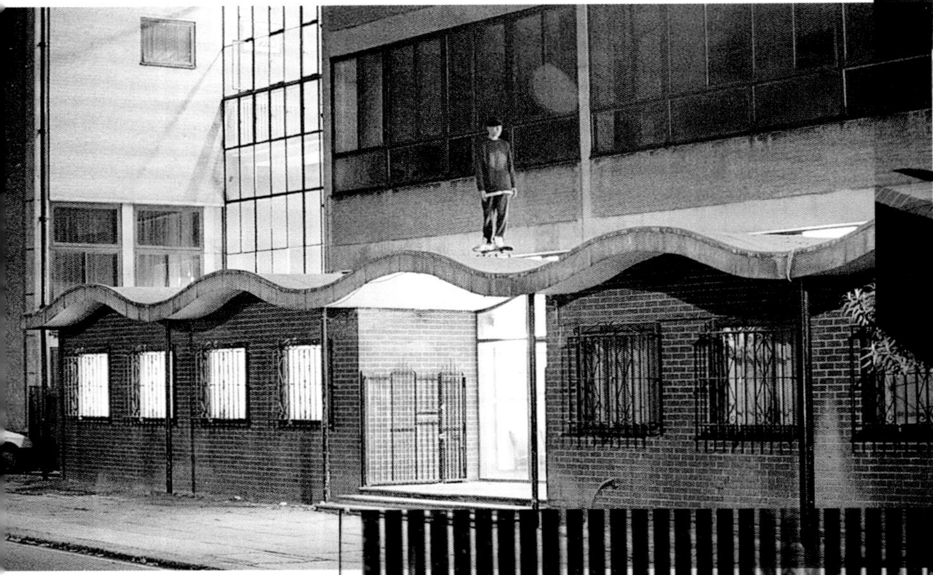
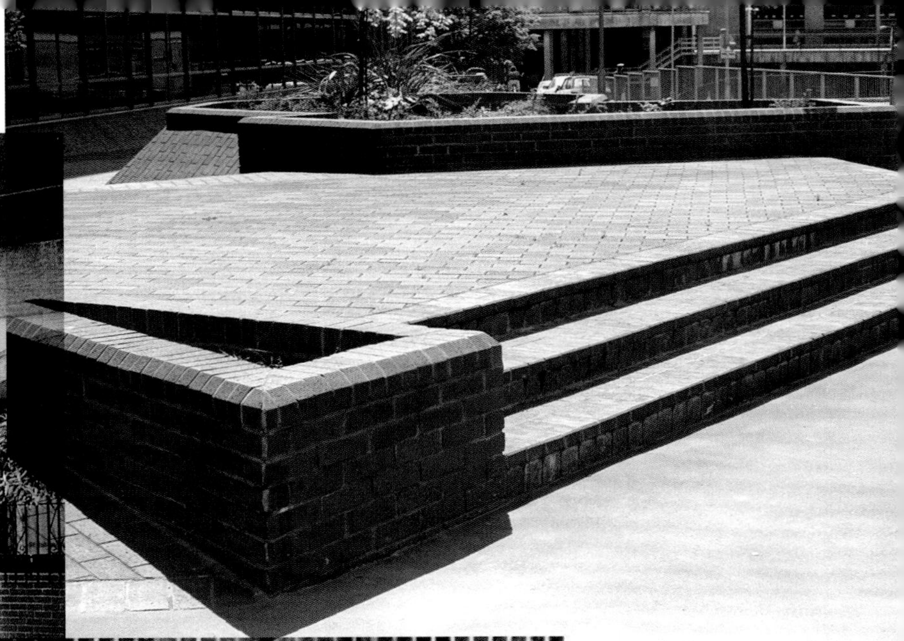
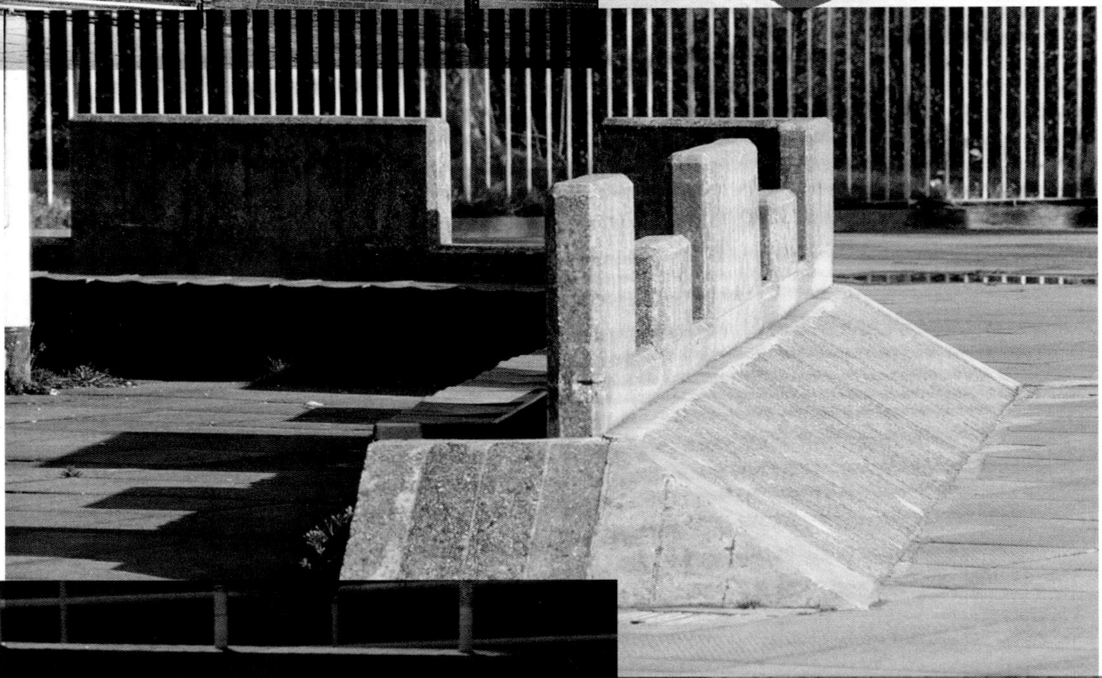
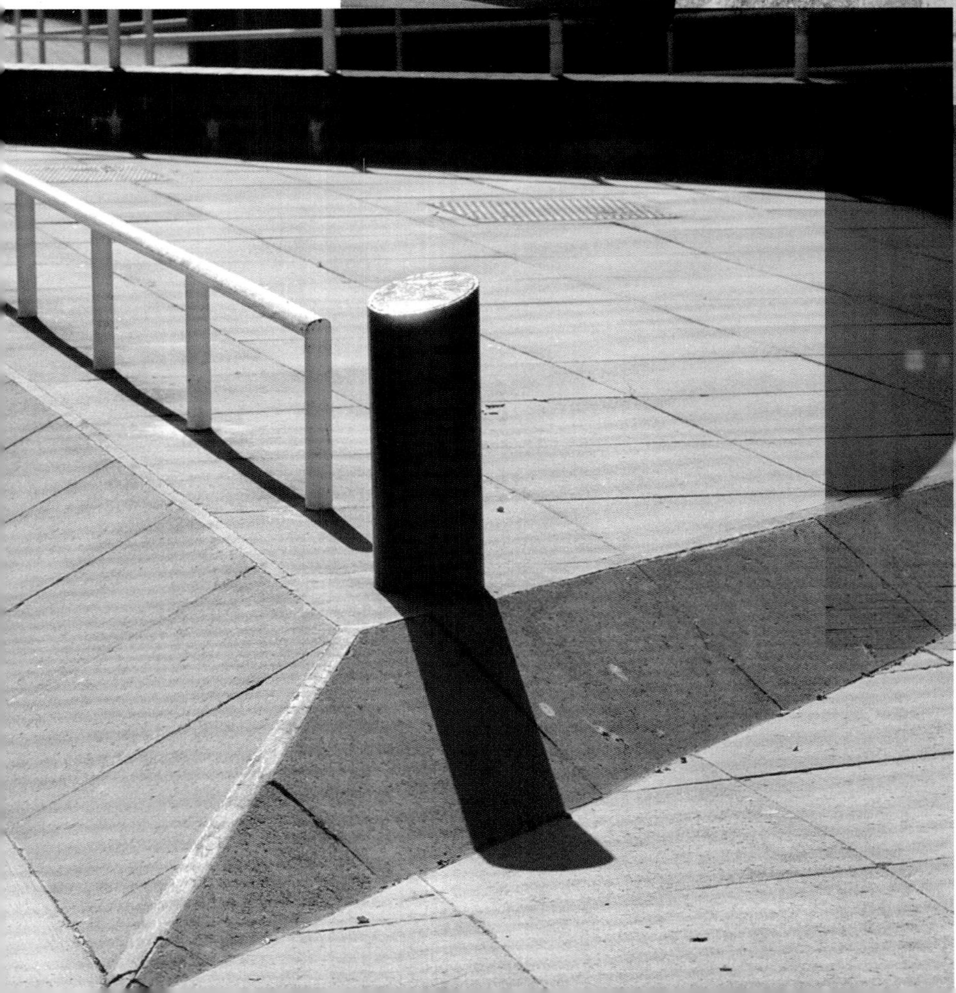
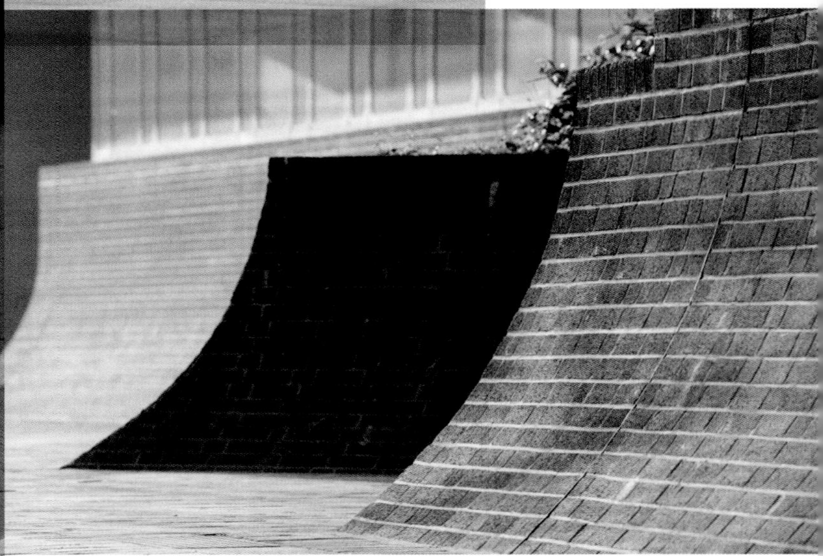

'I was responding to the starvation of terrain—the need for it. Looking for any banks even if they're not perfect banks—it was an obsession. I think that's something all skaters have, always looking for possibilities. So anything—even a bit of wood leaning up against a wall can be an inspiring thing for a skater, it can make you want to go and skate.

'I think that's something that TLB really understood—it was about showing possibilities. It was the idea of a magazine not just having awesome action shots; that's why he was always taking pictures of other things like a bench or some concrete or a texture.'

Ged Wells

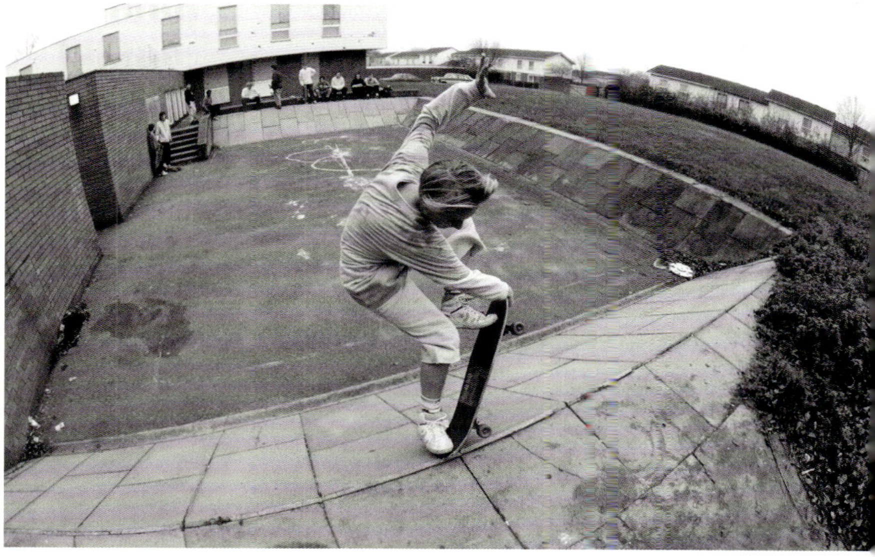

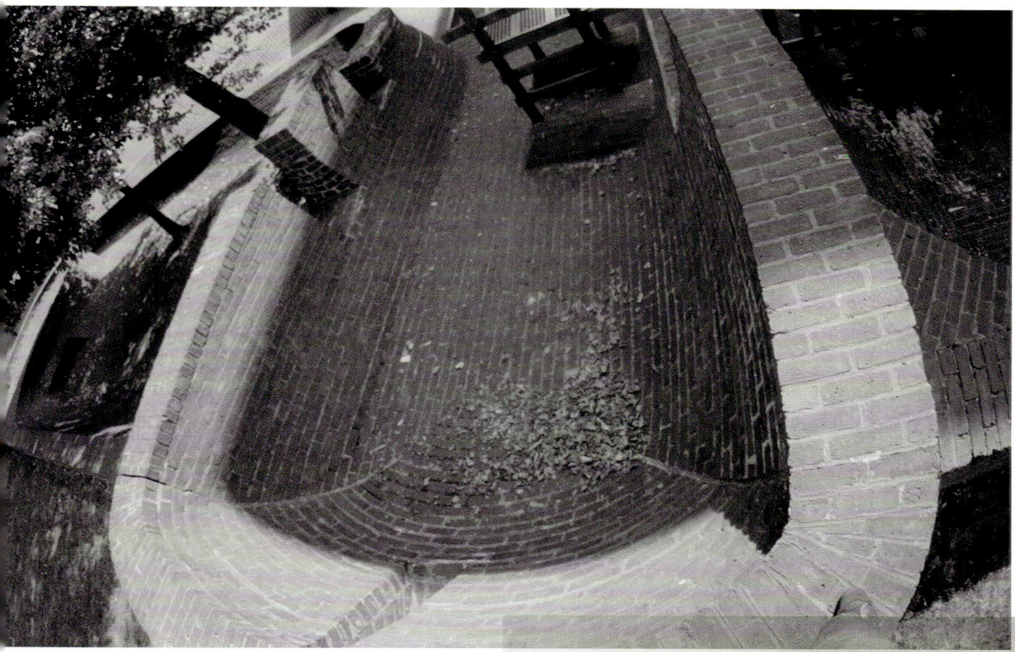

Previous spread left: Paul 'Rocker' Robson, Aberdeen contest, 1989 **Photo:** TLB, and **right:** Hugh 'Bod' Boyle, Madrid contest, 1989 **Photo:** Mike John

Above: Jim Houston, Basingstoke, 1989 **Photo:** TLB **All other photos:** Various skateable terrain photographed in the wild by TLB and Jay Podesta (below)

Overleaf left: Alex Moul, Oxford, 1989 **Photo:** TLB, and **right:** Sean Goff, Glasgow contest, 1988 **Photo:** Paul Sunman

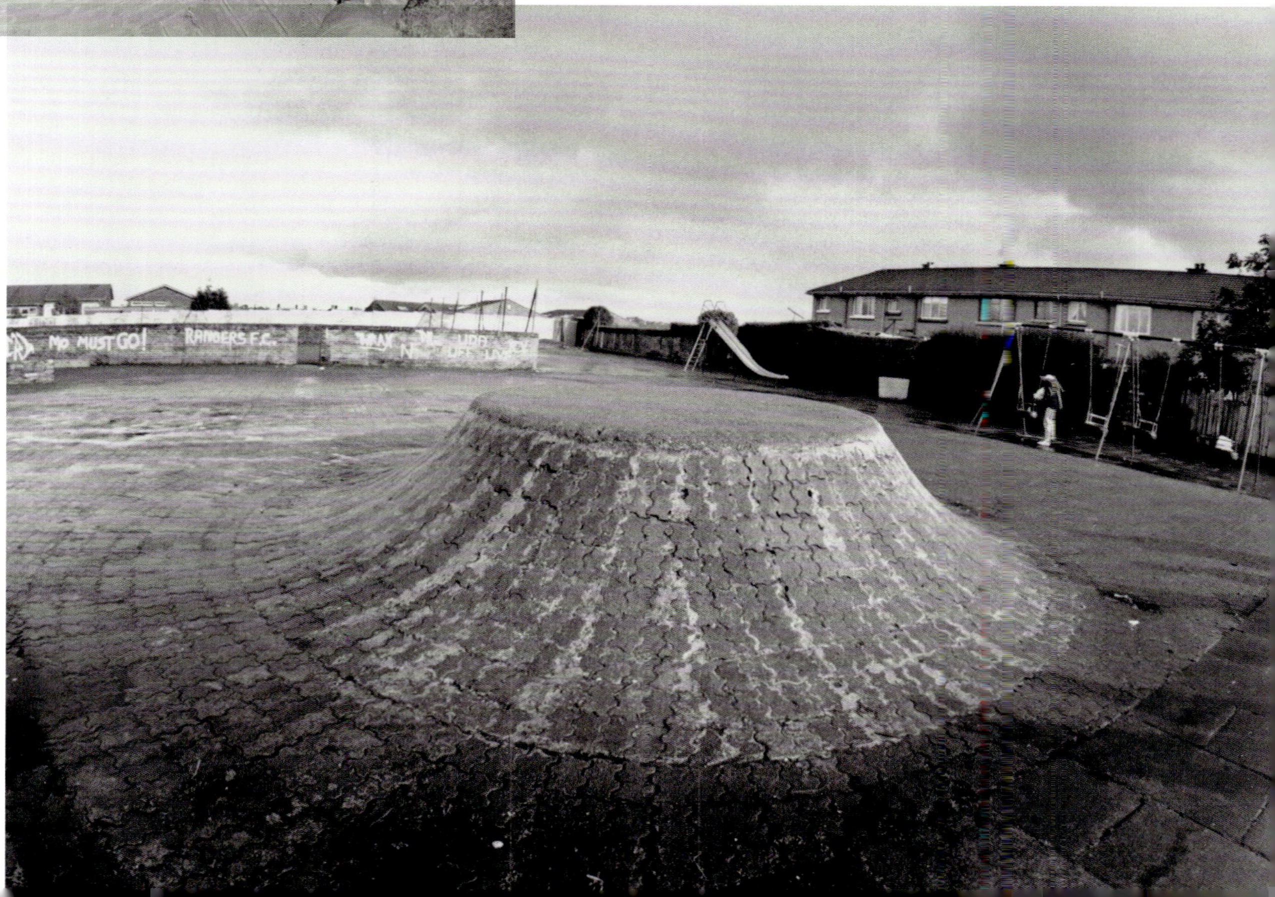

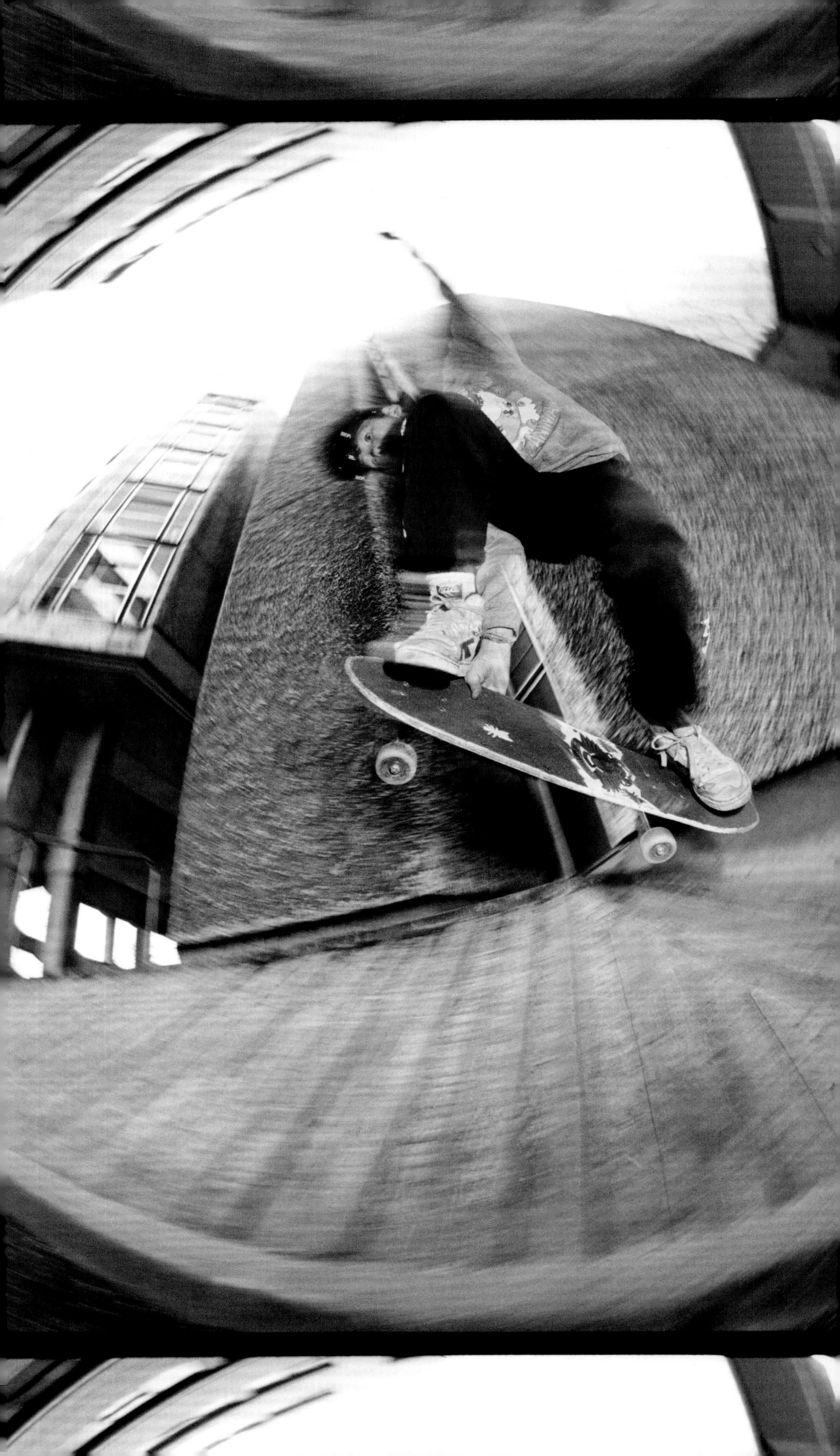

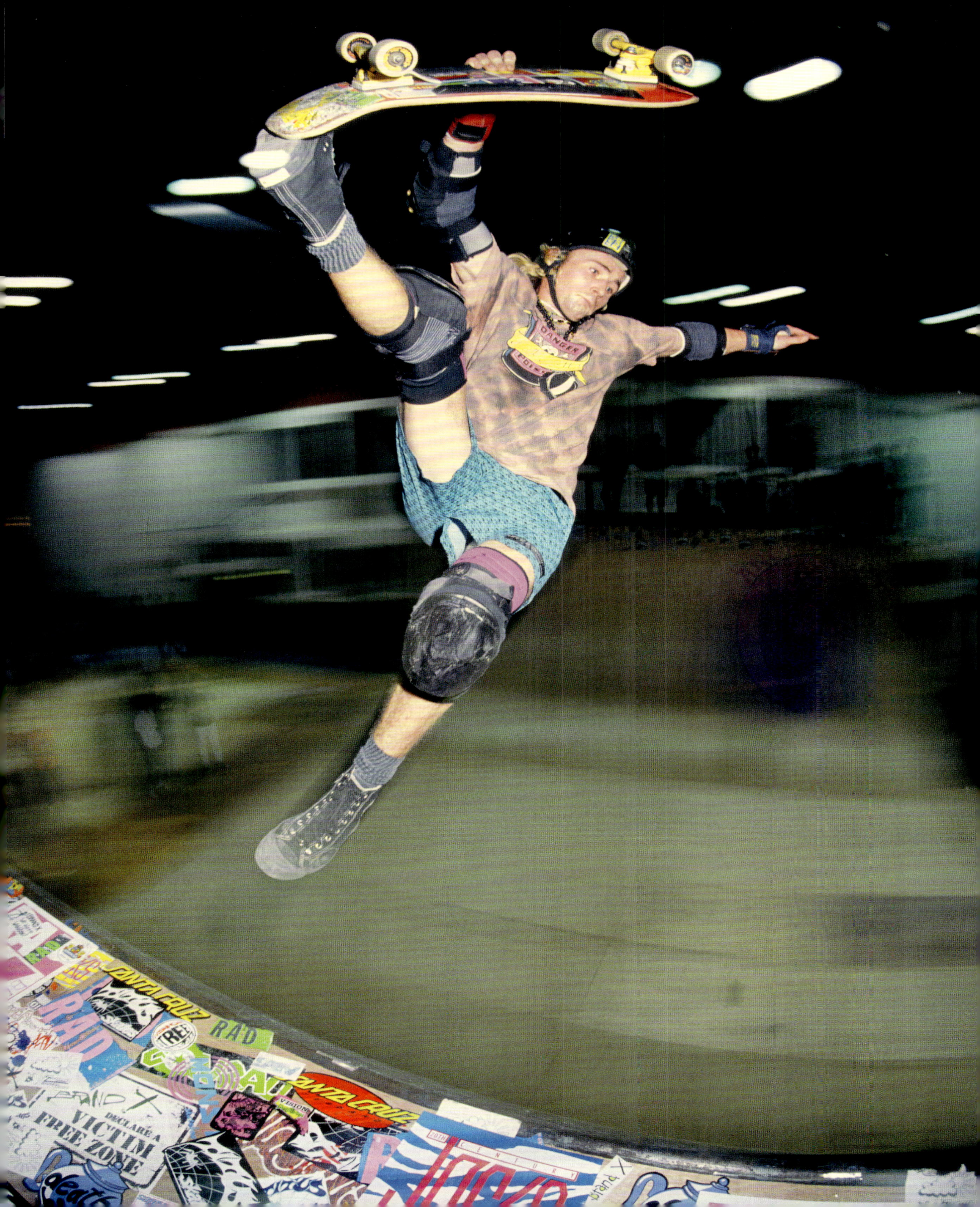

SANTA CRUZ
RAD
RAD
SANTA CRUZ
RAD
BRAND X
DECLARE A
VICTIM
FREE ZONE
brand X

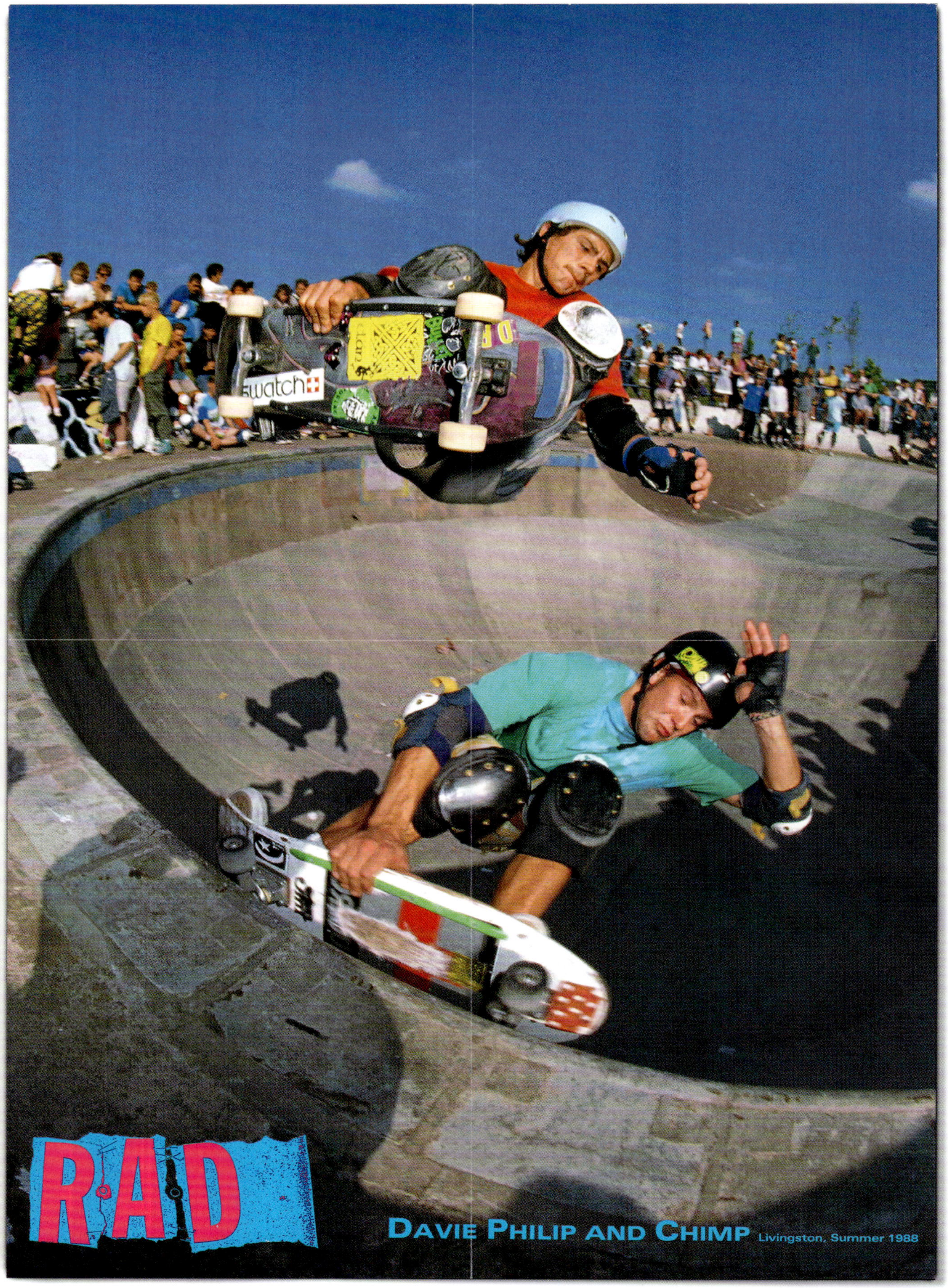

Left: Davie Philip and David 'Chimp' Robertson **Photo:** TLB **Opposite:** Tommy Guerrero, Goshen, Manchester, 1989 **Photo:** Mike John

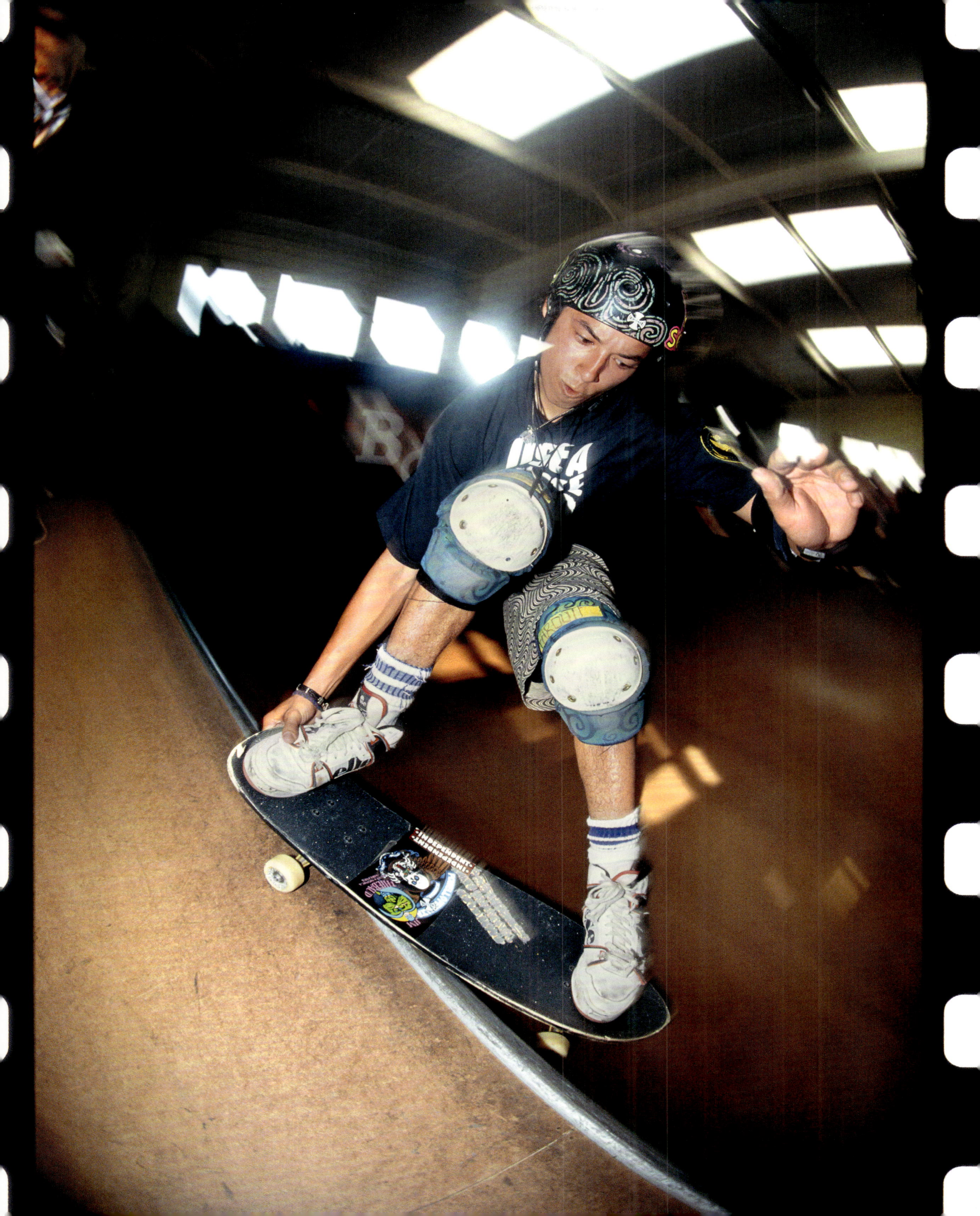

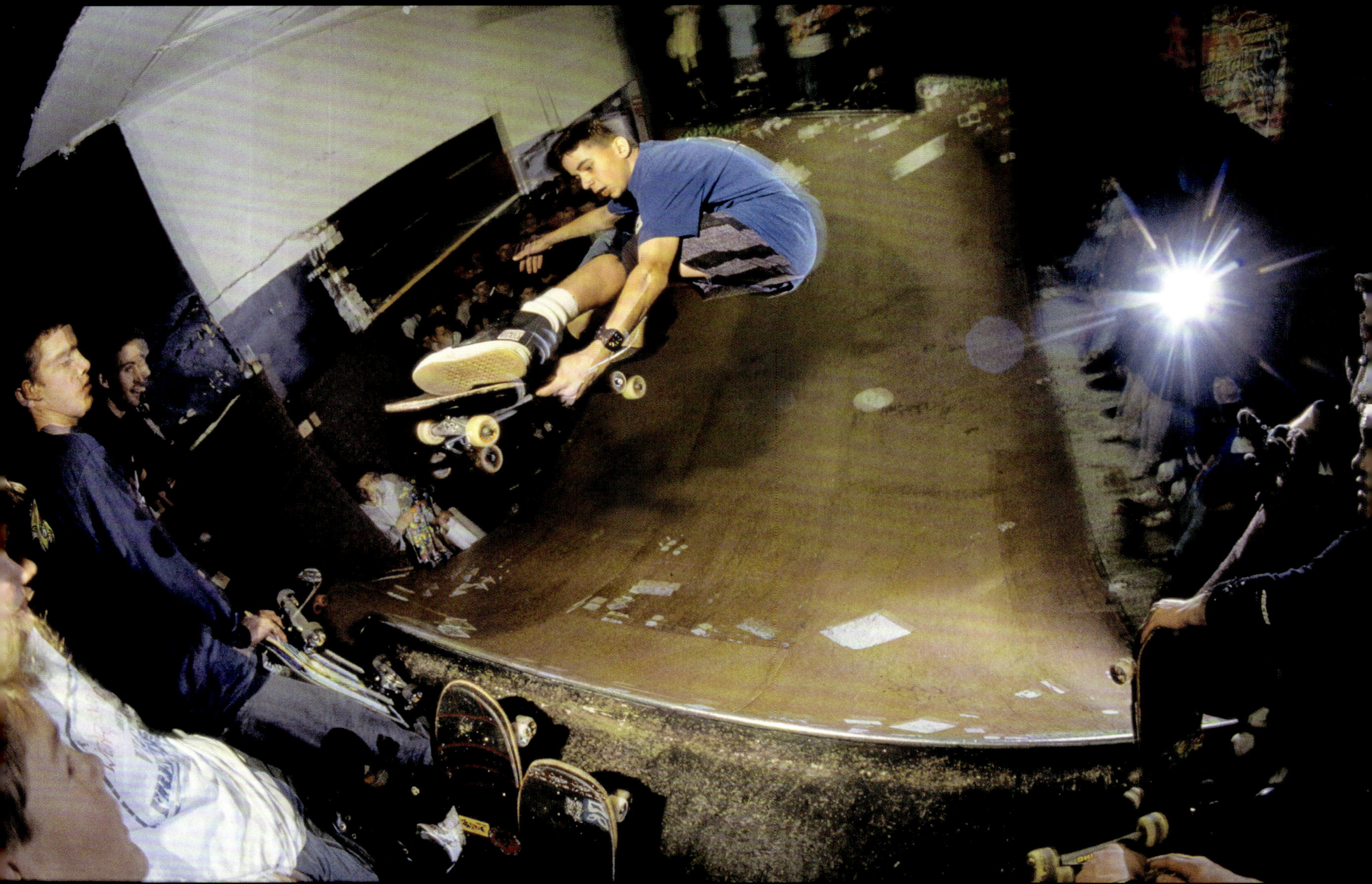

Opposite: Carl Shipman, Rollersnakes shop contest, Nottingham, 1990
Below: Brooklands, 1989 **Photos:** TLB

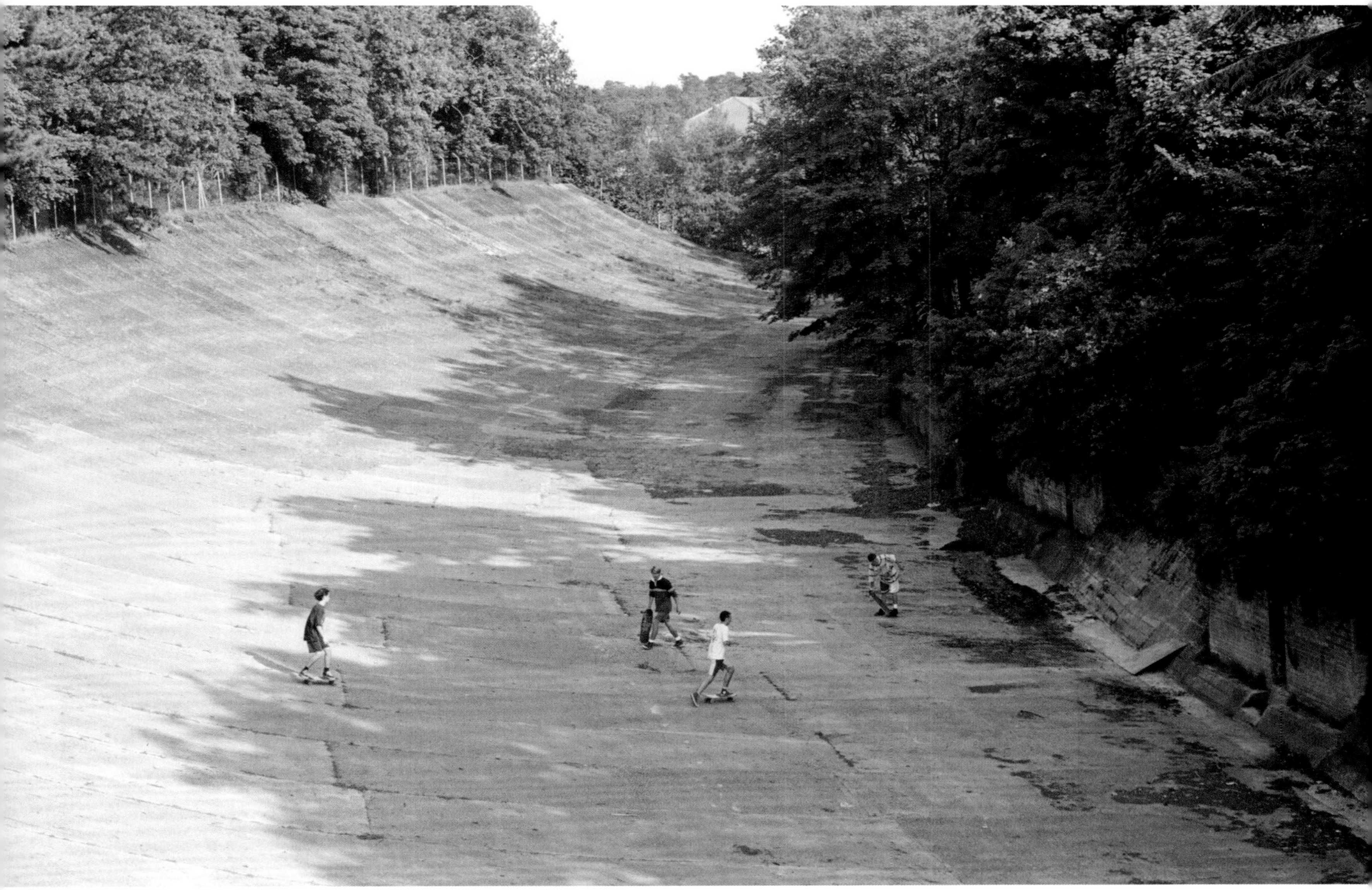

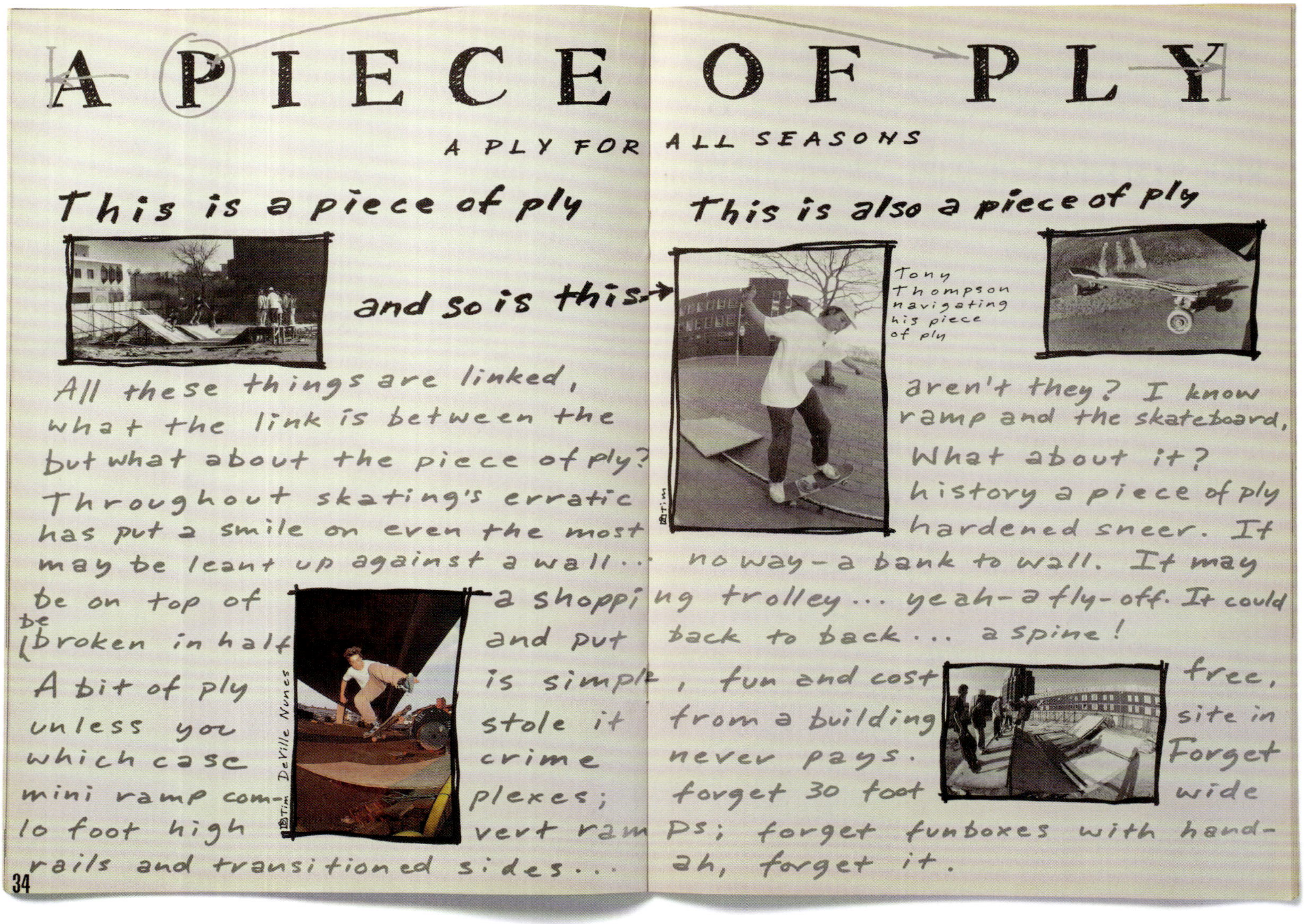

A PIECE OF PLY

A PLY FOR ALL SEASONS

This is a piece of ply

and so is this →

This is also a piece of ply

Tony Thompson navigating his piece of ply

All these things are linked, aren't they? I know what the link is between the ramp and the skateboard, but what about the piece of ply? What about it? Throughout skating's erratic history a piece of ply has put a smile on even the most hardened sneer. It may be leant up against a wall.. no way – a bank to wall. It may be on top of a shopping trolley... yeah – a fly-off. It could be broken in half and put back to back... a spine!

A bit of ply is simple, fun and cost free, unless you stole it from a building site in which case crime never pays. Forget mini ramp complexes; forget 30 foot wide 10 foot high vert ramps; forget funboxes with handrails and transitioned sides... ah, forget it.

Tim DeVille Nunes

34

Above: Issue 89, July 1990, graphic design by Ian Roxburgh
Opposite: Basingstoke, 1990
All photos: TLB

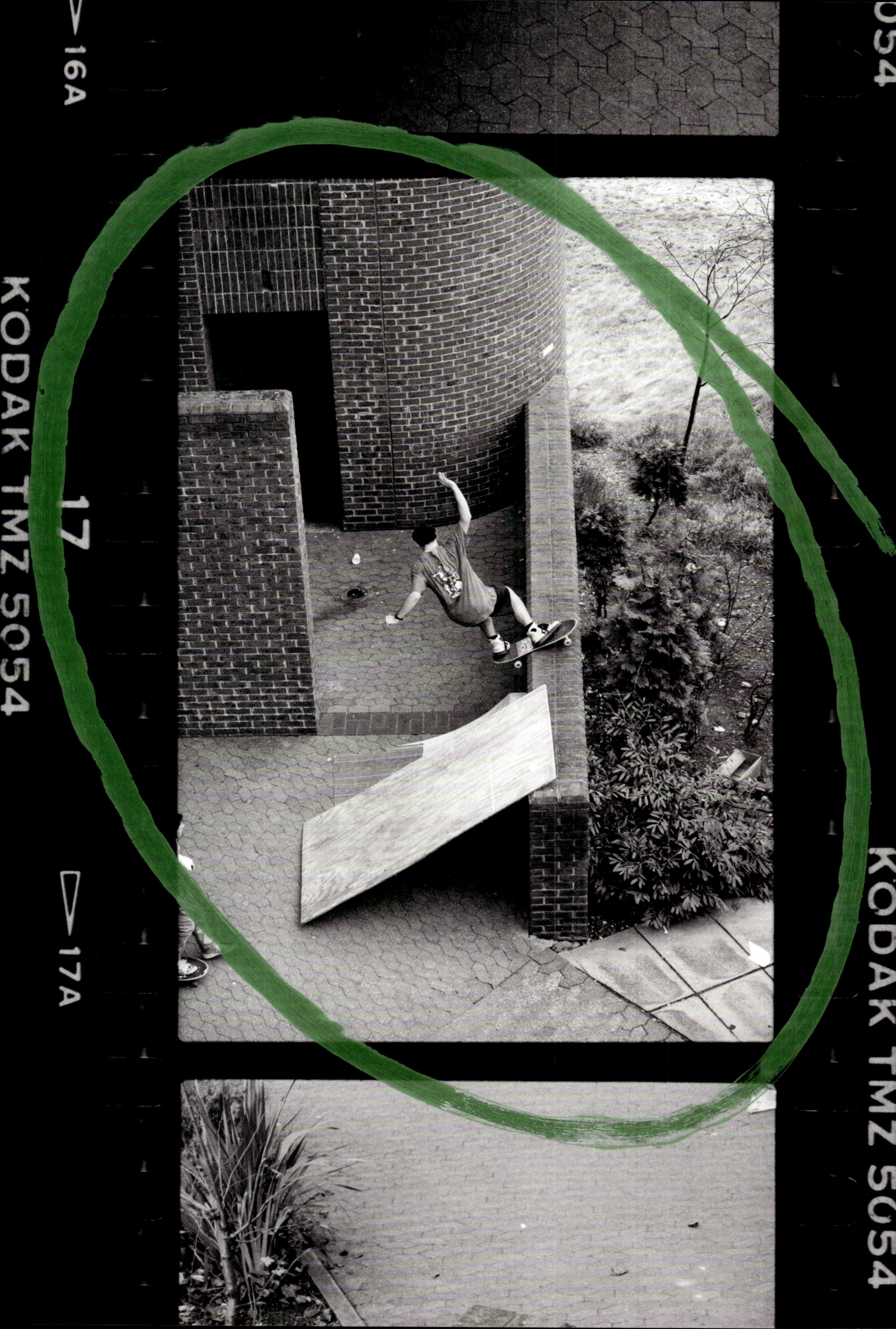

16A
KODAK TMZ 5054
17
17A
KODAK TMZ 5054

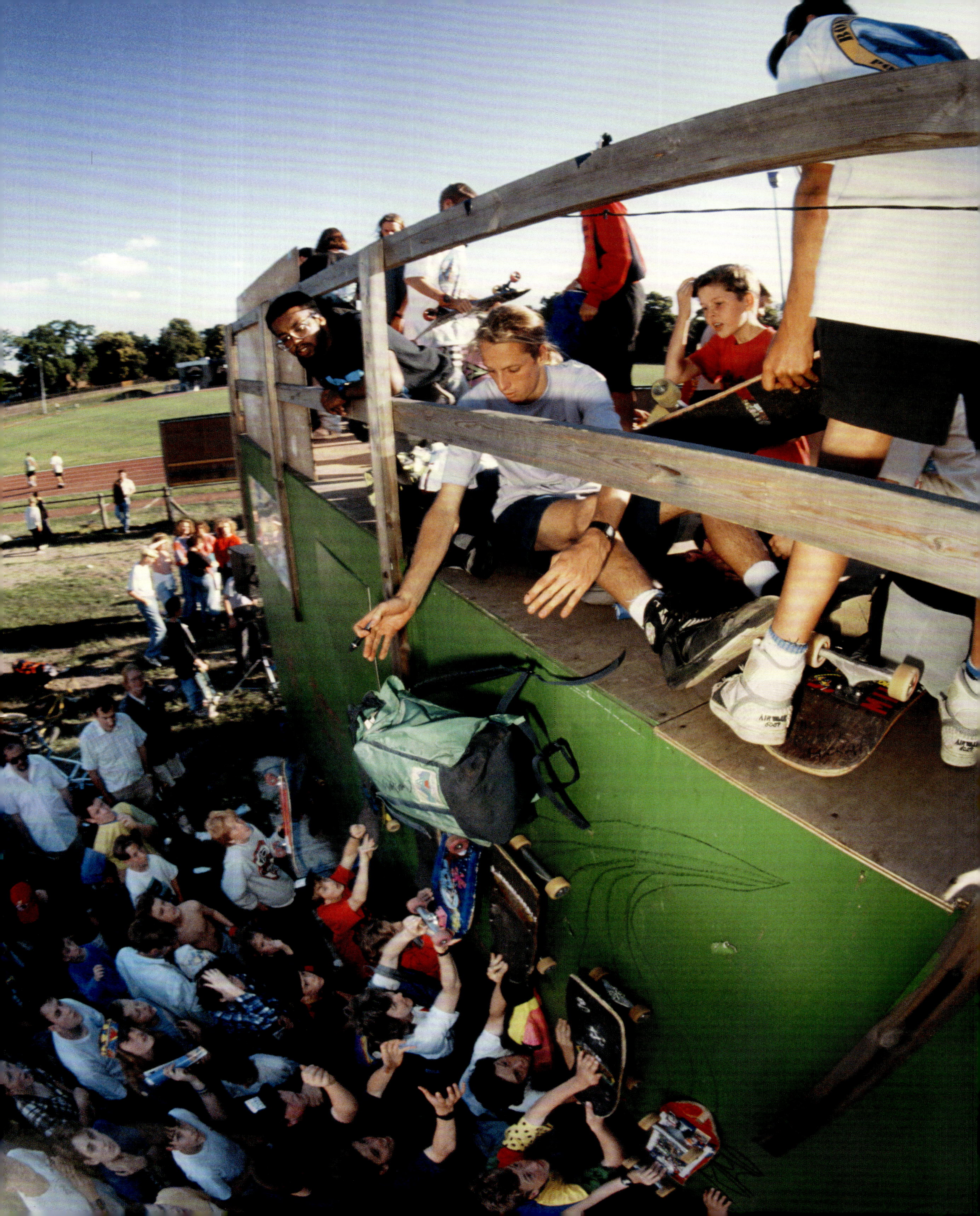

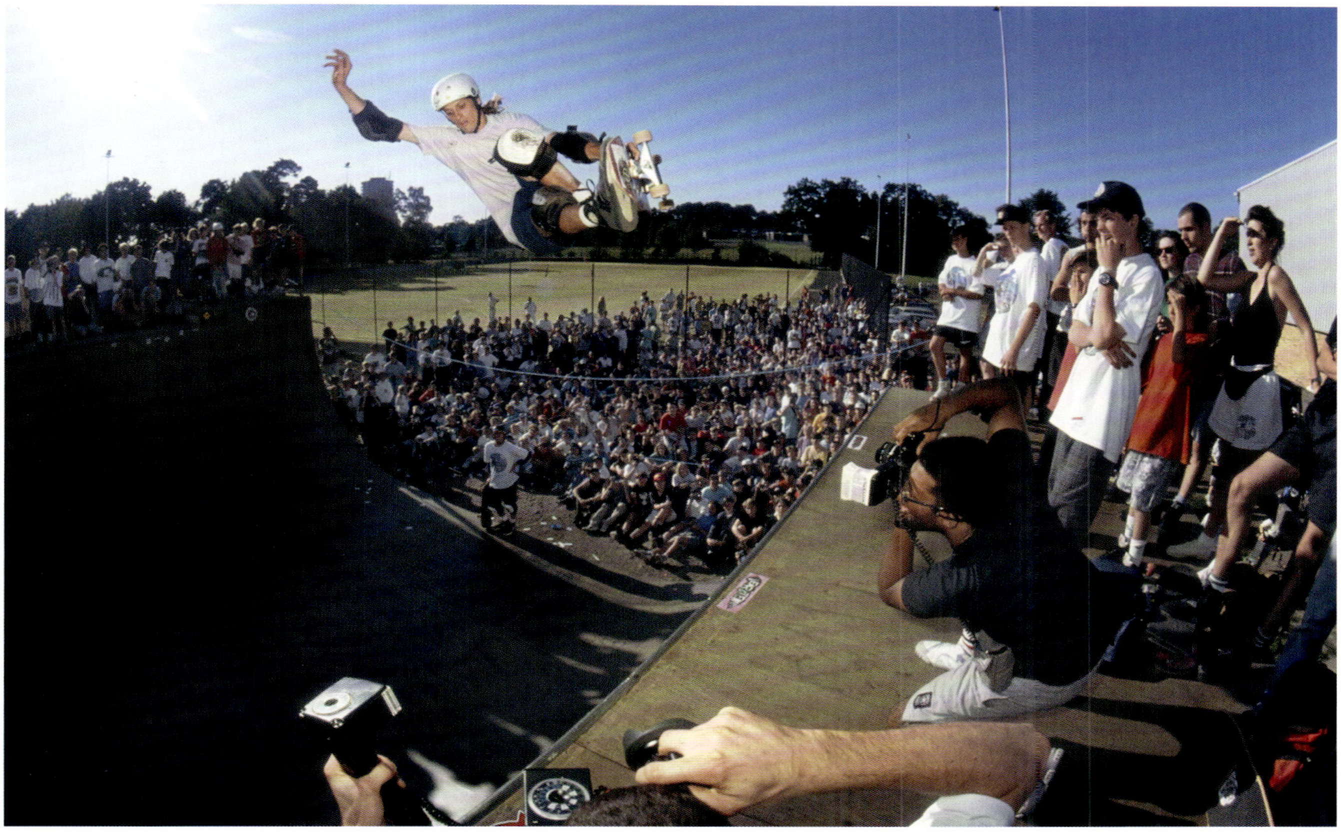

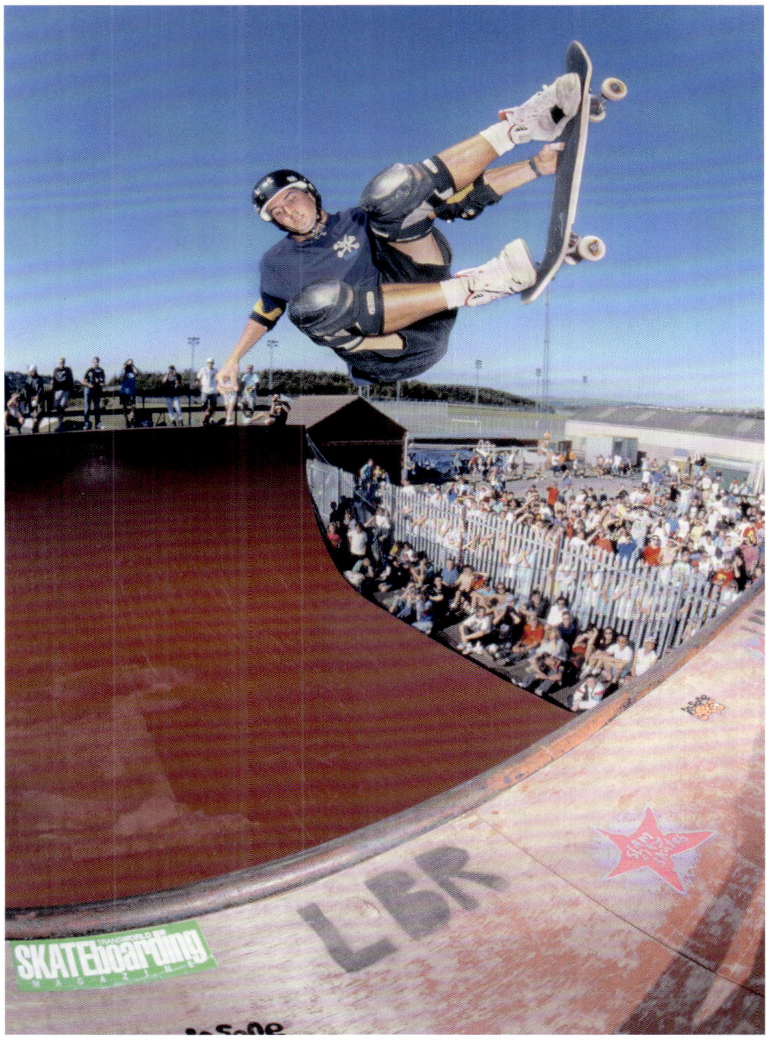

Opposite: Tony Hawk and fans, Bracknell, UK, 1990 **Above:** Tony Hawk, Bones Brigade demo, Bracknell, 1990
Photos: TLB **Right:** Ray Underhill, Bones Brigade demo, Swansea, Wales, 1990
Photo: Paul Sunman
Overleaf left: Curtis McCann, Mike Manzoori and Cookie in the line-up, Goshen contest, 1990, and **right:** Steve 'Wingy' Wilkinson, Goshen contest, 1990
Photos: TLB

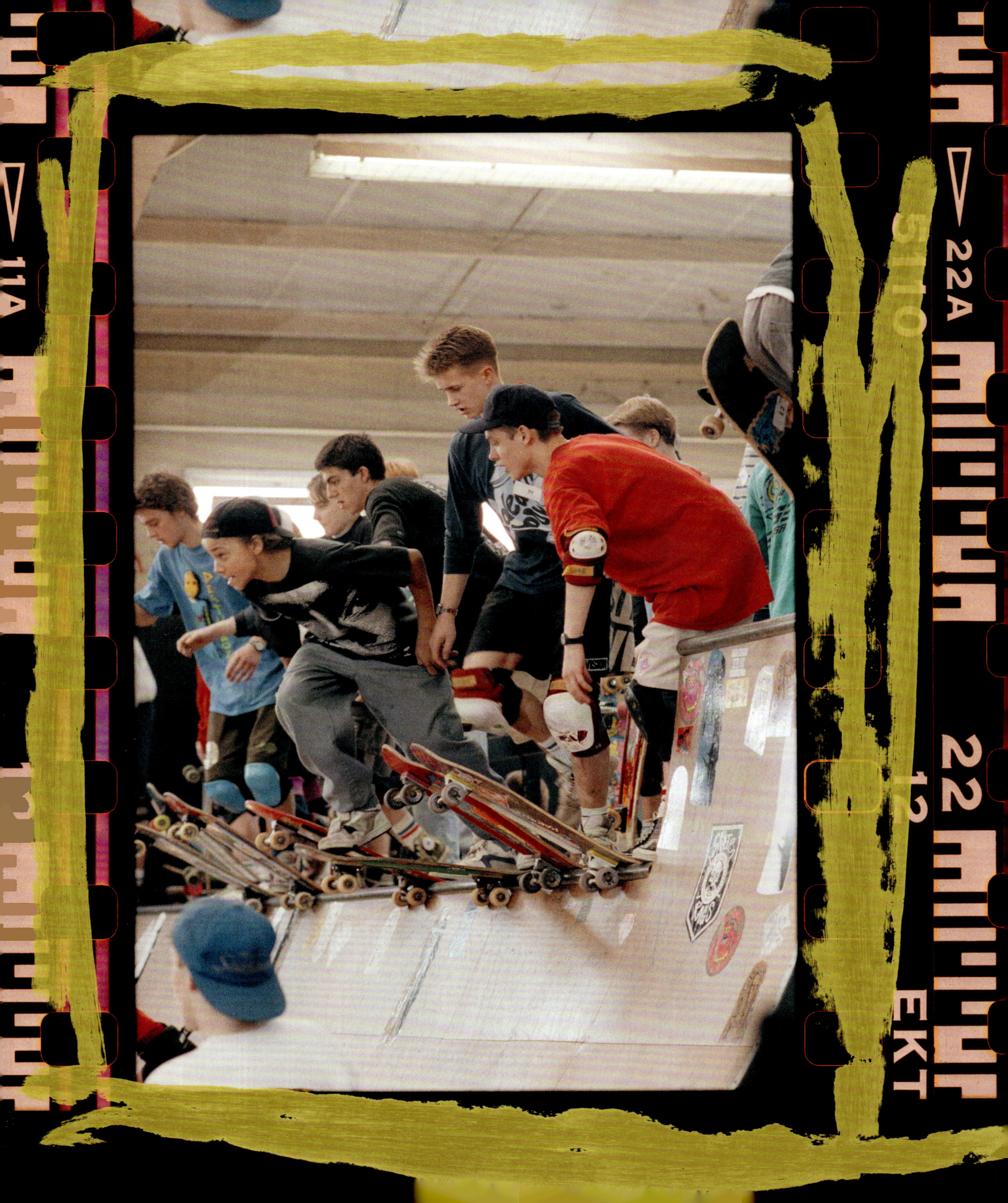

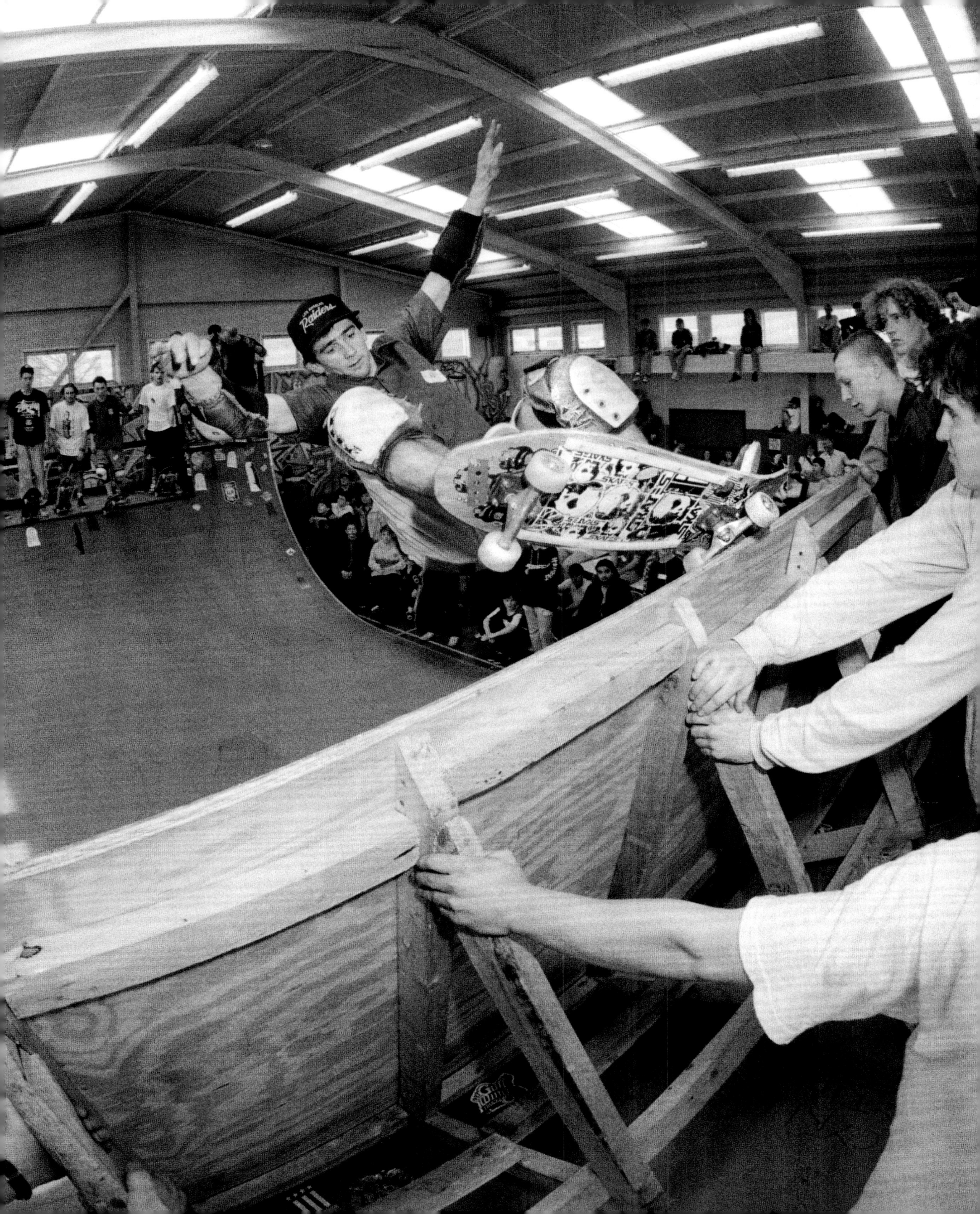
Raiders

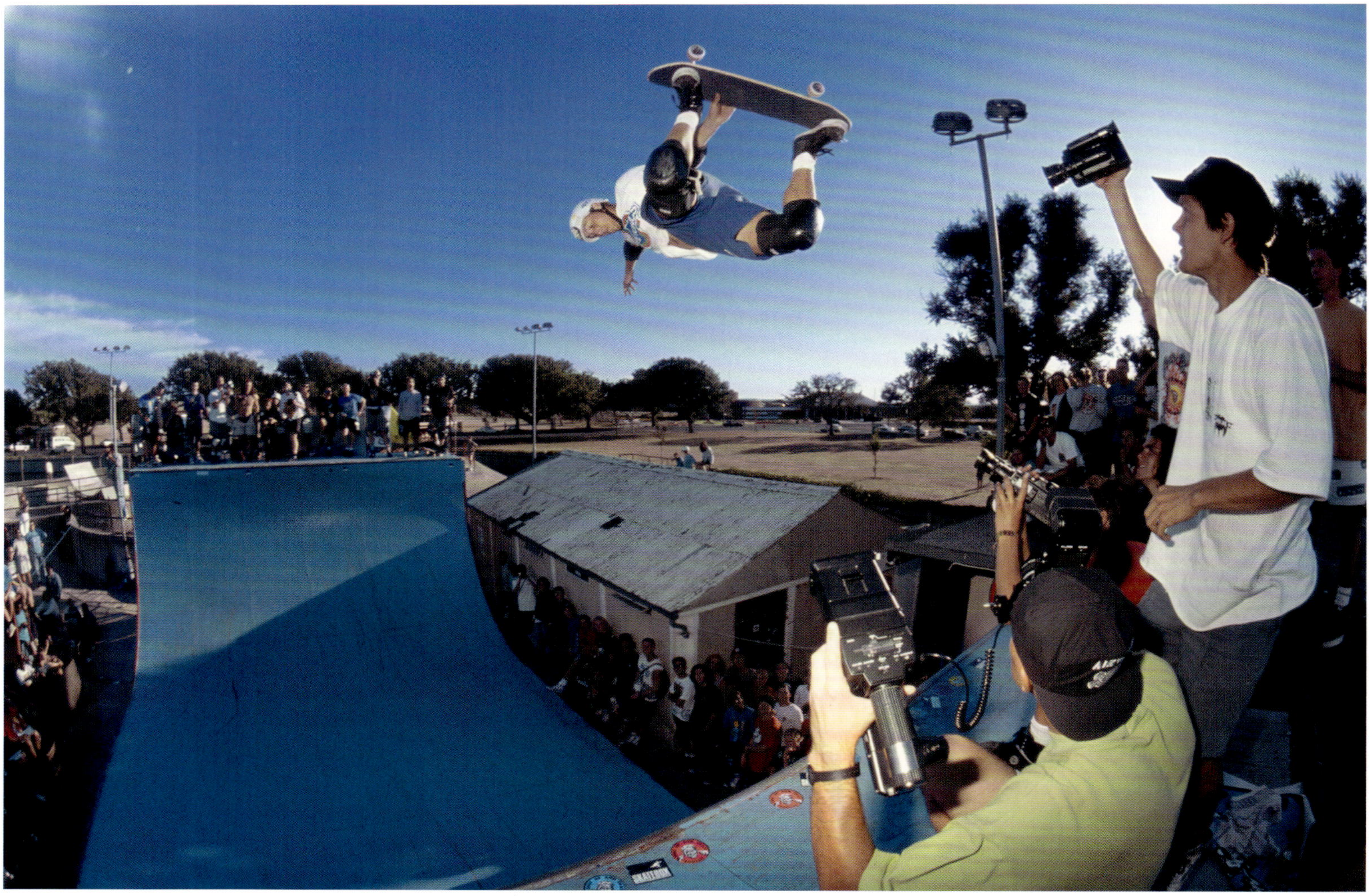

Above: Allen Losi **Opposite:** Craig Johnson, Southsea skatepark, Shut Up And Skate contest, 1990 **Photos:** TLB

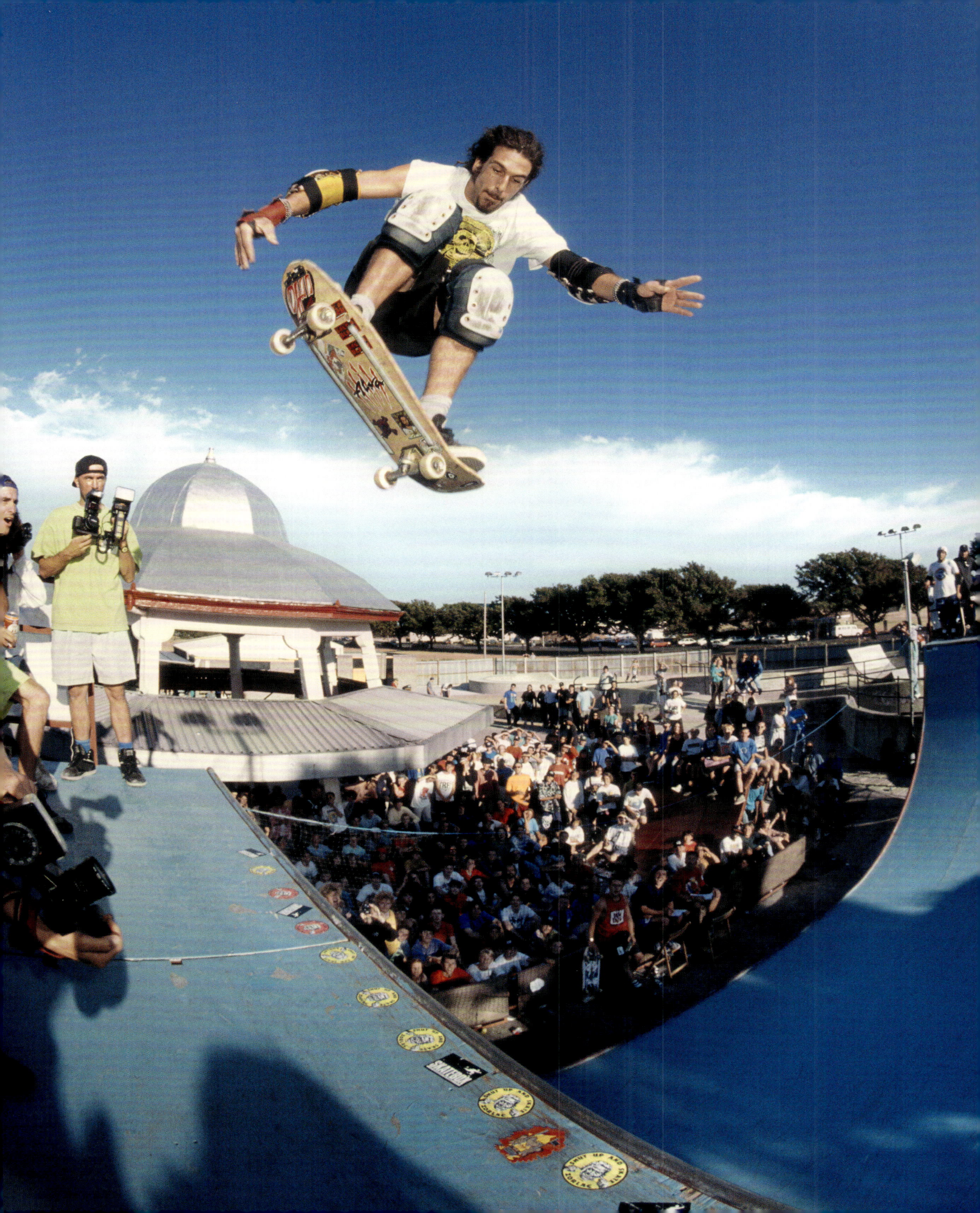

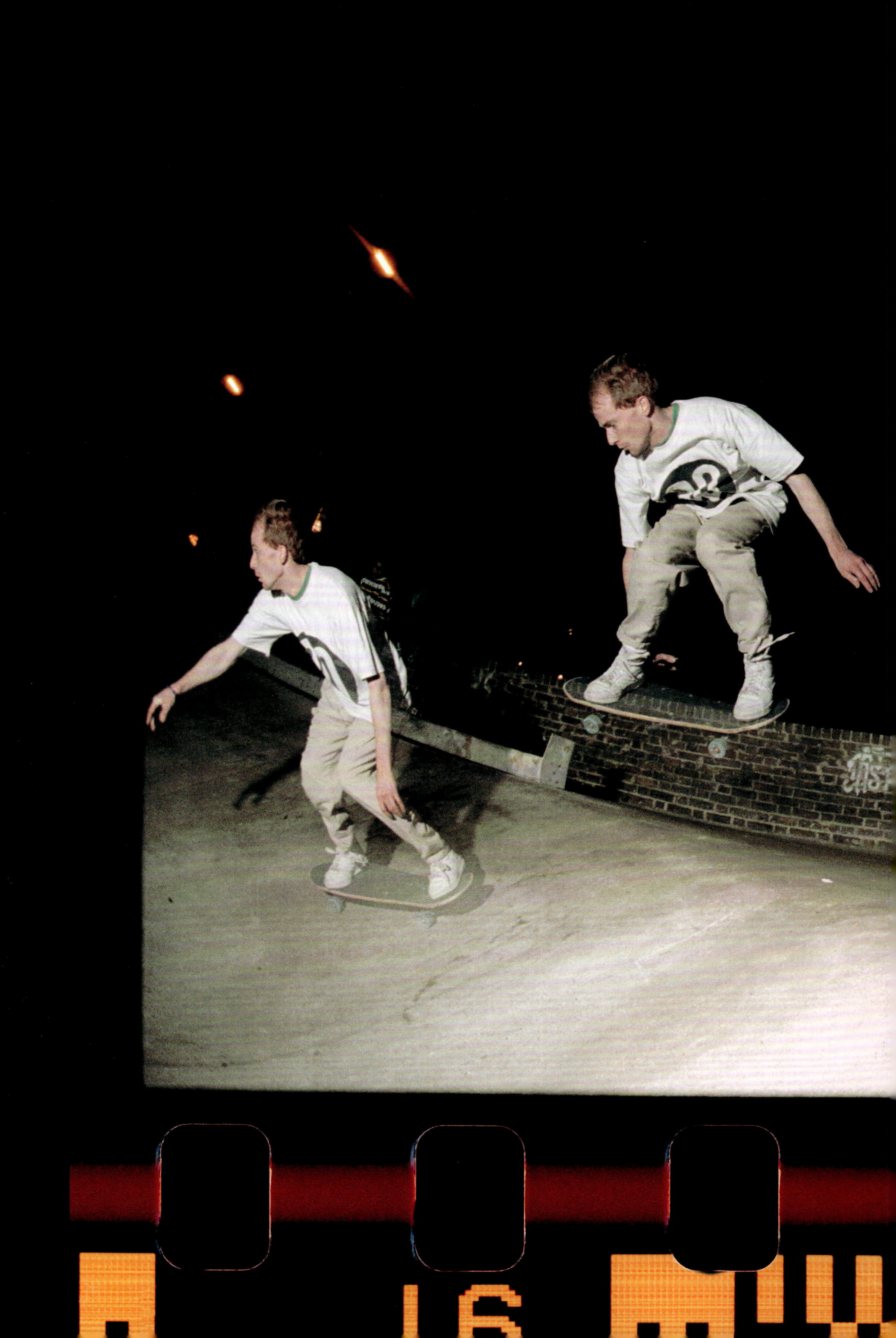

Rob Dukes, Stockwell, London, 1990 **Photo:** TLB

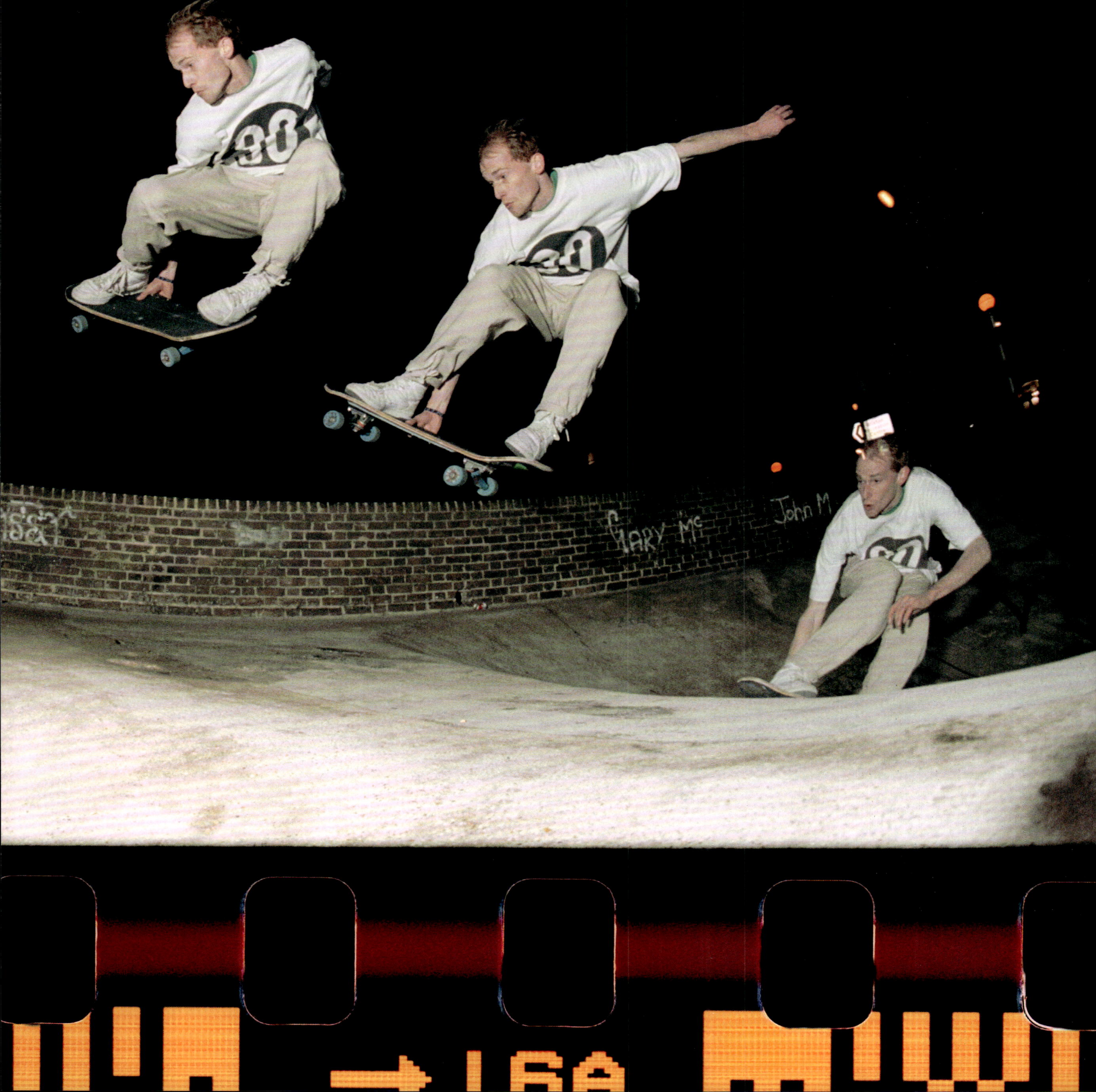
GARY Mc
John M
→16A

Below: Joe Milson's ramp, Newbury, 1990 **Opposite:** Ben Schroeder, Shrewsbury, 1990 **Photos:** TLB

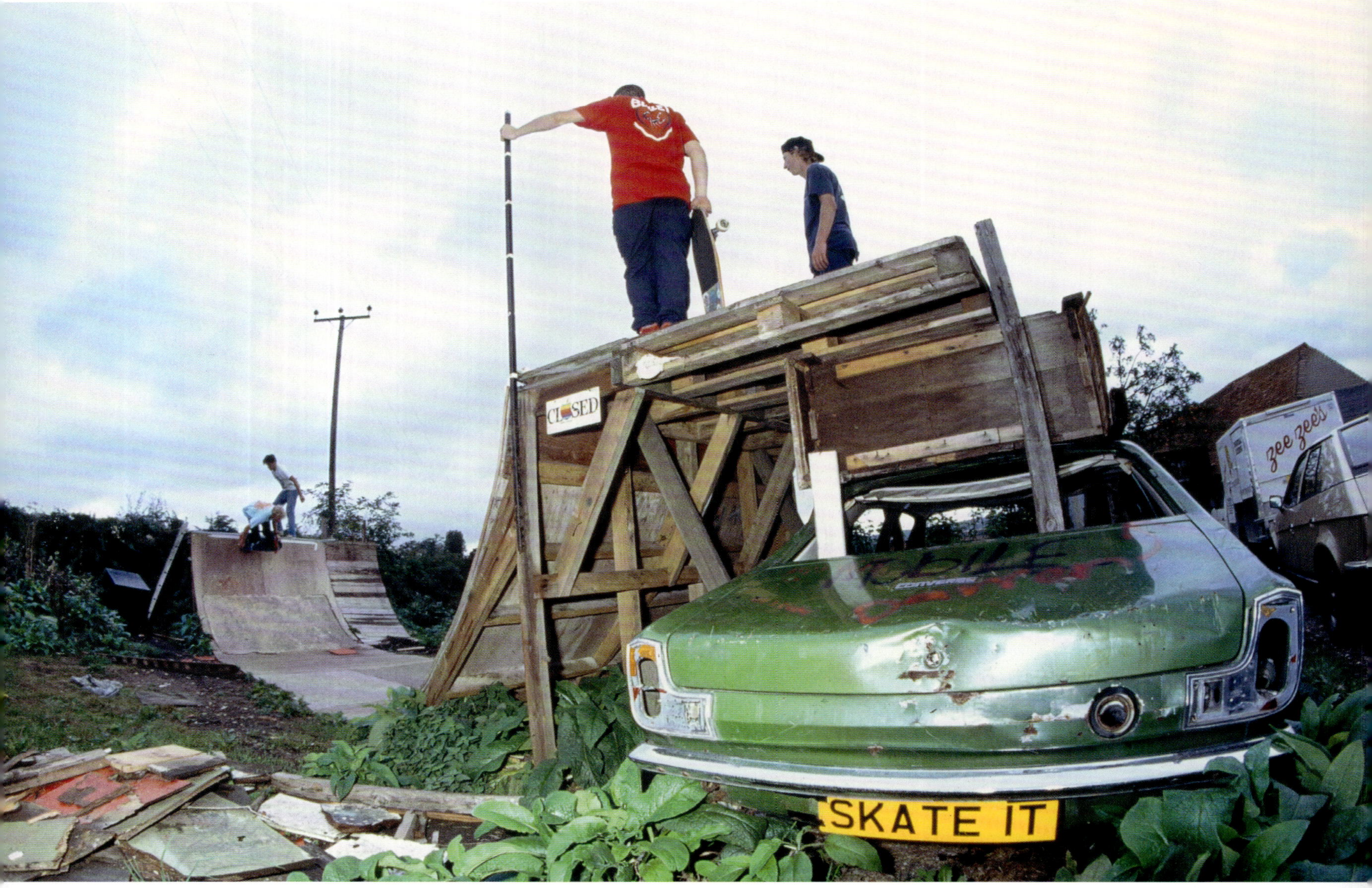

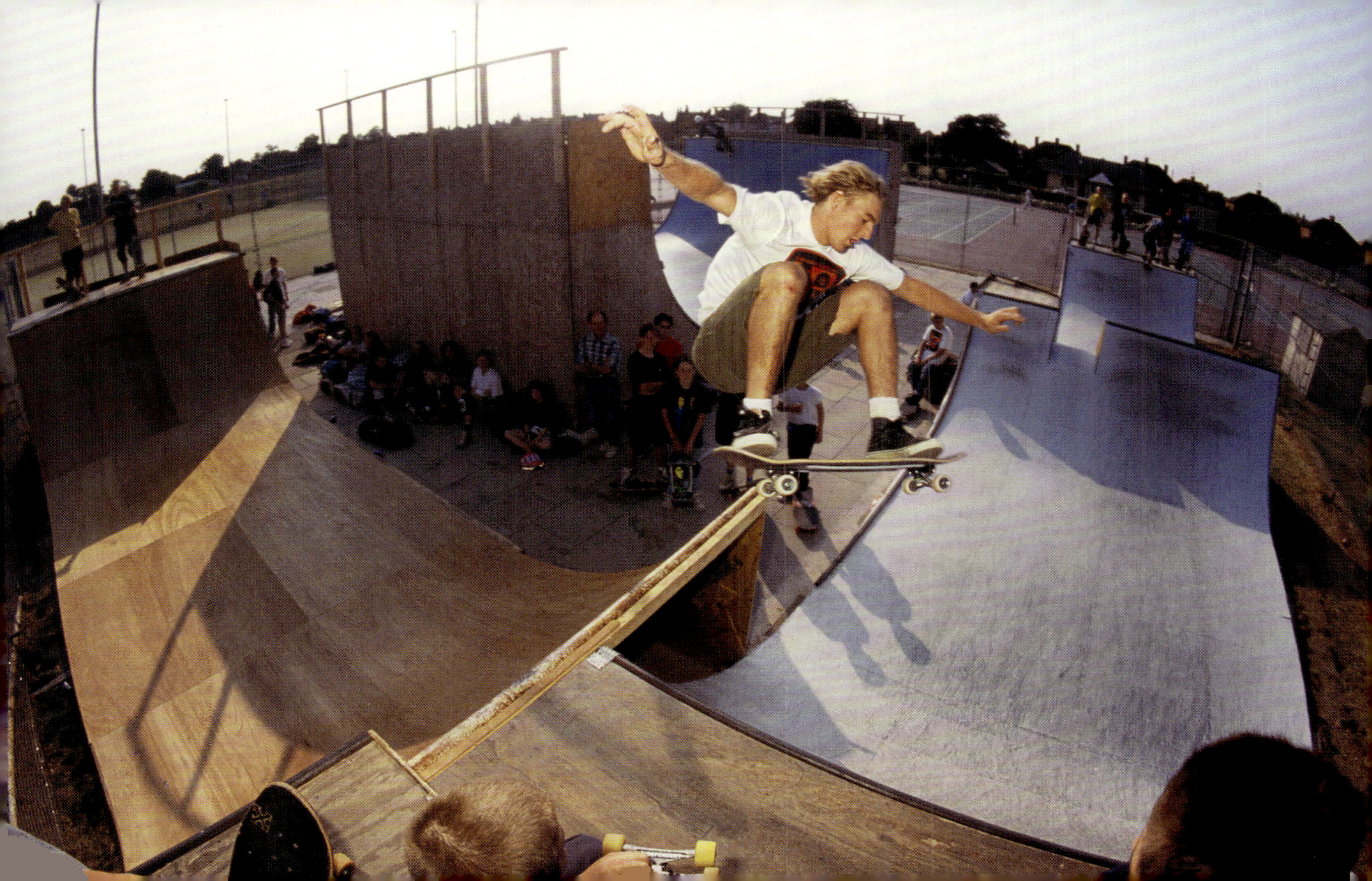

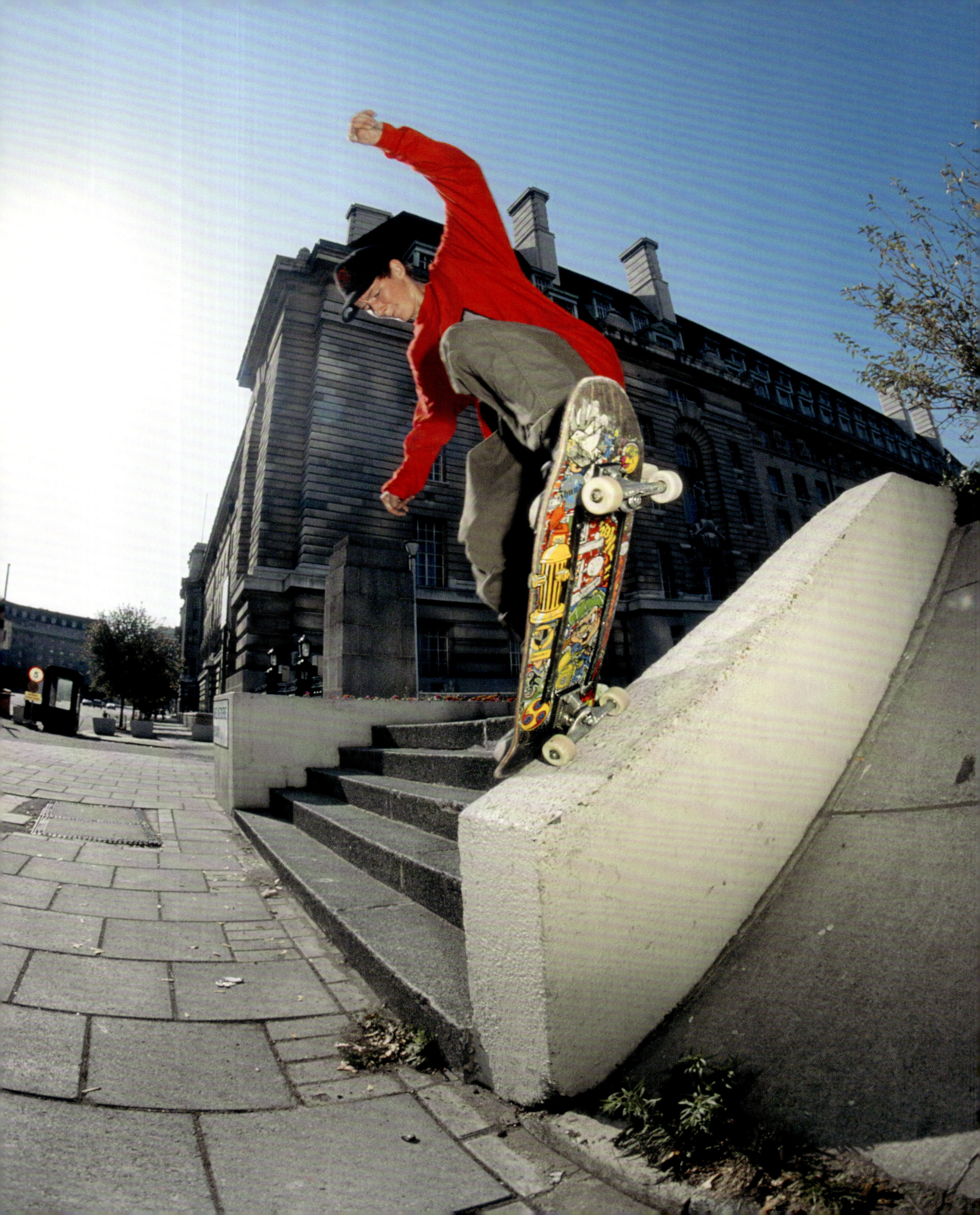

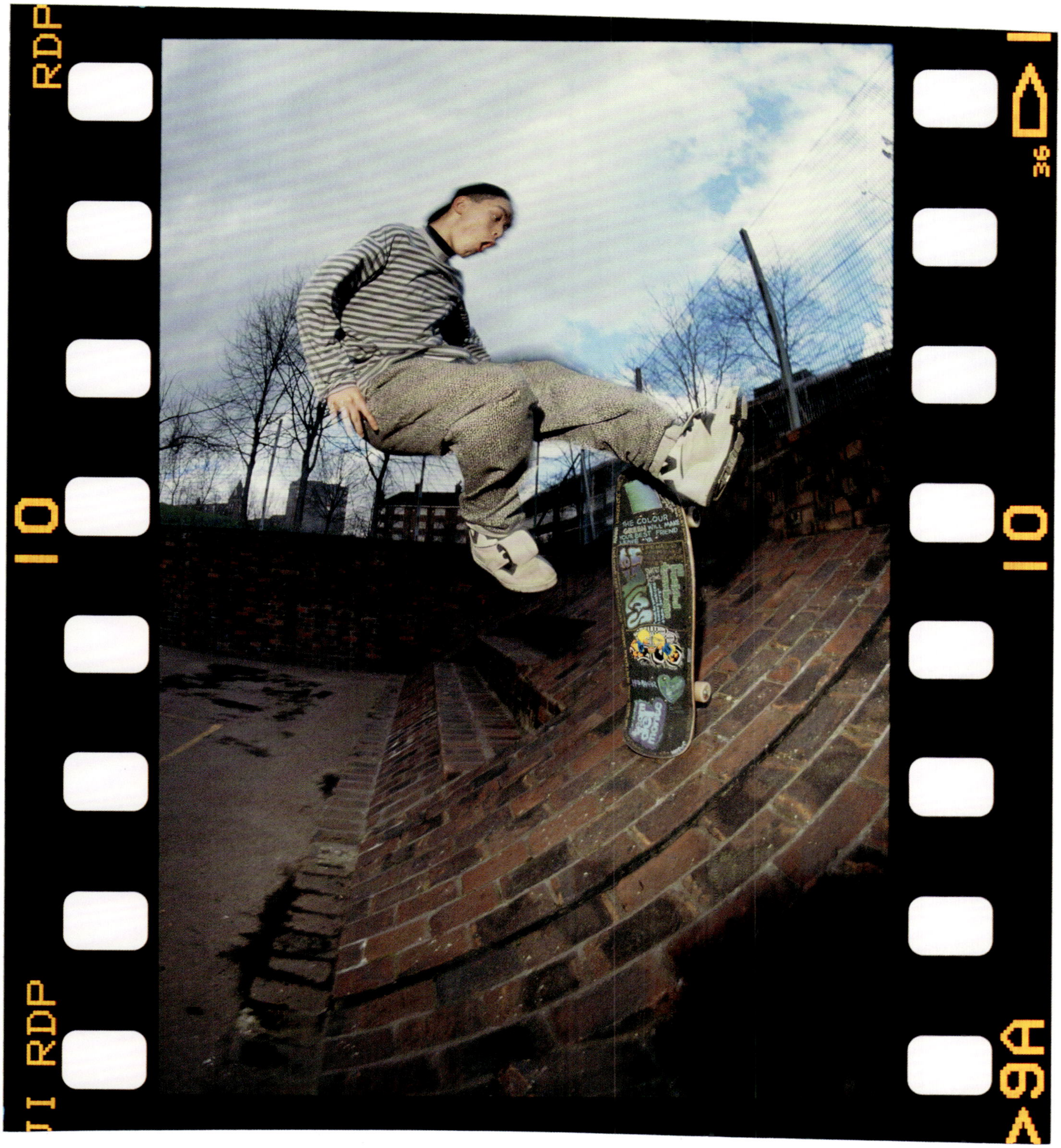

Opposite: Simon Evans, Southbank, 1990 **Right:** Ray Calthorpe, Archway, London, 1990 **Photos:** TLB

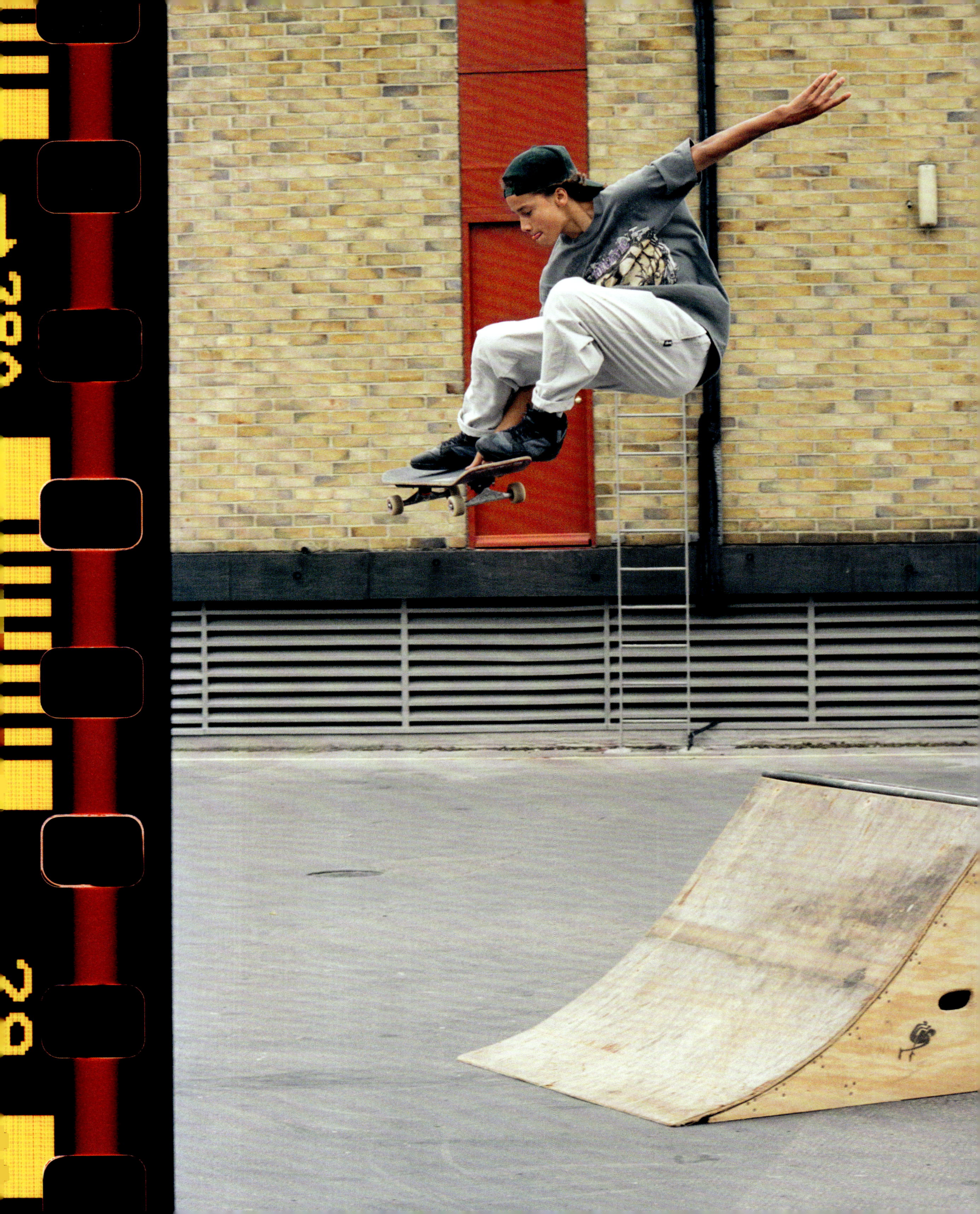

Opposite: Curtis McCann, Orpington, 1990 **Below:** Left to right: Matt McMullen, Curtis McCann, Warren Brown and Winstan Whitter, Orpington, 1990 **Photos:** TLB

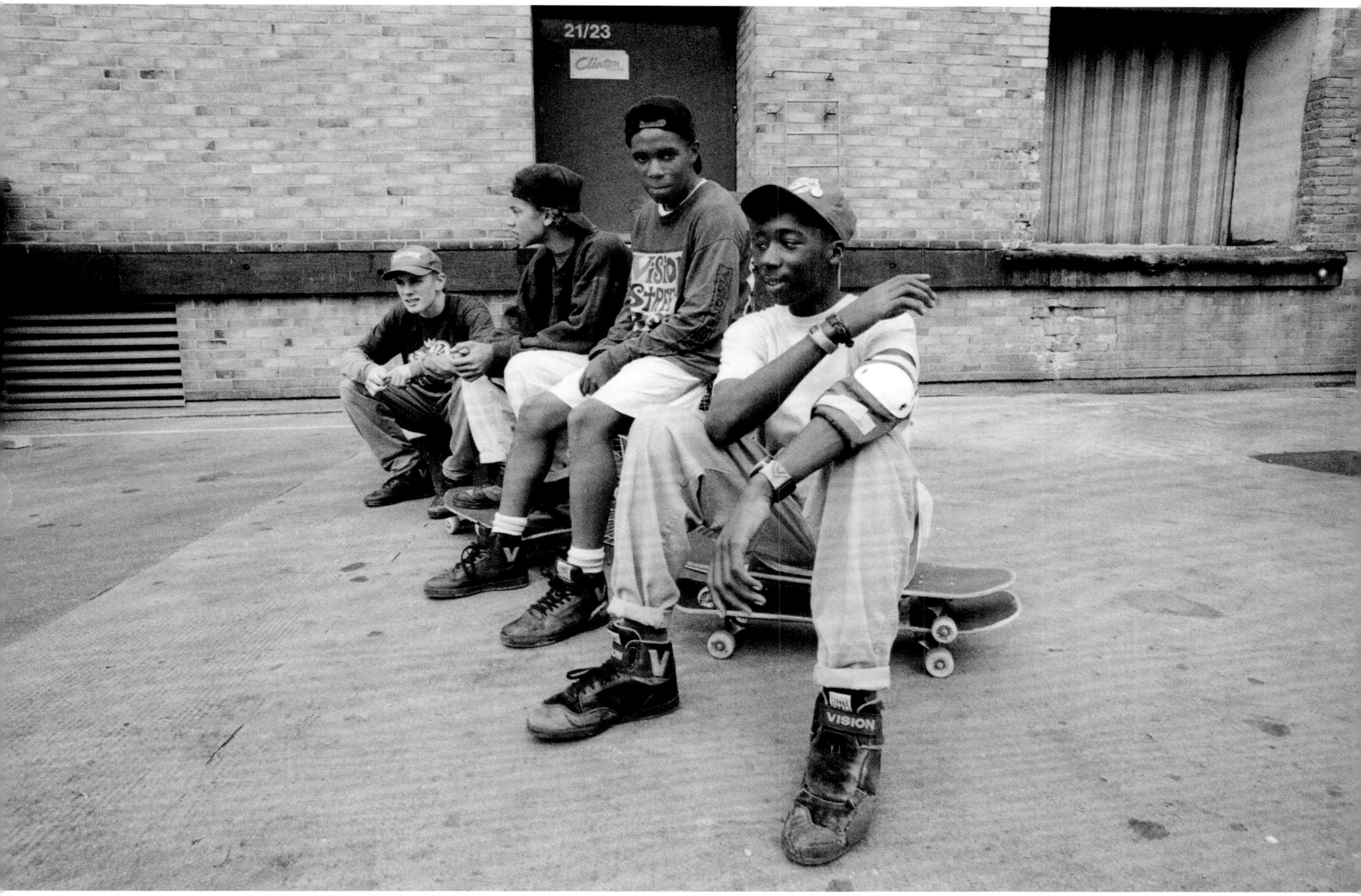

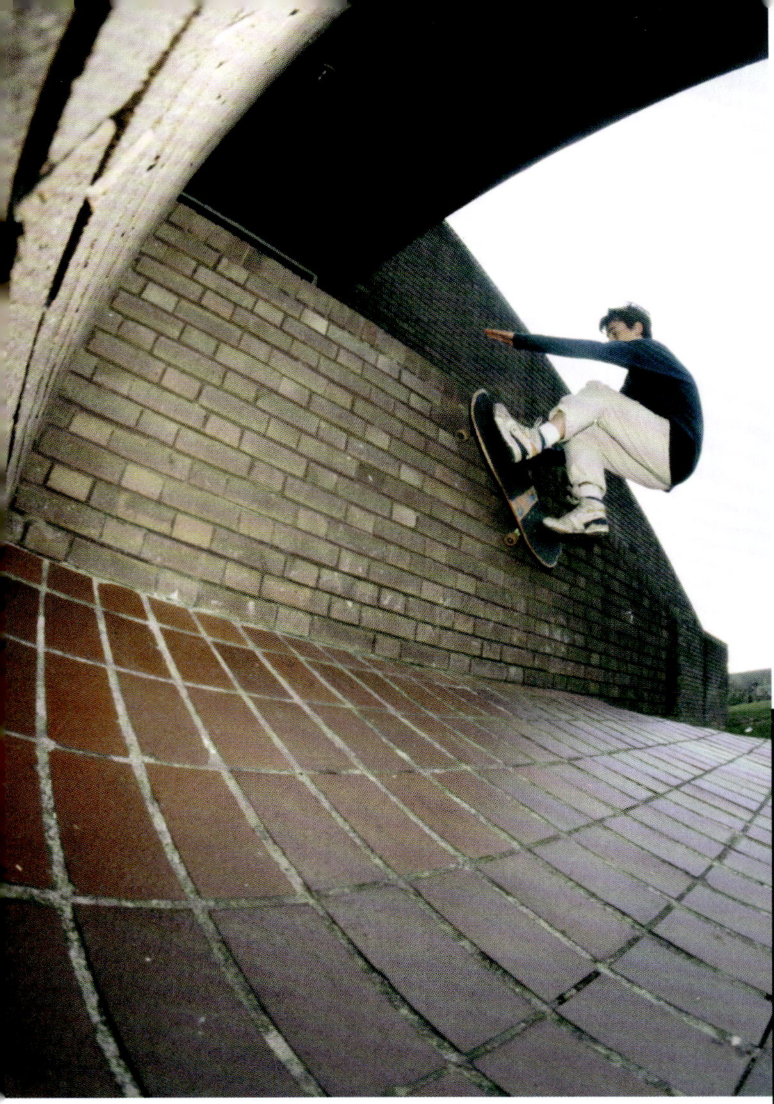

'With street skating, we'd go out with people and find spots around London. Maybe Ged had written a story and we'd go out to shoot photos around his idea that might involve looking at the environment in a different way. I always liked shooting things like that, stuff that was related to skateboarding but wasn't actual shots of skateboarding—random pedestrians and scuff marks on benches—things you'd notice if you were a skater. It's the idea of a city as a playground, finding things in the environment that were almost like skateparks. Street skating in a hall is different; it's obstacle skating.'

Vernon Adams

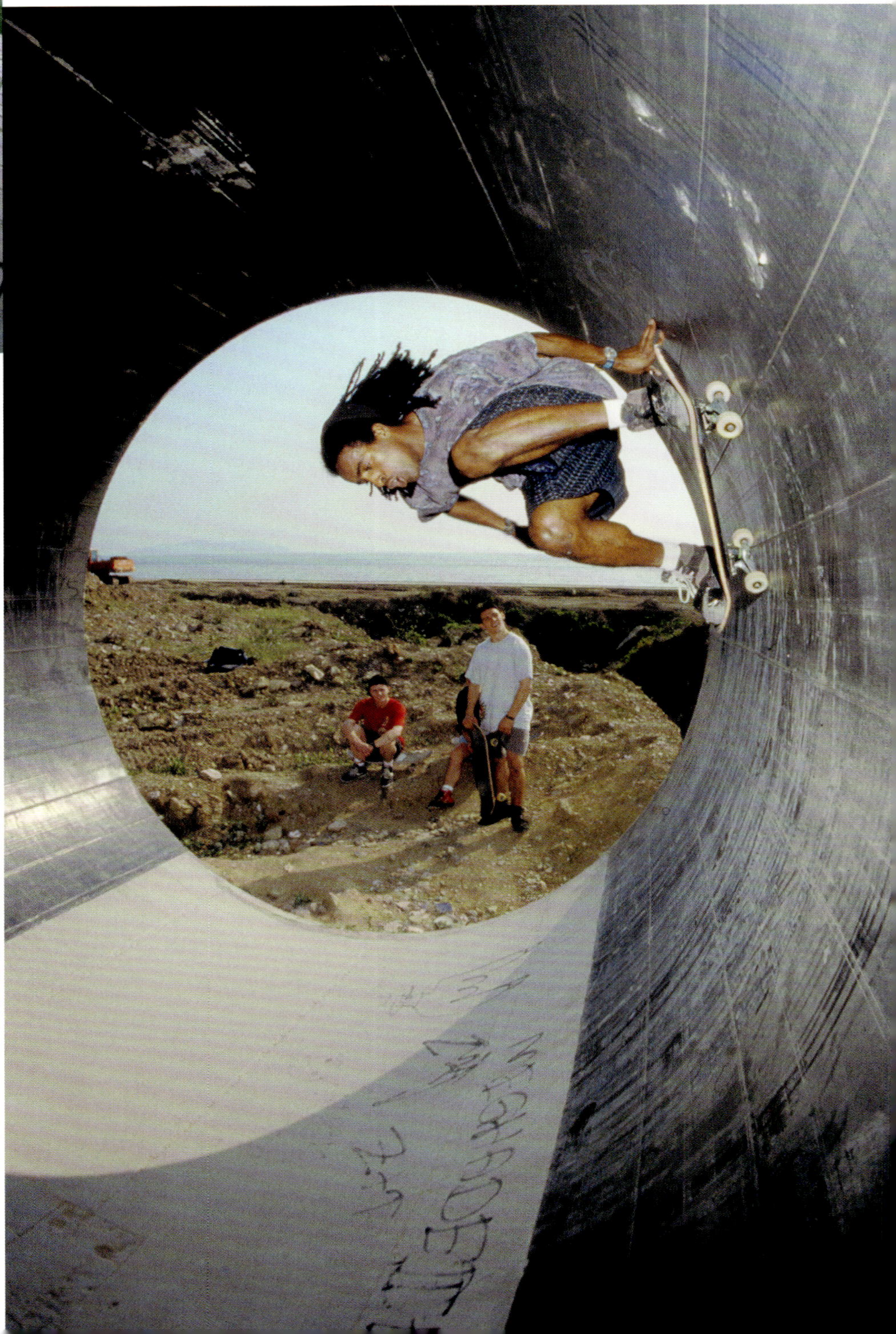

Above: Biddick banks, Tyne and Wear, 1990 **Right:** Neil Danns, Turkey, 1991 **Photo:** Shane Rouse **Opposite top:** Ged Wells, London, 1990, and **bottom:** Davy Van Laere, Broadmarsh banks, Nottingham, 1990 **Photos:** TLB

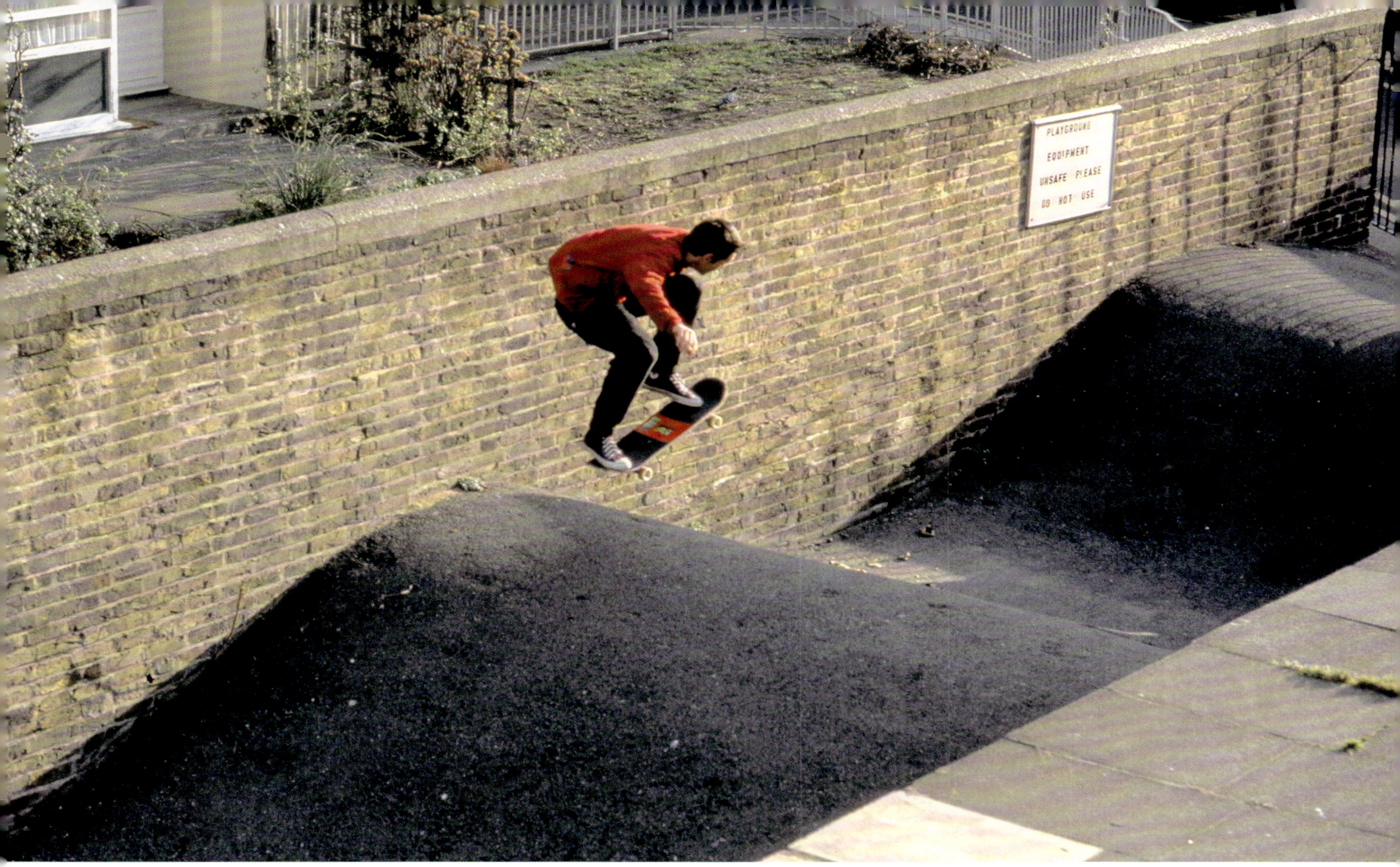
PLAYGROUND
EQUIPMENT
UNSAFE PLEASE
DO NOT USE

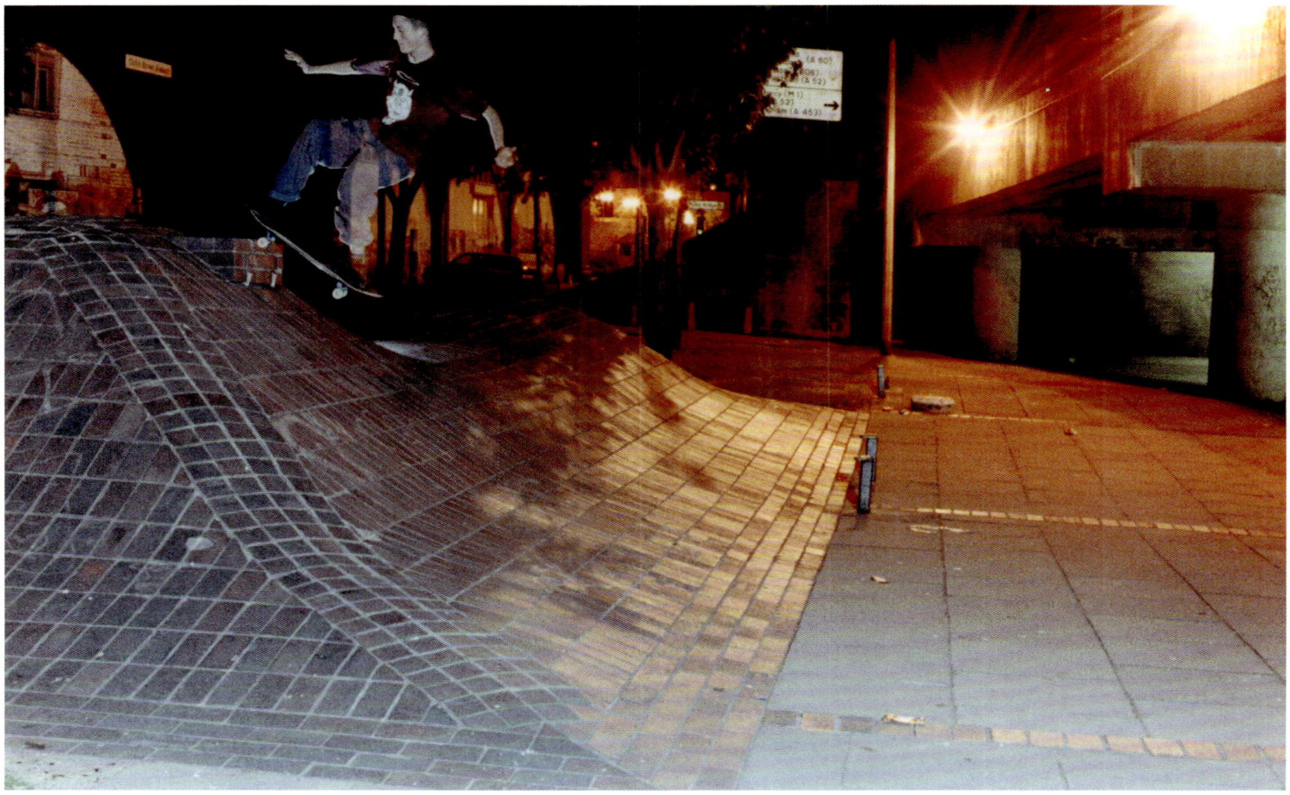

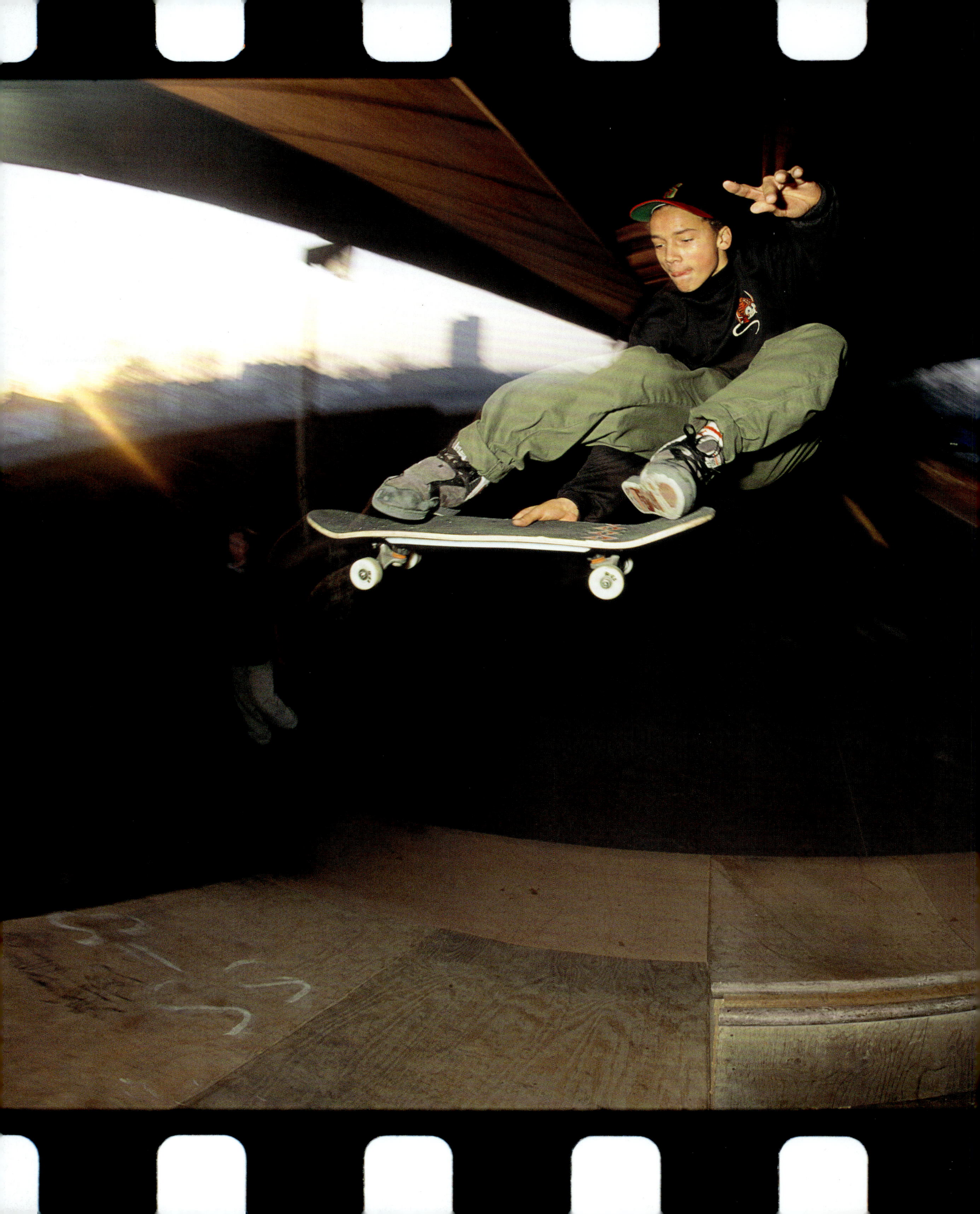

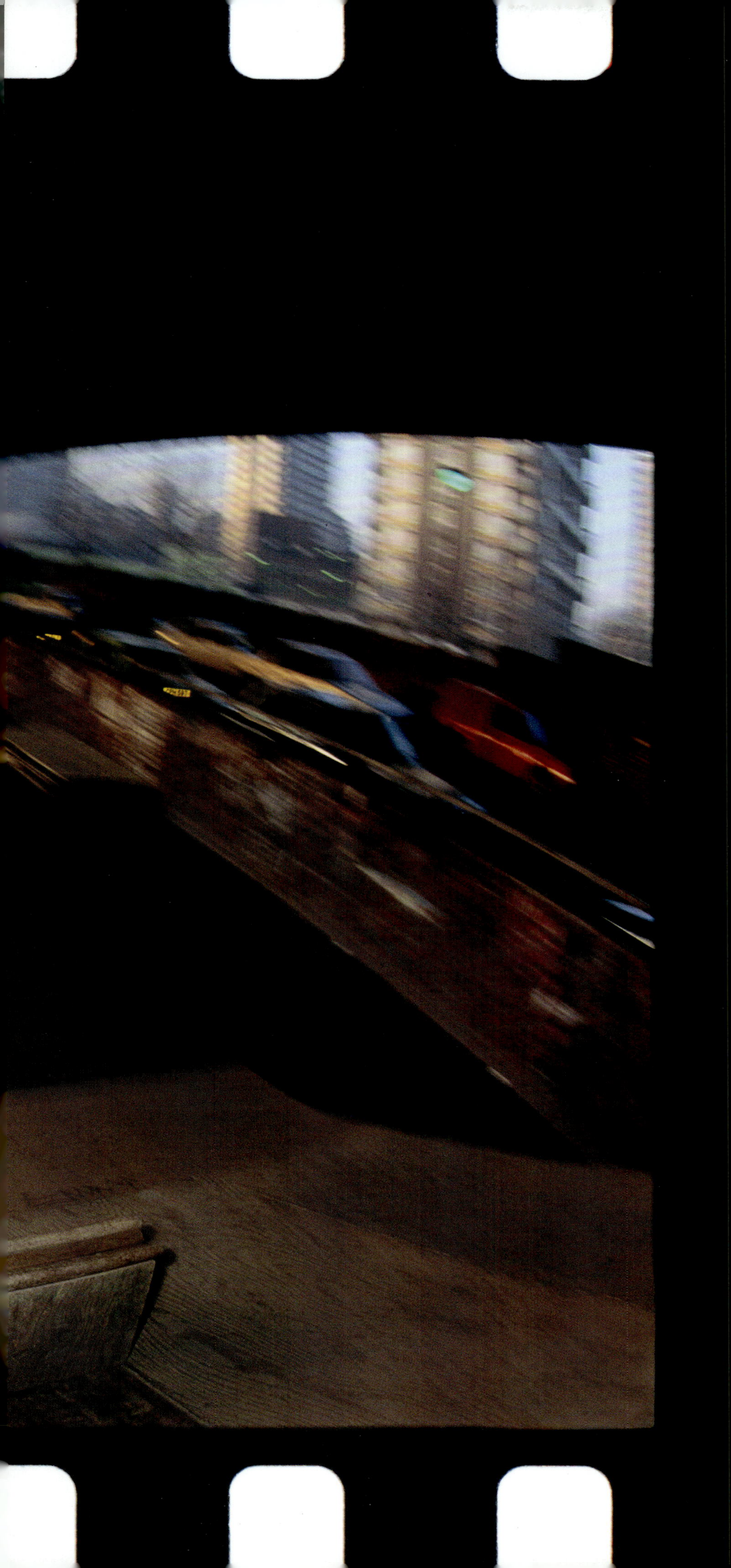

Curtis McCann, Meanwhile 2, London, 1990 **Photo:** TLB

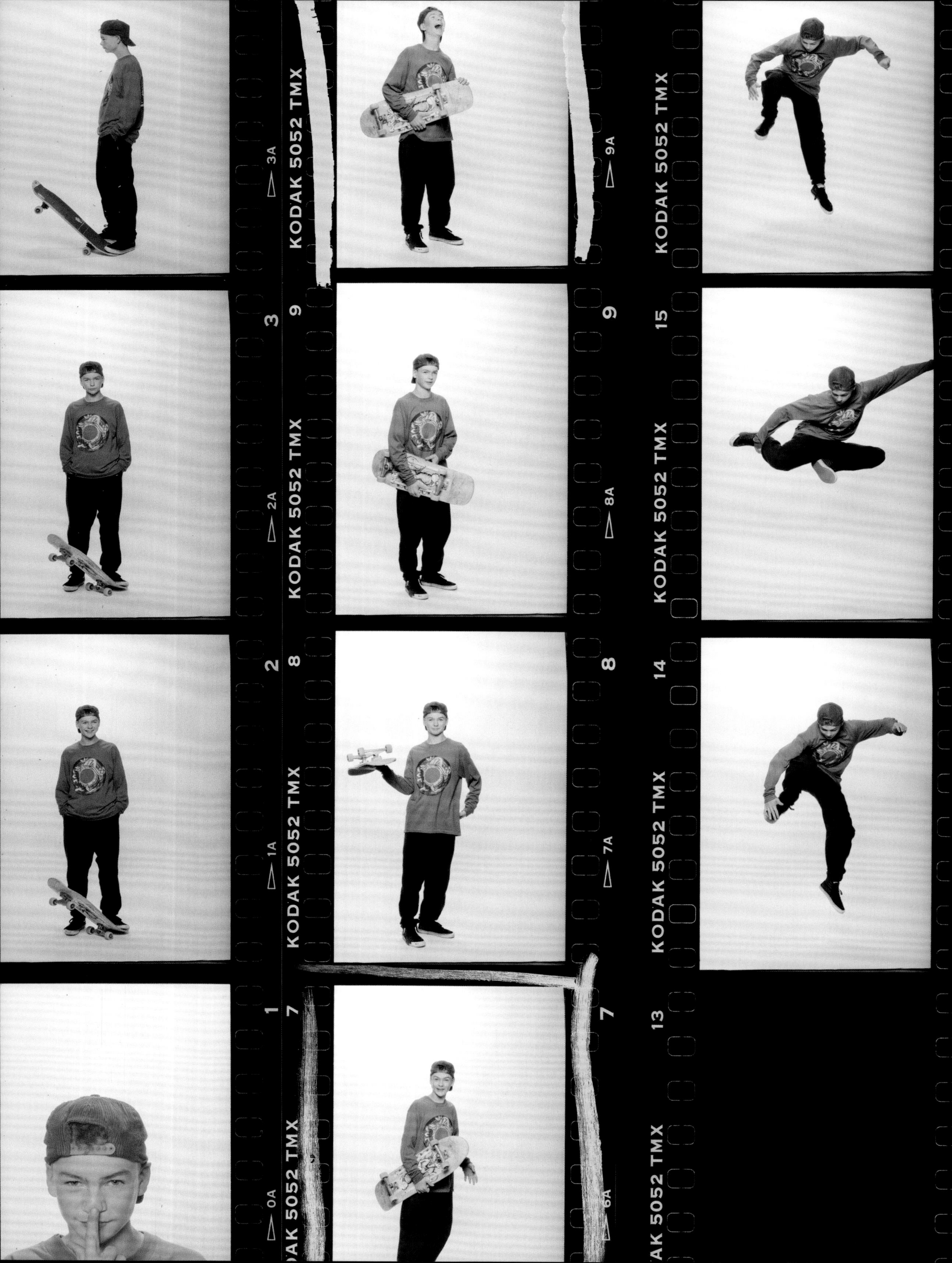
KODAK 5052 TMX

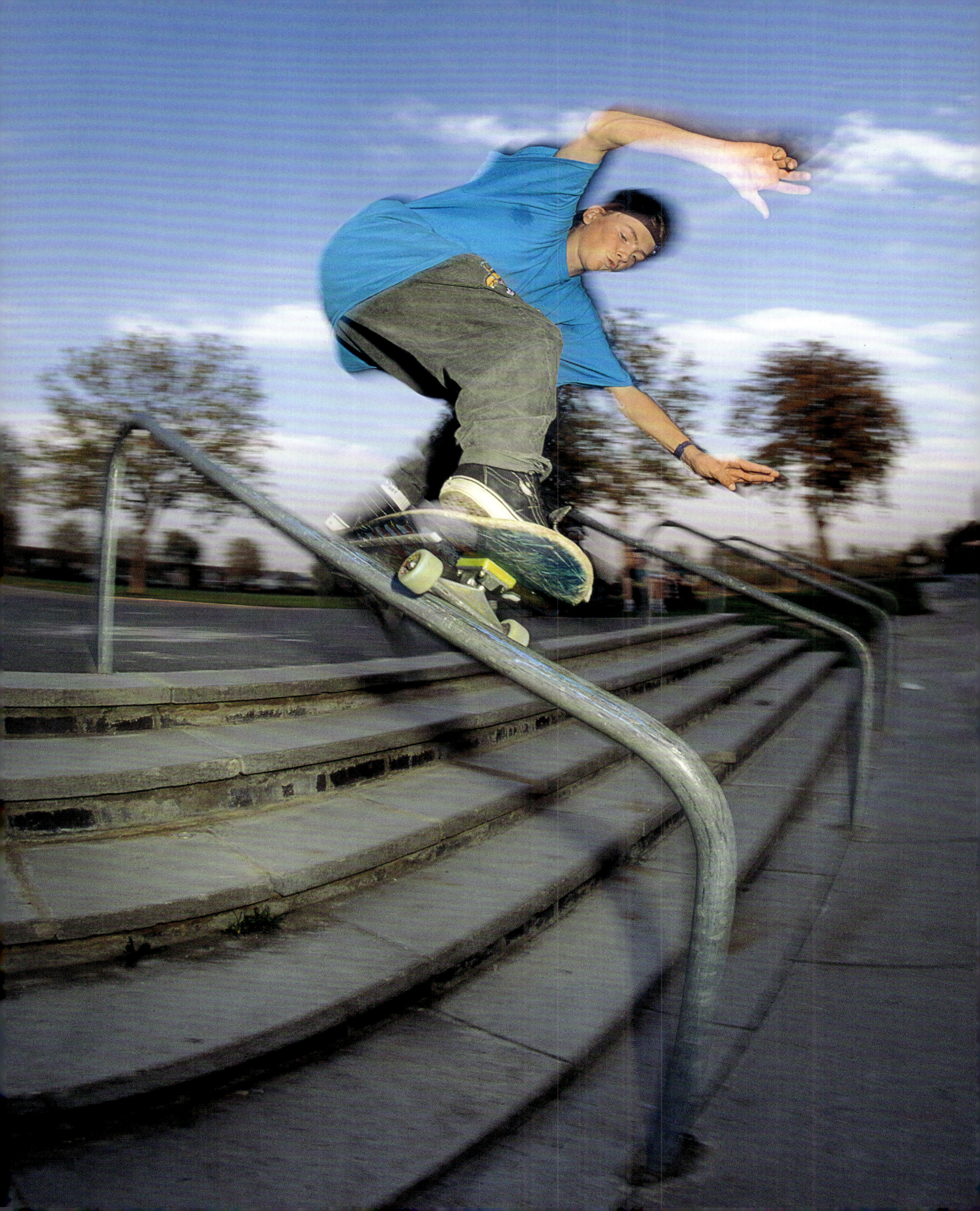

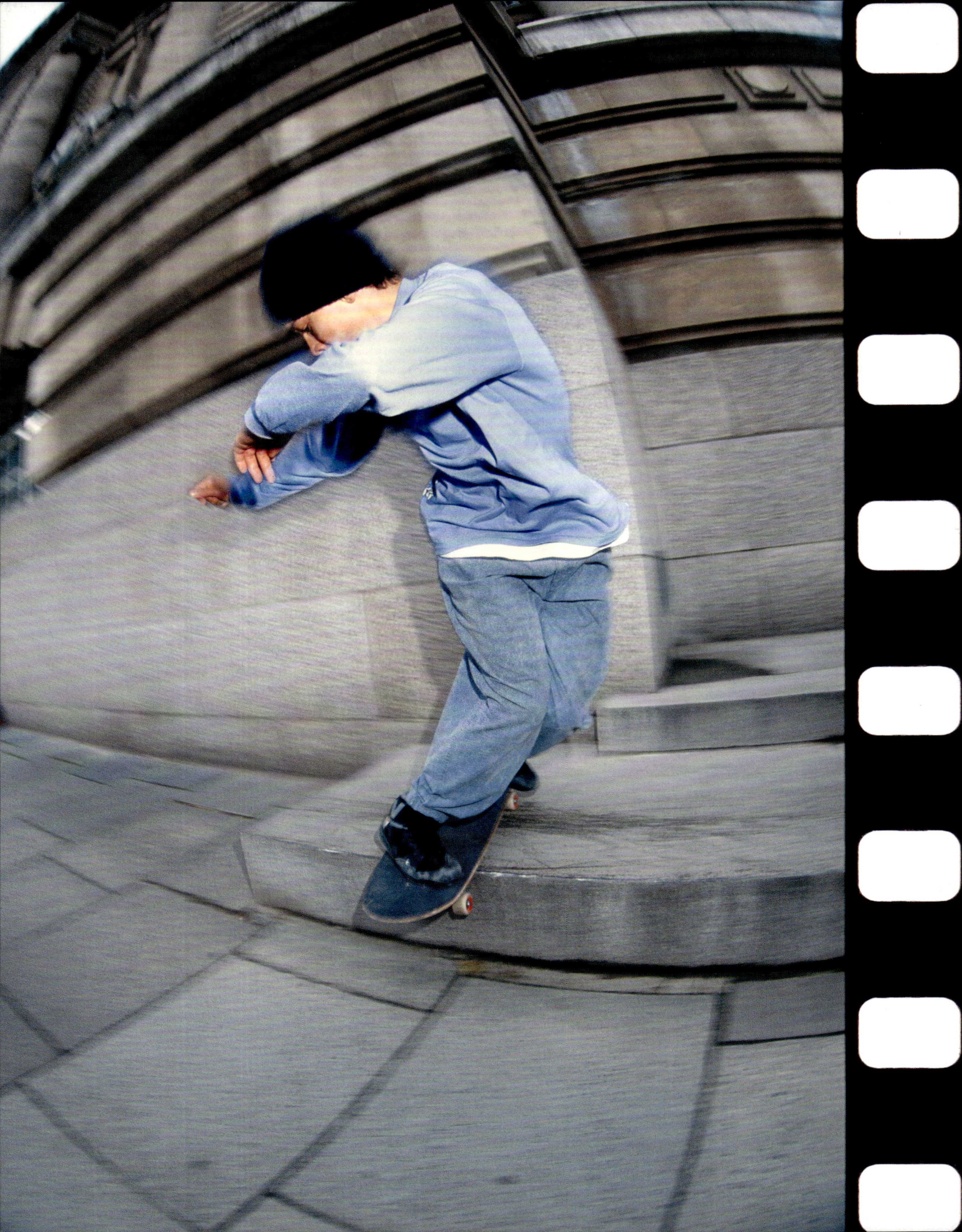

Previous spread left: Alex Moul, 1991, and **right:** Alex Moul, Harrow, 1991 **Photos:** TLB **Opposite:** Curtis McCann, Southbank, 1991 **Photo:** Jay Podesta **Right:** Tony Luckhurst, Southbank, 1991 **Photo:** TLB

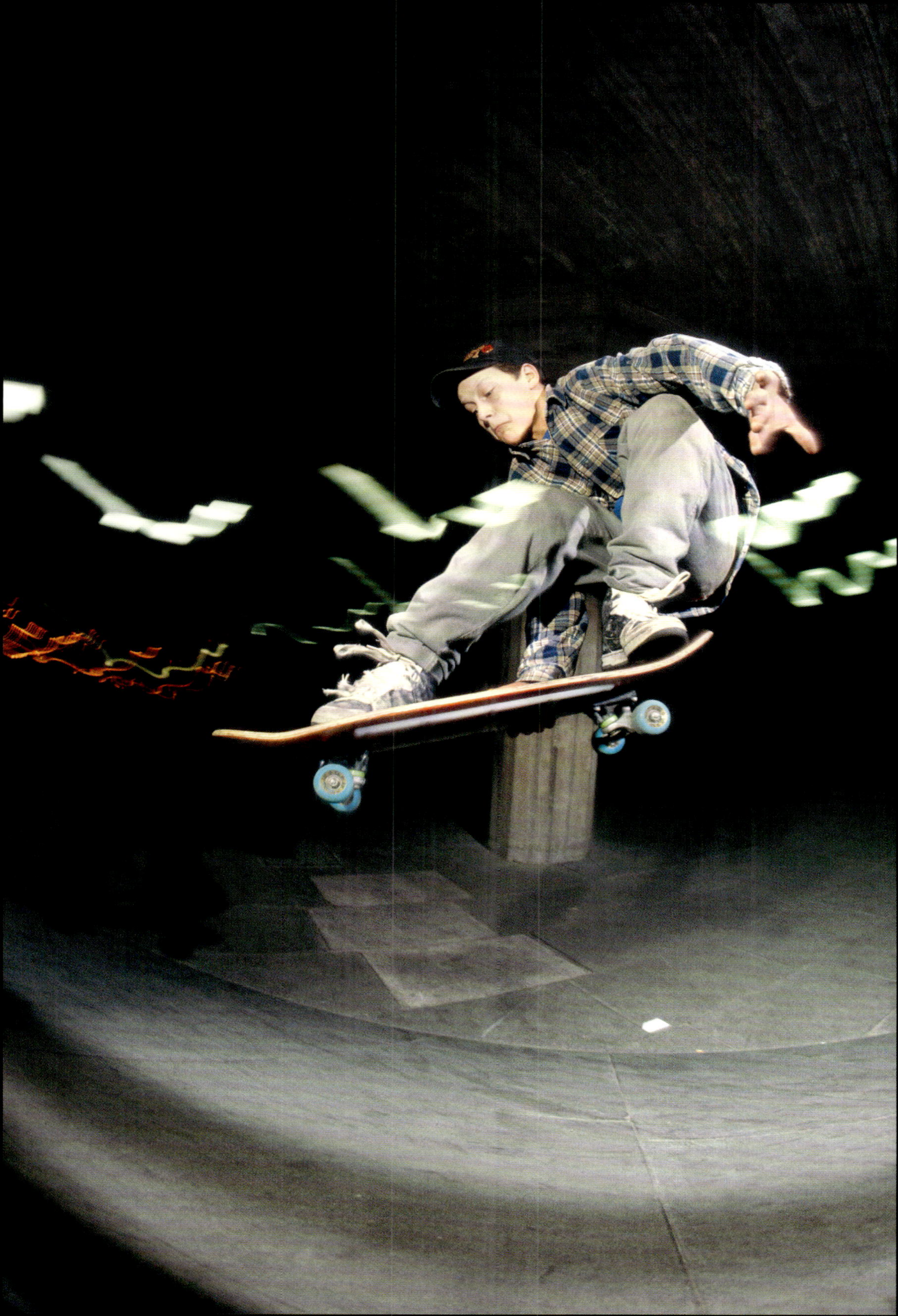

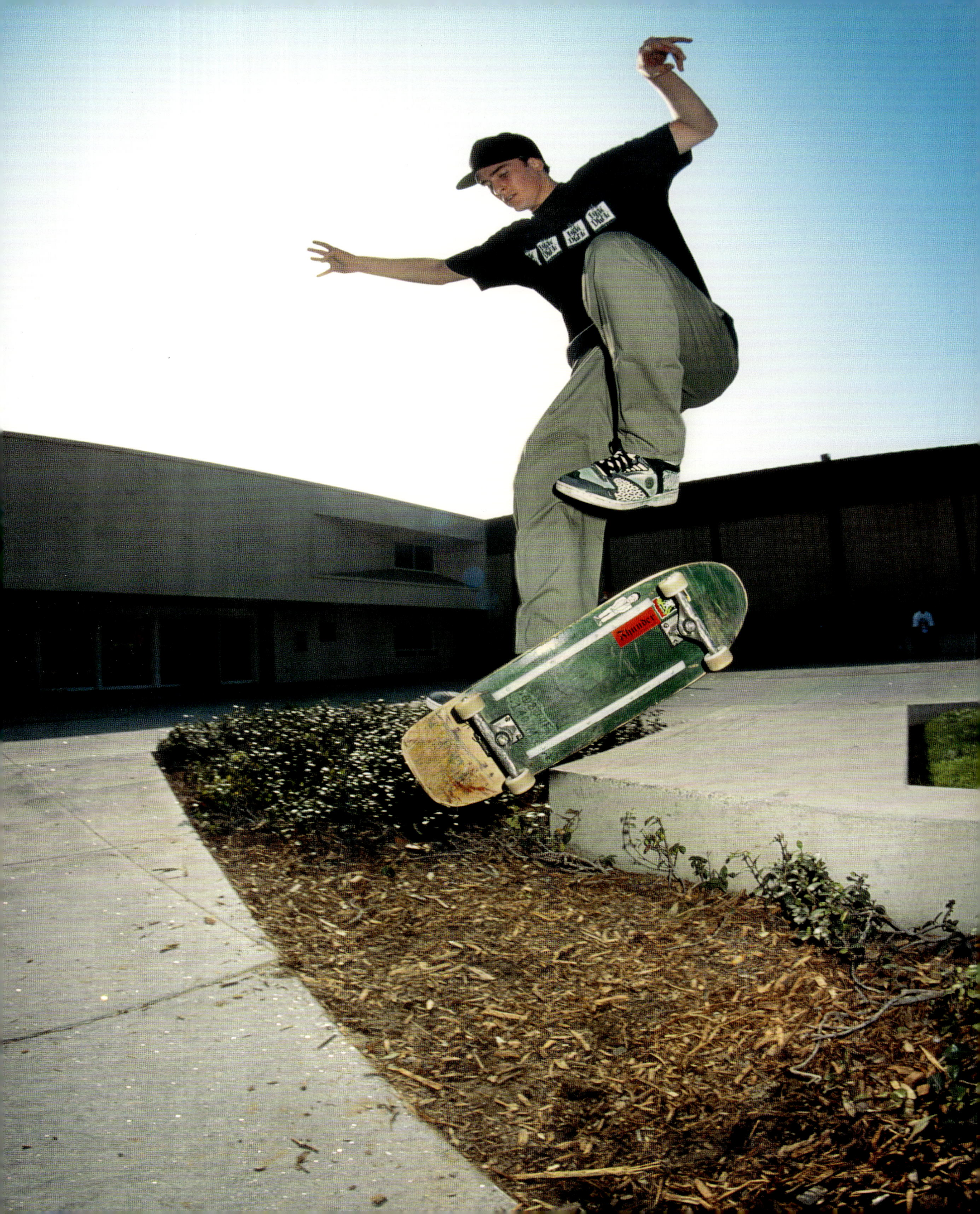

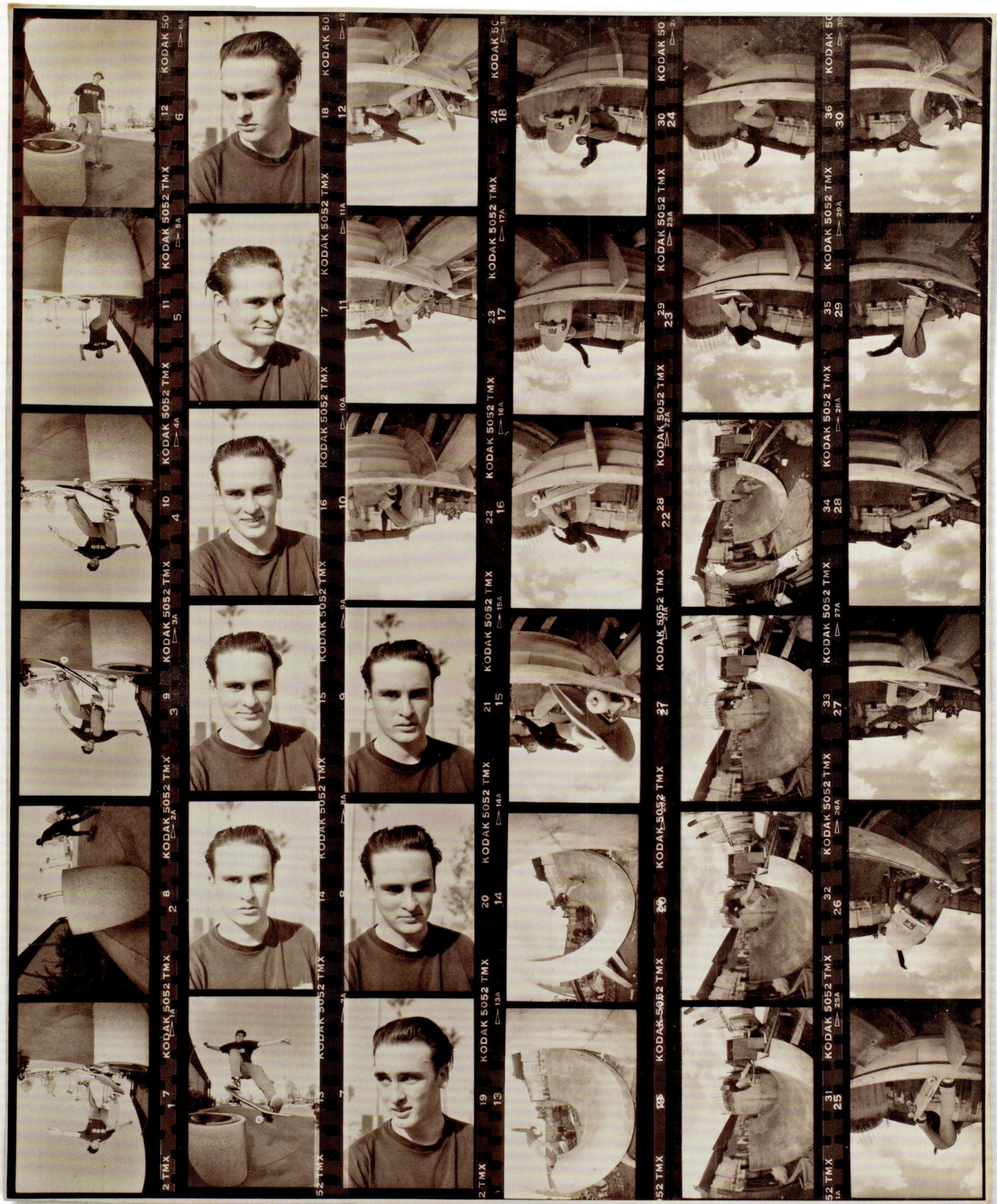

Opposite: Ed Templeton, USA, 1991 **Above:** Ed Templeton, USA, Ed Gill and Will Bankhead, London **Photos:** Paul Sunman

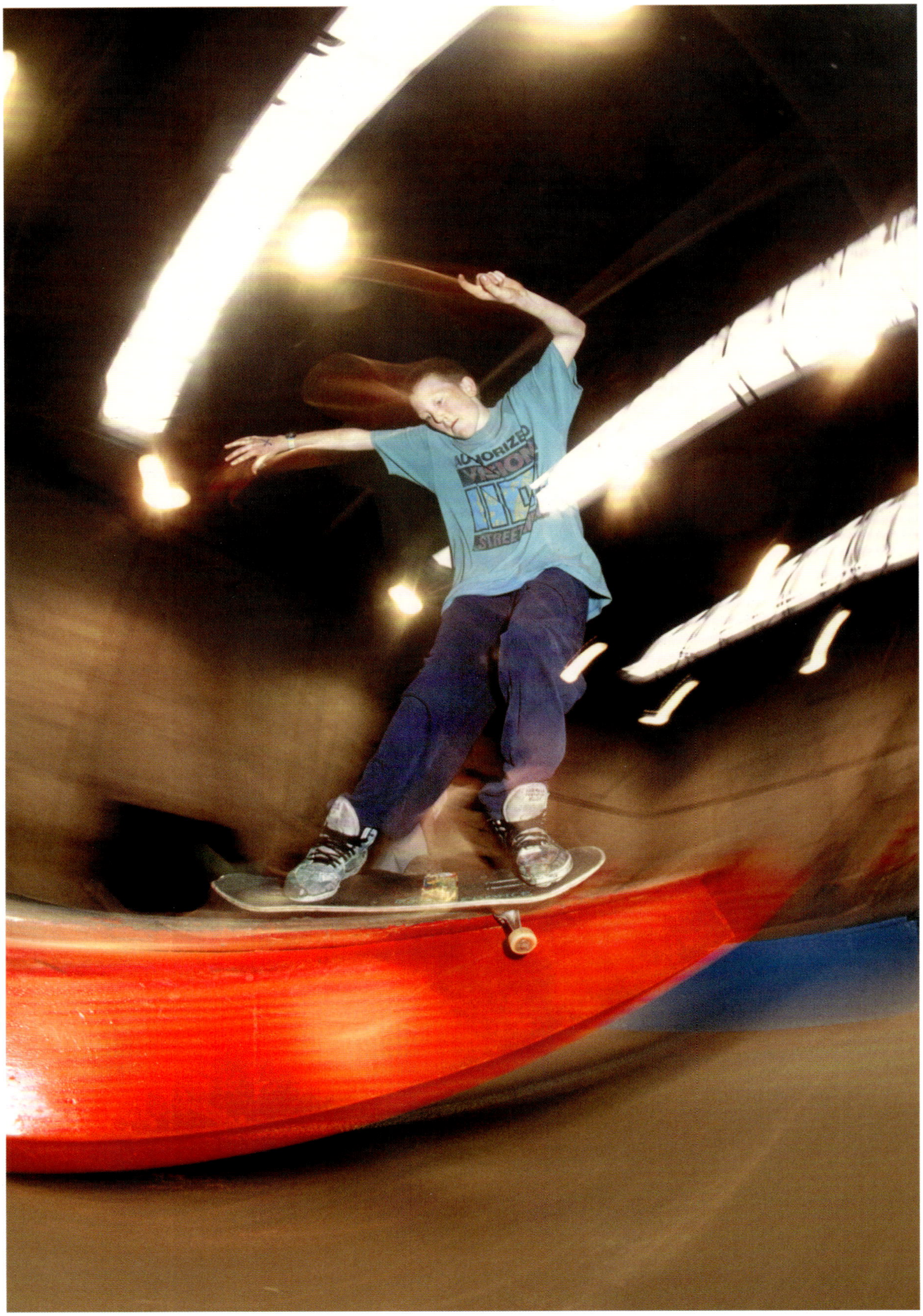

Left: Chris Atherton **Opposite:** Boots, Wigan, 1991 **Photos:** TLB

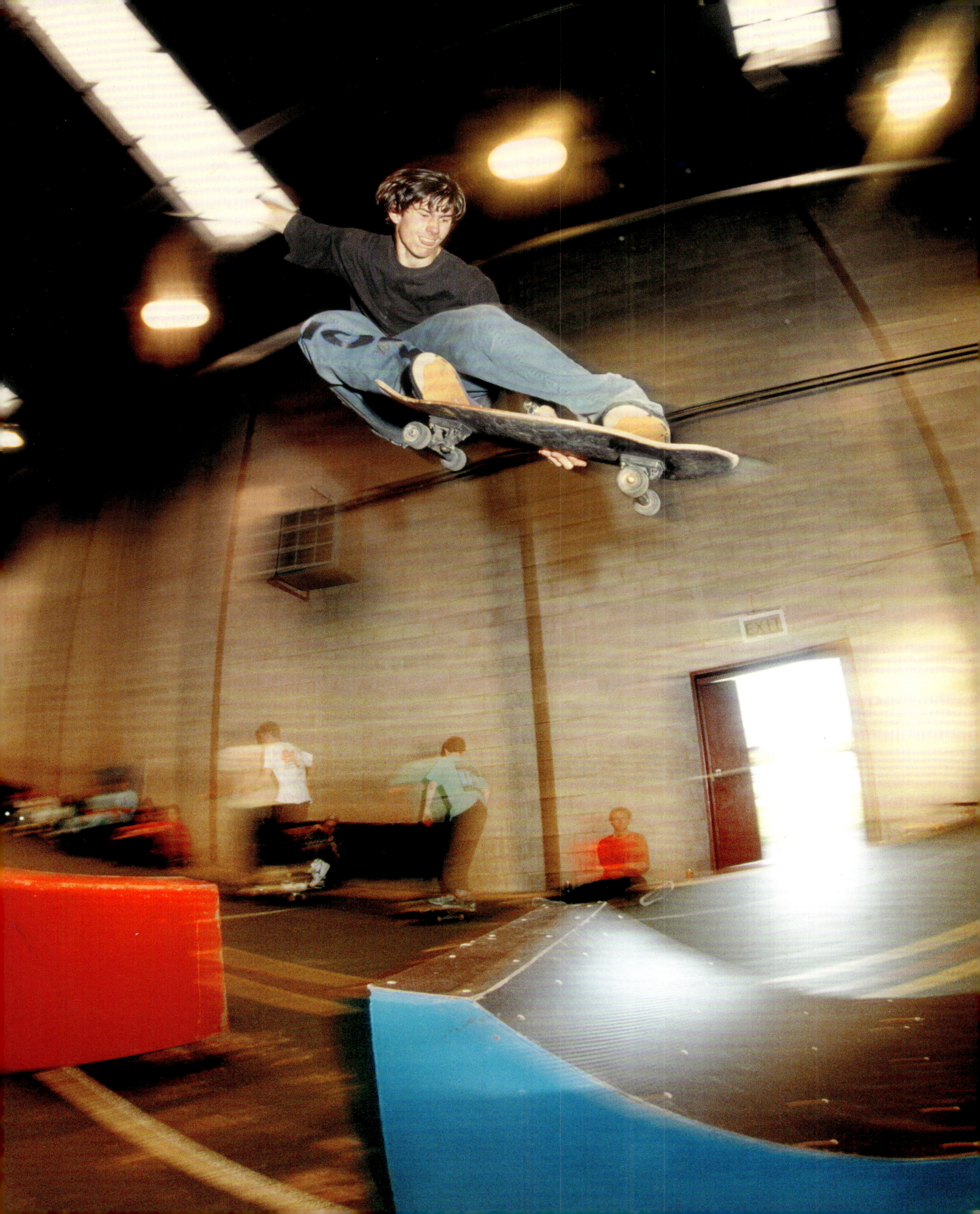
EXIT

Munster contest, Germany, 1990
Left: Allen Losi **Below:** Contest area overview **Opposite:** Sean Sheffey, Munster, 1991 **Photos:** Jay Podesta **Overleaf left:** Alan Petersen, Santa Cruz team demo, Rom skatepark, 1991 **Photo:** Jay Podesta, and **right:** Dave 'Dickie' Allen, Leigh-on-Sea contest, 1991 **Photo:** TLB

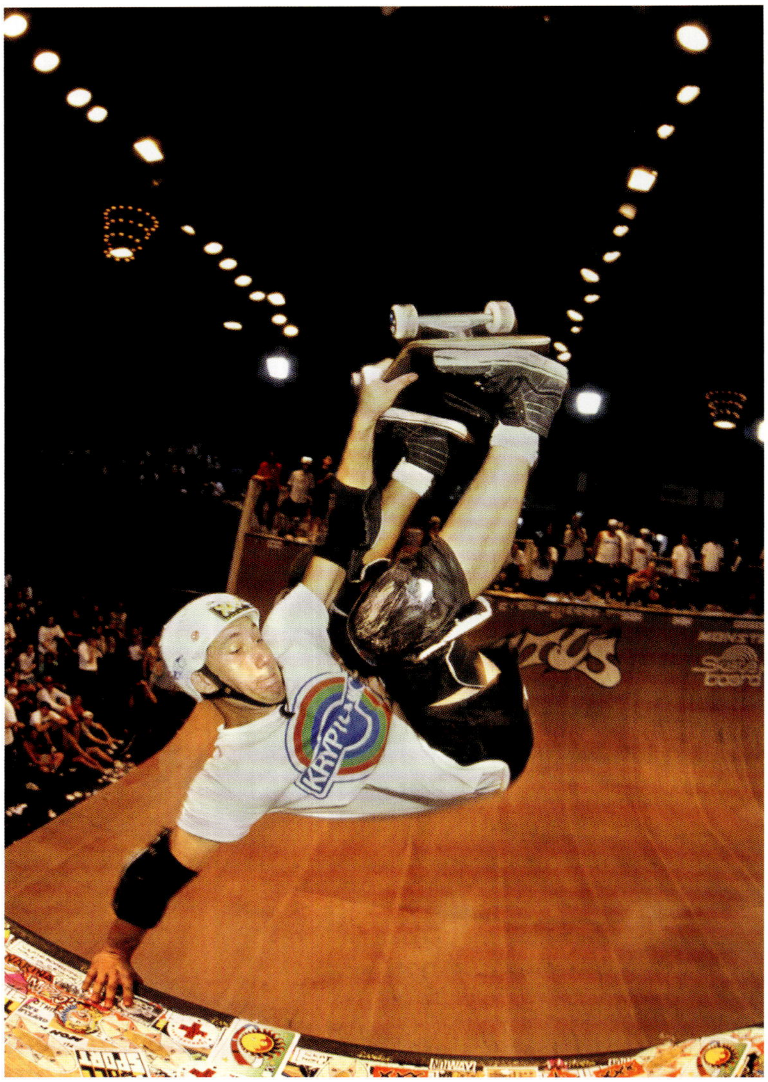

'So much happened in such a short space of time. I remember going to Palace in '85, '86, then by '88, '89 we were going off to big international competitions—then street skating hit. We went from nothing to World Industries in the blink of an eye.'

Vernon Adams

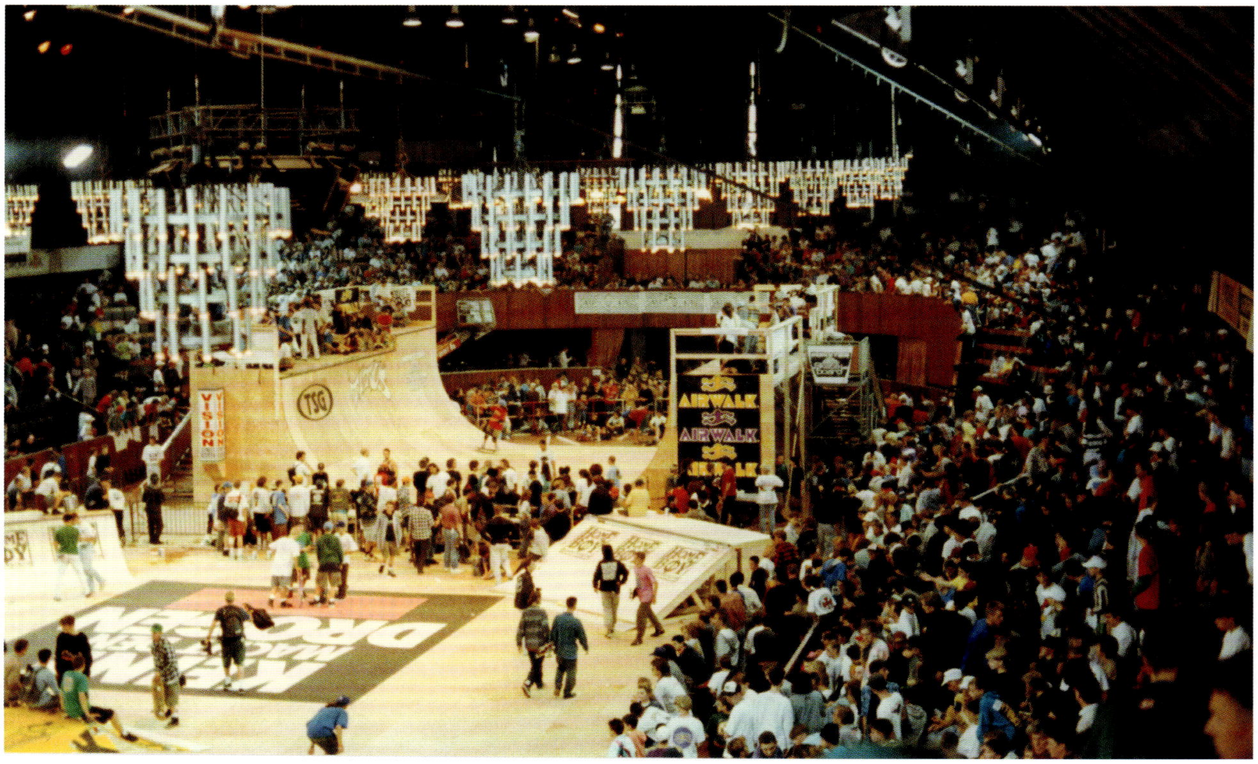

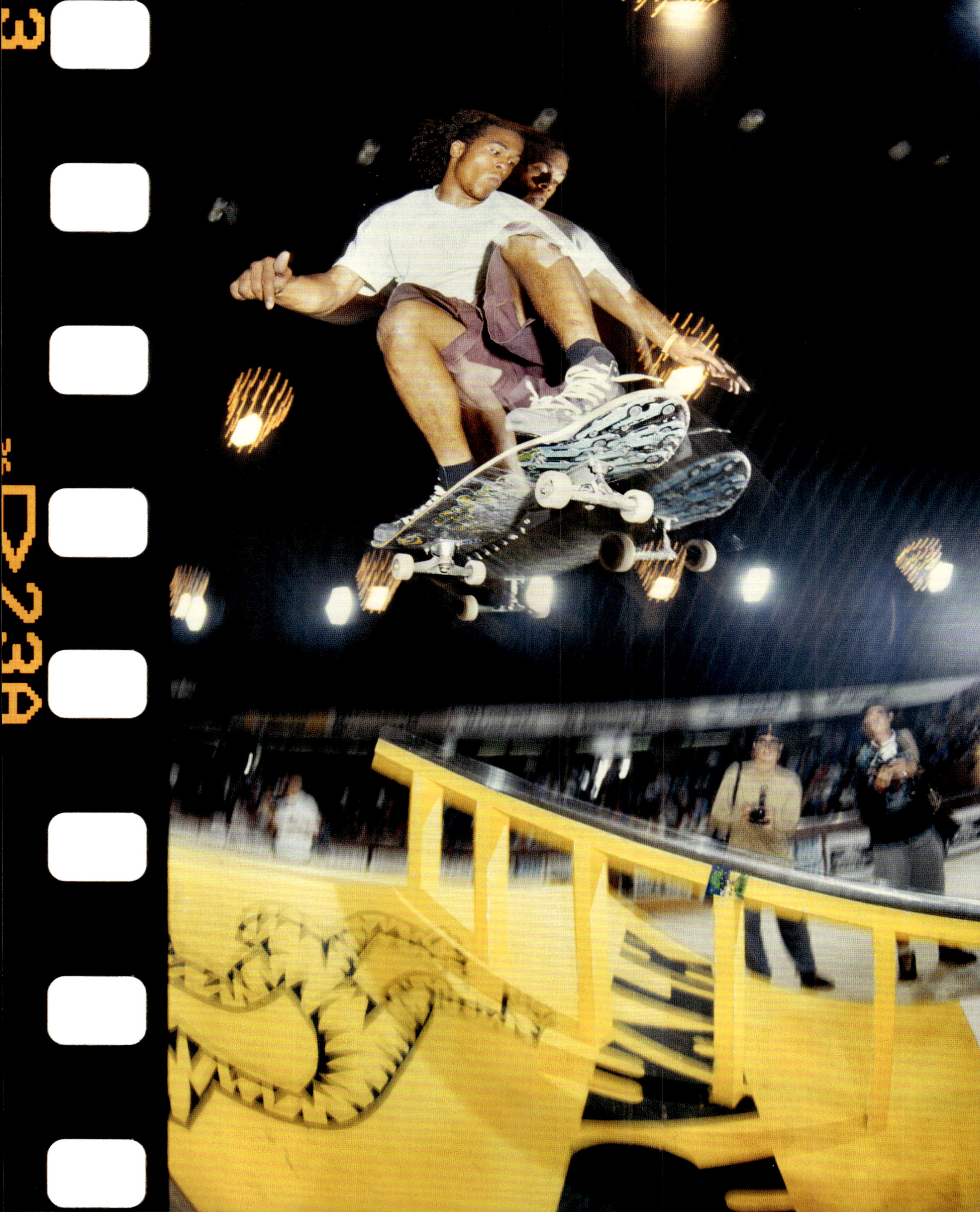

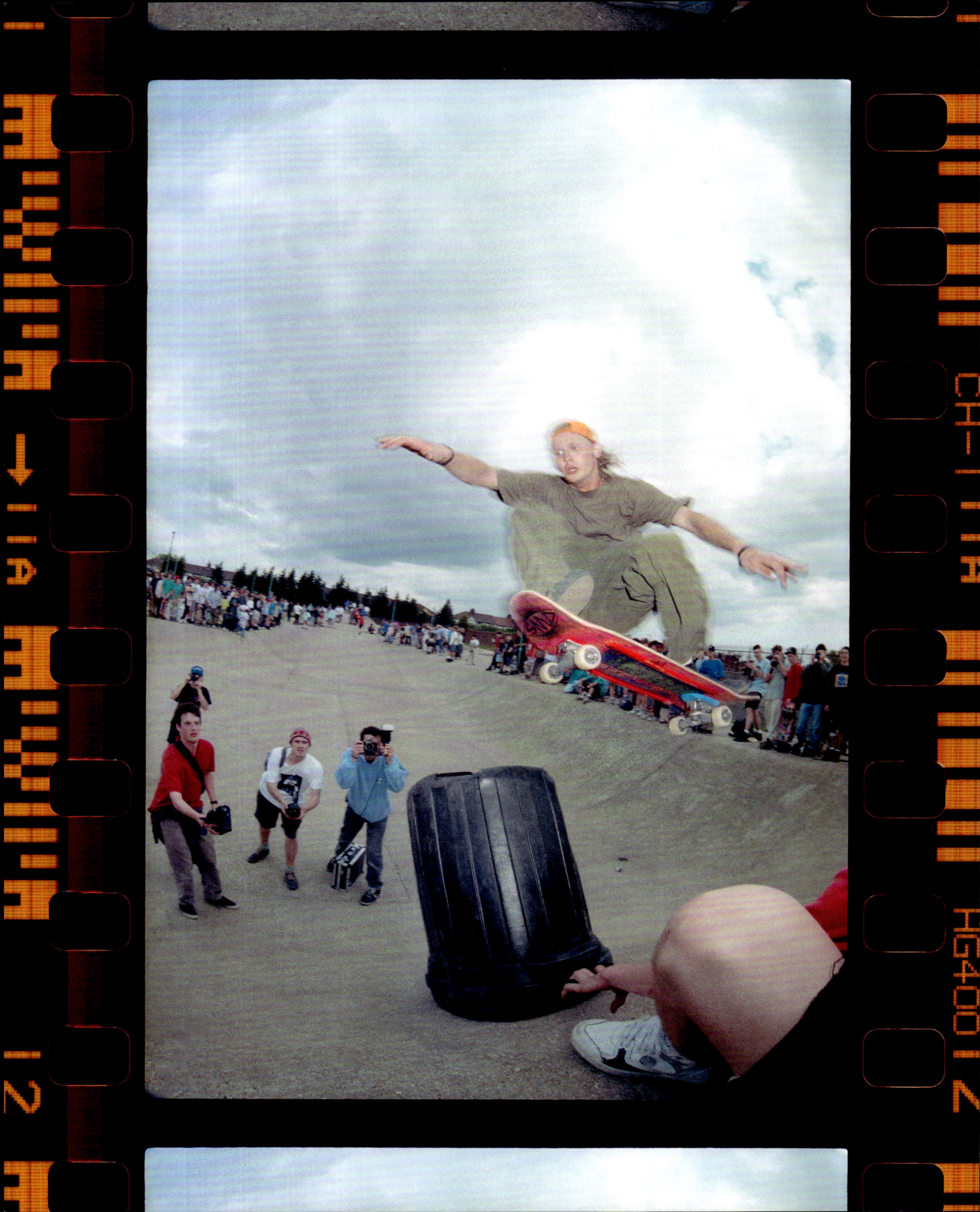

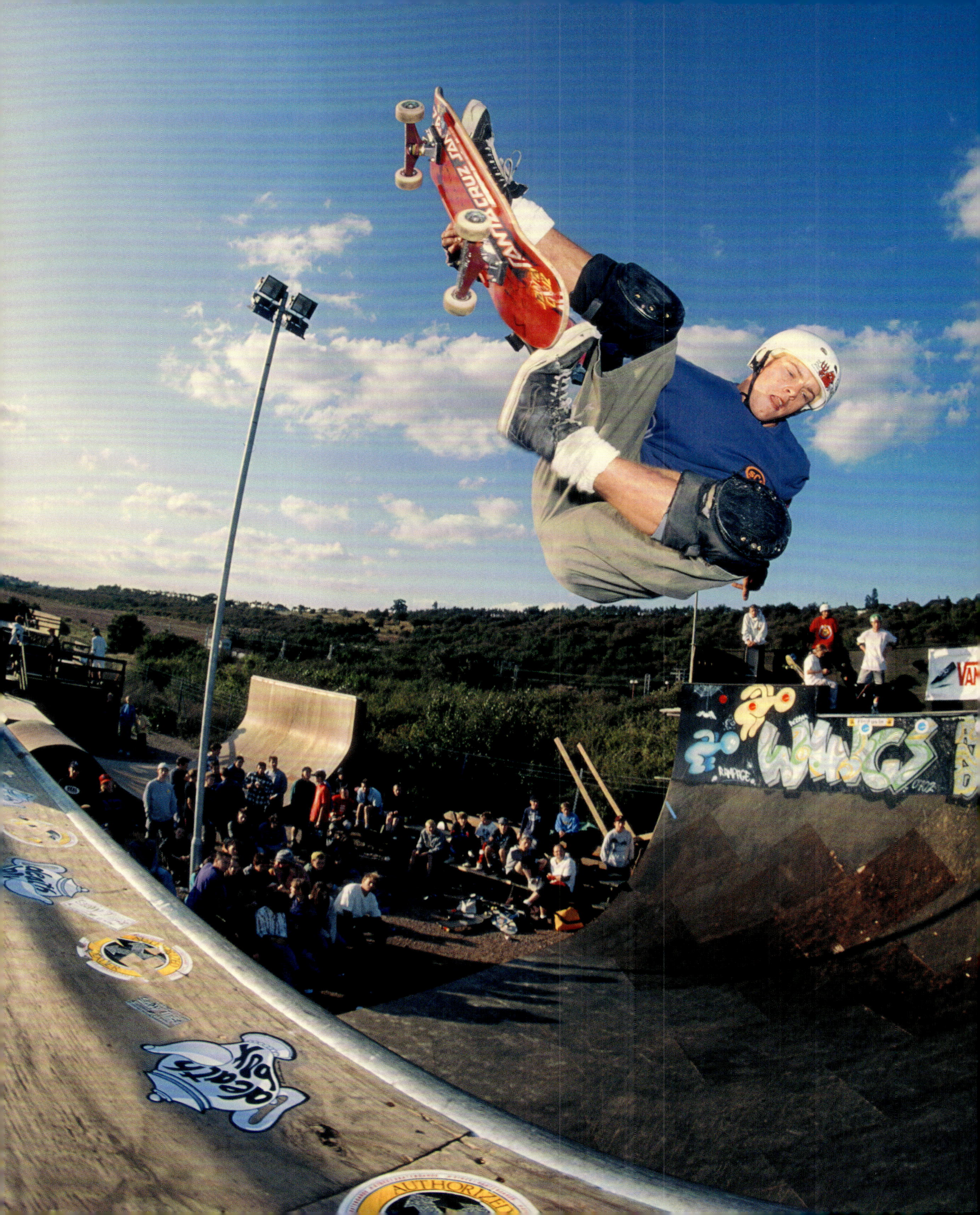

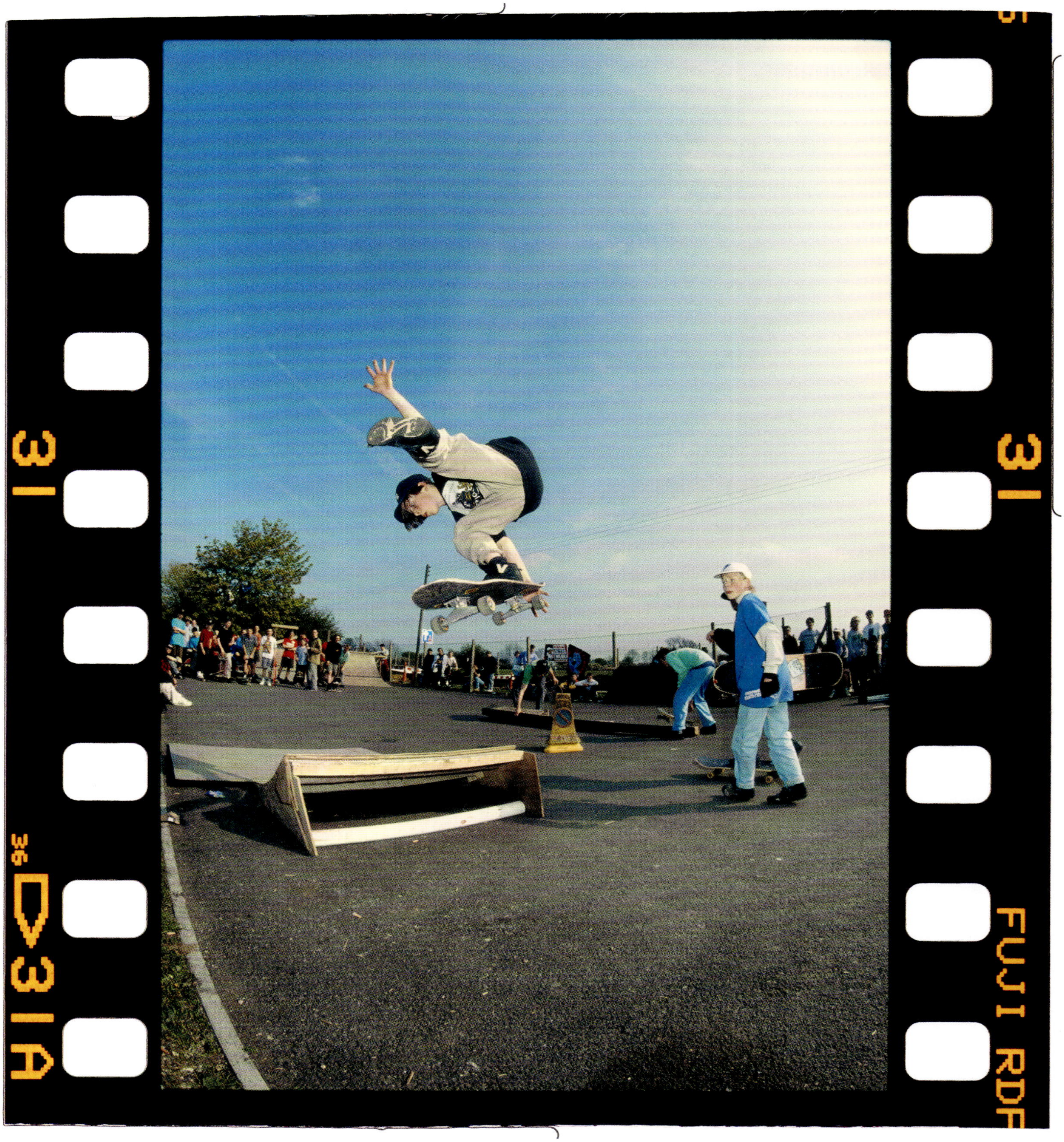

Above: Tom Penny, Botley, Oxford, 1991 **Opposite:** Dan 'Jagger' Ball, Birmingham, 1991 **Overleaf:** Bones Brigade demo, Bath, 1990 **Photos:** TLB

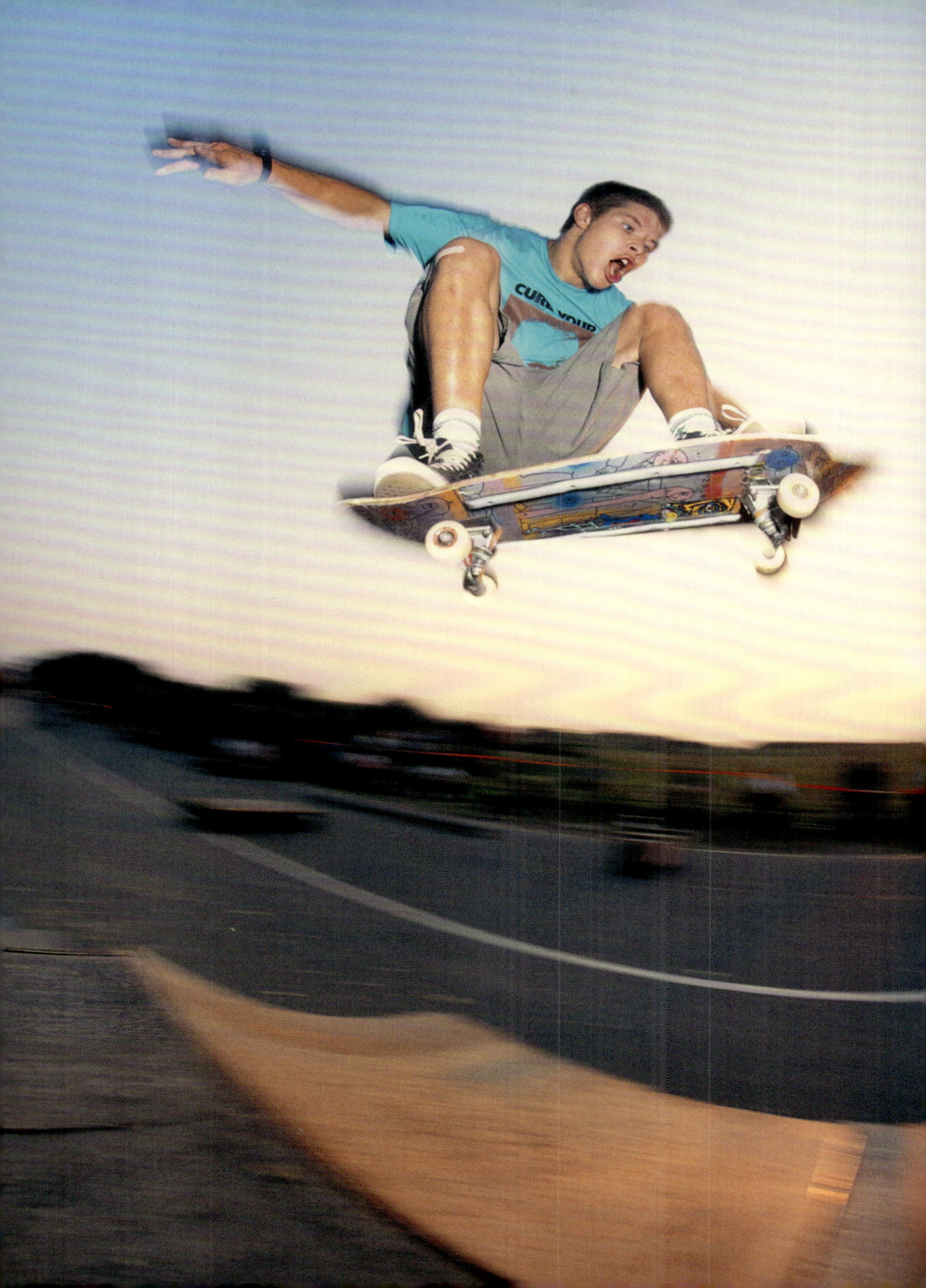

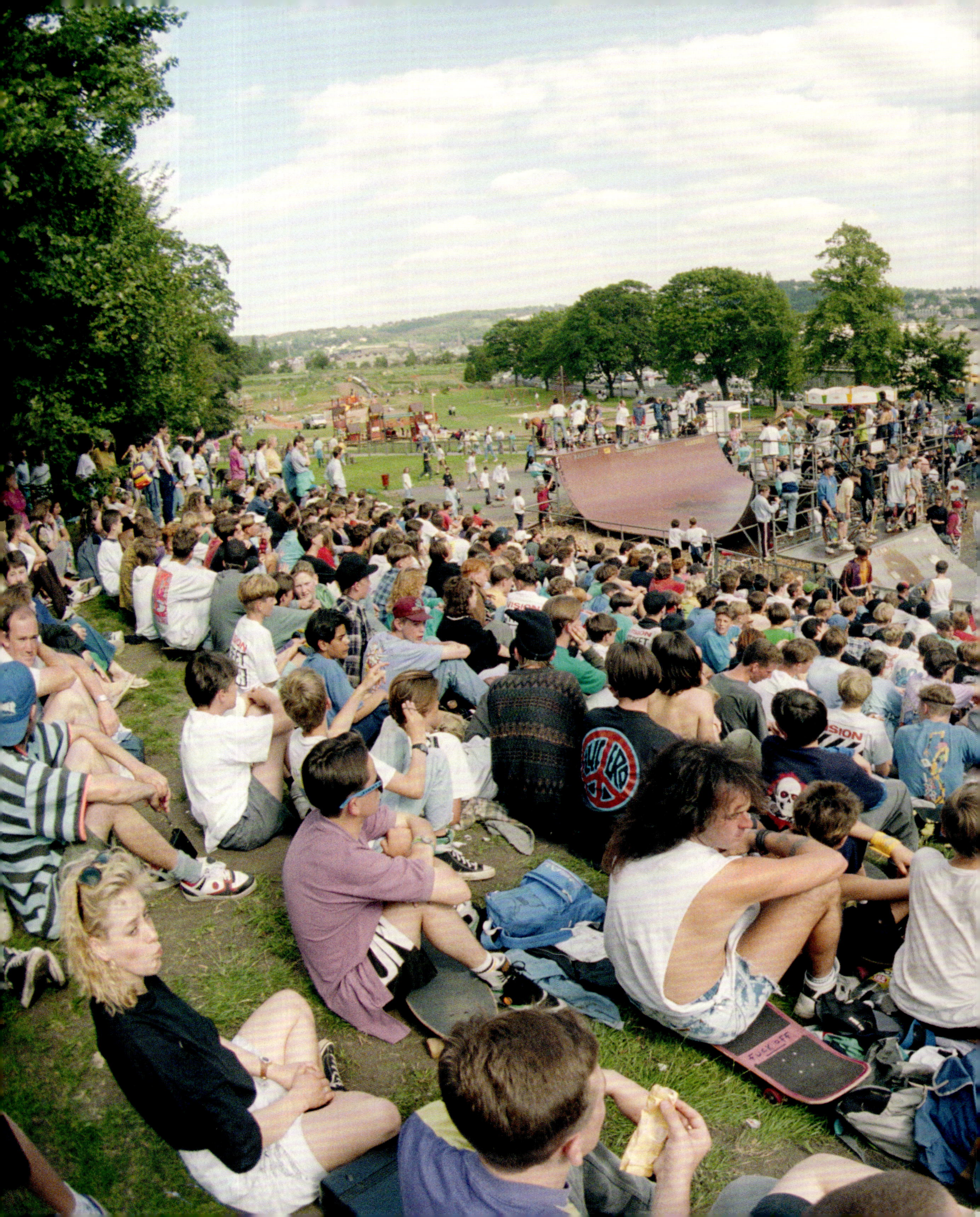
VISION
FUCK OFF

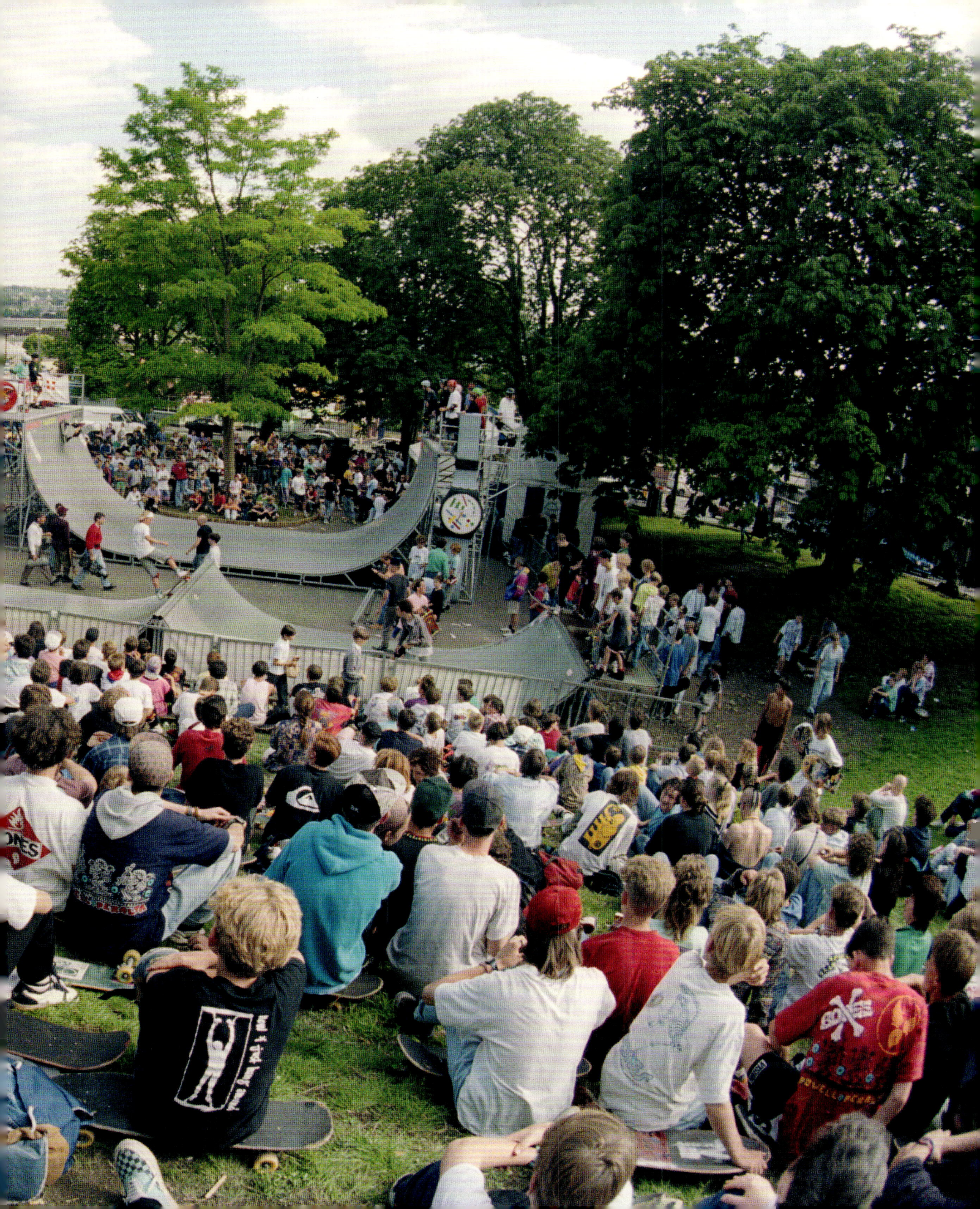
BONES

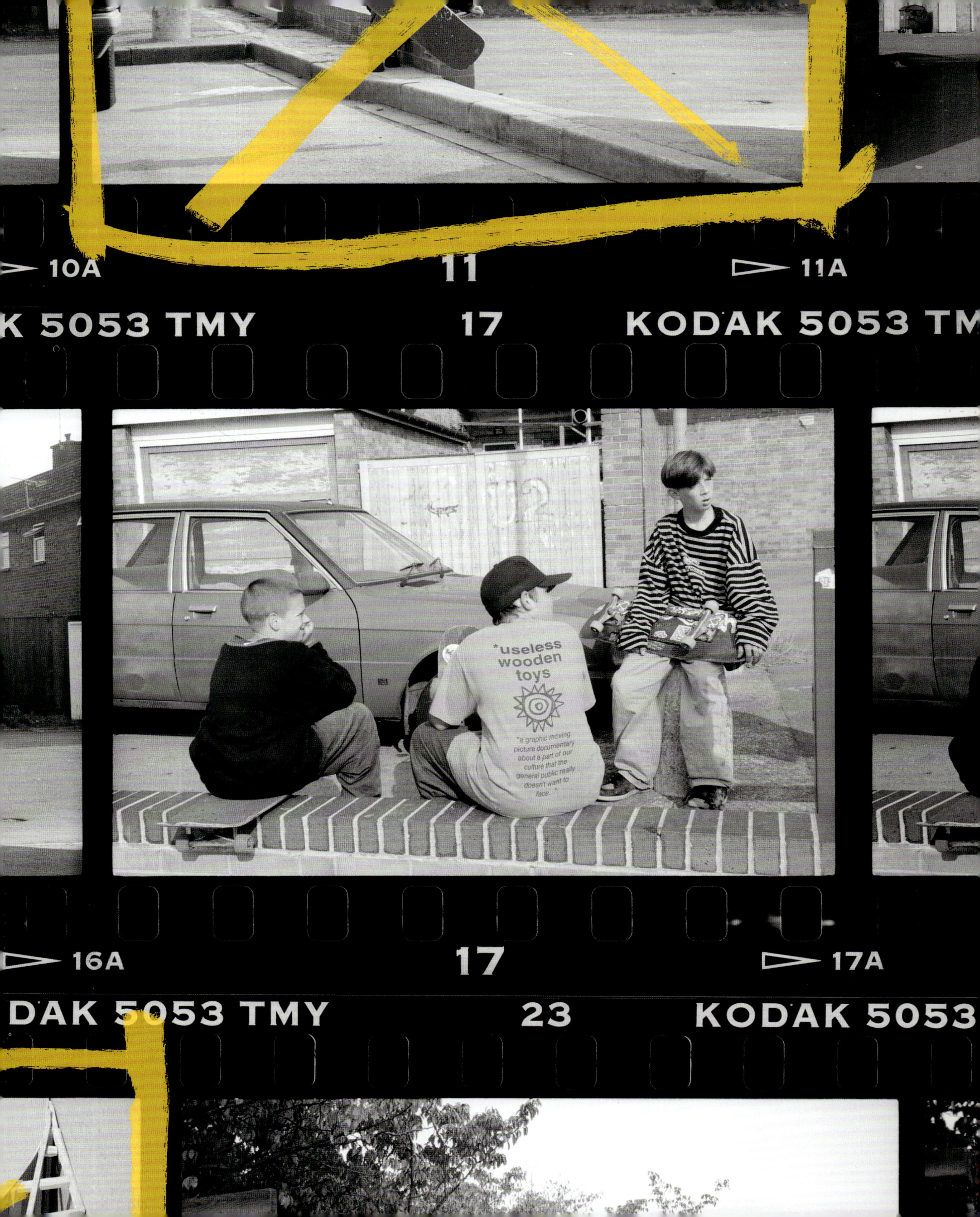
10A
11
11A
K 5053 TMY
17
KODAK 5053 TM
U2
*useless
wooden
toys
"a graphic moving
picture documentary
about a part of our
culture that the
general public really
doesn't want to
face..."
16A
17
17A
DAK 5053 TMY
23
KODAK 5053

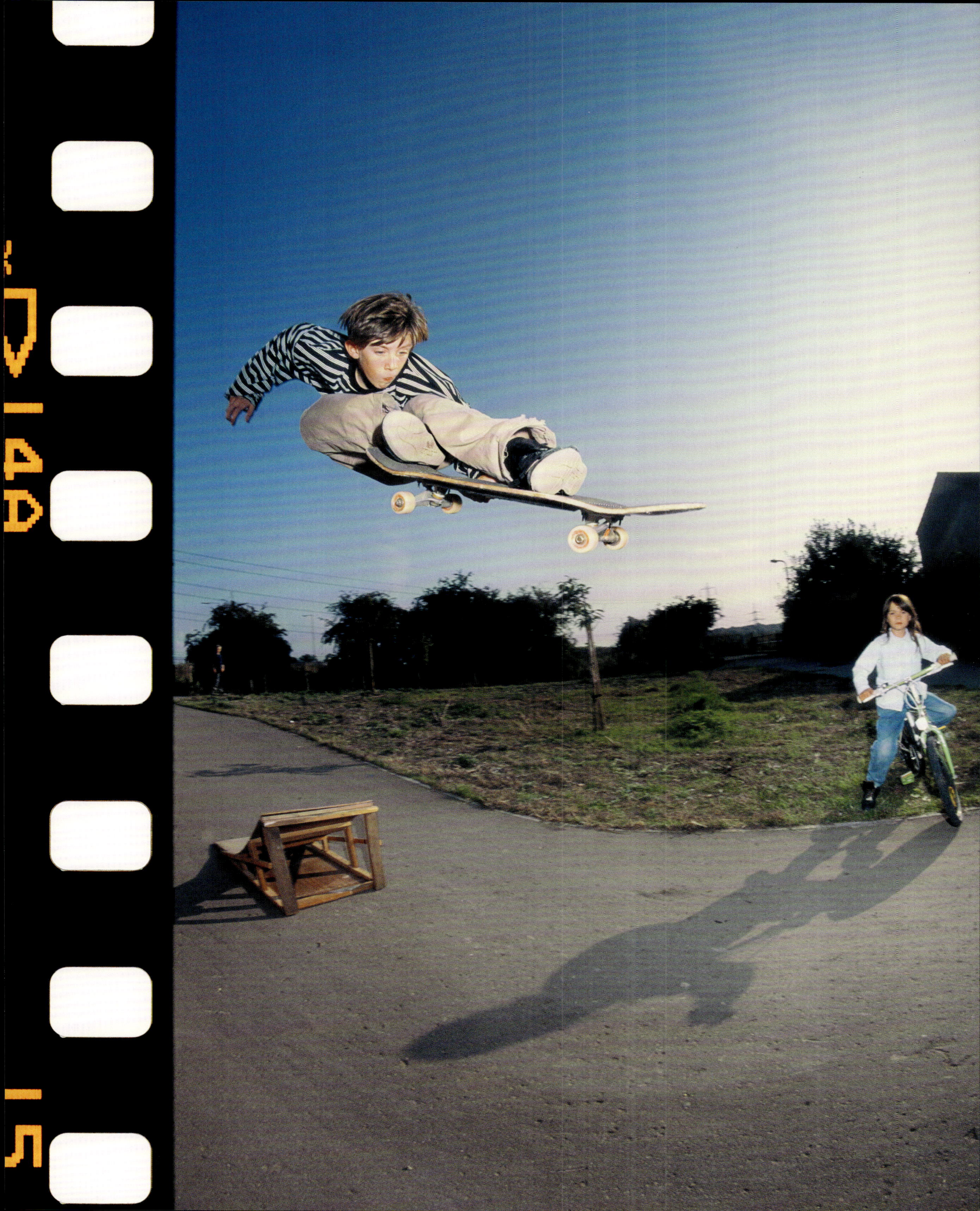

Previous spread left: Tom Penny, Justin Parker and friend, and **right:** Tom Penny, Oxford, 1991 **Below:** Tom Penny, Oxford, 1991 **Opposite** (left to right): Marc Bultitude, Simon Evans and Matt Stuart, 1991 **Photos:** TLB

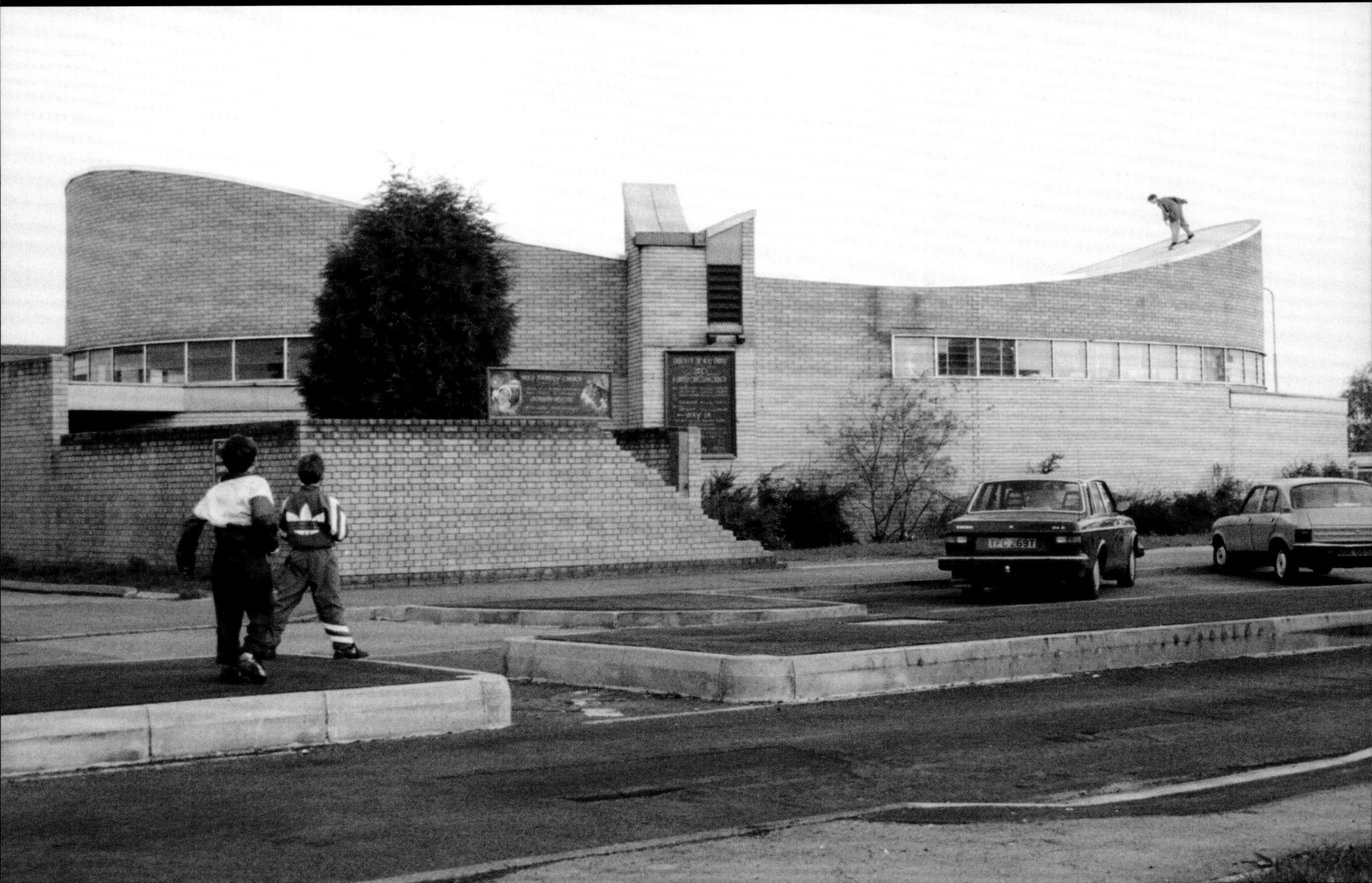

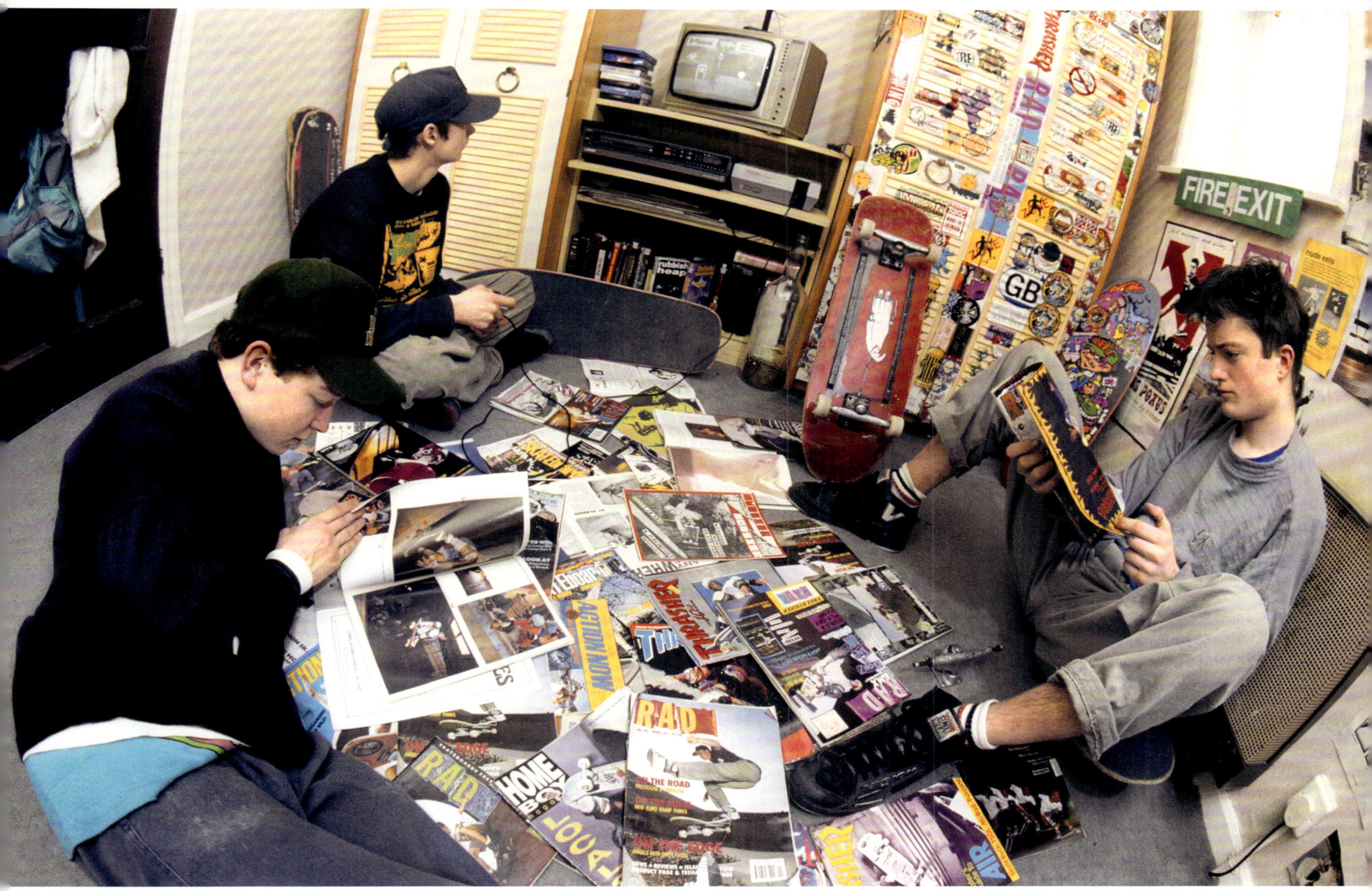

Overleaf top left: Lee Stewart, Fairfield Halls, Croydon, 1991, and **bottom left:** Margate, 1989 **Overleaf right:** John Farmer, Oxford Road, Manchester, 1991
Photos: TLB

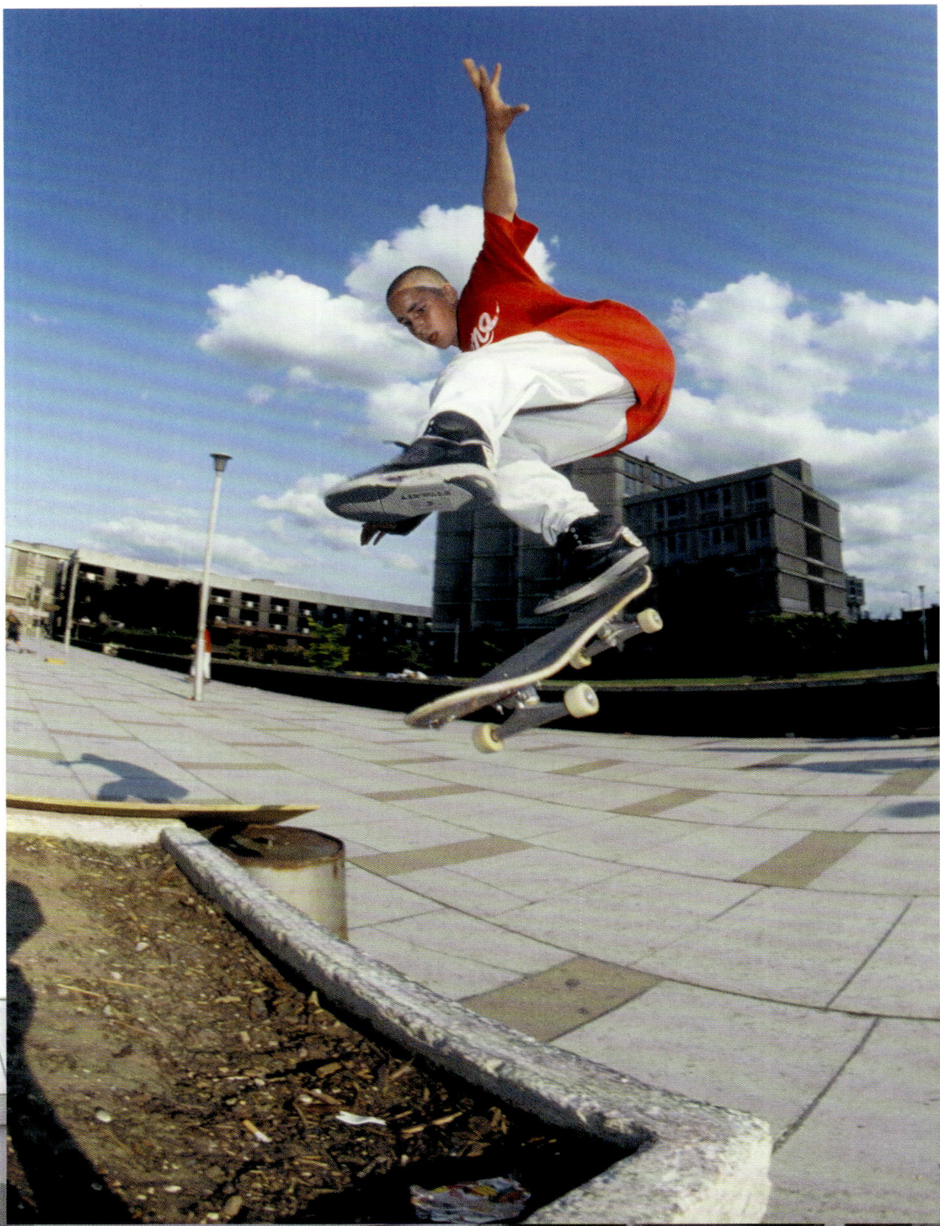

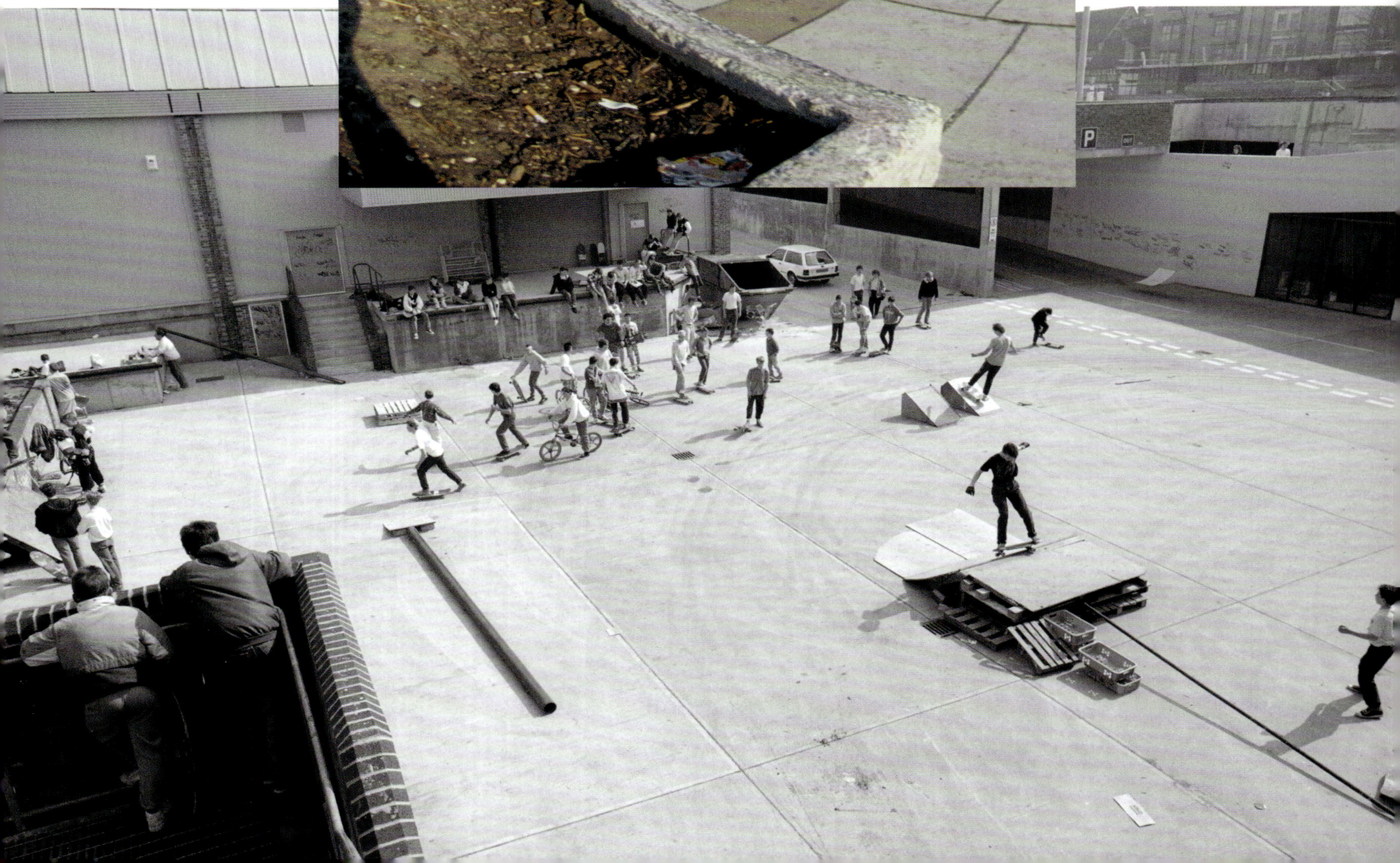

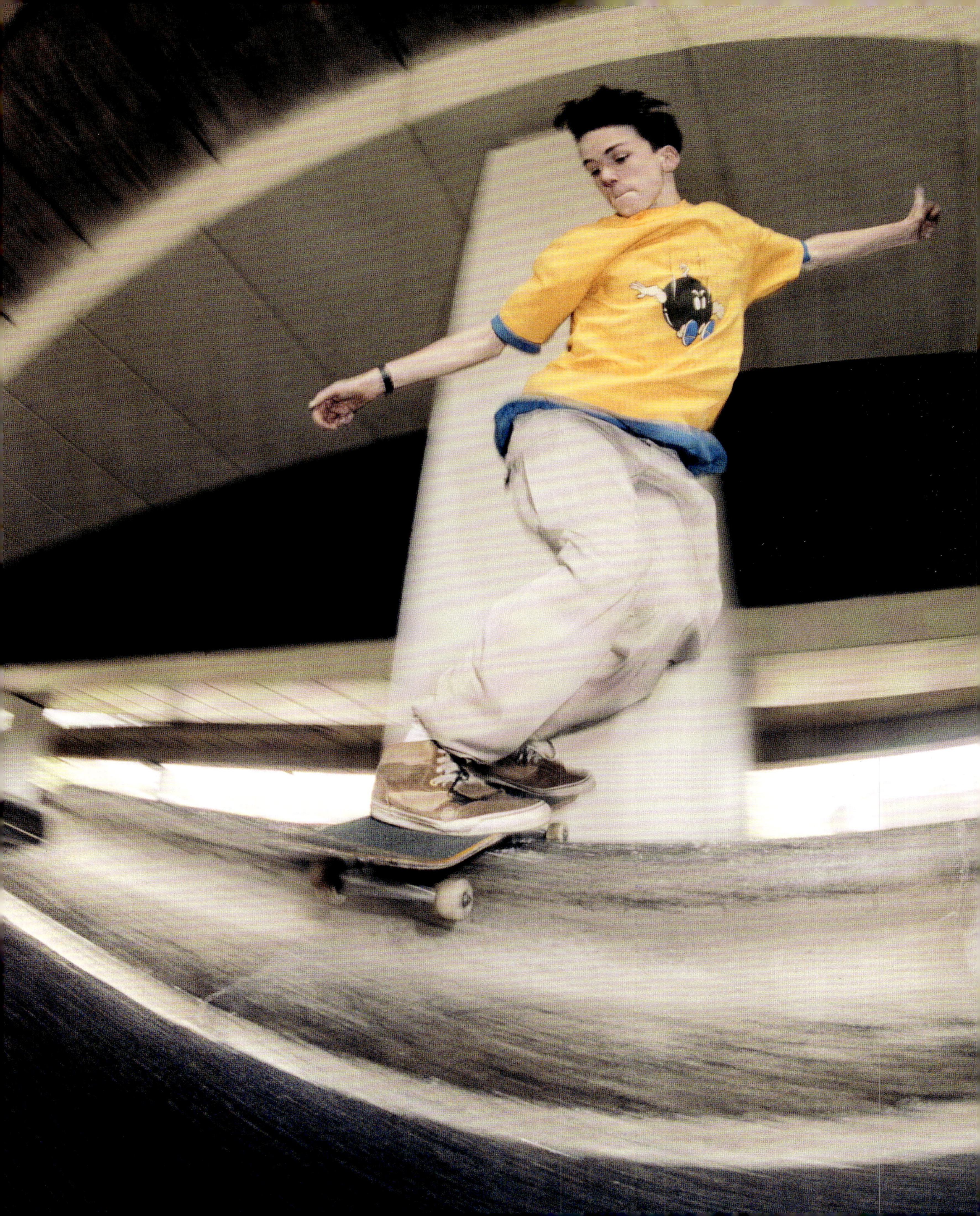

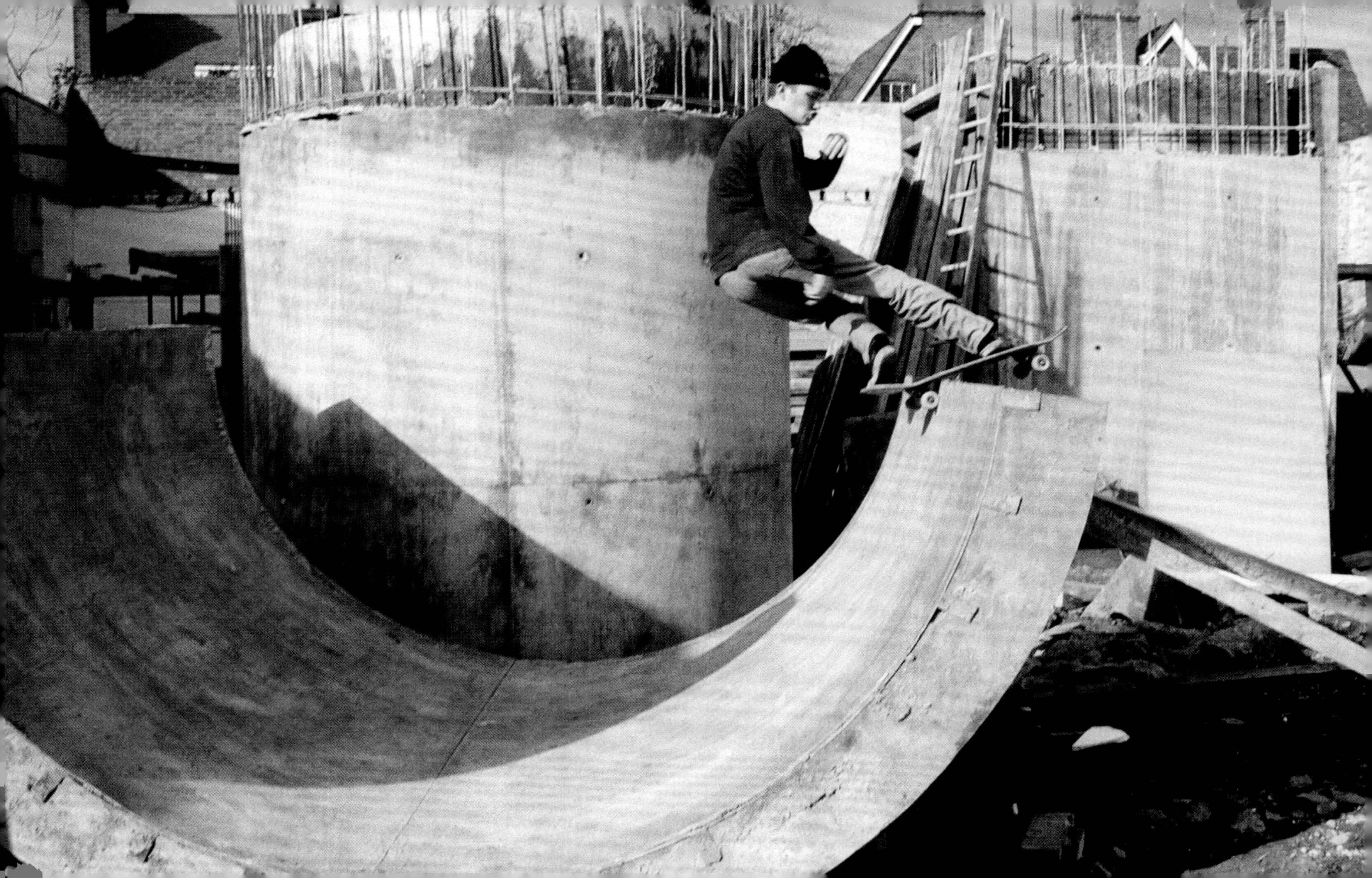

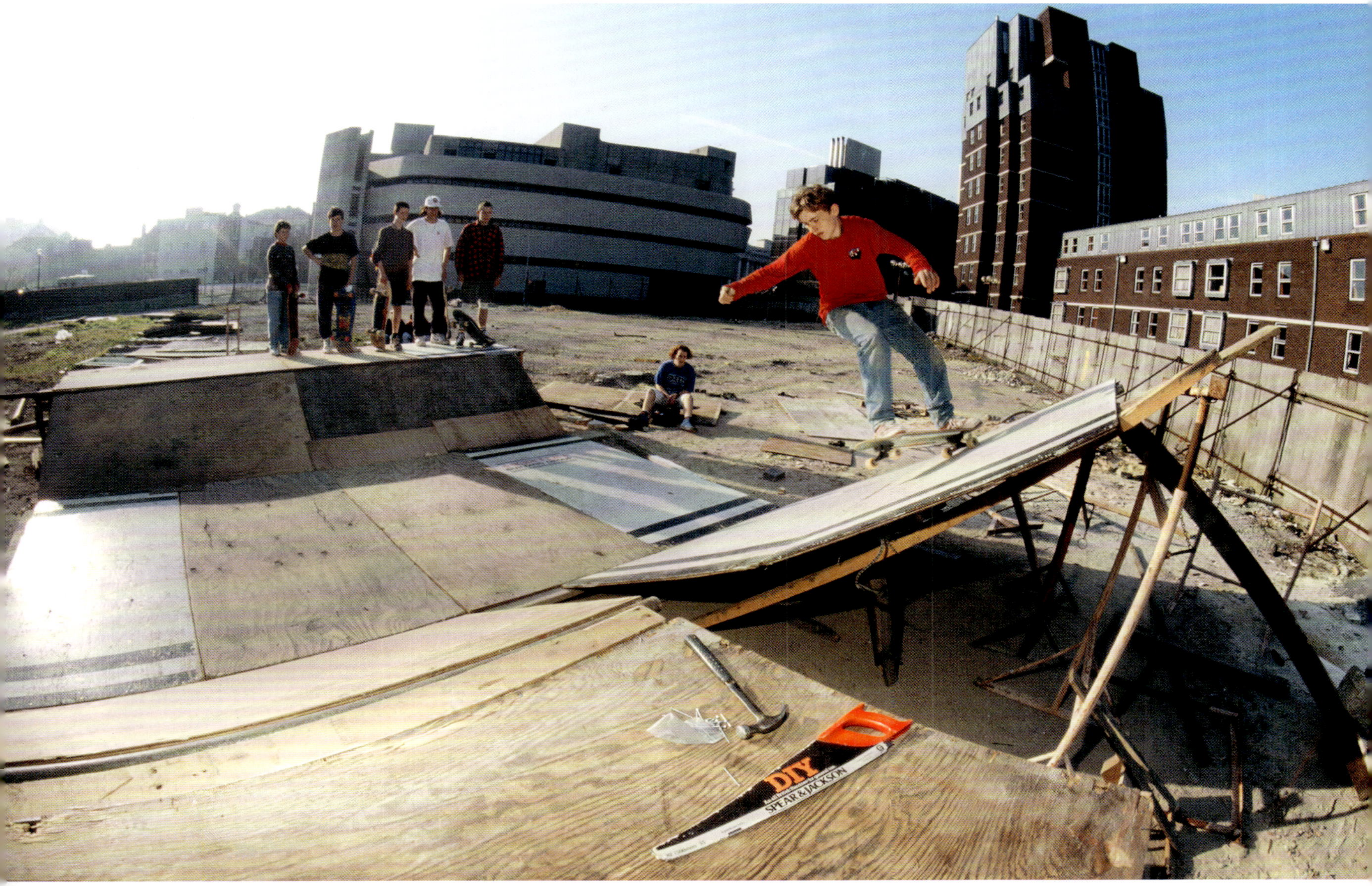

Opposite: Will Bankhead, Church Road building site, Wimbledon, 1991 **Photo:** Ed Gill **Above:** DIY mini ramp, Portsmouth **Photo:** TLB

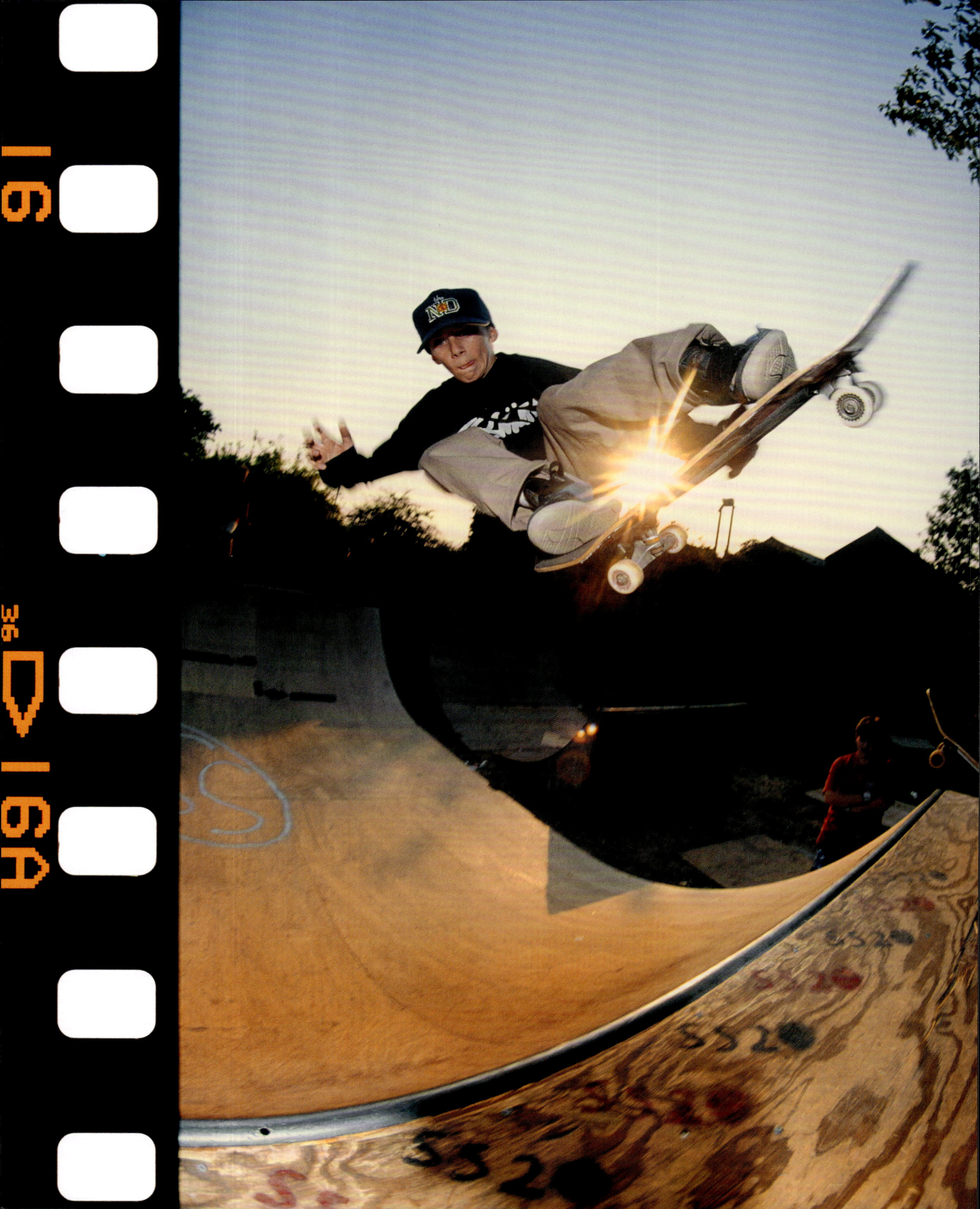

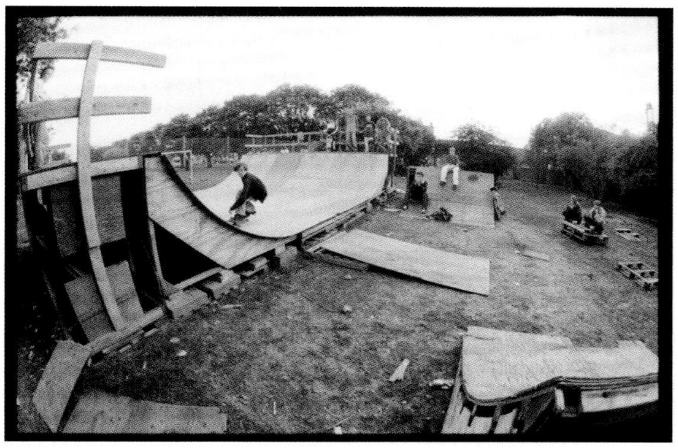

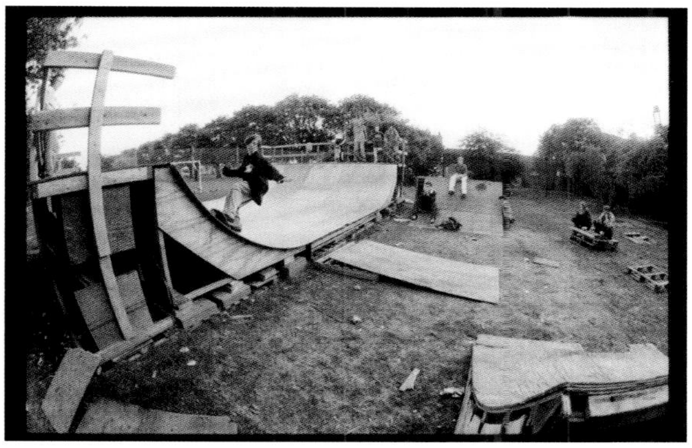

This spread: Tom Penny, Oxford, 1991 **Overleaf left:** Danny Wainwright, Cirencester, Gloucestershire, 1991, and **right:** Curtis McCann, Pioneer club, St Albans contest, 1991 **Photos:** TLB

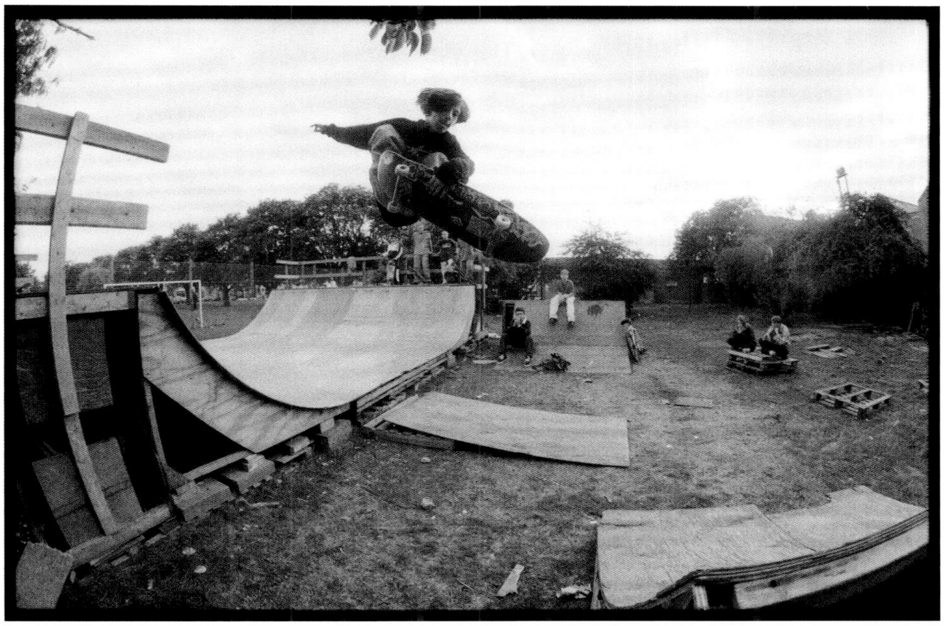

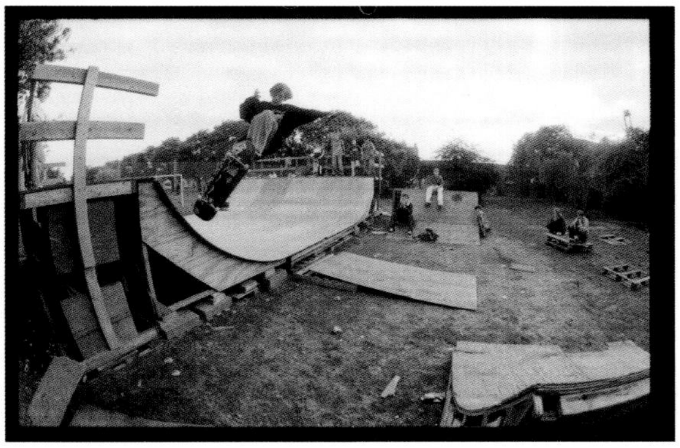

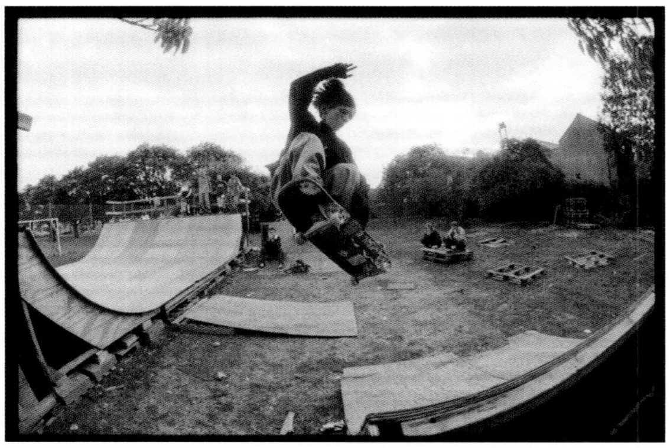

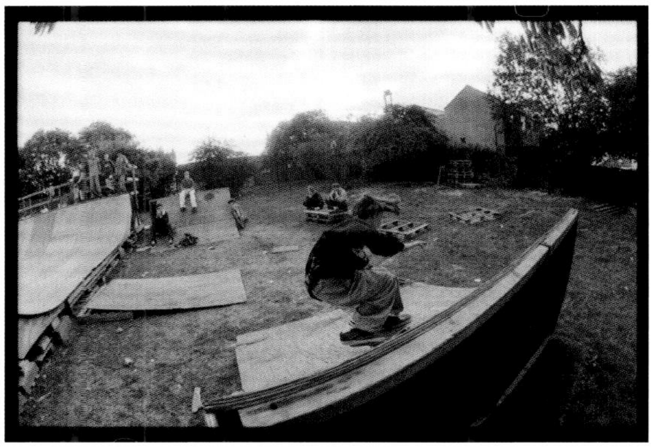

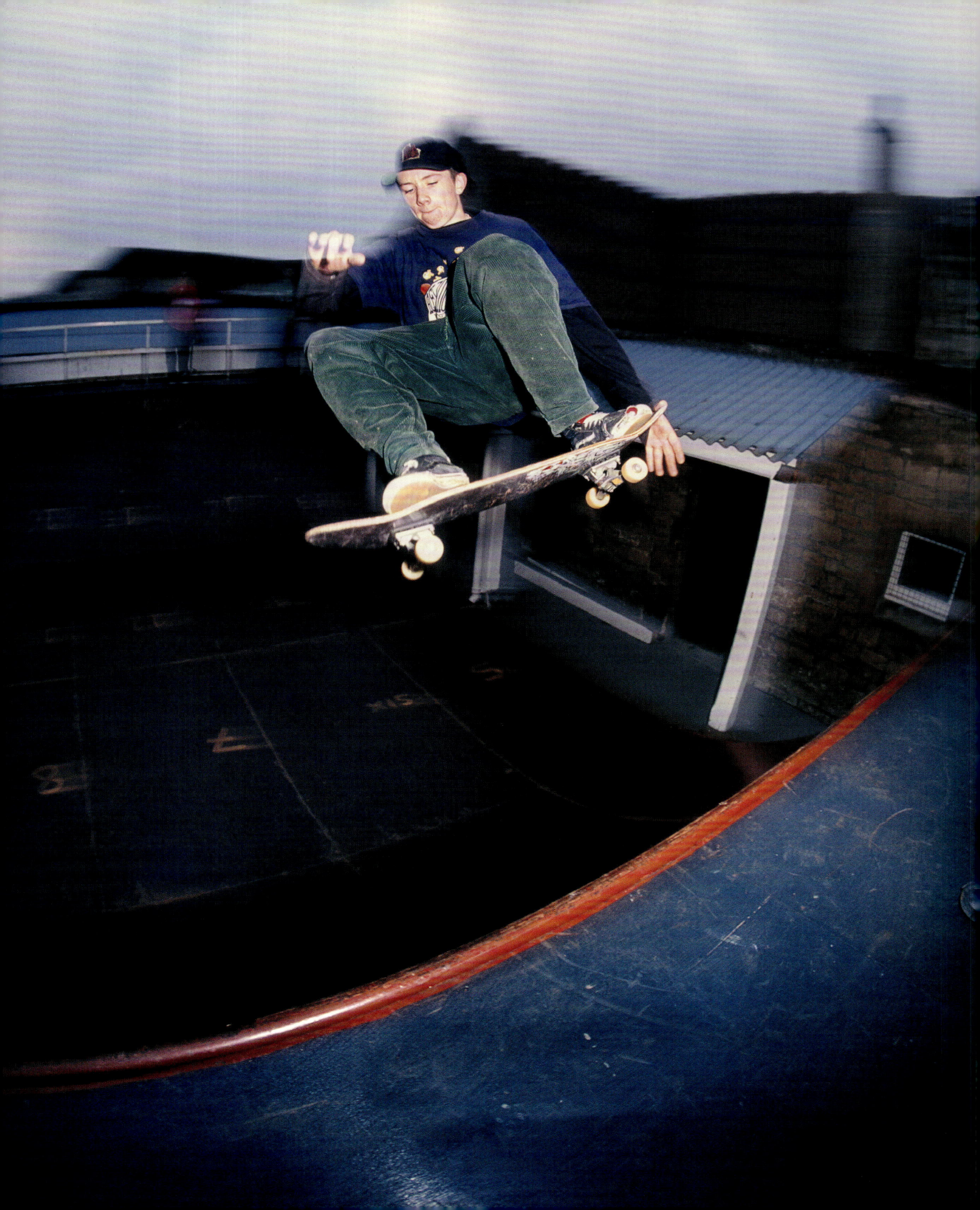

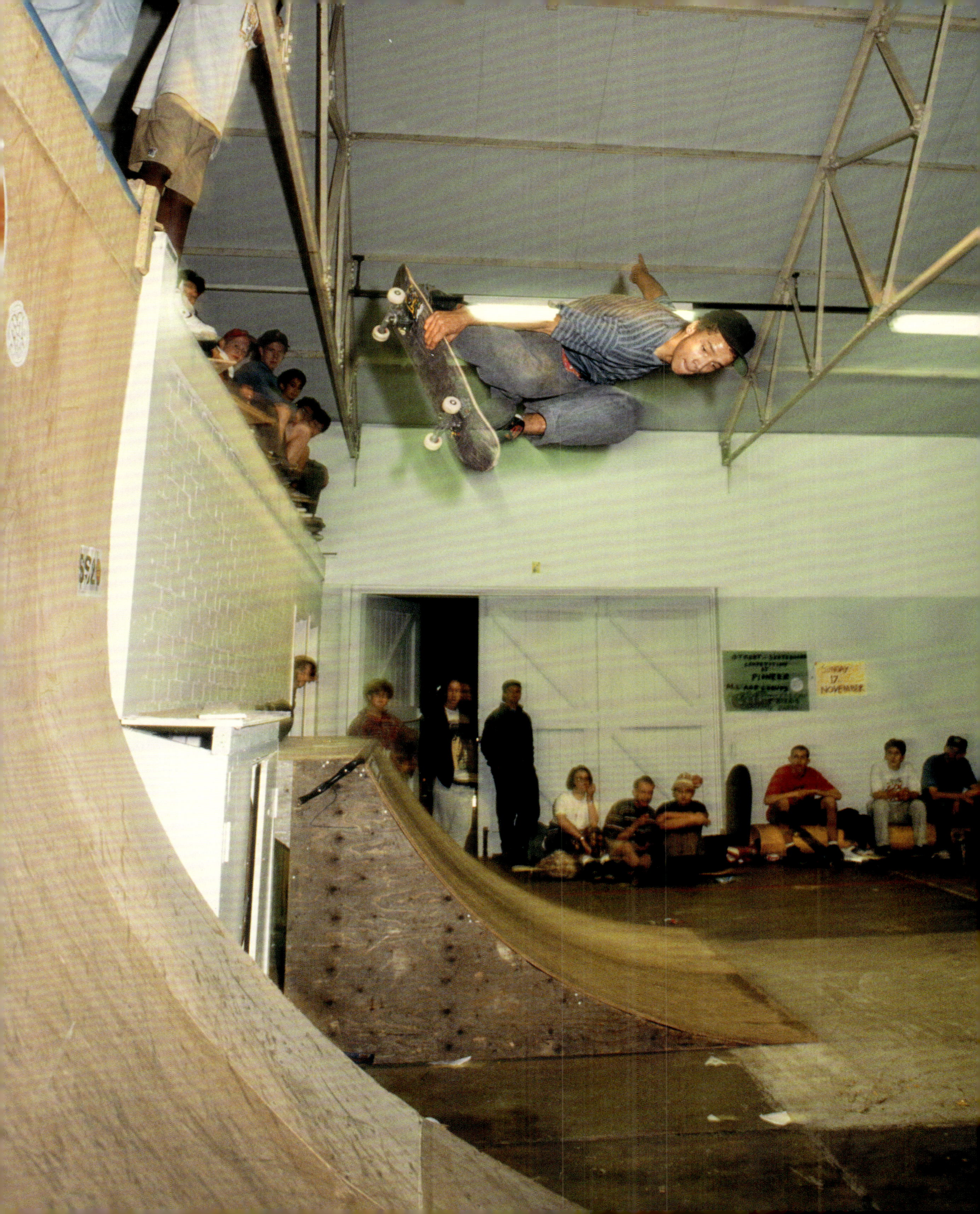
17
NOVEMBER

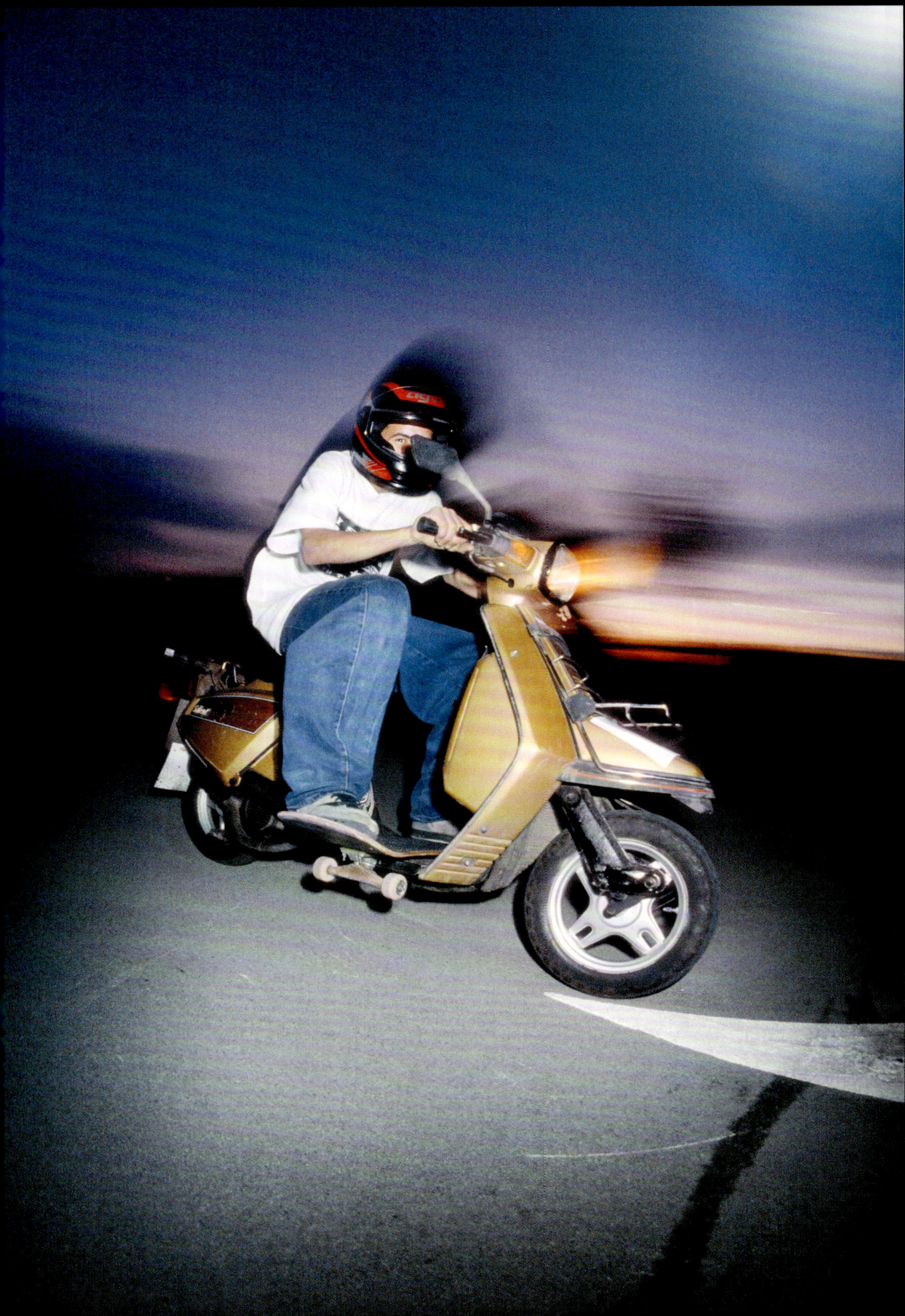

Left: Carl Shipman, 1992 **Photo:** James Hudson **Opposite:** Magazine cover collage by Ian Roxburgh, 1992 **Photos:** TLB

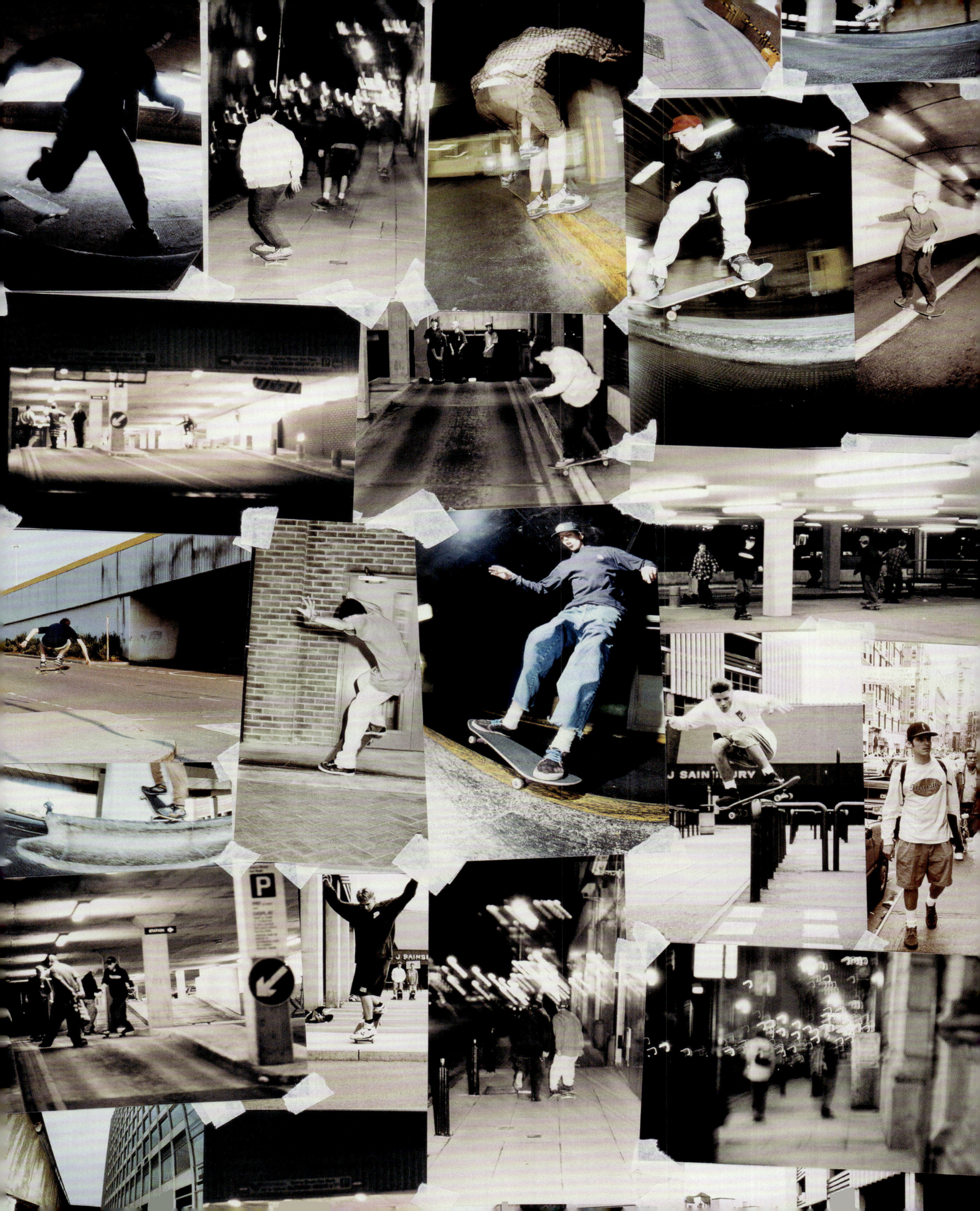
P

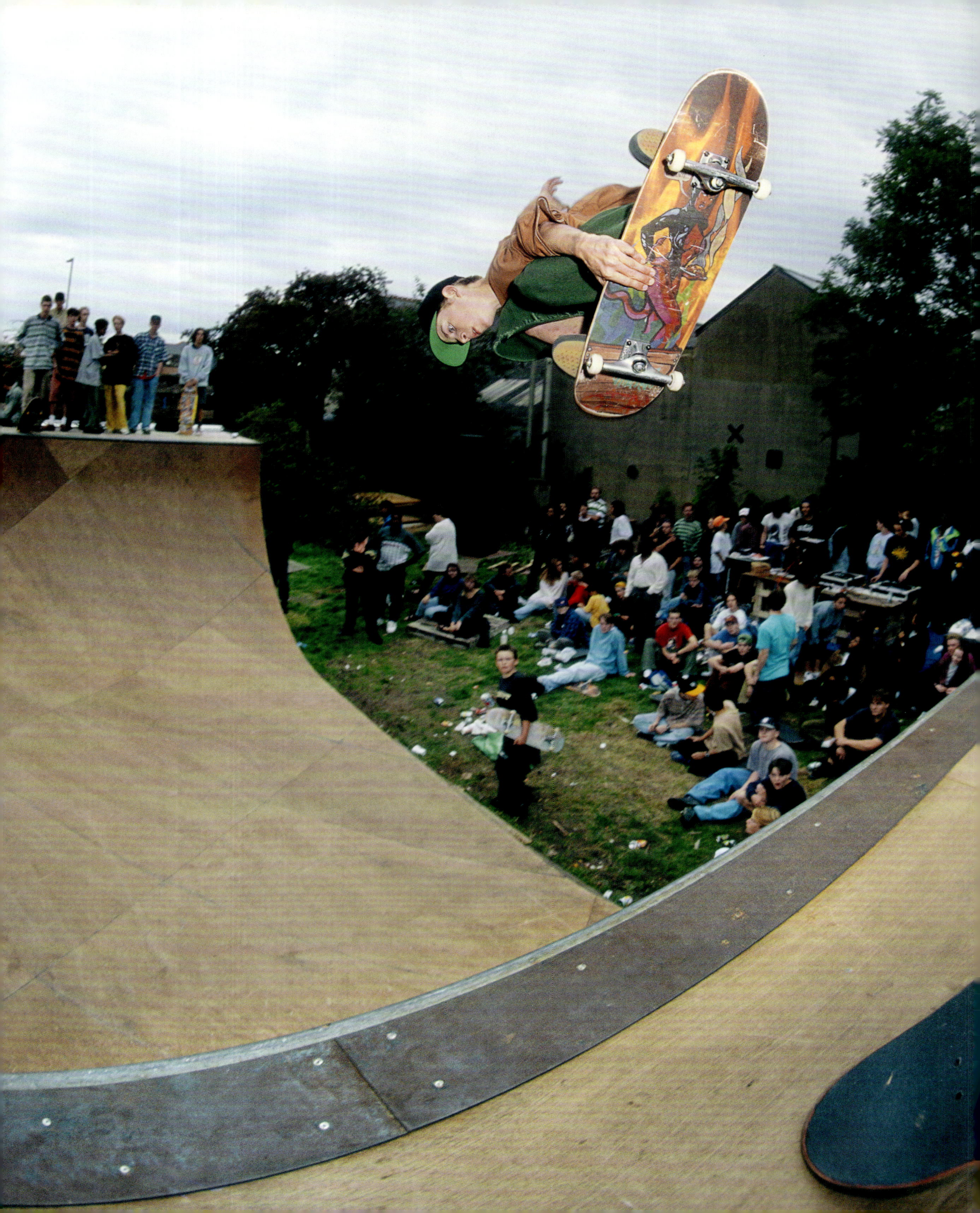

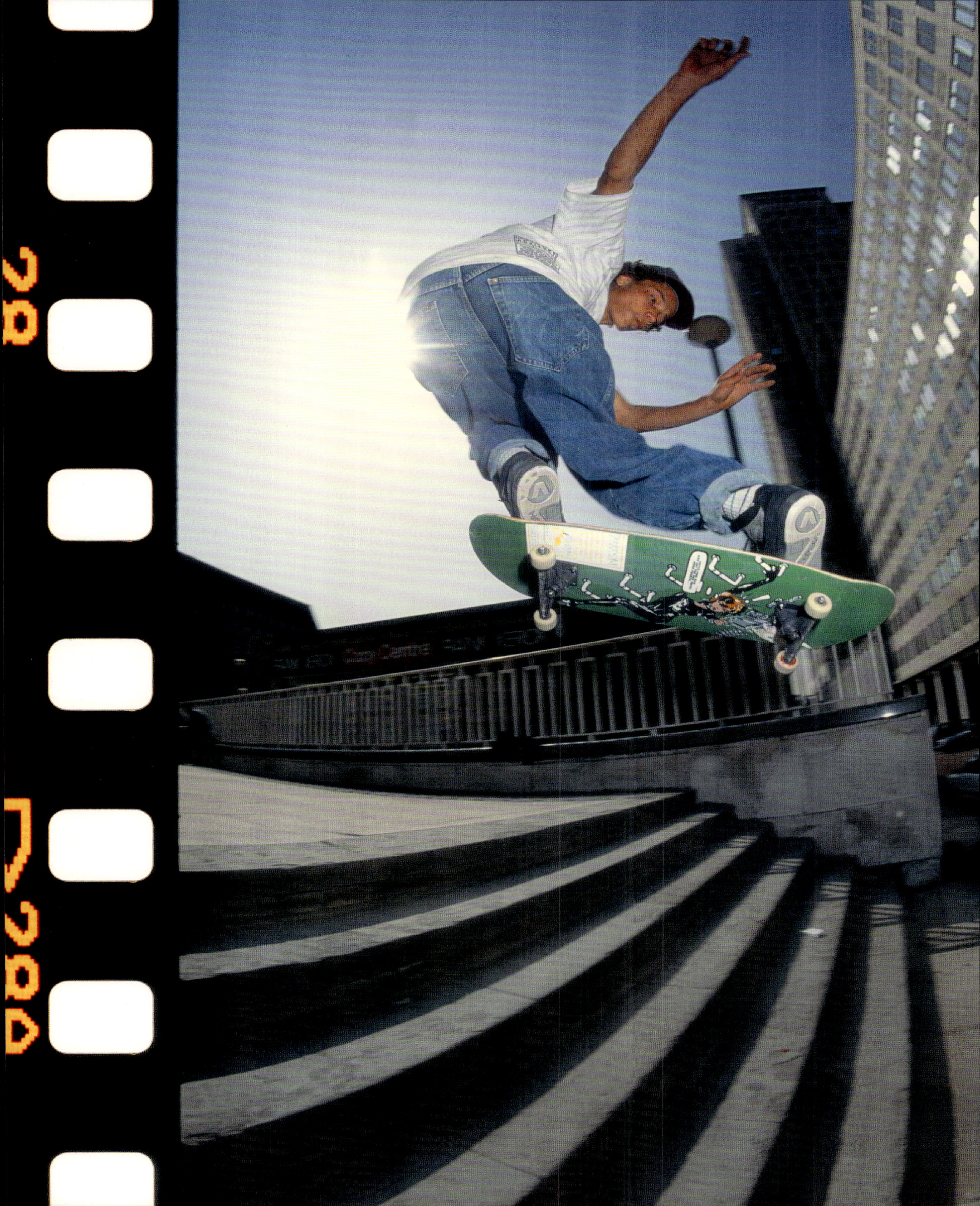

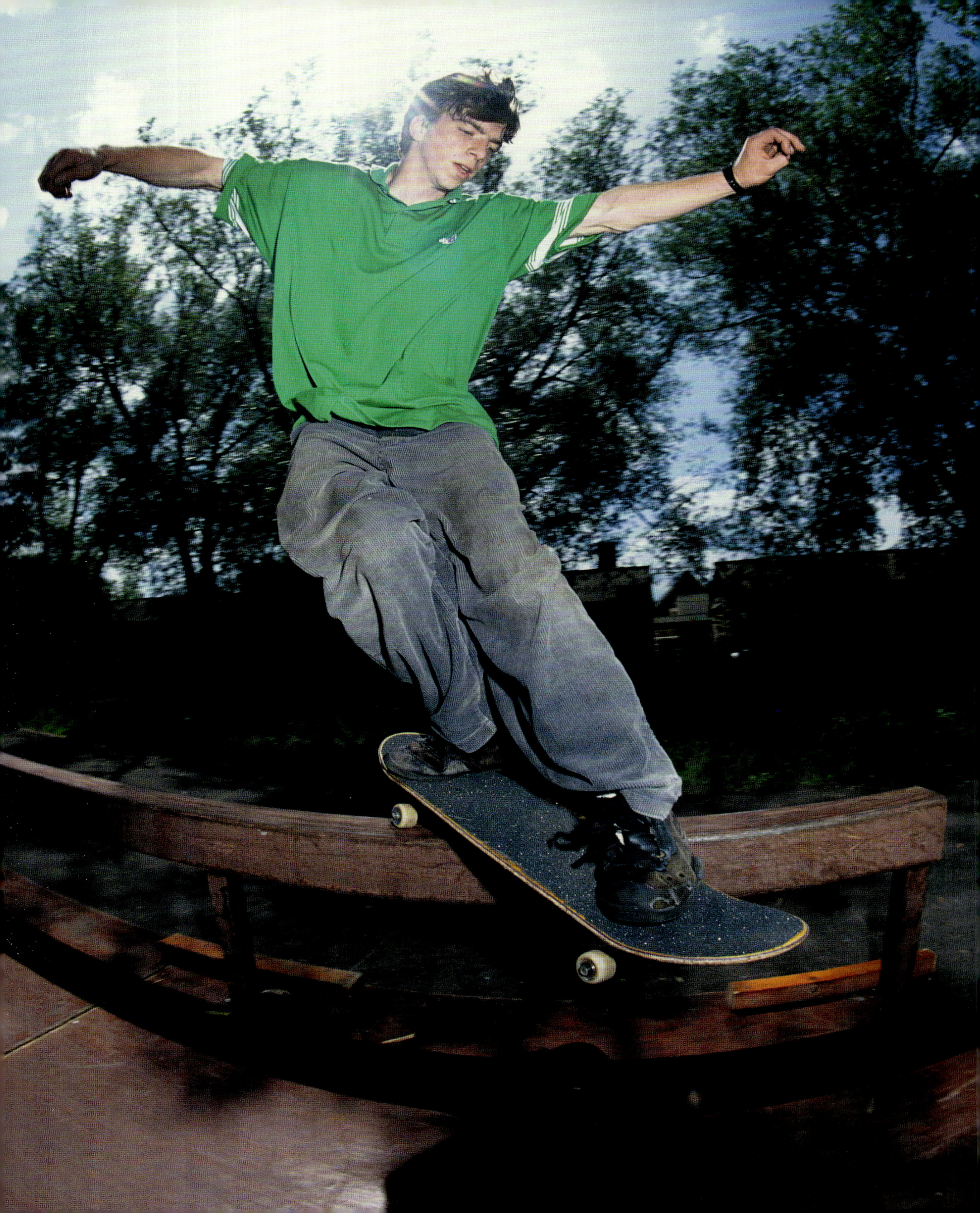

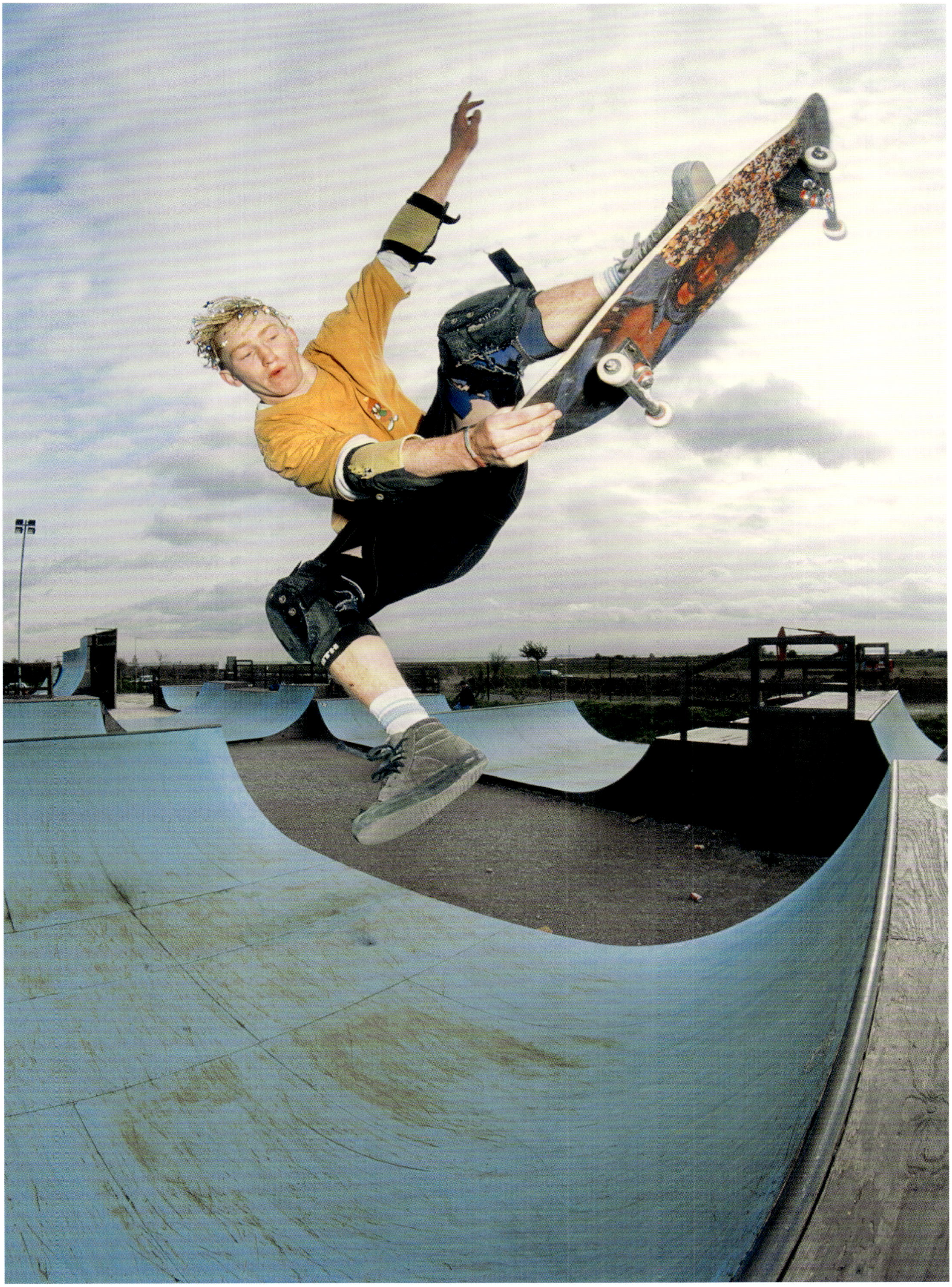

Previous spread left: Tom Penny, Oxford, 1992, and **right:** Curtis McCann, Shell Centre, London, 1992 **Opposite:** John Cattle, Winchester, 1992 **Right:** Sean Kelly (previously Ward), Leigh-on-Sea, 1992 **Photos:** TLB

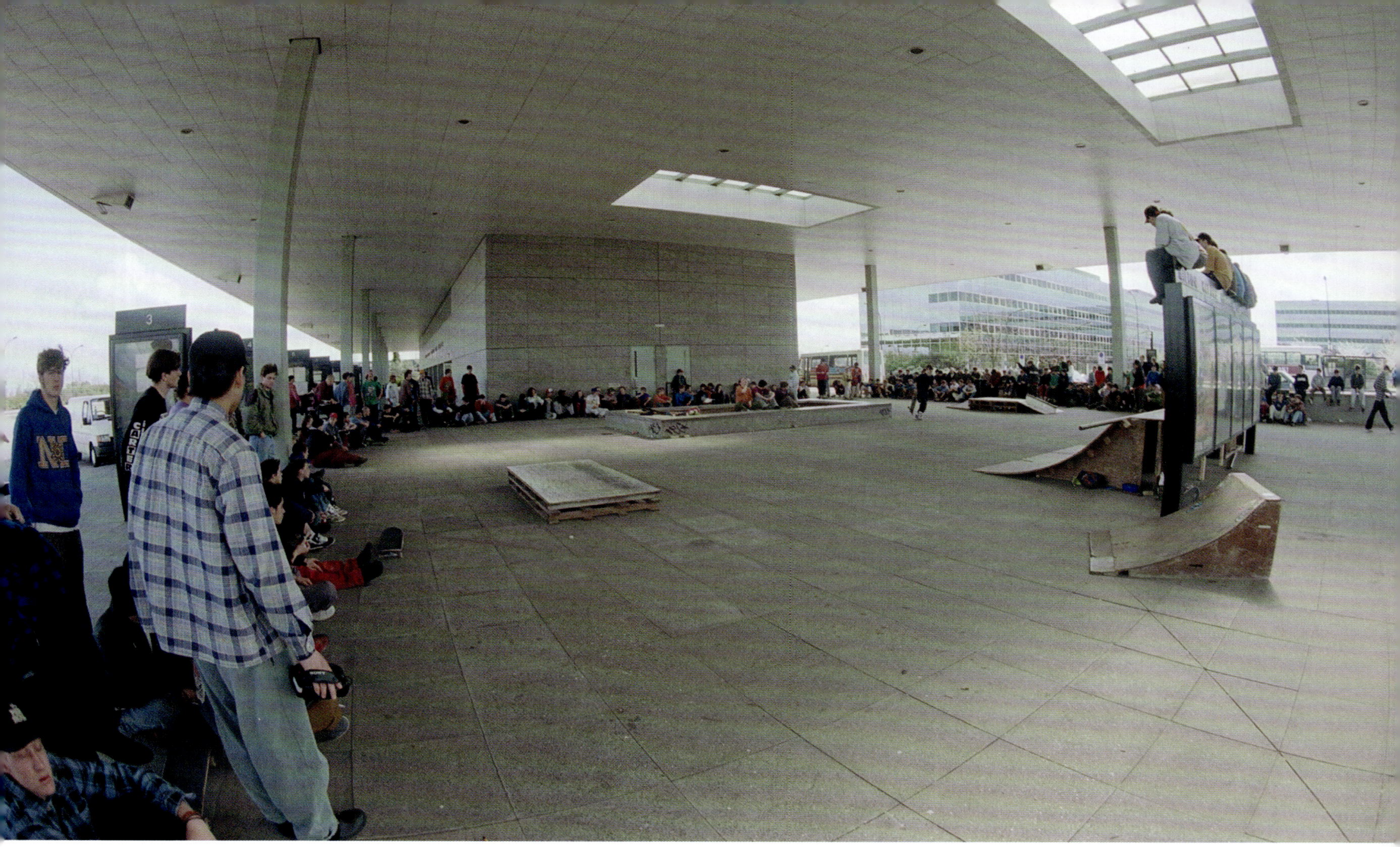

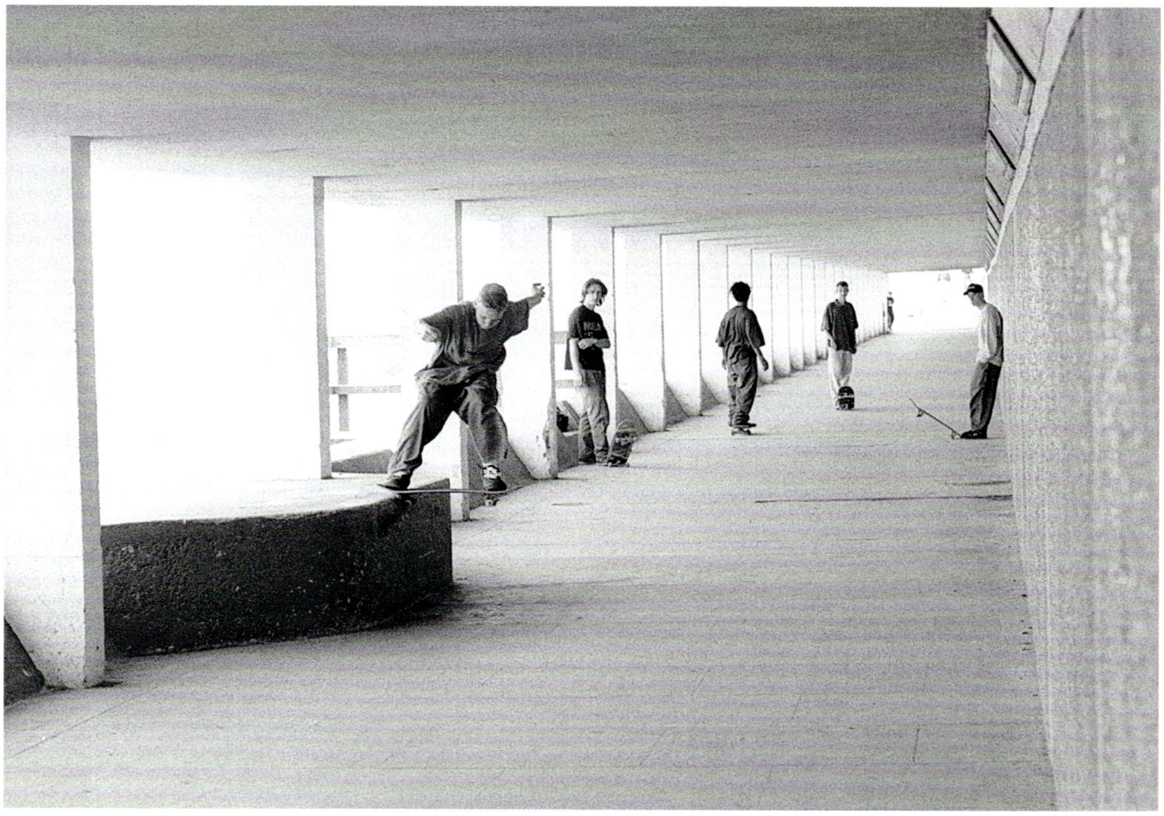

Clockwise from above: Milton Keynes bus station contest. Shell Centre London, Southbank crew with Rick Ibaseta and Salman Agah. Lewis Ashenden, Southbank. Bottle Alley, Hastings, 1992
Photos: TLB

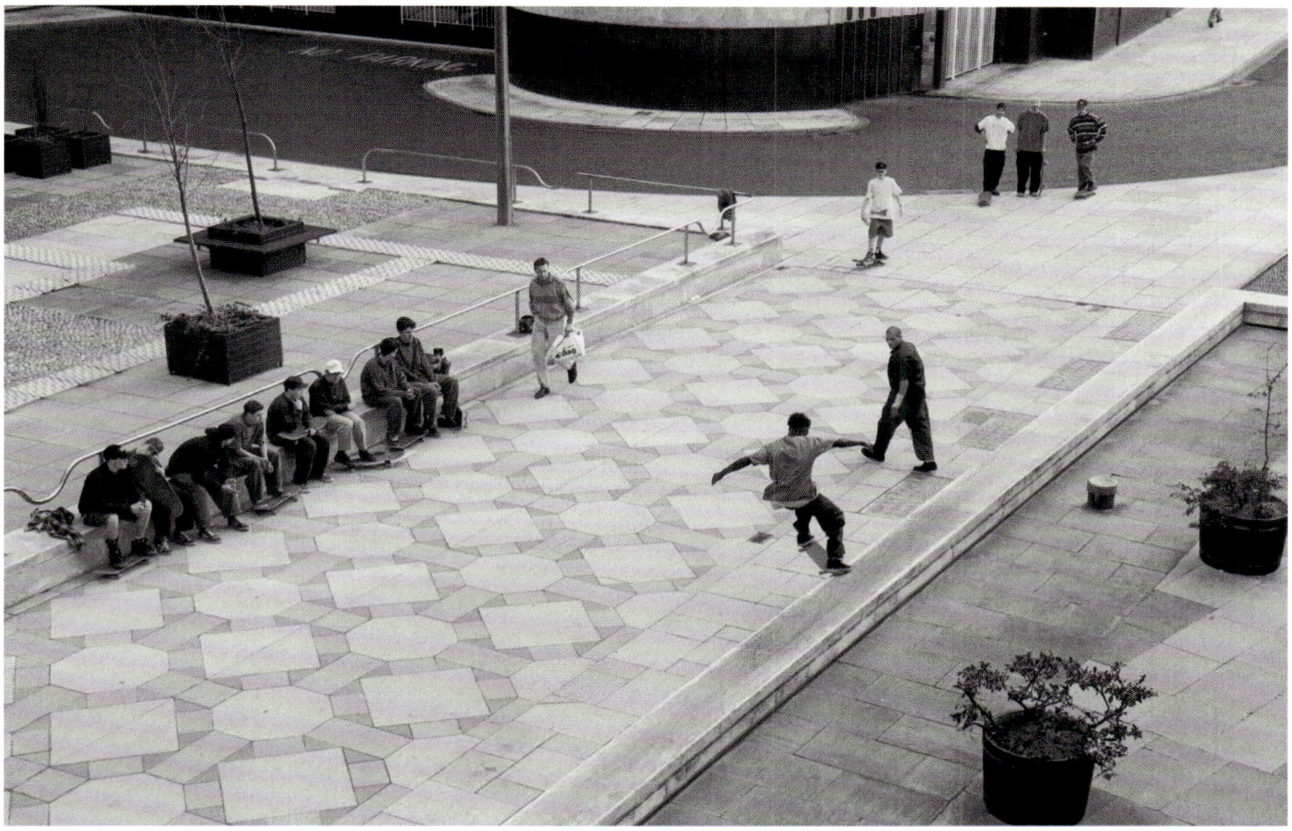

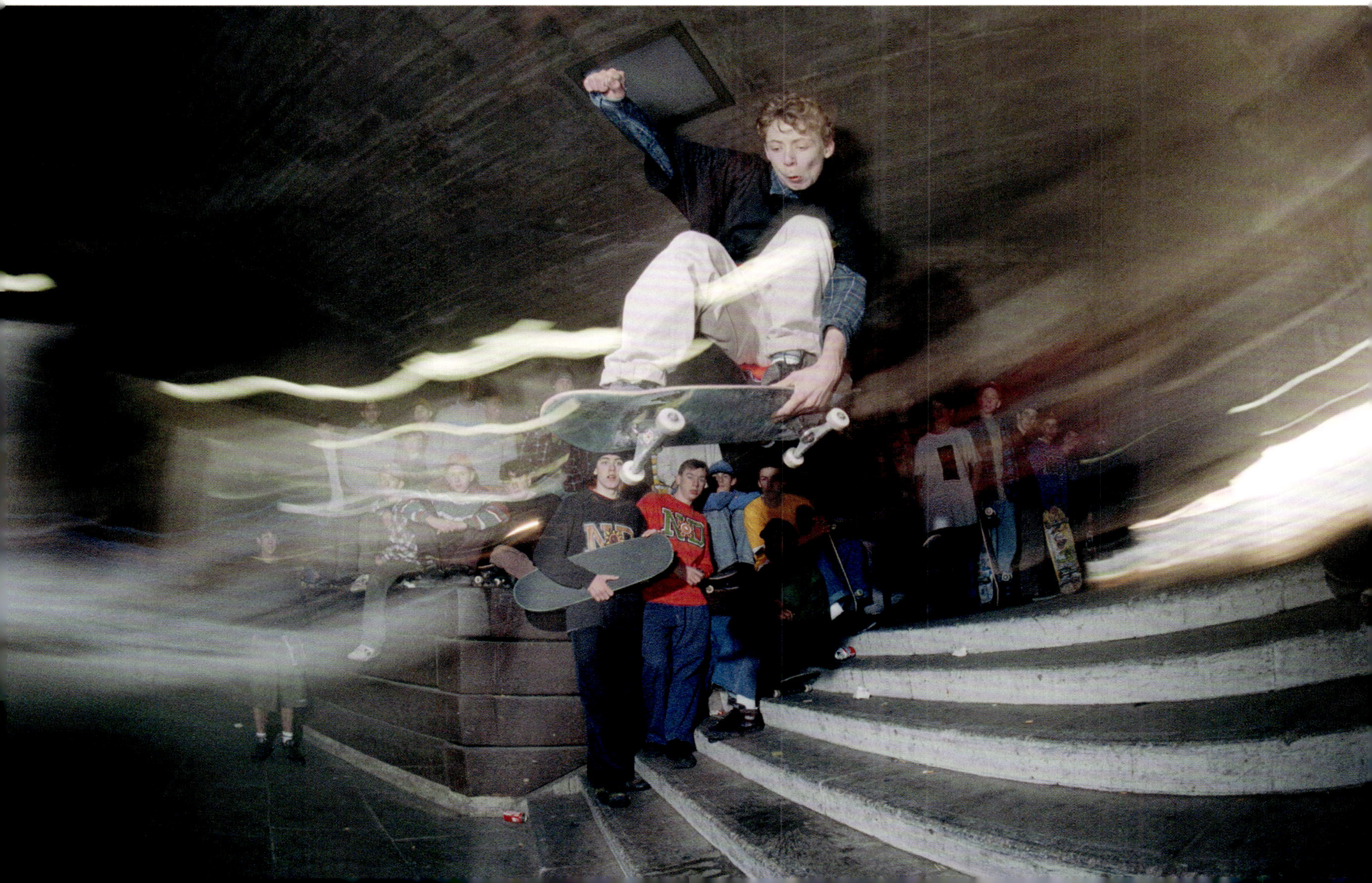

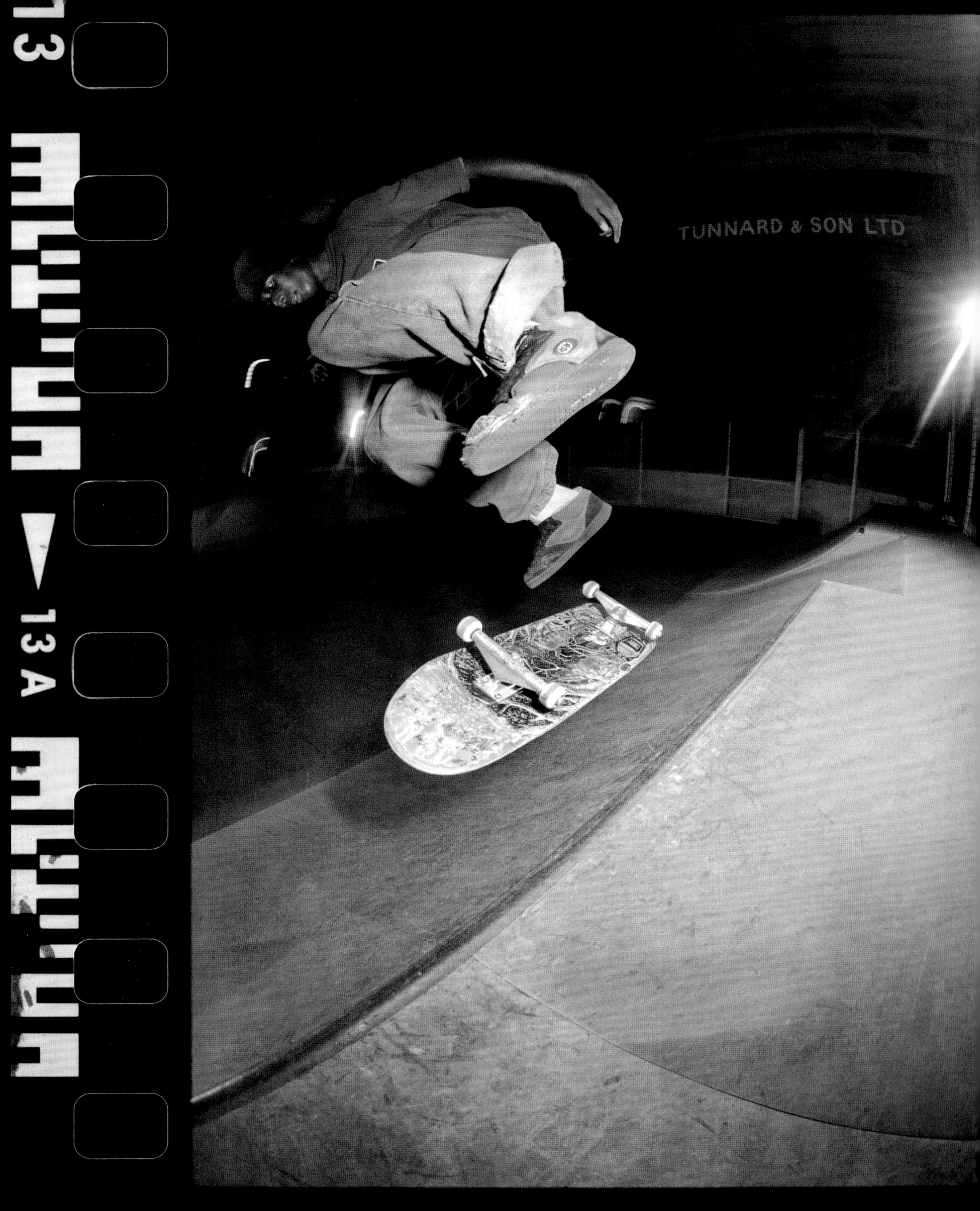
TUNNARD & SON LTD

Opposite: Winstan Whitter, Spitalfields, 1992 **Right:** Simon Evans, London, 1992 **Below:** Reuben Goodyear, Southbank, 1992 **All photos:** TLB

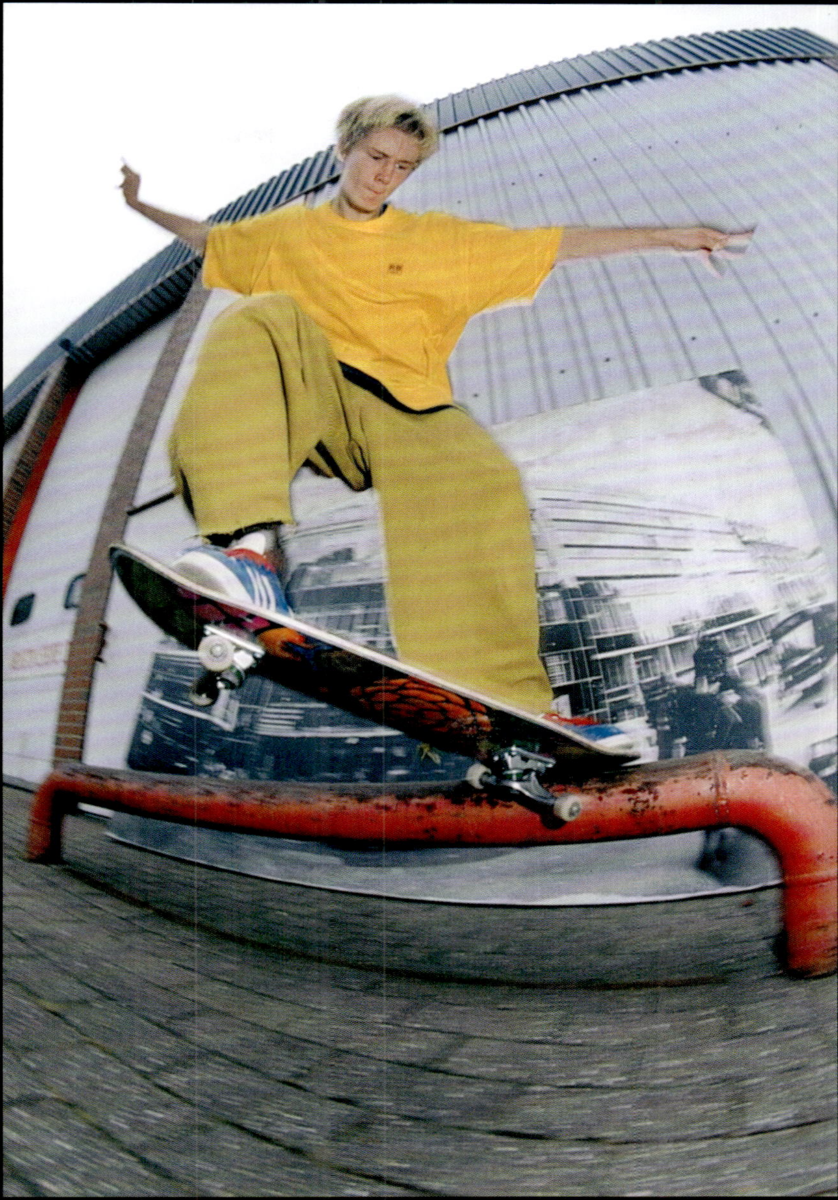

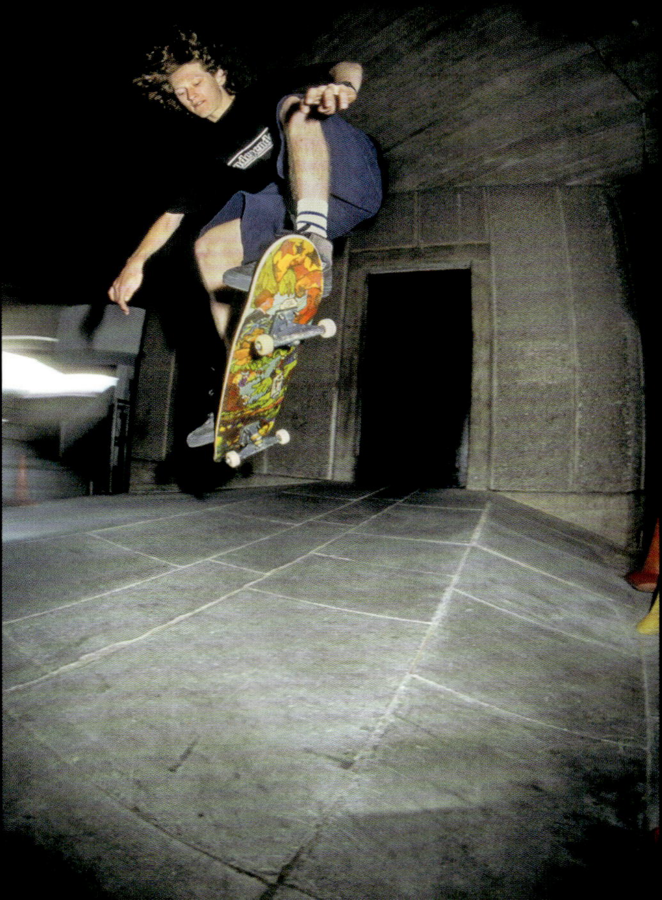

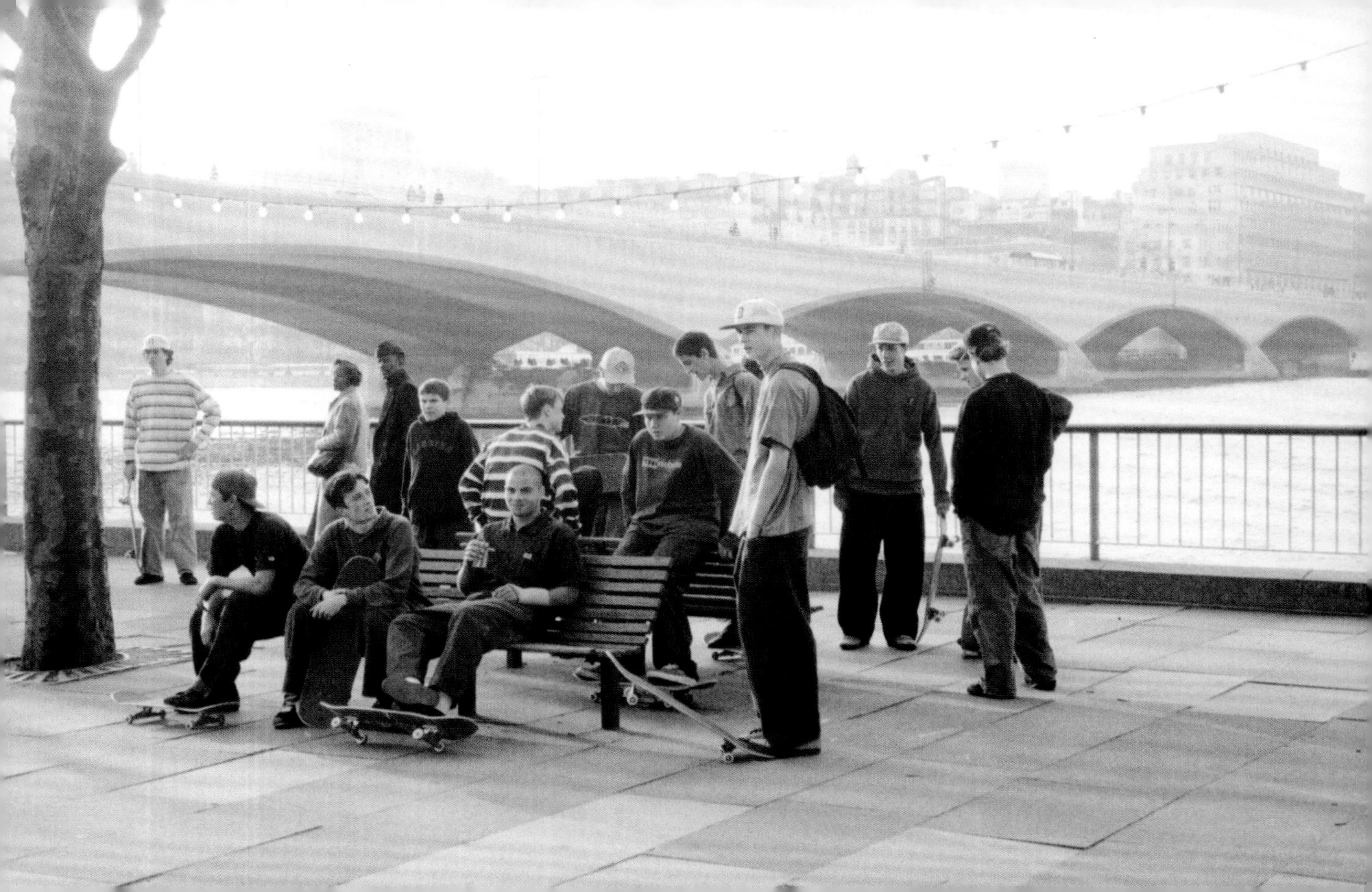

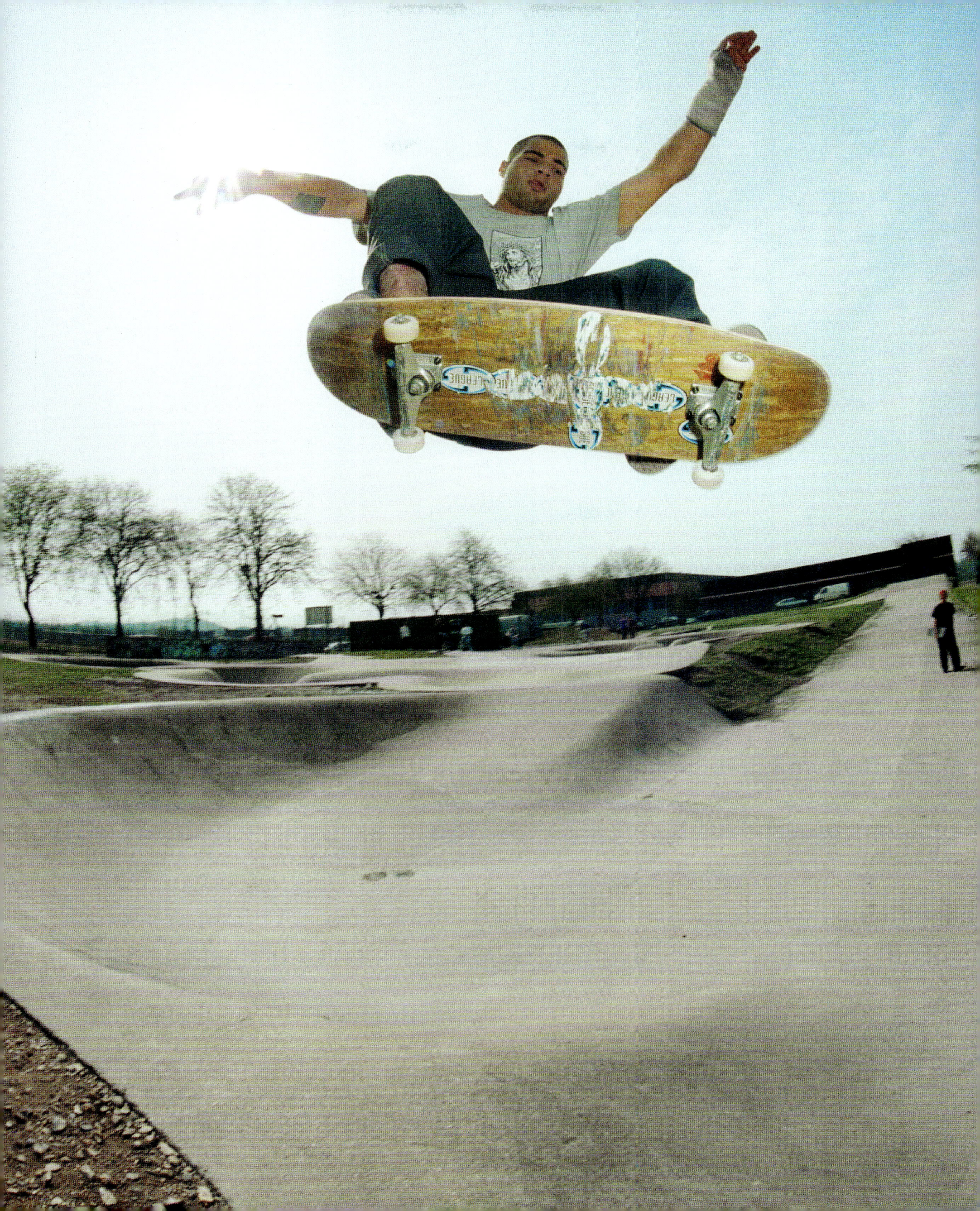

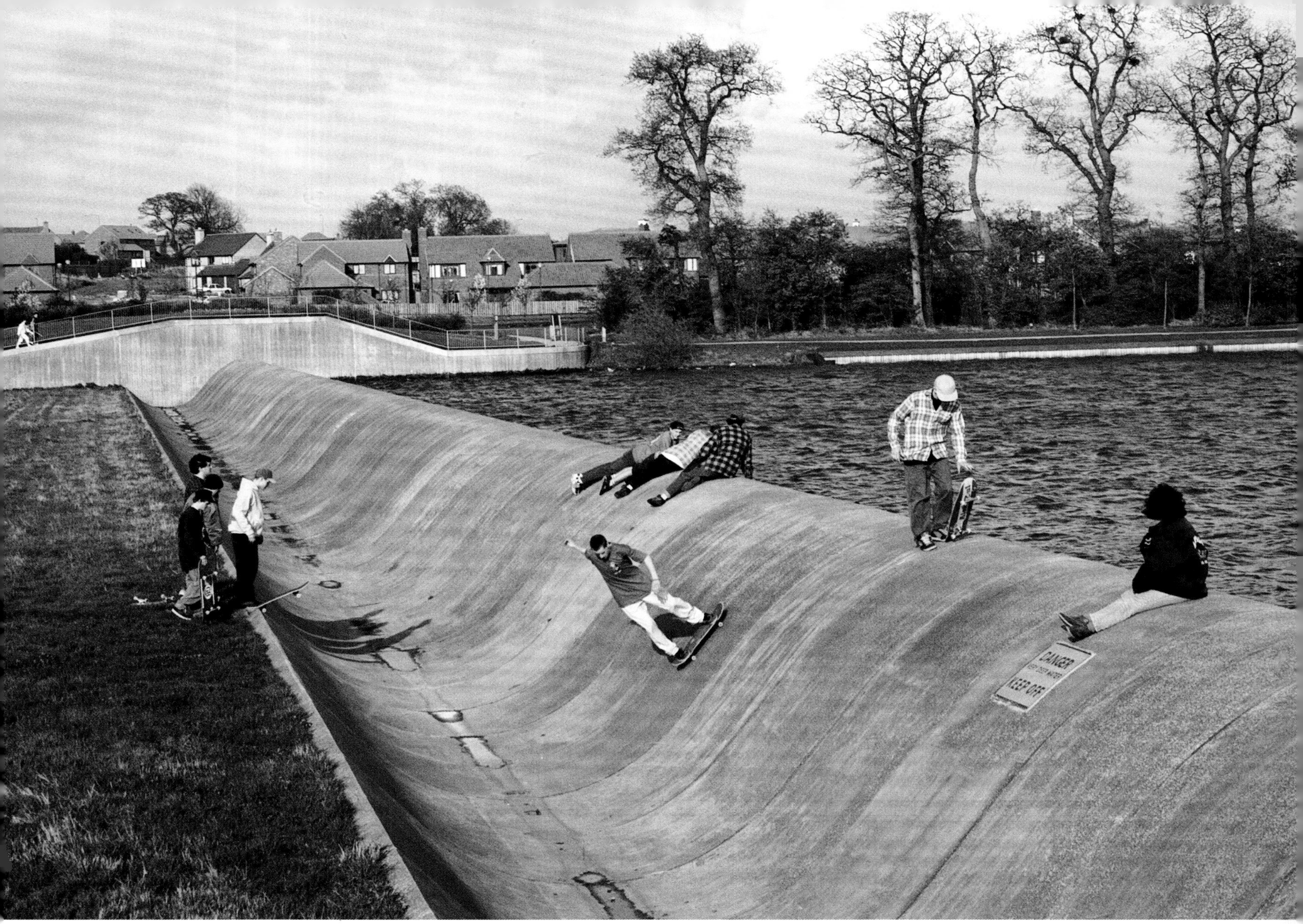

Clockwise from above: Caldecott reservoir, Milton Keynes, 1992 **Photo:** TLB. Howard Cooke, Livingston, Scotland, 1992 **Photo:** Percy Dean. Pete Hellicar, Nottingham contest, 1992 **Photo:** TLB **Overleaf:** Pioneer club, St Albans, contest, 1992 **Photos:** TLB

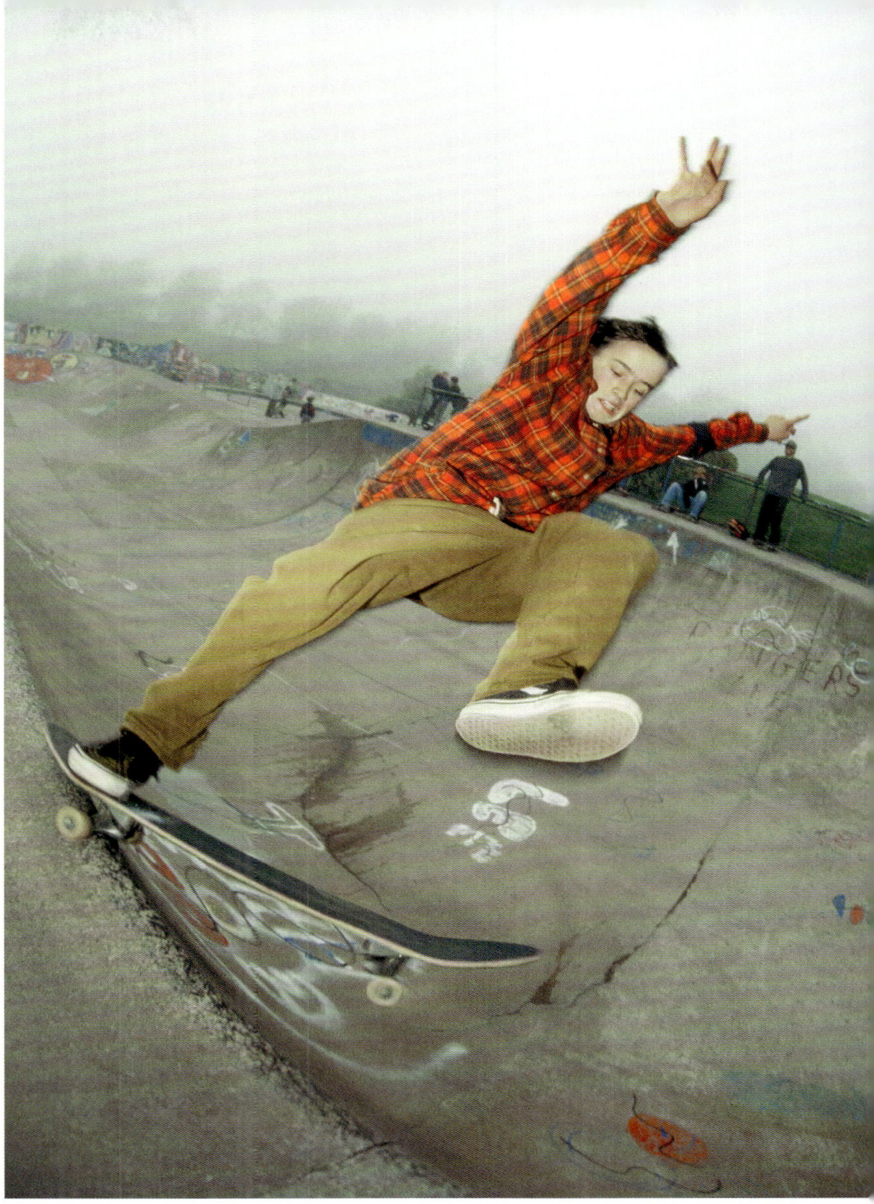

‘The magazine, especially at that time, was everything. It captured the whole culture. Not just the skateboarding—what people were wearing, music, different fashions. You know, who’s who, the contests—that was your source of information. That’s where you got everything. And it was SO important, something tangible, in print and you can hold it. You go into the newsagents and it’s there—and you’re in it! You’re like, FUCK this is crazy.’

Danny Wainwright

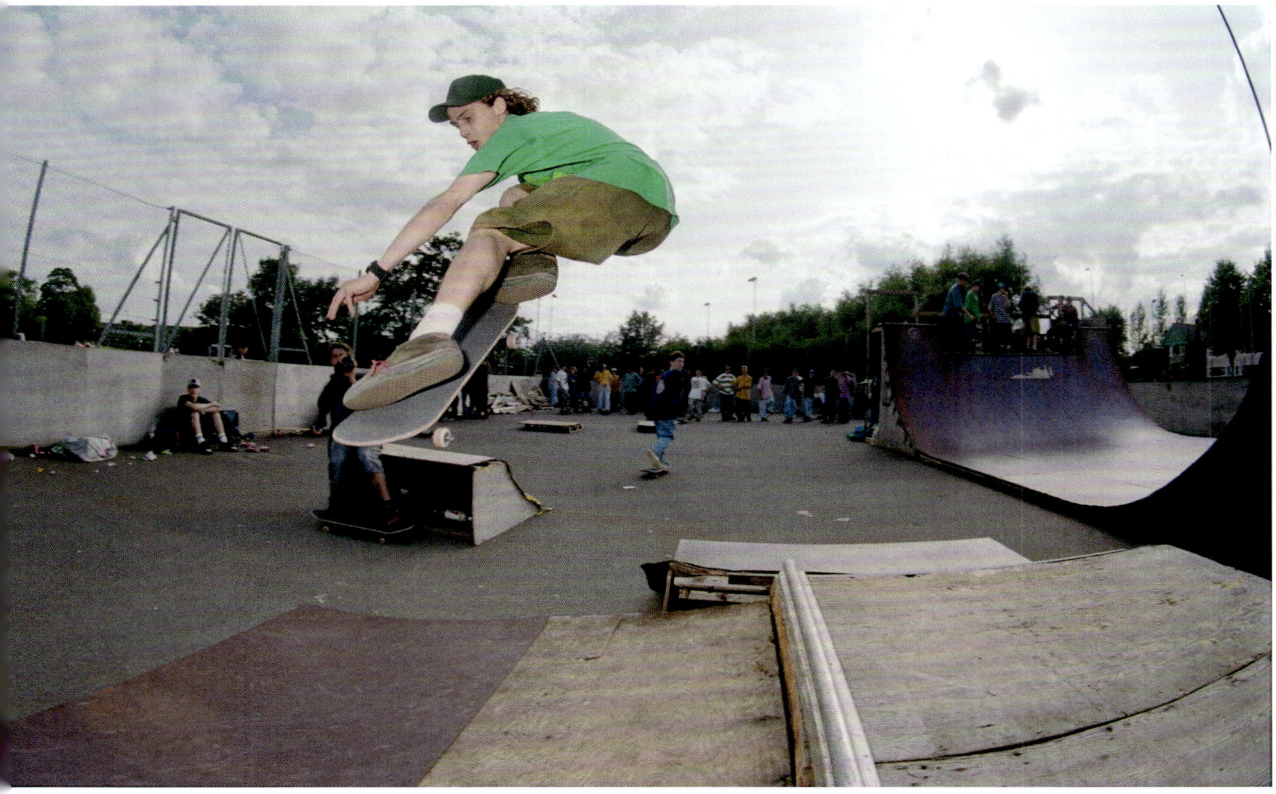

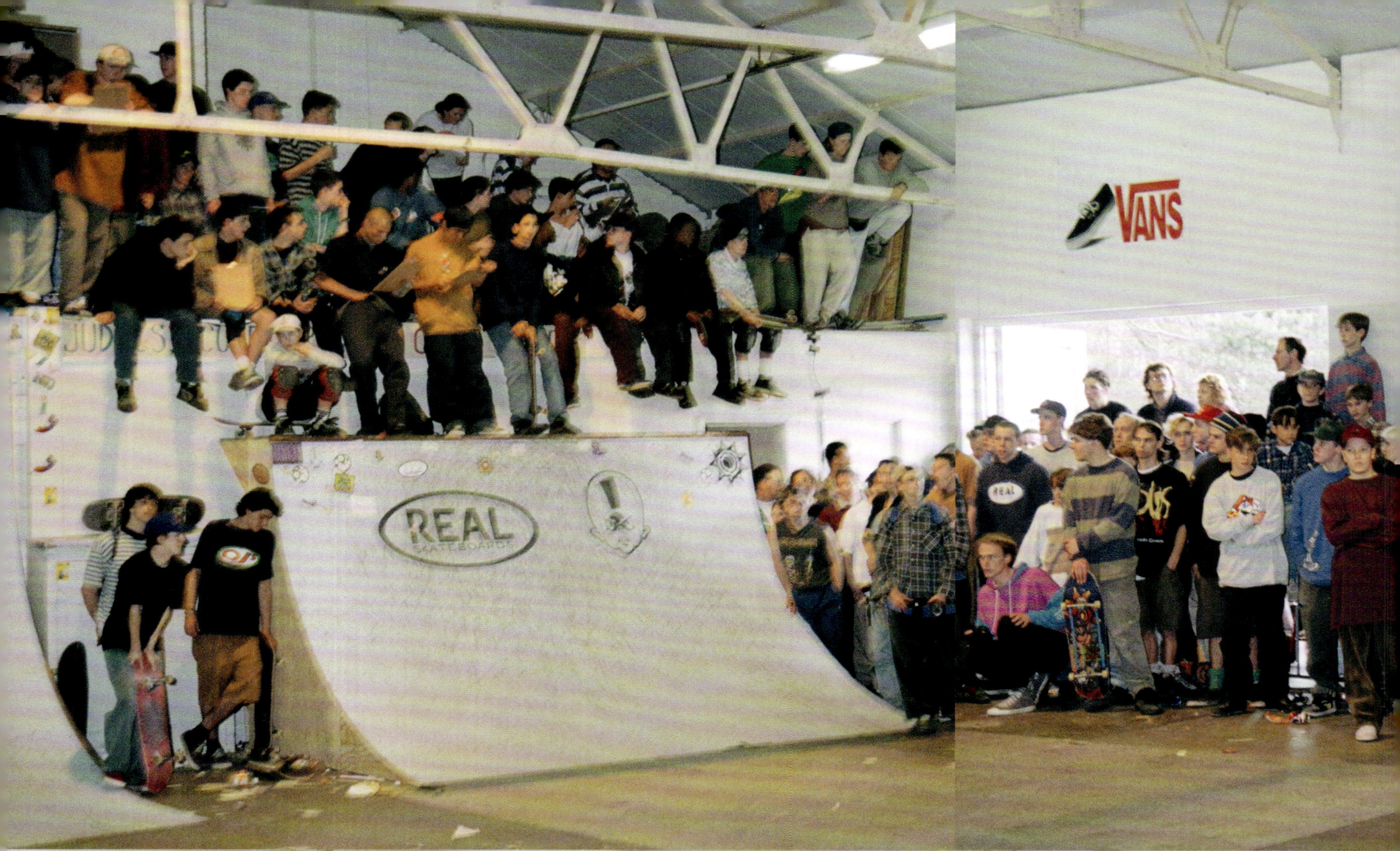
VANS
REAL

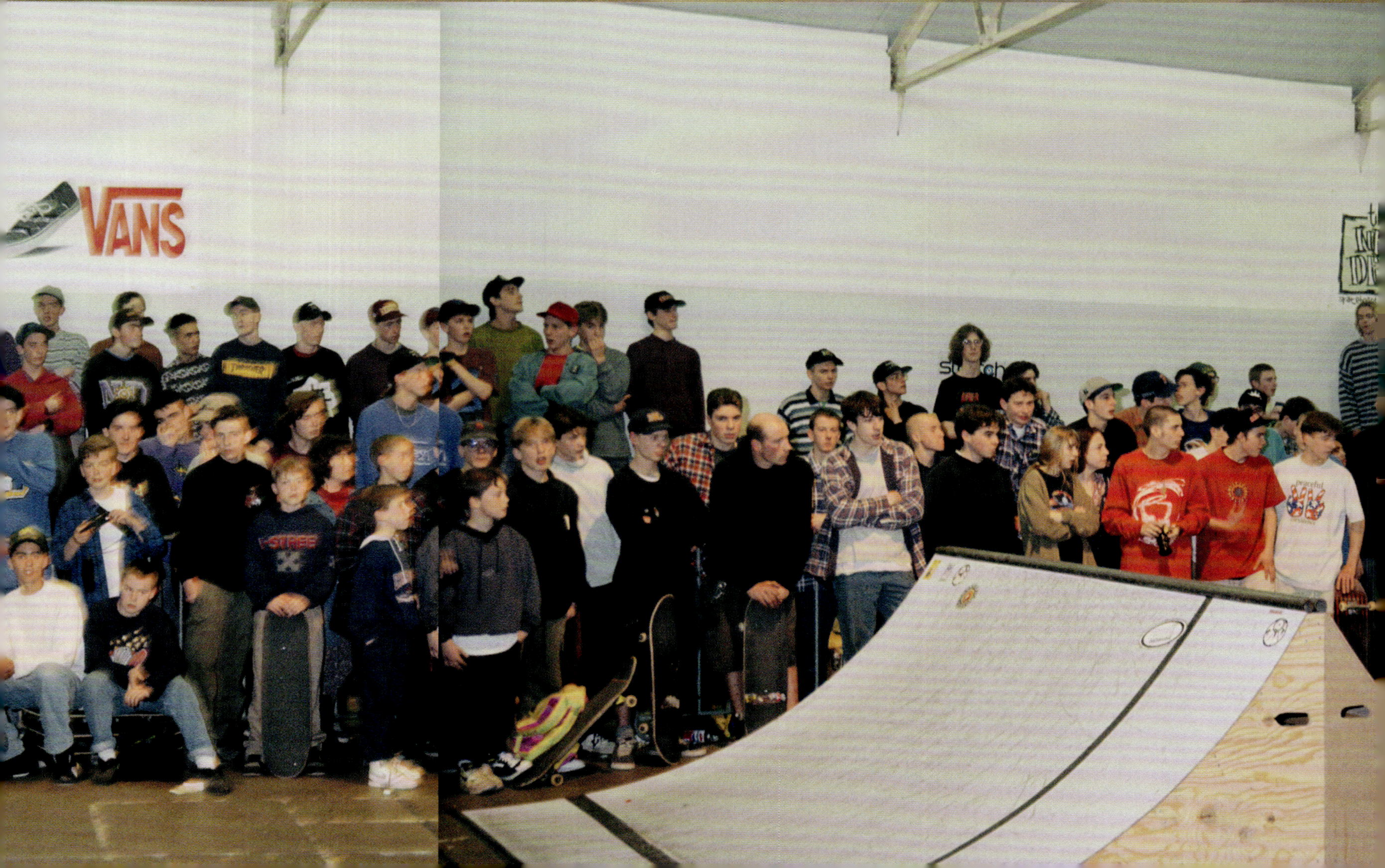
VANS

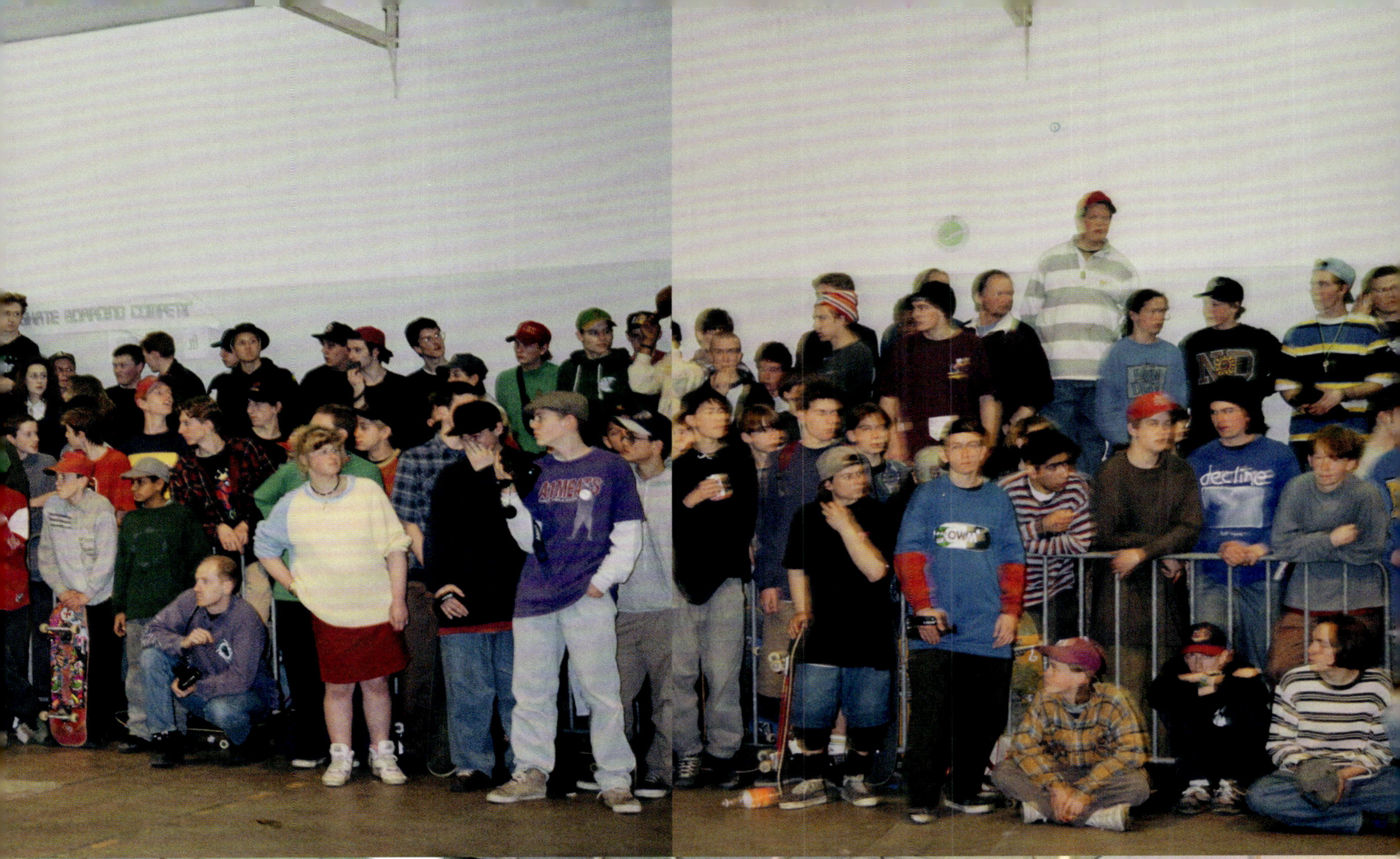
decline

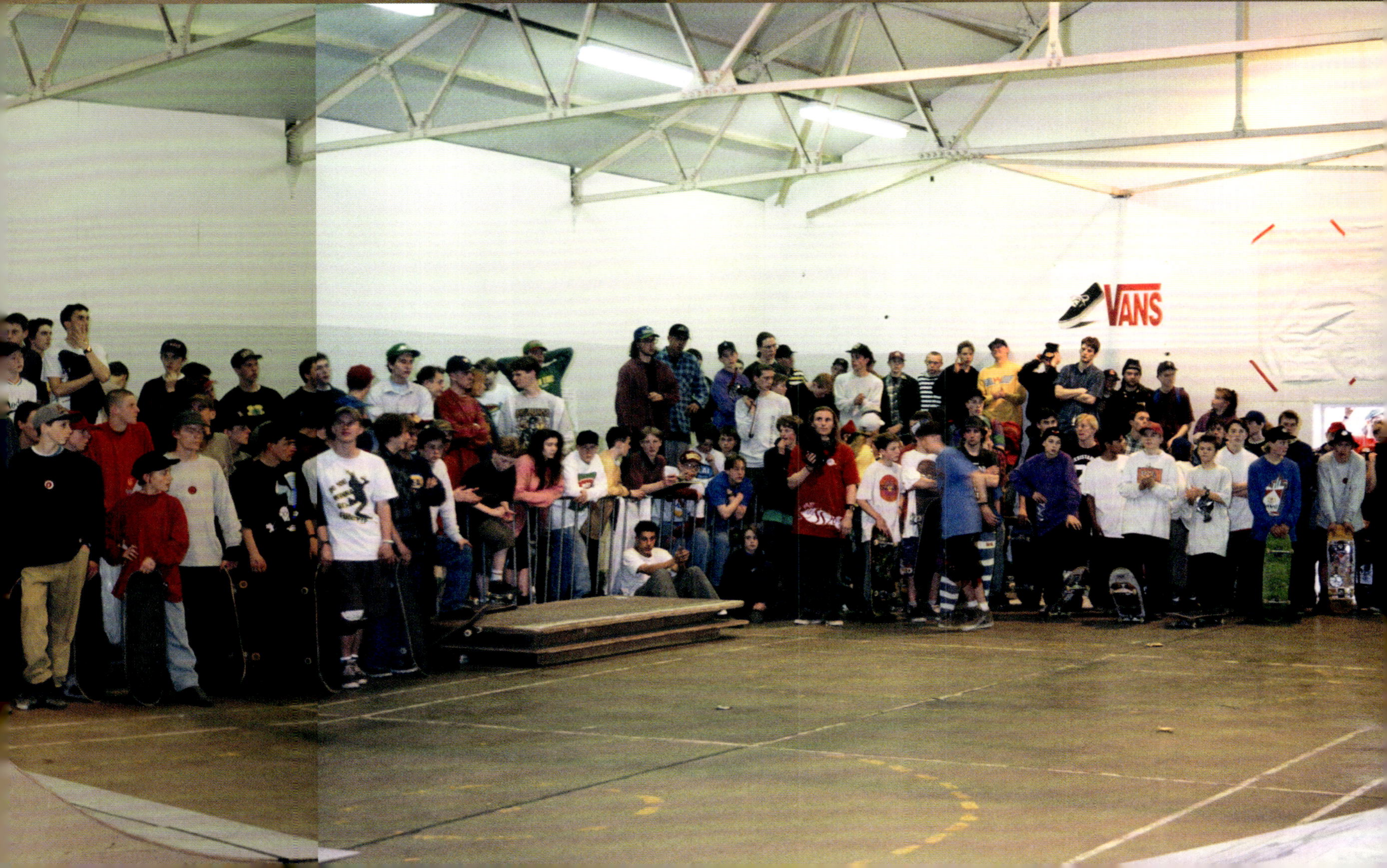
VANS

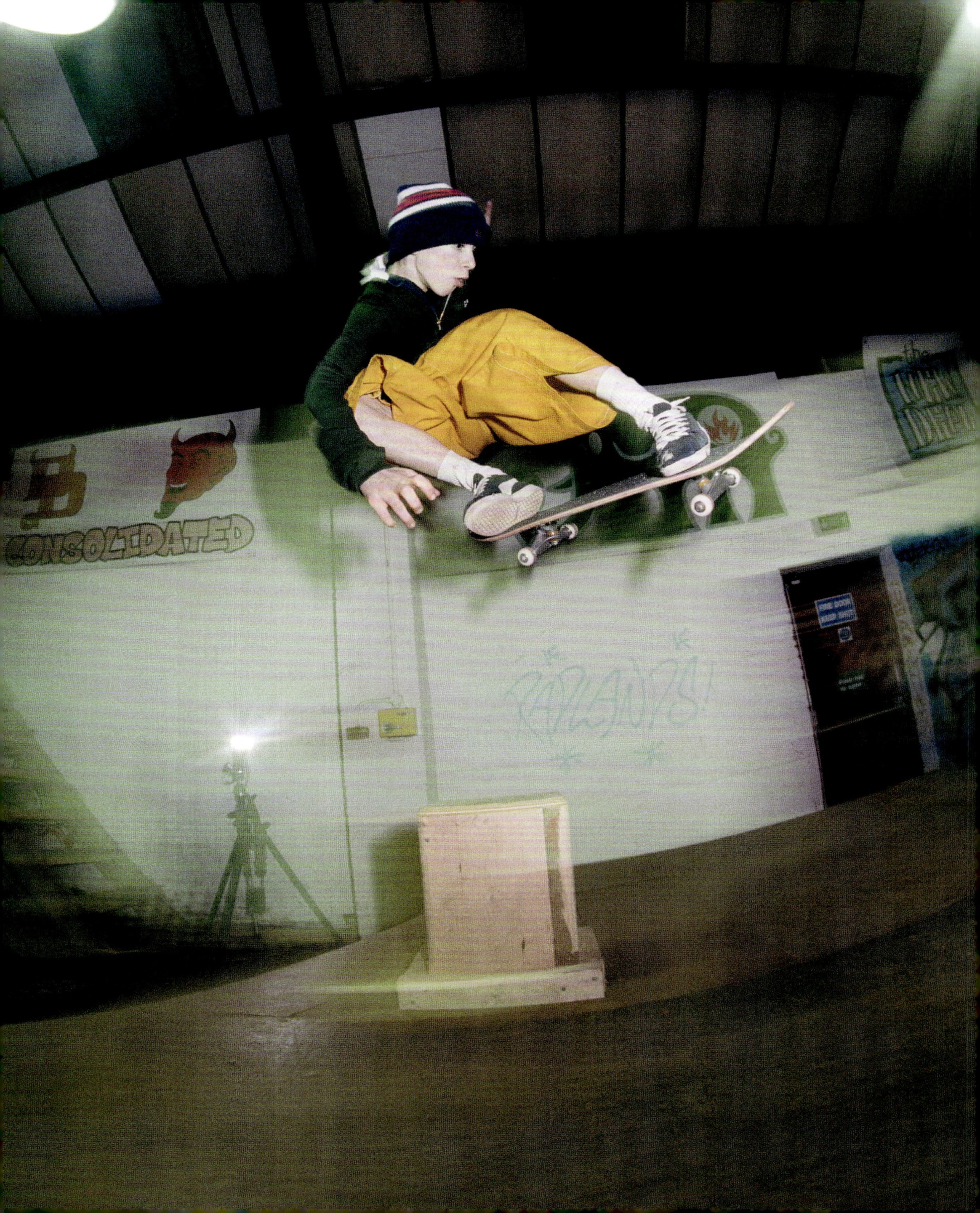
CONSOLIDATED

Photo Captions. all photos by Leo Sharp.

Sadly, most of my film came out shite, due To a shite flash on my camera, heres the best of a rotten bunch:-

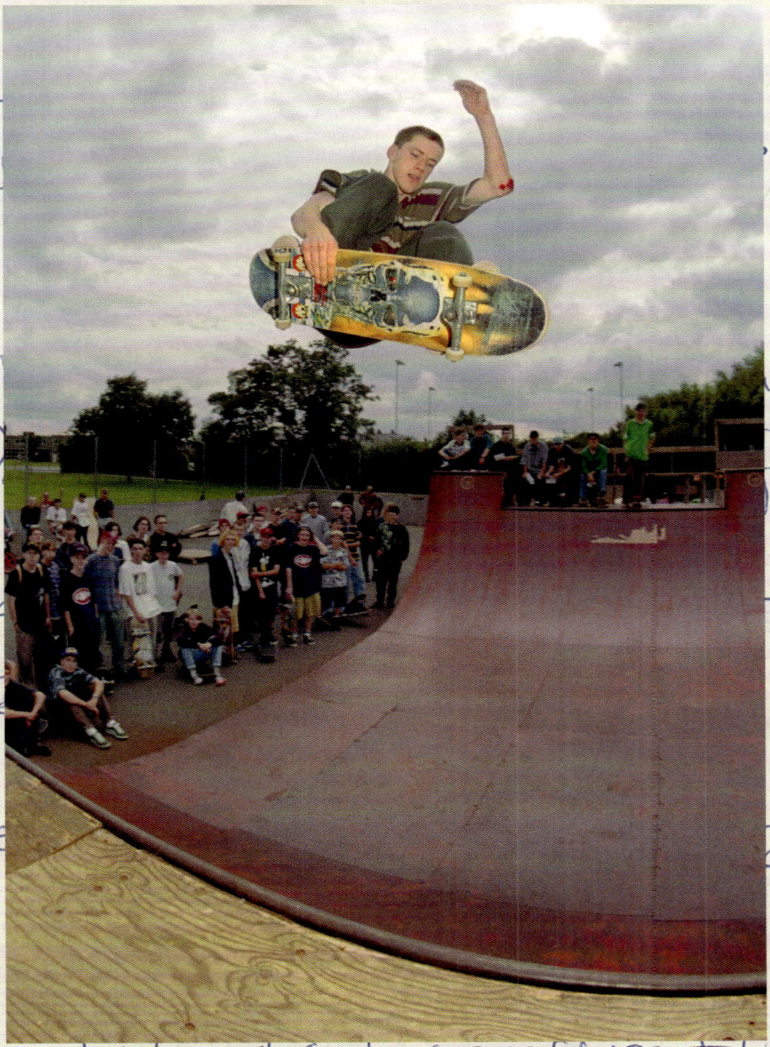

(1) The aggr… expected on the mellowes…

(2) Few others … s fly off as it's owner, D… at melon.

(3) A Talior-ma… the infamous Luckhurst rep…

(4) Hectic scene… t a look behind the camera.

(5) Robert Selley Tailgrabs his pressure flip switch-stance whilst strangling a would be snaker.

Opposite: Tom Penny, Radlands, 1992 **Photo:** TLB **This page:** Photo submission and contest report, Leo Sharp, 1992 **Inset:** Alan Rushbrooke, Nottingham contest, 1992 **Photo:** TLB

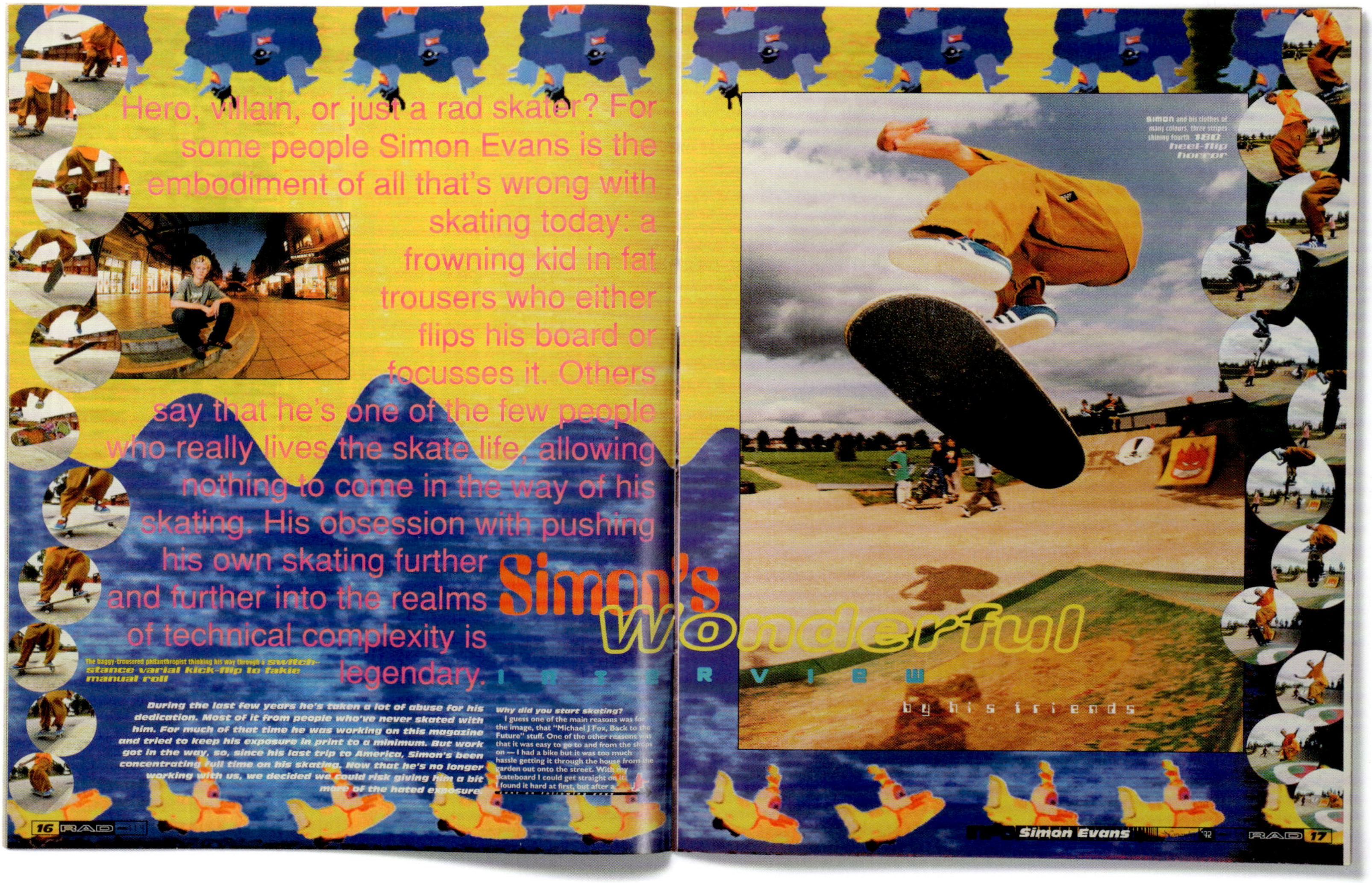

Hero, villain, or just a rad skater? For some people Simon Evans is the embodiment of all that's wrong with skating today: a frowning kid in fat trousers who either flips his board or focusses it. Others say that he's one of the few people who really lives the skate life, allowing nothing to come in the way of his skating. His obsession with pushing his own skating further and further into the realms of technical complexity is legendary.

The baggy-trousered philanthropist thinking his way through a switch-stance varial kick-flip to fakie manual roll

Simon's Wonderful Interview

by his friends

During the last few years he's taken a lot of abuse for his dedication. Most of it from people who've never skated with him. For much of that time he was working on this magazine and tried to keep his exposure in print to a minimum. But work got in the way, so, since his last trip to America, Simon's been concentrating full time on his skating. Now that he's no longer working with us, we decided we could risk giving him a bit more of the hated exposure.

Why did you start skating?

I guess one of the main reasons was for the image, that "Michael J Fox, Back to the Future" stuff. One of the other reasons was that it was easy to go to and from the shops on — I had a bike but it was too much hassle getting it through the house from the garden out onto the street. With my skateboard I could get straight on it. I found it hard at first, but after a

simon and his clothes of many colours, three stripes shining fourth 180 heel-flip horror

16 RAD

Simon Evans '92 RAD 17

'I think we probably just got confused. I remember standing on Earl's Court station—looking like a banana—and just realising, just clicking; "Oh my God, what the fuck? Oh. My. God". Basically we were fashion victims you know—let's burn the photo albums, secure the perimeter! It was—yeah, it was just foolishness, really!'

Simon Evans

Above: Simon Evans interview, Issue 114, November 1992, design by Steve Hicks
Opposite: Simon Evans, Kennington, 1992 **All photos:** TLB

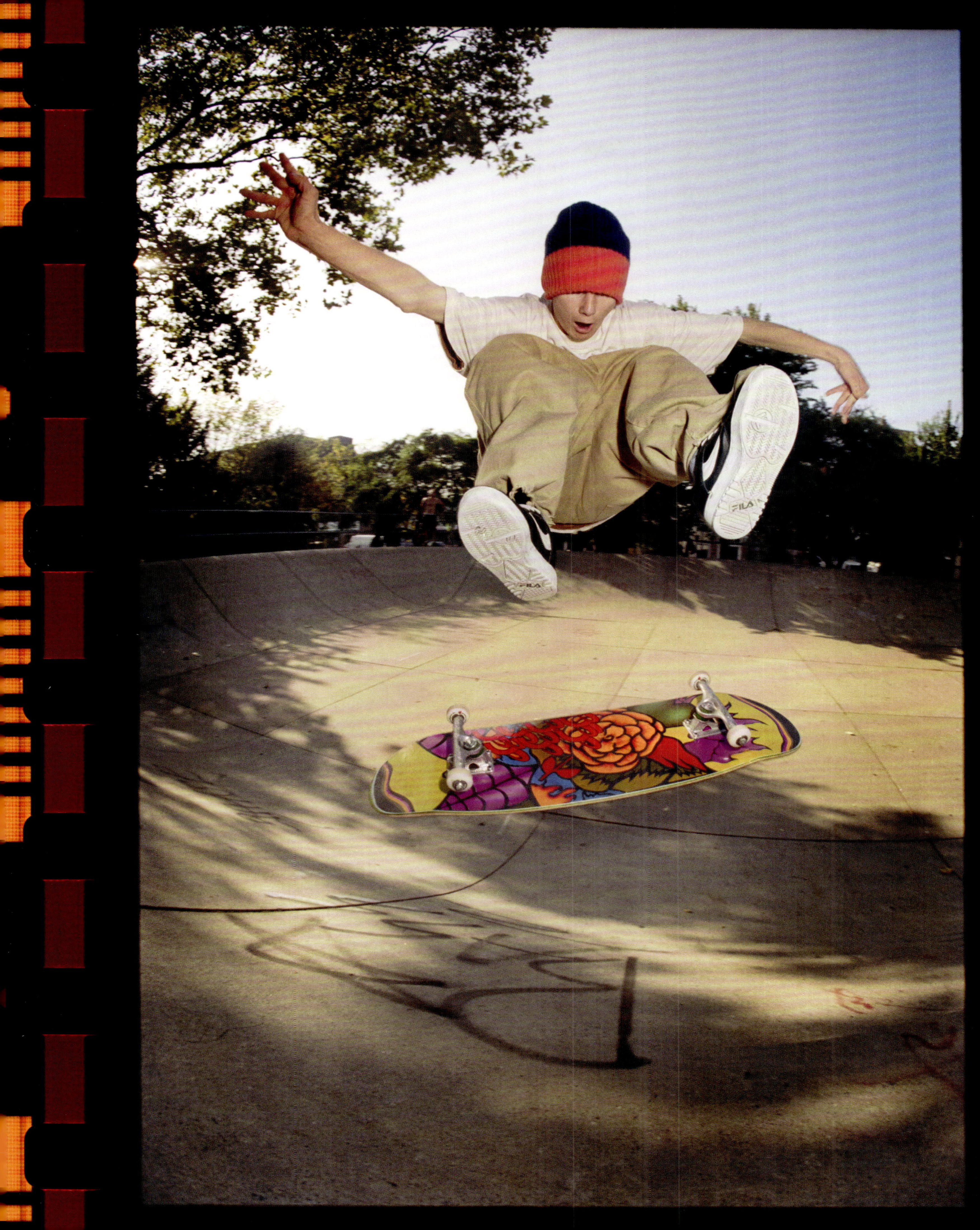

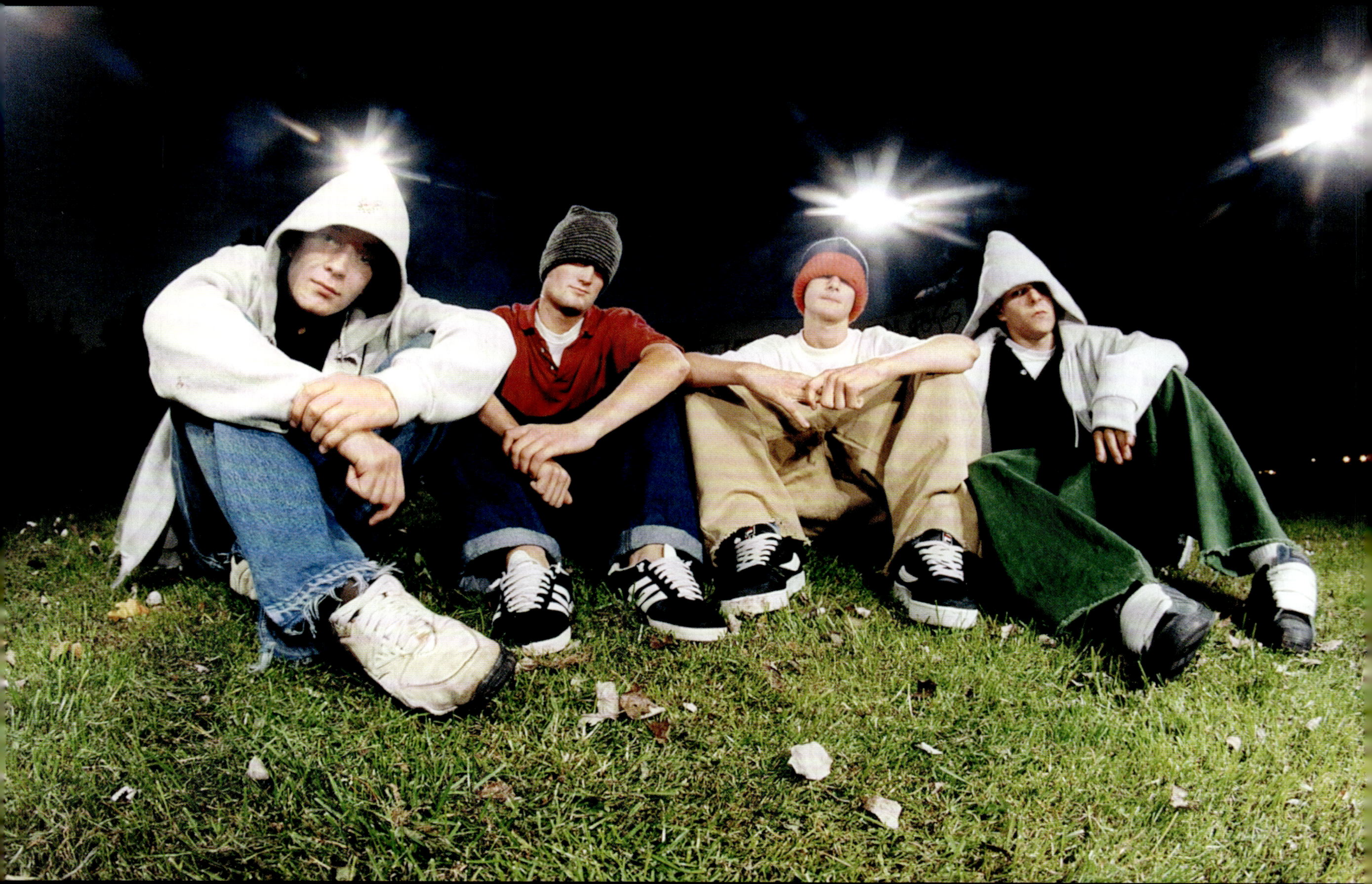

Opposite (from left): Marc Bultitude, Matt Stuart, Simon Evans and Sam Silverstone
Below: Simon Evans, St Anne's, Harrow
Photos: TLB, 1992

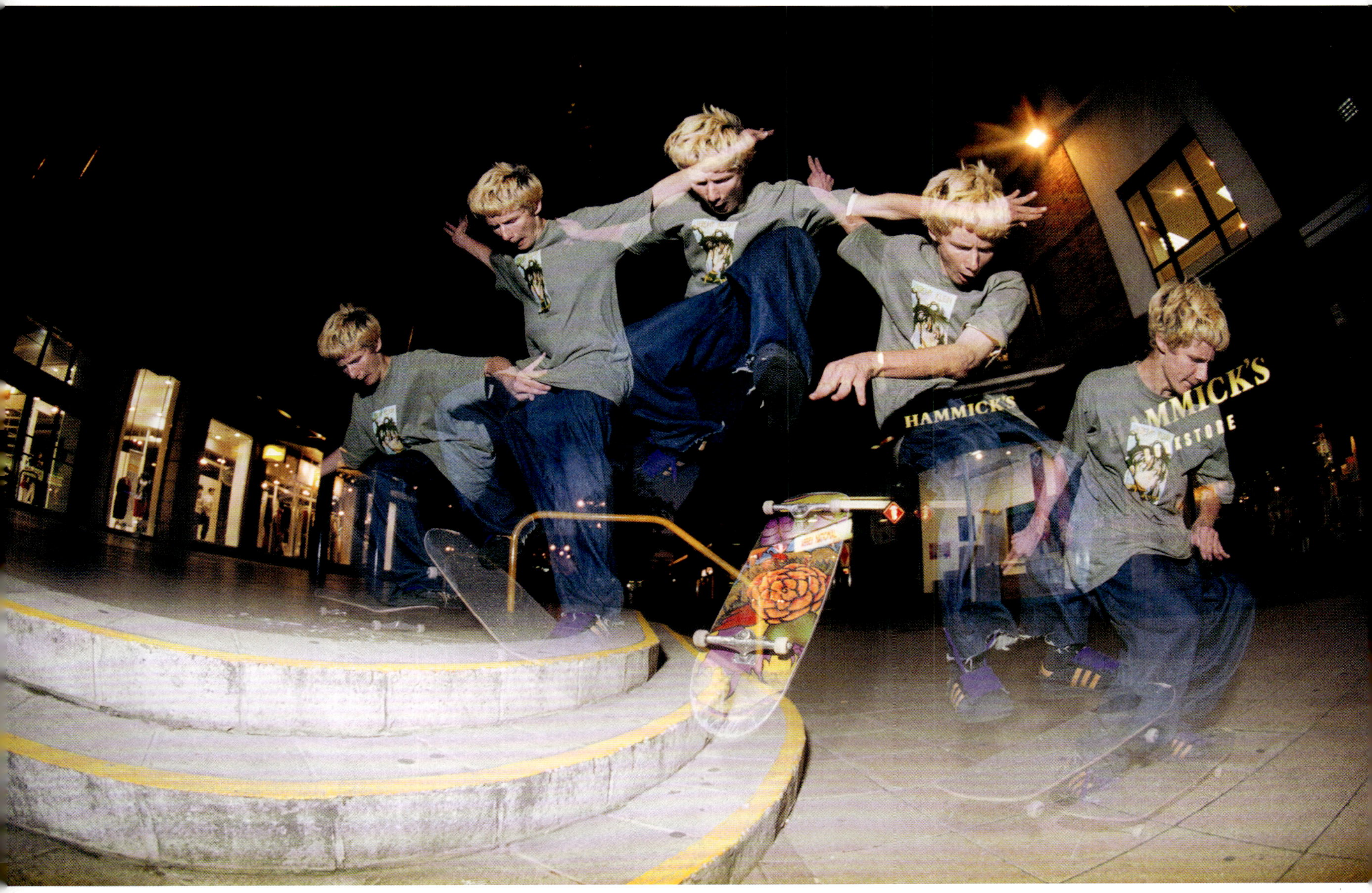

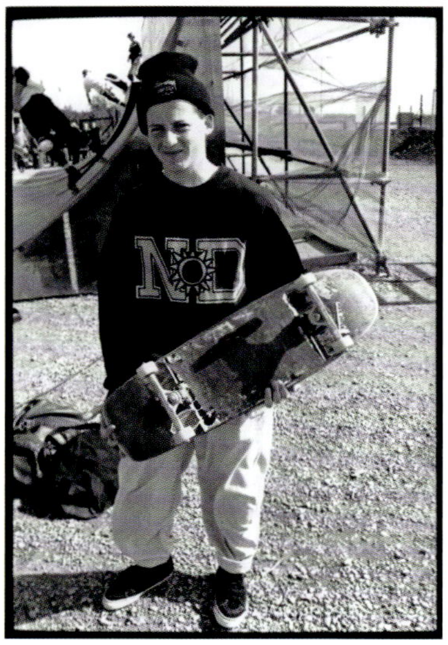

Top row: "Who's riding what? And why? How do they set up their boards and how long do they last? Questions by Simon Evans". From left: Peter Davis, Chris Atherton and Ed Loftus, 1991 **Below:** Chris Leng, Lloyds Square, Bristol, 1992. Tom Penny and Jeremy Fox in the crowd **Opposite:** Mike Manzoori, Birmingham, 1992 **Photos:** TLB

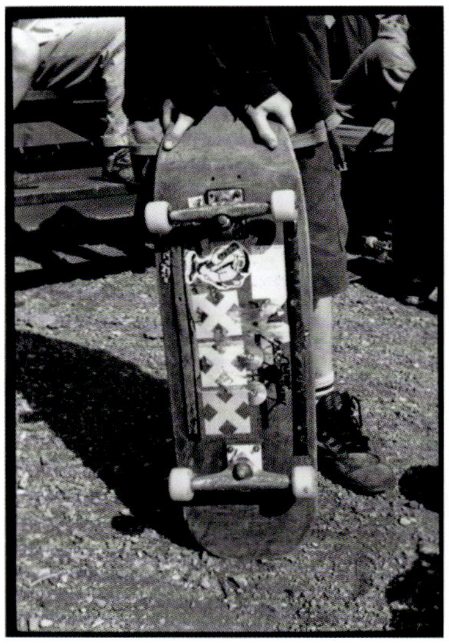

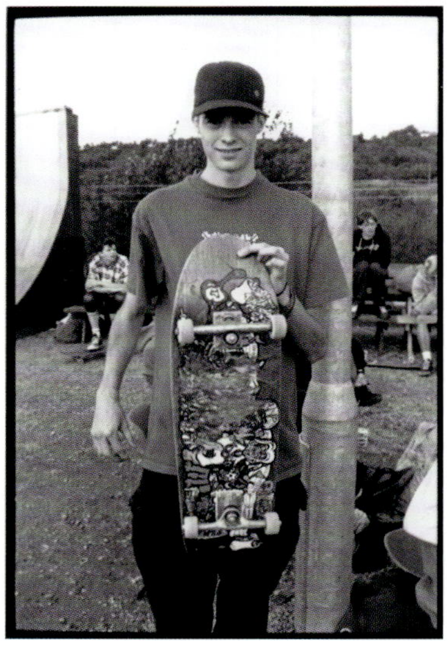

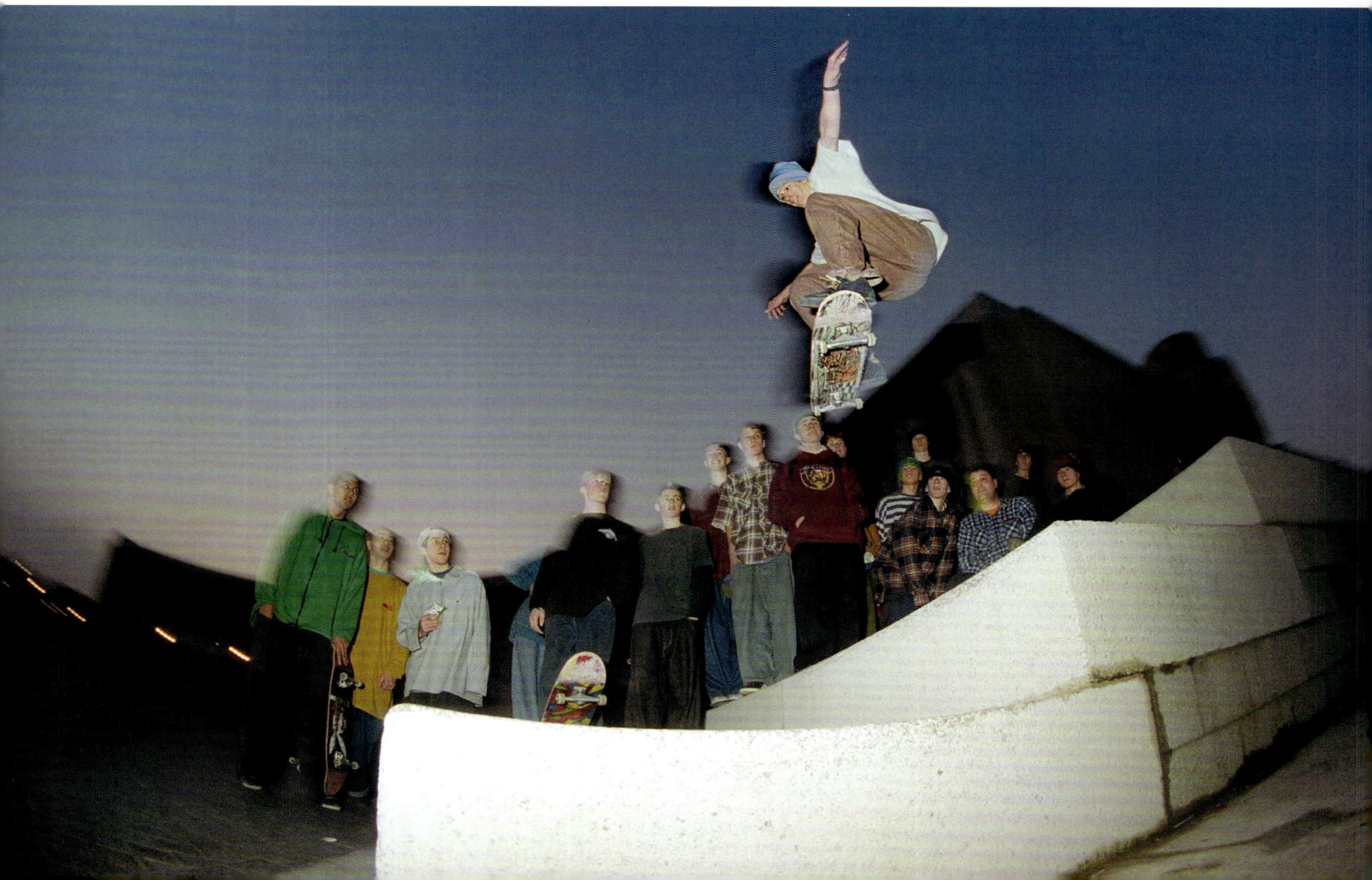

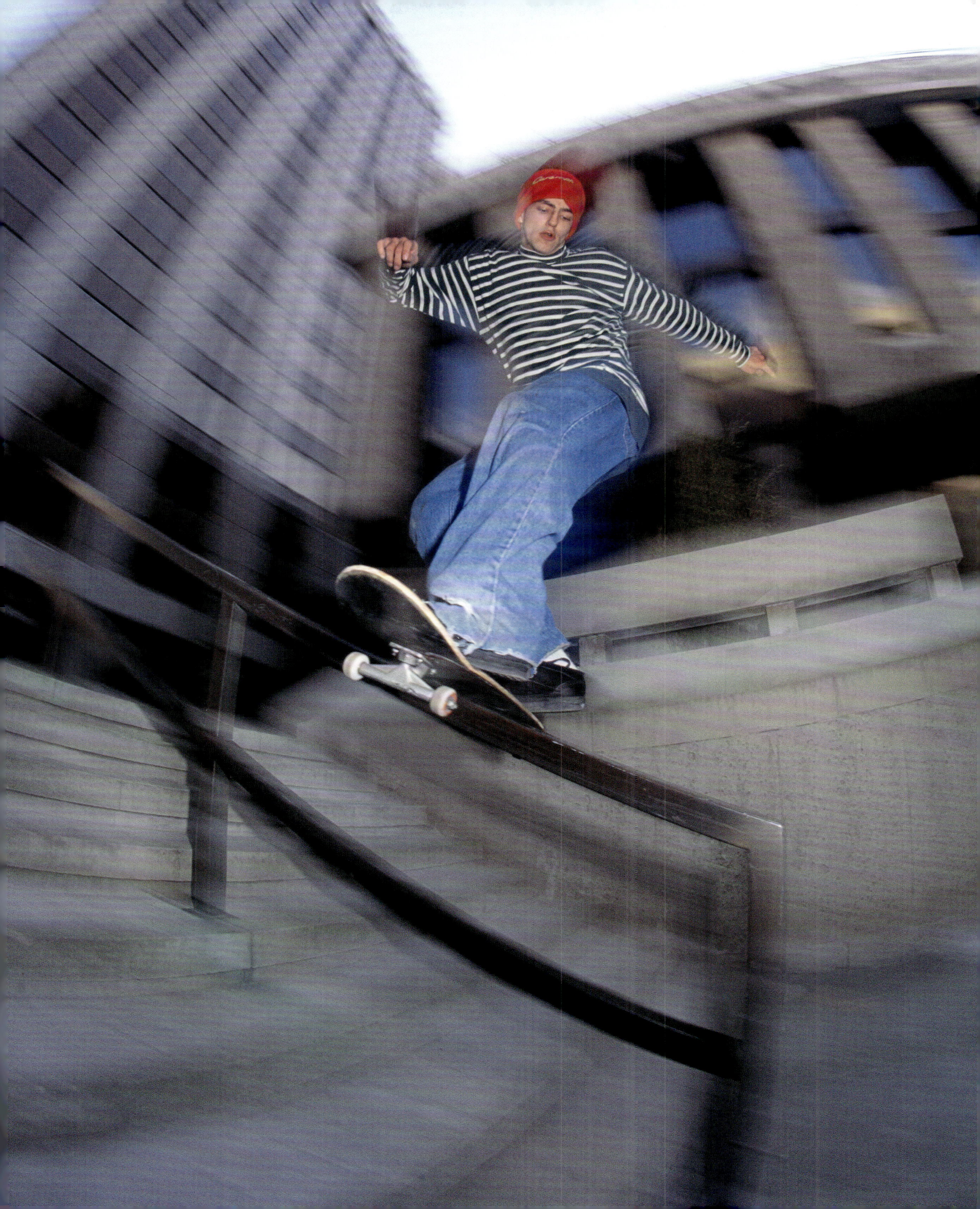

Below: Andrew Makkonen AKA Ben Jobe, Spitalfields, 1992 **Opposite:** Geoff Rowley, Radlands, Northampton, 1992
Following spread left: Leigh-on-Sea skatepark overview (top), Radlands skatepark (bottom), 1992, and **right:** Danny Wainwright, Radlands contest 1992
Photos: TLB

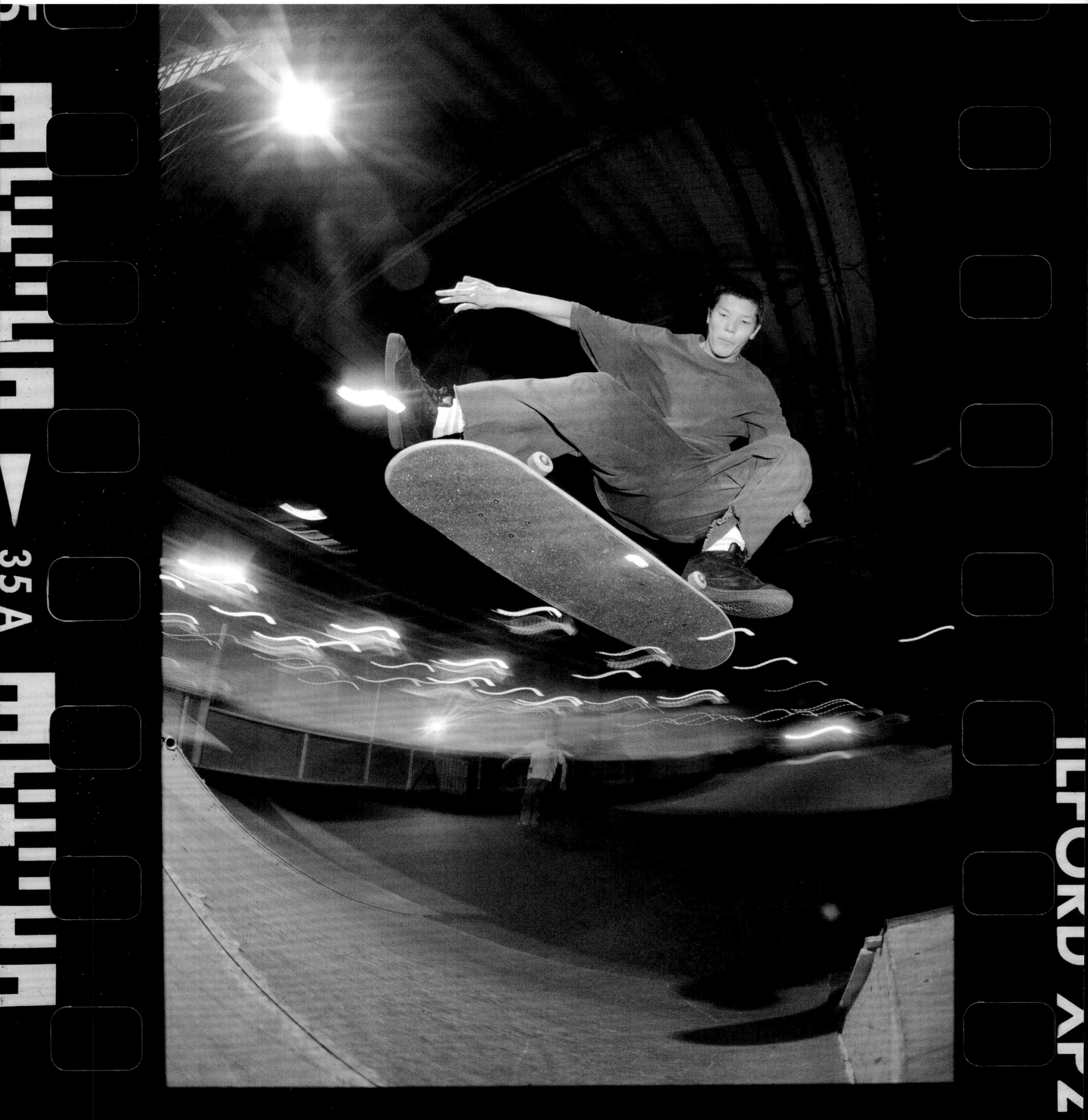

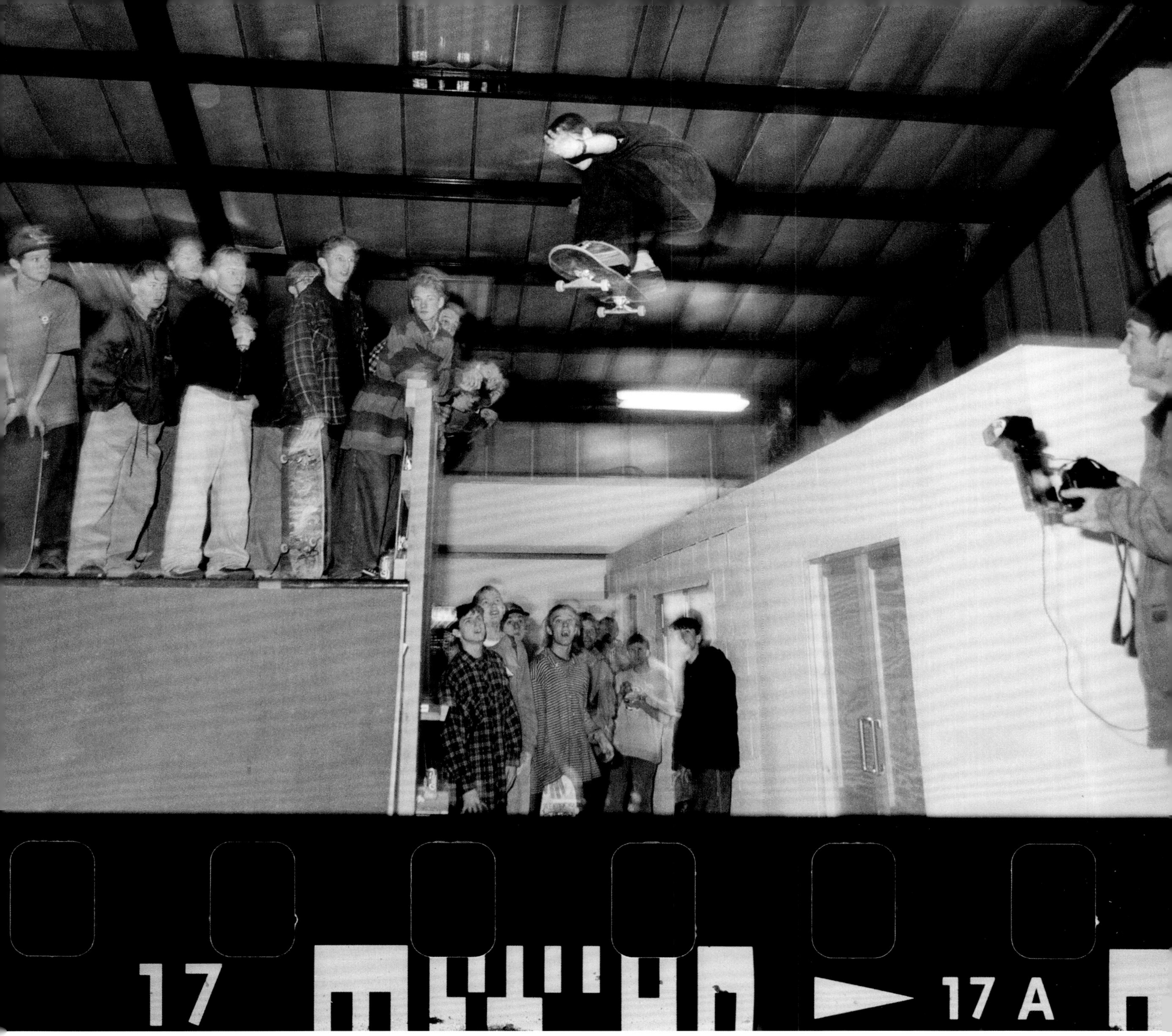

‘Oh, yeah. I mean, there were so many good skateboarders—really crazy good. Carl Shipman, Tom Penny and Geoff Rowley. Those guys were like, proper, special talents you know. They were just—yeah—those people were just fucking mad. And Mouly as well. Those people, Tom, Carl, Geoff, Alex, those guys were TITANS, you know? At the time, I was just like, whoa, that’s crazy!’

Simon Evans

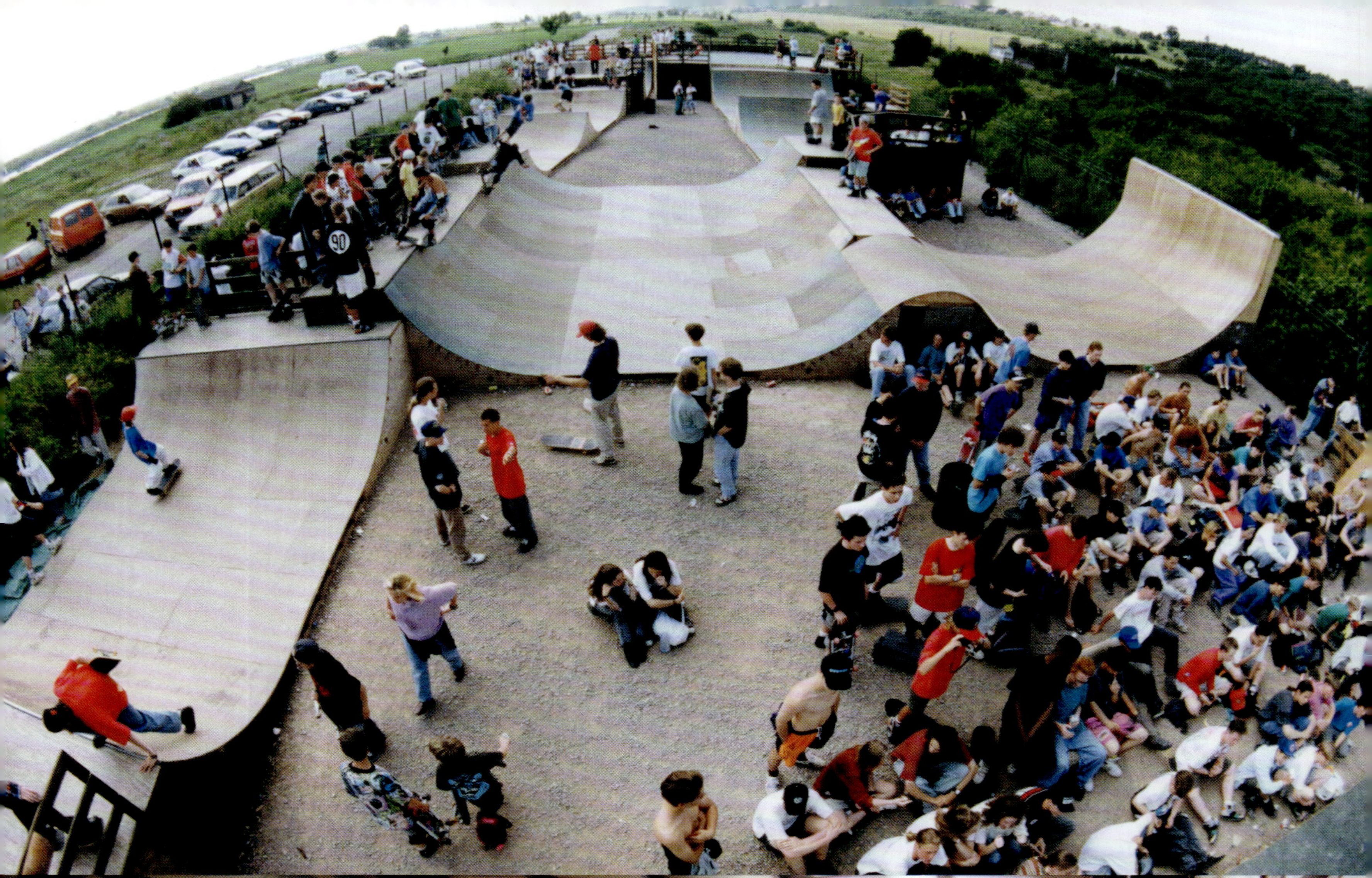

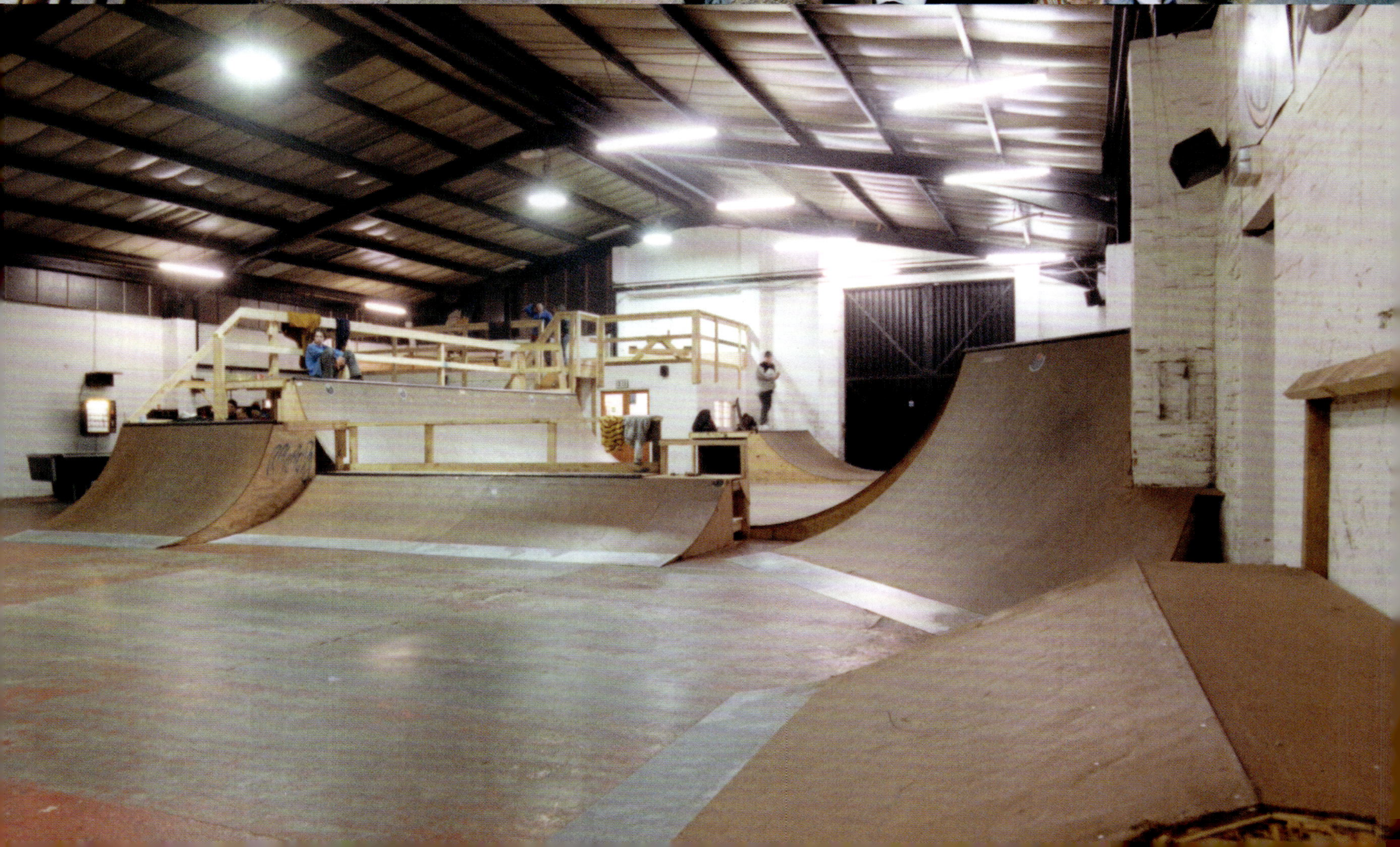

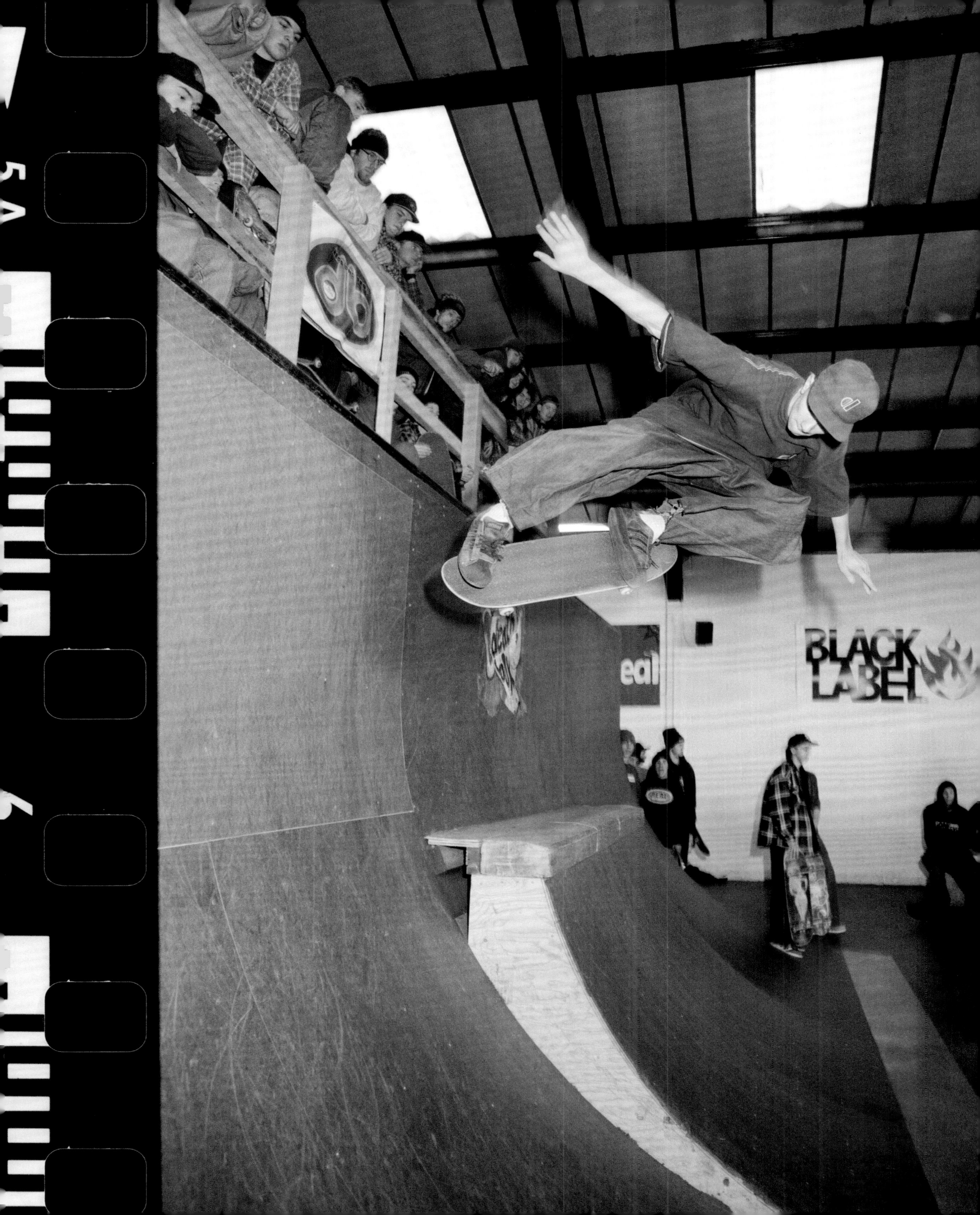
BLACK
LABEL

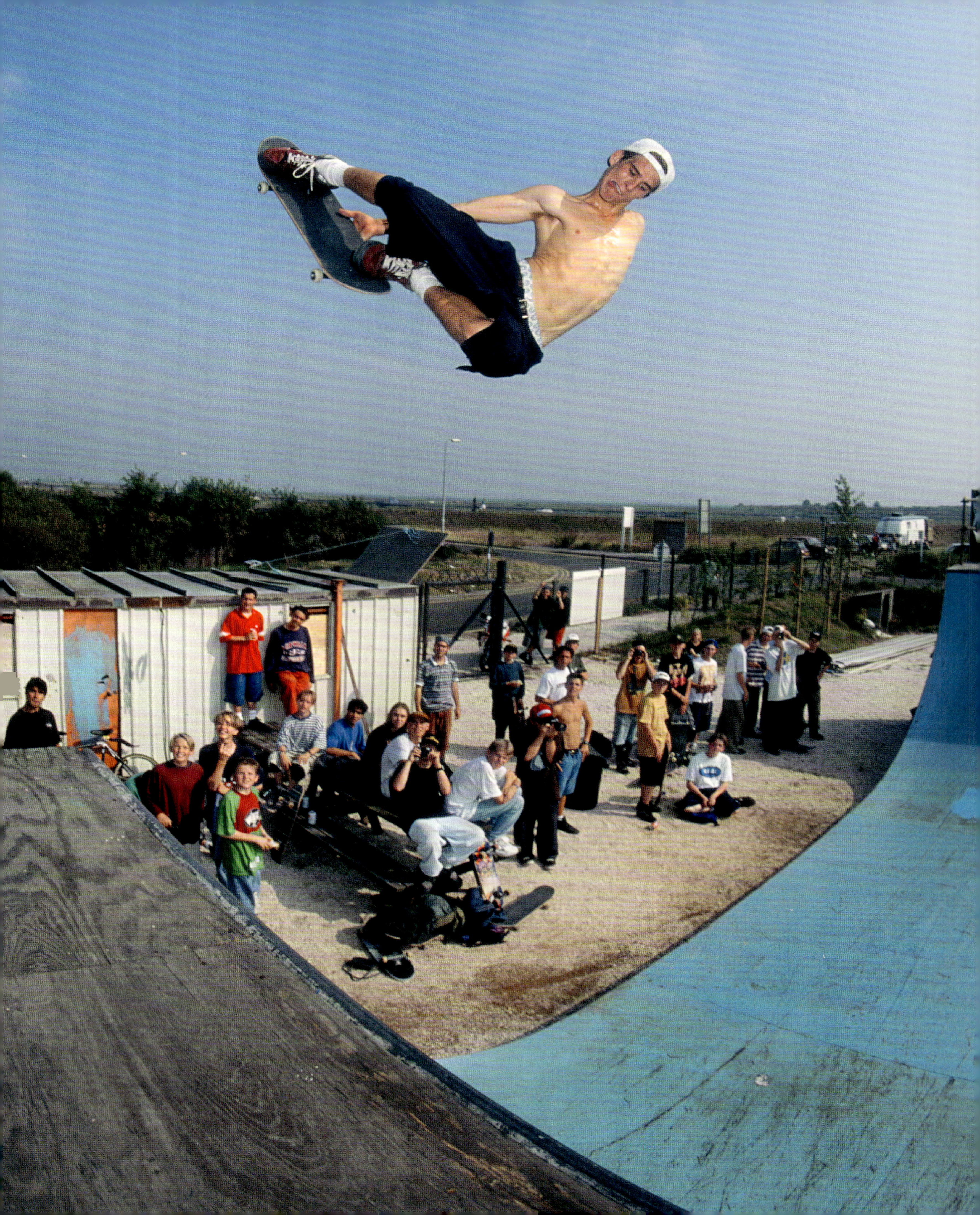

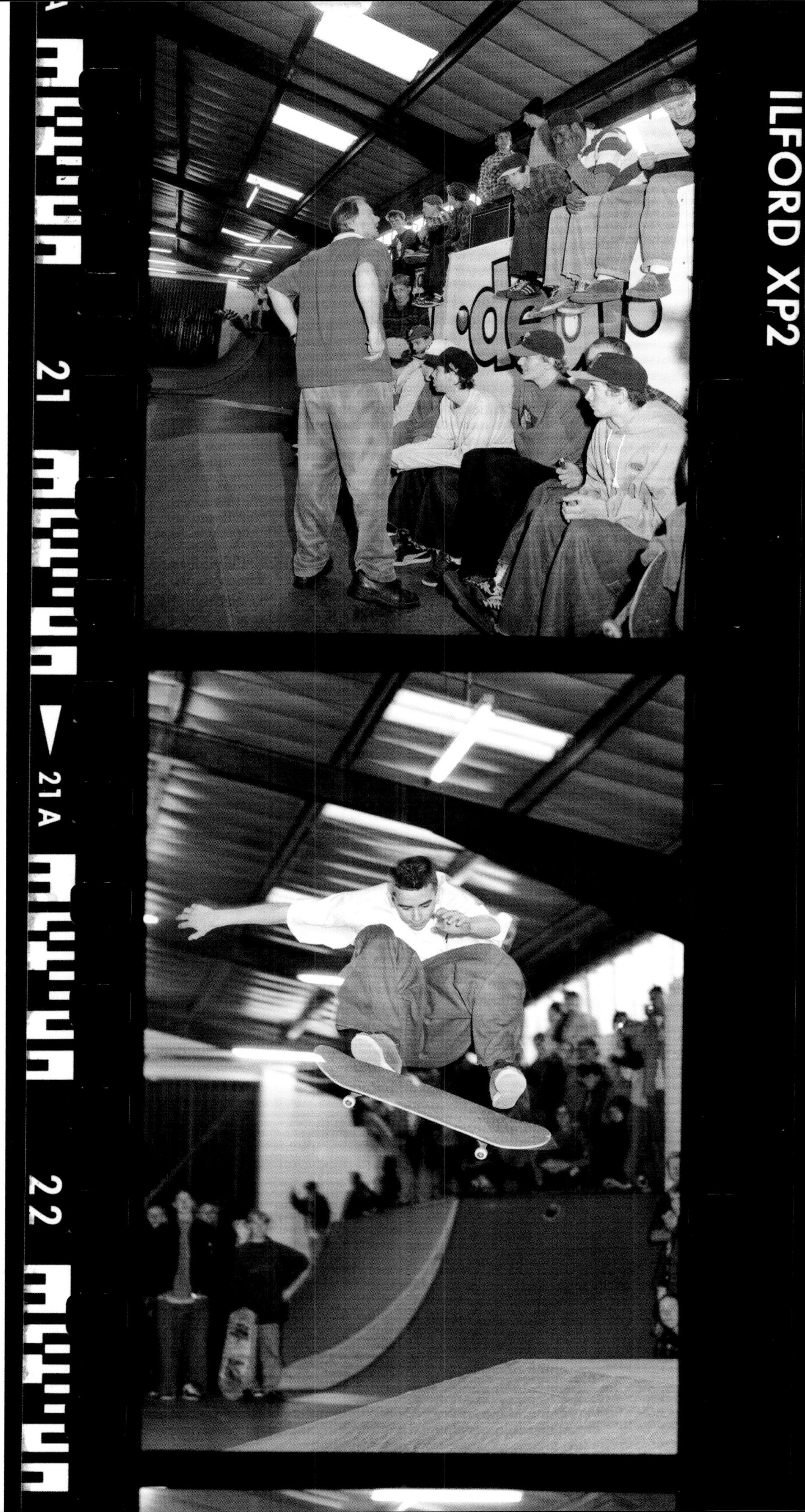

Opposite: John Cardiel, Leigh-on-Sea demo, 1992 **Photo:** Skin Phillips
Right top: Chris Ince and skaters including Kev Lamey, Jon Swann and Ali Cairns (far right) and **bottom:** Carl Shipman, Radlands, 1992 **Photos:** TLB

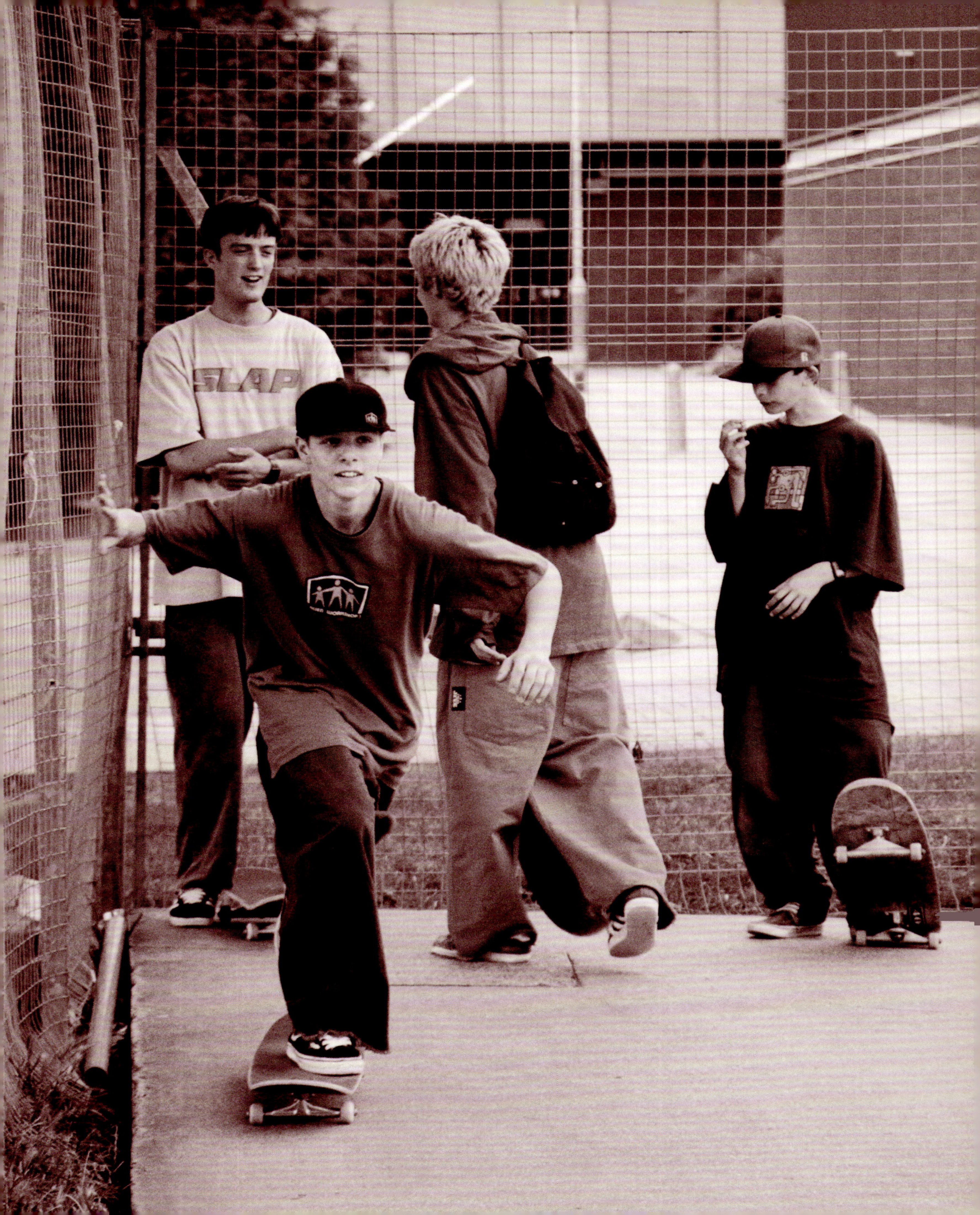
SLAP

PHAT & ALL THAT

FUTURE INFLUENCERS 1993–1995

By the early 1990s, *RAD* was a creative and successful publication with a loyal following and solid circulation. TLB and the collaborators who brought the magazine vividly to life had created a respected, lively channel of communication for the British skate scene. However, the nature of true success is a subjective matter and for the publishers (and owners) of the magazine, it had never generated enough income to fulfil their hard commercial expectations.

Throughout every stage of the magazine's life TLB never had direct ownership nor held any publishing rights. This would always prove to be the Achilles' heel of the *RAD* project, the title forever at the mercy of the commercial whims of its owners and, by the time 1993 rolled around, the magazine had already been bought and sold three times in its short life. Despite the ever-present uncertainties and then upheavals that came with each change of ownership, TLB managed to steady the ship and stay true to his ambitions, albeit with a heavy and personal financial burden.

In 1993, as skateboarding entered another downturn in its boom and bust cycle, the publisher made TLB aware of yet another plan to sell the magazine—only this time, it was offered to him to buy. Finally, a very real opportunity to take full control and become responsible for the magazine's destiny as a publisher and owner was in his sights. The tight group of loyal *RAD* magazine collaborators pulled together:

'We rushed around, raised some money and then got organised to take over RAD. *I foolishly tried to haggle, but someone else was interested and they (presumably) offered to pay more. So, suddenly we found ourselves with everything in place to carry on with the magazine, but no magazine to carry on with.'* TLB

Despite the huge sense of defeat for all involved and knowing that they were now working on what would be their last issue of *RAD*, TLB made a final statement via a cover image made up of skateboarders' portraits, as opposed to the typical action shot:

'The Spitalfields competition [in spring 1993] was a very strange time for me. I knew that we had lost the magazine and this would be the last issue I produced. I went round the edge of the arena taking portraits of the people watching. I wanted as many people as possible to be able to say they were on the cover of RAD *magazine. It was an attempt to do something directly about the feeling of inclusivity I wanted, and my belief that it was the readers' magazine, not ours.'* TLB

With the magazine sold from under them but spurred on by their original plan to buy and keen not to lose momentum, TLB and the close group of collaborators quickly formulated an idea for a new publishing project. For TLB, the whole purpose of starting again was simple: *'The original intent was to do whatever we needed to do to keep a decent skate magazine on the streets of Britain.'* (Quoted in *Gwarizm*, 2014)

To their frustration, publishing a new British skateboard magazine with national distribution proved to be an elusive endeavour. The all-powerful magazine distributors of the day made it quite plain that they had no interest in taking on another skateboard-focused publication whilst the *RAD* title existed in the market-place. TLB was again stifled in his ambitions—finally in a position to have full control of his own skateboarding publication he was being shut down by external forces that lacked vision. So what now?

Tim Leighton-Boyce

Fax/phone 081 677 6301

Wig Worland
Stony Stratford
Milton Keynes

Thursday, March 18, 1993

Wig,

Sorry I haven't … entire life
rushing round … wering
machine full o…

No doubt you' … uff rumours
here's my versi…

So now I'll cut …

Very soon now … agazine. I
thought every… … the real story:

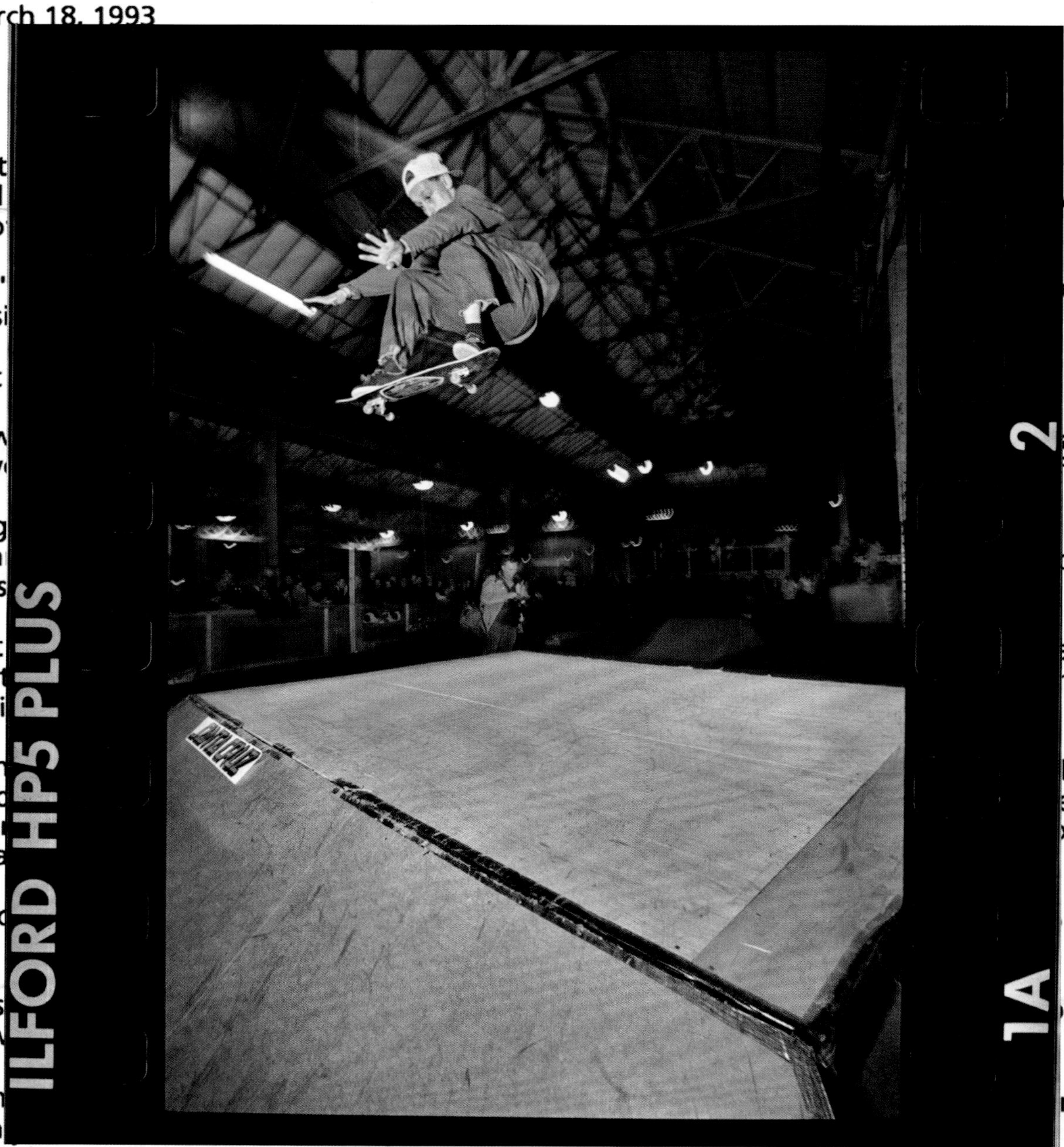

- A while ag… … certain markets, a… … puter magazines…
- I went out… … l team could take over … nobody else would be i…
- I was wron… … le that there was somec… … er people probably i… … ut if they had known tha…
- HHL did no… … increase our bid. I only…
- I went to s… … e no problem and that w…
- There seem… … ny who publish on… … into the R.a.D (they didn't know about the problem with the editorial). It became clear that they hadn't really done any research into the skate market either.
- It seemed to me that they had rushed into this without examining the project properly — and there is no way I would risk getting involved with anyone who acts like that. I've had enough bad experiences with previous publishers of the magazine.
- They offered to sell the magazine "back" to me. I was prepared to pay them as much as I had offered to HHL. Obviously the new people had paid far, far more. So they weren't into that.

So the R.a.D team now finds itself all set-up to take over producing a magazine, but without a magazine to produce. There seems no point in stopping now. So we're planning to launch another magazine this summer after we've had a chance to see what the new people do with R.a.D (who knows — we might learn

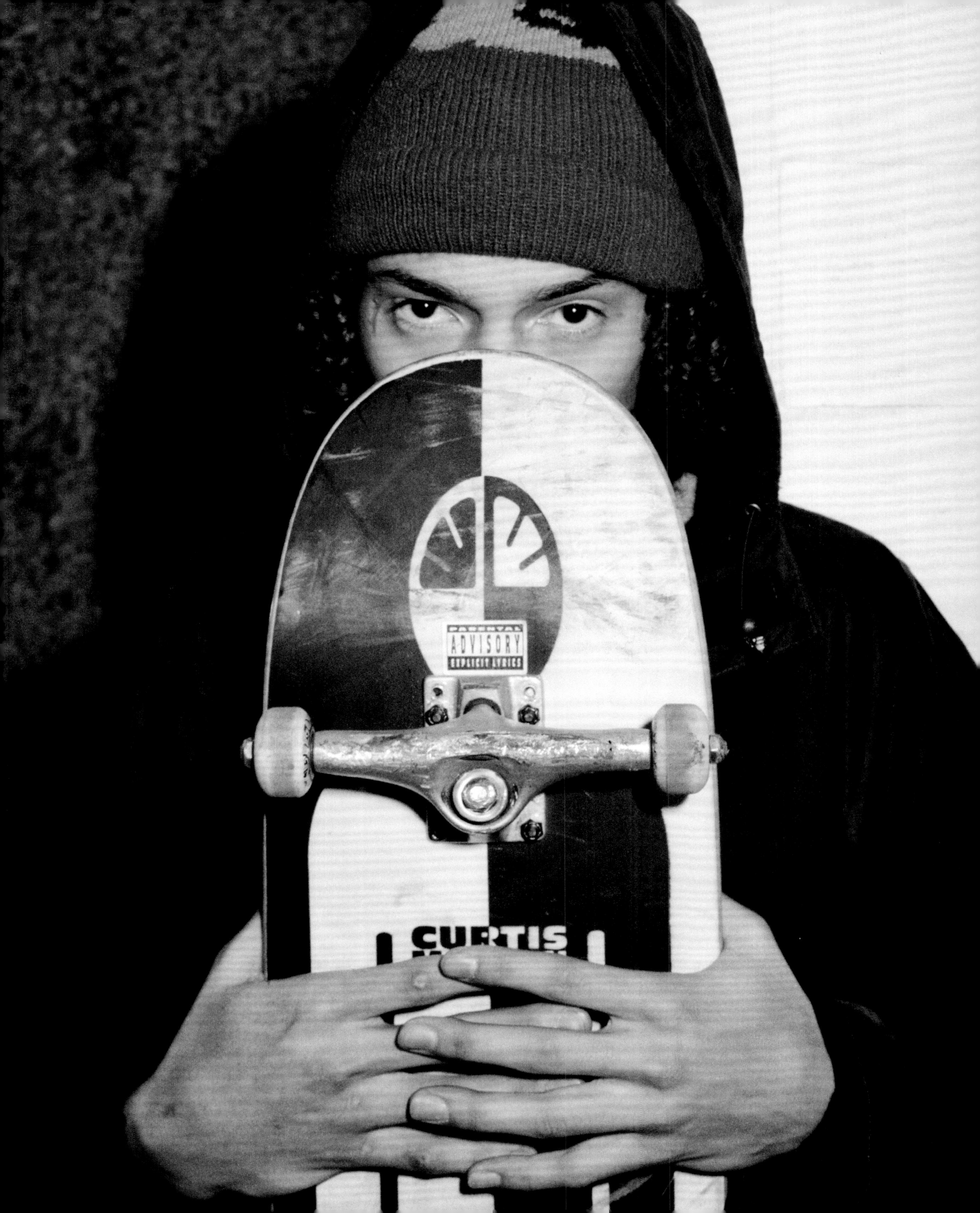
ADVISORY
CURTIS

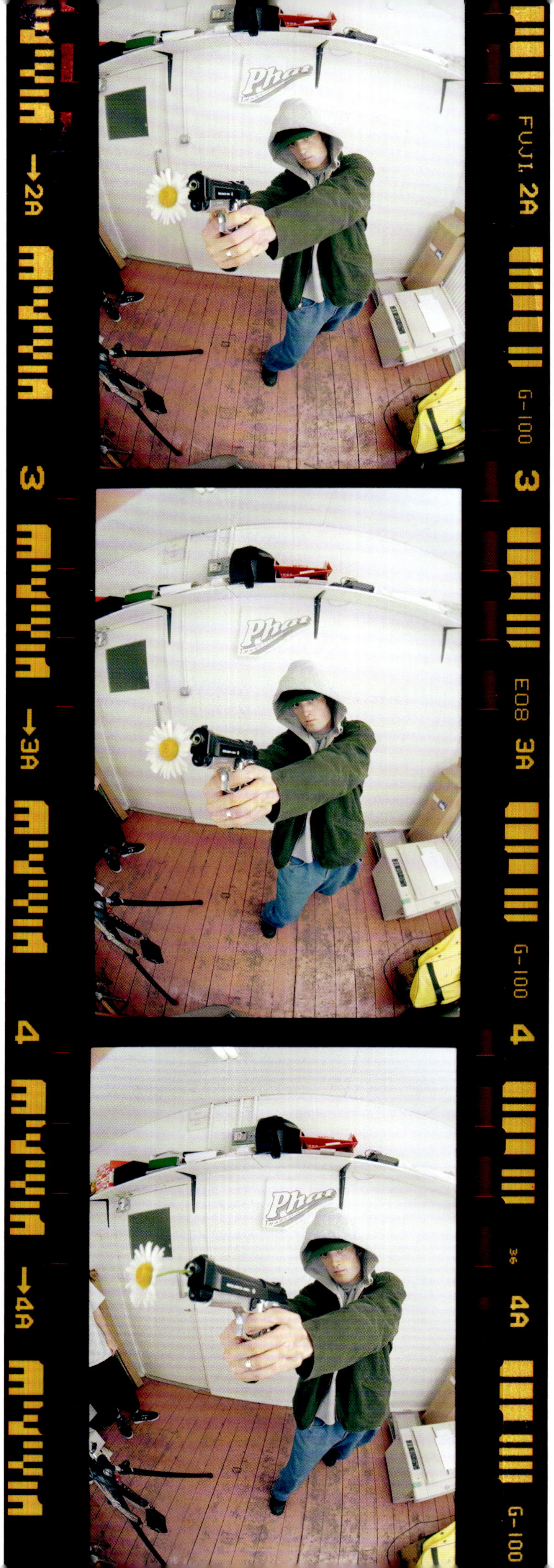

Beginning in the late 1980s, skate culture had steadily expanded its influence beyond its core participatory audience. No longer confined to the act of skateboarding alone, skate culture was being gradually co-opted into an emerging global 'street culture'. Many aspects of this developing culture were influenced by or were emanating from the skateboard scene and its creative movers and shakers around the world. Skateboarding was developing its own clothing and shoe brands, its own artists, musicians and dress codes. The average skateboarder had become—maybe always had been—a heavy, style-conscious and loyal consumer of highly specific products. The 'skater owned' and 'by skateboarders for skateboarders' tag had moved from the DIY culture into a wider commercial realm. This growing influence of skate-focused or skate lifestyle brands increased as the 1990s progressed and this was where TLB and close collaborator Gavin Hills could see potential for a new publication.

Their concept was to be a magazine with skateboarding at its heart but a broader scope to its editorial content. This new tack was not entirely dissimilar—and no less risky—than that taken by *Skateboarder* in 1980 when skateboarding had taken a dive in popularity and hard economics meant a pure love of the culture had not been enough to sustain a commercially viable publication. Under the new title *Action Now* they branched out to cover other new 'action / lifestyle sports' in the hope that they could broaden distribution, gain more advertising and turn a new audience on to skateboarding. The reality was that they failed to excite their core loyal skateboarding audience (who felt betrayed) and never managed to switch on a big enough new audience. TLB had prior experience—the adapt or die approach was not unlike that taken at *BMX Action Bike* magazine in 1987.

Obviously there existed potential pitfalls in trying to broaden the reach of a skateboarding magazine and gain new readers to ultimately appease a distributor. But TLB, Gavin Hills and the rest of the team knew that hovering around the edges of skate culture was a wider audience keen to buy into the scene and all its trappings. And perhaps, more crucially, there might be a larger pool of advertisers ready to speak to this broader customer base, potentially offering a more long-term commercial viability.

'The appearance of a RAD*-like UK-based title called* Phat *on a village newsagent shelf had me intrigued. Those glossy, easily damaged pages hurled multiple topics together—movies, girls, video games, music, skate and BMX—during the boom time for Pete Rock productions,* In Utero*, big clothes and World Industries... Operating as multiple fanzines in one,* Phat*'s modular approach to editorial, irreverence, information overload, and celebration of consumerism connected with every sub-culture I'd ever fixated on.'* Gary Warnett AKA Gwarizm, 2014

The new broader content convinced the distributor of the magazine's potential and earned them a place on the news-stands. Part of the new formula included more challenging, socially relevant editorial, but it was this aspect that unexpectedly and tragically proved to be their unravelling. The new magazine became a frustratingly short-lived experiment—just three lively issues before it imploded under duress from a baseless media furore:

'A victim of its own appetite for controversy and the dangerous assumption that reactionists would take time out to read the content before forming an opinion. A gun on the cover of August 1993's inaugural issue, previewing a provocatively written anti-firearm article, would lead to newspaper columns, radio show phone-ins and debates on corruption of young minds and gang culture's supposed rise—a precursor to the nation's alarmist attitude toward any youth in a hoody a decade later.' Gary Warnett

An unlikely and unprecedented amount of media heat was aimed squarely at the fledgling magazine and Gavin Hills (taking on the more public face of 'editor'). His built-in desire to court controversy and stick two fingers firmly up in the face of authority proved to be an unfortunate act of hubris. The all-important distributors, news-agents and then the commercial advertisers swiftly walked away.

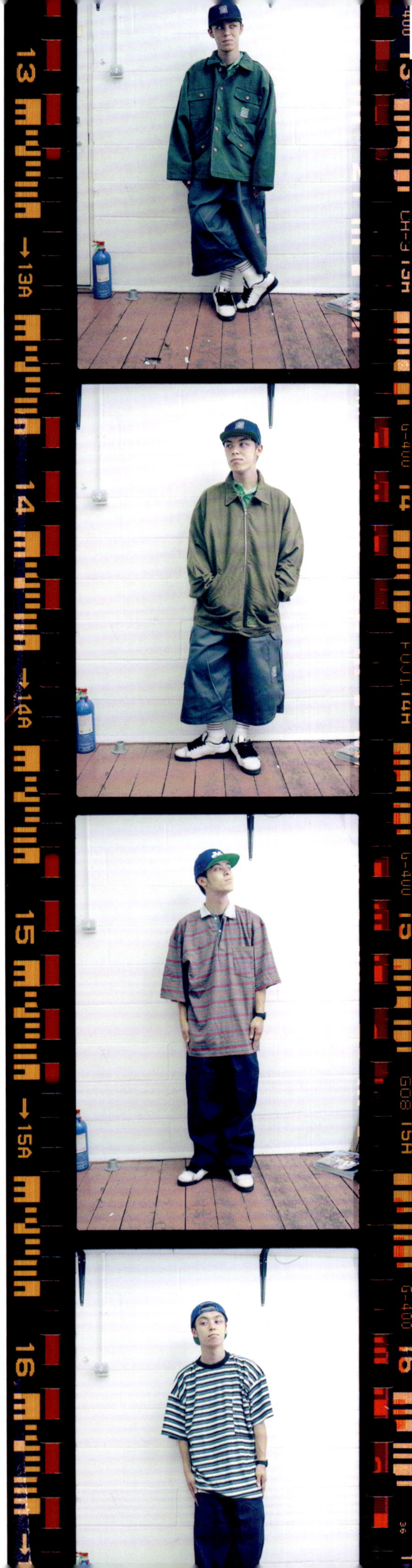

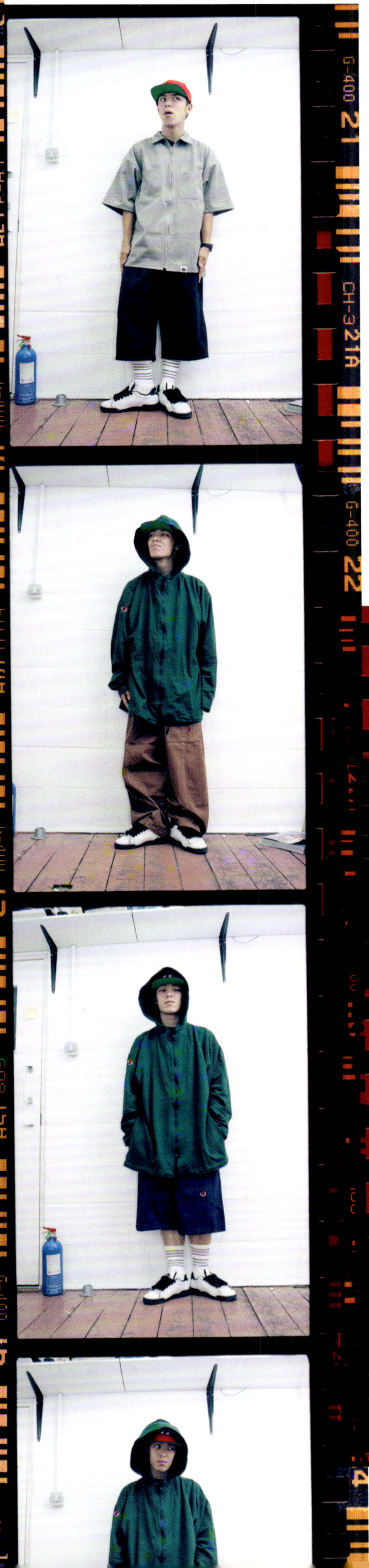

Opening spread: Matt Stuart, Sam Silverstone, Simon Evans and Toby Shaull, Harrow skatepark, 1993 **Photo:** TLB **Previous spread left:** Tony Luckhurst, Spitalfields contest, spring 1993 **Photo:** Wig Worland, and **right:** Curtis McCann, 1993 **Photo:** TLB **Opposite:** The infamous *Phat* magazine cover shoot, 1993, Matt Stuart **This page:** Ray Calthorpe, *Phat* magazine photoshoot, 1993 **Photos:** TLB

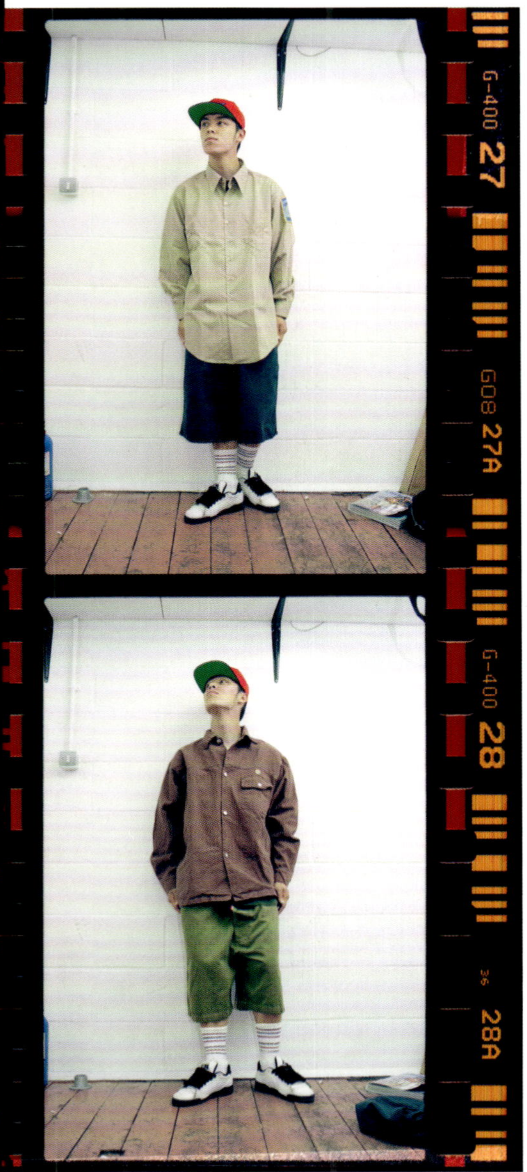

‘There are those who are not happy about handing over our beautiful country to these ignorant hoodlums’

Auberon Waugh on *Phat* magazine from the *Daily Telegraph*, 1993

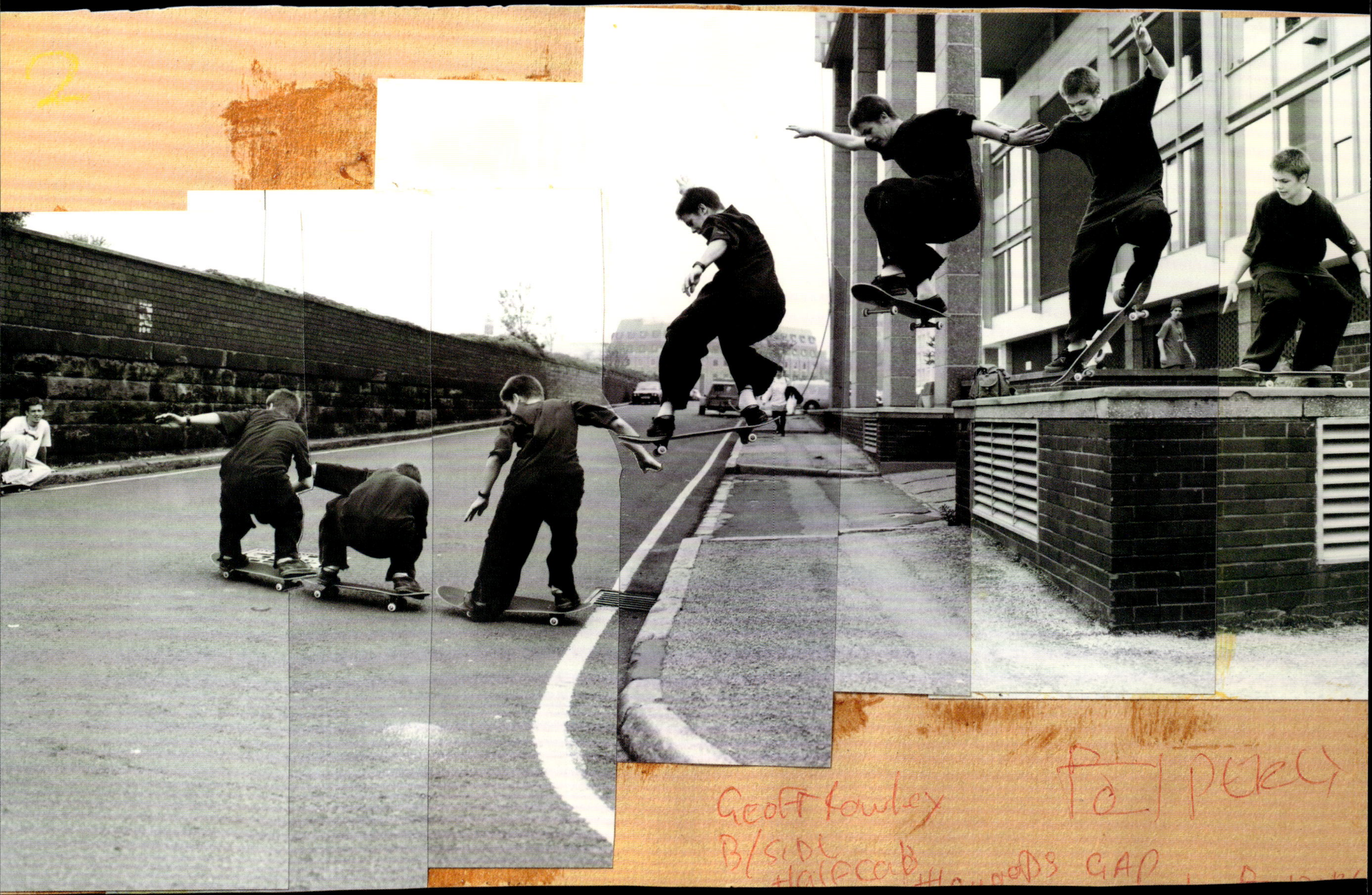

'I remember doing that [cover] shoot, saw the reaction and thought "What's their problem?", because I'd put a daisy in the end of the gun! To be fair, we knew we were being sensationalist: "Wouldn't it be cool to have a gangster kid on the cover"... "But we don't want anyone thinking we want people to get shot"... "OK, so we'll put a flower in the gun"... "Ahhh, brilliant idea!".' Steve Hicks, *RAD and Phat* designer

Losing control of *RAD* magazine and the implosion of the *Phat* project struck TLB a hard double blow. This would be the moment he decided to withdraw from his prominent and hitherto consistent role as an important figure in British skateboarding. This painful and significant decision would inadvertently open up a new chapter in the life of *RAD* magazine and ultimately the development of future British skateboard media.

As a respected voice of British skateboarding, *RAD* had outlived competition from the resurrected *Skateboard!* title and then the short lived *Skate Action* magazine. Now, with the premature demise of *Phat*, *RAD* stood alone—with it's new owner—as the only magazine committed to covering skateboarding in Britain. But where to now without its established, experienced and connected team of contributors, writers, and photographers? Struggling for a solution, the new owner and publisher hastily drafted in *Snowboard UK* magazine editors, Eddie Spearing and Mark Sturgeon, aka 'Stig', to try and keep the magazine on the news-stands:

'Out of the blue, the new RAD *owner calls us with an offer to edit and run the magazine, THE skate bible of bibles AND get paid to do so. Well, we were all over it. You see, we loved* RAD*. We grew up with* RAD *as long-time skaters since 1977 and we knew all about every magazine that there ever was about skateboarding. But deep down we knew we weren't really the right people for the job because of the way TLB had been kicked out.'* Eddie Spearing

RAD magazine struggled on its new path, only nominally supported by those within the culture who wanted to ensure that the well-loved title could sustain its important role at the centre of the British scene. Seeing the vital need for a reliable channel of communication—the glue holding the scene together—professional skateboarder, *RAD* alumnus and local skate shop co-owner Sean Goff stepped in:

'I thought of it as first aid [laughter]. I was the first person there [at RAD*] after Tim went, who had even a slight idea of how to represent skating; I did it to keep things going until someone came along with a magazine background who knew better. I asked Steve Douglas for help and he was really anti being involved. I think people felt a loyalty to TLB, which I totally understand. I think a lot of people felt "Fuck it, let it die".*

'I know Tim put a lot of effort into RAD *and when he couldn't get the magazine he vanished for a bit. Then* Phat *magazine came out. I had a lot of respect for what he was doing but wasn't happy to let* RAD *die. I thought "If you want to do something else, just do it". He'd been telling us that for years: "Get out there, do it for yourself". I totally understood how someone could get pissed off to the point where they'd had enough, but it didn't mean I had to agree with them. I saw a value in keeping* RAD *going when Tim stopped.'* Sean Goff

*'Because it was perceived that Tim had been kicked out of his own mag, sourcing advertising was difficult, getting imagery was difficult—we were not really accepted as we were "just" snowboarders. Talking with Paul Sunman at Slam City Skates, he said we would be unlikely to succeed as there was too much industry anti-*RAD *sentiment with TLB not being involved. So we knew it was going to be difficult but it became increasingly hard convincing advertisers—made worse from one issue to the next by the lack of content we were able to pull together for much the same reasons. Lack of advertising meant lack of investment from the publisher and being under-resourced meant there was a progressive decline in the quality of the content—which we were painfully aware of.*

'From time to time, better photographers would deem fit to drop us a few of their images. It was like being fed crumbs. We could not do justice to RAD *and we felt bad about it. On top of that, our own snowboard magazine was suffering.'* Eddie Spearing

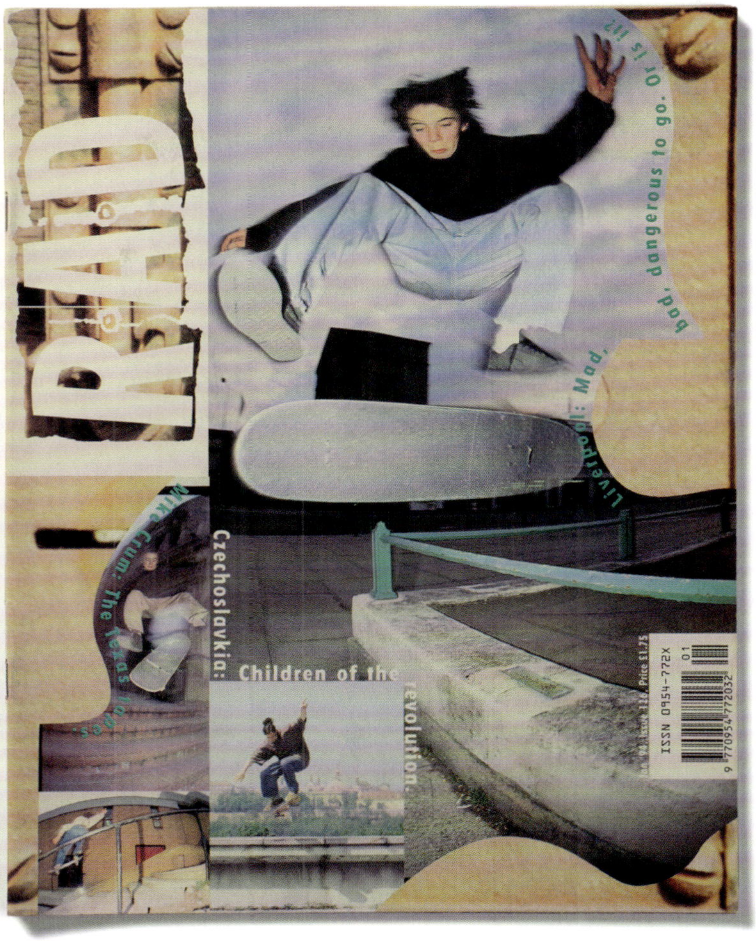

Opposite: Sequence collage as submitted before reproduction in *Phat* magazine, Geoff Rowley, Liverpool, 1993
Photos and collage: Percy Dean
Above: Issue 126, 1993. Cover design by Steve Billington featuring Joel O'Connor
Photo: Percy Dean

While Eddie and Stig attempted, with difficult odds, to re-establish *RAD*, events were taking place in a parallel universe that would determine its future. A new skateboarding magazine was being developed in Nottingham in surprisingly similar circumstances to TLB's initial publishing endeavours at Alpine Sports back in the late 1970s. Andy Horsley, a relatively recent but committed recruit to the world of skateboarding was about to begin his career in British skateboard media via the support of an established skate shop.

'Paul Haynes from Rollersnakes [in Nottingham] wanted a catalogue for the shops—like a mail order catalogue, but I don't think it was as grand as that. So I was working on that and I kept hassling him: "Maybe we should put in some more bits and bobs, interviews, skateboards and things like that." He pretty much gave me free rein to do what I wanted and I managed to push it until I thought if we were going to do that, we may as well just do a zine really—to have in the shops, in Nottingham and Derby and give away for free. It was like a photocopied zine—that's the way I was thinking—have a little magazine. Then because he was agreeing, I said: "Why don't we just make it bigger and on better paper and have a colour cover and stuff like that—do our own little mag, you know?"

'It was when we were looking towards doing the first issue of this, The System*, that Chris Forder, John Robson and I, went down to Spitalfields in London. At that comp I was handing out flyers: "If you take photos, if you do any journalism or anything like that to do with skateboarding please get in touch with us." And this is how much I didn't know about the industry or anyone involved in the industry—I handed one of them to TLB [laughs]. I didn't know who that was!'* Andy Horsley

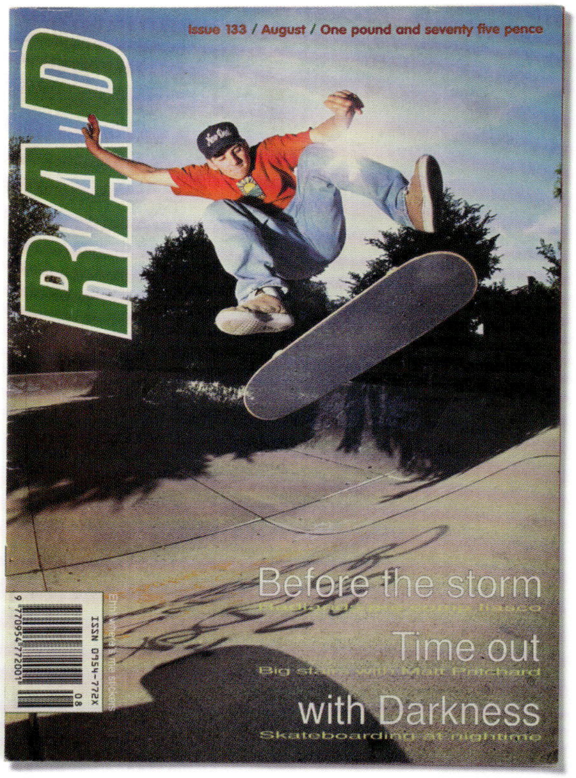

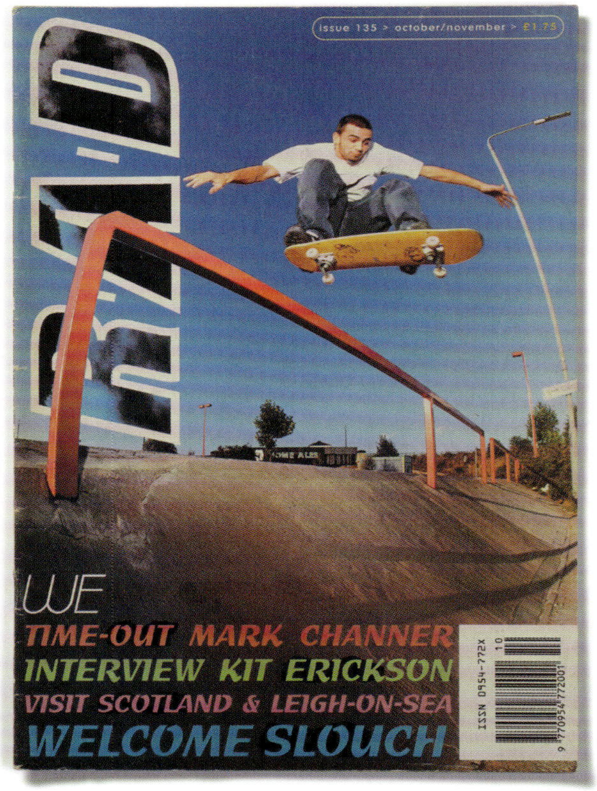

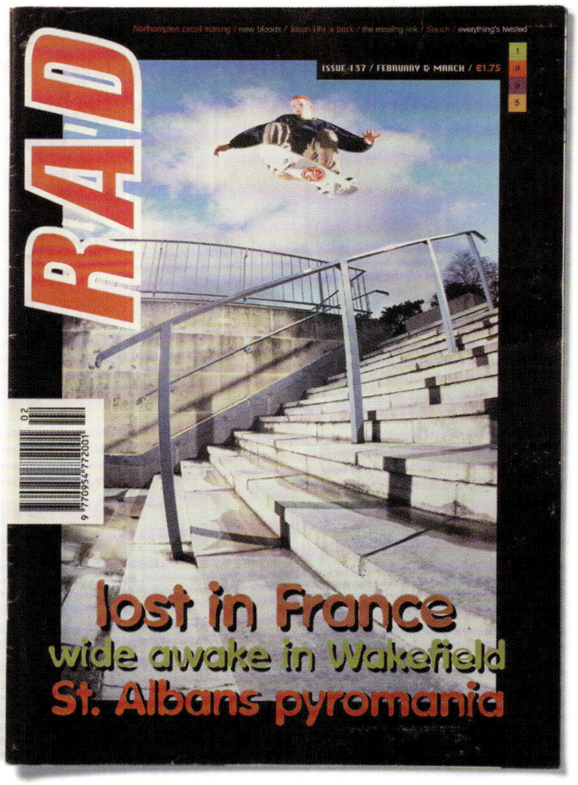

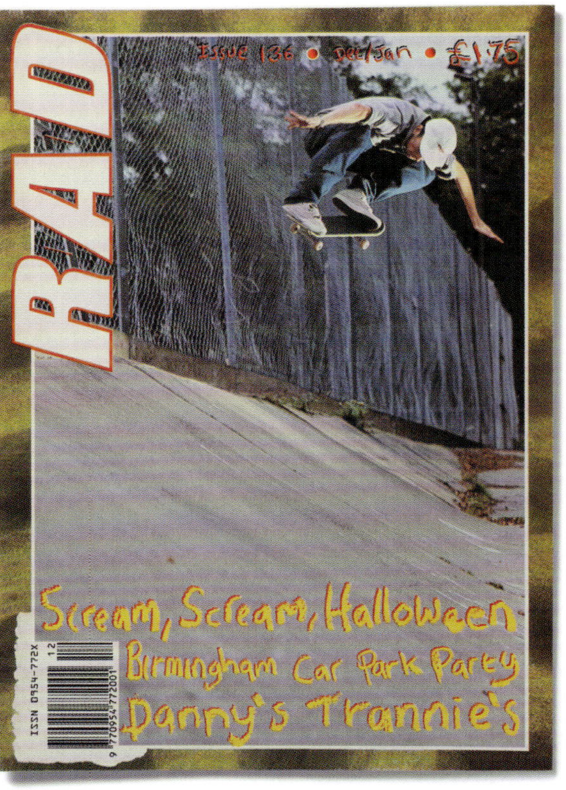

Clockwise from top left: Covers designed by Andy Horsley, 1994–95: Mark Channer, Kennington, 1994; Carl Shipman, Worksop, 1994; Danny Wainwright, Dean Lane skatepark, Bristol, 1994; Matt Pritchard, Cardiff, 1995 **Opposite:** Carl Shipman, Radlands, 1993 **All photos:** Wig Worland

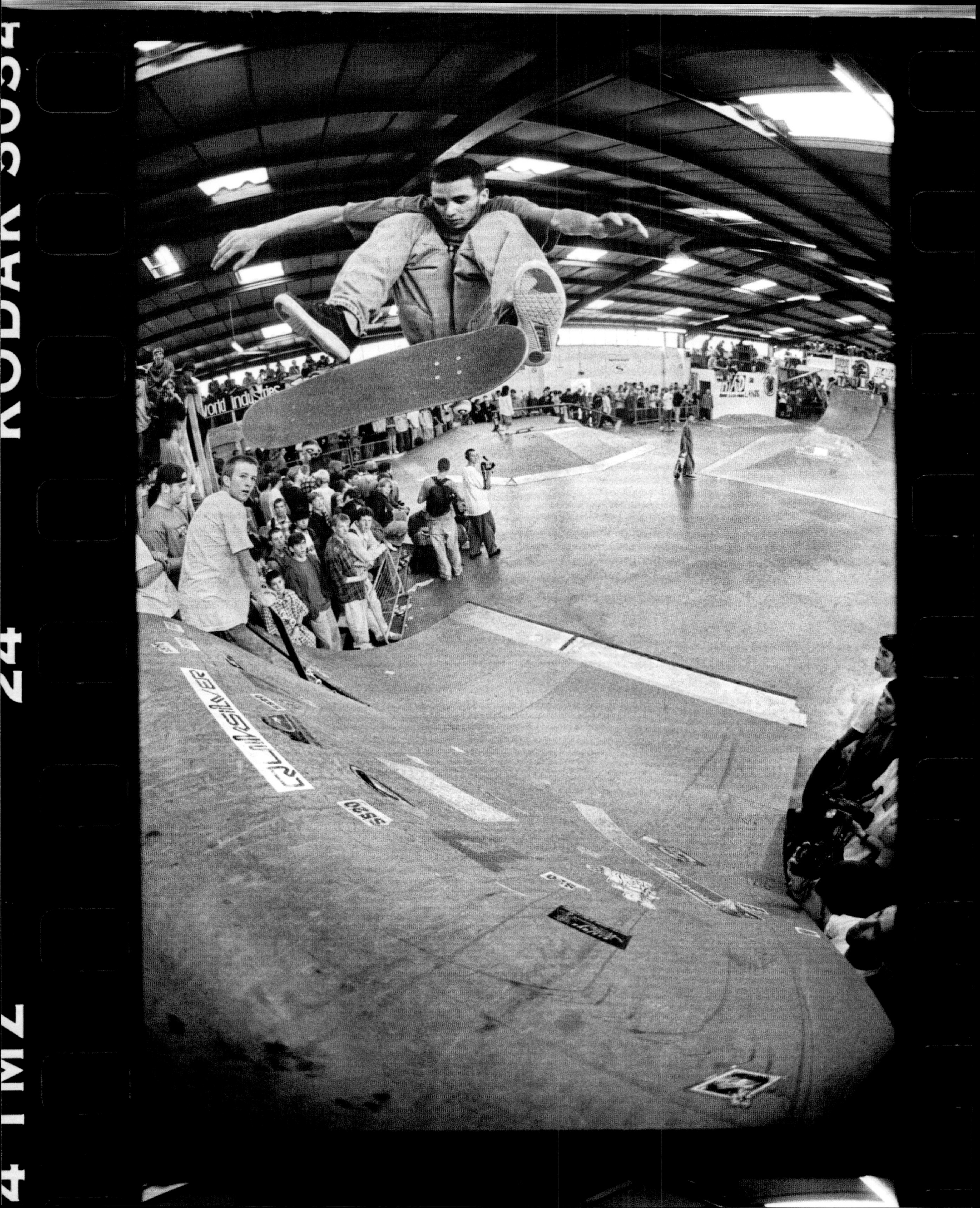
world industries

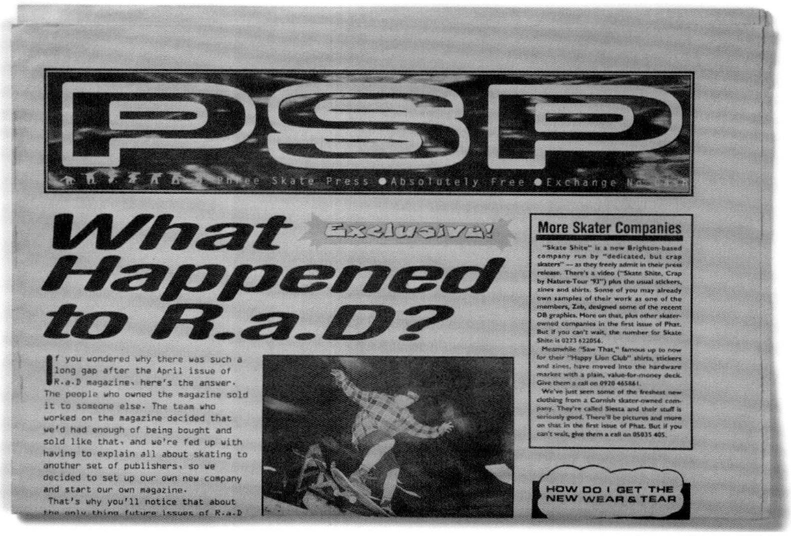

PSP

Three Skate Press ●Absolutely Free ●Exchange

What Happened to R.a.D?

Exclusive!

If you wondered why there was such a long gap after the April issue of R.a.D magazine, here's the answer. The people who owned the magazine sold it to someone else. The team who worked on the magazine decided that we'd had enough of being bought and sold like that, and we're fed up with having to explain all about skating to another set of publishers, so we decided to set up our own new company and start our own magazine.

That's why you'll notice that about

More Skater Companies

"Skate Shite" is a new Brighton-based company run by "dedicated, but crap skaters" — as they freely admit in their press release. There's a video ("Skate Shite, Crap by Nature-Tour '93") plus the usual stickers, zines and shirts. Some of you may already own samples of their work as one of the members, Zeb, designed some of the recent DB graphics. More on that, plus other skater-owned companies in the first issue of Phat. But if you can't wait, the number for Skate Shite is 0273 622056.

Meanwhile "Saw That," famous up to now for their "Happy Lion Club" shirts, stickers and zines, have moved into the hardware market with a plain, value-for-money deck. Give them a call on 0920 465861.

We've just seen some of the freshest new clothing from a Cornish skater-owned company. They're called Siesta and their stuff is seriously good. There'll be pictures and more on that in the first issue of Phat. But if you can't wait, give them a call on 05035 405.

HOW DO I GET THE NEW WEAR & TEAR

This was also the moment when Horsley made an all-important connection with a photographer capable of providing photographs that could elevate a humble local zine project into something more impactful and worthy of national attention.

'Andy came up to me [at Spitalfields], introduced himself and said "We're doing a new magazine called The System *and we need you to work for us; here's the address, send us some stuff." So I did—and they basically ran everything I sent. That must have been my entire portfolio at the time, shot during the previous two years—I sent him every decent picture I had and they used virtually all of them.'* Wig Worland

'When Wig started sending photos, that's when it starts to happen. We had enough momentum to put something together—which we did. Wig was coming backwards and forwards to Nottingham to shoot stuff and then I bought my first camera soon after that. That's when I started shooting photos, constantly harassing Wig, asking how the hell do you do it? Because I hadn't really picked up a camera before either; I was just winging it. So we're doing this zine and I didn't know where it was going to go as there were no real plans for it other than just to do it—obviously trying to make it better. And I was trying to take better photos for it, and travelling a bit for it.' Andy Horsley

Andy and Chris, with the addition of Wig and a small evolving network of photographers new and established were employing their skateboarder learn-by-doing savvy, developing their own network and publishing nous. At this point the only real competition to their concerted efforts was from *RAD* under its new ownership. Following the progress of their competition they were increasingly amazed by and then highly critical of the direction *RAD* was heading:

'Whilst we were developing The System, *RAD magazine was going through a pretty low period and wasn't at all good—this went on for about 8 months after TLB left. I was upset about that—it seemed wrong.'* Wig Worland

'Paul [Haynes] said to us: "Well, if you think you could do better than that, give the publishers a shout and see if you can go and speak to them." Thinking back, it's insane—I wouldn't do that now. But because of that we said: "Well, why not just give it a go?" I think maybe Paul rang up the guy at the publishers—or maybe we talked Wig into it because he definitely was the sensible one; we were just a bunch of stoners knocking up a skate thing. So we decided that we would do it—jumped in Paul Haynes' little red van and drove down to Oxford overnight. We went there and just told them.' Andy Horsley

'When we had the meeting with the new publishers, I basically said "You've got to let these guys take over RAD, *it's not going well and you've got to do something about it. These are the guys to do it and they're here now—you need to give them a job. It was an audacious move but amazingly they went for it.'* Wig Worland

'We were all for The System *guys taking over and even had a hand in setting up the initial connection. Stig and I had been in touch with them and then primed our publisher by suggesting that they would be the right people to get* RAD *back on track. The speed at which it happened surprised us, but we were so relieved with the outcome.'* Eddie Spearing

'Thankfully, Andy and Wig did a better job than we had been able to at RAD *and brought it back to life because they had the correct connections and skater respect that we did not have.'* Stig

Despite being instrumental in this significant editorial coup, and the opportunities it presented, Wig Worland was tempted away to America to work for *Transworld Skateboarding* magazine. In the 1980s and early '90s the opportunity to work in the US was a highly desirable rite of passage for any would-be professional skate photographer of the time. From the early 1980s onwards, British skate photographers had submitted photos to and been published in *Transworld Skateboarding* magazine. Worland continued the tradition, sending photographs out to California in the early 1990s.

*'*Transworld Skateboarding *was where any aspiring skateboard photographer wanted their work to end up because it had the best print quality of any skateboard magazine at the time. In the early 1990s,* TWS *(via Dave Swift and Grant Brittain) impressed with my black and white printing skills, offered me a job working in the mag's darkroom and then taking photographs for them in California just as soon as I could get there.'* Wig Worland

As an up-and-coming skate photographer, Wig had initially taken impetus from the pages of *RAD* magazine. He began submitting photos for inclusion and his first published photo had appeared in the magazine in 1989. Publication in other British skate magazines—until their eventual demise—had followed. The invitation to work in California gave Wig a chance to immerse himself more deeply at the cutting edge of skateboarding, honing his craft in the process.

During the period of transition to new ownership and a new editorial team at *RAD*, the all-important relationship between good-quality skate photography and magazine had suffered. Andy Horsley and Wig Worland brought with them a strong vision and practical understanding of the importance of the powerful imagery required to sustain a respected skateboard magazine.

'I was in America and Horsley was in the UK struggling with the magazine. He suggested that I come back to be the main photographer at RAD. *I thought about it and felt I could have a more significant influence on that magazine than I could at* Transworld. *That was a pivotal moment in my life.'* Wig Worland

With a new, tight-knit group of connected skateboarders and photographers ready to try and revive *RAD*, the magazine provided a more appealing forum for a new breed of contributors alongside the established photographers previously published in the original *RAD* and *Phat* magazines. A greater emphasis on high-quality imagery returned to the magazine and new voices would make full use of the opportunities presented.

Despite the steep learning curve that accompanied grasping the full requirements of putting together a commercially printed and nationally distributed magazine, confidence developed quickly—in parallel with frustrations with their publisher.

'We didn't have any budget beyond our wages for doing the mag. We'd kind of exhausted what we were doing and covering in our surrounding locale, and we needed to travel further and find new people and do new stuff, and the publisher just wasn't having any of it—obviously because he wasn't making nearly enough money.' Andy Horsley

‘Thankfully, Andy and Wig did a very much better job than we did at *RAD* and brought it back to life because they had the correct connections and skater respect that we did not have’ Eddie Spearing

Opposite: *PSP* newspaper published and distributed free to skateshops by the *RAD/Phat* team to maintain momentum and influence whilst *Phat* was developed, 1993 **Below:** Luke McKirdy, Worthing boating lake, 1994 **Photo:** Wig Worland

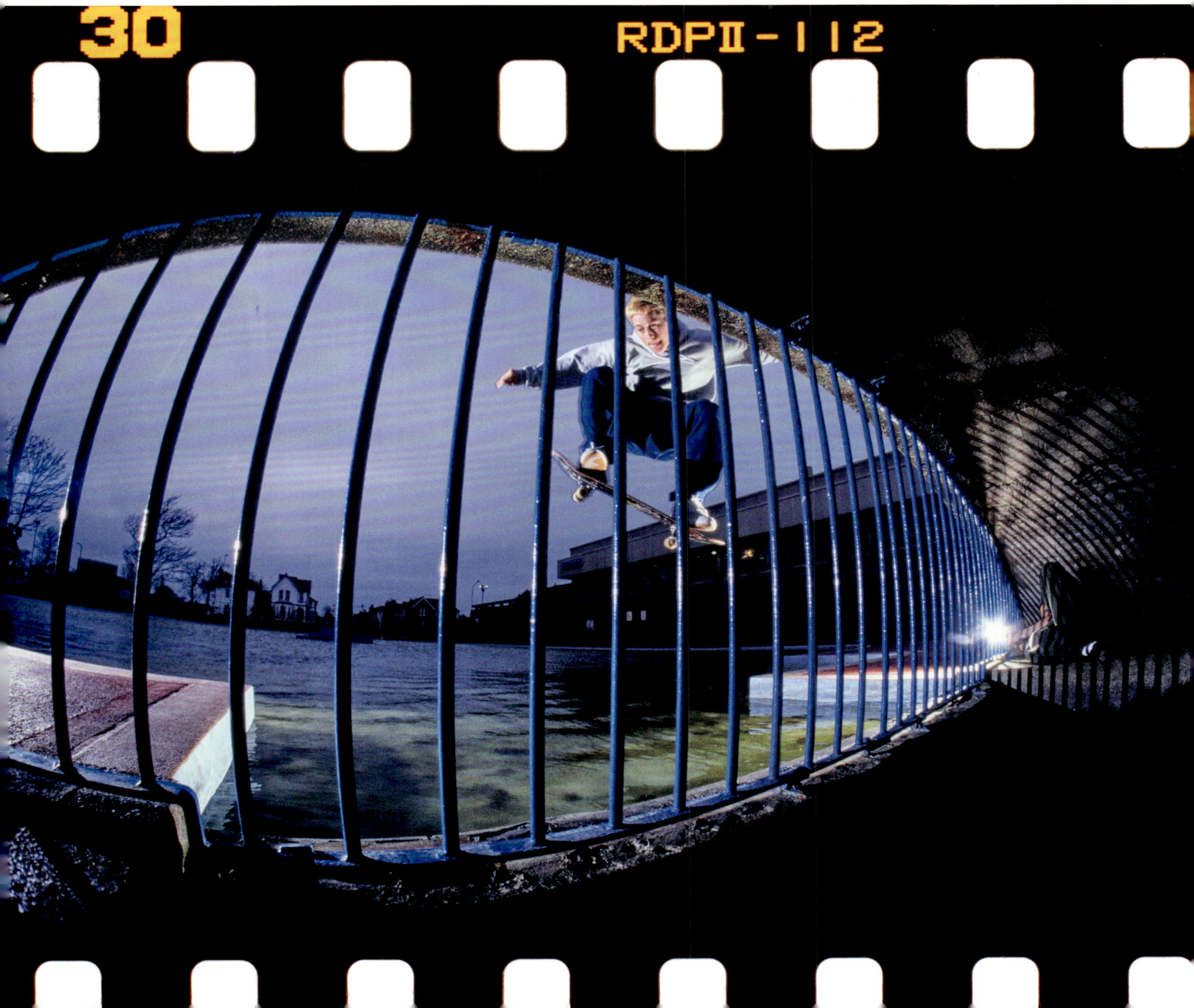

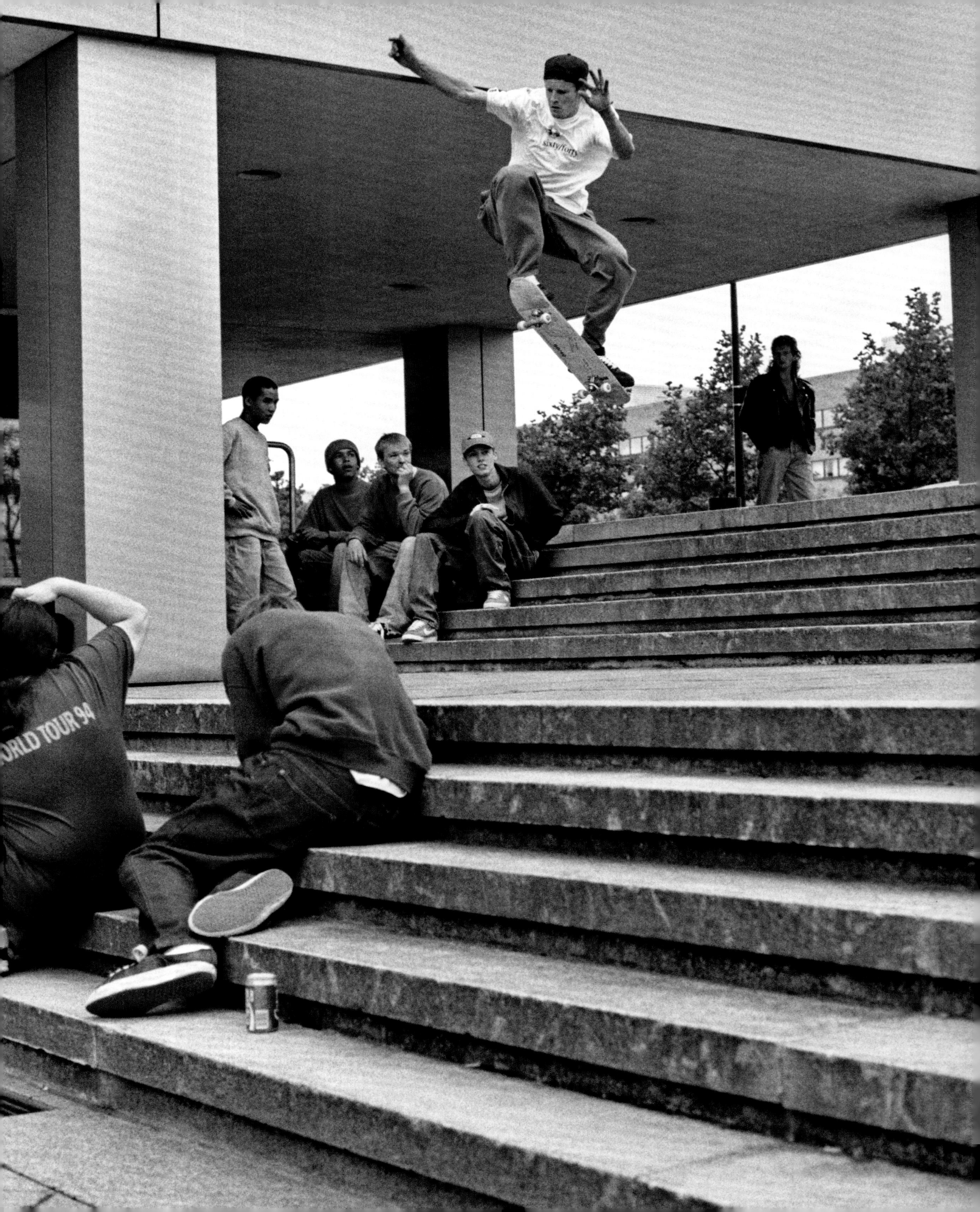
sixty/forty
ORLD TOUR 94

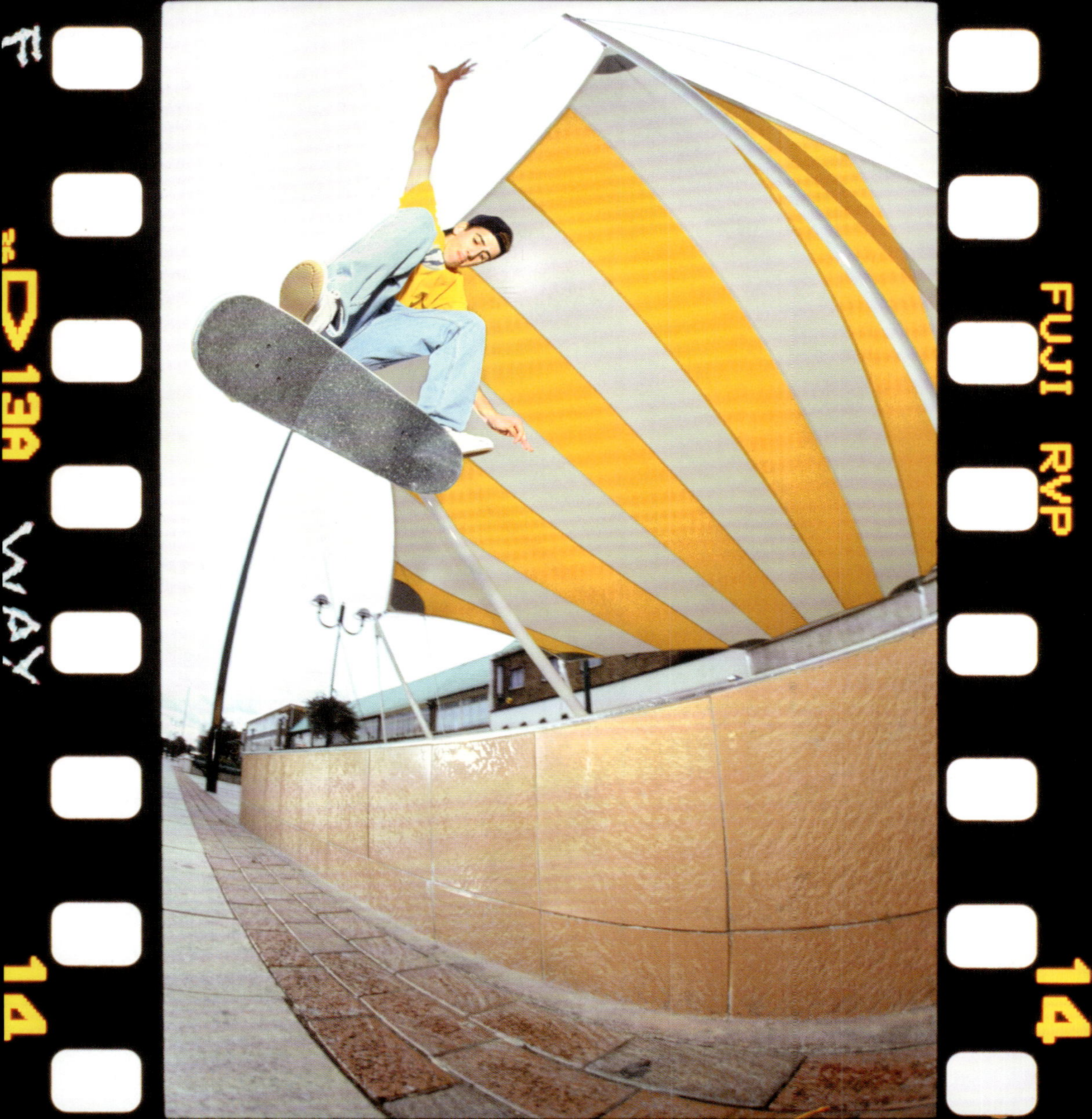
FUJI RVP
14

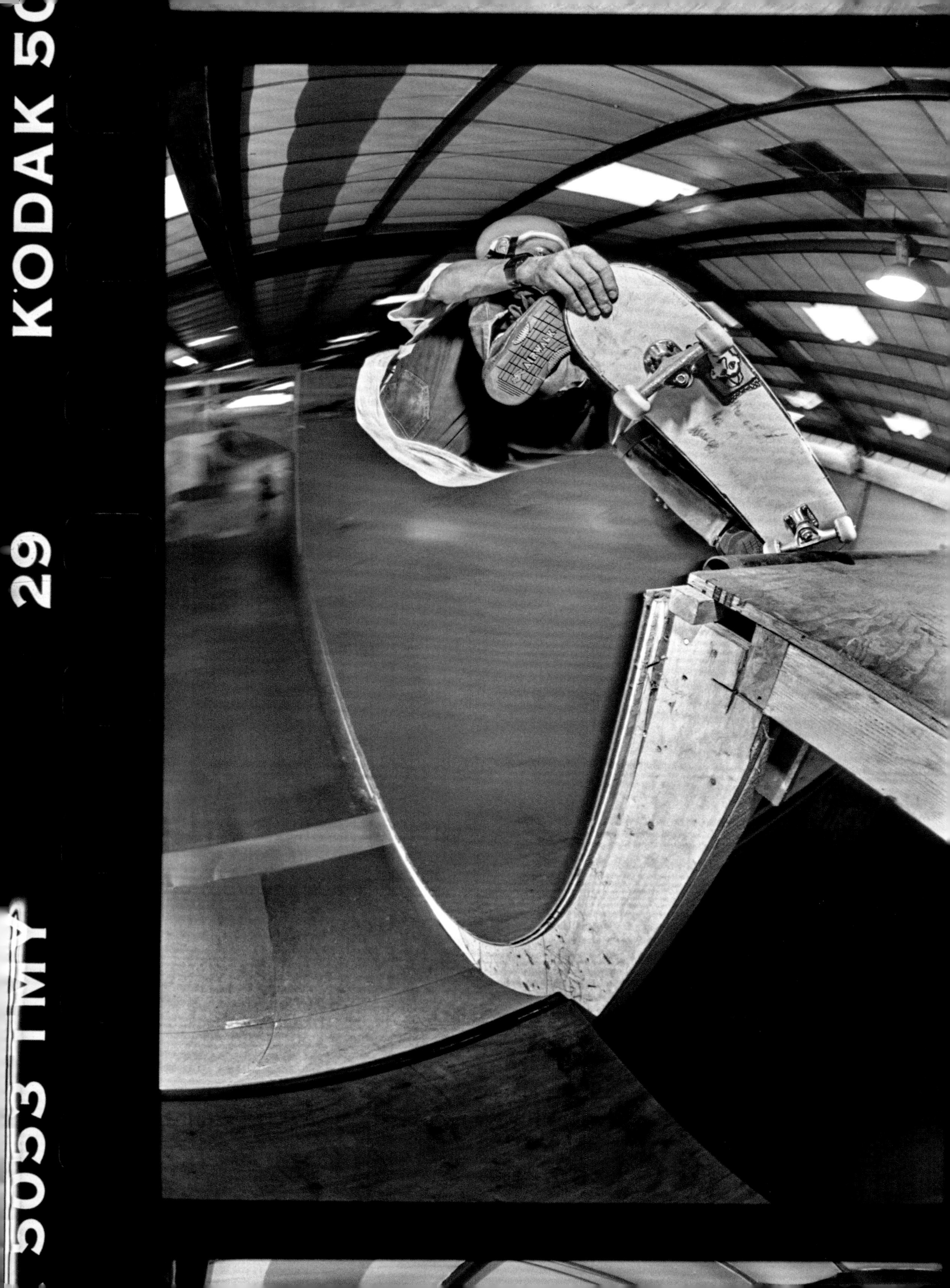
5053 TMY
29
KODAK 50

'Some of my friends I skated with were just looking at the ads, thinking about which boards they wanted to get, but I was already noticing the action pictures more. I was looking at the tricks and trying to learn how to do them, but I was also caught by the image of someone frozen in flight; the way they were tweaking something or how their face looked. So I wanted to learn how to do those things on a skateboard but also I was realising how cool it was to capture that with photography.'

Leo Sharp

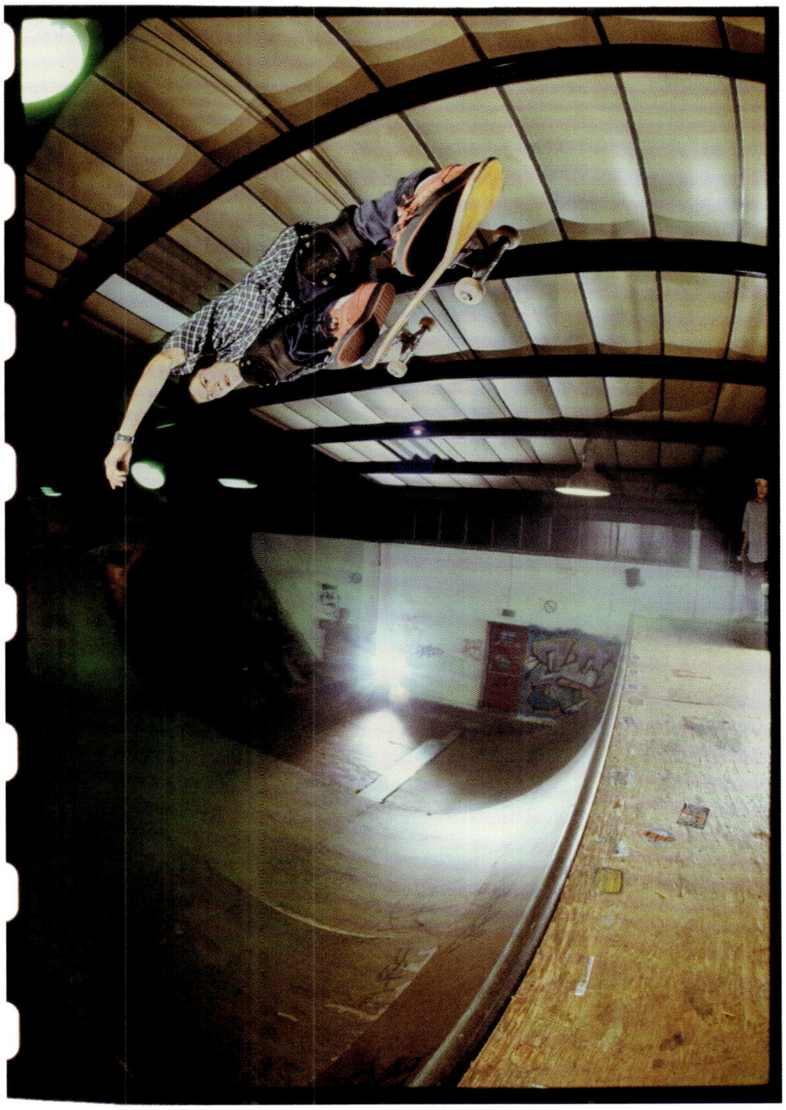

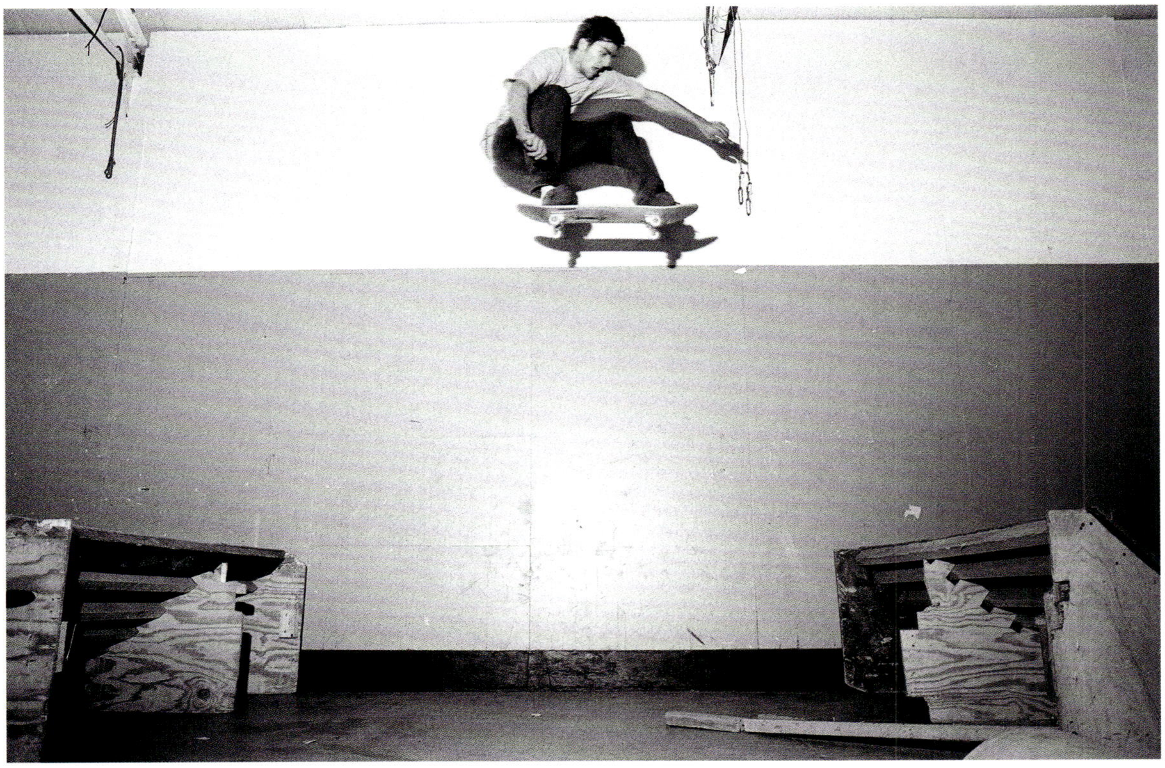

Previous spread left: Mathew Pritchard, Milton Keynes City Centre double set 1994, and **right:** Mark Channer, Hemel Hempstead, 1994 **Opposite:** Andy Scott, Radlands, 1995 **Above:** Rune Glifberg, Radlands, 1994 **Photos:** Wig Worland **Left:** Mike Manzoori, Pioneer Club, St Albans, 1993 **Photo:** Leo Sharp

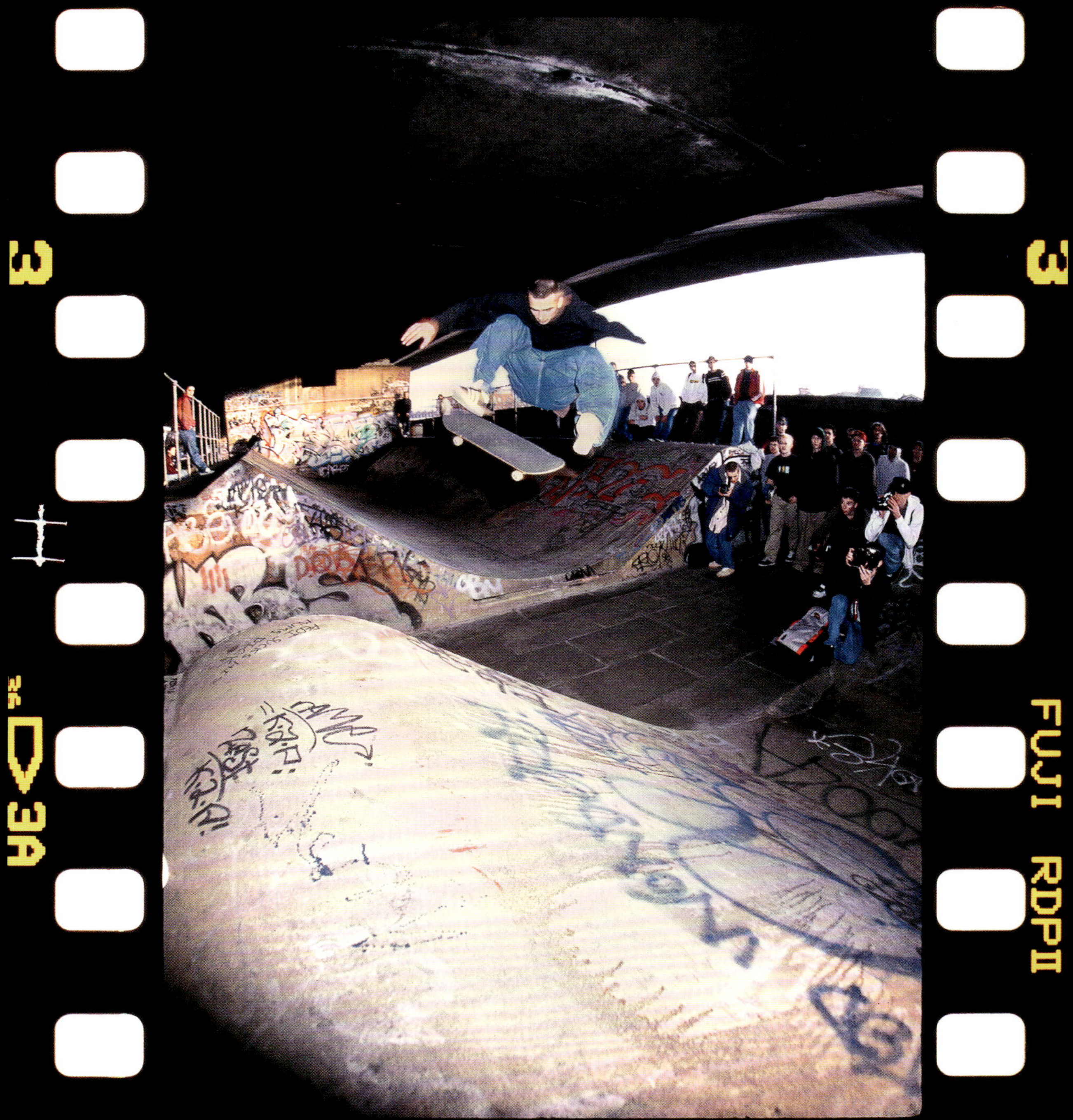

Left: Carl Shipman, Meanwhile 2, London, 1994 **Photo:** Andy Horsley **Opposite:** Mark Channer, Amersham, 1994 **Photo:** Wig Worland

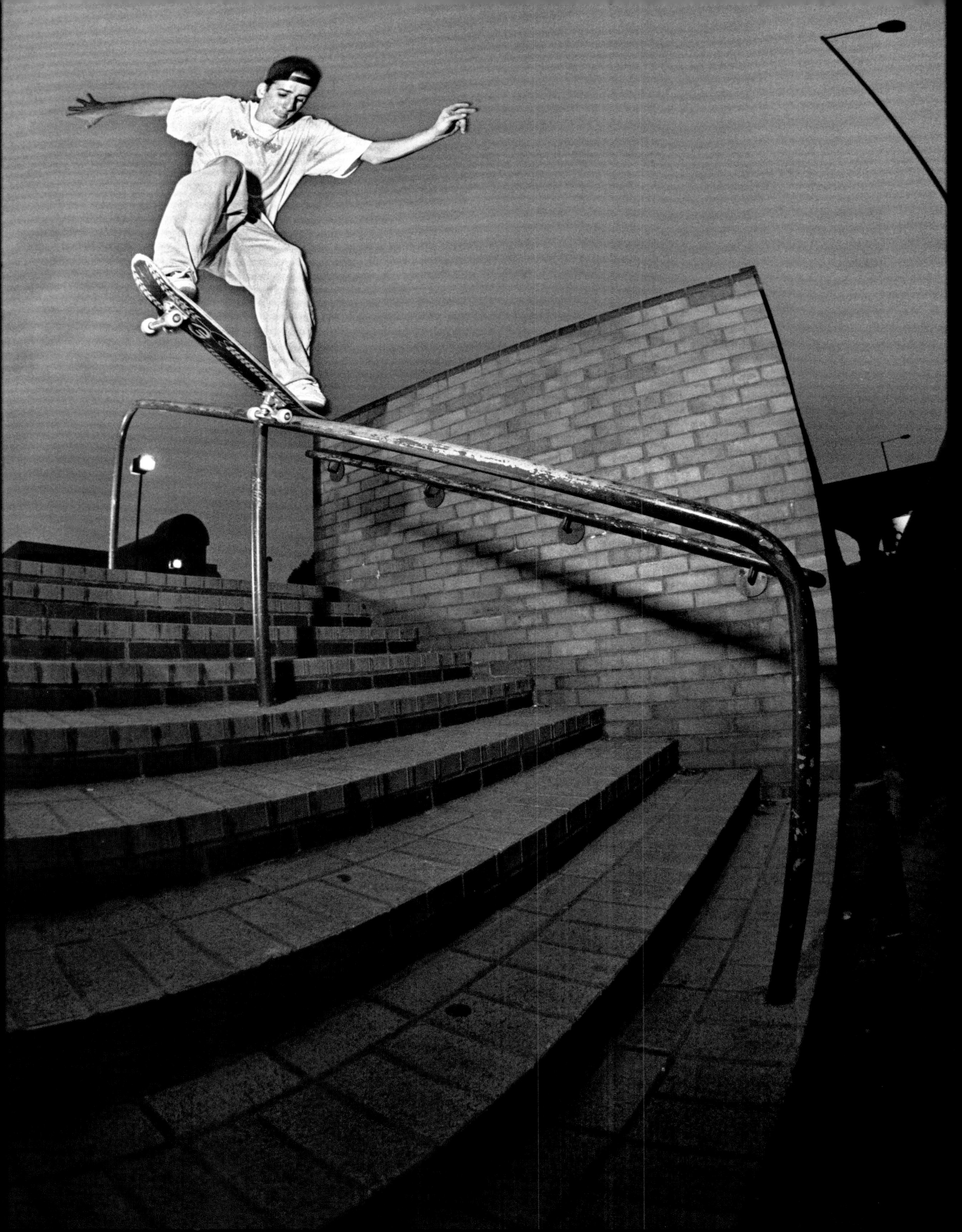

TRANSWORLD
SKATEboarding
MAGAZINE

P.O. Box 6
Cardiff-by-the-Sea
California 92007
(619) 722-7777
FAX (619) 722-0653

Feb. 6, 93

Hi Wig-

I read the letter you sent to Dave. I would really like to start using you more as our

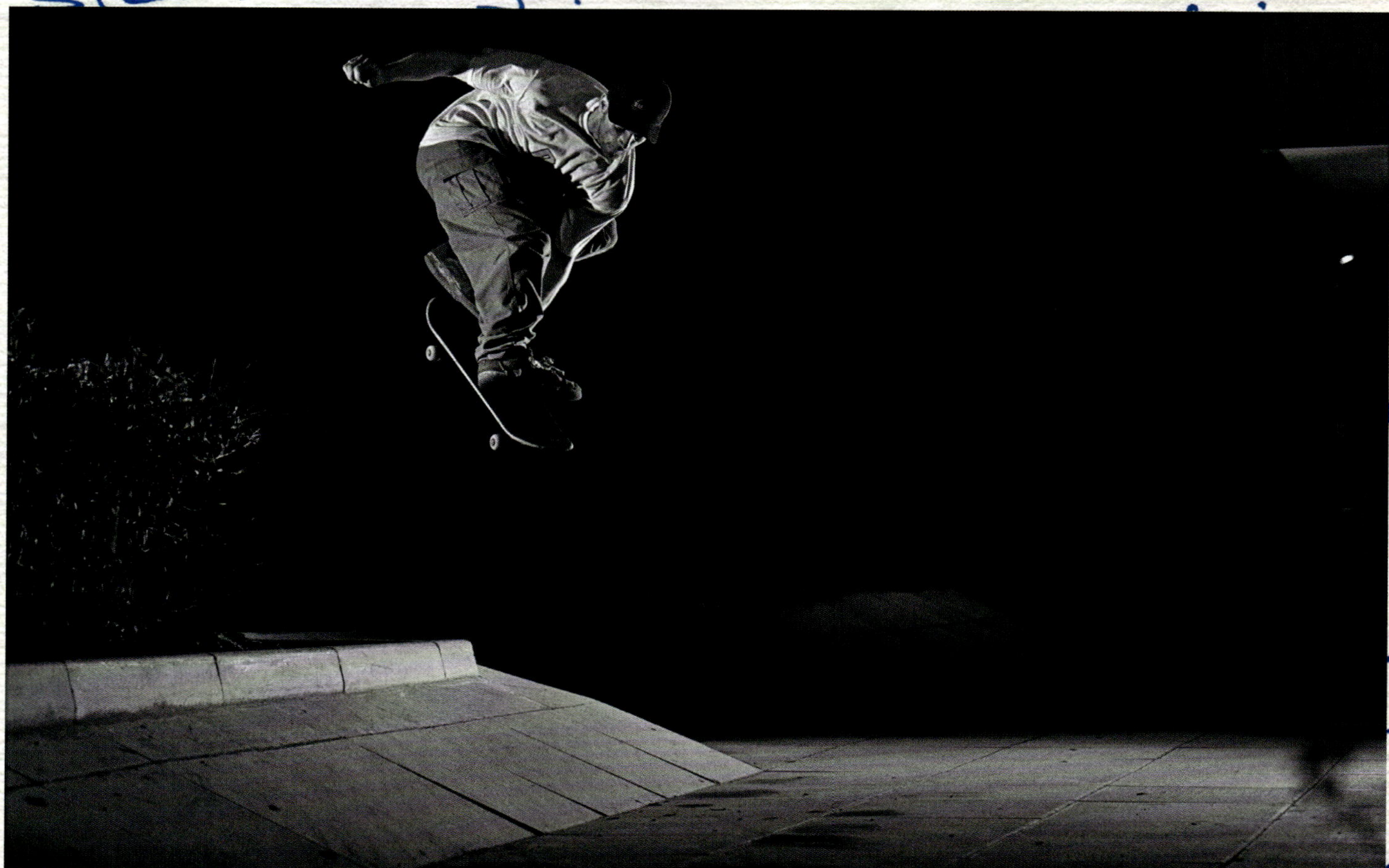

are much better, I like that grainy, contrasty b+w. So, we'll get something together soon. Let me know what you think.

Seeya-

Grant

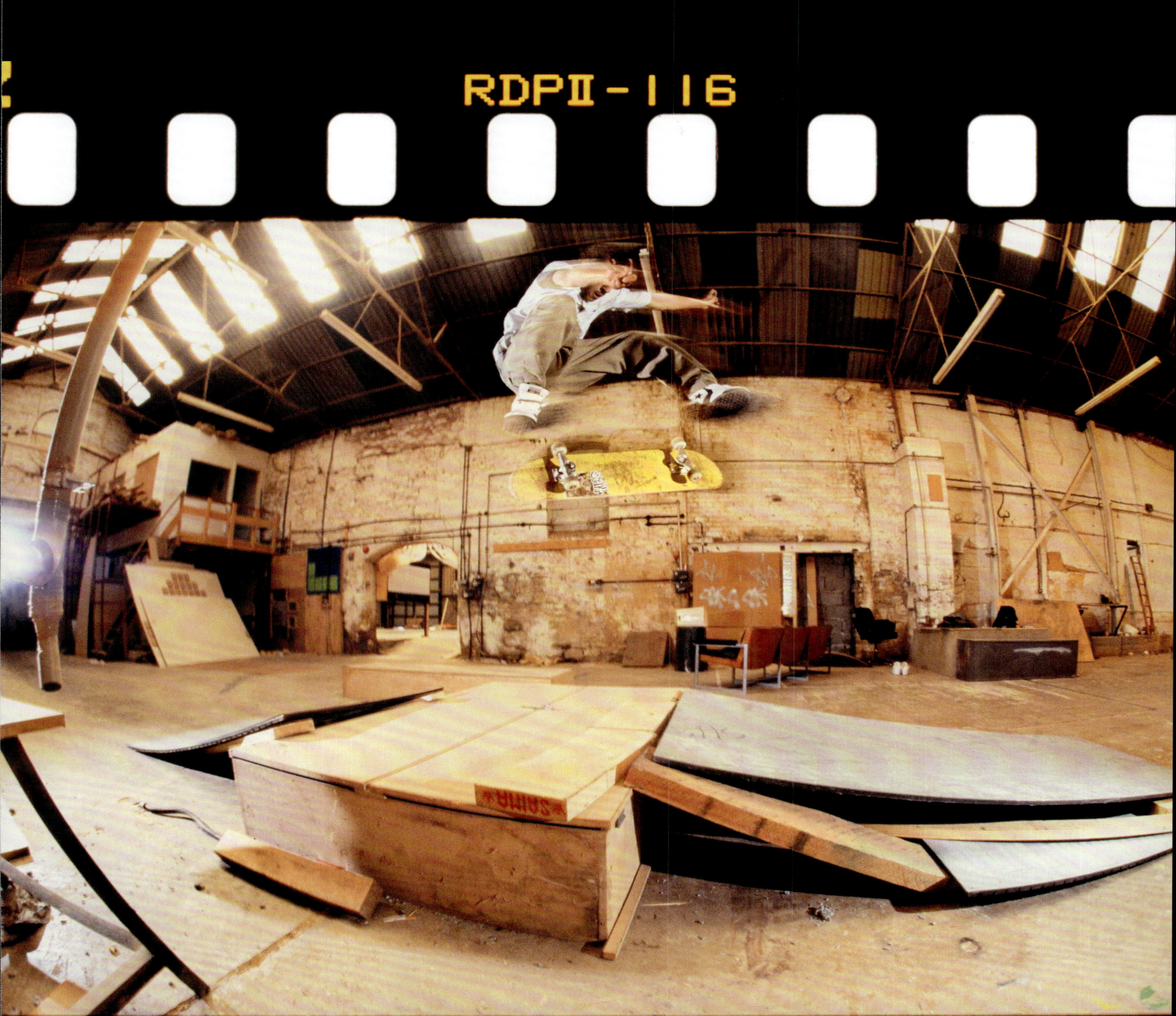

Opposite: Letter from J. Grant Brittain inviting Wig Worland to submit photos for publication in *Transworld Skateboarding*, and **inset:** John Dalton, John Moores University, Liverpool, 1994
Above: Flynn Trotman, Bath, 1995
Photos: Wig Worland

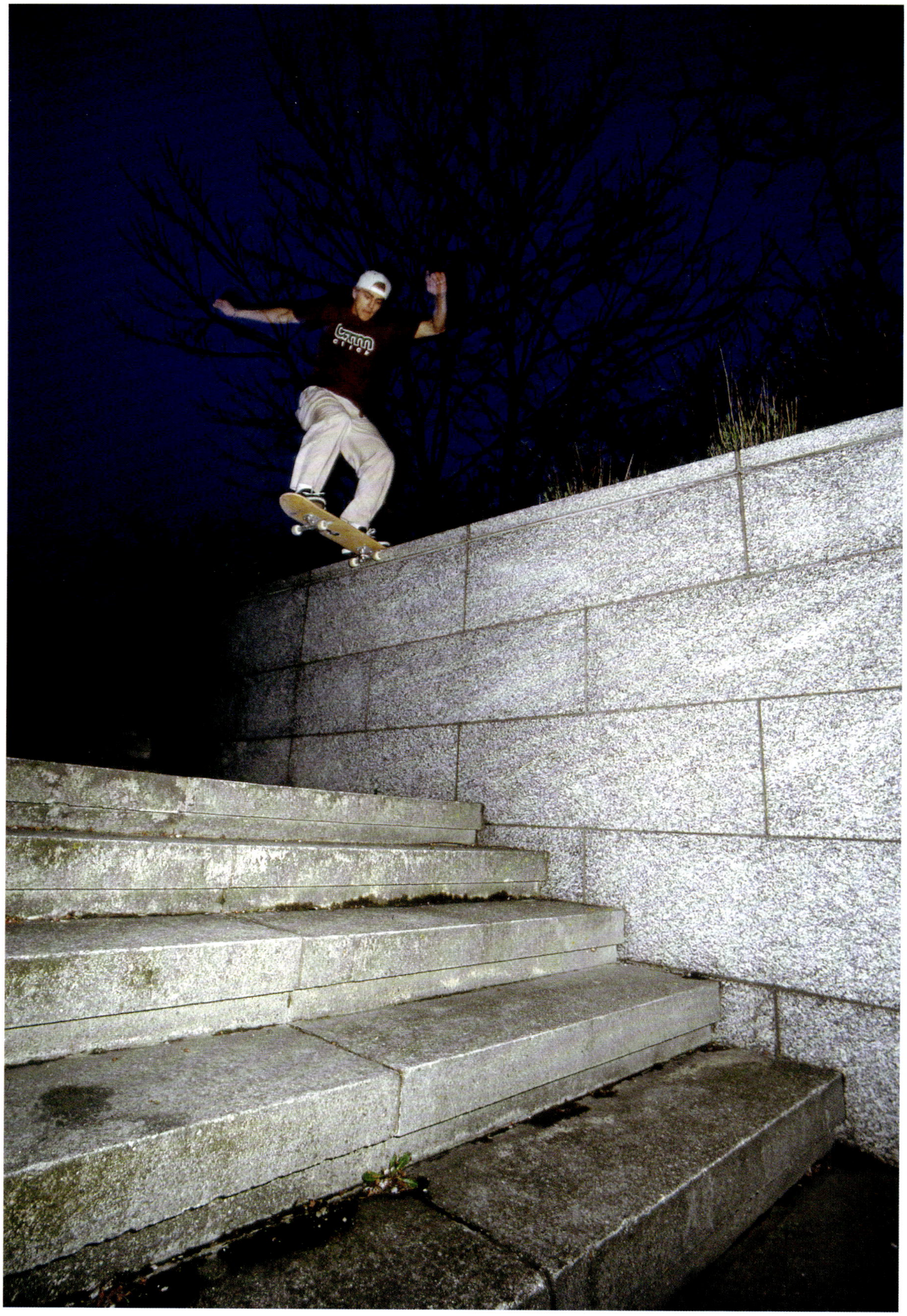

Left: Mike Manzoori, Milton Keynes, 1993 **Photo:** Leo Sharp **Opposite:** Neil Urwin, Five Bridges, Gateshead, 1994 **Photo:** Wig Worland

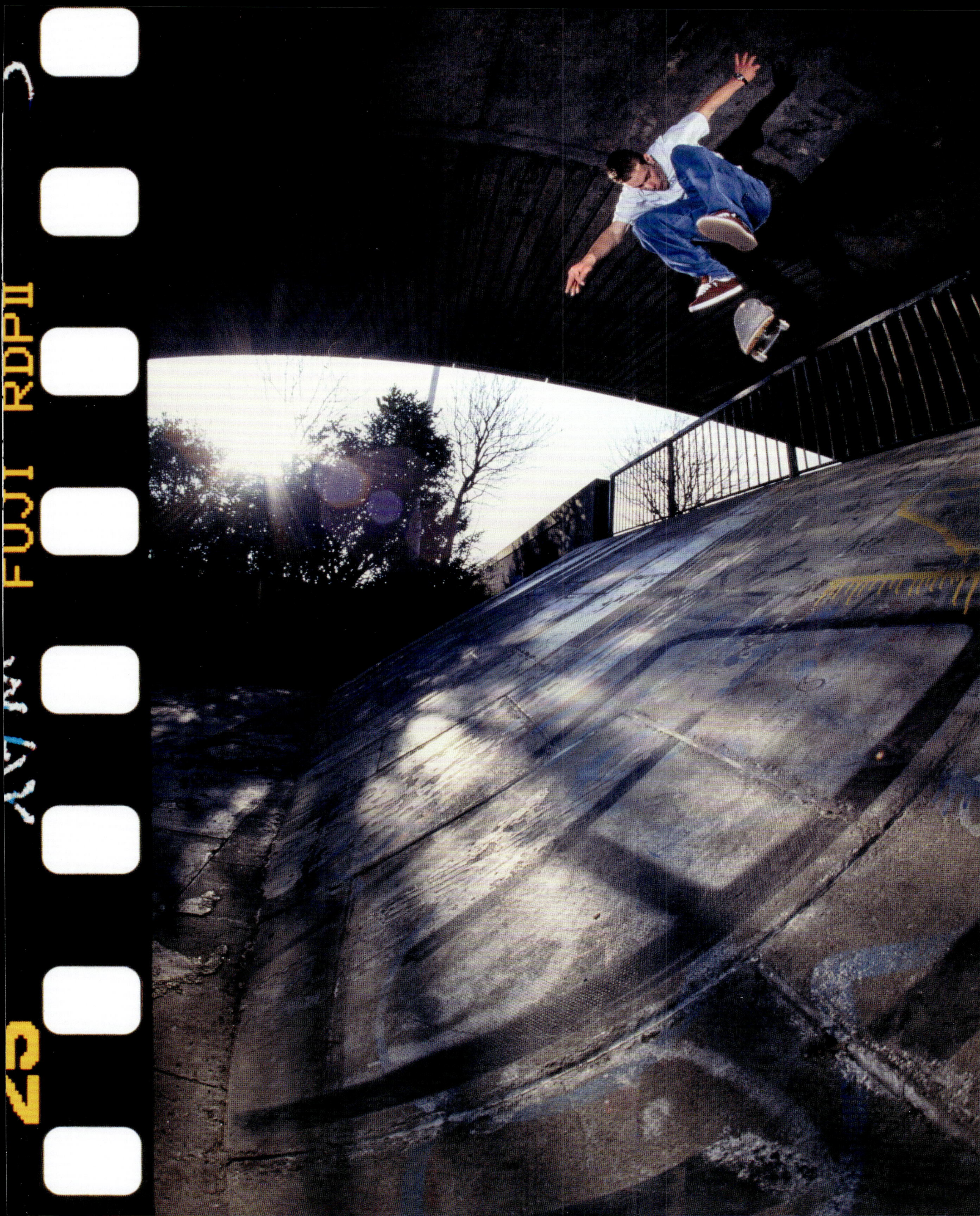
FUJI RDPII
23

'I thought purely about skating. I didn't think about how it would look. I didn't think about like, "Why is he putting a flash there or shooting with the fisheye?" No—it was like, "I'm gonna jump down this." We'd be like, "Alright, let's do it!" I trusted [Wig] 100%. I used to love hanging out and I used to love what would come back from those shoots.'

Danny Wainwright

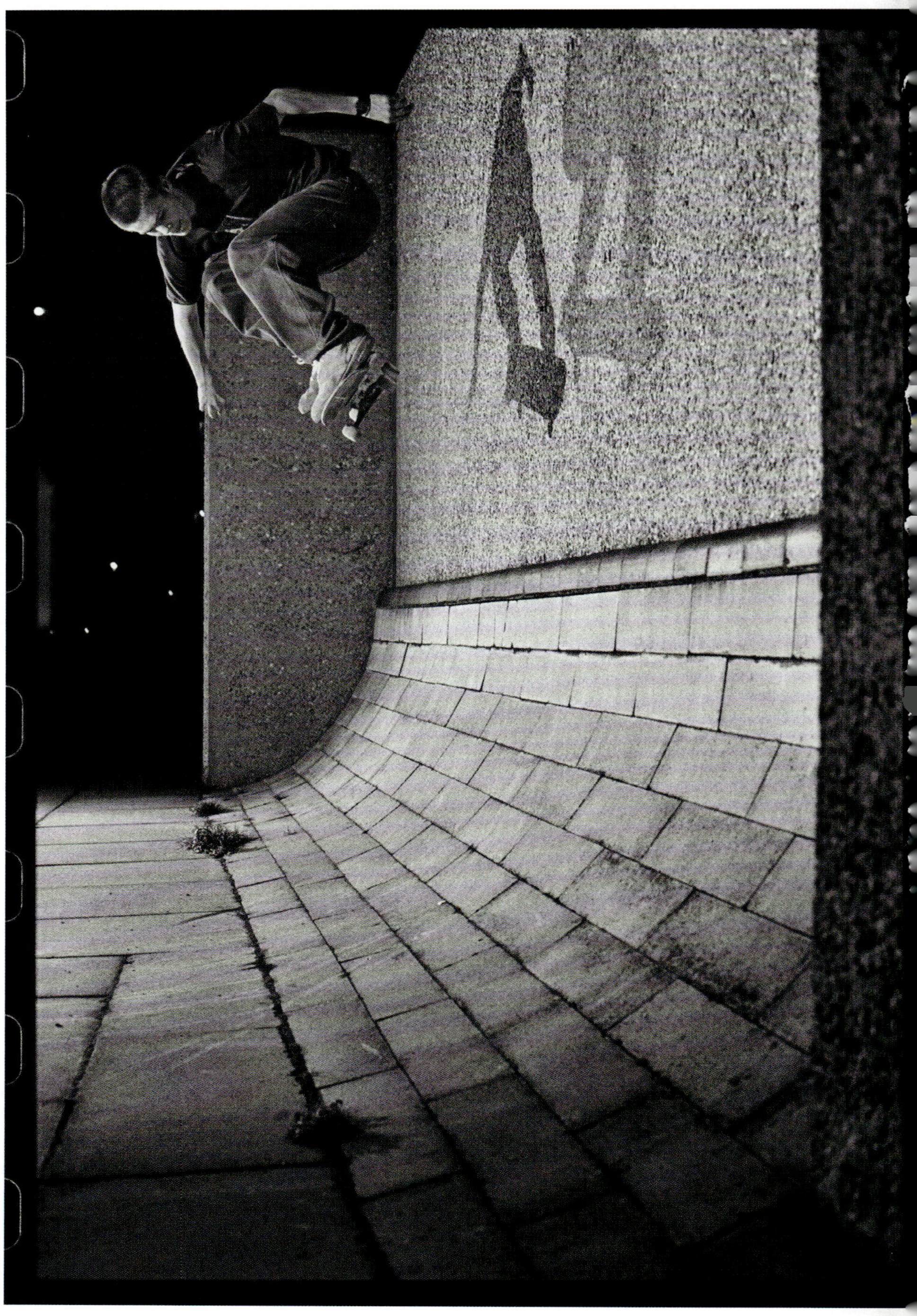

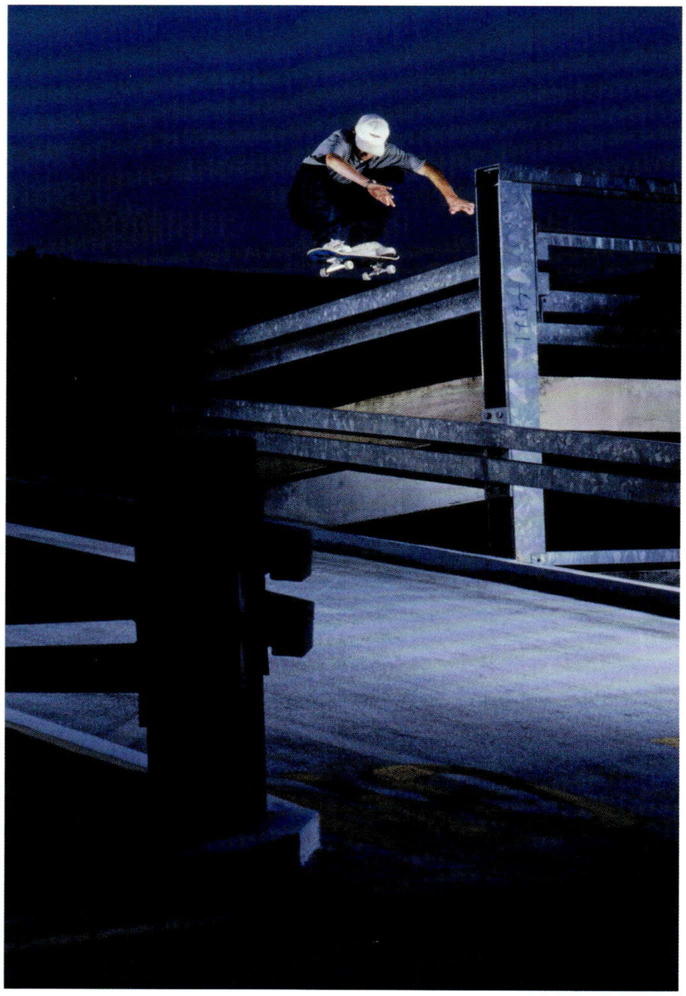

Above: Geoff Rowley, Chaloner Street, Liverpool, 1994 **Left:** Danny Wainwright, Stroud, 1994 **Opposite**: Neil Urwin, Barbican, London, 1995
Photos: Wig Worland

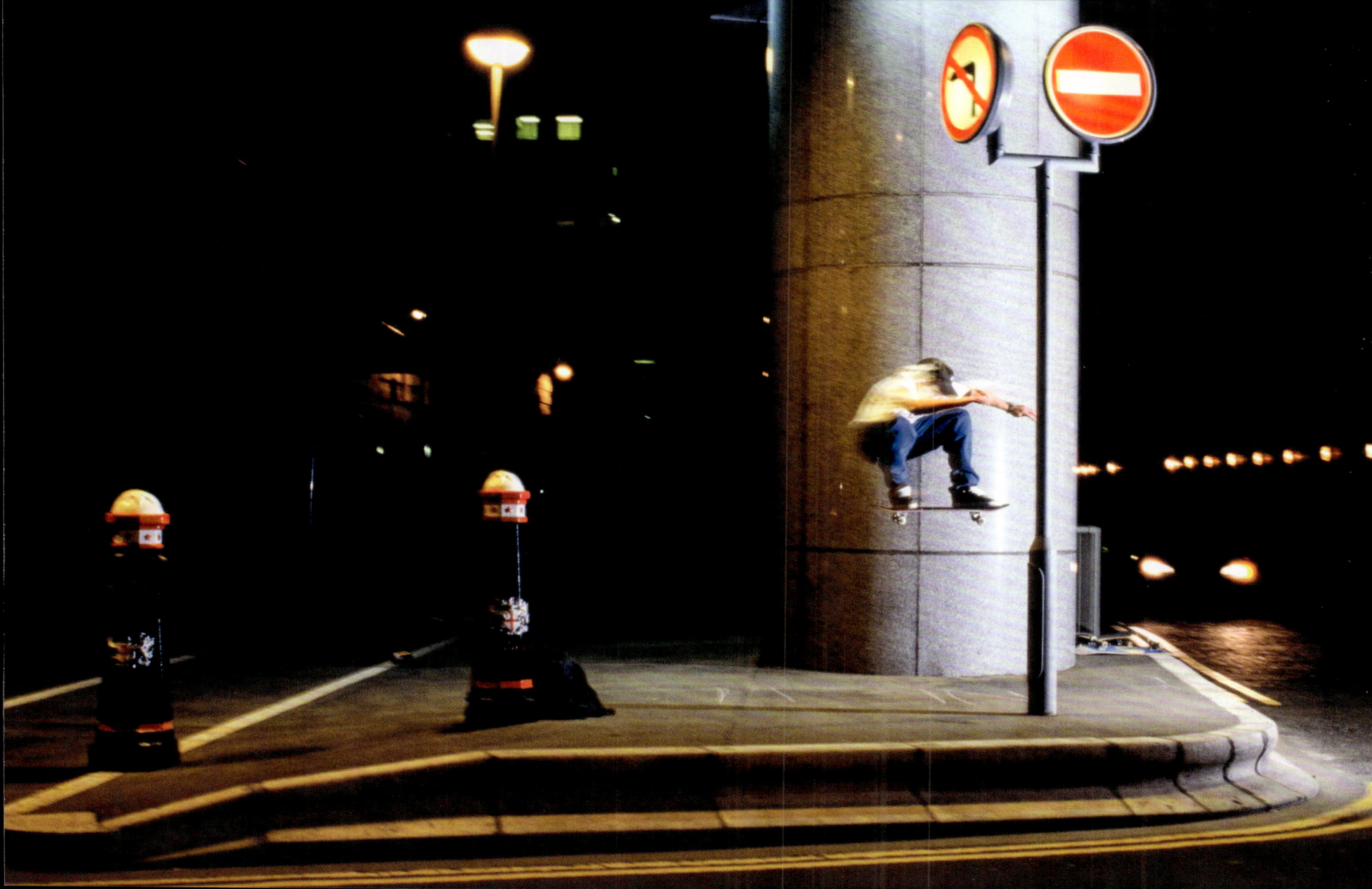

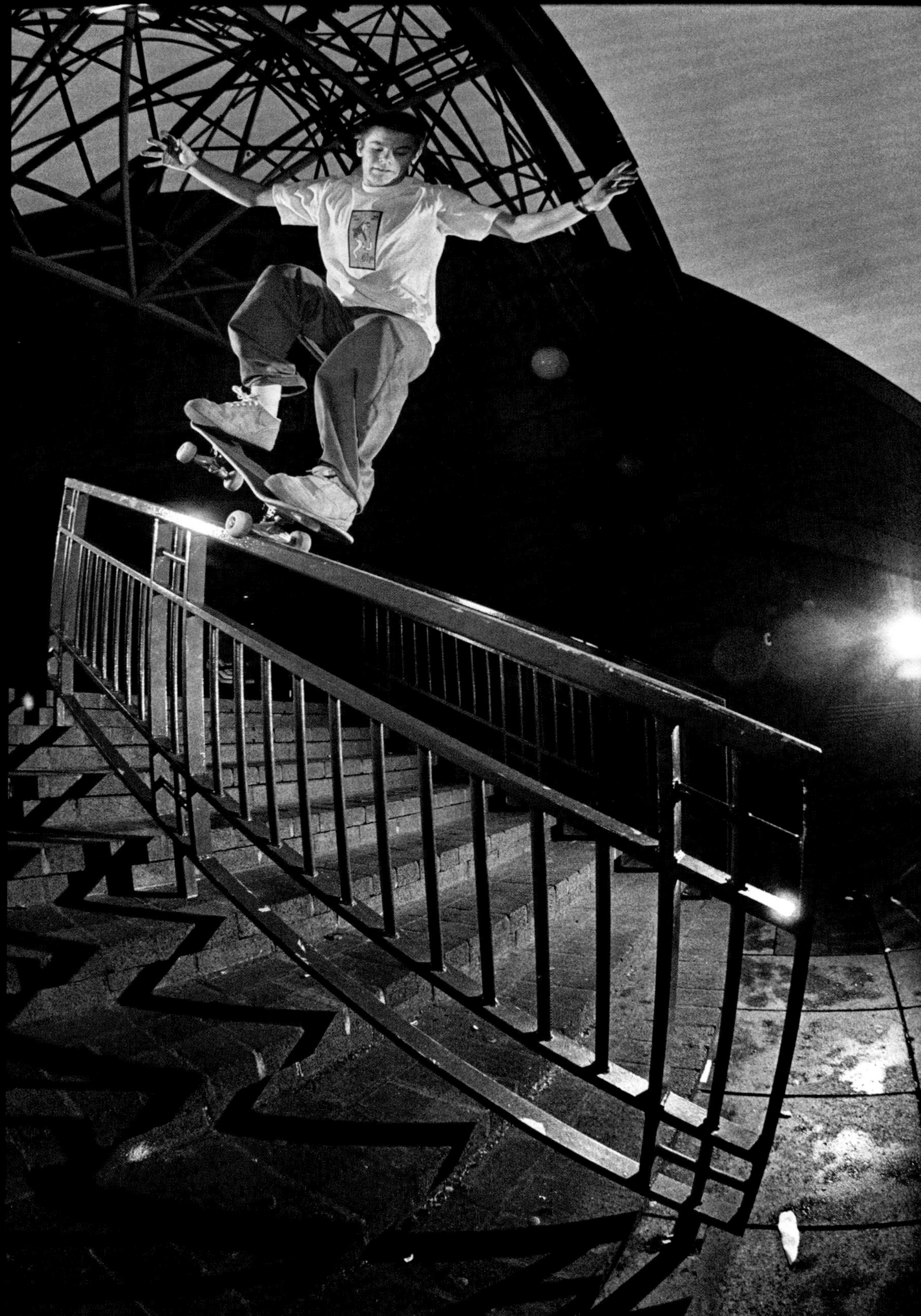

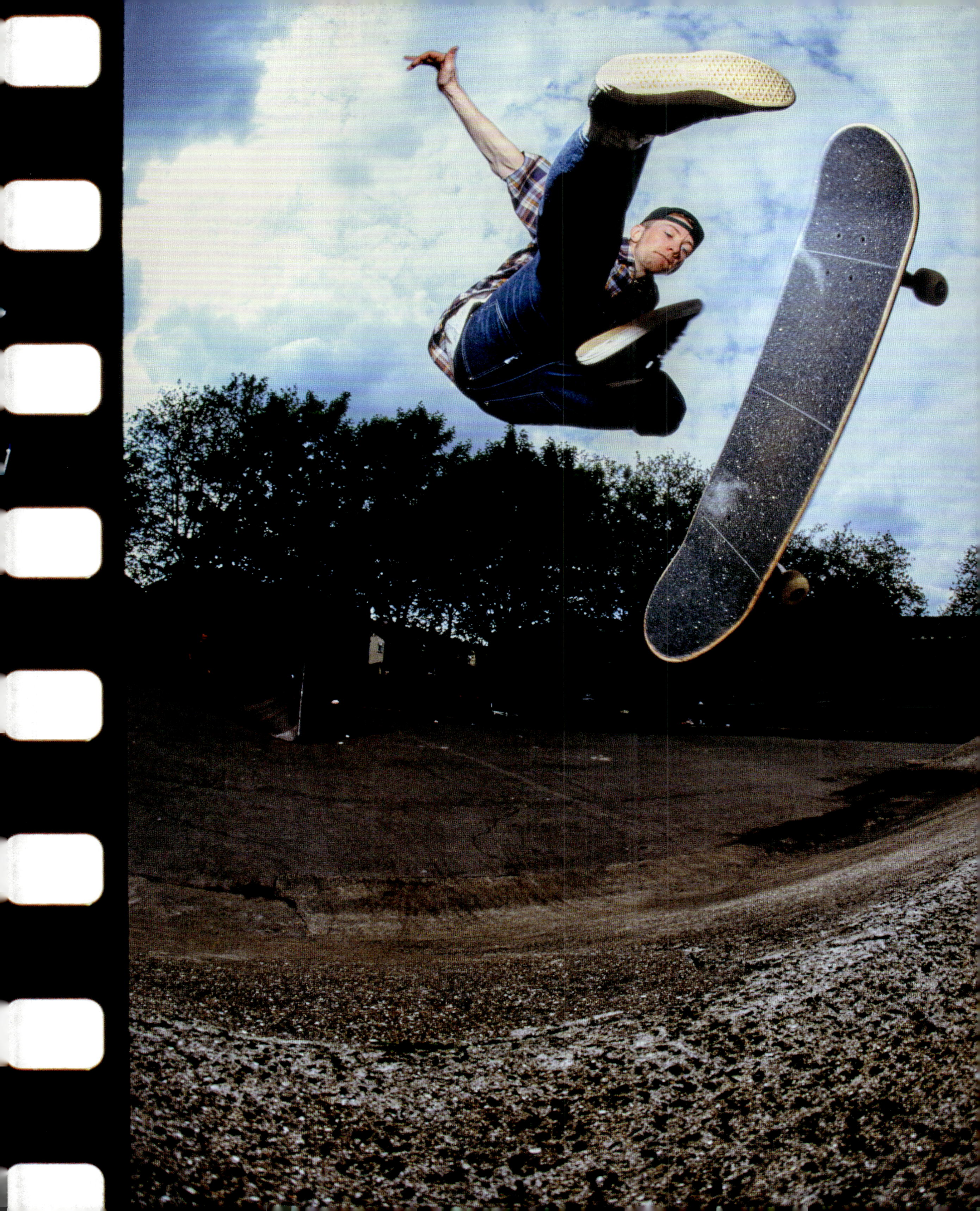

‘The skateboarding community owes TLB and the *RAD* magazine contributors a great debt for being there when nobody else was, showing us what skateboarding culture in the UK looked like at the time. There were a few people alongside TLB who shared that world and opened up its creative possibilities. It used to be so exciting when the magazine came out every month and it’s still incredible to see all that imagery today’ Wig Worland

Frustrations were not confined solely to the editorial team; advertising manager Jim Peskitt felt that more could be achieved with the resources available. He convinced Andy and Wig that they could all leave together, start completely afresh and build a new publishing enterprise based on what they had already achieved.

‘We had a massive meeting—I think we went to the pub first, 9 o’clock in the morning, and had a couple of pints each—then went in and just told the publisher. Screaming at him, “Well, if you don’t give us any money we can’t do anything”, and this, that and the other. Jim just laid it on the line and said, “Look we’re going to go off and start our own thing”. And the publisher said, “I’m very disappointed in you”. Like being in school again—well that made it easy.

‘And that was it. We’d already made what was going to be our final issue of the mag, but because we had to work another month’s notice we put together a spare issue of RAD *[which would never be published]. Just used all of the old photos at the bottom of the barrel, and made up articles, made up scene reports. It was amazing and so funny—we just went in full guns on it and made an issue of* RAD *but full of bullshit. And while we were knocking up this stray unpublished issue, we were really putting all our efforts into the first issue of the new magazine—*Sidewalk*—that we would publish ourselves. Our experience at* RAD *had enabled us to think that we could go out and do a magazine ourselves. We definitely needed* RAD *as a stepping stone. Otherwise there’d have been no* Sidewalk *magazine.’* Andy Horsley

What transpired was a new publishing company with a focus purely on board culture. This would be the right (and long-overdue) space in which a magazine covering skateboarding could flourish. And flourish it did; *Sidewalk* magazine became the voice of British skateboarding for the next 20 years plus. Whether conscious or not, the roots of this enterprise lay in the legacy of *RAD* and the groundwork put down by TLB and the magazine’s collaborators in establishing a confident British outlook on skateboarding culture. This sense of identity and self-assurance was carried forward by a generation that had previously been inspired by and informed of that culture in the pages of *RAD* magazine.

‘That singular point in our continuum, where Tim decides not to carry on with RAD*, in fact spawned a whole new horizon of action sports titles. Ponder on that one for a while...’* Eddie Spearing

Below: The last cover, June/July 1995.
Neil Urwin, Harrow-on-the Hill
Photo: Wig Worland

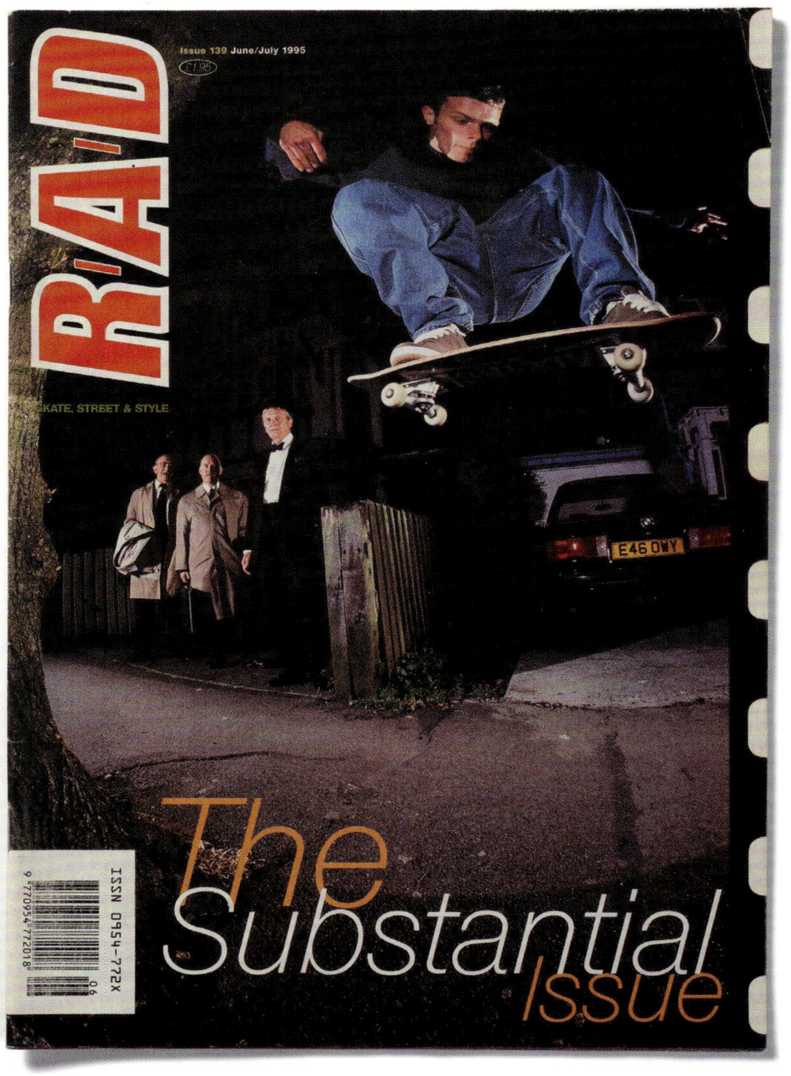

RAD STAFF AND CONTRIBUTORS 1987–1995
Credits as originally published

Editor / Photographer
Tim Leighton-Boyce
Editor
Stig
Editor and Designer / Editor and Design Bomb / Mr. Editor / Editor and Fool
Andrew Robert Horsley (does a bit of design)
Assistant Editor and Designer / Co-Editor and Layout Explosion / Editor 2 and chip eater
Chris Forder
Associate Editor / American Pie / American Spy / Contributing Editor
Skin Phillips
Editorial Assistants
Ray Calthorpe, Simon Evans, Matt Stuart
Contributing Editors
Ali, Appleman, Paul Browne, Dan Cates, Percy Dean, Simon Dodson, Douglas, Emmeline, Chris Fowler, Sean Goff, Harry, Jon, Jeff Kendall, Kris, Phraeser, Pin, Chris Pulman, Jon Robson, Russell, Alvin Singfield, Darren Ward, Warrington, Simon Woodstock
Consultant
Dave Currey
Assistant Editors / Designers
Christian Malcolm Forder (full names to please our mums), Nick Philip
Designer in Spirit
Nick Philip
Designer in Body
Derek Westwood
Designer in Waiting
Ian Lawson (Roxburgh)
Art Directors
Ian Lawson (Roxburgh) F.W.I., Steve Billington, Chris and Andy
Designers
Dan Adams, Steve Billington, Jeff Gurney, Steve Hicks
Guest Designers
Ian Lawson (Roxburgh) F.W.I., Ian Middleton
Assistant Designers
Frances Aghajani
Jason Snelling
Art Assistants
Rico Gusman, Andy Holmes
Cartoonists
James Maxwell, Graham 'Mac' McEachran, Sketchy, James Watmough

Contributing Photographers
Don Brider, J. Grant Brittain, Percy Dean, Bryce Kanights, Steve Keenan, Jeff Kendall, Marney, North, Chris Ortiz, Skin Phillips, Leo Sharp, Alvin Singfield, Dave Swift, Bryan Temmerand, Wig (don't go) Worland, Wig (come back) Worland
Senior Photographers
Dobie Campbell
'Mad' Mike John
Jay Podesta
Paul Sunman
Photographer at Large
'Mad' Mike John
Photographic Technician / Chief Photographer / Photo Diva / Photographic Wizard / Mr. Photographs / Mr. Co-Editor
Wig Worland
Mr. Photographers / Photographic burdens
Andy, Michael Blabac, Percy Dean, Ben Etheridge, Leo Sharp, Andy Shaw
Photographic Flashes
J. Doff
Who takes shots of other bald men?
Andy, Leo, Percy
Technical Editors / Senior Contributors
Shane O'Brien
David Slade
American Correspondents
Steve Douglas
Skin Phillips
American Representative
Steve Douglas
Bike Correspondent / Bike Type / Bandit Correspondent
David Slade
Senior Engineering Department
Vernon Adams, Paul Browne, Gavin Hills, Ged Wells
Product Placement Consultant / New Product Section
Vernon Adams
New Age Strategists
Gavin Hills, Kojak Hills
Teenage Mutant Tester / New Kid On The Deal
Simon Evans
Young And Trendy Club
Ricky Spangle
Videographers
Lee Dainton's friends
Wayne Fenlon
Steve Williams

Senior Ryters [sic]
Simon Evans, Gavin Hills
Chief Journalists / Journalistic Auras
Cates, Harry, Jon
Contributing Editorial Sparks
Ben, Douglas, Matt Fowler, Kris, Woodstock
Who puts pen to paper like hot sideburns?
Benny, Dan, Harry, Jon, Joyce
Mr. Journalists
Benny, Dan, Joyce, Justin, Ben Powell, Chris Pulman, Jon Robson, Tommy Boy, Simon Woodstock
Skateboarder and Nintendo champion
Harry
Journalist and intense sleeper
Jon Robson
Editorial nuisances
Ben Bodilly, Dan, Geoff, Ben Powell, Chris Pulman, Jon Weatherall
Ad manager and father
Jim Peskett
Contributors
Dan Adams, Moreau Alexis, JB Allstars, Jeff Ames, Appleboy, Graham Arden, Chris Aylen, Alex Baldock, James Baldock, William Bankhead, Tim Barnett, PD Baron, Paul Beards, Ben Bodilly, Robert Boerleider, Florian Böhm, Bod Boyle, Don Brider, Andy Brown, Angry Brown, Don Brown, Paul Browne, Ian Budd, Marc Bultitude, Phil Burgoyne, Raymond Calthorpe, Jamie Cameron, Mike Cameron, Thomas Campbell, Corin Casey, Simon Casey, Phil Chapman, John Chennels, Roger Clapham, Gary Clegg, Jeremy Cloot, Jeye Cloth, Evan Commbrinck, Patrick Cowan, Dave Currey, Percy Dean, Steve Douglas, Martin Drayton, Tom Dubern, Paul Duffy, Stuart Duncan, Dward, C. Edwards, Twiss Enwright, Edward Erskine, Simon Evans, Tim Evans, Stefan Fiedler, David Foldvari, Jeremy Fox, Franco, Ben Funnell, Ed Gill, Dave Glover, Sean Goff, Jem Gordon, Claus Grabke, Ian Guy, Timothy H, Fraser Hamilton, Nico Hardcore, Jay Hardy, Marcus Hardy, Harry, Rodga Harvey, James Holder, Dan Hollenbeck, Andy Hopper, Duncan 'Wurzel' Houlton, Andy Howell, James Hudson, Tim Hughes, Steve Ince, Andy Irvine, JaH, Alyn Jones, Spike Jonze, Bernadette Josiah, Thomas Kalak, Radek Kalhous, Steve Keenan, Christian Kline, Dan Kuhns, Ian 'Meanie' Lawton, Simon Levene, Jorg Ludewig, Scott Madlin, Chris Massey, Curtis McCann, Danny McCourt, Allan McNaughton, Bob Milk, Sonny Miller, Joe Millson, Ryan Monihan, Morbid, Alan Morrison, Geoff Nas, Damien Neary, Nico, Dave North, Tim Norton, Shane O'Brien, James O'Grady, Luke Ogden, Kenny Omond, Windy Osborn, Richard Ouwens, Michael Pankhurst, James Parry-Jones, Stephanie Pearson, Rick Peck, Perry, Nick Philip, Davie Philips, Pin, Jay Podesta, Chris Pulman, Steve R, Mark Richards, Tony Roberts, John Robson, Shane Rouse, Lee Reynolds, Marcus Rieger, Keith Russell, Colin Schenk, Sam Scott-Hunter, Simon Shanks, Leo Sharp, Frankie Shea, Adam Shillaber, Sam Silverstone, Sin, Alvin Singfield, Sketch, David Slade, Snoz, Eric Steel, Matt Stuart, Daniel Sturt, Paul Sunman, Jonathan Swan, Sean Sweeney, Peter Tarry, Brian Temmerand, Bill Thomas, Jamie Turnbull, Davy Van Laere, Matt Waddams, David Walsh, Warrington, Russell Waterman, Mark Waters, Ged Wells, Simon White, Kevin Wilkins, Andy Williams, Steve Wilshire, Jonnie Wilson, Woody, Mark Wright, Tobin Yelland

Every attempt has been made to credit all those involved in the original magazine. Sincere apologies for any omissions or misspellings in this abridged list.

Front cover photograph: Eric Dressen, Dean Lane, Bristol, 1987
Photo: Tim Leighton-Boyce

ISBN: 978 1 78884 258 7

The right of Dan Adams to be identified as author of this work has been asserted by him in accordance with the Copyright, Designs and Patents Act 1988

A CIP catalogue record for this book is available from the British Library

The author and publisher gratefully acknowledge the permission granted to reproduce the copyright material in this book. Every effort has been made to trace copyright holders and to obtain their permission for the use of copyright material. The publisher apologises for any errors or omissions in the text and would be grateful if notified of any corrections that should be incorporated in future reprints or editions of this book.

Compiled and designed by Dan Adams

MIX
Paper | Supporting responsible forestry
FSC® C008047

Printed in China
for ACC Art Books Ltd,
Woodbridge, Suffolk, UK

www.accartbooks.com

ACC ART BOOKS

ACKNOWLEDGEMENTS

Sincere thanks are due to the following people for their enthusiasm for all things *RAD*, and their support to help make this book a reality.

First and foremost, huge thanks to Sebastian Palmer at New Balance Numeric. Without his belief in the *RAD* project and his continued support, this book would not have been possible. Thanks also to Dave Mackey at New Balance Numeric.

The skate photographers. To each and every photographer who has ever picked up a camera and made skateboarding look so exciting, dynamic and radical. Not least of all, Tim Leighton-Boyce for his steadfast commitment to skateboarding and providing a visual (and emotional) landscape to the British skate scene, particularly in the 1980s when we needed it the most.

All the *RAD* magazine contributors 1987–1995 from across the nation and around the world.

Realising this book has been a long haul, helped along the way by supportive and encouraging friends, family and colleagues. Huge thanks to Wig Worland for the technical (and emotional) support, Paul Sunman for letting us use Slam City Skates HQ to develop the very first phase of the project way back when. My former studio colleagues for listening to me babble on about skateboarding and books, and to my family, Hester, Sam and Nelle for putting up with the struggle. Aaron Probyn for his encouragement and providing a much needed workspace. My mother Suzanne Adams for her support and allowing her home to be used as a photo archive. To my late father Dennis Adams for helping me repair ramps back in the day when he would have preferred that I was playing cricket.

For their efforts and contributions to the project along the way, THANK YOU to: Richard Hart, James Davis, Joel Lardner, Matt Barr, Laurence Johns, Seth Curtis, Winstan Whitter, Sam Griffin, Tamsin Murray Leach, Hester Hettinga, Neil MacDonald, James Hudson, Ben Coseley, Paul Sunman, Kate Shearman, Tamsin Blanchard, Idea Digital, Martin Rogers, Kirstin Munro, Iain Borden, Chris Parkinson, Andy Holmes, Rob Ashby, Jacob Sawyer and Mark Jackson at Slam City Skates, James Bowthorpe, Mackenzie Eisenhower, Neil Macdonald, Mon Barbour and Ian Roxburgh at SS20, Sophie Warwick, Mat Scott and India May at Hempstead May, Tony Campbell, Jason Jules, James Smith and the team at ACC, everyone who committed their time to being interviewed, and lastly to the photographers who have generously made their archives available to share with this project.

THANK YOU to EVERYONE who has ever bought, read, looked at, interacted with, contributed to or been featured in *RAD* magazine. The response to the *Read And Destroy* social media has been an enjoyable and humbling experience, allowing us—the former *RAD* contributors and creators—to understand, perhaps for the first time, just how much the mag meant to the fans back in the day. THANK YOU for the comments, likes, enthusiasm and support. The magazine was always about the readers.

Thank you to skateboarding and in particular the skateboarders whom I have had the personal pleasure of rolling with, watching and being blown away by over the years (I only wish I had your talent). Skateboarding rules.

info@read-and-destroy-archive.com
@readanddestroy

This project was made possible by the generous and enduring support of New Balance Numeric.

new balance numeric

BAD
magazine

Read and Destroy. You'
do it (destroy your precon
tear, blaze, etc.). Open yo
Enjoy life while you can.
There are no rebates.